CATO THE CENSOR

Cato the Censor

ALAN E. ASTIN

OXFORD
AT THE CLARENDON PRESS
1978

Oxford University Press, Walton Street, Oxford OX2 6DP

OXFORD LONDON GLASGOW
NEW YORK TORONTO MELBOURNE WELLINGTON
IBADAN NAIROBI DAR ES SALAAM LUSAKA CAPE TOWN
KUALA LUMPUR SINGAPORE JAKARTA HONG KONG TOKYO
DELHI BOMBAY CALCUTTA MADRAS KARACHI

© *Oxford University Press 1978*

British Library Cataloguing in Publication Data

Astin, Alan Edgar
  Cato the censor.
    1. Cato, Marcus Porcius, b. B.C.234 2. Rome –
  Biography
  I. Title
  937'.04'0924   DG253.C3   77–30281
  ISBN 0–19–814809–7

*Printed in Great Britain
at the University Press, Oxford
by Vivian Ridler
Printer to the University*

TO

J., A., AND N.

PREFACE

IN this book I have sought to provide a study of Cato as complete and as coherent as the often fragmentary evidence permits, excluding only the strictly agricultural content of the *De agricultura*. The first six chapters examine his career in sequence, and then a further six deal with several broad topics which cut across the chronological pattern. The detailed arrangement of the material has presented a number of problems, especially because many of the topics are to some extent interrelated and because a considerable amount of evidence bears upon more than one of them. The result is inevitably something of a compromise, but the sequence I have adopted, particularly for the topics in Chapters 7 to 12, is strongly influenced by a desire to avoid a great deal of repetition and cross-referencing. Another major problem has lain in the frustrating deficiencies of the information available to us. It is not hard to find questions—especially concerning Cato's role and attitudes in the conduct of foreign affairs—which clamour for answers which the evidence cannot provide. All too soon the point is reached at which the links between evidence and conjecture are too tenuous for the latter to be a reasonable basis for interpretation. Yet I hope to have shown that, without undue speculation, there is much which can be said; that Cato was, at least in some respects, less extreme, less idiosyncratic, and more positive than some scholars have supposed, though not as sophisticated as others have suggested; and that he was not only a remarkable personality but in a number of ways a figure of considerable historical significance.

Two lesser problems have concerned citations in the original languages and the construction of the General Index. Throughout I have had very much in mind the needs of readers who have no knowledge of Latin and Greek, but I have not attempted to maintain the use of translation and paraphrase in Chapter 7, where it would have been inappropriate to the discussion of stylistic features of Cato's speeches, or in the more technical arguments in the Appendices. As for the General Index, it quickly became apparent that if this was to be manageable a considerable measure of selection would be necessary. Various names and topics have therefore been omitted; in particular I have not included the ancient authors who provide information or comment. The result inevitably contains some anomalies and inconsistencies, but I hope that the combination of the two indexes and the arrangement of material in the body of the book will enable any significant topic or item to be found fairly readily.

Although I have been preparing this book for many years, most of it was written during study leave from the Queen's University in 1974–5, and the greater part of it during six months in 1975 when for the second time I enjoyed the generous hospitality and facilities of the Institute for Advanced Study at Princeton. I cannot express too warmly my gratitude to the Institute for the opportunity it afforded me and for a memorable experience. The book was largely written by the autum of 1975 and was completed in the spring of 1976. Much of the material in Chapters 7 and 8 was first presented in papers read to audiences at Cambridge, at Princeton, at Carleton University in Ottawa, at the State University of Ohio in Columbus, and at an informal conference of 'the Hibernian Hellenists' at Ballymascanlon, Co. Louth. I benefited greatly from the helpful comments offered on all those occasions.

From the many to whom I owe thanks there are some whom I must single out for mention. The Queen's University of Belfast, besides granting me study leave in 1974–5, assisted me to visit Spain in 1970. Dr. T. J. Cornell kindly allowed me to photocopy large portions of his thesis on the *Origines*. The fact that the thesis is unpublished raised the question of how far it would be useful to cite it; but since it is in my opinion an important contribution to which I am considerably indebted, and from which I also dissent on some points, I decided that in Chapter 10 it is preferable and proper to give a number of quite specific references. On military matters I have enjoyed valuable discussions with Col. C. E. Thompson and I particularly appreciated his comments upon a draft of Appendix 4. I am most grateful to Betty Horton and Sandy Lafferty in Princeton and Pauline Roberts in Belfast for the outstanding quality of their work on the typescript. In the reading of proofs my colleagues Mary Smallwood, Raymond Davis, John Salmon, and Richard Talbert have been most generous of their time and have offered many helpful observations; and the last three have been both a tolerant and a stimulating audience over many a departmental coffee break. Finally I thank the Oxford University Press for all the help and encouragement I have received.

A. E. A.

The Queen's University, Belfast
December 1977

CONTENTS

ABBREVIATIONS

CAH *Cambridge Ancient History.*

ESAR i T. Frank, *An Economic Survey of Ancient Rome*, i: *Rome and Italy of the Republic*, Baltimore, 1933.

FGrH F. Jacoby, *Die Fragmente der griechischen Historiker*, Berlin and Leyden, 1923– .

HRR i² H. W. G. Peter, *Historicorum Romanorum Reliquiae* i², Leipzig, 1914.

ILLRP A. Degrassi, *Inscriptiones Latinae Liberae Rei Publicae*, 2 vols., Florence, 1963–5.

ILS H. Dessau, *Inscriptiones Latinae Selectae*, 3 vols., Berlin, 1892–1916.

Janzer B. Janzer, *Historische Untersuchungen zu den Redenfragmenten des M. Porcius Cato*, Würzburg, 1937.

Jordan H. Jordan, *M. Catonis praeter librum de re rustica quae exstant*, Leipzig, 1860.

Kienast D. Kienast, *Cato der Censor. Seine Persönlichkeit und seine Zeit*, Heidelberg, 1954.

MRR T. R. S. Broughton, *The Magistrates of the Roman Republic*, 2 vols. and suppl., New York, 1951–60.

*ORF*³ H. Malcovati, *Oratorum Romanorum Fragmenta*³, Turin, 1967.

RE Pauly–Wissowa–Kroll, *Real-Encyclopädie der classischen Altertumswissenschaft.*

TLL *Thesaurus Linguae Latinae.*

Titles of periodicals are abbreviated in accordance with the system used in *L'Année philologique.*

I

The New Man from Tusculum

MARCUS PORCIUS CATO was born in 234 B.C.,[1] a native of Tusculum. Tusculum, situated about 15 miles south-east of Rome, was a Latin town which had long since acquired the status of a Roman *municipium* and the full privileges of Roman citizenship. It was left to modern scholars to argue, seriously and powerfully, that although Cato himself came from Tusculum his forefathers did not, and that his grandfather was not even a Roman citizen; that his family was Sabine, had received Roman citizenship only in his father's generation, and had but recently taken up residence in Tusculum. The evidence from which all this has been inferred need not, however, lead to these unexpected conclusions, and in view of the acrimonious disputes which studded Cato's career the total absence of direct evidence for such a background is highly significant. Far more probably Cato's Tusculan origin—one of the most frequently attested facts about him—is to be understood to imply that he came from a long line of Tusculan, and therefore Roman citizens.[2]

Cato did spend much of his youth in Sabine territory, on an estate which he inherited from his father. Its proximity to a villa once owned by M'. Curius Dentatus, famed for his military successes and personal integrity, is represented by Cicero to have been a source of inspiration to

---

[1] Cicero clearly indicates birth in 234 and death in 149 at the age of eighty-five: *Brut.* 61; 80; 89; *De sen.* 10; 14; 32; so also Pliny, *Nat. hist.* 29. 15. Death at age ninety is stated or implied by Livy, 39. 40. 12; Plut. *Cato Mai.* 15. 5; Val. Max. 8. 7. 1; but birth as early as 239 is ruled out by Cato's own statement that his first military service was at age seventeen and when Hannibal was in Italy (p. 6). On Cato's early career see esp. Fraccaro, 'Sulla biografia di Catone Maggiore sino al consolato', *Opusc.* i. 139 ff. (with supplements to the original publication in *Atti e mem. della Accad. Virgiliana*, n.s. 3 (1910), 99 ff.); Gelzer, *RE*, s.v. *Porcius*, no. 9, cols. 108 ff.; Kienast, pp. 33 ff.; Ruebel, *The Political Development of Cato Censorius*, pp. 30 ff. Plut. *Cato Mai.* 1. 3 says that his third name was originally Priscus but was changed to Cato in recognition of his ability; but this is probably a misunderstanding of *priscus* used to differentiate this Cato from his namesake Uticensis: Drumann–Groebe, *Gesch. Roms* v². 102. According to Plut. *Cato Mai.* 1. 1 Cato himself referred to his great-grandfather as a Cato.

[2] For references and discussion see Astin, 'Cato Tusculanus and the Capitoline Fasti', *JRS* 62 (1972), 20 ff., against Fraccaro, op. cit., pp. 169 f., and others. For Tusculum and its status see esp. McCracken, *RE*, s.v. *Tusculum*, cols. 1463 ff. and Taylor, *Voting Districts*, pp. 79 f. and 301 f.

Cato whenever he revisited his property.[3] The idea may well have its origin in Cato's own writings, possibly in a speech designed to extol his own virtues in contrast to the failings of some opponent; certainly he used, in just such a context, a reference to farming and 'Sabine rocks' to symbolize the austerity and industry of his youth.[4]   When, how, and why the family acquired this property is unknown. Presumably it was purchased, though it is conceivable that it originated in part with Curius Dentatus' distribution of small lots of conquered Sabine land to Roman citizens in 290.[5] Possession of a Sabine estate would have been convenient for the transfer of livestock to higher ground in summer; and it may well be that a Tusculan family which with rising status and prosperity wished to acquire additional land had little choice but to seek it outside the very restricted territory of Tusculum itself.[6] But that invites other questions about Cato's family background.

'His ancestors', says Plutarch, 'seem to have been men of no note whatsoever, but Cato himself praises his father, Marcus, as a brave man and a good soldier; and he says that his great-grandfather, Cato, often won prizes in recognition of his valour and received from the public treasury because of his bravery the price of five war-horses which he lost in battle. The Romans used to call those who had no family distinction but were coming into public notice through their own achievements "new men", and such they called Cato; but he himself used to say that in terms of office and glory he was indeed new, but in respect of the deeds and virtues of his ancestors he was extremely old.'[7] That his ancestors were undistinguished in the sense that none had become a Roman senator is obvious; but lack of distinction is a relative matter. Two writers, Velleius Paterculus and Valerius Maximus, use expressions which, if taken literally, would suggest that the family did not even belong to the governing class of Tusculum; but since both are emphasizing Cato's remarkable rise to the peak of office and influence they are only too likely to have chosen their words with more concern for rhetorical contrast than for historical

---

[3] Nepos, *Cato* 1. 1; Plut. *Cato Mai.* 1. 1, cf. 2. 1 ff.; Cic. *De sen.* 55, cf. 24, 46; *Rep.* 3. 40.

[4] *ORF*[3], Cato fr. 128, from a speech *De suis virtutibus contra Thermum*.

[5] Val. Max. 4. 3. 5; Colum. *De re rust.* 1, *praef.* 14; 1. 3. 10; 'Plut.' *Apophth. Man. Cur.* 1; Frontin. *Strat.* 4. 3. 12; cf. Pliny, *Nat. hist.* 18. 18; 'Victor', *De vir. ill.* 33. 5. Forni, 'Manio Curio Dentato', *Athenaeum*, n.s. 31 (1953), 197 f., defends the authenticity of Curius' assignments, *contra* Frank, 'On Rome's Conquest of Sabinum, Picenum and Etruria', *Klio*, 11 (1911), 365 ff.

[6] Tusculum probably had only about 50 square kilometres in total: McCracken, *RE*, s.v. *Tusculum*, cols. 1482 f.

[7] Plut. *Cato Mai.* 1. 1 f.

exactitude. Similarly a reference by Plutarch to 'when he was still poor' seems likely, from the context, to be contrived and unreliable, and in any event poverty itself is a relative term.[8] Cato's own claim, in a speech 'concerning his own virtues, against Thermus', that he had spent his entire youth in frugality, rigour, and industry ('in parsimonia atque in duritia atque in industria') proves neither poverty nor humble status;[9] and his failure in the passage reported by Plutarch (quoted above) to mention his grandfather along with his father and great-grandfather proves not impoverishment but only a lack of distinction in military and public service on the part of the grandfather; and this could be accounted for in a host of ways, not least plausibly by physical infirmity or an early death. On the other hand the accident-prone great-grandfather is a figure of some significance, inasmuch as he regularly served as a cavalryman and therefore was at least moderately wealthy. He may even have been enrolled in the Roman equestrian order, the *equites equo publico*, though this is by no means necessarily the case.[10] In any event a man who started with sufficient property to serve as an *eques* and who won extensive public recognition of his valour is virtually certain to have enhanced both the status and the wealth of his family.

Cato, then, came of a family which enjoyed at least moderate wealth. That much can be stated with confidence and indeed is an almost necessary assumption to explain his ability to embark on a public career; but also it is a plausible guess that the wealth was considerable, and that the family had either long belonged to or had recently made its way into the local aristocracy of Tusculum; and it is conceivable that some members may have belonged to the Roman equestrian order.

Thus Cato was born a Roman citizen, to a family of at least moderate prosperity, and at a time when the Roman state was entering upon one of the most decisive transformations in its history. Not that the past history of Rome had been other than one of frequent and remarkable change. Over the centuries an extraordinary complex of political institutions had been evolved, replete with checks and balances and with intricate subtleties of legal and quasi-legal authority. The once tiny hill-settlement had

---

[8] Vell. 2. 128. 2; Val. Max. 3. 4. 6; Plut. *Cato Mai.* 21. 3. In the latter passage the antithesis between early poverty and later affluence looks like a gloss to explain a seeming discrepancy between the dictum that 'it was shameful to quarrel with a servant about one's belly' and Cato's severe insistence on excellent service when he was entertaining friends to meals. In Livy, *Per.* 48 the phrase 'nam pauper erat', in explanation of the modest funeral he gave his elder son *c.* 152, is an obvious and ludicrous gloss; cf. p. 105.

[9] *ORF*[3], Cato fr. 128.

[10] So Kienast, pp. 33 f., though with less caution about the inference.

vastly extended its territories and had absorbed numerous neighbouring peoples into its body politic. All the remaining peoples of the entire Italian peninsula, from poor and hardy tribes in the hills to Greeks in flourishing maritime cities, had been brought one by one under the sway of Rome, bound to her by treaties which interfered little with their internal affairs but which placed their military resources wholly at her disposal. Yet until recently Rome's awareness of the world had been largely confined to Italy and still it extended only a little beyond it; her peoples remained mostly self-sufficient communities of peasant farmers, her army a citizen militia drawn from these communities. Merchants and traders there were, especially in the Greek coastal towns, but most of the population was barely, if at all, involved in this wider commerce. In the city itself, although tenement blocks and two aqueducts attest its growth, the gleaming marble and the magnificent buildings of imperial splendour still lay in the future. It was a society lacking in grace and elegance, virtually without a literature of its own, and as yet knowing little of Hellenic literature or culture.

In all this Rome stood on the threshold of an astonishing transformation. In Cato's lifetime the horizons of her vision were to recede to take in the entire Mediterranean world; she was to become not merely a world power but the dominant power; she was to acquire vast wealth, destined to affect her society profoundly; her upper classes were to discover, enthuse over, and adapt to their own purposes the literary, artistic, and intellectual heritage of the Greeks; a virile and varied Latin literature was to come into being and a tradition of literary activity was to be created which was to continue for centuries. Cato was a witness to these momentous changes, but he was more than that. He experienced them, was himself part of the society that was changing; his career was intimately intertwined with them, and it is arguable that he himself had no small influence on the form and direction which some of them took.

It was a transformation which sprang from war and the consequences of war. Already the First Punic War had seen Rome in conflict beyond the confines of Italy—against Carthage, one of the major non-Italian powers—had led her to annex Sardinia, Corsica, and Sicily, and in the latter had widened and deepened her contacts with Hellenic culture considerably beyond those provided by the Greek cities in Italy; when Cato was born Livius Andronicus and Naevius were just beginning to draw upon the Greek dramatic tradition for the entertainment of Roman audiences. Further, the pressures of this war had encouraged the growth of a mercantile class capable of handling state contracts on a major scale;[11] and its outcome had initiated the flow of foreign revenue into the Roman economy. Soon was to come the convulsive experience of Hannibal's invasion and the Second Punic War, obliging Rome to become a world power in order to survive, leading on to the wars with Philip, Antiochus, and Perseus and to the hegemony of the Hellenistic East.

Warfare, it is always to be remembered, was a central preoccupation of Roman society, a normal part of life. It is tempting to think of the interval between 241, when the First Punic War ended after twenty-three years of protracted agony and monstrous casualties, and the outbreak of the Second Punic War in 218 as a period of peace, briefly interrupted by Illyrian wars in 229–228 and 219 and by a Gallic invasion in 225. The reality is that despite the meagreness of the sources for this 'interlude' there are only five years in which active warfare is not positively attested. Roman forces were repeatedly employed in the conquest of Sardinia and Corsica and against the Ligurians and the Gallic tribes (notably the Boii) of northern Italy, as well as in the two Illyrian campaigns; and at least thirteen Roman commanders celebrated public military triumphs. Nor were these the remote activities of a professional army. The troops who fought in these recurring campaigns were a citizen militia, maintained by annual levies; and their officers were drawn from those who administered public affairs. The Roman governing class itself was in no small measure a military aristocracy, in which long service as a junior officer was a prerequisite for a political career, and in which the major public offices combined civil and military functions. This was the class into which Cato was to make his way. Military prowess counted for much, and it was no irrelevance when he boasted of the martial qualities of his father and great-grandfather; but more relevant still were those of Cato himself, and there was no lack of opportunity to display them.

In 218 B.C., as Cato was almost of age to be eligible for military service and to embark on civic activity, war broke out afresh between Rome and Carthage, a traumatic, decisive war which was to drag on for seventeen years. Within the year Hannibal had crossed the Alps and defeated the Roman armies at the Ticinus and the Trebia. The massacre at Trasimene in 217 was followed in 216 by the catastrophe of Cannae, which to all appearances brought Rome to the brink of total disaster. Recovery was slow and arduous. Roman armies toiled and fought in Italy

---

[11] Badian, *Publicans and Sinners*, pp. 16 ff., points out that public contracting must have begun in much earlier times and that the evidence concerning the Second Punic War implies that the use of large-scale military contracts was already well established.

and Cisalpine Gaul, in Spain and Sicily, and ultimately in Africa. The demands on manpower were enormous—and the opportunities for military talent innumerable. It can be no accident that during this war and in its aftermath there are found in office several men with names new to the high positions of state, and yet more in the lower ranks of the senatorial class. Evidently the pressure of the conflict had prised open a little wider the door which gave access to the preserves of the aristocracy, enabling a rather larger number of individuals and families to attain public office and senatorial status, principally no doubt in virtue of the prominence they had won in war. One such individual was M. Porcius Cato.

'He was far more desirous', says Plutarch, 'of high repute in battles and campaigns against the enemy, and while he was yet a mere stripling the front of his body was covered with wounds.' So also Livy: 'In war he was the bravest of fighters and distinguished himself in many remarkable combats.'[12] But he had more to commend him than personal bravery and physical prowess; the man whose later exploits in Spain and Greece earned him the reputation of 'a consummate commander' (*summus imperator*) was both acquiring experience and displaying his talent in the early years of the Hannibalic war, at first in the ranks, soon as a military tribune. Soundly based though these generalizations unquestionably are, there is a frustrating lack of detail. Cato first enlisted, as he himself stated, 'at the age of seventeen, at the time when Hannibal, enjoying the favour of fortune, was setting Italy aflame'—perhaps in 217, more probably in 216, and possibly at the emergency levy held after Cannae.[13] By 214 he was in Campania during the operations of Q. Fabius Maximus and M. Claudius Marcellus, probably in Marcellus' army. Later in that year Marcellus took his army to Sicily, where Cato served as a military tribune in a protracted campaign dominated by the siege of

---

[12] Plut. *Cato Mai.* 1. 8; Livy, 39. 40. 6.

[13] Plut. *Cato Mai.* 1. 8 = ORF[3], Cato fr. 188; cf. Nepos, *Cato* 1. 2: 'primum stipendium meruit annorum decem septemque.' The year is widely held to have been 216, though Münzer, 'Atticus als Geschichtsschreiber', *Hermes*, 40 (1905), 65, prefers 217, while Gelzer, *RE*, s.v. *Porcius*, no. 9, col. 108, and Malcovati, *ORF*[3], p. 12, admit both years as possible. The fact that in *De sen.* 10 Cicero mentions no military service earlier than 214 may support 216 rather than 217; for in that passage his dominant interest is in Cato's contacts with Fabius Maximus, and 217 was the year when Fabius took command as dictator after Trasimene. Fraccaro, *Opusc.* i. 149 f., argues plausibly that Cato was first recruited at the special levy after Cannae mentioned in Livy, 22. 57. 9 ff., cf. 23. 14. 2 ff., though he relies too readily on Mommsen's inferences about the *tirocinium* at this date, *Röm. Staats.* i[3]. 506 n. 2. Silius Italicus, *Punica* 7. 691 ff. has Cato serving under Fabius in 217, and in 10. 13 ff. has him serving at Cannae in 216. The latter is certainly incorrect and no reliance can be placed on the former.

Syracuse.[14] When he left Sicily is not known: the most likely guess is in 211 with his commander, but the legions which had accompanied Marcellus stayed on until 209 and Cato might have remained with them. On the other hand it is quite possible that in 209 he was present in the army of Q. Fabius Maximus at the recapture of Tarentum. So it is reported by Cicero (followed by Plutarch), and although much suspicion and controversy have been aroused by Cicero's use of the setting for some patently fictitious material there is no strong argument for denying entirely Cato's presence at Tarentum in 209. In any event it is not easy to believe that Cato saw no military service between 211 and 207.[15] There is firm ground again in 207, in which year Cato was in the army of C. Claudius Nero and won high praise for his contribution at the battle of the Metaurus—the battle in which the destruction of Hasdrubal's relieving army finally removed any lingering possibility that Hannibal might recover the initiative in Italy.[16] Whether or not Cato continued on active service thereafter cannot be determined. Nothing at all is known of his situation in the following two years, and 204 marks the beginning of a new phase altogether, for Cato became a quaestor and thus formally embarked on a senatorial career.

To recognize the fundamental importance of military talent and achievement is not to imply that these alone sufficed for an aspirant to senatorial status. With useful personal qualities Cato was amply endowed. 'No art of conducting either private or public business was lacking to him', says Livy. 'Some men were advanced to the highest offices by knowledge of the law, others by eloquence, others by military reputation: his versatile nature was so adapted to everything alike that you would say

[14] Cic. De sen. 10, which alone mentions Cato in Campania and says that he served with Fabius, is superficially contradicted by Nepos, Cato 1. 2, which says that he was military tribune in Sicily in that year; similarly 'Victor', De vir. ill. 47. 1, without the date. But in 214 Marcellus' army was with Fabius in Campania before it went to Sicily, so Cicero's basic information is probably correct even if he has inferred too much about Cato's service under Fabius. Plut. Cato Mai. 3. 3 mentions service as a military tribune but without details. Whatever the precise import of ORF³, Cato fr. 129, 'quid mihi fieret, si non ego stipendia omnia ordinarius meruissem semper', it cannot mean that Cato never served as military tribune.

[15] Cic. De sen. 11, 39, and 41; Plut. Cato Mai. 2. 3. Reasons for doubting the report have been the assumption that Cato would have remained in Sicily till 209, the silence of other sources, especially Nepos, Cicero's use of the story as part of his contrived emphasis on links between Fabius and Cato, and above all Cicero's use of the setting for the 'Nearchus' story, which is virtually certainly fictitious; hence it is suggested that Cato's presence at Tarentum is itself fictitious. But Cicero is at least as likely to have used a genuine setting for his contrived effects, and there is no evident reason why anyone else should have invented the story. For various arguments see esp. Münzer, 'Atticus', Hermes, 40 (1905), 64 f.; Fraccaro, Opusc. i. 152 f. and 171 ff.; Gelzer, RE, s.v. Porcius, no. 9, cols. 108 f.; Ruebel, The Political Development of Cato Censorius, pp. 41 ff.   [16] Nepos, Cato 1. 2.

that whatever he was doing was the one thing for which he was born.'[17] Versatility, amply confirmed by his career and writings, was matched by energy, drive, and initiative. Personal charm and affability, though perhaps not lacking, are not much in evidence; rather the dominant impression is of a forceful and somewhat irascible personality.[18] The 'rustic' virtues of a robust physique, hard work, endurance, and indifference to material advantage were emphasized by a calculated and largely consistent display of austerity, by an oft-proclaimed scorn of ostentatious luxuries. In the expression of scorn he was an adept, lashing his victims with an asperity and a caustic wit which found lasting fame in collections of his sayings; and he had a special gift for aphorism and hyperbole. Indeed, his exceptional command of language and powers of delivery were the principal elements in an eloquence which established him as the outstanding orator of his age.[19]

According to Plutarch this eloquence was developed and perfected by constantly placing it at the disposal of all in the towns and villages who wished to avail themselves of Cato's services as an advocate.[20] Whether this is derived from an authentic source, such as one of Cato's own writings, or from the imagination of some later writer it is not possible to tell. Diligent performance of the duties of patronage, with the concomitant strengthening and extension of his *clientela*, could reasonably be inferred of any Roman of standing and particularly of a *novus homo* with senatorial ambitions. Whether in Cato's case it was, as Plutarch seems to suggest, a major factor or even *the* major factor in bringing him to the notice of a powerful patron and thereby launching him on a public career is perhaps more questionable. For much of the war period Cato was on military service, and therefore not present to offer himself as an advocate in the towns and villages; and the army would have presented him with more frequent and more immediate opportunities of establishing close personal contacts with men of influence. What is certain is that a *novus homo* needed such contacts, and that Cato had them.

---

[17] The opening of the vivid character-sketch in Livy, 39. 40. 4 ff.

[18] *Comitas* and *facilitas* are ascribed to Cato in Cic. *Pro Mur.* 66, but it is possible that this owes more to Cicero's immediate rhetorical purpose than to his knowledge about Cato. Similar hesitation must be felt about the picture of conviviality in Cic. *De sen.* 46, which is the source of Plut. *Cato Mai.* 25. 3 f.; but cf. Livy, 34. 5. 6: 'oratorem non solum gravem sed ... etiam trucem ... cum ingenio sit mitis.' In contrast Livy, 39. 40. 10 and the epigram in Plut. *Cato Mai.* 1. 4:

πυρρόν, πανδακέτην, γλαυκόμματον, οὐθὲ θανόντα
Πόρκιον εἰς ἀίδην Φερσεφόνη δέχεται.

[19] For collected dicta see pp. 187 f.; for Cato as an orator, Ch. 7.

[20] Plut. *Cato Mai.* 1. 5; cf. 3. 2.

To start with, there is a strong possibility that he was assisted into public life by a distant relative. Three families of Porcii make their first appearance in the Roman aristocracy in these years; and although Cato was the first Porcius to reach the consulship, he was not the first to become a senator or to hold curule office. Of the other 'new' Porcii one, P. Porcius Laeca, was slightly younger than Cato, holding the praetorship (his highest office) in the year in which Cato was consul; but L. Porcius Licinus was his senior by a considerable number of years and a person of some significance.[21] He is mentioned first as having fought with distinction during the siege of Capua in 211, at which time he was already a *legatus*. His aedileship, in the next year, attracted special attention by the munificent expenditure with which he and his colleague, Q. Catius, celebrated the Plebeian Games. When he achieved the praetorship in 207 he received command of two legions in Cisalpine Gaul. With these he shadowed and harassed the invading Carthaginian army until he was able to join forces with Livius Salinator at the Metaurus. There he was in charge of the Roman centre at the decisive battle in which Hasdrubal was killed and his army destroyed—the battle in which Cato also distinguished himself under the command of Claudius Nero. There can be no proof that these Porcii were related to each other, but the almost simultaneous emergence of three men each bearing a name unknown in the earlier history of Rome can hardly be a coincidence. It looks very much as if Cato was assisted in his entry into public life by the patronage and success of a kinsman whom he himself was soon to outshine.

Much more important than Porcius Licinus, however, was L. Valerius Flaccus, sprung from one of the most distinguished of the ancient patrician *gentes* and son of P. Valerius Flaccus, consul in 227, who had himself been prominent in public affairs. Tradition was explicit that Valerius encouraged Cato to transfer his activities to Rome itself and helped to launch him on his career, and although Plutarch's account of this—the only extended account—patently incorporates some imaginative embroidery, the authenticity of the basic tradition is beyond doubt.[22] The close association between the two men is evident in their careers.[23] Although Valerius, not surprisingly, was slightly ahead of Cato in the earlier stages, he was Cato's colleague in the consulship in 195, like Cato was a military tribune during Acilius Glabrio's campaign against Antiochus in 191 and like

[21] *RE*, s.v. *Porcius*, nos. 19 (Laeca) and 22 (Licinus).
[22] Plut. *Cato Mai.* 3. 1 ff., cf. fr. *ex Comm. in Hesiodum* 28; Nepos, *Cato* 1. 1; 'Victor', *De vir. ill.* 47. 1.
[23] For Valerius' career see *RE*, s.v. *Valerius*, no. 173, and below, pp. 23 f.

Cato was placed in charge of an outflanking movement at Thermopylae; he and Cato were unsuccessful candidates for the censorship in 189 and were the successful candidates in 184, whereupon Cato appointed him *princeps senatus*. Though the personal relationship between them became very close, virtually nothing is known of its nature. Plutarch and Livy both record that Cato actively campaigned to have Valerius elected as his colleague in the censorship, and Plutarch's picture is of patronage and encouragement which developed into friendship;[24] but that is all. Indeed Valerius is almost indistinguishable as a character. It is his one-time client whose personality has impressed itself upon the historical tradition and who as consul, military tribune, and censor appears as very much the dominant partner. No doubt there is substance in this: Cato was almost certainly the more eloquent, the more outwardly dynamic, the more colourful and therefore the more prominent in public image; but it would be rash to infer too much, to suppose that in these high offices the original roles had been reversed and that Valerius was a colourless character carried to such eminence by his association with Cato.[25] Moreover Cato's greater prominence is enhanced because he outlived his patron by more than thirty years (Valerius died of plague in 180), and was active in public affairs to the end; and even more because much of the later tradition was strongly influenced by Cato's own extensive and varied writings. These conveyed to subsequent generations both a vivid awareness of his personality and his own accounts—apparently quite untinged with modesty[26]—of the events in which he was involved. The fact is that Valerius enjoyed the prestige of his ancient and illustrious lineage, demonstrated in successful action that he too had military talent, and as aedile won great popularity by lavish expenditure on entertainments and by fairness and efficiency in the distribution of cheap corn. The power wielded by such a man in the essentially aristocratic society of Rome would have been very considerable. His contribution to the partnership was less spectacular than Cato's but perhaps no less substantial, even in the later years; as for the earlier years, Cato's association with Valerius 'brought him much honour and influence', says Plutarch, 'so that he first obtained a military tribunate and then became quaestor'.[27]

[24] Livy, 39. 41. 1 ff.; Plut. *Cato Mai.* 3. 1 ff.; 10. 1; 16. 7 f.; 17. 1.

[25] Thus Kienast, p. 74, suggests that Valerius probably lacked initiative. Cf. Marmorale, *Cato Maior*[2], pp. 38, 'uomo mediocre', and 89, 'uomo di scarso rilievo'.

[26] Livy, 34. 15. 9: 'haud sane detractor laudum suarum'. Similarly Plut. *Cato Mai.* 14. 2; 32. 3 = *Compar.* 5. 3.

[27] Plut. *Cato Mai.* 3. 3. On Valerius' career and general influence see further pp. 23 f.

2

Cursus Honorum

THE decade from 204 to 195—from Cato's quaestorship to his consulship —was studded with events portentous for the future of Rome. The Second Punic War was brought to a triumphant conclusion, carrying Scipio Africanus to the heights of fame and adulation. Roman control was firmly and finally re-established throughout Italy and the work of reconstruction was begun. Veteran troops were settled on lands confiscated from communities which had sided with Hannibal, and a new programme of colonization was initiated. In the north, where Hannibal's Gallic and Ligurian allies were still in arms, Rome was quickly drawn into long and tedious wars which ultimately ensured the further extension of her rule. Similarly the retention of the Spanish territories taken from the Carthaginians—in itself a substantial new commitment—was to lead to the inexorable advance of Roman power across the Iberian peninsula. Furthermore, as soon as Rome had put an end to her struggle with Carthage she embarked upon a war to curtail the power of Philip V of Macedon, thereby entering into a major involvement in the East. When in 197 Philip was defeated at Cynoscephalae by Titus Quinctius Flamininus some believed that this involvement was ended, that the communities of Greece and the East would be left to their own devices. That was a delusion: the intervention had created a situation of obligation, awareness, and interest from which total disengagement was not possible. In the following decades Roman ambassadors and Roman armies were repeatedly drawn back across the Adriatic and the reality of Roman control became increasingly evident. Rome had entered unmistakably upon the era of imperial domination. Meanwhile the same years saw on the internal scene not only the triumphant return of Scipio but a series of acrimonious disputes and the meteoric rise of Flamininus.

Between these momentous events and the relatively scanty information about Cato the links are few and tenuous. Yet these were important years for Cato too, not only as a citizen of this evolving state but in a personal sense. The new man from Tusculum advanced steadily and without electoral rebuff through the ascending sequence of public offices, until in 195, with his patron and friend Valerius Flaccus as his colleague, he was invested with the supreme power of the consulship. Already in these years, when Cato had not yet attained the abiding eminence of consular status, when the struggle for office and influence had yet to be won, there are the first indications of his characteristic interests and public attitudes. The material is slender—for most of the evidence on these matters, especially on his rhetorical and literary interests, stems from the second half of Cato's life, from the post-consular years. Nevertheless there is enough to give the first hints of what was to come.

Cato's quaestorship has been the subject of long and needless controversy, even as to its date. It is virtually certain that the year was 204: the only conceivable alternative—that he was quaestor in 205 and remained in office as proquaestor in 204—has little to commend it (though acceptance of it would not necessarily affect the general picture in matters of substance).[1] He was sent to Sicily, to serve under P. Cornelius Scipio, the future Africanus. Since the early months of 205 Scipio had been based at Syracuse, preparing the expeditionary force with which he was shortly to invade the Carthaginian homeland. As the winter of 205/4 was devoted to the equipping and training of this force Scipio spent a considerable amount of time in Syracuse, and in his hours of leisure he evidently enjoyed the cultural opportunities offered by the greatest Greek city in the West. To him came Cato as quaestor, and when Scipio at last set sail for Africa Cato sailed with him. It is Cato's relationship with his eminent commander which is the principal focus of interest.

---

[1] 204 is stated or clearly implied by Cic. *Brut.* 60; *De sen.* 10 and 45; Livy, 29. 25. 10. Nepos, *Cato* 1. 4, presupposes that Cato was still in office in 204, but for the quaestorship itself 205 is indicated by 1. 3 ('quaestor obtigit P. Africano consuli') and 2. 2 ('Africanus . . . cuius in priore consulatu quaestor fuerat'); it is also the natural inference from Plutarch's story (discussed below) that Cato returned to Rome to support Fabius Maximus' complaints about Scipio, since these seem to have occurred early in the consular year corresponding to 204. Most modern discussions assume that the date of the quaestorship was consciously falsified in one direction or the other in order to establish or discredit some particular view about Cato. This seems unnecessary and implausible. It is easy to see Nepos' references as the result of imprecision by himself or by some predecessor, blurring the fact that by the time Cato arrived Scipio had passed from consulship to proconsulship. The story of Cato's visit to Rome, certainly fictitious, is probably the product of uncritical inference (see below); it is most unlikely that it occurred to whoever first set out the story in the form found in Plutarch that this version had implications for the date of his quaestorship. Other references to the quaestorship: Cic. *De sen.* 32; 'Victor', *De vir. ill.* 47. 1; cf. Pliny, *Nat. hist. praef.* 30; Frontin. *Strat.* 4. 7. 12. For discussion of Cato's quaestorship and its date see esp. Münzer, 'Atticus als Geschichtsschreiber', *Hermes*, 40 (1905), 68 ff.; Fraccaro, *Opusc.* i. 156 ff. and 173 f.; Gelzer, *RE*, s.v. *Porcius*, no. 9, cols. 109 f.; Marmorale, *Cato Maior*[2], pp. 41 ff.; Della Corte, *Catone censore*[2], pp. 19 ff.; Kienast, pp. 16 ff. and 38 f.; *MRR* i. 307 with n. 4; Ruebel, *The Political Development of Cato Censorius*, pp. 46 ff.

Any conclusion regarding that relationship is dependent upon two different but related stories concerning serious complaints levelled against Scipio's conduct, even though in one of these, the affair of Pleminius, Cato is not even mentioned. In 205 Scipio had taken advantage of an opportunity to recapture for Rome Locri, a Greek city in the south of Italy. Soon afterwards he was obliged to intervene in a violent dispute between the man he had placed in charge of Locri, Q. Pleminius, and two military tribunes. He found in favour of Pleminius, whom he confirmed in his appointment. It seems clear, however, that from the start Pleminius had exercised no restraint over the rapacity and brutality of his troops, and himself had been guilty of gross maltreatment of the Locrians. Scipio's confirmation of Pleminius' appointment did nothing to ameliorate the situation, with the result that by the beginning of the next consular year Locrian envoys were imploring the intervention of the Senate. There was a storm of protest, not least from the not inconsiderable number of Scipio's personal and political enemies. Q. Fabius Maximus demanded not only the immediate arrest of Pleminius but that Scipio should be recalled and deprived of his command. The attack was reinforced by rumours that Scipio, preferring Greek dress to military uniform, was idling away his time amid books and philosophers, grossly neglecting his duties, and allowing the discipline of the army to become dangerously lax. After much debate a more moderate proposal was adopted: a special commission was appointed with instructions to deal with the situation at Locri itself, to determine the degree of Scipio's responsibility for events there, and to investigate the general charges of neglect of duty. Provision was made for his recall, and if necessary his arrest, if the commission found against him. In the event the Locrians pressed no charges against Scipio himself, and a massive display of his assembled forces easily convinced the commission of the thoroughness of his military preparations. Shortly after its visit he embarked for the invasion of Africa.

This episode is narrated at length by Livy and mentioned with minor variations in a few lesser sources.[2] Neither Livy nor the lesser sources include any mention of Cato. Plutarch, however, has the following story:

When he was sent out with Scipio as quaestor for the war in Africa, he saw the man indulging in his customary extravagance and lavishing money without

---

[2] Livy, 29. 8–9 and 16–22; Diod. 27. 4; Val. Max. 1. 1. 21, cf. 3. 6. 1; App. *Hann.* 55; Dio, fr. 62; Zon. 9. 11. For discussions of the Pleminius affair see esp. Grosso, 'Il caso di Pleminio', *GIF* 5 (1952), 119 ff. and 234 ff.; Toynbee, *Hannibal's Legacy* ii. 613 ff. (both arguing that Africanus was guilty).

stint upon his soldiery. He therefore made bold to tell him that the greatest
cause for complaint was not the matter of expense but the fact that he was
corrupting the native frugality of his soldiers, who resorted to luxurious
pleasures when their pay exceeded their actual needs. Scipio replied that he had
no use for an excessively parsimonious quaestor when the winds were bearing
him under full sail to the war; he owed the city an account of his achievements,
not of its moneys. Cato therefore left Sicily, and joined Fabius in denouncing
before the Senate Scipio's waste of enormous moneys and his boyish addiction
to palaestras and theatres, as though he were not commander of an army but
master of a festival. As a result of these attacks tribunes were sent to bring
Scipio back to Rome, if the charges against him should turn out to be true.
Then Scipio convinced the tribunes that victory in war depended on the
preparations made for it; showed that he could be agreeable in his intercourse
with his friends when he had leisure for it, but was never led by his sociability
to neglect matters of large and serious import; and sailed off to the war.[3]

Beyond reasonable doubt Cato's alleged return to Rome is fictitious.
It is unbelievable that such outrageous conduct on the part of a
quaestor, above all a quaestor whose subsequent public career was as
polemical as it was famous, should pass unmentioned in other sources;[4]
or that a quaestor who had done this should not only return to his post
but be given a position of command in the invasion of Africa by the very
general whom he had criticized and who is alleged previously to have
virtually dismissed him. Furthermore, if Plutarch's story were true it
would most naturally be understood to imply that Cato's quaestorship
was in 205, which is otherwise much less probable than 204. There are
two other peculiar features about the story: the Pleminius affair is not
mentioned at all, although there is clearly a relationship between it
and Plutarch's account; and the principal charge regarding Scipio's
conduct in Syracuse is rather different from that given by Livy, with the
emphasis on improper expenditure of public money.

How much truth, if any, underlies this story of conflict between proconsul and quaestor? Years later, in the 180s, Scipio was at the centre
of a bitter public dispute. It was inevitable that the accusations of lax
discipline should once again be raked up: Livy explicitly states that they
were.[5] It is most improbable that Cato, who was deeply implicated in
these later attacks on Scipio, refrained at that time from commenting

---

[3] Plut. Cato Mai. 3. 5 ff.

[4] Nepos, Cato 1. 3, says, 'quaestor obtigit P. Africano consuli, cum quo non pro sortis
necessitudine vixit; namque ab eo perpetua dissensit vita'; but this falls well short of Plutarch's
account.

[5] Livy, 38. 51. 1. On these later attacks see pp. 60 ff. and 70 ff.

adversely on what he had seen when he was in Sicily; and he is more than likely to have asserted that he had remonstrated with Scipio—whether he had actually done so or not. Significantly, the heart of the controversy in the 180s was Scipio's failure to account fully for public moneys, and the response which Plutarch alleges he made to Cato in Syracuse is suspiciously close in spirit to the events and issues of those later years. If such assertions, whether true or baseless, were made in the 180s and recorded in Cato's speeches or elsewhere, it would be but a short step for someone to infer that Cato had associated himself with Fabius' attacks (or indeed Cato himself may have implied so), and then for Plutarch or some predecessor to infer that Cato had returned to Rome at that time.[6] In short, the story reported by Plutarch is in part patently fictitious and for the rest could easily have been so much influenced by what was alleged during the bitter controversy of the 180s that it cannot be used as evidence for the actual state of affairs during Cato's quaestorship.

It does not follow that all was concord and harmony between Cato and Scipio in 204. To judge by Cato's conduct when he himself commanded armies he believed in a regime of strict discipline, austerity, and constant endurance training, and further that the commander himself should ostentatiously share the rigours to which the troops were subjected. Thus it is likely enough that he had reservations about Scipio's methods and manner of life (from a military point of view; if palaestras and theatres were explicitly mentioned the reference need have been only to neglect of duty and to their seeming contrast with martial qualities and training; a more general cultural criticism could have been implicit but cannot properly be inferred); nor is he likely to have made great efforts to conceal his opinions. It would be no surprise if the personal relationship between the two was none too cordial.[7] The experiences of 204 may have induced

---

[6] Similarly Della Corte, *Catone censore*[2], p. 252, though he probably attributes too much to Plutarch's own inventiveness. Plutarch's story follows a more general remark about Cato's admiration for Fabius, an idea which he probably owes to Cicero's picture in the *De senectute*. It is impossible to say whether there is any substance in this. The only concrete evidence of association, apart from the fictitious story about the quaestorship, is that Cato is said to have served under Fabius in 214, which is probably a misunderstanding, and again in 209, which may be correct though it is often doubted (see p. 7); and even if both are correct such service would prove little. It is conceivable, though unattested, that there were complimentary remarks about Fabius somewhere in Cato's speeches or writings, but it is also possible that Cicero was exercising his imagination for the purposes of the dialogue, with no more substantial basis than the military service.

[7] Cf. Nepos, *Cato* 1. 3, cited above, p. 14 n. 4; but this too could be a retrojection from the later disputes. For Cato as a commander see Ch. 3, esp. pp. 35 ff.

in Cato an unfavourable opinion of Scipio, perhaps even active disapproval and dislike. If so, they were a significant prelude to the great dispute of the 180s which destroyed Scipio's public life and assisted Cato to the censorship. It is an attractive, even a probable hypothesis; but it is well to remember that it is conjecture only, conjecture for which Plutarch's story does not provide a reliable basis.

So far Cato's quaestorship has proved a disappointment. Plutarch, whose brief report is the only narrative account, has been found to be an insecure witness; the potential drama of the conjunction of two of the most remarkable yet contrasting personalities of the age remains without substance; above all there is no evidence of the oft supposed 'cultural clash' between the philhellene Africanus and a Cato reacting with revulsion against the proconsul's predilection for Greek manners and culture.

There is however one further item. At the end of his quaestorship Cato went from Africa to Sardinia (presumably on a mission on behalf of Scipio, though no reason is stated); from there he brought back to Rome and established in residence Quintus Ennius. Only the bare fact is reported, with a brevity as tantalizing as the scarcity and imprecision of information about the subsequent relationship. Ennius is termed a *familiaris* of Cato, whom his praises 'raised to the heavens'; and according to one late source Ennius gave Cato instruction in Greek literature.[8] Possibly the association came to an end after some years: Ennius devoted a special work to the praise of Africanus, and he certainly found a new patron in M. Fulvius Nobilior, whose martial achievements as consul in 189 were celebrated in the *Ambracia* and who was publicly criticized by Cato himself for taking the poet in his entourage on the campaign. Moreover it was not Cato but another Fulvius, probably a son of Nobilior,

---

[8] Nepos, *Cato* 1. 4, reports the basic fact; cf. 'Victor', *De vir. ill.* 47. 1, suffering from obvious oversimplification and perhaps guessing about the instruction in 'Greek letters'. Cic. *De sen.* 10 ('familiaris'); *Pro Arch.* 22 ('in caelum . . . tollitur'). In the view of Badian, 'Ennius and his Friends', *Ennius*, Fond. Hardt, *Entretiens* xvii. 151 ff., the tradition that Cato brought Ennius to Rome is a fiction. He points out that no explanation is given as to why Cato should have returned from Africa by so indirect a route as via Sardinia, suggests that since Cato later governed Sardinia the coincidence is suspicious, and argues that there is cumulative significance in Cicero's failure to mention the matter in three passages: *De sen.* 10; *Tusc.* 1. 3 f.; *Brut.* 57 ff. This argument from silence is the essence of the case. In the opinion of the present writer, however, none of these passages is such that if Cicero had known and believed the story his failure to mention it is remarkable; hence neither individually nor collectively do they constitute sufficient evidence to be set against the clear and explicit statement of Nepos. Cf. esp. the remarks of Jocelyn and Suerbaum in the discussion at the Fondation Hardt, op. cit., pp. 200 ff.

who obtained for Ennius his Roman citizenship.[9] A subsequent estrangement, however, does not alter the basic and significant facts that Cato assisted Ennius to settle in Rome and at least for a time maintained a personal association with him.

The arrival of Ennius in Rome, it has been said, was an event as momentous for the foundations of Roman poetry as had been the first production of a play by Livius Andronicus, a generation before.[10] For three decades, till his death in 169, Ennius was to produce a stream of compositions, mostly in verse, but of astonishing variety: tragedies, comedies, *fabulae praetextae* (plays with Roman themes), *saturae* (verse miscellanies), poems with subject-matter as diverse as philosophy, gastronomy, and Roman victories, and above all the eighteen books of the *Annals*. He effected striking advances in the literary exploitation of the Latin language, in style, in structure, in metre, and in subject-matter. Yet there was no chauvinistic preoccupation with what was distinctively Latin. Ennius was a Messapian, from Rudiae in Calabria, a district much influenced by Greek culture. He probably received a formal Greek education, and his familiarity with Greek, Oscan, and Latin led him to describe himself as a man with three hearts. He taught in Latin, but also in Greek; he wrote plays on Roman subjects, but also Latin versions of the Greek classics; he composed his monumental epic on the annals of Rome, but drew attention to his debt to Homer; he wrote to praise the Romans Scipio and Fulvius, but translated into Latin a philosophical work attributed to Epicharmus, a gastronomic poem by Archestratus, and even that extraordinarily imaginative exercise in mythological interpretation, the 'Sacred Writing' of Euhemerus. Ennius it was who discarded the native Saturnian metre and instead employed the Greek hexameter for a Roman epic; in so doing he exemplified and encouraged that characteristic readiness of Latin writers to draw directly and heavily on Greek literature without a trace of embarrassment, so that a literature which was distinctively Roman was almost invariably shot through with unmistakable Hellenic influences. This was the 'semigraecus', no youngster with unformed outlook but already thirty-five years of age, whom Cato brought from Sardinia and established in Rome—the

[9] Vahlen, *Ennianae poesis reliquiae*, pp. xii ff.; Warmington, *Remains of Old Latin* i, pp. xx f.; Jocelyn, 'The Poems of Quintus Ennius', in Temporini, *Aufstieg und Niedergang* i. 2, pp. 987 ff. Cato's criticism of Fulvius: Cic. *Tusc.* 1. 3. On Ennius' citizenship and the Fulvii see esp. Badian, op. cit., pp. 183 ff.

[10] Vahlen, op. cit., p. x. For what follows see esp. works cited in previous note; also Skutsch, *RE*, s.v. *Ennius*, no. 3.

earliest indication we have of Cato's relationship to the development of Roman culture.

After his quaestorship Cato is soon heard of again, in connection with a curious event in 202. The plebeian aediles of that year abdicated because they were *vitio creati*, in other words because there had been some procedural flaw in their election. This is remarkable enough in itself, in that only one other case seems to be recorded in which plebeian magistrates resigned for this reason; but in addition this resignation came only after the aediles had held office for eight months or more, long enough to have celebrated the Plebeian Games in November and to have dedicated three statues paid for from fines which they had imposed in the exercise of their duties. No explanation is recorded for the long delay. Presumably at the time of the election the *vitium* was either not alleged or was not accepted as such by the presiding magistrate; and possibly thereafter the two aediles long resisted the challenge to the validity of their position; if so a dispute may have rumbled on for many months.[11] In any event the episode looks suspiciously like a symptom of political struggle, of which there are at this time other signs including other electoral difficulties.[12] Cato, it appears, delivered a speech on the subject: two fragments are quoted from an oration entitled *De aedilibus vitio creatis*—undated, it is true, and with no mention of the circumstance, but beyond reasonable doubt to be assigned to this occasion.[13] Probably he was calling for the

---

[11] Livy, 30. 39. 8. An associated problem is that 'the dictator' is stated to have celebrated the *ludi Cerialia*, which fell in April and should have been conducted by the plebeian aediles; yet these aediles were still in office in November. It has been suggested that Livy's notice is confused, perhaps reversing the festivals celebrated by the aediles and the dictator; but such confusion would itself demand explanation, and in any case the data about fines and statues also suggest that these aediles were in office for a considerable time. Almost certainly the dictator concerned was not the one appointed in 203 but the one appointed late in 202 to conduct the elections. Since the elections were delayed the year ended without the appointment of new curule magistrates, and probably also without new plebeian aediles. Thus the *Cerialia* celebrated by the dictator were probably those of 201, not 202. See esp. Scullard, *Roman Politics*[2], pp. 80 f. and 278 f.; Kienast, p. 39 ff.; *MRR* i. 318 n. 1.

[12] Scullard, op. cit., pp. 79 ff.; Livy, 30. 39. 4 f.

[13] *ORF*[3], frs. 217 and 218. Fraccaro, *Opusc.* i. 161; Scullard, op. cit., p. 256; Kienast, pp. 39 ff. All three writers note that the subject of Cato's speech *De Laetorio*, *ORF*[3], fr. 108, could have been one of these aediles, L. Laetorius, and that the speech could even have been connected with the same episode; but there is no link other than the coincidence of name. Janzer, p. 45, and Malcovati, ad loc., tentatively assign the *De Laetorio* to Cato's censorship; see p. 82 n. 17. In connection with the *De aedilibus vitio creatis* Fraccaro and Scullard allude to the question of whether Cato was an augur, though both doubt that he was and Kienast, p. 41, concludes that he definitely was not; cf. *MRR* i. 457 and ii. 462. The central evidence is Cic. *De sen.* 64, where the reading *in vestro collegio* is almost certainly to be preferred to *nostro*. Cato's complaint of negligence by the augurs, Cic. *De divin.* 1. 28 = *HRR* i[2], Cato fr.

resignation of the aediles, but the few words which survive, warning that the excellence of the standing corn did not necessarily guarantee a plentiful supply of grain, are not irreconcilable with the opposite view: conceivably, though less probably, he meant that removal of the incumbent aediles might prove detrimental, whether because of a loss of efficiency or because the gods might be angered.[14] When so little is known nothing is to be gained by speculation on the character of the speech, the time and place of delivery, the audience addressed, the nature of Cato's concern— whether political, religious, or administrative—or the significance of the episode for his own standing and public career. One matter, however, does invite further comment: the fact that the text of this speech was known later in antiquity.

This is not necessarily the earliest of Cato's speeches to have survived, but it must have been among the earliest and is certainly the earliest which is attested as having done so. Thus around this time Cato started to keep records of at least some of his speeches, though probably copies did not pass into circulation until later. From previous generations there survived only a few funeral orations and one or two other speeches which may have been authentic, and those probably in family archives rather than as copies in circulation. In contrast a great number of Cato's speeches were 'published'. More than 150 were known to Cicero and nearly eighty titles are known today. Cato himself reproduced at least two of these speeches in his historical work, the *Origines*, though for sheer lack of evidence it remains uncertain whether he himself published any or all of the remainder. At the least, however, he preserved them, and when he began to do so he took an essential initial step in one of his own substantial—if in this case possibly unwitting—contributions to Roman cultural history; for he was paving the way for the emergence of the published speech as a major form of literature.[15]

Cato's aedileship—he was plebeian aedile in 199—has sometimes been suggested as the most appropriate setting for another speech, known only by a single fragment. The speech was an assertion of the principle that

---

132, is difficult though not impossible to reconcile with his own membership of the college. The fragment of an undated speech *De auguribus*, *ORF*[3], Cato fr. 220, and Cic. *De sen.* 38 give no help either way.

[14] Fr. 217: 'nunc ita aiunt, in segetibus, in herbis bona frumenta esse. nolite ibi nimiam spem habere. saepe audivi inter os atque offam multa intervenire posse; verumvero inter offam atque herbam, ibi vero longum intervallum est.' Fr. 218 is a single word only, 'neminisque'.

[15] See Ch. 7, esp. pp. 132, 134 ff., and 155 f.

the plebeian aediles enjoyed a sacrosanctity similar to that of the tribunes of the plebs, a principle which occasionally seems to have been challenged.[16] There is, however, no special evidence or circumstance to link the speech with this or any other particular year, nor is there any further indication of its content or argument. Of the aedileship itself it is known that Cato and his colleague, C. Helvius, found reason to repeat the Plebeian Games and to give further games in connection with the associated *Epulum Iovis*. Their efforts brought the reward they almost certainly envisaged. For a decade past tenure of the plebeian aedileship had almost guaranteed a subsequent praetorship, and increasingly in recent instances the praetorship had come in the year immediately following the aedileship. Both Cato and Helvius were among the four praetors elected for 198.[17]

For his year as praetor Cato was allotted the governorship of Sardinia, a province which included also Corsica, though the latter is not mentioned in the passages referring to his tenure of the post. The 2,000 Italian and Latin infantry and 200 cavalry which he took with him were to replace veteran troops due for discharge.[18] Presumably they constituted part of a garrison for the maintenance of order rather than a campaigning army, for although one late source asserts baldly that Cato 'subjugated' Sardinia, the province was not at this time a theatre of war. His troops are likely enough to have been put to some practical use in an island where long after this date the endemic brigandage and predatory raids of the hill peoples could not be suppressed by the Roman governors; but all that is known of Cato's activities concerns civilian administration, and this is probably a fair reflection of the general character of his governorship.[19] He organized the dispatch of substantial supplies of food and clothing for the Roman army then operating against the Macedonians in Greece. The activities of money-lenders were curtailed with a sharpness, perhaps even a harshness, which corresponds to other indications of his intense disapproval of usury, and usurers (that is presumably Roman or Italian usurers) were actually expelled from the island. Cato himself adopted an ostentatiously austere style of life, drastically reducing the demands made on the provin-

---

[16] *ORF³*, Cato fr. 219: 'aedilis plebis sacrosanctos esse'. Fraccaro, *Opusc.* i. 162 f.; Mommsen, *Röm. Staats.* ii³. 472 n. 2 and 486; Scullard, *Roman Politics²*, pp. 256 f., rightly stressing the uncertainty about the date.

[17] Livy, 32. 7. 13; cf. Nepos, *Cato* 1. 3; Sen. *Epist.* 86. 10.

[18] Livy, 32. 8. 5 ff. Afzelius, *Die röm. Kriegsmacht*, pp. 76 and 78, followed by Toynbee, *Hannibal's Legacy* ii. 133 n. 4 and 652, conjectures that the garrison of 5,000 allied troops sent to Sardinia in 200 (Livy, 31. 8. 9 f.) was maintained at that level in and beyond 198.

[19] 'Victor', *De vir. ill.* 47. 1 says 'in praetura Sardiniam subegit', but the silence of Livy and Plutarch is decisive against large-scale military activity. Nepos, *Cato* 1. 4 is not to be taken as a hint of such action. On Sardinian brigandage see Strabo, 5. 2. 7.

cials for the maintenance of the governor and his staff.[20] Plutarch appears to conjure up a startling and improbable vision when he says that as Cato made his circuit of the cities on foot he was followed by a single public servant carrying his clothing and bowl for sacrifices; but the point lies in the reference to a *public* servant, and the context is an emphatic assertion that in contrast with other governors Cato avoided virtually all expenses which would have been met out of public funds: 'he achieved an incredible contrast in economy'—a claim which, whatever the later embellishment in detail, may well have originated with Cato himself.[21] In any event no Roman praetor will have walked about Sardinia without a military escort, without lictors, and without at least a few personal servants of his own. For Plutarch this austere restraint in demands for maintenance indicates Cato's good-natured attitude towards the provincials, but he is at least as likely to have been motivated by a strong sense of propriety as by a spirit of leniency. Plutarch himself states that in the administration of justice and the enforcement of authority his undoubted integrity and uprightness ('sanctus et innocens' says Livy)[22] were combined with an inexorable rigour.

It is likely that during this period of his career Cato was involved with new legislation concerning *provocatio*—the procedure by which Roman citizens were able to appeal against the infliction of capital punishment or scourging at the behest of a magistrate. A *lex Valeria*, traditionally but questionably dated to the very foundation of the Republic, had laid down that no magistrate should inflict these penalties in face of the exercise of *provocatio*. During the second century B.C. this law was modified by three separate *leges Porciae*, the authors and dates of which are not known.[23]

---

[20] Livy, 33. 27. 2 ff.; Plut. *Cato Mai.* 6. 2 ff. On Cato and usury see further p. 54 and Appendix 5.

[21] Plut. loc. cit. Fraccaro, *Opusc.* i. 163 ff., thinks that at least the first part of Plutarch's account is derived from one of Cato's speeches. Cf. the similar sentiments in ORF³, Cato fr. 173, cf. 132.

[22] Livy, 32. 27. 3; cf. 'Victor', *De vir. ill.* 47. 1: 'praetor iustissimus'.

[23] Cic. *Rep.* 2. 54; *Rab. perd.* 8; *Verr.* 2. 5. 162 f.; *Pro Corn. ap.* Ascon. p. 78C; Livy, 10. 9. 4; Sall. *Cat.* 51. 21 f. and 40. There is much uncertainty and controversy about the fundamental nature, the practical mechanisms, and the legislative history of *provocatio*, including the *leges Porciae*. Recent opinion leans markedly towards the view that a law of 300 was the only authentic *lex Valeria de provocatione*, though *provocatio* itself was almost certainly more ancient than this. For recent discussions and surveys of earlier literature see esp. Bleicken, *RE*, s.v. *provocatio*, esp. cols. 2447 ff.; Martin, 'Die Provocation in der klassischen und späten Republik', *Hermes*, 98 (1970), 72 ff., esp. 87 ff.; Ruebel, *The Political Development of Cato Censorius*, pp. 133 ff.; Lintott, 'Provocatio', in Temporini (ed.), *Aufstieg und Niedergang* i. 2, pp. 226 ff., esp. 249 ff.; Bauman, 'The Lex Valeria de Provocatione of 300 B.C.', *Historia*, 22 (1973), 34 ff.

At least one of them was the work of a Porcius Laeca, as is indicated by coins issued by a member of that family;[24] and it is often supposed that Cato was the Porcius responsible for another. An obscure and possibly slightly corrupt fragment from a speech delivered (almost certainly) in 184 reveals Cato claiming that some action, or more probably he himself, had been of great benefit to 'the shoulders'—an obvious reference to legislation connected with scourging.[25] Such a claim, coupled with the fact of a relevant law named *Porcia*, does indeed suggest Cato's authorship. On the other hand, if so famous a person successfully promulgated important legislation in this field it is remarkable that no ancient source, not even Cicero, records the fact. Nor is it easy to see when Cato is likely to have done this: he did not hold the tribunate of the plebs; and although his praetorship and consulship are not demonstrably excluded enough is reported about his activities in the latter office to suggest that total silence concerning a *lex Porcia de provocatione* would be surprising, while praetorian legislation is distinctly uncommon. It is possible therefore that Cato was an active supporter of one of the *leges Porciae* rather than its originator,[26] in which case a likely proposer is P. Porcius Laeca as tribune of the plebs in 199; other possibilities are Laeca as praetor in 195 or L. Porcius Licinus as praetor in 193, and he too could have held a tribunate earlier in the 190s. Yet the uncertainty does not extend to the central fact that Cato, whether as advocate or as author, was ranged in support of a law designed to protect and strengthen the citizen's right to exercise *provocatio*; for the principal and perhaps the only provision of the law was the introduction of penalties for the violation of that right.[27] The slender evidence for Cato's involvement affords no indication of his motive, but in the general context of his career and actions this seems likely to have been not so much a direct

---

[24] Crawford, *Roman Republican Coinage* i, no. 301.

[25] ORF³, fr. 117: 'si em percussi, saepe incolumis abii; praeterea pro re publica, pro scapulis atque aerario multum rei publicae profuit.' The comment of Festus, p. 266L, confirms the obvious inference from 'pro scapulis', though the precise import of the fragment as a whole remains uncertain. Among emendations which have been proposed is the plausible *profui* for *profuit*. On the speech *si se M. Caelius . . .* see p. 86.

[26] So Kienast, pp. 90 f., against De Sanctis, *Storia*, iv. 1², pp. 516 f. and 566; Janzer, p. 49; McDonald, 'Rome and the Italian Confederation (200–186 B.C.)', *JRS* 34 (1944), 19; Scullard, *Roman Politics²*, p. 112 n. 4; Gelzer, *RE*, s.v. *Porcius*, no. 9, col. 111; Bleicken, *RE*, s.v. *provocatio*, col. 2448. Scullard, Gelzer, and others also attribute to Cato a *lex Porcia*, apparently *de sumptu provinciali*, mentioned in the *lex Antonia de Termessibus* (*ILS* 38; *c.* 68 B.C.). While this attribution is possible there is no sound reason for singling out Cato from among plenty of other possible Porcii.

[27] Cic. *Rep.* 2. 54: 'neque vero leges Porciae . . . quicquam praeter sanctionem attulerunt novi.' See esp. Lintott, op. cit., pp. 249 ff.; also Martin, op. cit., pp. 87 ff.

and sympathetic concern to champion the common people as a deep conviction that what was provided by law should be enforced and not flouted, that violation of laws and abuse of public powers should be checked and punished.[28]

Down to this time, indeed down to 195, the known public careers of Cato and of his patron L. Valerius Flaccus reveal no formal link; knowledge of their association is confined to the generalities mentioned in the previous chapter. Valerius had in fact enjoyed a career rather similar to that of Cato, though a year or two ahead of him at each step.[29] He may be the Valerius Flaccus mentioned as a military tribune in connection with a Roman victory in 212, but the first firm date is his curule aedileship in 201. His colleague, curiously enough, was Lucius Quinctius Flamininus, elder brother of that Titus Flamininus who was soon to outstrip and outshine Lucius himself. Seventeen years later Valerius as censor at the least acquiesced when Lucius Flamininus was expelled ignominiously from the Senate by Cato; but in 201 the two aediles seem to have worked together harmoniously and profitably. The *ludi Romani* were celebrated with magnificent and sumptuous dramatic entertainments, and occasion was found to repeat two days of the festival. To the proconsul Scipio went the credit of having sent a vast supply of grain, but it was the curule aediles who were seen to sell it to the populace at a very low price and whose scrupulous fairness in this operation won them great goodwill. As so often in this period, generosity in the aedileship brought its reward: both men became praetors in 199, the earliest possible date. In fact Valerius had probably further enhanced his reputation and prospects by service as a *legatus* in a successful military campaign in Cisalpine Gaul. Another indication of Valerius' high standing at this time is that immediately after his election to the praetorship his younger brother, Gaius, was elected to the curule aedileship for that same year, for Gaius' election was secured in the face of a formidable constitutional obstacle. As *flamen Dialis* Gaius was burdened for life with a number of inconvenient taboos and in particular was not permitted to take oaths, so could not take the oath which was a necessary preliminary to his assumption of the aedileship. The problem was resolved by an ingenious arrangement which enabled Lucius to take the oath on his behalf, but that was after his election; his success in the election itself, despite the obvious difficulty ahead, points not only to his own ambition and determination but to the popularity

---

[28] See pp. 326 ff.

[29] Evidence for his career collected in *RE*, s.v. *Valerius*, no. 173 and in *MRR* i under the years mentioned below.

and influence of Lucius.[30] Of Lucius' praetorship we know only the bare
fact that he governed Sicily. There is a brief mention that in 196 he was
elected to a priesthood, filling a vacancy in the college of *pontifices*.
Otherwise nothing more is heard of him or of Cato until their election
to the consulship of 195—the first specific event in which they are linked
together.[31]

Once again the sources offer nothing with which to answer obvious
and pertinent questions. They do not preserve the names of defeated
candidates in the consular elections; they give no hint as to whether either
consul played any part in debates prompted by growing fear and uncertainty as to the intentions of Antiochus III, whose sweeping successes
in Asia had been followed by the establishment of a European bridgehead
at Lysimacheia in the Thracian Chersonese; nor is either consul mentioned
in connection with the consequent decisions to take military action against
Nabis of Sparta and political action against the influence of Hannibal
in Carthage. The silence may correspond to the facts, but equally it may
be fortuitous. As it happens, Cato as consul is attested in only three
areas of activity.[32] The most substantial of these, his campaign in Spain,
will be examined in the next chapter. The least illuminating is the conduct
of the rite known as the *ver sacrum*, the 'sacred spring'. This was the
fulfilment of a vow made by order of the Senate and People in the critical
days after the disaster of Trasimene in 217 B.C. In a modified form of an
ancient Italic/Sabellian practice it had been vowed that if the Roman
people should be preserved in the wars with Carthage and the Gauls
all swine, sheep, goats, and cattle born in the spring of a year yet to be
designated would be sacrificed to Jupiter. The *pontifices* now decreed
that the time had come for the vow to be fulfilled, and the consuls of 195
were instructed to attend to this before departing for their respective
provinces.[33] Subsequently the Pontifex Maximus, P. Licinius Crassus
Dives, persuaded the *pontifices* and through them the Senate that there
had been a flaw in the procedure; in consequence the consuls of the next
year were instructed to repeat it. This has been interpreted as a subtle

[30] Livy, 31. 50. 6 ff. For Gaius' appointment as *flamen* in 209 and the consequent dispute
about his membership of the Senate see Livy, 27. 8. 4 ff., whence Val. Max. 6. 9. 3; also
Münzer, *RE*, s.v. *Valerius*, no. 166.

[31] Livy, 33, 42, 7. Numerous other references to their consulship in *MRR* i. 339.

[32] Cato's opposition to a proposed *lex Iunia* concerning usury has sometimes been
associated with this year, since a P. Iunius Brutus was one of the tribunes. More probably
this occurred a few years later; see pp. 54 f. and 321 ff.

[33] Livy, 33. 44. 1 ff.; Briscoe, Commentary on Livy, Books XXXI–XXXIII, ad loc. The
vow in 217: Livy, 22. 9. 10 ff.

political move to discredit Valerius and Cato, and that possibility cannot be excluded; but there is no obvious reason why Crassus, whose pontificate was marked by several episodes of this kind, should not have been genuinely concerned about a technical flaw in the procedure.[34] The original action in 195 certainly shows no more than the consuls of the year performing an entirely normal role as agents of the wishes of Senate and People.

The third area of activity does however show Cato taking a personal stand. Two tribunes, M. Fundanius and L. Valerius, chose this moment to propose the repeal of the *lex Oppia*. This law, introduced in 215 in the darkest days of the Second Punic War, had laid down that no woman should own more than half an ounce of gold, or wear a multi-coloured garment, or ride in an animal-drawn vehicle in the city or a town or within one mile thereof, except for certain religious purposes. The proposal to repeal this measure excited intense controversy; two other tribunes, Marcus and Publius Iunius Brutus, announced that they would use their veto; the city was thronged with the partisans of either side and, according to Livy's vivid account, the streets were packed with women appealing to men of every rank to remove the restrictions; many *nobiles* came forward to speak for or against the proposal; and among the opponents was the consul Cato. In the event the Bruti, besieged by even greater crowds of women, withdrew their threatened veto and the repeal was approved with overwhelming support.[35]

Livy takes this opportunity to present a pair of contrasting speeches, first Cato's and then a vigorous reply put into the mouth of the tribune L. Valerius. Neither speech is to be taken as an authentic version of what was actually said, or as a record of the arguments actually used; indeed in this instance it seems probable that the text of Cato's speech was entirely unknown to Livy and perhaps was not preserved at all.[36] Some have sought

[34] Livy, 34. 44. 1 ff. Earlier Crassus had clashed with Gaius Valerius, Lucius' brother, compelling him in 209 to become *flamen Dialis* and in the following year disputing his claim to membership of the Senate: Livy, 27. 8. 4 ff.; Val. Max. 6. 9. 3. But Crassus is also known for the exercise of his authority in matters of pontifical law in four other cases, including two which aroused much controversy: Livy, 28. 11. 6 f. (206); 31. 9. 5 ff. (200); 36. 2. 3 (191); 37. 51. 1 ff. (189); cf. also his observance in 205 of the obligation to remain in Italy, 28. 38. 12, and his lasting reputation as an expert in pontifical law: Livy, 30. 1. 6; Cic. *De sen.* 27 and 50.

[35] Livy, 34. 1–8; Zon. 9. 17; Val. Max. 9. 1. 3.

[36] No fragments or other traces of the speech are found in the grammarians and lexicographers, or elsewhere. Pais, 'L'orazione di Catone a favore della Lex Oppia', *Atti d. R. Acc. d. Arch. Lett. e B. Arti di Napoli*, 1 (1910), 123 ff., and Kienast, pp. 23 ff., argue that Livy's version is based upon an authentic speech, but most scholars have rightly taken the opposite view. See esp. Tränkle, *Cato in der vierten und fünften Dekade des Livius*, pp. 9 ff.; Fraccaro, 'Le fonti per il consolato', *Studi storici*, 3 (1910), 132 ff. = *Opusc.* i. 179 ff.; Scullard, *Roman Politics*[2], p. 257; Ruebel, *The Political Development of Cato Censorius*, pp. 60 ff.

to identify certain particular phrases and ideas as items which Livy might have found in other of Cato's speeches, but that is a hazardous procedure and affords no basis for a sound interpretation. Even the emphatic theme of the fear of a growth in luxury, coupled with determined opposition to any such growth, though no doubt introduced by Livy as a genuine element of characterization, does not take us far. It is a feature of Cato's outlook which is well enough attested by other words and actions, and it seems an obvious inference that it was a major reason for his wish to retain the *lex Oppia*. But when it comes to probing deeper into his apprehensions, to asking what consequences he feared from an increase in luxury, no answer is offered by Livy in this speech. Nevertheless, if the speech itself is a Livian composition and has little value as evidence, Cato's intervention in favour of retaining the *lex Oppia* is a fact of considerable interest. It shows that by this date his concern about the spread of luxury was serious and well established, not merely a topic for tart witticisms but sufficient to induce him to exploit his consular authority in a public stand in the face of great popular pressure; and it shows him seeking to use the sanction of law for a new and distinctive purpose. There is more than one strand in the history of Roman sumptuary legislation: some was certainly directed against practices akin to bribery; it was in response to a desperate military and financial crisis that the *lex Oppia* itself, the first in the series of sumptuary laws, placed restraints on private extravagance; corresponding traditional attitudes and prejudices there certainly were, finding expression from time to time in the *regimen morum* of the censors;[37] but the attempt to retain the *lex Oppia* when its original *raison d'être* was no longer relevant marks the beginning of another and perhaps the major strand. It introduced the concept of sumptuary law in its most direct sense: the legal restraint of expenditure on 'luxuries' as something desirable in itself, as a social rather than an economic measure, in the belief that such restraint could be achieved by explicit restrictions laid down in formal legislation. Cato was not necessarily personally responsible for the emergence of the concept, and he was certainly not alone in adopting it—as is witnessed by the two Bruti in 195 and by the subsequent enactment of various sumptuary laws;[38] but the direct intervention, unsuccessful though it was, of a consul who was also an exceptionally powerful personality and a forceful orator was an event of no small significance in the emergence of the concept

[37] Kübler, *RE*, s.v. *sumptus*; Lintott, 'Imperial Expansion and Moral Decline in the Roman Republic', *Historia*, 21 (1972), 631 f.; cf. Mommsen, *Röm. Staats.* ii³. 375 ff.
[38] See further pp. 93 f.

as an important element in Roman social attitudes. At the least it showed that Cato himself regarded legal restriction as a suitable means of giving expression to the views revealed later in his actions as censor and in many of his utterances; probably it was more than that, the first step towards the acceptance of sumptuary legislation half a generation later. None of this answers the crucial question as to why Cato wanted restrictions of this kind, what consequences he feared in the absence of such restraints; but that will be more appropriately discussed in another context.[39] For the moment the discussion must return to Cato's consulship.

[39] Ch. 5, esp. pp. 94 ff.

3

The Consul in Spain

THE year of his consulship was the only occasion on which Cato commanded an army in active warfare. Though he had had troops under his command when he was praetor in Sardinia in 198, there was no serious fighting;[1] and after his consulship he never again held an independent command. That is no adverse reflection on his achievement or ability. In the second century B.C. underemployment of military talent and a rapid turnover of generals were constant failings of the Roman Republic, products of idiosyncrasies in the constitutional mechanisms and the structure of public life; in particular re-election to the consulship was not permitted within the space of ten years.[2] Indeed, Cato might easily have been deprived, not by decision but by luck, of this one opportunity in 195; for just as in 198 it had been the drawing of lots which had assigned him to essentially civilian tasks in Sardinia, so now it was the lot which sent him to Spain instead of to Cisalpine Gaul, where his colleague L. Valerius Flaccus had to be content with minor operations, insufficient to earn him a triumph.[3]

By good fortune there is in Livy a remarkably full account of Cato's operations. This account, which has close linguistic and factual correspondences with fragments of Cato's speech 'Concerning his consulship', *De consulatu suo*, is unquestionably derived in the main from Cato's own writings, possibly from that same speech, more probably from his historical work, the *Origines*. The result is not only more detailed but patently more authentic than the conventional literary battle-pieces which Livy

[1] 'Victor', *De vir. ill.* 47. 1 says 'Sardiniam subegit', but this must be a misunderstanding; the silence of Livy and Plutarch is decisive. Livy, 32. 8. 6 ff. reports replacements for the garrison troops but no other military details. Nepos, *Cato* 1. 4, is not evidence of military activity.

[2] Astin, *Lex Annalis*, p. 19 n. 6.

[3] Sortition: Livy, 33. 43. 2 and 5; Nepos, *Cato* 2. 1; Plut. *Cato Mai.* 10. 1. Valerius' campaign: Livy, 34. 22. 1 ff.; 34. 42. 2; 34. 46. 1; cf. Orosius, 4. 20. 15. Münzer, *RE*, s.v. *Valerius*, no. 173, col. 18, rightly suspects that the casualties inflicted in the two victories ascribed to him have been greatly exaggerated, since, unlike his three predecessors, he was not awarded a triumph. Livy says explicitly that for the most part the province was undisturbed.

so often offers to his readers—though for obvious reasons the highly favourable judgements on Cato's activities must be examined with some caution: Cato was certainly not one to disparage his own achievements, as Livy himself observes. Plutarch, in another context, puts it less elegantly but more bluntly: always unstinting in praise of himself.[4]

Modern critics have not always thought highly of Cato's performance.[5] His initial victory, which led to the submission of rebel tribes north of the Ebro, has been rated as no more than a successful tactical exercise, presenting no real difficulty or danger to two well-trained and properly led legions, against a horde of barbarians inferior in tactics and in number and frequently defeated by the Romans in the past; a battle which, despite a complexity of tactical movements, was by no means as remarkable, either in itself or as an example of a battle of manœuvre, as Cato's own account would seem to have implied. His subsequent actions in the south have been judged cautious and undistinguished, marked by lack of initiative (despite the unusual size of the forces at his disposal), by inability to quell the rebellious Turdetani or to deprive them of the support of an army of Celtiberian mercenaries, and by a failure to capture the Celtiberian stronghold of Segontia (Siguenza), and perhaps by another failure at Numantia. An adverse critic might be tempted to add that extensive new rebellions north of the Ebro suggest a lack of caution in embarking on the southern campaign, for which the north was apparently stripped of Roman troops within weeks of the conquest; certainly it has not passed without comment that yet further rebellions broke out as soon as Cato left Spain. Nevertheless, so disparaging an assessment considerably under-rates many aspects of Cato's achievement: the formidable nature of the

---

[4] Livy, 34. 15. 9; Plut. Cato Mai. 14. 2. Livy's account: 34. 8. 4–21. 8; see Appendix 2. The speech De consulatu suo: ORF³, Cato frs. 21–55; on the date and probable circumstances of its composition see below, p. 60. The versions of Appian, Iber. 39 ff. and Zon. 9. 17 are shorter and cruder but not in serious contradiction with Livy, and they preserve a few additional details. Plutarch's material in Cato Mai. 10 consists almost entirely of anecdotes. Comparatively little is added by the numerous other references to the campaign, many of which are collected by Schulten in Fontes Hispaniae Antiquae iii. 177 ff. For discussions of the campaign as a whole see esp. Götzfried, Annalen der röm. Provinzen beider Spanien, pp. 50 ff.; Fraccaro, 'Le fonti per il consolato', Studi storici, 3 (1910), 129 ff. = Opusc. i. 177 ff. (with an additional excursus); Schulten, Numantia i. 322 ff.; id., Gesch. der Numantia, pp. 29 f.; De Sanctis, Storia iv. 1², pp. 447 ff.; Gelzer, RE, s.v. Porcius, no. 9, cols. 112 ff.; Marmorale, Cato Maior², pp. 54 ff.; Della Corte, Catone censore², pp. 28 ff.; Kienast, pp. 43 ff.; Schlag, Regnum in Senatu, pp. 31 ff.; Tränkle, Cato in der vierten und fünften Dekade des Livius, pp. 16 ff. It has not been possible to consult Del Pozzo, Il console M. Porcio Catone in Spagna nel 195 a.C.

[5] See esp. De Sanctis and Schlag, locc. citt., and Scullard, Roman Politics², p. 110. Kienast, loc. cit., offers a more favourable estimate.

task confronting him, his success in the training and leadership of troops, his tactical expertise, the justification which can be found for his strategic moves, and the total effect of his campaign.

In the first place, his actions and achievement must be judged in relation to the considerable difficulty of large-scale military operations in the Iberian peninsula, especially offensive operations aimed at conquest and subjugation.[6] Over much of this huge area terrain and climate create formidable problems for the maintenance and movement of large field armies and considerable dangers to troops dispersed in garrisons—not to mention the virtually impossible demands in manpower required for effective garrisoning. Conversely, conditions are eminently suited to guerrilla warfare, in which the Spaniards proved themselves highly skilled, and the suppression of which, as the modern world has come to recognize, is often a long and costly business. Politically the Spaniards lacked elaborate and centralized direction; but this had advantages as well as disadvantages, for while the Romans could exploit tribal dissensions and rivalries, their victories in the field and the capture of particular strongholds (and Spain was dotted with hundreds, indeed thousands of hill-forts and strongholds) could rarely be truly decisive or give effective political control of large areas.[7] Nor does the lack of political cohesion mean that the Spanish tribes were mere barbarian hordes, incapable of matching the tactics and equipment of the Italian invaders. They did not have the elaborate military organization of the Romans, but for a generation they had fought as their allies and auxiliaries; their weaponry was as good, if not better; their cavalry was effective and more numerous; and over the years not a few Roman armies suffered massive defeats at their hands. Nor did the Romans necessarily enjoy obviously superior morale and determination.

The Romans had gone to Spain in the first place in order to drive out the Carthaginians, and they had remained in order to keep them out. Even when Carthage had been decisively defeated and, almost simultaneously, there arose prospects of new commitments in the East, it is

---

[6] On this and on what follows see esp. Bell, 'Tactical Reform in the Roman Republican Army', *Historia*, 14 (1965), 404 ff., esp. 410 ff. On weapons see also Schulten, *RE*, s.v. *pilum*. To Bell's arguments for his main contention, that the cohort was used as a tactical unit, at least in Spain, long before the Marian reforms, add *ORF*³, Cato fr. 35, from the account of the Spanish campaign in the *De consulatu suo*: 'interea unamquamque turmam manipulum cohortem temptabam quid facere possent.'

[7] In the long run the contrast was plainly to the advantage of the Romans. While the Spaniards could be conquered piecemeal, strong unitary political organization enabled the Romans to draw constantly upon their reservoir of manpower and to maintain substantial armies in the field over long periods. Cf. Strabo, 3. 4. 5.

improbable that they ever seriously considered abandoning the areas which had come under their control. Spain had played too dramatic a part in the strategy of the Hannibalic war; an involvement of seventeen years' duration was already too close in spirit to permanent acquisition; and Rome had begun to exploit for herself and no doubt to depend upon the resources which had become available to her.[8] Not surprisingly, peoples who had fought alongside the Romans in order to liberate themselves from the Carthaginians quickly became restive under this new domination. 'He had greater difficulty in subduing the enemy', says Livy, 'than those who had first gone to Spain, because the Spaniards defected to the latter through weariness with Carthaginian rule, but he had to claim them back into servitude from the liberty which they had acquired.'[9] Granted that this assessment, probably stemming from Cato himself, is unlikely to be an understatement of his difficulties, none the less in general terms the point is plausible enough. To suggest that because of past defeats the morale of Cato's opponents was poor and that they were lacking in confidence would be to misread the probabilities of a situation in which grim determination might more reasonably be expected. And in any case the balance of success prior to Cato's arrival lay overwhelmingly with the Spaniards.

The great rebellion broke out in 197. M. Helvius, praetor in Hispania Ulterior, sent word of a massive rising, apparently at first centred on the middle Baetis valley but expected to spread rapidly throughout Baeturia and Turdetania, even to some of the coastal cities.[10] Indeed, before the year was out it had spread also to Citerior, where the proconsul C. Sempronius Tuditanus was severely defeated with heavy losses and himself died of wounds received in the battle.[11] The praetors assigned to Spain for the

[8] References collected in *ESAR* i. 127 ff., and iii. 126 ff.

[9] Livy, 34. 18. 1 f.

[10] Livy, 33. 19. 7 and 21. 6 ff. Sumner, 'Proconsuls and *Provinciae* in Spain, 218/7–196/5 B.C.', *Arethusa*, 3 (1970), 85 ff., esp. 92 ff., argues that despite references in Livy to the separate provinces of Ulterior and Citerior the appointments in 197 and 196 continued to be to two army commands without this territorial designation. Although this would be an explanation for certain problems in Livy's reports, these problems are not such as to justify rejection of his explicit evidence that provision was made for this division with effect from 197 (32. 28. 2 and 11; cf. 32. 27. 6 f.) and his subsequent frequent references to Ulterior and Citerior. On the other hand, although the praetors of 197 had been instructed to determine the boundary it is quite likely that circumstances prevented them from completing the task, and that military exigencies sometimes led commanders to ignore the demarcation.

[11] Livy, 33. 25. 8 f. Sumner, op. cit. pp. 93 f., suggests that Sempronius' defeat may have occurred in southern Spain, in the region where Helvius reported the revolt; but there is no positive reason to suppose this and it is beyond doubt that a serious situation did develop in the north.

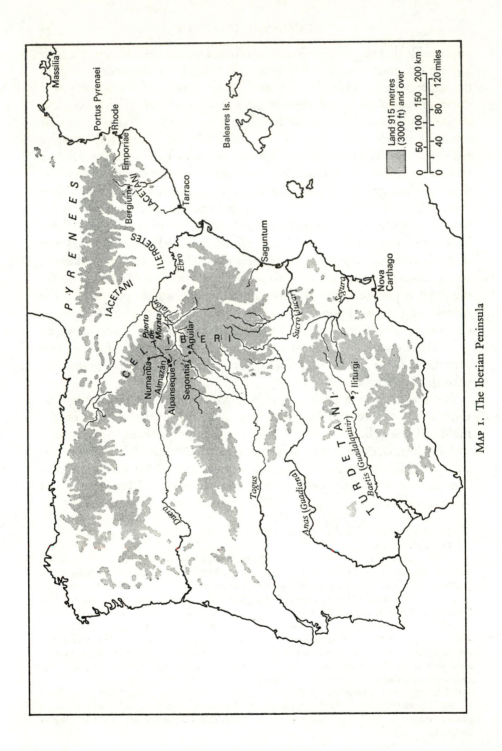

MAP 1. The Iberian Peninsula

following year, Q. Fabius Buteo and Q. Minucius Thermus, were given additional forces and ordered to depart immediately for their provinces;[12] but by the later part of 196 (the beginning of the new consular year in March according to the Roman calendar, which at this time was several months in advance of the seasons)[13] the gravity of the situation impelled the Senate to make exceptional arrangements which, incidentally, show that by now the danger seemed even greater in Citerior than in Ulterior. One of the new consuls was to take command in Citerior with a full consular army of two legions supported by 15,000 allied troops, 800 cavalry, and twenty-five warships. Further reinforcements were decreed for the two armies already in Spain, and in addition to the praetor sent to Ulterior another praetor was appointed to Citerior as assistant to the consul but with command of the existing praetorian army.[14] This highly unorthodox arrangement, by which a praetor was assigned as a direct subordinate of a consul in the one *provincia*, almost in the manner of a *legatus*, highlights not only the alarm with which the situation was viewed but also one of the major features of the strategic situation. The Romans might wish to treat their Spanish territories as two provinces, but one of these, Citerior, was in reality a comparatively narrow coastal strip some 450 miles long. This enormous front, which might reasonably be regarded as being on exterior lines, was effectively split into two major sectors by

[12] Livy, 33. 26. 1 and 3 f. Fabius, here assigned to Ulterior, is not mentioned again, but Minucius, here and in 33. 43. 8 assigned to Citerior, is later (34. 10. 5 f.) said to have been the successor of Helvius, i.e. in Ulterior. The latter is usually assumed to be an error, though De Sanctis, *Storia* iv. 1², p. 432, believes Ulterior to be correct and Sumner, op. cit., pp. 94 ff., argues that Minucius did succeed Helvius in his command, though the territorial division was not specified. According to Livy, 34. 17. 1, the command of Minucius' army was later taken over by Manlius, who in 195 was assigned to Citerior with Cato; and this is differentiated from the army of Ap. Claudius from Ulterior. There is a possibility that Turda (or Turba), the scene of Minucius' victory, was in Ulterior (Livy, 33. 44. 5 f.; see below) but that is by no means certain and in any case in the circumstances it would not necessarily be a decisive argument. Schulten, *RE*, s.v. *Turba*, is convinced that it was in Citerior.

[13] The solar eclipse of 14 Mar. 190 (by the extrapolated Julian calendar) is reported by Livy, 37. 4. 4, to have occurred on 11 Quinctilis; thus the Ides of March on which the consuls of '190' entered office actually fell on 18 Nov. 191 (Julian). In 196/195 the discrepancy, though presumably not identical, must have been similar, so Cato and Valerius entered office in the later part of 196. Beloch, 'Die röm. Kalender von 218–168', *Klio*, 15 (1918), 382 ff., wrongly attempted to discredit this and similar synchronisms. See esp. De Sanctis, *Storia* iv. 1², pp. 358 f.; Holleaux, 'Le consul Fulvius', *BCH* 54 (1930), 1 ff. = *Études d'épigraphie* v. 249 ff. Two recent studies of the Roman calendar in this period: Marchetti, 'La marche du calendrier romain de 203 à 190', *L'Antiquité classique*, 42 (1973), 473 ff.; Derow, 'The Roman Calendar, 190–168 B.C.', *Phoenix*, 27 (1973), 345 ff.

[14] Livy, 33. 43. 1–8. These special arrangements tell more heavily than Schlag allows against her suggestion, *Regnum in Senatu*, pp. 33 f., that the impression of a great war in the north is misleading, created by Cato's own exaggerations.

the great Celtiberian mountain ranges; and in 196 the Romans were hard pressed in both sectors. In the north the peoples of the Ebro valley had won sweeping successes, the Romans apparently retained control only of a number of coastal towns, and the few inland allies who remained loyal were under the severest pressure. The extent of the rebellion in the south is not documented but the rebels probably had close contact with others further west in Ulterior, and it was certainly necessary for the Romans to safeguard the vital areas of the Jucar valley and Carthago Nova. The peculiar arrangements for Citerior in 195 may therefore be seen as a recognition of the strategic realities. It was evidently after these decisions had been taken that news came of a substantial victory won by Q. Minucius Thermus, at a town called Turda (or Turba) in the southern sector. Livy asserts that in consequence there was less fear about Spain, where a huge war had been expected, and that all concern was now centred on Antiochus, but this may be his own interpretation and at best a half-truth.[15] As subsequent events demonstrate, the crisis in Spain was far from over and no changes were made in the allocation of forces. Hence, while the praetor Ap. Claudius Nero was assigned to Ulterior the fortune of the lot destined Cato for Citerior with the praetor P. Manlius as his subordinate.

Cato did not set out for his province for some months. In the interval he and Flaccus conducted the *ver sacrum*, and presumably also the Latin festival, and he involved himself in the controversy surrounding the repeal of the *lex Oppia*; but these were not the true causes of the delay. The preparations for the assembling and especially the marine transportation of an army of more than 25,000 men must necessarily have taken some time; and Cato could not possibly have hazarded this force at sea until the recognized sailing season opened in the spring. Even so there is a hint that he was subsequently alleged to have been dilatory, since in a fragment of his speech *De consulatu suo*, 'Concerning his consulship', delivered some years later, he claims with suspicious emphasis to have received the highest praise because he had been able to make ready so

---

[15] Livy, 33. 44. 4 f. There is uncertainty and disagreement as to whether the site of Minucius' victory was named Turda or Turba, whether or not it is to be identified with the Turta mentioned by Cato in *ORF*[3], frs. 40 and 41, and whether it was in Citerior, near Saguntum, or in Ulterior. The question is complicated by the disagreement as to whether Minucius was assigned to Citerior or Ulterior (see above), and also by the belief of some scholars that the Turdetani against whom Cato later campaigned were not those of the Baetis valley but a tribe of the same name living near Saguntum (see p. 41 n. 32). See esp. Schulten, *RE*, s.v. *Turba*, no. 1; McDonald, edition of Livy, xxxi–xxxv (O.C.T. vol. 5), ad loc.

many ships, so great an army, and so many supplies as would have been thought beyond the capabilities of anyone, and 'because I made those preparations so very rapidly'.[16] In fact it seems to have been during April (i.e. by the Julian calendar) and more probably in the first half of the month, that the expedition assembled at Luna, north of Pisa. No one can now judge whether a slightly earlier date would have been possible in the prevailing circumstances, but the possible margin cannot have been large.[17]

When the expedition left Luna Cato announced a date for a rendezvous at Portus Pyrenaei, which beyond reasonable doubt is the modern Port-Vendres (a choice which suggests that he was well informed about the situation which would face him); but the rendezvous was probably intended only for stragglers since the bulk of the fleet evidently sailed together, perhaps making rather slow progress at first but assisted by favourable winds once past Massilia.[18] When it had re-formed at Port-Vendres it moved on into Spanish waters, into the gulf of Rosas. It paused to expel a Spanish garrison from Rhode (Rosas), but its real destination was Emporiae (Ampurias) where, probably in middle or late May, the entire expedition disembarked, significantly only a few miles south of the Pyrenees, at the very gateway to Spain. Although the small Greek section of this double town was loyal and served as a temporary base for Cato, the larger Spanish section was evidently at least sympathetic to the rebels.[19] Far inland the Ilergetes were still loyal but under extreme pressure and quite unable to provide help; on the contrary, soon after his arrival Cato received a deputation from their king desperately pleading for military assistance and insisting that if it were not given immediately they would be compelled to join the rebels. Cato did not dare divide his forces but in order to prevent the defection had to organize an elaborate deception to make the Ilergetes believe that he was doing so. No doubt also a number of other coastal towns, such as perhaps Tarraco, were still in Roman hands; but to all intents and purposes the rebels controlled the entire territory between the Ebro and the Pyrenees.

After a short pause at Emporiae while he assessed the situation Cato moved his troops away from the town, which obviously could not have

---

[16] *ORF*³, Cato fr. 28. For the speech see also p. 60.   [17] See Appendix 3.

[18] Livy, 34. 8. 4 ff.; *ORF*³, Cato frs. 29–30. For the principal sources for Cato's campaign see p. 29 n. 4. The account which follows is necessarily derived mainly from Livy, 34. 8–21, and references to this and lesser sources are given only on special points. On Portus Pyrenaei see Jannory, *RE*, s.v. *Portus Veneris*, no. 1, esp. cols. 415 f.

[19] Almagro, *Las fuentes escritas*, esp. pp. 49–60, discusses the topography of Emporiae in relation to the data in Livy, 34. 9. 1 ff. and other sources. See also Hübner, *RE*, s.v. *Emporiae*.

accommodated such a large force for any length of time. Already a
Spanish army, almost certainly larger than his own,[20] was in the field to
oppose him, but he was far from ready for a major encounter. The terrain
and the conditions, the enemy's strength and military methods were all
still unfamiliar; though it is possible (but by no means certain) that many
of Cato's troops had seen recent service in Cisalpine Gaul, there were many
raw recruits among them; and Cato himself clearly regarded his army
as insufficiently experienced and felt a need to familiarize himself with the
capabilities of the various units. He therefore moved carefully for some
time, skilfully avoiding large-scale actions, constructing a number of
camps, and at length establishing a strong permanent camp to serve as
a base a few miles from Emporiae; and throughout this period an extensive
training programme was undertaken.[21] One aspect of this was stern
discipline: an anecdote records an instance of calculated public severity
which apparently had occurred earlier, during the voyage to Spain.[22]
But most of our information is concerned with more positive steps.
Whether or not considerations of principle underlay Cato's ostentatious
personal austerity—he used few personal servants and drank the same
coarse wine as the ships' rowers—he can hardly have been unaware of the
salutary impression it was likely to make on the troops.[23] Similarly when
he began by dismissing the Roman corn contractors with the bold assertion
that 'the war would nourish itself' from the grain then on the threshing-
floors of the Spaniards he may have been motivated as much by a desire
to inspire confidence in his men as by concern for the Roman treasury.[24]

[20] De Sanctis, Storia iv. 1[2], p. 435 supposes the Spaniards to have been numerically
inferior. This is a priori improbable, though no trust can be placed in Appian's figure of
40,000 (Iber. 40) which is probably connected with the 40,000 casualties reported by Valerius
Antias, whereas in the version followed by Livy, 34. 15. 9, Cato himself mentioned no
specific number of casualties.

[21] Livy, 34. 9. 12 f. and 13. 2 f.; ORF[3], Cato fr. 35; cf. 66. Afzelius, Die röm. Kriegsmacht,
p. 36, indicates uncertainty as to whether Cato was assigned two new legions or two which
had been enrolled previously. In view of Livy's silence about a levy at 33. 43. 3 f. he assumes
the latter and further supposes them to have been two raised in 198 and used in Cisalpine
Gaul. On the other hand Livy, 34. 13. 3, 'exercebat ea res novos milites', shows that Cato's
troops included a considerable number of inexperienced recruits. Cato's forces at Emporiae
did not include the seasoned troops already in Spain; these were placed under the command
of Manlius and, in Ulterior, of Claudius: Livy, 34. 17. 1. Cf. De Sanctis, Storia iv. 1[2], p. 434,
who takes Cato's legions to have been newly recruited. On the castra hiberna see Appendix 3.

[22] Frontin. Strat. 4. 1. 33. Note also Cato's views on punishment for theft, reported in
Frontin. Strat. 4. 1. 16, probably from the De re militari.

[23] Livy, 34. 18. 3 ff.; Plut. Cato Mai. 4. 4; 10. 6; Inst. Traian. 6; Val. Max. 4. 3. 11; Pliny,
Nat. hist. 14. 91; Frontin. Strat. 4. 3. 1; 'Plut.' Apophth. Cat. Mai. 27; Apuleius, Apol. 17 =
ORF[3], Cato fr. 51; cf. App. Iber. 39; Cassiod. Var. 9. 25. 10 = Trogus, fr. 16L.

[24] Livy, 34. 9. 12.

Drill and training had begun immediately upon disembarkation, and were assuredly rigorous ('he said that he had no use for the soldier who plied his hands on the march and his feet in battle and whose snore was louder than his battle-cry');[25] and now Cato undertook a series of forays and raids, skirmishing, plundering, and burning crops: 'Meanwhile I was testing the capabilities of each squadron, maniple, and cohort in turn; in light engagements I was observing the quality of each man; if anyone had performed especially well I rewarded him fairly, so that others should wish to do the same, and before the assembled troops I praised him profusely.'[26] The activities, then, served various purposes: training, raising morale, harrying the enemy, keeping him in a prolonged state of expectancy, and thoroughly reconnoitring the field of operations.

The effectiveness of Cato's methods was shown in the army's performance when, after this comparatively short interlude, he did take the initiative and force a major battle; and it was particularly evident in the difficult manœuvres with which he began. About 20,000 men marched by night in good order to the far side of the enemy's camp, and by dawn were deployed in the chosen position. The execution of such a manœuvre is notoriously difficult, involving serious risks of confusion and mistiming; simple errors can all too easily leave units exposed to assaults when they are in disarray or on unfavourable ground. Success implies thorough reconnaissance, together with a high degree of efficiency in organization and discipline. Indeed, some words of Livy's suggest that Cato's programme had specifically included training in night marches.[27]

According to Livy Cato chose his position in order to leave his troops, cut off from the sea by the enemy encampment, with no hope of survival except in victory. Although this may be no more than the introduction by Livy of a stock dramatic theme it is also possible that it has a more respectable origin, going back to Cato himself. Just possibly he may have made the point to his troops before the battle, and in any case it is likely enough to have appeared in *post eventum* accounts, as a *de facto* consequence of the manœuvre if not as its declared motive.[28] But clearly such a motive

[25] Plut. *Cato Mai.* 9. 5; 'Plut.' *Apophth. Cat. Mai.* 7. On Cato's belief in the efficacy of the battle-cry see also Plut. *Cato Mai.* 1. 8; *Coriol.* 8. 3; 'Plut.' *Apophth. Cat. Mai.* 23.

[26] *ORF*³, Cato fr. 35.

[27] Livy, 34. 13. 3. For the number of troops likely to have been deployed see Appendix 4, p. 314, though the present point would not be seriously affected even if there were several thousand fewer.

[28] Livy, 34. 14. 3 f. and 16. 1; a slightly different and probably distorted version in App. *Iber.* 40. The sources for the battle itself are Livy, 34. 14–16 and App. *Iber.* 40; cf. *ORF*³, Cato frs. 36–8. On topographical considerations and some possible sites for the battle see Appendix 4.

is insufficient in itself to account for so complex and risky an operation; and more solid military advantages may be discerned. Cato had cut himself off from the coast, but he had also blocked the enemy's line of retreat, precluding an orderly withdrawal or avoidance of a pitched battle; and if the enemy were defeated their flight would be in the direction of the coast so that they would have little hope of escape in substantial numbers and little chance of effectively regrouping in territory where it might be difficult or dangerous for the Romans to follow. Plainly Cato was determined to force a major engagement in which he could make full use of his concentrated field army, and to make the battle as decisive as possible. In addition he selected a favourable tactical position; and it is not at all surprising that the most favourable location, and conversely the enemy's most vulnerable side, was to be found on the side away from the Roman camp.

By marching at night Cato was able to occupy his chosen ground unhampered by the enemy; he was also exploiting the element of surprise, since he could reasonably hope that his unexpected appearance would cause the battle preparations of the Spaniards to be hasty and unsystematic.[29] At dawn three cohorts were immediately sent forward close to the enemy camp, no doubt partly to enhance the consternation and confusion, but especially to exploit it. For the principal function of these cohorts was to simulate flight and thereby induce the enemy to hasten out in pursuit. This too was necessarily a difficult manœuvre, demanding high morale and good discipline if it was not to lead to dangerous consequences. The stratagem was successful, the enemy poured out into the open ground between their camp and the Roman line, and Cato launched his cavalry on both wings. His intention was to exploit the supposed confusion and prevent the Spaniards from forming an effective line against his infantry, whom he held back for the time being. But it seems that the Spanish deployment was more efficient and rapid than he had anticipated. On the left the Roman cavalry had moderate success, certainly containing the enemy (and it was undoubtedly important to contain their cavalry), but not enough to cause confusion or to prevent the Spaniards forming a line; those on the right were repulsed in disorder by the Spanish cavalry. This reverse in turn induced panic in some of the Roman infantry on that flank—possibly their own cavalry were driven back on them, and they

---

[29] To create surprise it was not essential for the Roman march to have been totally undetected. The Spaniards almost certainly heard the Romans on the move during the night, but Cato's previous night marches (Livy 34. 13. 3) had probably accustomed them to this and made it easier to achieve surprise on this occasion in respect of his objective and deployment.

were now exposed to harassment by enemy cavalry. Cato was obliged to intervene personally to avert a rout. At the same time he initiated a counter move, sending two cohorts on his left on a flanking march to threaten the Spanish right from the rear. (It is an interesting comment on the composition of the Roman army that a movement of this kind should have been undertaken by infantry.) Such a movement by 1,000 or so detached infantry presupposes that the assault by the Roman cavalry on that flank had achieved sufficient success to cover their march. By developing this threat to the Spaniards' rear Cato sought both to divert them from exploiting their own success on their left and to cause uneasiness and distraction in the infantry line; and for this latter reason he wished the two cohorts to be seen in the rear before the infantry clashed.

The infantry equipment of both sides included javelin-type missiles, the Roman *pila* perhaps having been in part modelled on the corresponding Spanish weapons. Cato's successful occupation of the ground of his choice—presumably facing down a slope—must have given the Romans some protection and advantage in the exchange of missiles which constituted the first part of the infantry battle. One purpose in holding back the Roman infantry was certainly to retain this advantage, whereas a premature charge could have been seriously disrupted by the missiles. When the missiles were exhausted hand-to-hand fighting began, though it is not known whether it was the Romans or the Spaniards who first attacked the others' line; what is clear is that at this stage both lines held. But this was a situation for which Cato was prepared. Despite the difficulties on his right flank and the dispatch of the two cohorts to his left he had managed to keep very substantial forces in reserve—at least the whole of his second legion and three other cohorts. The legion was still held back, but fresh troops, very probably these three cohorts, possibly led by Cato in person, were now thrown in massed formation against the enemy line and crashed through at the first assault.[30] With their line disrupted and menaced by the two cohorts closing in from the rear, the Spaniards broke and fled to their camp.

A final stage was yet to come. If Cato's victory was to be as decisive and as politically effective as he wished, the destruction of the enemy forces needed to be complete, and therefore their camp, which they were

---

[30] Reserve cohorts are mentioned both by Livy, 34. 15. 1, and by Appian, *Iber.* 40, who mentions three. On Appian's use of the word τάξεις see Bell, 'Tactical Reform', *Historia*, 14 (1965), 406 f., who notes that this could have been the rear line of a legion in *triplex acies*. Appian also says that Cato led the assault in person, which is plausible, though there are touches of dramatic exaggeration in his account, such as that the battle lasted all day and the pursuit all night.

not yet too demoralized to defend, had to be taken. The Roman forces which had been engaged in the battle carried their pursuit to the walls but were unable to break in; presumably they were physically weary and by this time the units would have lost cohesion in the pursuit. But Cato still had in reserve his entire second legion, apparently deliberately held back so that a fresh and co-ordinated force should be available for just this situation. It was marched at quick step but in strict formation towards the camp and was directed to assault the left gateway, which was comparatively thinly defended; it may be inferred that the other defenders, preoccupied with the repulse of the attacks already in progress, either failed to notice the seriousness of the new danger or felt unable to spare men to reinforce the threatened sector. The garrison at the gate was unable to withstand the attack, and there followed the inevitable panic and grim massacre. The men of the second legion cut down the Spaniards as they struggled to escape from their own camp, which was already being plundered by the rest of the victors.

Cato followed up his victory without delay, demonstrating its decisiveness and driving home the lesson of how vulnerable the Spaniards were in the wake of their defeat. Within a few hours the Roman army, now able to range widely and freely, was plundering the countryside. Spanish Emporiae and some neighbouring peoples immediately surrendered, together with numerous individuals from other states who had taken refuge in Emporiae after the battle. Cato's treatment of them was calculated to show that quick submission would bring safety. Those survivors of the battle who had fled to Emporiae were fed and then sent off to their homes. Still making the most of his opportunity Cato at once began a march through the hostile areas. As the Roman army advanced, city after city— or tribe after tribe—hastened to surrender; the rebel alliance crumbled and collapsed, until by the time Cato reached Tarraco he could claim that the entire area north of the Ebro had submitted to him.

While Cato was conquering the north there were developments in the south. M. Helvius, praetor in Ulterior in 197, who had been detained in his province by illness, was now recovered and with an escort of 6,000 men supplied by Ap. Claudius Nero marched across country to the area held by Cato, where he embarked for Rome. On his march, near the town of Iliturgi, he met and defeated a large force of Celtiberi and captured Iliturgi itself.[31] Also in the south the two praetors P. Manlius and Ap. Claudius

---

[31] Schulten, 'Iliturgi', *Hermes*, 63 (1928), 288 ff., and *Fontes Hispaniae Antiquae* iii. 181, cf. 80 f., argues that the town captured by Helvius was not the well-known Iliturgi in Ulterior but another of the same name in Citerior, probably Ildum, north of Saguntum. Vallejo,

Nero had combined their forces in a campaign against the rebel Turdetani (probably to be understood as including the Turduli of eastern Ulterior) over whom they won a victory. But despite these successes the war was not going well for the Romans; for, so far from submitting, the rebels had procured the assistance of 10,000 Celtiberian mercenaries. Claudius, who is not mentioned again, may have returned to the western part of his province, perhaps when he was rejoined by the troops who had escorted Helvius; but Manlius found himself under severe pressure from the reinforced rebels and was obliged to appeal to Cato for help.[32]

Cato's response was to commit his entire army to a southern campaign, thus stripping of troops the area he had only just conquered. At first sight he appears to have been guilty of a major error of judgement, not to say reprehensible complacency, since inevitably there were rebellions. It is more reasonable, however, to suppose that although he recognized the dangers of his action he considered it to be the imperative response demanded by the gravity of the situation in the south, as reported to him. (It is virtually certain that he afterwards depicted the purpose of his march as 'to save' Manlius and his troops.[33]) Supposing that to have been his assessment, it is impossible to be sure that it was correct, but at least there is no ground for supposing it to have been unreasonable. Admittedly at the end of the campaign Cato did divide his forces and was able to restore

'Cuestiones hispánicas', *Emerita*, 11 (1943), 142 ff., shows that Schulten's case is not beyond question but offers little positive argument for the alternative.

[32] The Turdetani lived in the Baetis (Guadalquivir) valley, in Ulterior. Some scholars, sceptical as to whether Cato went so far, have taken his opponents to have been a more northerly tribe, supposedly of the same name, living near Saguntum; and it is certainly possible to make a plausible reconstruction of Cato's movements on this basis. On the other hand the evidence for the supposed northern Turdetani is slender and rests mainly on what may be an erroneous transcription by Livy at 21. 6. 1; it is doubtful whether they existed at all. Moreover if Cato was engaged with the well-known Turdetani of Ulterior, although the distances he covered would have been considerable, this would accord with other evidence. Most specifically, the Baetis is expressly mentioned in the anecdote in 'Plut.' *Apophth. Cat. Mai.* 24, which clearly refers to the episode in the campaign against the Turdetani reported in Livy, 34. 19. 3 ff. Also the rebellion reported by Helvius in 197 had been in an adjacent area of the Baetis valley; and Manlius, whom Cato was aiding, had conducted his operations against the Turdetani in co-operation with Ap. Claudius, praetor in Ulterior, which would most naturally be taken to imply that they were against the familiar southern Turdetani. There is an associated question regarding Turda (or Turba), the scene of Minucius Thermus' victory, and whether or not this is identical with the Turta mentioned by Cato in *ORF*[3], frs. 40 and 41 (above, p. 34 n. 15). For a useful review of opinions see Fraccaro, *Opusc.* i. 224 n. 12; also Schulten, *RE*, s.v. *Turdetaner* and *Turduler*; Vallejo, 'Cuestiones hispánicas', *Emerita*, 11 (1943), 153 ff.

[33] *ORF*[3], Cato fr. 40, quoted below.

order in the north with a much depleted army, but it is certainly arguable that at the beginning such a division would have been unwise, indeed rash, courting defeat in both sectors. In fact the sequence of events shows that he was both aware of and concerned about the risks inherent in his decision, and that he took what steps he could to minimize defections in the north. A premature report of his departure brought about the rebellion of seven groups of the Bergistani, a remote mountain tribe. They quickly capitulated in face of Cato's swift reaction, but no sooner had he returned to Tarraco than they rebelled again. This time the entire population was sold into slavery: deterrence by stern example replaced the previous policy of conciliation. Cato then attempted a general confiscation of arms. However, as was to be demonstrated repeatedly in the following decades, the right to bear arms was of central importance to the self-esteem of many Spaniards. Where the ruling was enforced many warriors preferred suicide to life without arms; thus there was a danger that this move would be self-defeating and actually provoke rebellion. Cato summoned the leading men of every community to a conference on the problem. Whether he really expected these people themselves to suggest effective ways of forestalling rebellion it is impossible to say; it is tempting to suppose that in reality they became hostages for the fulfilment of his demand that all the towns north of the Ebro should destroy their walls. This operation was carefully planned and skilfully executed:

For he sent letters in all directions with orders that they should be delivered to everybody on the same day; and in these he commanded the people to raze their walls immediately, threatening the disobedient with death. The officials upon reading the letters thought in each case that the message had been written to them alone, and without taking time for deliberation they all threw down their walls.

Success was almost total. The few recalcitrants were quickly coerced; one city only, Segestica, said to have been important and wealthy, had to be taken by storm.[34]

[34] The second rebellion of the Bergistani has sometimes been taken to be either a doublet of the first or identical with the rebellion which occurred after Cato's southern campaign. This has led some to conclude that the razing of city walls also occurred after the southern campaign. See Appendix 2, pp. 304 ff. The affair of the city walls was a popular anecdote: Livy, 34. 17. 5 ff.; 'Victor', De vir. ill. 47. 2; Frontin. Strat. 1. 1. 1; App. Iber. 41; Zon. 9. 17. 5 f. (whose version is quoted in the text); Polyaen. 8. 17; Plut. Cato Mai. 10. 3 = Polyb. 19. 1 (this last referring to the Baetis in error for the Ebro). Only Livy has the full context of the attempt at general disarmament and the conference, though Zonaras mentions disarmament and Polyaenus hostages.

'And so I next set out to Turta [probably = Turdetania] to save them.'[35] The route and precise destination are unknown,[36] but it was a long march, scarcely less than 300 miles. The junction with Manlius was effected, he and his troops were extricated from their difficulty, and Cato found himself at the head of an unusually large army. He has been severely criticized for his caution in this situation and for his failure to employ these troops, their morale high after the victory at Emporiae, in a vigorous offensive (a Hannibal or a Caesar would have known how to use such forces and such opportunities, it is asserted);[37] but the criticism seems ill founded. In the short time available—the campaigning season must already have been well advanced[38]—a few marches and raids, the capture of a few towns or hill-forts would scarcely have changed the basic situation, and would only have prolonged to little purpose Cato's undesirable absence from the north. It is clear that the enemy were established in strong defensive positions, inaccessible or hazardous to a Roman assault, and from which they refused to be drawn out into a set-piece battle; yet only if Cato could bring about such a battle could he hope to make decisive use of his huge field army. Successful skirmishing with the Turdetanian outposts there may have been, but it had little practical effect; and he did not have the time for a long period of waiting or manœuvre. Recognizing that his best hope of significantly changing the situation would be to deprive the Turdetanians of their Celtiberian mercenaries, he made approaches to the Celtiberians. He first sought to induce them to change sides, offering them twice the amount they were receiving from the Turdetanians. When his officers expressed indignant disapproval he replied that if they were victorious they would pay out of the enemy's resources, not

---

[35] *ORF*[3], Cato fr. 40: 'itaque porro in Turtam proficiscor servatum illos.'

[36] Livy, 40. 39. 2, mentions in connection with a campaign in 180 a *saltus Manlianus*, which clearly has to do with a key pass on the main line of advance into Celtiberia. Schulten, *RE*, s.v. *Manlianus saltus*, holds that this probably was the Puerto de Morata, where the Jalón river breaks through the mountains to the north-east of Celtiberia; which is plausible, though there seems to be no other evidence. However, in that article and elsewhere Schulten repeatedly indicates his belief that the name was derived from P. Manlius in 195, and therefore that Manlius, and he assumes also Cato, marched south by way of the Jalón valley. This argument has no force. In the first place, as De Sanctis, *Storia* iv. 1[2], p. 437 n. 153, rightly observes, the name could have been derived from L. Manlius Acidinus, who was in Citerior from 188 to 186 and in 186 fought in Celtiberia. In the second place the use of the Jalón route southwards by either Manlius or Cato seems improbable, since it was almost certainly less direct and more difficult than the coastal route; and to reach it Manlius would have had to pass through extensive territories not yet reconquered by Cato.

[37] De Sanctis, *Storia* iv. 1[2], p. 438. He assumes that Ap. Claudius and his army remained with Cato and therefore possibly overestimates the forces at Cato's disposal.

[38] Appendix 3, p. 310.

their own, and if they were defeated there would be no one either to ask or to be asked for the payments.[39] As an alternative he offered to let the Celtiberi return home without interference, undertaking that it would not be held against them that they had been allied to enemies of Rome. On the other hand, 'if they wished to become enemies they could easily do so now',[40] and in that case they should nominate a day and a place on which they would engage in armed combat with him—a challenge which seems something of a forlorn and wistful hope. The Celtiberians asked for time to consider the proposals, which the Turdetani naturally pressed them to reject. According to Livy (from Cato?) there were such divisions of opinion that they were unable to give an answer; but since that meant that they stayed where they were, and Cato could not afford to wait indefinitely, this scarcely differed from a delayed refusal. Cato led off a number of light-armed cohorts to plunder, probably in a further attempt to draw the enemy out. Then he marched against Segontia—almost certainly Siguenza, commanding a major route through the Celtiberian mountains—because he was informed that the mercenaries had left their possessions and equipment there; but the mercenaries still refused to be drawn (a reminder, it may be observed, of their good discipline and morale).

This move against Segontia is usually held to have resulted in a considerable reverse, not only because it did not achieve the desired reaction by the mercenaries but also on the ground that despite the massive forces at his disposal Cato failed to capture the town. This may be so, but there is reason to be cautious since the facts are not at all clearly established. All the positive information about the episode is contained in a single sentence of Livy's: 'When the consul was unable to draw the enemy out to battle, he first led a force of several light-armed cohorts to plunder in the fields of a region not previously attacked, and then, having heard that all the baggage and equipment of the Celtiberi had been left at Segontia, he led them there to attack it.'[41] Although Livy, adapting and polishing his material, could have distorted details it is worth noting precisely what he does and does not say, particularly on three points. First, Livy's words clearly mean that the force led against Segontia consisted of the limited number of light-armed cohorts ('aliquot expeditas

---

[39] Plut. *Cato Mai.* 10. 1 f.; 'Plut.' *Apophth. Cat. Mai.* 24; cf. Frontin. *Strat.* 4. 7. 35. For the episode as a whole, Livy, 34. 19. 2 ff.; Zon. 9. 17. 7.

[40] *ORF*[3], Cato fr. 42.

[41] Livy, 34. 19. 9 f.: 'Consul ubi hostes ad pugnam elicere nequit, primum praedatum sub signis aliquot expeditas cohortes in agrum integrae regionis ducit, deinde audito Seguntiae Celtiberum omnes sarcinas impedimentaque relicta, eo pergit ducere ad oppugnandum.'

cohortes') which had just been used on the plundering march[42]—and this is a very different matter from attacking the town with a consular army. Second, Livy's brief mention of the march to Segontia—'eo pergit ducere ad oppugnandum'—is not incompatible with the possibility that the town was not actually assaulted. It would be entirely comprehensible if Cato, with only limited forces, had decided against an assault once it had become clear that the mercenaries were not going to attempt to come to the defence. But third, supposing it to have been attacked, Livy does not say that it was not captured. Since the passage is centred entirely on the question of whether the mercenaries could be enticed into battle it says nothing specific about the fate of Segontia itself; silence need not mean Roman failure. Indeed an indication to the contrary might be seen in an anecdote, recorded in the *Strategemata* of Frontinus, which it is tempting to associate with this march:

Marcus Cato, when in Spain, saw that he could gain possession of a certain town, if only he could assault the enemy when they were off their guard. Accordingly, having in two days accomplished a four days' march through rough and barren districts, he overpowered the enemy, who were fearing no such thing. Then, when his victorious men asked the reason for so easy a success, he told them that they had won the victory as soon as they had accomplished the four days' march in two.[43]

The aptness of the anecdote to the march on Segontia is evident, especially if it was undertaken by light-armed cohorts, though the identification can never be more than an attractive hypothesis. In view of this, and of the contrary possibility that Cato did not actually attempt an assault, it would be rash to conclude that Cato experienced a humiliating reverse at Segontia.

Since the Celtiberian mercenaries held firm it was obvious that there could be no quick solution. Faced with this stalemate Cato left the greater part of his army with Manlius, paid all the troops, and set off back to the Ebro with only seven cohorts. It may have been at this stage that he went to Numantia, at which his presence is attested only by the title of a speech of exhortation which he addressed to his cavalry.[44] If so, he evidently crossed the watershed between the area of Segontia and the

---

[42] It is tempting to connect this point with the small size of the strongly built camp at Aguilar, some 20 km east of Siguenza, which is much too small for a consular army and which Schulten, *Numantia* iv. 191 ff., is strongly inclined to associate with Cato; but though the form of the camp is of an early type its precise date cannot be determined.

[43] Frontin. *Strat.* 3. 1. 2.   [44] *ORF*[3], Cato fr. 17, from Gell. 16. 1. 1.

Duero valley, proceeding along this at least as far as Numantia, until he crossed over again towards the Ebro; and it has been held that remains of a Roman camp at Alpanseque, mid-way between Siguenza and Almazán, and of two camps at Renieblas near Numantia are to be associated with this march.[45] Reasons for the selection of this circuitous route could perhaps be found in a last effort to tempt the Celtiberian mercenaries to return home, and in the wish not to expose his small force to possible ambush, for example in the Puerto de Morata, where the river Jalón breaks through the mountains towards the Ebro. But although this has often been confidently accepted as Cato's route, it is not really certain that he returned to the Ebro this way rather than by the Jalón valley or even, since he may have rejoined Manlius well to the south or east, by the coastal route.[46] The visit to Numantia could equally well have been an unrecorded extension of the earlier activity at Segontia rather than part of the march back to the Ebro. In any event there is no justification for supposing that Cato—with only seven cohorts and some cavalry!—was so unwise as to attempt to capture Numantia and thereby met with a further reverse.

Despite the small size of his force Cato had further successes in the north. In part this was the re-establishment of control in some of the previously conquered areas, where his absence in the south had opened the way for some restlessness; but it is also possible that some of the tribes which now went over to the Romans had not been within the

---

[45] Schulten, *Numantia* iv. 33 ff. and 196 ff. Though superficially attractive the association with Cato is neither established nor free from difficulty. Schulten is too ready to exclude the possibility that the camps could have been constructed by other commanders between Cato and Fulvius Nobilior (in 153; almost certainly responsible for camp III at Renieblas); the argument from silence about operations in this area is weak. Also the camp at Alpanseque is exceptionally small (4·7 hectares, compared with 12·4 at Aguilar, 12·5 at Renieblas (I), and the 40 to 60 required for a consular army) and it evidently contained some stone buildings, which is surprising if it was essentially a stage on the route from Siguenza to Numantia. Schulten unconvincingly supposes that at Renieblas Cato transferred from a stone winter camp (I) to a summer camp (II). One of these, probably I, may well be Cato's, in which case he certainly delayed some time in the vicinity; but that is not proof that with such slender forces he actually attempted to capture Numantia. Moreover though Renieblas, 6 km from Numantia, is an excellent and much used base for operations in the area, it is not a convenient base for a direct assault.

[46] Livy, 34. 20. 1 ff., names several tribes with which Cato had dealings after his return north. Fatás Cabeza, 'Sobre Suessetanos y Sedetanos', *AEA*, 44 (1971), 109 ff., argues that several of these are to be identified with peoples living in the area of the upper Ebro, near or north of Saragossa, and links this with Cato's return by one of the inland routes. Supposing these identifications to be correct, however, it is still possible that he returned by the coastal route and then moved up the Ebro, especially as one of the tribes named, the Ausetani, did live nearer the coast: Hübner, *RE*, s.v. *Ausetani*.

scope of the earlier operations.[47] In any event there is little doubt that inter-tribal disputes were a significant factor in this, encouraging some tribes to turn to the Romans in the hope of protection and support against their rivals, a situation which Cato was not slow to exploit. Supplementing his own force with contingents from the 'allies', and in particular from the Suessetani, one of two large tribes which had ostentatiously proclaimed or returned to their allegiance, he proceeded to deal rapidly with their more successful rivals and persecutors, the Iacetani or Lacetani, 'a remote and forest-dwelling people'. He captured their principal fortress (at the expense of mostly Suessitanian casualties, possibly deliberately and cynically conserving his own men)[48] and moved on to Bergium, where many raiders had taken refuge. Here he was able to secure the support of a discontented group within the town, who by seizing the citadel as the Romans assaulted the walls facilitated his victory and secured immunity for themselves from the severe penalties inflicted on the rest of the population. With that, his last recorded military action as consul, Cato seems to have re-established control in the north. After completing administrative arrangements for the exploitation of highly profitable iron and silver mines in the area he was succeeded in his command and set off for Rome, to celebrate a triumph.[49]

Cato boasted that he had captured more towns than he had spent days in Spain.[50] His reports on the campaign were greeted with three days of public thanksgiving, followed, on his return to Rome, by the award of a triumph.[51] It is more than likely that an uninhibited exposition of his own successes helped to induce the Senate's astonishing decision to disband

[47] There is uncertainty and disagreement about both the names and the locations of several peoples mentioned in Livy, 34. 20, especially 'Sedetani' or 'Edetani' and 'Iacetani' or 'Lacetani', and possibly 'Suessetani' or 'Cessetani'. Fatás Cabeza, op. cit., pp. 109 ff., argues plausibly for the first in each instance. Cf Schulten, *RE*, s.v. *Iaca, Lacetaner,* and *Suessetaner*; Hübner, *RE*, s.v. *Cessetani* and *Edetani*.

[48] The subjection of the Lacetani mentioned in Plut. *Cato Mai.* 11. 2 is almost certainly a different and later episode (on which see pp. 51 f.) involving the tribe of that name in Catalonia, which is an additional reason for regarding the people mentioned in Livy, 34. 20. 2 ff. as different. A tribe living well north of Saragossa would fit well with Livy's description of the latter.

[49] Livy, 34. 21. 7 f. Cato mentioned these mines, among other notable features of the area, in the fifth book of his *Origines*: *HRR* i², fr. 93. On their exploitation, probably through publicani, see esp. Badian, *Publicans and Sinners*, pp. 32 f. For his departure, including the affair of the Lacetani mentioned in Plut. *Cato Mai.* 11. 2, and victory celebrations see below, pp. 51 ff.

[50] Plut. *Cato Mai.* 10. 3; 'Plut.' *Apophth. Cat. Mai.* 25.

[51] Livy, 34. 21. 8, 42. 1 and 46. 2. Refs. to triumph in *MRR* i. 344, to which add Vell. 2. 128. 2; Seneca, *Epist.* 87. 10. *ORF*³, *Cato* fr. 19 is a brief fragment from the speech *ad populum de triumpho*: 'asperrimo atque arduissimo aditu'.

his army, a decision the error of which was glaringly exposed by the rebellions which flared up after his departure.[52] Cato may well have overestimated the thoroughness of the conquest and underestimated the resilience of the Spaniards; but miscalculations of that kind are peripheral to the real issues in assessing his military capacity. A century and a half later none other than Julius Caesar made a similar miscalculation in Gaul, yet few would deny his brilliance as a general. More pertinent questions are whether, in the given circumstances, with the given resources, and in the time available more could have been expected from Cato; whether errors were committed; whether the operations were conducted efficiently and skilfully; whether the tasks performed demanded more than routine competence or presented no serious difficulty to the side with major initial advantages, provided only that common sense was exercised; and whether the operations did have important and lasting effects.

Unquestionably there were certain respects in which the Romans had the advantage over the Spaniards, notably in their strict discipline and in the elaborate military organization which gave them both cohesion and flexibility. But these advantages gave no automatic guarantee of success; they did not save Tuditanus in 197, nor yet many another Roman commander over the next sixty years. Only if such advantages were exploited skilfully and to the full could the Romans hope to defeat their Spanish opponents, who, as has been seen, themselves enjoyed certain advantages. The known events of the operations around Emporiae permit no reasonable doubt that Cato did indeed exploit his advantages to the full and that he showed uncommon efficiency and skill in a situation where a mistake could easily have had serious consequences. As for the southern operations, it has been argued earlier in this chapter that there is no reason to question the soundness of Cato's decisions and movements, and that there is little evidence for the reverses which some suppose him to have suffered. Even if these reverses did occur, they were minor and incidental to the main operations. It is true that Cato failed either to entice the enemy into a set-piece battle or to detach the Celtiberians from their alliance with the Turdetani, but the time available was so short that it is difficult to see what more could have been done. Moreover, the primary purpose of these operations was to rescue Manlius from an exposed and dangerous situation. That objective was attained, and attained without excessive set-backs elsewhere. And when Cato returned to the north he accomplished a great deal with a very small force. Finally, though the total achievement of the campaign may have been exaggerated

[52] Livy, 35. 1. 1.

by Cato himself, it was none the less considerable. When Cato arrived the rebels had won sweeping successes and the Roman position was, to say the least, difficult. This was especially so in the north, where the Ilergetes were in imminent danger of being forced to abandon their alliance with Rome, and where Rome's effective positions had been reduced to a few toe-holds on the coast. When he departed the rebellion had been contained in the south and virtually extinguished in the north; huge areas had been brought back under control or subjugated for the first time; and though new rebellions were to flare up, some of them almost immediately, the Roman position was never again so seriously threatened and the hold on the territories conquered by Cato was never in serious danger of being loosened.

Later generations readily accepted that Cato was an outstanding general: in a succession of writers from Cicero to Fronto he is repeatedly characterized by such phrases as 'summus imperator' and 'optimus imperator'.[53] Yet the truth is that although military affairs undoubtedly bulked large in his career and in his thoughts, for only a single year in his long life was he in command of an army engaged in active warfare. The military distinction won in earlier years had probably contributed substantially to his rise to the highest offices; but that distinction was won not as a commander but as a daring fighter and an able junior officer. A few years after his consulship he was to lead a difficult and successful outflanking operation at Thermopylae, which he did not hesitate to claim as decisive in the defeat of Antiochus;[54] but again this was the exploit not of the commander of an army but of a bold, competent subordinate carrying out his commander's orders with efficiency and initiative. Of course it is highly unlikely that Cicero and his successors troubled themselves with such precise considerations or with a critical assessment of evidence. Their references to Cato as a great general are probably based upon a bare knowledge of his victories and triumph, his authorship of a military handbook—the first written in Latin[55]—and the self-evaluations to be found in his own writings. Even so, the actual facts of the campaign of 195—the only truly relevant evidence—suggest that, with due allowance for a degree of overstatement, there is considerable justification for these ancient designations. A single campaign, in a single season, is not sufficient to establish a man as one of the really great

[53] See esp. Cic. De orat. 3. 135; Rep. 2. 1; Brut. 65; 294; Nepos, Cato 3. 1; Livy, 39. 40. 6; Seneca, Epist. 87. 10; Pliny, Nat. hist. 7. 100; Quintil. Inst. 12. 11. 23; Fronto, Ad V. Imp. 2. 1. 20 = Haines ii. 150.

[54] Below, pp. 57 ff.   [55] Below, p. 184.

commanders, to rank him with a Scipio Africanus or a Caesar. Cato lacked opportunity, and therefore historians lack evidence to determine whether his talents were of that order. But the challenge of Spain was far from negligible, and was met with competence, skill, sound judgement, and conspicuous success. There is no good reason to suppose that his performance could have been bettered, or to doubt that he possessed very considerable expertise and ability in military matters.

4

From Consul to Censor

1. Return from Spain

THE public thanksgivings for Cato's victories were probably not without an accompanying note of discord. Two writers, Nepos and Plutarch, allege that Scipio Africanus, who had been elected consul for 194, attempted to force Cato to leave Spain as soon as possible because he himself wished to succeed to the command. In further details their accounts diverge, Nepos stating that the Senate rejected Scipio's proposal, Plutarch that Scipio did succeed Cato, that he complained about Cato's execution of some Roman deserters, and that he failed to persuade the Senate to change any of the arrangements which Cato had made.[1] These accounts are unquestionably in error, since Africanus did not go to Spain and almost certainly did not seek to go: his ambitions were now directed towards the East rather than the West and towards a possible war with the Seleucid king, Antiochus the Great.[2] It is possible that Africanus put forward some proposal which would have affected Cato's position or the arrangements he had made, or which Cato later asserted to have been directed against himself; but more probably there has been confusion with Africanus' cousin and near-homonym, P. Cornelius Scipio Nasica, praetor in 194, who was assigned Further Spain and therefore was one of Cato's successors. With that correction Plutarch's account, though not entirely free of difficulties, makes reasonable sense:

While Cato was still in Spain Scipio the Great, who was hostile to him and wished to take Spanish affairs out of his hands, contrived to have himself appointed as his successor in that province. Then he set out as quickly as possible and brought Cato's command to an end. But Cato, who had taken five cohorts of legionaries and 500 cavalry as an escort, subdued the tribe of the Lacetani and put to death 600 deserters who were handed over to him. When Scipio

---

[1] Nepos, *Cato* 2. 2; Plut. *Cato Mai.* 11. 1 f.

[2] Livy, 34. 43. 3 ff.: Scipio argued that one of the consuls of 194 should be assigned to Macedonia to prepare for war against Antiochus. Cf. McDonald, 'Scipio Africanus and Roman Politics', *JRS* 28 (1938), 156 f.; Scullard, *Roman Politics*², pp. 116 ff. Ruebel, *The Political Development of Cato Censorius*, pp. 71 ff., accepts Nepos' version.

was enraged at these actions Cato ironically said that Rome would be at her greatest when the famous and great did not yield the prizes of virtue to the men of lower rank, and when those of humble origin, like himself, vied in virtue with their superiors in birth and fame. However, since the Senate voted that none of Cato's arrangements should be modified or changed, Scipio's term of office detracted more from his own glory than from that of Cato, and was spent vainly in inactivity and idleness.[3]

The nub of the accusation Scipio is said to have made is that Cato had abused his position because his action against the Lacetani and the deserters was taken after he had been succeeded; while on the other side the passage not only records a scornful riposte to the charge but implies a complaint about the manner in which Scipio had hastened to take over, castigating his motives both for that haste and for an effort to persuade the Senate to change Cato's administrative arrangements. Although it is unlikely that these mutual recriminations were entirely the product of pure invention by later generations, there can be no knowing how far they correspond to what actually happened in 194, and whether they were first exchanged in the immediate aftermath of Cato's departure or in the course of later rivalries and disputes—for Cato and Nasica were twice to stand as rival candidates for the censorship. Probably there was a quarrel in 194, but whatever form it took it was by no means the dominant feature of Cato's return to Rome.

Cato returned to celebrate a triumph, granted in public recognition of substantial victories and a highly successful period of command. Of his triumphal speech to the people only one brief fragment remains. He must have given an account of his achievements, and the solitary fragment, emphasizing the extreme physical difficulties which had to be overcome in some operation, is in keeping with the self-laudation which is to be expected.[4] Probably a first airing was given also to at least some of those boasts about his personal conduct which are in the main preserved as isolated sayings or comments: that he was content to have the same food and wine as the rowers on the voyage and as his own slaves, that he used kid skins as coverlets, spent only 500 asses on his personal expenses, had with him only five personal slaves, and at the end left his horse in Spain

---

[3] Plut. loc. cit. Note that Cato's jibe would have had an added significance in relation to Nasica, who when the Mater Idaea was brought from Asia to Rome in 204 had been chosen to receive the goddess on the ground that he was the best and noblest man in Rome. For Nasica's career see Münzer, *RE*, s.v. *Cornelius*, no. 350, cols. 1494 ff.

[4] *ORF*[3], Cato fr. 19: 'asperrimo atque arduissimo aditu'. Triumph: Livy, 34. 46. 2; for other refs., *MRR* i. 344, and Vell. 2. 128. 2 and Sen. *Epist.* 87. 10.

to save the state the cost of bringing it back.[5] Particularly striking are his claims about the distribution of booty: that he himself had taken nothing from the enemy's country but his food and drink, that so rigorously and so scrupulously had he abstained from all personal enrichment that one of his slaves who had rashly bought three captives at the auction hanged himself rather than face Cato's wrath; that he had never divided any spoils among a few friends and thereby 'snatched them away from those who had captured them', and that 'it was better for many Romans to go home with silver in their possession than a few with gold.'[6] It is a subject on which his views remained strong and consistent, for it figured in at least four speeches later in his career[7]—evidence enough of his confidence that his claims about his own conduct were beyond reasonable challenge. His actions in 194 certainly seem to conform to those claims. He did retain some *manubiae*, to provide for the erection of a shrine to Victoria Virgo, vowed during the Spanish campaign,[8] and no doubt much went into the state treasury; but in addition to much booty already distributed in Spain each soldier was given at the triumph a donative of a pound of silver, or, to use Livy's more precise formulation, 270 asses, and according to custom threefold for each cavalryman.[9] In so far as figures are recorded for other donatives in the immediately preceding period this is quite exceptional. It had been surpassed only at Africanus' triumph over Carthage, when the rate was 400 asses per man, the next best was 120, and the remainder less than a third of the amount given by Cato; even Titus Flamininus, triumphing from Macedonia shortly after Cato's celebration, distributed only 250 asses per man.[10] No doubt Cato's generosity was made possible by the very large amount of booty which he brought home, perhaps including proceeds from the mines, but it seems more than likely that it was facilitated also by the restraint which as a matter of principle he deliberately imposed upon

---

[5] Plut. *Cato Mai.* 4. 4; 5. 7; 10. 6; *Inst. Traian.* 6; Frontin. *Strat.* 4. 3. 1; Pliny, *Nat. hist.* 14. 91; Val. Max. 4. 3. 11; Apul. *Apol.* 17 = *ORF*³, Cato fr. 51; cf. Livy, 34. 18. 3 ff.; App. *Iber.* 39; Cassiod. *Var.* 9. 25. 10.

[6] Plut. *Cato Mai.* 10. 4 ff.; *ORF*³, Cato fr. 173; 'Plut.' *Apophth. Cat. Mai.* 26; 27. On the rules and conventions which applied to booty see Schatzman, 'The Roman General's Authority over Booty', *Historia*, 21 (1972), 177 ff.

[7] *ORF*³, Cato frs. 98; 173; 203; 224–6. Schatzman, loc. cit., argues also that Cato attempted to secure the passage of legislation on the matter, but this is an uncertain inference from the fragments. It is at least as likely that the speeches dealt with particular cases rather than proposals for general legislation.   [8] Livy, 35. 9. 6.

[9] Livy, 34. 46. 2 f.; Plut. *Cato Mai.* 4. The omission of any mention of centurions, who usually received a double share, is presumably accidental.

[10] There is a convenient collection of data in *ESAR* i. 127 ff.

himself and his officers. It certainly helped to mark out his triumph as distinctive and to secure his newly won position as one of the outstanding men in the state.

2. From 194 to 191

Consulship and triumph did not set the bounds either to Cato's ambition or to his progress. In the next few years the tide of success carried him forward, and several times brought him to public notice. Probably he went off almost immediately to serve as *legatus* to Ti. Sempronius Longus in his successful campaigns against the Boii and Ligurians in 194–193.[11] Since Cato's elder son was born a year or two later (almost certainly 192 or 191), it was probably about this time that he married Licinia. Said to be 'of noble birth rather than rich', she almost certainly came from a senatorial family of distinction, so that Cato's marriage probably marks an important advance in the process of acceptance into the ranks of the aristocracy.[12] Before the end of 193 he was able to dedicate the shrine to Victoria Virgo, a public reminder of his achievements in Spain; and in this same period, most probably late in 192 or early in 191, Cato delivered a speech against a proposed 'Junian law concerning usury', *Dissuasio legis Iuniae de feneratione*. Since the evidence is slim and fragmentary it is perhaps not surprising that both the proposal and Cato's objections have been the subject of some controversy; but a possible explanation is that recent attempts to enforce existing legal restrictions on usury had served only to point up the unrealistic character of those restrictions at a time when there was a considerable demand for loans. The Junian law may well have been an attempt to set a maximum rate of interest which was both realistic and enforceable. If so, Cato, consistent with the prejudices against usury manifested in his words and actions on other occasions, could well have regarded a proposal to modify the prevailing restrictions as a dangerous concession, a weakening of the authority of law, a positive encouragement to a disreputable practice.[13] So much can never be more

---

[11] Plut. *Cato Mai.* 12. 1. Plutarch's mention of Thrace and the Danube (Ister) is a puzzle which leaves no doubt that there is an error of some sort, but that is not a sufficient reason to reject outright the statement that Cato was a *legatus* to Sempronius. On the latter's campaign see *MRR* i. 343 and 348 f.

[12] Plut. *Cato Mai.* 20. 2; Pliny, *Nat. hist.* 7. 62; *RE*, s.v. *Porcius*, no. 9, cols. 143 f., no. 14, cols. 167 f.; cf. Kienast, pp. 47 f., and, for speculative discussion, Ruebel, *The Political Development of Cato Censorius*, p. 93. On the basis of Cato's age Kienast puts forward the suggestion that this may not have been Cato's first marriage; but the total absence from Plutarch, Gellius, and other sources of any mention of an earlier marriage makes this unlikely.

[13] *ORF*³, Cato frs. 56–7. See Appendix 5.

than conjecture; but at least, since the *lex Iunia* is never mentioned again, it seems certain that the proposal was defeated, that Cato was on the winning side. Meanwhile a fresh, more promising, and very different opportunity to advance his standing had presented itself. In the autumn of 192 Antiochus the Great, ruler of the Seleucid kingdom centred upon Syria and Mesopotamia, had crossed with an army into Greece. A great eastern war, long looming, had become inevitable.

3. *Cato in Greece*

The circumstances which led up to this war were varied and complex. Antiochus' ambitions to re-establish his control over former Seleucid dominions in Asia Minor, and even in Thrace, began to conflict with the interests of Rome's allies and protégés, and therefore with those of Rome, just as Rome was seeking to resolve her relations with Macedonia and Greece. An extended period of intrigue, of diplomacy, public and private, of efforts to win diplomatic and propaganda advantages, of poses and manœuvres to gain the favour and confidence of the Greeks, fostered a steadily deepening climate of mutual suspicion, distrust, and fear between Antiochus and the Romans. Eventually the Aetolians, bitterly resentful at what they regarded as Rome's treacherous betrayal of their interests and on that account eager for Antiochus' support in war, managed to create a situation which faced Antiochus with the choice of intervening or of standing aloof while his only committed partisans in Greece were suppressed by the Roman intervention they were patently provoking. Perhaps by now under the firm impression that in the end the Romans intended war unless he submitted to unacceptable humiliation, he crossed to Greece and in effect entered into war with Rome.[14]

In fact Antiochus was at that moment inadequately prepared for a major campaign in Greece, but it is unlikely that this was realized in Rome. Rather he was the most powerful of the Hellenistic monarchs, formidable by reason of his reputation, his successes, and the vastness of his territories, and now the more alarming because he had at his court Hannibal, an almost symbolic object of Roman fear and hatred. The predominant sentiment at Rome had probably been no more in favour of deliberately embarking on a war of aggression than had been Antiochus himself; but if there was to be war the Roman senators were not disposed

[14] See esp. Badian, 'Rome and Antiochus the Great', *CPh* 54 (1959), 81 ff. On Rome's dealings with Antiochus and the subsequent campaigns see also De Sanctis, *Storia* iv. 1², pp. 117 ff.; Scullard, *Roman Politics*², pp. 117 f. and 123 ff.; and, for a useful short account, Errington, *The Dawn of Empire*, pp. 156 ff.

to regard it as anything but a grave and formidable undertaking, nor were they slow to appreciate the opportunities for winning military renown. When the consul Manius Acilius Glabrio took his army to Greece in 191 he had among his senior officers at least four men of consular rank, among them Cato and L. Valerius Flaccus. Despite some discrepancy in the sources about their status, Cato and Valerius almost certainly went as military tribunes, a most unusual position for ex-consuls.[15] According to one author, Frontinus, Cato was *tribunus militum a populo*, which implies that he had actually sought election to the position, though that detail may be no more than an assumption made by Frontinus himself. However that may be, Cato went, and benefited greatly from a combination of good fortune, personal ability, and vigorous self-advertisement.

One of Glabrio's immediate concerns was to ensure that the bulk of the Greek states continued to reject invitations to ally themselves to Antiochus. The key figure in this was Titus Flamininus, who was still in Greece and whose reputation as 'liberator' of the Greeks was more convincing than that of Antiochus in the same role.[16] Nevertheless, while the Roman army was crossing the peninsula from Apollonia to Thessaly Cato was sent to visit several cities. When Plutarch says that he 'brought over' Corinth, Patrae, and Aegium, three cities of the Achaean League, he claims too much, since the loyalty of the Achaeans, never seriously in doubt, had been dramatically confirmed some time before, in the presence of Flamininus himself, by a formal declaration of war upon Antiochus.[17] It should be remembered, however, that the exaggerated claim may stem from Cato's own subsequent version of events; and indeed the potential of the Greek communities for division and unrest was such that the new command may have thought such a visit would be a wise precaution to reinforce the pro-Roman commitment. On the

[15] The point is really settled by Polyb. 20. 10. 10, where Valerius is termed χιλίαρχος; also App. *Syr.* 18, which is derived from Polybius, terms both Cato and Valerius χιλίαρχοι. Cato is mentioned as tribune also in Cic. *De sen.* 32; Plut. *Cato Mai.* 12. 1; 29. 3 = *Compar.* 2. 3; Frontin. *Strat.* 2. 4. 4; 'Victor', *De vir. ill.* 47. 3. Livy, 36. 17. 1 terms both men *legati*; cf. also Zon. 9. 19. 9; Phlegon Trall. fr. 36 (*De mir.*), III. 1. That Cato and Valerius were tribunes is widely accepted, though Kienast, pp. 48 f., argues that they were probably *legati*. However Kienast rightly rejects the cynical view stemming from Mommsen, *Röm. Forsch.* ii. 460 n. 91, that Cato and Valerius accepted the status for political reasons, wishing to influence the conduct of the war or to prepare for the subsequent political attack on Glabrio. The two other ex-consuls among Glabrio's officers were L. Quinctius Flamininus and Ti. Sempronius Longus: Livy, 36. 1. 8; 36. 22. 7 and 24. 1.

[16] Livy, 36. 31–5; Plut. *Flam.* 15 f.; *Cato Mai.* 12. 4. For refs. to his extensive activities in the previous year see *MRR* i. 351.

[17] Plut. *Cato Mai.* 12. 4. Achaea: Livy, 35. 48–50, esp. 50. 2; Gelzer, *RE*, s.v. *Porcius*, no. 9, col. 117.

other hand the real reason for these visits may have been simply that the towns lay conveniently on Cato's route to his principal objective, Athens. There he addressed the Athenian people, speaking in Latin. He afterwards asserted that the Athenians were astonished at the speed and pungency of his speech, since 'what he himself set forth with brevity the interpreter would repeat to them at great length and with many words'. One fragment survives, pouring ironical scorn on Antiochus' appeals for support: 'Antiochus wages war with letters, he campaigns with pen and ink.'[18] Evidently Cato stayed some time at Athens, taking the opportunity to indulge his curiosity about Greek society and customs, but the visit cannot really have been very prolonged since he had rejoined Glabrio before the battle against Antiochus.

As the Roman army advanced south through Thessaly the king, seriously outnumbered and inadequately supported even by his Aetolian allies, withdrew within the pass of Thermopylae, where he established himself in an extremely strong position. The principal weakness of this famous defensive position was that it could be outflanked if the enemy could make his way with but a moderate force through the adjacent mountains—as the Persians had done in 480 and the Gauls in 279. To guard against this danger detachments of Aetolians held three forts on ridges commanding the principal paths. Consequently during the night preceding his frontal attack in the pass itself Glabrio sent contingents with orders to dislodge the Aetolians and take Antiochus in the rear. In the event Valerius Flaccus, with 2,000 men, failed to take the two forts against which he had been sent and made no progress; it was Cato, with another 2,000 men, who drove the Aetolians from the third fort, Callidromos, and successfully carried out the operation. Plutarch gives a dramatic but essentially plausible account, which beyond reasonable doubt stems from Cato himself, of how the detachment made its way with great difficulty and danger over arduous and often pathless terrain, for a time losing its way in the dark, and ultimately found itself high on the mountainside above the Aetolians. He then describes a daring dawn raid on an enemy outpost, followed by a bold charge, led by Cato in person, which caused the Aetolians to flee headlong and leave Antiochus' army exposed to the outflanking force.[19]

[18] Plut. *Cato Mai.* 12. 5 ff.; Pliny, *Nat. hist.* 29. 14; *ORF*³, Cato fr. 20.

[19] Plut. *Cato Mai.* 13 f.; cf. 29. 3 = *Compar.* 2. 3. Other refs. to Cato's part in the battle: Livy, 36. 17. 1; 36. 18. 8; App. *Syr.* 18 f.; Cic. *De sen.* 32; *Pro Mur.* 32; 'Victor', *De vir. ill.* 47. 3; 54. 2; Frontin. *Strat.* 1. 2. 5 (incident erroneously referred to Spain); 2. 4. 4; Zon. 9. 19. 9 f. = Dio fr. 19; Phlegon Trall. fr. 36, III. 1; *ORF*³, Cato fr. 49. On the battle and the topography see esp. Pritchett, *Studies in Ancient Greek Topography* i. 71 ff.

Cato did not hesitate to claim that the defeat of Antiochus at Thermopylae was entirely due to his exploit. 'Likewise when very recently I dispersed and allayed the very great turmoil, threatening from Thermopylae and Asia', he said (irrelevantly, in a speech about his consulship) soon after his return to Rome;[20] and it is clear that either one of Cato's speeches or his own account in his *Origines* is the source of the boasts recorded by Plutarch:

Cato was always, it seems, unstinting in praise of himself, and did not shun outright boasting as the sequel to great achievement; but these actions he invests with extreme importance. He says that those who saw him at that time, pursuing the enemy and striking them down, thought that Cato owed less to the Roman people than the Roman people owed to Cato; and that the consul Manius, still flushed with the heat of victory, threw his arms around Cato, himself still hot, and embraced him for a long time, crying out in joy that neither he nor the whole Roman people could adequately reward the benefits conferred by Cato.[21]

It is quite possible that Cato's claims were to a considerable extent justified by the facts—that Livy and other sources are essentially correct in indicating that the tide of battle was flowing in favour of Antiochus until Cato's troops appeared in his rear, or at least that the appearance of these troops was the decisive factor in the forcing of his position.[22] Yet it is equally, indeed more significant that this was the version proclaimed by Cato and that it was this version which imposed itself on the tradition. The process began almost immediately. Shortly after the battle Glabrio sent Cato to report the victory to the Senate and People at Rome. According to Livy Cato was not the first to be sent: L. Cornelius Scipio had set out a few days before him. Whether or not that is so, Cato was clearly determined to be first with the news and, making all possible speed, succeeded, with the result that the first account of the victory heard at Rome was the account given by Cato in person; and it is clear that Cato was in no doubt as to who should be given the chief credit.[23] Not that Cato, a *legatus*, could eclipse the consular commander: it was Glabrio who, after handing over his army to the new consul, L. Scipio, returned in 190 to celebrate a triumph, resplendent with booty, in public recognition of his success.[24] Nevertheless Cato had unquestionably

[20] ORF[3], Cato fr. 49.   [21] Plut. *Cato Mai*. 14. 2.
[22] Livy, 36. 18. 8; 'Victor', *De vir. ill*. 54. 2; cf. App. *Syr*. 19; Frontin. *Strat*. 2. 4. 4; Zon. 9. 19. 10; Plut. *Cato Mai*. 29. 3 = *Compar*. 2. 3.
[23] Livy, 36. 21. 4 ff.; Plut. *Cato Mai*. 14. 3 f.; Phlegon Trall. fr. 36, III. 1.
[24] Livy, 37. 7. 7; 37. 46. 1 ff.

managed to win for himself a major share of the credit for Glabrio's victory and once again to project himself in a position of special prominence just when the two men were about to come into open rivalry in their ambition to reach the censorship.

4. The Disputes of 190–184[25]

The effort to attain the censorship is one of the two principal features of Cato's career over the next few years. He failed in 189 but succeeded at the next election, in 184, on both occasions offering himself in partnership with his friend L. Valerius Flaccus. On each occasion the competition was intense, both in the vigour of the contest and in the eminence of the candidates, whose names happen to be recorded;[26] and in 189 one of Cato's rivals was his recent commander, M'. Acilius Glabrio, whose name links this aspect of Cato's career with the other marked feature of these years. Repeatedly Cato was involved in clashes with leading political figures, sometimes in the Senate, several times in connection with judicial processes. One of these figures was Q. Minucius Thermus, consul in 193, whom Cato attacked sharply in two speeches, one virtually certainly and possibly both during the discussions in the Senate in 190 when Minucius was refused a triumph in connection with his campaigns in Liguria.[27] In the earlier part of the next year Cato appeared as a prominent witness against his former commander, M'. Acilius Glabrio, who was accused by two tribunes of having given an inadequate account of his handling of the booty from his campaign. No doubt this was the occasion of a speech In M'. Acilium Glabrionem, the one fragment of which shows Cato taking the opportunity to emphasize his own excellent handling of

[25] See the final section of this chapter for a summary account, in chronological sequence and incorporating the main conclusions of this section, of the known events of Cato's career from 190 to 184.

[26] 189: Livy, 37. 57. 9 ff. 184: Livy, 39. 40. 1 ff.; cf. Plut. Cato Mai. 16. 4 f.

[27] Livy, 37. 46. 1 f. There can be little doubt that Cato's De falsis pugnis, ORF[3], fr. 58 (translation at the end of Appendix 6) was connected with this, and the De decem hominibus, ORF[3], frs. 59–63, could have been. In any case it belongs at about this time, since Minucius was killed in 188. Janzer, pp. 18 ff., Scullard, Roman Politics[2], p. 248, and Gelzer, RE, s.v. Porcius, no. 9, cols. 119 f., are all inclined to regard the fragments as coming from a single speech; Malcovati, ORF[3], ad loc., and Kienast, p. 51, rightly accept that the differences in title indicate two speeches, despite the coincidence that ten men were mentioned in each. The crucial point is that the ten men mentioned in fr. 58 were beaten but survived, whereas those mentioned in fr. 59 had been executed. Frs. 64 and 65, designated In Q. Thermum, could come from either speech, and frs. 182–4, Contra or In Thermum, could come from these speeches or from the later speeches against L. Thermus.

military matters in Spain, presumably in contrast to the alleged deficiencies of Glabrio.[28] It was probably at about this same time that Cato himself was the defendant in a tribunician prosecution. The precise charge is not known but it was connected with his consulship some years previously, for the speech which he delivered, of which an unusually large number of fragments have been preserved, was entitled *Dierum dictarum de consulatu suo*.[29] The great majority of the fragments fairly clearly concern the Spanish campaign, which must have been described in considerable detail, but there are a few general remarks about the disreputable motives and false accusations behind the prosecution, and Cato also managed to slip in his claim to have put an end to the danger from Antiochus.[30] Either the case was dropped or it ended in acquittal.[31] Then about two years later, beginning in 187, Cato was involved in the attacks and prosecutions directed against Lucius Scipio and his brother Africanus.

The accusations and prosecutions directed against the two Scipios in the 180s constitute a notoriously difficult and complex episode. The various accounts and references not only differ widely in scale, character, and points of detail, but positively conflict on almost every point of substance. Behind them clearly lies a complicated history of carelessness, cavalier speculation, and colourful fabrication, extending even to the names of the participants. Events have been telescoped and distorted, gaps filled by surmise and invention, narratives enlivened with dramatic detail, and patently incompatible versions combined to produce bewildering confusion. The difficulties are such that no reconstruction could ever be regarded as beyond dispute, but fortunately at least the main outline

[28] Livy, 37. 57. 12–58. 1; *ORF*[3], Cato fr. 66. Kienast, p. 53, rightly protests at the general readiness to assume that Cato was the real instigator of the prosecution, though his arguments are insufficient to prove his positive contention that the actual instigators were Titus Flamininus and M. Claudius Marcellus, the two successful candidates in the censorial elections.

[29] *ORF*[3], Cato frs. 21–55. That a single speech is in question has been generally accepted since Fraccaro's arguments in 'Le fonti per il consolato', *Studi storici*, 3 (1910), 147 ff. = *Opusc*. i. 188 ff. A few undesignated fragments are assigned to this speech by conjecture only.

[30] *ORF*[3], Cato fr. 49, generally accepted as giving the *terminus post quem* for the speech, though Leo, *Gesch. der röm. Literatur* i. 283 n. 2, regards it rather as evidence of revision. The actual date cannot be determined precisely. Fraccaro, *Opusc*. i. 190 ff., improbably placed it during the contest for the censorship of 184; others prefer a date around 190. See Malcovati, *ORF*[3], ad loc.; Gelzer, *RE*, s.v. *Porcius*, no. 9, cols. 120 f.; Kienast, pp. 54 f.; Scullard, *Roman Politics*[2], pp. 258 f.; Janzer, pp. 6 ff. (attempting a more elaborate analysis than the evidence permits). Much has been made of the possible identity of censors mentioned in fr. 50: 'censores qui posthac fiunt, formidulosius atque segnius atque timidius pro re publica nitentur.' There are, however, too many uncertainties about this for it to be used as primary evidence about the date.

[31] It is known that although Cato was prosecuted many times he was never convicted: Plut. *Cato Mai*. 29. 5 = *Compar*. 2. 5; Pliny, *Nat. hist*. 7. 100; 'Victor', *De vir. ill*. 47. 7.

of events does seem to have been established fairly clearly.[32] It seems probable that the sequence of events was approximately as follows.

When Lucius Scipio, with Africanus as his legatus, succeeded Glabrio in 190 he carried the war against Antiochus into Asia. At Magnesia he won a decisive victory which enabled Rome to impose stern but not unduly harsh terms. These included the immediate payment to Lucius of 500 talents of silver, to be used to pay the troops. This was the first instalment of the full war indemnity which the Romans were to receive over a period of years. In addition Lucius acquired enormous booty which enabled him to reward his soldiers liberally and also to celebrate his triumph at the end of 189 with a display of treasures even more magnificent than those which had been carried in his brother's triumph over Carthage.

In 187 it was the question of booty, or rather of the status of the 500 talents, which provided the basis for the attacks on the Scipios. Two tribunes, the Petillii, said to have been instigated by Cato,[33] demanded in the Senate that account should be given of the 500 talents. The point at issue was whether the money was to be treated as booty, in which case no account was necessary, or as war indemnity belonging to the state, in which case a proper accounting was required. The tribunes were claiming that it was the latter but the Scipios evidently wished to treat it as the former and indignantly rejected the tribunes' claim as presumptuous interference.[34] Although the responsibility lay with Lucius, Africanus intervened, possibly feeling that he was the real target, and dramatically tore up the account books in front of the Senate. It was a magnificent gesture but unwise, for it destroyed vital evidence. Though taken no further in the Senate the dispute was quickly transferred to a different field.

Another tribune, C. Minucius Augurinus, summoned a *contio* to

[32] By Scullard, *Roman Politics*[2], pp. 142 f., 151 f., and esp. Appendix IV, who lists earlier bibliography, including the important studies by Fraccaro. Note also Kienast, pp. 57 ff.; Gagé, 'La rogatio Petillia', *RPh* 27 (1953), 34 ff., against whom Siena, 'A proposito di una nuova interpretazione delle fonti sul processo dell'Africano', *RFIC* 35 (1957), 175 ff.; Schatzman, 'The Roman General's Authority over Booty', *Historia*, 21 (1972), 177 ff.; Balsdon, 'L. Cornelius Scipio', *Historia*, 21 (1972), 224 ff. The most important among the numerous sources are Polyb. 23. 14; Livy, 38. 50–60 (with confusion of several versions); Gell. 4. 18 and 6. 19.

[33] Livy, 38. 54. 1 ff.; cf. Dio, fr. 65; Plut. *Cato Mai.* 15. 2 (though Plutarch regards the Petillii as accusers of Africanus, not of Lucius).

[34] Kienast, pp. 62 f., takes the view that the Scipios were patently in the wrong and that the issue was in no sense a matter of definition; but see Schatzman, op. cit., esp. pp. 192 ff. There is more to be said for Kienast's suggestion, pp. 61 f., that the dispute may have arisen in the first instance out of the attacks on Cn. Manlius Vulso on his return from Asia.

initiate judicial proceedings against Lucius, who was now in a most awkward position. Faced with a public demand to render account of the money, he could scarcely reverse the attitude he had taken in the Senate, especially as the account books had now been destroyed; but his public refusal to render an account was bound to arouse suspicions and rumours of peculation; and even without such suspicions he might still be held to be patently in the wrong. The next step was that Minucius imposed an enormous fine, and probably also demanded a large sum as surety, pending Lucius' appeal in the next stage of the procedure; with the result that Lucius was threatened with imprisonment if he did not pay.[35] When he refused to comply, the weakness of his position was demonstrated by the refusal of eight of the other nine tribunes to intervene to save him from the imminent humiliation. Fortunately for him one tribune, Ti. Sempronius Gracchus, agreed to do so and interposed his veto. What happened next is uncertain. It is possible but unlikely that Lucius paid the fine, and very unlikely that he was reduced to the total poverty portrayed in one account.[36] Probably an impasse had been reached and for the time being the whole matter temporarily fell into abeyance. Lucius not only remained a senator but in 186 gave magnificent public games for ten days, in fulfilment of a vow which he alleged he had made in Asia.[37] In 184 there was a new attack, this time directed specifically at Africanus himself. Though much is obscure, it seems that a tribune named M. Naevius initiated proceedings against him before the People; that the accusations may have been concerned with his own private dealings with Antiochus rather than with the 500 talents; and that Scipio, after a highly emotional reminder of his great services to Rome, withdrew from the assembly, whereupon the people dispersed. But once again it was a splendid gesture which could be only a short-term victory. His scornful defiance of a tribune, coupled with his refusal even to attempt to answer the accusations, necessarily weakened his position for the future. He left Rome and settled at Liternum, a virtual exile; and there he died the next year.

To seek one single motive for a number of disputes spread over several years, or even for one such dispute, is likely to result in caricature. It is wise to recognize from the outset that the disputes in which Cato was involved from 191 to 184 will have involved many motives, rational and irrational, calculating and emotional, about most of which there is no hope of finding evidence. Nevertheless there are three types of possible

---

[35] Kienast, pp. 64 f., believes that the case reached the point of conviction and fine, rather than simply the demand for surety.

[36] Dio, fr. 63; cf. Zon. 9. 20; Val. Max. 4. 1. 8.   [37] Livy, 39. 22. 8 ff.

motivation which it is plausible to consider: political expediency, notably in the form of attempts by rival candidates for the censorship to discredit each other; partisan and factional conflicts between individuals and groups, notably between Cato and the Scipios; and a genuine concern about improprieties in the conduct of public affairs. These are not necessarily mutually exclusive, for a man may care deeply about the misdemeanours of those who are also his rivals for office, and likewise may encounter among those rivals men with whom he has had long and bitter feuds. In the episodes of 191–184 all three elements probably played some part in varying degrees, though the element of partisan conflict may have been less important than has sometimes been supposed.

In most of these disputes Cato is known to have made accusations of serious misconduct in the conduct of public affairs. Thus he accused Q. Minucius Thermus of at least three abuses. While the speech entitled 'Concerning fictitious battles', *De falsis pugnis*, was presumably principally an allegation that Minucius was claiming a triumph on false pretences, the one surviving fragment is a scathing attack on him for having ten allied officials beaten because the supply arrangements they had made were allegedly inadequate.[38] The other speech against Minucius also dealt with an alleged outrage in the exercise of power over allied peoples, in this case the execution of ten men allegedly without opportunity for trial or defence.[39] Cato's evidence against Acilius Glabrio was that he had not displayed in his triumph gold and silver vessels captured in Antiochus' camp, clearly with the implication that Glabrio had appropriated them for himself, a practice which was not illegal but of which Cato strongly disapproved.[40] And the attack on Lucius Scipio concerned the failure to account for money which could very reasonably be regarded as belonging to the state and therefore subject to account, rather than as booty.[41] All these, abuse of power, misappropriation of booty, failure to observe the proprieties and obligations of public duty, are matters about which Cato protested repeatedly during his career and about which the genuineness of his concern cannot reasonably be doubted. It is unreasonable to assume that in these instances the accusations were no more than excuses for attacking rivals for office or personal enemies, that a determination

[38] *ORF³*, Cato fr. 58; translation in Appendix 6.

[39] *ORF³*, Cato fr. 59; also 60–3.

[40] Livy, 37. 57. 12 ff. Schatzman, 'The Roman General's Authority over Booty', *Historia*, 21 (1972), 191 f., points out that the purpose of the action taken by the tribunes against Glabrio seems to have been not to convict him of peculation but to force him to render an account of his booty.

[41] Scullard, *Roman Politics²*, pp. 142 and 292 f.; Schatzman, op. cit., esp. pp. 192 ff.

that such misconduct should be punished and stamped out was not itself
a major motive for his actions.

However, there is a strong case to be made for the view that rivalry
for office was also a major factor in these events. Highly contentious
rivalries in connection with consular elections are well attested in this
period, but it is on the censorial elections that Cato had his eyes. In this
connection the clearest instance is the attack on Acilius Glabrio, which
actually took place in the period when the candidates, Glabrio and Cato
among them, were actively seeking support; furthermore according to
Livy Glabrio had much the brightest prospects of success, and the tribunes
who initiated the proceedings against him, P. Sempronius Gracchus and
C. Sempronius Rutilus, ended them as soon as he announced that he was
withdrawing his candidature. Livy's account takes the political and
electoral motivation entirely for granted, and indeed the inference
seems obvious and inevitable. There is no specific evidence that Cato
was the prime mover in the affair, that his influence stimulated the two
tribunes to action; indeed Livy speaks of the silent resentment of the
nobiles at the popularity of the 'new man' Glabrio, and it should be
remembered that besides Cato, Valerius Flaccus, and Glabrio there were
three other candidates, P. Cornelius Scipio Nasica, T. Quinctius Flamininus, and M. Claudius Marcellus (the last two of whom were in due course
elected). But at least Cato was a principal witness, and according to
Livy he was directly blamed by Glabrio, whose withdrawal from the
contest was intended especially to bring odium upon him. Even when
allowance has been made for possible elaboration by Livy or his source, he
was undoubtedly in receipt of a tradition according to which Cato was
a central figure in the episode.[42]

It has often been suspected that the prosecution which obliged Cato
to defend himself in the speech 'Concerning his own consulship', *Dierum
dictarum de consulatu suo*, was itself a political manœuvre of the same kind,
designed to impede his candidature for the censorship and possibly even
the direct counterpart to the attack on Glabrio. That Cato himself asserted
that the accusations against him were false, audacious, and malicious is
scarcely to be taken as reliable evidence, but one fragment does seem
significant: 'Those who become censors hereafter will strive on behalf
of the state more fearfully, more slowly and more timidly.'[43] Without
any wider context this remark cannot be fully understood; but the fact
is that Cato had occasion to work into his speech, the principal purpose

---

[42] Livy, 37. 57. 12 ff. See also p. 60 n. 28.
[43] *ORF*[3], Cato fr. 50. On his accusers: frs. 22-4.

of which was to rebut accusations relating to his own consulship, an assertion that some fact or event would have an adverse influence on the conduct of certain future censors. That strongly suggests (though it does not prove) that the remark derived its real relevance from the immediate circumstances, that the proceedings were close in time to censorial elections and quite possibly that they were regarded as directly related to those elections.

In other instances a connection with the censorial elections is entirely conjectural. No source links the refusal of a triumph to Q. Minucius Thermus or Cato's criticisms of him with these elections, and when the elections came Minucius was not a candidate. Yet a faint suspicion persists. Minucius had returned from his praetorship in Spain to celebrate a triumph, became consul in 193, and from 193 to 190 had been left in charge of a Ligurian war in which he had apparently won significant successes. He therefore had a standing and a record which might seem to mark him out as a possible candidate for the censorship of 189, if, that is, the Senate had not refused him a triumph in 190. But in the absence of direct evidence it can be no more than a faint suspicion, especially as the fragments of Cato's speeches suggest that there may have been ample grounds for acting against Minucius even if no element of political rivalry entered into the case. It is positively unlikely that electoral manœuvring was behind the attack on Lucius Scipio in 187, which is too early to be plausibly construed as a preliminary to the next censorial elections, still three years away; but it possibly was important in the affair of Africanus in 184. Assuming that this preceded the censorial elections, its outcome can hardly have failed to damage the prospects of Lucius Scipio, who was one of the candidates.[44] It is unfortunate that so little can be discovered about this affair, even as to the particular charges brought by the tribune Naevius or the names of persons associated with him. There are however two suggestive points. There is a persistent though regrettably imprecise tradition that Cato was the principal author of Scipio's downfall;[45] and the timing is striking, just when Cato and Valerius were making their second bid for the censorship, but after a very considerable lapse of time since the events to which the charges must have been related. Thus there are real grounds for the suspicion that at least the timing of the re-newed attack on Africanus was influenced by considerations of political expediency.

[44] Livy, 39. 40. 2.
[45] Livy, 38. 54. 1 f.; Plut. Cato Mai. 32. 4 = Compar. 5. 4; Dio, fr. 65; Gell. 4. 18. 7. See further below.

The third type of motivation which must be considered is the pursuit of longer-term rivalries and hostilities between individuals and factions (as opposed to immediate disputes over particular issues). The episodes of 187 and 184 especially are often seen as the culmination of just such a prolonged hostility between Cato and the Scipios, especially Scipio Africanus; but before examining this particular view it will be as well to dispose of another, more general theory. Cato, the 'new man' from Tusculum, has sometimes been portrayed as the representative of the landed gentry, or even of the peasantry, as a leader of a 'rural opposition', championing their interests and values against the dominating oligarchy, which itself had become overbearing and corrupt in consequence of the great wars.[46] It is a portrayal which has been challenged, and rightly so.[47]

Most 'new men', men who were the first in their families to attain the great public offices of Rome, were likely to come from the landed gentry, the local aristocracies of the towns; for such local aristocrats had extensive landed estates, the form of wealth which was the essential economic basis for a senatorial career; they had social and community ties with powerful patrons; and their service in the Roman armies, often as middle-rank officers, could bring them to the notice both of the public and of influential friends. Such a one was Cato, certainly no peasant;[48] but because he sprang from the landed gentry it does not follow that he saw himself as their special representative, nor indeed is there evidence that they saw themselves as a distinct and coherent class with interests to be championed against the dominant section of the senatorial aristocracy. If such a view were taken as axiomatic, naturally there are particular items in Cato's career which could be interpreted to conform to it, but there is virtually nothing either in his background or in his actions to compel that interpretation. If Cato attacked instances of corruption and misgovernment his targets were necessarily to be found among the aristocracy; it does not follow that he regarded the whole senatorial aristocracy, or the dominant elements within it, as guilty of such offences, or that he was an enemy of the aristocracy as such. In fact the only explicit evidence that Cato played such a role is Livy's comment,

[46] Such a concept, owing much to Mommsen, permeates the articles of Fraccaro concerning Cato collected in *Opusc.* i. Also De Sanctis, *Storia* iv. 1², pp. 564 ff.; Della Corte, *Catone censore*², e.g. pp. 13 f.; 43 ff.

[47] Kienast, *passim*, though he goes too far in another direction, interpreting many of Cato's actions as positively intended to protect the interests of the senatorial aristocracy. He overestimates the extent to which that aristocracy is likely to have felt threatened by the growth of equestrian wealth and influence: see Appendix 6.

[48] It has often been observed that Cato's *De agricultura* reveals interests and an outlook far removed from those of a peasant farmer. See further Ch. 11.

'nor would you easily say whether the *nobilitas* did more to press upon him than he to harry the *nobilitas*', but this is scarcely to be regarded as an authoritative assessment. It occurs in Livy's vivid and succinct character sketch immediately after reference to Cato's numerous speeches, prosecutions, and feuds, and therefore may reflect Livy's literary skills, with a touch of anachronism, rather than a careful historical judgement.[49] Some support for an 'anti-aristocratic' attitude might be drawn from the fact that both Livy and Plutarch speak of widespread 'noble' opposition to Cato's candidature for the censorship,[50] from his riposte to Scipio (Nasica) on his departure from Spain, contrasting 'the famous', ἔνδοξοι, like Scipio with men of humble origin, δημοτικοί, such as himself,[51] and from his decision to exclude the names of all commanders from the narrative in the later books of the *Origines*.[52] All of this, however, is susceptible to an alternative explanation, and has to be set against Cato's long and harmonious co-operation with L. Valerius Flaccus, a man of the most aristocratic lineage, his marriage with Licinia, preferred for her nobility of birth, and his son's marriage to a member of the great patrician family of the Aemilii, a daughter of L. Aemilius Paullus, who himself had close links with the Scipios.[53]

The truth about Cato's attitude to the aristocracy is simple and obvious. He was a *novus homo*, seeking not to undermine the aristocracy but to establish his own position as a full and accepted member of it. As such he inevitably encountered opposition and conflict; as such his candidature for the censorship, the most eminent office of all, was bound to meet much aristocratic prejudice; as such he naturally sought to play down considerations of noble birth and distinguished ancestry, to emphasize instead, as in his rejoinder to Scipio Nasica, the worth of personal qualities and achievement[54]—for though in the *Origines* he might suppress the names of military leaders (foreigners as well as Romans, it should be noted, and probably individuals of all ranks) he was far from reticent about his own achievements. Nor did he hesitate to claim credit for the achievements of his ancestors along with his own: 'I ordered the book to be brought out', he says in his speech *De sumptu suo*, 'in which was written

---

[49] Livy, 39. 40. 9.   [50] Livy, 39. 41. 1 ff.; Plut. *Cato Mai.* 16. 4.
[51] Plut. *Cato Mai.* 11. 3, quoted above, pp. 51 f.
[52] Nepos, *Cato* 3. 4; Pliny, *Nat. hist.* 8. 11 = HRR i², Cato fr. 88. See pp. 213 and 232 f.
[53] Licinia: Plut. *Cato Mai.* 20. 2. The son's marriage: below, pp. 104 f. Paullus: Astin, *Scipio Aemilianus*, pp. 12 f.
[54] Note the emphasis on personal achievement in ORF³, Cato fr. 252: 'iure, lege, libertate, re publica communiter uti oportet: gloria atque honore, quomodo sibi quisque struxit.' Since there is no title or context, the point of the passage is uncertain; possibly Cato was opposing some attempt to secure election to office contrary to the rules of eligibility.

my speech on that matter over which I had a legal contest with M. Cornelius. . . . The services of my ancestors were read through; then those things which I myself had done for the state were read.'[55] Similarly it was Cato himself, according to Plutarch, who extolled the martial services of his father and great-grandfather, and described himself as 'new in respect of office and glory, but exceedingly old in the deeds and virtues of his ancestors'.[56]

The significance of Cato's *novitas* is neatly summarized by Cicero, comparing Cato's situation with his own: 'Since he considered that he was commended to the Roman people by his virtue and not by his lineage, since he wished the beginning of his stock and of his family name to be born and propagated from himself, he took upon himself enmities with men of very great power.'[57] The *novus homo* might decry the advantages of birth and status enjoyed by many of his competitors, but they were advantages he coveted. Clashes and disputes with particular members of the senatorial aristocracy were inevitable in the pursuit of such far-reaching ambition, but the aim was acceptance into the governing class, not a general assault upon it.

If the clashes and disputes of the years between Thermopylae and Cato's censorship are not to be seen as manifestations of an attitude or policy of hostility towards the senatorial aristocracy as such, there remains the question of whether they were manifestations of a long-term quarrel with a particular group within the aristocracy. For, as was mentioned previously, the episodes of 187 and 184 are often seen as the culmination of a prolonged hostility between Cato and the Scipios, especially Scipio Africanus; and some of the other episodes have been interpreted in that context as attacks on supporters and associates of Scipio, on the 'Scipionic faction'. Sometimes this feud is seen as the expression of a cultural, almost an ideological conflict of outlook and policy between the 'philhellene' Africanus and a Cato doggedly resisting the spread of Hellenic influence— which is almost a caricature of both men. The fact is that no ancient source states or implies, either in a general reference to the hostility or in connection with particular events, that there was any such ideological dispute between them; nor are any known clashes naturally suggestive in themselves of such a basis for hostility. It is entirely a modern inference which is derived in no small measure from an erroneous and much oversimplified interpretation of Cato's attitude to the Greeks and their culture, a topic which will be examined in another chapter.[58]

---

[55] *ORF*³, Cato fr. 173.   [56] Plut. *Cato Mai.* 1. 1 f.   [57] Cic. *Verr.* 2. 5. 180.
[58] Ch. 8.

The 'cultural clash' is not the only area in which modern hypothesis has taken the feud motive too far. From time to time the attacks on Q. Minucius Thermus and Acilius Glabrio have been seen as manifestations of the feud, as attacks on members of the 'Scipionic group'. Such a view is closely associated with an insufficiently flexible interpretation of Roman politics in this period, which tends to assign individuals too firmly to a particular group, with insufficient allowance for the complexity of inter-relationships, of cross-ties, and of obligations in more than one direction. There is still much to be said for the view that there was a tendency for Roman politicians to operate in factional groups and that these groups tended to be centred upon particular families, but there was also a con-siderable fluidity in the relationships.[59] In view of all this three questions need to be asked about the attacks on Minucius and Glabrio. Is there any positive evidence that they were attacked *because* they were associates of Africanus, or is that motive only a modern inference? Does it seem necessary or reasonable to supply such a motive by inference? Can these men be shown with reasonable probability to have been associates of Africanus at the time of the attacks?

To the first question the answer is simply that there is no such evidence; it is a matter of modern inference. Part of the answer to the second question is clear from what has already been said earlier in this chapter: in both instances powerful and sufficient motives can be identified with near certainty and without recourse to the hypothesis that the men were attacked *because* of a close association with Africanus. However, the hypothesis is not necessarily incorrect because sufficient motive can be identified without it. It is conceivable that in the decision to act against these particular individuals Cato's other motives were powerfully re-inforced by an intense hostility towards a faction to which they belonged —which leads to the third question. It is certainly the case that in 202 Minucius had served with distinction as a military tribune under Scipio Africanus and seems to have been entrusted with important missions; and that as tribunes of the plebs in 201 Minucius and Glabrio had acted together with great vigour to protect Africanus' interests against the attempts of the consul Cn. Cornelius Lentulus to supersede him in the African command and to overthrow his peace settlement with Carthage.[60] Thereafter there is no satisfactory evidence about Minucius' relationship to Scipio; he may have remained an unwavering supporter: but the case

[59] Astin, *Politics and Policies*, esp. pp. 7–9.
[60] App. *Lib.* 36; 44; Frontin. *Strat.* 1. 8. 10; Livy, 30. 40. 9 ff.; 30. 43. 2 f. Minucius: Münzer, *RE*, s.v. *Minucius*, no. 65. Glabrio: Klebs, *RE*, s.v. *Acilius*, no. 35.

of Glabrio shows that he need not have done so. Glabrio's first attempt
to secure the consulship was at the elections for 192, when one of his
plebeian rivals was none other than Gaius Laelius, indisputably the closest
and most loyal of Africanus' associates and explicitly stated by Livy to
have been supported in his candidature by Africanus himself.[61] Neither
Glabrio nor Laelius was successful on that occasion, and since Glabrio was
elected for 191 and Laelius for 190 it is probable that Glabrio's election
was at the expense of Laelius. Furthermore, though Glabrio evidently
took Lucius Scipio as one of his officers in the campaign against Antiochus,
none of his other known officers seems to have been especially closely
associated with Africanus, and the two who were entrusted with the
vital outflanking operation at Thermopylae were none other than
Valerius Flaccus and Cato himself. Thus the notion that the attack on
Glabrio in 189 was in any degree motivated by a feud with the 'Scipionic
group' is not only unnecessary but improbable.

There remain the attacks on the Scipios themselves, in which it is
unquestionably conceivable that motives of concern for public propriety
or of political expediency should have been intertwined with a deep-
seated hostility. To admit the possibility, however, is not to establish
the fact, nor does it mean very much without some understanding of the
nature of any such hostility; yet the evidence is tantalizingly imprecise,
not to say vague, not only about the nature and particular manifestations of
this hostility but even about the nature and extent of Cato's involvement
in the episodes of 187 and 184. There are four sources which state or
imply that Cato was a leading instigator of the attacks on the Scipios.[62]
Although Lucius is mentioned, the form of words used in these sources
directs attention principally towards Africanus, though clearly including
the affair in the Senate in 187, in which Africanus is regarded as the real
target. When however it is asked what Cato actually did these sources
reveal only (*i*) that he incited the Petillii against Africanus, (*ii*) that he
incited the Petillii to introduce a bill, a *rogatio*, directed against Lucius
Scipio and in support of this *rogatio* delivered a speech 'concerning the
money of king Antiochus', *de pecunia regis Antiochi*, (*iii*) that he deterred
two other tribunes, the Mummii, from vetoing the Petillian *rogatio*, (*iv*)
that when the action in the Senate was dropped Cato co-operated with the
accusers of Lucius. Cato's name is never linked with that of the tribune
Naevius, though in view of the obvious telescoping of events in the

---

[61] Livy, 35. 10. 3 and 10.
[62] Livy, 38. 54. 1 f. and 11; Plut. *Cato Mai.* 15. 1 f.; 32. 4. = *Compar.* 5. 4; Gell. 4. 18. 7;
Dio, fr. 65.

sources and the tendency to confuse the actions of the Petillii with those of Naevius, the references to attacks on Africanus can reasonably be taken to cover the episode of 184. But even when the scope of the evidence is thus extended it remains scanty in the extreme, especially as the introduction of a *rogatio* by the Petillii, and with that the threatened veto of the Mummii, is almost certainly fictitious.[63] Furthermore Cato's speech is mentioned only by Livy (no fragments survive), and only in the context of this probably fictitious episode of the Petillian rogation. On the other hand Livy does say that the speech was extant in his day, and his form of words does leave open the possibility that the association with the alleged *rogatio* is only a matter of inference, that Cato did indeed deliver a speech 'concerning the money of king Antiochus', but not in support of a particular *rogatio*. If that is so, it is the only specific action attributable to Cato throughout the whole affair of the Scipios. Otherwise there are only the vague assertions that he incited—or rather was believed to have incited—the Petillii to act and that he co-operated with the accusers of Lucius (i.e. presumably with C. Minucius Augurinus). Nevertheless, despite this lack of precision in the evidence, it remains probable that Cato was a major force, perhaps *the* major force in the affair: there was clearly a strong tradition that he was; it is plausible that his role was mainly that of inciting others, with few specific public interventions of his own; and it would complement the generalized statements about hostility between Cato and Africanus.

Several sources refer in general terms to this hostility, some stating and others implying that it was intense and of long duration: Cato was at variance with Africanus all his life, says Nepos (overlooking the fact that Cato survived Africanus by thirty-five years); he could not bear Africanus, says the elder Pliny; he had many struggles with him, says Plutarch; he was the chief of Africanus' *inimici*, says Livy, wont to carp at his greatness.[64] Yet only this last passage even hints at an underlying reason for prolonged enmity, and when the details are sought it transpires that remarkably few outward manifestations of it are known. Prior to 187 only two supposed examples are mentioned (both as it happens by Plutarch): the story of the quarrel between Cato and Africanus during the former's quaestorship; and the story of Africanus' attempt to supplant Cato in Spain.[65] Both stories are, to say the least, gravely distorted and

---

[63] Scullard, *Roman Politics*[2], pp. 294 f.

[64] Nepos, *Cato* 1. 3; Pliny, *Nat. hist. praef.* 30; Plut. *Cato Mai.* 15. 6; Livy, 38. 54. 1. Note also Dio, fr. 65; Gell. 4. 18. 7; Plut. *Cato Mai.* 3. 5; 11. 1; 32. 4 = *Compar.* 5. 4; *Flam.* 18. 3.

[65] pp. 12 ff. and 51 f.; cf. Ruebel, *The Political Development of Cato Censorius*, p. 93.

highly suspect; much of the former is patently fictitious, the latter is most probably the garbled product of confusion between P. Scipio Nasica and P. Scipio Africanus. It was pointed out in a previous chapter that although the open quarrel of 204 must be rejected it might reasonably be conjectured on *a priori* grounds that the personal relationship between Cato and his commander was none too cordial; but also that this is only a conjecture, for which there is no reliable evidence. Otherwise, apart from the attacks on the Scipios in 187 and 184, the only other incident recorded is that Cato as censor deprived Lucius Scipio of his public horse, in other words of his membership of the equestrian order. This was done as an insult, says one source; it was thought that Cato did this in order to spite Africanus, says another; but even if some such motive were accepted as the primary reason for Cato's action, it would, of course, reflect the situation only *after* the disputes of 187 and 184, and would reveal nothing about any earlier hostility. As it happens, there is reason to believe that the removal of Lucius from the Order was 'without ignominy', and consequently there is a real possibility that Cato's primary motive lay in his insistence on the standards of physical fitness required of *equites*.[66]

In view of this surprising lack of specific evidence there must be a cautious reserve about those passages which refer in general terms to deep and long-standing enmity, a suspicion that they are indeed generalizations, projecting backwards the intense and exacerbated antagonisms of the 180s and exaggerating the significance of any earlier ill-feelings. That is not to discount the *a priori* probability that there was an antipathy between the two men, and especially that Cato disliked Scipio. Cato disapproved of self-praise (though very inclined to indulge in it himself), scorned the honour of statues, believed in the virtues of restraint and austerity, and deplored the display of luxury and extravagance by men and women alike; and he constantly championed the strict observance of the proprieties in the conduct of public affairs. It is likely enough that he viewed with some disfavour the flamboyant, ambitious Africanus, ostentatiously communing with Jupiter,[67] quick to recall his services and achievements, flaunting them in his very name; and married to a woman whose public appearances were characterized by brilliant displays of spectacular extravagance.[68] There are grounds enough to suspect an underlying antipathy, which could have done much to encourage and

---

[66] 'Victor', *De vir. ill.* 53. 2 ('ignominiae causa'); Plut. *Cato Mai.* 18. 1. See further p. 81.
[67] See esp. Scullard, *Scipio Africanus*, pp. 19 ff.
[68] Polyb. 31. 26. 1 ff.

intensify attacks on the Scipios when these were prompted by other motives; but there must be grave doubts about a long-standing feud sufficiently intense to constitute a major factor in political life or itself to be a principal cause of political conflict.

5. *Cato's Career from 190 to 184*

It is now possible to set out in sequence the known events of Cato's career from his return from Thermopylae to his election to the censorship, incorporating brief accounts of the disputes discussed in the preceding section.

When Q. Minucius Thermus returned in 190 from his Ligurian campaign he was refused a triumph by the Senate. Among those who opposed Minucius was Cato who, besides accusing him of making spurious claims, alleged that he was guilty of at least two very serious abuses of power. It is possible that some of the objectors, including Cato, were looking ahead to the censorial elections of 189 and took the opportunity to undermine the standing of a possible candidate; but there is neither evidence nor need for such a hypothesis. Assuming that Cato believed his accusations to be well founded they are quite sufficient in themselves to account for his involvement. The situation was rather different, however, in the action taken in the next year against M'. Acilius Glabrio. Cato is likely to have disapproved strongly of the personal appropriation of valuable booty, and therefore to have been ready enough to appear as a principal witness in a case formally intended to compel Glabrio to submit accounts but probably really designed to expose his failure, despite his lavish largesses, either to distribute or to hand to the treasury booty of considerable value. But neither the course of events nor the explicit statements of Livy admit any reasonable doubt that motives of political expediency played a considerable part in this action, forcing Glabrio to withdraw his candidacy for the censorship when the contest was already under way. Whether this happened before or after Cato himself had been unsuccessfully prosecuted cannot be determined, but it is highly probable that a similar motive, the desire to discredit Cato's candidacy, played no small part in that prosecution. In the event the censors elected were T. Quinctius Flamininus and M. Claudius Marcellus. The three defeated candidates, Cato, Valerius, and Scipio Nasica, were all to try again.

In the same year, 189, Cato was sent as a *legatus* to the consul M. Fulvius Nobilior, evidently in connection with negotiations with the Aetolians, against whom Fulvius was prosecuting the war which they had begun in alliance with Antiochus.[69] Although Cato subsequently criticized Fulvius there is nothing to show whether or not he had any role in the attempts instigated by M. Aemilius Lepidus in 187 to condemn Fulvius' conduct at Ambracia and to deny him a triumph. A speech in which Cato referred to these events is to be dated after the triumph and probably as late as 178.[70] Similarly, tempting though it is to conjecture his attitude, there is no evidence to link Cato with the objections to the triumphs of Lucius Scipio at the end of 189 (on the ground that Thermopylae, not Magnesia, had been the decisive victory against Antiochus) and of Cn. Manlius Vulso in 187; indeed he may still have been in Aetolia with Fulvius at the time of Lucius' triumph in 189.[71]

Likewise, in a very different aspect of public affairs, virtually nothing is known of Cato's actions or role in connection with the so-called 'Bacchanalian conspiracy' of 186.[72] Allegations that the Bacchic cult, which had become widespread, had given rise to numerous acts of crime, sexual abuse, and even ritual murder prompted the Senate into a vigorous campaign of punishment and repression. The matter was serious enough to be the major preoccupation of the consuls of the year. Large numbers of persons were executed or otherwise punished, and the Senate found it necessary to require the Italian allied states to institute the same measures and restrictions in their territories. Attempts have been made to attribute to Cato a definite role in all this, but the only evidence is a single uninformative word from an undated speech entitled *De coniuratione*, which may mean that Cato participated in the debates about this particular 'conspiracy' but reveals nothing about his attitude or recommendations.[73] Meanwhile, however, he had certainly been involved in the attack made on the Scipios in 187, first by the Petillii and then by Minucius Augurinus, and probably he was the principal instigator.

[69] *ORF*[3], Cato fr. 130; cf. Frontin. *Strat.* 2. 7. 14. Refs. to Fulvius' campaigns collected in *MRR* i. 360, 366, and 369.

[70] *ORF*[3], Cato frs. 148–9. Fr. 148 is later than the triumph since it refers to gifts to the troops which Livy, 39. 5. 17, shows were made on the day of the triumph. On the question of whether or not these fragments were taken from the same speech as fr. 150, see p. 110 n. 22. Probably there was only one speech, *c.* 178, but a separate one in the years 187–184 cannot be positively excluded. For Lepidus' opposition to Fulvius see Livy, 38. 42. 8–44. 6; 39. 4–5. See esp. Fraccaro, 'Catoniana', *Studi storici*, 3 (1910), 272 ff. = *Opusc.* i. 247 ff.; Scullard, *Roman Politics*[2], pp. 266 f.   [71] Livy, 37. 58. 6 ff.; 38. 44. 9–50. 3.

[72] The principal sources are Livy, 39. 8–19 and the inscribed copy of the *SC de Bacchanalibus*, *ILLRP*, no. 511 = *ILS* 18. For a cautious view and references to earlier discussions see Scullard, *Roman Politics*[2], p. 147. See also Tarditi, 'La questione dei Baccanali', *PP*, 9 (1954), 265 ff.; Toynbee, *Hannibal's Legacy* ii. 387 ff.; and esp. Cova, 'Livio e la repressione dei Baccanali', *Athenaeum*, n.s. 52 (1974), 82 ff.

[73] *ORF*[3], Cato fr. 68.

It is unlikely that this latter affair looked forward to the censorial elections of 184. More probably a long-standing dislike of the Scipios, reinforced by the ostentatious celebration of their recent successes—Lucius, in emulation of his brother, now flaunted the name Asiaticus as a permanent reminder of his achievement—gave added impetus to a genuine disapproval of their high-handed disregard of the responsibility to account for 500 talents of public money. The arrogant and impetuous defiance with which Africanus met the demand for an account, tearing up the account books in front of the Senate, served only to inflame passions and exacerbate the issue: it led directly to new tribunician action and a renewed demand before the People, and to the verge of a major humiliation which was averted only by a last-minute tribunician veto—which itself was perhaps obtained only with some difficulty and embarrassment. Probably the dispute then ground to a halt. For Lucius' critics, Cato prominent among them, impasse was failure, for Lucius himself and for Africanus it was victory of a kind; but from such an episode there must have been a formidable legacy—the legacy of an unresolved conflict and of angry resentment. Whatever the case may have been before, mutual hostility must now have been deep-seated, intense, and bitter.

In the next year, 186, Lucius was busy reviving his popularity with lavish games which he suddenly announced that he had vowed in Asia four years before. Possibly he was 'reminded' of this 'obligation' by the similar games given in that year by M. Fulvius Nobilior, the conqueror of Aetolia;[74] and both displays may have looked forward to the censorial elections of 184, when both men were candidates. If so their hopes proved vain. It is likely that before the vote was taken Lucius Scipio's prospects, and perhaps also those of his cousin Scipio Nasica, had been irretrievably damaged by the downfall of Africanus. No doubt the charges brought by the tribune Naevius alleged misconduct of which he and his associates believed Africanus to be guilty; no doubt Cato, probably the moving force, genuinely wished to see wrongdoing punished; but it is difficult to reject the suspicion that at this date the real impetus stemmed from a combination of personal animosity and political ambition.

The five patricians and four plebeians who sought the censorship in 184 were L. Valerius Flaccus, P. Scipio Nasica, L. Scipio Asiaticus, Cn. Manlius Vulso, L. Furius Purpurio, M. Fulvius Nobilior, Ti. Sempronius Longus, M. Sempronius Tuditanus, and Cato himself. They competed 'summa contentione' says Livy, and he and Plutarch report the contest in very similar terms, which may even be derived ultimately from Cato

74 Livy, 39. 44. 1 f. and 8 ff.

himself.[75] It is alleged that there was a concerted effort against Cato by a large section of the aristocracy, and that all the other candidates except his ally Valerius worked together to keep him from office (presumably by all directing their principal abuse at him). Even if there is exaggeration in this, it seems clear that he staked his candidature on a declared intention to conduct a stern and severe census, a distinctive approach in which his record and personality would have given him much credibility. He accused his rivals of unwillingness to exercise the severity of which he asserted the state stood in urgent need.

He exhorted the people, if they were wise, to choose not the most agreeable physician but the one who was most in earnest. He himself, he said, was such a physician, and of the patricians one, Valerius Flaccus: with him and him alone as colleague he thought he could achieve something effective, cutting and searing the hydra-like luxury and softness.[76]

Cato himself may have had in mind especially the recent massive and ostentatious inflow of wealth and luxury from the eastern wars, especially the spectacular booty brought by Manlius Vulso;[77] but however this was viewed, the feeling that, despite the military successes, all was not well with the state had had not a little to feed upon in recent years. Not only practical misfortunes but the disfavour of the gods might be seen in the floods, earthquake, and serious fire of 192, the twelve inundations by the Tiber in 189, and the plague of 187.[78] The trouble over usurers in the late 190s implies considerable monetary and economic problems;[79] in 189 the prosecution of grain dealers for hoarding betrays difficulties of supply and points to hardship;[80] 187 had seen difficulties with the Latin states over their losses of population to Rome, 186 the alarms and fears engendered by the 'Bacchanalian conspiracy' and the ruthless measures of repression, which dragged on into 184.[81] In 185 a serious slave uprising in Apulia had necessitated the intervention of a praetor, and his investigation into a 'conspiracy' of shepherds whose brigandage was infesting the public highways and pastures resulted in the conviction of some 7,000 men—which indicates a menace of no small proportions.[82] All this is known despite the scantiness of such information in sources whose

[75] Livy, 39. 40. 1 ff. and 41. 1 ff.; Plut. *Cato Mai.* 16.
[76] Plut. *Cato Mai.* 16. 6 f.; cf. Livy, 39. 41. 3 f.; 'Plut.' *Apophth. Cat. Mai.* 22.
[77] Livy, 39. 6. 7–7. 5.   [78] Livy, 35. 21. 5 f.; 35. 40. 7 f.; 38. 28. 4; 38. 44. 7.
[79] p. 54 and Appendix 5.   [80] Livy, 38. 35. 5 f.
[81] Livy, 39. 3. 4 ff.; 39. 8–19; 39. 41. 6 f.
[82] Livy, 39. 29. 8 ff., on which see also p. 248 n. 30.

dominant interests are military campaigns and the quarrels of the aristocracy.

To what extent such events, and especially the most recent of them, enabled Cato to elicit a favourable response to his promises of severity it is impossible to tell; nor is it possible to assess how far his cause was advanced by the deliberate discrediting of his opponents, by disunity among them, by the aid of the patrician Valerius (and perhaps of other senatorial supporters, despite the picture of concerted hostility), by the recollection of his achievements, or by the sheer force of his powerful personality. No doubt all contributed in some degree. The outcome was the election of Cato and Valerius, who embarked upon a censorship which Livy was to characterize as 'renowned and full of quarrels'.[83]

[83] Livy, 39. 44. 9: 'nobilis censura fuit simultatium plena.'

5

The Censorship[1]

THE censorship was the most senior, the most select, and the most prestige-laden of the Roman magistracies. To be elected to it was in itself an outstanding achievement and a coveted prize, all the more so for a *novus homo*, the first of his line even to become a senator. But it was also an office with important duties and extensive powers, affording its holder an opportunity unique in his career to exercise direct authority in many aspects of the life of the *res publica*. Cato is not likely to have been indifferent to the honour and distinction conferred by his office, but he had not sought it for that alone. His promises of a stern censorship were not empty words uttered to entice votes. There is no mistaking the thoroughness with which he set about his duties or the vigour with which he exercised the powers he had striven so hard to gain.

The evidence about Cato's use of these powers is drawn in part from narrative sources, in part from fragments of his speeches. Although his censorship is mentioned by many ancient authors the significant narrative sources, aside from a few brief comments and anecdotes, consist of two accounts which, though succinct, fortunately preserve much detail. One of the accounts is by Livy, the other by Plutarch. Though each of them supplies some particulars omitted by the other, the two narratives are in broad agreement and actual discrepancies are concerned not with the actions of the censors but with details of the offence for which they expelled a certain individual (Lucius Flamininus) from the Senate.[2] The fragments of the speeches present a more varied picture.[3] Some are

---

[1] Select bibliography: Fraccaro, 'Ricerche storiche e letterarie sulla censura del 184/183', *Studi storici*, 4 (1911), 1 ff. = *Opusc.* i. 417 ff. (for the remainder of this chapter indicated by *Opuscula* references only); De Sanctis, *Storia* iv. 1², pp. 585 ff.; Janzer, pp. 30 ff.; Schmaeling, *Die Sittenaufsicht der Censoren*, ch. 2, *passim*; Marmorale, *Cato Maior*², pp. 87 ff.; Della Corte, *Catone censore*², pp. 54 ff.; Scullard, *Roman Politics*², pp. 153 ff.; Gelzer, *RE*, s.v. *Porcius*, no. 9, cols. 126 ff.; Kienast, pp. 68 ff. A number of views relating to Cato's censorship which are not accepted in this chapter are discussed briefly in Appendix 6.

[2] Livy, 39. 42. 5–44. 9 and 52. 1 f.; Plut. *Cato Mai.* 17–19. The order of events is virtually identical in the two accounts, suggesting that they ultimately go back to a common source, despite the differences regarding the offence of L. Flamininus (on which see further below). The sources are discussed at length by Fraccaro, loc. cit.   [3] *ORF*³, Cato frs. 69–127.

explicitly attested as belonging to the censorship, but others are assigned to it by conjecture only. While some of the latter can be accepted as almost certainly censorial, others could also be plausibly associated with other occasions, and some, which have been assigned to the censorship for tenuous reasons, would be more properly designated as being of unknown date and circumstance. Even so, the number of useful fragments is considerable and their value is the greater in that for the most part they supplement rather than duplicate the narrative sources. With this background in mind it is possible to begin with a short survey of the known events of the censorship.

It is clear that the two censors, Cato and Valerius, acted in full harmony. There is no hint of disagreement, of one vetoing any act of the other, and when a dispute arose over the public contracts they stood firmly together. Only in placing contracts for some of their public works are they recorded as acting separately, and that is likely to have been for reasons of practical convenience. Nevertheless the sources, mentioning Cato constantly, Valerius only occasionally, unmistakably reflect the belief, which there is no reason to question, that Cato was the dominating partner, that he was responsible for the spirit in which this censorship was conducted: 'He [sc. Cato] exercised that power with severity (*severe*)', says Nepos; 'a noble censorship', says Livy, 'and full of quarrels, which occupied Marcus Porcius, to whom that severity (*acerbitas*) was ascribed, through his whole life'.[4]

In the review of the Senate Cato and Valerius expelled seven men as unworthy to be members.[5] One of these was a former consul, Lucius Quinctius Flamininus, brother of Titus Flamininus, the 'liberator of Greece' who himself had been censor in 189. In the most vehement of his censorial speeches Cato declared that at a banquet during his campaign in Cisalpine Gaul Lucius had carried out an execution, whether with his own hand or through the agency of a lictor, merely to gratify the whim of a paramour, probably a boy named Philippus. In most versions of the story the victim is said to have been a criminal already condemned to death, but Livy asserts that in the speech (which Livy implies that he himself had consulted) Cato described the victim as a Boian chieftain who had come to seek Roman aid and protection.

---

[4] Nepos, *Cato* 2. 3; Livy, 39. 44. 9. Fraccaro, *Opusc.* i. 437, holds that the lot assigned Cato priority and the responsibility for the concluding ceremony of the *lustrum*; but as the comparable case of Scipio Aemilianus shows, this is not proved by Cato's subsequent judicial dispute *De lustri sui felicitate* (pp. 105 ff.); cf. Astin, *Scipio Aemilianus*, pp. 119 and 325 ff.

[5] Livy, 39. 42. 5 f.; Plut. *Cato Mai.* 17. 1; *Flam.* 19. 1; Nepos, *Cato* 2. 3. Only Livy states the precise number.

Since Lucius, supported by Titus, was denying the accusation Cato
concluded his speech with a challenge to a judicial contest as to the
facts, a challenge which Lucius did not take up.[6]

According to Plutarch another of the expelled senators was a certain
Manilius who had been thought to have good prospects of reaching the
consulship. It is possible that this man was really a Manlius who had
already held the praetorship, but this is no more than a tentative conjecture
and he cannot safely be identified with any other known individual.[7]
Plutarch goes on to say that 'Manilius' was expelled because he had
kissed his wife while his daughter was looking on, a statement which
has given rise to comments on the seriousness of Cato's moral stance

[6] Livy, 39. 42. 5–43. 5 (n.b. 'longe gravissima oratio'); Plut. *Cato Mai.* 17. 1 ff. and *Flam.*
18–19 (with only slight differences which might be expected between the two accounts and
no contradiction in substance); Cic. *De sen.* 42; 'Victor', *De vir. ill.* 47. 4; *Val. Max.* 2. 9. 3;
4. 5. 1; cf. Seneca, *Controv.* 9. 2 (25) (not naming Cato); *ORF*[3], Cato fr. 71. Livy also reveals
the main features of the version given by Valerius Antias, by strongly criticizing his errors.
Livy himself is distinctive in identifying the victim as a Boian chieftain, in being the only
source to say explicitly that he was executed by Lucius personally, and in naming the lover
as Philippus (for which some support may be found in *ORF*[3], fr. 71). Plutarch mentions
versions given by Livy, Cicero, and Valerius Antias, and by 'many others', and there is no
reason to doubt that he had himself consulted at least the first two; but since his own
accounts contain details, including the challenge, not found in any surviving source it is
certain that he based them primarily on some work now lost. The various versions of the
story are discussed by Münzer, 'Atticus als Geschichtsschreiber', *Hermes*, 40 (1905), pp. 73 f.;
Fraccaro, *Opusc.* i. 426 ff.

[7] Plut. *Cato Mai.* 17. 7, also *Coniug. praec.* 13; cf. Amm. Marc. 28. 4. 9. Fraccaro, *Opusc.* i.
433 f. argues that the statement that 'Manilius' was thought to have good prospects for the
consulship implies that he was of praetorian standing; yet no Manilius is among the praetors
of recent years, all of whom are known. He therefore suggests that the name was really
'Manlius' (a correction which presents no difficulty) and the person perhaps A. Manlius
Vulso, who it has been conjectured was suffect praetor in 189. This hypothesis has been
received with considerable favour. However, if it is correct Manlius Vulso made a remarkable
recovery in public esteem after his expulsion, for he was consul in 178. Another possible
candidate might be P. Manlius (see *MRR* i. 382 with note), whose second praetorship in 182
is a most unusual phenomenon and could be his 'come-back' after the expulsion; but since
his first praetorship was as far back as 195 it is not easy to envisage that in 184 his prospects
for the consulship were considered strong. L. Manlius Acidinus, cos. 179, is excluded from
consideration by the appointments he held in 183.

In view of all these difficulties it is worth considering whether Plutarch's comment has not
been taken too literally or accepted too confidently. In any case it does not necessarily imply
that the expelled senator was of praetorian status. Perhaps there was a more junior Manilius—
or Manlius—who was widely regarded as exceptionally promising until Cato's censorship.
Alternatively the remark may be an exaggeration—or a retrojection from the fact that the
expelled senator did subsequently become consul, in which case he would certainly have been
A. Manlius Vulso. But the whole question of identity is too open for any conjecture to be
useful as an element in assessing the character and objectives of Cato's censorship, though
this has sometimes been attempted. For a brief discussion of the episode with references to
cult practices see Schönberger, 'Der glückliche Cato', *RhM* 112 (1969), 190.

and comparison with his own remark that the presence of his young son put him on his guard against indecencies of speech just as much as did the presence of the Vestal Virgins.[8] So it may be, but more probably, if it is to be taken literally at all, this was a minor item among more serious complaints, preserved in isolation as a severe moral *exemplum*; and possibly the remark itself was never intended to be taken literally as the genuine reason for the expulsion but originated in scornful and humorous sarcasm: for Cato seems to have followed it up immediately with a joke about never embracing his own wife except when there was loud thunder, and that he was a happy man when Jupiter thundered.[9]

Conceivably the name of a third expelled senator may be preserved in the title of a speech *De moribus Claudii Neronis*, which is plausibly regarded as censorial, though not actually attested as such.[10] Although Claudius was presumably one of the patrician Nerones, nothing further is known of him and it cannot even be taken for granted that he had entered the Senate. Thus, supposing the speech to have been censorial, it is not possible to be sure that Cato was dealing with him as a senator rather than as an *eques*.

How many *equites* were deprived of their horses at the *recognitio* is not recorded, but the most distinguished of them was certainly Lucius Cornelius Scipio Asiaticus, the brother of Africanus.[11] The accusations mentioned by Plutarch that this action was a deliberate insult were probably inevitable but perhaps unfounded. An *eques* might lose his status because of unworthy conduct, because his horse was inadequately cared for, or because he was no longer physically fit for cavalry service: in the latter case the removal of the horse was not regarded as a punishment and was 'without ignominy'.[12] All three principles were certainly applied by Cato during his *recognitio*, but although one late and brief source says that Scipio lost his horse 'ignominiae causa',[13] the fact that he was not expelled from the Senate suggests that there was no major complaint of unworthy behaviour; and since it is unlikely that his horse was inadequately maintained the stated reason and perhaps the true reason was probably his physical disability.[14] In another case, however, that of

---

[8] Plut. *Cato Mai.* 20. 7.   [9] Plut. *Cato Mai.* 17. 7.

[10] *ORF*[3], frs. 83–4; see esp. Scullard, *Roman Politics*[2], p. 261. Janzer, p. 37, too confidently identifies Claudius as the Ap. Claudius Nero who was praetor in 195; similarly Kienast, p. 94.

[11] Livy, 39. 44. 1; Plut. *Cato Mai.* 18. 1; 'Victor', *De vir. ill.* 53. 2.

[12] Mommsen, *Röm. Staats.* ii[3]. 399 f.; Gell. 4. 12. 2 f.; 6. 22. 1 f.

[13] 'Victor', *De vir. ill.* 53. 2.

[14] 'Victor', *De vir. ill.* 53. 1: 'infirmo corpore'; Fraccaro, *Opusc.* i. 492 f.; Kienast, p. 149 n. 73; cf. Scullard, *Roman Politics*[2], p. 159. See also p. 324.

Lucius Veturius, against whom Cato alleged both unworthy conduct and physical unsuitability, he sought to present the latter as well as the former as a matter of disgrace and ignominy. Most of the surviving fragments of the denunciation of Veturius are concerned with his neglect of a sacrifice, evidently a family cult which Cato believed to have public significance, but the comment of Gellius, who knew the speech, makes it clear that Veturius was alleged to be much too fat for cavalry service and that Cato treated this as a serious accusation against him.[15] Two other fragments are probably part of this attack: 'He cannot keep his seat on an agitated horse' and 'How can such a body be useful to the state when everything between gullet and genitals is devoted to the belly?'[16]

Since a collection of Cato's sharply worded denunciations of senators and *equites* survived along with other of his speeches, it is possible that the names of a few more of those removed from the orders are preserved in the titles of other orations (for example, *In Q. Sulpicium*); but as there is nothing to connect these specifically with the censorship they could equally well have been composed in connection with judicial or political disputes on other occasions.[17] It is also possible but similarly uncertain that the censorship was the occasion of an attempt to persuade the Senate to approve an increase in the equestrian order from 1,800 to 2,200 men.[18] Otherwise, nothing more is known about the *recognitio equitum*, and with regard to the review of the Senate the only other item is that Cato appointed his colleague Valerius Flaccus to be *princeps senatus*.[19]

In the general registration of citizens and property there is good reason to suppose that Cato took seriously his right—or duty—to downgrade

---

[15] Gell. 6. 22. 1 ff. = *ORF*[3], Cato fr. 78. The fragments, though mostly brief, are more numerous than those of most speeches: frs. 72–82.

[16] Frs. 79 (= Plut. *Cato Mai.* 9. 6) and 80; in neither case is Veturius named.

[17] Livy, 39. 42. 6; *ORF*[3], Cato frs. 108 (Laetorius); 109 (Annius); 110 (Q. Sulpicius). No certain identifications are possible. For the possibility that the *Contra Annium* was actually delivered *c.* 152 see Astin, *Scipio Aemilianus*, p. 39 n. 2. The brief fragment about Laetorius seems to be a witty and sarcastic progression which would be comprehensible as part of an attack on his performance as an *eques*: 'asinum aut musimonem aut arietem'. Fraccaro, *Opusc.* i. 442, believes the speeches in support of the censorial *notae* to be an innovation by Cato, but this must remain uncertain since, with a very few exceptions, Cato's speeches in general were in any case the earliest to survive.

[18] *ORF*[3], frs. 85–6. *ORF*[3], fr. 123, *Contra C. Pisonem* ('video hac tempestate concurrisse omnes adversarios'), seems more likely to have been connected with a prosecution brought against Cato, though Janzer, p. 51, and Malcovati, ad loc., tentatively assign it to the censorship; cf. Scullard, *Roman Politics*[2], pp. 151 and 272, who believes that it was not censorial but that it was Piso who was being prosecuted—which is possible.

[19] Livy, 39. 52. 1; Plut. *Cato Mai.* 17. 1. See also pp. 324 f.

those who had neglected their farms or vineyards, though specific instances are lacking:

If anyone had allowed his land to run to waste and was not giving it sufficient attention and had neither ploughed nor weeded it, or if anyone had neglected his orchard or vineyard, such conduct did not go unpunished but was a matter for the censors, who made such a man an *aerarius*. Likewise [if an *eques* neglected his horse] ... There are authorities for both punishments and Marcus Cato attested them frequently.[20]

A chance anecdote does preserve the name of one man who was reduced to the *aerarii*, a certain L. Nasica, though his offence had nothing to do with property: he answered one of the censors' formal questions with a light-hearted witticism.[21] Cato's reaction at least illustrates the attitude of serious purposefulness with which he conducted the proceedings and his consequent view of such levity as disrespectful and outrageous. But it is Cato's treatment of 'luxury' property which figures prominently in the sources. Ornaments, women's clothing, and vehicles valued at more than 15,000 asses and slaves under the age of twenty who had been purchased since the previous censorship for 10,000 asses or more were all assessed at ten times their actual value and then made subject to a special tax of 3 asses in 1,000.[22] Furthermore Cato is known to have delivered a censorial speech, presumably both explanatory and hortatory, 'concerning clothing and vehicles', *De vestitu et vehiculis*.[23] A speech 'concerning statues and pictures' may have dealt with the same general topic, though alternatively it may have been concerned with another practice about which Cato complained vociferously during the censorship, the setting up of statues to Roman women, presumably wives of governors, in the provinces.[24]

In carrying out their responsibilities for public works both censors showed much energy, initiative, and indeed severity. They required all privately owned buildings which encroached upon public land to be

[20] Gell. 4. 12. 1 f. = ORF[3], Cato fr. 124.

[21] Cic. *De orat.* 2. 260. Gell. 4. 20. 2 ff. does not name Cato but shows that the story was used by Scipio Aemilianus in his own censorial speech to warn of the need for respect and solemnity in the presence of the censors. The joke itself is untranslatable: 'Ridicule etiam illud L. Nasica censori Catoni; cum ille "ex tui animi sententia tu uxorem habes?" "non hercule" inquit "ex mei animi sententia." '

[22] Plut. *Cato Mai.* 18. 2 ff.; Livy, 39. 44. 1 ff. (with some details, lost in corruptions and lacunae, restored from Plutarch); Nepos, *Cato* 2. 3.

[23] ORF[3], fr. 93.

[24] ORF[3], Cato fr. 94: *De signis et tabulis*. Malcovati, ad loc., following Janzer, p. 41, assigns the fragment concerning provincial statues (fr. 95, untitled but from the censorship) to the same speech. On this and other aspects of these fragments see esp. Scullard, *Roman Politics*[2], p. 260.

demolished within thirty days, and they acted vigorously to shut off supplies of water diverted from the public system to private houses and land (except perhaps in a few cases where limited rights had been granted in return for a rental).[25] This must be the context of a speech 'against L. Furius concerning the water', *In L. Furium de aqua*. Cato evidently alleged that Furius had paid a high price for some land in the expectation that he would be able to irrigate it with illegally diverted water, and at least in this instance Cato did not content himself with cutting off the supply but also imposed a fine.[26] More positively the censors included among their contracts for new work provision for the fountain basins of the water system to be paved with stone. This same concern with practical features of life seems to characterize the whole programme of public works. The sewer system, which had been badly neglected, was not only cleaned and repaired but extended to completely new districts, including the Aventine. This, too, seems to have been discussed in one of Cato's speeches, though the two fragments reveal nothing more.[27] Perhaps they are from an address to the Senate arguing his case for the requisite funds, for the cost was enormous—probably 6,000,000 denarii.[28] While Valerius let a contract for a new road at Formiae and a causeway or mole at 'the Neptunian waters' (site unknown), Cato himself arranged for the construction of two business buildings (*atria*) and, on the site of four shops which he purchased for the state, a basilica, the first building of its kind in Rome and known as the Basilica Porcia.[29] A speech 'That a basilica should be built' was presumably part of the effort to overcome the considerable opposition to the project which Cato encountered in the Senate. The nature of the objections is not recorded but it is a fair guess that they were primarily financial, especially in view of the heavy costs of the public works programme as a whole.[30]

It was over financial matters that Cato and his colleague became

[25] Livy, 39. 44. 4; Plut. *Cato Mai.* 19. 1. On rights in respect of the water-supply see Frontin. *De aquis* 2. 94 ff.; cf. *ORF*[3], Cato fr. 103; Mommsen, *Röm. Staats.* ii[3]. 436.

[26] *ORF*[3], Cato frs. 99–105; fr. 102 for speculation in land. Charisius four times uses the words *de multa* when introducing fragments of this speech. Scullard, *Roman Politics*[2], p. 161, and Kienast, p. 78, *contra* Fraccaro, *Opusc.* i. 443 and 451, lean towards identifying this Furius with Purpurio, cos. 196. That is possible but it is right to be cautious about too ready an identification with the one distinguished L. Furius known in the period. Fraccaro, op. cit., pp. 451 ff., examines the fragments in detail.

[27] Livy, 39. 44. 5; *ORF*[3], frs. 126–7.

[28] *HRR* i[2], Acilius fr. 6 = Dion. Hal. 3. 67. 5, for 1,000 talents spent on the sewers by censors, rightly taken to be almost certainly those of 184.

[29] Livy, 39. 44. 6 f.; for the basilica also Plut. *Cato Mai.* 19. 3; *Cato Min.* 5. 1; 'Victor', *De vir. ill.* 47. 5; Ps. Ascon. p. 201 Stangl. It was destroyed by fire in 52: Ascon. *In Mil.* p. 33C.

[30] *ORF*[3], fr. 87 (the few surviving words add nothing); Plut. *Cato Mai.* 19. 3.

involved in a much greater controversy.[31] They were responsible for
assigning by auction a great number of public contracts, not only for
their own new public works but for the maintenance of existing public
properties and for the collection of numerous rentals and imposts (*vectigalia*). Tackling this task with a typically thorough concern to secure
the most favourable possible arrangements for the state, Cato and Valerius
set about leasing the contracts for the public works at the lowest possible
figures and those for *vectigalia* at the highest possible. After the auction
the successful contractors began to complain, obviously seeking a revision
of the contracts to give them more favourable terms. Their case was taken
up by Titus Flamininus, who persuaded the Senate to order the contracts
to be annulled and new ones to be made. No doubt Plutarch is right to
imply that Titus was acting out of anger at the humiliation of his brother
Lucius, but his ability to carry a majority in a Senate which had already
been persuaded to approve vast expenditure on the censors' public works
suggests that he was able to exploit an issue more substantial than a
personal feud. Probably the argument was that the margins of profit
allowed to the contractors were dangerously narrow, so narrow that
they might imperil the fulfilment of the contracts and lead to defaults.
Just such a default was referred to with disapproval by Cato himself,
probably but not certainly during his censorship, in his speech against
Oppius, a contractor who had found it preferable to forfeit the land he
had pledged as security rather than deliver the wine he had contracted to
supply.[32] On the other hand the censors had simply taken full advantage
of a situation in which keen competition for contracts led bidders to
risk narrow margins. Obliged to start the whole procedure afresh, Cato
and Valerius were able to exclude from the auction all those who had
been successful on the first occasion and yet to reassign all the contracts
on terms which were only slightly more favourable to the contractors.
It has been suggested that this episode was the occasion of Cato's *Ad
litis censorias*, 'On censorial litigation', a speech obscure in purpose but
particularly interesting for a fragment in which Cato pledges his utmost
efforts to combat negligence.[33]

[31] Livy, 39. 44. 7 f.; Plut. *Cato Mai.* 19. 1 f.; *Flam.* 19. 6 f. On this episode see esp. Badian,
Publicans and Sinners, pp. 35 ff.; also below, pp. 325 f.

[32] *ORF*[3], Cato fr. 106: 'vinum redemisti, praedia pro vini quadrantilibus sexaginta in
publicum dedisti, vinum non dedisti.' The speech is not stated to have been censorial,
though it is widely assumed that it was and that Cato was excluding Oppius from the auction
for new contracts: Fraccaro, *Opusc.* i. 454 f. and 497; Janzer, pp. 44 f.; Scullard, *Roman
Politics*[2], p. 162; Kienast, p. 79.

[33] *ORF*[3], frs. 121–2; Scullard, *Roman Politics*[2], pp. 162 and 263 f.; note Fraccaro, *Opusc.* i.
450 f.

During the dispute about the contracts Titus Flamininus also incited a tribunician move to impose a heavy fine on Cato. The fine was certainly not paid, and it is likely that the whole attempt was dropped before it even reached the stage of formal proceedings. That is the most probable interpretation of one of Cato's speeches which is generally taken to be connected with this affair, *Si se M. Caelius tribunus plebis appellasset*, 'If M. Caelius, tribune of the plebs, had summoned him [sc. to face an accusation before a gathering of the people]'. The fragments reveal a vigorous personal attack on the character and manners of Caelius but nothing of the substance of the dispute.[34]

This review of the events of the census may be rounded off by noting briefly several other speeches which may have been censorial, though none of them is certainly so. The purpose of two of them is clear. 'That booty should be assigned to the public account', *Uti praeda in publicum referatur*, is self-explanatory, and the one fragment comments sarcastically upon the use of statues of deities from booty to adorn private houses.[35] 'That spoils should not be affixed unless captured from an enemy', *Ne spolia figerentur nisi de hoste capta*, was obviously directed against those who displayed among their household exhibits trophies which had been purchased or which were otherwise not authentic personal trophies.[36] The others, however, are extremely obscure: two, *De Indigitibus*[37] and *De agna musta pascenda*,[38] may have something to do with temples and sacred precincts, while the third is simply *De fundo oleario*, 'Concerning an olive farm', with a single uninformative fragment.[39]

The most pervasive characteristic of all this censorial activity is perhaps the rigorous thoroughness with which it was performed. Every function, every responsibility inherent in the office of censor seems to have been approached with a determination to carry it out to the letter. It is the most striking application of a concept which is to be seen at many points

---

[34] *ORF*[3], frs. 111–20. The best interpretation of the problems presented by this speech and its title is that of Till, 'Zu Plutarchs Biographie des älteren Cato', *Hermes*, 81 (1953), 440 ff., rejecting the earlier suggestions of Fraccaro, *Opusc.* i. 237 ff. and 457 f., Janzer, p. 46, and Scullard, *Roman Politics*[2], pp. 262 f. (where there is a useful review of the evidence). Kienast, p. 79, in the main follows Till.

[35] *ORF*[3], fr. 98; see Malcovati, ad loc., and Janzer, p. 43; but the positive grounds for regarding this as censorial are slight.

[36] *ORF*[3], fr. 97; Fraccaro, *Opusc.* i. 441 f.; Janzer, pp. 42 f.; Scullard, *Roman Politics*[2], pp. 157 and 261.

[37] *ORF*[3], fr. 88, the text of which is mutilated. Fraccaro, *Opusc.* i. 450 n. 145; cf. Janzer, p. 40.

[38] *ORF*[3], frs. 89–92. Janzer, p. 40; Scullard, *Roman Politics*[2], pp. 161 and 262.

[39] *ORF*[3], fr. 107. Janzer, p. 45, and Malcovati both place it among the censorial speeches, but on slender grounds.

in Cato's career. Public office and public service were for him duties to be performed in the interests of the *res publica*, with strict attention to the particular tasks and proper procedures, and with equally strict avoidance of all personal material gain from the opportunities afforded by public offices and commands. Nor was this a concept relevant only to the relatively infrequent years of public office. It was a duty, at least for 'a great and illustrious man', always to put his time to good use and to be active in the public interest.[40] Such an attitude, indicated in the assessments given by several writers in antiquity (especially but not only Plutarch)[41] is not to be dismissed as posthumous idealization. It is apparent in the fragments of the speeches, where the phrase *pro re publica* is an important standard of judgement alongside scrupulous abstention from personal material gain in public affairs;[42] likewise in the dicta, in Cato's statements about the use of leisure,[43] and in the reports of his conduct in office, ranging from his general approach during the praetorship and censorship to such details as the sale of his horse in Spain to save the state the expense of shipment; and it can be seen again in his frequent participation in prosecutions for misconduct in office, which it would be unreasonably cynical to attribute wholly or even predominantly to personal and factional animosities rather than to genuine indignation at the alleged offences.[44] If the seeming harshness of the censorship was above all the product of the remorseless logic of unbending conscientiousness, it was a conscientiousness deeply rooted in Cato's temperament and it characterized his entire career. If further explanation is sought for this conscientiousness, it may be conjectured that it lies in a combination of literal-mindedness and reactions under-standable in a *novus homo*, making him a particularly enthusiastic champion of the traditional ideals and responsibilities of the class into which he had won his way.

In two fragments of speeches this conscientious attitude is directly associated with Cato's attitude to the office of censor. About 190 or 189, in his speech 'On his consulship', he said, 'Those who become censors hereafter will strive for the state more fearfully, more slowly,

[40] *HRR* i², Cato fr. 2 = Cic. *Pro Planc.* 66.

[41] Plut. *Cato Mai.* 8. 15, cf. *De se . . . laudando* 14; *Cato Mai.* 6; 10; 24. 11; *An seni sit . . .* 27; Cic. *Parad. Stoic.* 12; *Rep.* 1. 1; Livy, 39. 40. 10 ff.; Justin, *Epit. Trog. praef.* 5.

[42] The *res publica*: *ORF*³, Cato frs. 21; 50; 64; 83; 117; 173; 176. On improper gains from office: frs. 98; 132; 133; 173, thence 203; 177; 185; 224–6.

[43] *HRR* i², fr. 2; Cic. *Rep.* 1. 27, cf. *De off.* 3. 1; *Carmen de moribus* fr. 3, from Gell. 11. 2. 6; Colum. *De re rust.* 11. 1. 26; Pliny, *Nat. hist.* 19. 24.

[44] Plut. *Cato Mai.* 15. 1; Quint. *Inst.* 12. 7. 4; Livy, 39. 40. 8; 'Victor', *De vir. ill.* 47. 7; Ampel. 19. 8.

more timidly', which, whatever the precise reference, implies a belief that the office demanded boldness and vigour, applied without fear or favour.[45] The other fragment, from the speech 'On censorial litigation', is a direct comment on Cato's own censorship, or at least upon some aspect of it: 'I know that negligence is wont to get a grip upon good fortune: to prevent this, as far as lay within me I have not spared my labour.'[46] Both passages, and especially the mention of negligence, may imply criticism of preceding censorships, the last three of which seem to have been conducted with a mildness which Cato could well have viewed as negligence. The censors of 199 had expelled no senators at all, and the few expelled in 194 and 189—three and four respectively —were all of junior rank, not having held curule office. Furthermore Livy mentions that both in 194 and in 189 very few *equites* were deprived of their horses, and that in 194 no severity was shown towards any *ordo*.[47]

If Cato did consider his predecessors guilty of neglect it will certainly have reinforced his own natural determination to be wholly conscientious; but his claim that he was unsparing in his labour to prevent Rome's favourable fortunes being impaired by negligence is a reminder that it was not a mere mechanical conscientiousness. Cato did not perform his duties to the full only because they were the long-established duties of the office. There was also a positive belief that his efforts were in the interests of the state. Nor could a conscientious censorship be merely the strict and efficient application of a given set of rules. Obviously many aspects of the censors' work did demand above all the efficient exercise of administrative skills: such were the recording of many thousands of property-declarations, the preparation of a list of around a quarter of a million citizens, the leasing of numerous contracts, and the planning of public works; but a conscientious censorship meant even more than able and thorough organization. Many of the tasks by their very nature called for personal judgements: judgements as to what criteria required the removal of a senator or an *eques* from his order, judgements as to what kind of neglect or misbehaviour demanded the downgrading of a citizen, judgements even as to the merits of particular projects in the field of public works. Many though not all such judgements flowed directly from the *regimen morum*, which was regarded as an

---

[45] *ORF*[3], fr. 50. For this speech see p. 60.

[46] *ORF*[3], fr. 122; Scullard, *Roman Politics*[2], pp. 263 f. Janzer, pp. 51 f., rightly notes the similarity of the idea about good fortune to that expressed in fr. 163, the exordium of the speech on behalf of the Rhodians in 167.

[47] Livy, 32. 7. 2; 34. 44. 4 f.; 38. 28. 2; cf. Fraccaro, *Opusc.* i. 483; Scullard, *Roman Politics*[2], p. 157 n. 4.

integral part of the censorial duties. It goes without saying that judgements
of this kind were reached within the framework of long established
and respected traditions, but it is also the case that much was left to the
discretion of the censors themselves, subject only to each other's veto;
and in conscientiously performing their duties on behalf of the state
they were often making judgements as to what was in the interests of
the state.

The largely unfettered discretion of the censors, especially in the
regimen morum, meant that in the formulation of such judgements as
to what was beneficial to the state a considerable role might be played
by their personal opinions, their temperament and attitude, indeed by
their personal prejudices, though of course these opinions, attitudes,
and prejudices must themselves have been influenced by traditional
standards, sometimes no doubt accepted uncritically or with a modicum
of rationalization. So it was with Cato's censorship. For example, a
markedly practical, utilitarian outlook is apparent, in the whole programme of public works, in the concern with the water supply, in the
stress on the proper care of farms and property. This is carried through to
the *recognitio equitum*, in which Cato had in mind not only the *regimen
morum* but the historic role of the equestrian order as a body of serving
cavalrymen. The criticisms of L. Veturius embraced both his neglected
ritual and his manner of life, but the latter was expressed in terms of his
consequent inability to serve the state effectively on horseback; while
there seems little doubt that physical infirmity alone was in question in
the case of L. Scipio Asiaticus. A similar concern with practicalities may
well be the explanation of the attempt to enlarge the equestrian order
(whether or not the proposal was made during the censorship). It has
been plausibly suggested that Cato's attitude towards the *equites* may have
been conditioned in part by his own military experiences, including
personal encounter with the formidable cavalry of Carthage, the failure
of the cavalry on his own right wing at Emporiae, and whatever
circumstances led him to deliver a special exhortation to his cavalry at
Numantia.[48]

Cato's emphatic statement of the censors' duty to take action against
those who had neglected their farms or vineyards corresponds to another
of his personal attitudes. Several anecdotes and dicta indicate a firm
conviction that those who owned property had a responsibility to ensure
that it was carefully managed and maintained, and if possible increased,
that to allow an inheritance to be seriously diminished was especially

[48] Scullard, *Roman Politics*[2], p. 160; cf. Janzer, pp. 37 f.; Kienast, p. 75.

reprehensible.[49] Similarly, whatever may be thought about the 'Manilius' story, Cato's sense of outrage at the conduct of Lucius Flamininus may have been heightened (though not primarily caused) by his own strong views on sexual morality. His assertion that every adultress might be regarded as a poisoner, reminiscent of his equation of usury and murder, is probably an exercise in hyperbole, but at the least it springs from a powerful disapproval which is reflected in other passages concerned with sexual misconduct.[50] More central to the case of Flamininus was Cato's concept of the responsibilities of public office. Flamininus' action was a flagrant misuse of power, with no pretence at formal procedure and very probably in direct and inexcusable breach of *fides*.[51] But Cato had other ideals also, centring upon concepts of integrity and justice and shading off one into the other: an insistence that public office should not be a means to personal material gain gave rise to the demand that officials should take for themselves neither booty not perquisites from the provinces; but the question of booty was linked also with a concern that the state should get its proper due, while the avoidance of perquisites was linked with avoidance of arbitrary exaction and extortion, with observance of the legal rules, with a concern for justice and proper order.[52] This underlying concern with justice, proper procedure, and the law was probably another factor contributing to Cato's attitudes towards various concerns of the censorship: whether *equites* were fit to fulfil their prescribed role as cavalry, the requirement that farms and vineyards be maintained in good order, the neglect of a ritual by Veturius, the improper diversion of public water, and the encroachment of private buildings on to public land. And the whole concern about integrity, justice, and avoidance of personal gain may have some bearing on Cato's attitude towards luxury.

[49] Plut. *Cato Mai.* 8. 11; 21. 8; cf. *ORF*[3], fr. 246.

[50] *ORF*[3], fr. 240. More closely related to the Flamininus case is the scorching attack on the sexual misconduct of an unnamed man in frs. 212–13, from *De re Floria*. Cf. also frs. 221–2; Plut. *Cato Mai.* 20. 7 f.; Cic. *De orat.* 2. 256.

[51] See pp. 79 f. and esp. n. 6. On Cato's concern with *fides* see *ORF*[3], frs. 58 and esp. 238 = Cic. *De off.* 3. 104: 'Fidem in Capitolio vicinam Iovis optimi maximi, ut in Catonis oratione est, maiores nostri esse voluerunt.'

[52] Many of the fragments display these interrelationships. To the references on p. 87 n. 42 add *ORF*[3], frs. 58 and 59 (attacks on Q. Minucius Thermus, above p. 59; see esp. fr. 58, translation p. 327), and the passages linking Cato with the legend of M'. Curius and his refusal of Sabine gold: Cic. *Rep.* 3. 40; *De sen.* 55; Plut. *Cato Mai.* 2. 1 ff. On booty, note esp. the fragments of *Uti praeda in publicum referatur* (fr. 98) and *De praeda militibus dividenda* (frs. 224–6); also Cato's claims about his own conduct in fr. 173 (thence 203), his handling of booty in Spain (p. 53), and the grounds of his accusations against Glabrio and L. Scipio (pp. 59 ff.).

The attack on luxury, which is another prominent feature of the censorship of 184, is something more than a particular facet of Cato's conscientious thoroughness. Although this attack had its basis in the *regimen morum* Cato gave that concept a distinctive and seemingly unprecedented application when he systematically overvalued particular categories of property and then imposed a special tax upon them.[53] Moreover, the action of the censors corresponds closely to a hostility towards luxury evinced in a considerable number of Cato's words and actions at other times in his career, which confirms that the steps taken in 184 sprang not merely from a highly literal interpretation of censorial duties but from deep-rooted and enduring convictions—a fact which likewise tells heavily against the suggestion that the primary purpose of the measures was to raise revenue to finance the public works.[54] One indication of Cato's attitude is his opposition, some years after the censorship, to the partial repeal of the sumptuary law known as the *lex Orchia* (enacted not earlier than 182), which restricted the number of guests at banquets. A fragment of Cato's speech on this occasion refers with evident disapproval to the great increase in expenditure on meals, and other fragments which may come from this speech point to the simpler customs of the past.[55] The theme is echoed in a protest at the erection of statues to two cooks,[56] in the dictum 'Great concern about food, great unconcern about virtue',[57] in the retort to a well-known epicure that 'he [Cato] could not live in company with a man whose palate was more sensitive than his heart',[58] in the statements in a work actually entitled *Carmen de moribus* that one who devoted himself to dinner parties used to be stigmatized as an idler and that men used to pay more for horses than for cooks,[59] and in the similar complaint, in

---

[53] Cato's innovation differed in principle from a device which had been used previously, namely assessing a person at a multiple of the declared value of his whole property; though presumably that was the origin of Cato's idea. Mommsen, *Röm, Staats.* ii³. 395 f.

[54] Suggested by Kienast, pp. 79 and 86.

[55] *ORF³*, Cato fr. 139: 'qui antea obsonitavere ⟨aere⟩, postea centenis obsonitavere.' Also frs. 140–6; Macrob. *Sat.* 3. 17. 2 f., probably indicating 182 rather than 181 for the law, which is known only from references to Cato's speech. On the problems raised by two passages of Festus which as they stand imply another speech *opposing* the initial law and then that Cato *urged* partial repeal, see esp. Fraccaro, 'Catoniana', *Studi storici*, 3 (1910), 250 ff. = *Opusc.* i. 233 ff., who is almost certainly correct in restoring the titles to indicate a single speech. See also Janzer, pp. 53 ff.; Scullard, *Roman Politics²*, pp. 265 f.

[56] Fronto, *De Fer. Als.* 2 = ii. 2H = *ORF³*, fr. 96 (*In Lepidum*).

[57] Amm. Marc. 16. 5. 2 = *ORF³*, fr. 146.

[58] Plut. *Cato Mai.* 9. 7; *Quomodo adulescens* 1. Note also the untranslatable joke directed at a hearty eater which is reported by Macrobius, *Sat.* 2. 2. 4 = Jordan, p. 111, *Dicta* no. 83.

[59] *Carm. de mor.* fr. 2 = Gell. 11. 2. 5.

a speech to the People, 'that they would see the state changing for the worse especially when it was found that good-looking boys were being sold for more than fields and jars of pickled fish for more than a teamster'.[60] Just as this dictum widens the area of complaint from culinary extravagance to the prices paid for good-looking boys, the *Carmen* also complains, by reference to ancestral modesty, about unnecessary expense in dress.[61] The wearing of expensive clothing by women and the use of vehicles were two matters in which the censorial measures appear to be a direct reflection of restrictions in the *lex Oppia*, the repeal of which Cato had tried to prevent in his consulship;[62] and a fragment of a speech delivered in 152 shows disapproval of extravagance in the construction and decoration of villas and houses.[63]

The same attitude is evident in the claims made by Cato about his own manner of life. Indeed, according to Plutarch he made such claims in respect of many of the topics just mentioned:

For he says that he never wore clothing costing more than 100 drachmas; that even when praetor and consul he drank the same wine as his slaves; that as for meat he procured for his dinner 30 *asses'* worth from the market, and did that for the sake of the state, so that his body should be strong for military service; that when he received from a legacy a multi-coloured Babylonian tapestry he sold it immediately; that none of his farmsteads was plastered; that he never paid more than 1,500 drachmas (presumably = denarii) for a slave, since he wanted not the young and dainty but the hard-working and sturdy, such as grooms and herdsmen; and these he thought it necessary to sell when they became rather old and not to feed them when they were useless. He said that in general nothing which was superfluous was cheap, but that what one did not need, even if bought for an *as*, he considered expensive; and that he bought lands for sowing and pasturing rather than for sprinkling and sweeping.[64]

Much of this, and perhaps the whole, is shown by some remarks of Aulus Gellius to have been derived from a speech delivered twenty years or more after Cato's censorship, probably the speech entitled *De sumptu suo*, 'Concerning his own expenditure':

Marcus Cato, a man of consular and censorial rank, says that though the state and private individuals were abounding in wealth, his villas were plain

---

[60] Polyb. 31. 25. 5a; see Jordan, p. 97, *Dicta* 2; reproduced in whole or part in several other sources.
[61] Loc. cit.: 'Vestiri in foro honeste mos erat, domi quod satis erat.'
[62] pp. 25 ff.
[63] *ORF*³, fr. 185, though the principal point of this is that it attacks the improper acquisition of wealth.
[64] Plut. *Cato Mai.* 4. 4 ff.

and unadorned, and not even plastered, up to the seventieth year of his age. And afterwards he uses these words on the subject: 'I have neither building nor vase nor vestment which is costly, nor a high-priced slave or maidservant. If I have anything to use,' he says, 'I use it; if not, I do without. So far as I am concerned, each may use and enjoy what is his own.' Then he adds: 'They find fault with me because I lack many things; but I with them because they are unable to do without.'[65]

The context is probably a speech in self-defence against an accusation that he had violated a sumptuary law, and beyond question the tone of the passage is one of defence and self-justification; consequently it must be admitted that Cato almost certainly had powerful immediate motives for portraying his manner of life as modest and economical. Nevertheless the picture could hardly have been presented as it was unless it bore some resemblance to the truth, unless in broad terms it reflected Cato's known attitudes and practice. Similarly a fragment from the censorial speech 'Concerning clothing and vehicles' would have made little sense unless there had been a fair consistency in his attitudes: 'For, since honour [= public office] is given me on account of those *mores* which I have had previously, it would be utterly wrong if, when it has been given, I should then change them and become a different kind of person.'[66]

Such an accumulation of evidence places it beyond reasonable doubt that Cato's hostility to luxury and extravagance was not an artificial pose or an ephemeral enthusiasm but a matter of genuine conviction. Its most dramatic manifestation was no doubt in the censorship, but it was in evidence on many other occasions over a long period of years. Also, it was by no means a curious idiosyncrasy, peculiar to Cato. Although his forceful personality and his verbal skill may have made him its most prominent and influential exponent there were many who were sympathetic. To start with there was his colleague Valerius, whose approval was essential for the censorial measures; two tribunes, Marcus and Publius Iunius Brutus, took part in the opposition to the repeal of the *lex Oppia*; and of the two sumptuary laws of the period the *lex Orchia*, probably of 182, was introduced by a tribune named C. Orchius, acting on the recommendation of the Senate, while the more severe *lex Fannia* was put forward by C. Fannius Strabo, one of the consuls of 161, 'with the consent of all orders'.[67] More important than the part played by the few individuals named is the fact that sumptuary laws were

---

[65] Gell. 13. 24. 1; see also p. 107.   [66] ORF[3], fr. 93.

[67] Macrob. *Sat.* 3. 17. 2 ff.; Gell. 2. 24. 2 ff.; other refs. collected in *MRR* i. 382 and 443. Note also Plutarch's reference to the stern attitude of the elder Ti. Gracchus in his censorship in 169: Plut. *Ti. Grac.* 14. 4.

passed, and moreover received the prior recommendation of the Senate; for that implies that at least on occasion fairly widespread support could be aroused, as indeed does the fact of Cato's election to the censorship, especially if he is correctly reported as having declared one of his principal purposes to be an attack on 'hydra-like' luxury.[68]

Before the possible reasons for Cato's attitude are discussed it should be noted that his hostility was not at all directed against wealth as such, but strictly against luxury and extravagance. The censorial measures were imposed only on a limited group of items, ones which could be viewed as luxuries, not on valuable property in general, and it has been observed already that Cato regarded it as the duty of property-owners to maintain and if possible to increase their wealth, a duty which with much success he set himself to fulfil in person by amassing a substantial fortune of his own. That does not mean that his proclaimed readiness 'to do without' was hypocritical, for it was a readiness to do without unnecessary and extravagant expenditure, not to do without wealth. Such a dictum as that 'what one did not need, even if bought for an *as*, he considered expensive'—a characteristic aphorism which in any case is not to be taken literally as a solemn statement of principle—is a claim to be content with simplicity, not with poverty; and the underlying attitude is that wealth should be accumulated instead of being spent, not that it should be disdained.

What then lay behind Cato's hostility to luxury, a hostility sufficiently deep to endure over many years and to show itself as a major characteristic of his censorship, inducing him to introduce novel and remarkable measures? His actions show that he regarded great expenditure on luxuries as a concern of the state, as in some sense contrary to the interests of the state; but in what sense? No doubt it would be a mistake to seek a single answer, or one couched wholly in terms of reasoned argument; no doubt there was a compound of motives and ideas, some no more than emotional prejudices; but it is impossible to believe that Cato maintained his attitude and manner of life for so long or took his extraordinary censorial measures without any thought about why all this was, in his view, in the interests of Rome.

One element in Cato's thinking on this may have been his strong beliefs about the obligations of property-owners. To allow an inheritance to diminish was shameful, to maintain and enlarge it a duty. To one who held such views lavish expenditure on items for which there was no practical need is likely to have seemed a wasteful dissipation of wealth

[68] Plut. *Cato Mai.* 16. 7.

and property, avoidance of such expenditure a means of conserving and increasing it. If it be objected that this is a matter of standards of private conduct, or at most of the social conventions of a particular class, rather than a concern of the state, it may be answered that Cato is unlikely to have drawn the distinction between private and public at the point where it would be drawn in many societies today, or even to have thought in terms of so sharp a division. Though such a view of the responsibilities of wealth can scarcely have been uninfluenced by social conditioning and emotional prejudices, rational argument could readily be supplied in the sense that the prosperity of individuals was collectively beneficial to the state as a whole. In the censorship such identification of private conduct and prosperity with public interest was encouraged, indeed presupposed by the very concept of the *regimen morum*, and not least by the traditional responsibility for investigating whether farms and vineyards were in good order or suffering from neglect. Yet plausible though it is to suppose a connection in Cato's mind between his views on the management of property and his hostility to luxury, the one would scarcely seem an entirely sufficient explanation of the other even if the surviving evidence gave no indication of any further explanations. In fact it points towards two.

A second and much more important factor underlying Cato's attitude to luxury was his view of proper conduct in public office. He was not hostile to wealth as such, but he was extremely hostile to its acquisition by improper means, whether by defrauding the state or by making exactions from subject communities. To him it seemed that indulgence in expensive luxuries was a major stimulus to avarice, and that avarice led to corruption, to extortion, and to the personal appropriation of booty or other wealth which should properly have passed to the state or to rank-and-file soldiers. In the *Carmen de moribus* avarice was castigated as the supreme vice,[69] and the interrelationship in Cato's thinking between luxury, avarice, and misconduct in office is apparent in the fragments of several speeches. In one he speaks of a man 'who does not consider his belly to be an enemy, who feasts in the name [i.e. at the expense] of the state, not in his own, who gives pledges foolishly, who builds greedily'; in another, extravagant and richly decorated houses are seen as constructed from the spoils of office; in another he says of his opponent's conduct of a public mission, 'But if he did everything deceitfully, everything for the sake of avarice and money, such abominable crimes as we have

---

[69] Fr. 1 = Gell. 11. 2. 2: 'avaritiam omnia vitia habere putabant: sumptuosus, cupidus, elegans, vitiosus, inritus qui habebatur, is laudabatur.'

never heard of or read of, he ought to suffer punishment for his acts.'[70]
In a major passage elsewhere, though he makes no explicit reference
to luxury, he insists upon his own refusal to curry favour by giving
rein to the avarice of his subordinates at the expense of either subject
peoples or the state:

Never have I lavished my own money or that of the allies in order to win
favour. . . . Never have I imposed prefects on the towns of your allies, to
plunder their property and children. . . . Never have I granted a travel-order
to enable my friends to gain large sums by means of the warrants. . . . The
money intended for the wine-distribution I have never shared out among my
attendants and friends nor have I made them rich to the detriment of the state.[71]

In the speech demanding that 'booty be assigned to the public account'
he complained of statues and pictures being held back to furnish private
houses, while in the one 'on dividing spoils among the soldiers' he spoke
of fraudulent and avaricious conduct, referred to someone becoming
rich, and dramatically linked corruption and luxury in the assertion that
'those who commit private theft pass their lives in confinement and
fetters, those who plunder the public in gold and purple.'[72] Obviously
there is in all this no suggestion that he regarded a love of luxury as the
sole cause of avarice and corruption, but it is equally clear that he believed
it to be a factor of no small importance.

Another significant element in Cato's thinking is suggested by his
reported intention to use the censorship 'to cut and sear the hydra-like
luxury and softness'.[73] There can be no doubting the substantial role of
military matters in his outlook or the importance he attached to them
in public affairs. He had lived through the long military agony of the
Second Punic War, the terrible threat of defeat by the army of Hannibal.
Martial prowess had been a major factor in his own success and in his
entry into a governing class which was in no small measure a military
aristocracy. One can point to the many dicta with military associations,[74]
to the assertion in the Preface to the De agricultura that 'from farmers
come the bravest men and the sturdiest soldiers',[75] to his composition of
a military handbook, the De re militari,[76] and to the last four books
of the Origines, where the narrative dealt principally with wars and where

[70] ORF[3], frs. 133; 185; 177.
[71] Part of ORF[3], fr. 203, itself extracted from fr. 173, a full translation of which is on
pp. 135 f.   [72] ORF[3], frs. 98; 224–6.
[73] Plut. Cato Mai. 16. 7: τὴν τρυφὴν καὶ τὴν μαλακίαν ὥσπερ ὕδραν τέμνων καὶ ἀποκαίων.
[74] Most directly associated with the Spanish campaign, but also Jordan, pp. 100 ff., Dicta
nos. 19, 20, and 28, from Plut. Cato Mai. 9. 5 and 1. 8; refs. to other versions given by Jordan.
[75] De agr. praef. 4.   [76] pp. 184 f.

military terminology is much in evidence;[77] and in the censorship itself there is the concern about the military role of the *equites*. It is more than likely therefore that Cato regarded the spread of luxuries as enervating, as damaging to the physical and moral strength of a military people. No doubt such a belief could not have been sustained in every particular in the face of a rigorous logical scrutiny, but that does not mean that it was not held. It would have been natural and understandable, and indeed there are some positive indications, few but significant, that it was held by Cato. The most direct items are in Plutarch. Apart from the reference to the softness which was to be combated in the censorship, Plutarch says that Cato was admired because whereas other men were broken by labours and softened by pleasures, he was victor over both; that when he purchased meat for his dinner it was 'for the sake of the state, so that his body should be strong for military service'; that the basis of his concern about the reaction to the lectures of Carneades on his famous visit in 155 was a fear that 'the young men might come to love a reputation based on speaking more than one based on deeds and military affairs'.[78] It is Plutarch too who supplies the reproach to the fat *eques*, probably Veturius, 'How can such a body be useful to the state when everything between gullet and genitals is devoted to the belly?'[79] Nor is it likely that Plutarch is superimposing or reproducing what was only a post-humous interpretation, for most of these remarks are probably derived ultimately from Cato himself, and there is some evidence outside Plutarch.[80] A passage of Gellius attests that in the case of Veturius Cato did make his corpulence a matter of complaint, hence evidently castigated him for making himself unfit for cavalry service by self-indulgence; and a fragment of Cato's *Origines* concerning the supposed Spartan origin of certain Sabine customs associates Roman military success with having followed the Sabines in many of their 'severe' practices.[81]

It is a reasonable guess that other aspects of Cato's character and opinions were in some way associated with his hostility to luxury and extravagance, but to pursue this would be to pass into the realm of almost unfettered speculation. The three aspects of his attitude which have been examined,

[77] Nepos, *Cato* 3. 3 f., confirmed by many fragments, esp. from books 4 and 5.

[78] Plut. *Cato Mai.* 4. 3; 4. 4; 22. 5. The episode in 155 is discussed on pp. 174 ff.

[79] Plut. *Cato Mai.* 9. 6.

[80] Note also the complaint Cato is alleged to have made to Africanus in Sicily: that the most important point was not the expense which he was incurring but 'that he was corrupting the native frugality of his soldiers, who resorted to luxurious pleasures when their pay exceeded their actual needs': Plut. *Cato Mai.* 3. 5. On this episode and the possibility that the tradition has been influenced by the recriminations of the 180s, see pp. 13 ff.

[81] Gell. 6. 22. 1 ff. = *ORF*[3], Cato fr. 78; *HRR* i[2], fr. 51.

though probably not the whole truth, are at least firmly attested, and they can be shown both to have been important to him and to have been associated in his mind with the issue of luxury. Together they go far to explain not only the nature of his hostility to luxurious extravagance but the sense in which he regarded this as detrimental to the state, and thus why he was convinced that in his censorship he had a responsibility to take firm action.

Cato's work in the censorship is often represented as misguided and doomed to inevitable failure, as a futile attempt to turn back the clock, to take Rome back to an era of sobriety, modesty, and austerity which, if it had ever existed, was now irrecoverable.[82] Although sometimes allowed to be by no means an ignoble ideal, it is seen as a negative and conservative approach, illusory and unprofitable. The *mores* of Rome could not be fundamentally redirected in eighteen months at the behest of a pair of censors, especially when the most powerful sanctions available to them bit no more deeply than expulsion from the Senate or the equestrian order; and the changes which were occurring certainly could not be reversed in direct opposition to all the pressures and implications of the new situation of world power in which Rome found herself. What was required, it is said, was a readiness to seek new approaches, not to cling to the old; new policies to adjust the constitution to new aims, to cope with the economic consequences of vast new wealth, to create a more satisfactory relationship with the Italians and the Latins, and to establish a balance between Rome's concerns in the East and those in the West. Only thus could she be given a stable basis on which to manage her new responsibilities, only by such radical means could the Republic be saved from ultimate collapse.

In assessing Cato's censorship much of this is beside the point. The functions of the censorship were very wide but they were not universal. They had nothing to do with foreign affairs, with Rome's political relationships with eastern states, Italian allies, or subject peoples, nor with such matters as the redistribution of land or, except in rare and special cases, with constitutional reform. Further, if these matters are viewed in the wider context of Cato's career, contrasting a supposedly backward-looking moral emphasis exemplified in the censorship with the alleged real demands being made upon statesmanship at this time, it still seems

---

[82] Fraccaro, *Opusc.* i. 506 ff.; De Sanctis, *Storia* iv. 1², pp. 587 f.; Scullard, *Roman Politics*², pp. 153 ff. and 164 f.; Marmorale, *Cato Maior*², p. 86; Della Corte, *Catone censore*², p. 60. See Appendix 6 for discussion of other aspects of the views of these and other writers which are not accepted in this chapter.

that they are being viewed from a long-term historical perspective not available to Cato and his contemporaries. In theory it is always possible to imagine a statesman of such vision and penetrating intellect that he will foresee with accuracy the implications of a situation for generations ahead. Practical experience tells a different story, and it is unreasonable to expect in Cato and his contemporaries the insight to formulate policies to cope with matters in which even the issues emerged only gradually over a period of generations and for some of which effective solutions were never found in the century and a half for which the Republic continued. The same may be said of economic problems. In a society unfamiliar with economic theory, not habituated to thinking in terms of economic abstractions, the acquisition of great new wealth, whether in large immediate amounts or in long-term sources of revenue, will not easily have been seen as creating deep-seated economic problems. Even the social problems being generated by the increased flow of wealth into investment agriculture—of which Cato undoubtedly approved —were not easily foreseeable in such a context, especially as for a considerable time other factors permitted the transformation of the agricultural scene to proceed without serious disruption of the peasantry, thereby masking its full implications until the last few years of Cato's life, or even later.[83] Indeed, within the terms in which the question must actually have presented itself to Cato, namely how this wealth should be used, he showed himself in several respects alert and forward-looking. He discouraged wasteful expenditure, whether on the frivolous extravagances of private individuals or on the excessive profit-margins for contractors; he strove to ensure that a full and proper share of the revenue reached the state treasury, both from booty and from public contracts; and he arranged for an enormous amount of this new wealth to be spent on extensive and useful public works, thereby initiating a period of frequent large-scale expenditure of this kind. In fact it is misleading to lay great stress on the backward-looking element in Cato's censorship, on his supposed wish to re-establish the austere and fast-fading *mores* of Roman society as it had once been. This notion is in considerable measure the counterpart to a belief that one of Cato's principal objectives was to protect Roman society against Greek influences: the aggressive assertion of antique and specifically Roman values is seen as a form of resistance to hellenism. In point of fact, as will be argued in another chapter, Cato's attitude towards the Greeks and their culture was much more complex than this and in no

[83] pp. 240 ff. and 257.

way justifies the assumption that anti-hellenism was a constant factor underlying his activities;[84] and if no such *a priori* assumption is made there is little reason to see anti-hellenism as a significant feature of the censorship. It was natural for Cato, as for all Romans, to appeal to the authority of the *maiores* to reinforce his case, and there are several instances of him doing this.[85] If such appeals are likely to have idealized or oversimplified the past, nevertheless Cato did indeed seek to maintain certain standards of conduct which could fairly be represented as traditional, as accepted ideals of the past. But standards accepted in the past are not *ipso facto* irrelevant to the present. If the real areas of Cato's concern have been identified correctly in this chapter they were as relevant and realistic for his generation as for past generations, and were far from unimportant. There was nothing backward-looking or peripheral about wishing to stop officials improperly enriching themselves at the expense either of the state or of subject peoples, nor about indignation at corruption and the abuse of magisterial power, at the violation of obligations of *fides* or alliance, at the setting aside of proper procedures and legal duties. It was no nostalgic preoccupation with the past but a question of contemporary relevance which gave rise to his concern (possibly but by no means certainly a mistaken concern) at the adverse effect of luxury and self-indulgence on military efficiency, especially in the officer-class, upon which the whole edifice of Roman power and prosperity was constructed.[86] It might be argued that when it came to restraining expenditure on luxuries Cato overlooked the fact that the more austere standards of the past had probably been dictated largely by poverty, that now the wealth was there and was bound to be spent. But the issue was how it was to be spent: Cato's wish was to discourage its use in ways which he regarded as at best wasteful and at worst damaging to the interests of Rome.

It is a more pertinent observation that he looked upon these issues as essentially matters of moral standards and personal conduct rather than of economic, social, or legal structures, and that in any case exhortation, personal example, and the limited sanctions of the censorship were quite inadequate to effect profound changes in public and private

---

[84] Ch. 8, *passim*.

[85] e.g. *Carm. de mor.* frs. 1 and 2 = Gell. 11. 2. 2 and 5; *ORF*³, frs. 58; 172; 238; Cato, *De agr. praef.* 1; Gell. 6. 3. 52; and the passages linking Cato with the M'. Curius legend, probably ultimately derived from some statement of his own: Cic. *Rep.* 3. 40; *De sen.* 55; Plut. *Cato Mai.* 2. 1 ff.

[86] Cf. also Ennius, fr. 467, 'Moribus antiquis res stat Romana virisque.' The ancient standards are relevant to the quality of the men of the present.

conduct. Both statements are true so far as they go; neither is a valid criticism. Fundamentally the extent of private extravagance, luxury, and avarice, corruption, extortion, and the abuse of power was bound to be determined largely by the standards and values of individuals and by a climate of social opinion which was a collective expression of those standards and values. Laws might be imposed, but in the Roman context their enactment would presuppose at least a moderate degree of public acceptance of particular standards, and their effective enforcement would depend as much on the social climate as on the legal sanctions. In the last resort what mattered was whether certain kinds of behaviour were widely regarded as so shameful that the man who indulged in them was gravely jeopardizing his standing and his social and political acceptability, and also, if he violated the law, that he had little chance of escaping a conviction which besides carrying a legal penalty was generally regarded as a deep disgrace. This is not the place to embark on the complex question of why such attitudes as Cato's did not prevail in the public affairs of the late Republic (for even if historians have sometimes underestimated the efforts made to control misconduct, there is no denying that corruption, extortion, and personal extravagance all occurred on an enormous scale). Some would no doubt argue that the creation of such a climate of opinion was simply not possible in the context of a predominantly oligarchic government and an empire over subject peoples; and certainly there were great obstacles to its creation, such as the practical difficulties of supervising distant officials, the vast scope and discretion of magisterial power as traditionally conceived, the close-knit personal relationships among the relatively small group of those who exercised power, and the fact that in most respects neither the aristocracy nor the mass of Roman citizens were likely to feel a strong short-term self-interest in the maintenance of high standards in these matters. Possibly the basic situation made it inevitable or at least very likely that in the end standards such as Cato was championing would not predominate; but neither he nor his contemporaries can be expected to have viewed the question with the eyes of a modern social theoretician, or to have advocated changes which in second century Rome would have been literally unthinkable —such as the abandonment of all extra-Italian territories. He was right to see the areas of his concern as matters of personal conduct and of private and public *mores*; and within the terms of his own age and society he pursued them by the appropriate means.

For it can hardly be denied that it was appropriate, indeed essential to make use of personal example, exhortation, and the opportunities offered by the censorship. Moreover the sanctions of the censorship were not necessarily mild and ineffective: it can have been no light matter to suffer one of Cato's excoriating denunciations, as a preliminary to being downgraded with ignominy; and the depth of humiliation inflicted by expulsion from the Senate is evident from the reaction of Titus Flamininus to his brother's expulsion. It is true that the deterrent effect of Cato's actions must have been limited by the short duration of the censorship and by uncertainty as to whether subsequent censors would reproduce his severity; but it is not true that apart from exhortation and example he relied only on these sanctions. 'From youth right up to extreme old age,' says Nepos, 'he did not cease to incur enmities for the sake of the *res publica*', or, as another author puts it, he was an 'assiduous accuser of evil men'. Both these and other sources clearly mean not just outspoken condemnations but legal prosecution,[87] and a number of such prosecutions happen to be specifically attested. For forty years, from his evidence against Glabrio in 189 to a speech against Sulpicius Galba in the last months of his life, instances can be found of Cato initiating or supporting legal proceedings against men accused of misconduct in office. His attack, like his personal example, was sustained, and his weapons included the sanctions provided by law.[88]

If then Cato's censorship is viewed as a whole, the conclusion must be that although he did indeed strive against the spread of luxury and the growth of corruption it would be misleading to assess his censorship only by reference to that aspect, let alone to represent it as a doomed, backward-looking attempt to preserve an antique Rome while failing to come to terms with the realities of the present. In the first place the administrative operations which constituted no small part of the censorial duties were conducted with extreme thoroughness and, so far as can be judged, a high degree of efficiency. There was a massive and practical programme of public works, coupled with strict control of the terms of public contracts. The *regimen morum*, somewhat neglected in recent censuses, was applied with renewed vigour in what the censors conceived to be the interests of the state. In this Cato's censorship was consistent with his attitude throughout his career. Though he had his prejudices and no doubt sometimes erred in his judgements, the issues which were the focus of his concern were important and contemporary, seen by him essentially as questions of personal *mores* and of a climate of social opinion,

---

87 Nepos, *Cato* 2. 4; 'Victor', *De vir. ill.* 47. 7; Plut. *Cato Mai.* 15. 1; Quintil. *Inst.* 12. 7. 4; Ampel. 19. 8.

88 Toynbee, *Hannibal's Legacy* ii. 516, underestimates this aspect of Cato's activity.

which indeed in a real sense they were, and which in any case is how Cato and his contemporaries must inevitably have seen them. To his contemporaries, at least, he did not appear as an isolated curiosity, trying almost single-handed to reverse the irresistible march of history. Even in the matter of luxury and extravagance the subsequent passage of the sumptuary laws shows that there were many who held views similar to his; and it is surely no accident that though Cato's personality and methods evidently gave his censorship a peculiar severity and con-tentiousness, nevertheless the three succeeding censorships resembled it in many respects, in marked contrast to the three which had preceded it.

With benefit of hindsight the historian can say without fear of contra-diction that there was a sense in which Cato's efforts in the field of *mores* proved of no avail, in that Rome was to experience the age of Lucullus and Pompey, of Verres and Brutus; applying modern modes of thought he can assert confidently that there were deep-seated structural and economic factors at work which (so far as can be seen) Cato failed to comprehend. But the likelihood of any contemporary having com-prehended them is remote, and the failure to do so is not to be taken as a symptom either of stupidity or of lack of imagination. If Cato is to be properly understood, it is necessary also to consider his career in terms of its contemporary context, his censorship in terms of the nature, functions, and limitations of the office of censor. Seen in those terms Cato emerges as thorough and efficient, and concerned not with the past but with contemporary and important issues which he tackled with vigour and consistency, using all the means which he can reasonably be expected to have employed.[89]

---

[89] Plutarch, *Cato Mai.* 19. 4, says that the Roman People erected a statue of Cato in the temple of Salus (Hygieia) and inscribed on it not his military commands or his triumph but 'that when the Roman state [πολιτεία = *res publica*] was in decline and inclining to a worse condition he was appointed censor and by useful guidance and wise practices and teachings set it right again'. In the following sentence Plutarch makes it clear that he supposes this statue to have been erected in Cato's lifetime (for he assumes it to have been later than the dicta in which Cato expressed scorn for such honours). If this were correct it would be further evidence both that Cato as censor did give expression to a strong body of opinion and that his concerns were regarded as fully relevant to contemporary problems. However, while a publicly authorized statue of a living senator is a possibility which cannot be ex-cluded at this date, it would be surprising, especially in view of the silence in other sources; and an inscription in such terms, and moreover omitting mention of the consulship and triumph, is extremely improbable. It is much more likely that Plutarch uncritically assumed to have been contemporary a statue of whose existence he had heard but which was erected long afterwards. Cf. Fraccaro, *Opusc.* i. 435. Note also the literary evidence on republican statues collected by O. Vessberg, *Kunstgesch. der röm. Rep.*, esp. pp. 26 ff.; also Mommsen, *Röm. Staats.* i³. 447 ff.

6

The Later Years

THE censorship was the last magistracy and almost the last public appointment of any kind held by Cato. Nevertheless for a further thirty-four years, to the very end of his life, he remained active and influential. Apart from his writings, most of which were probably composed in this period of his life, his frequent participation in public affairs is well attested, especially by dicta and by numerous fragments of his speeches. Many of these dicta and fragments can be linked confidently with events recorded in the narrative sources, some of which actually mention Cato's involvement, though others do not do so. A number, however, are less securely associated with a particular context or even a particular date, and in some cases there is no evidence at all for either. Part of the explanation may lie in the sketchy and fragmentary nature of the narrative sources for the years after 167, Livy's account of which is lost; but in other instances the episodes concerned simply found no place in the accounts given by the narrative historians. The cumulative effect of all this is that although a considerable amount of information survives about Cato's post-censorial career, it affords a picture which is patchy and often fragmented. Consequently a review of all this information in sequence— so far as that would be possible—would be confusing and disjointed. In this chapter it will, therefore, be set out under four headings, corresponding to broadly definable categories of activity or events, with an attempt to make the chronological sequence clear within each section.

1. Family Affairs

A little is known about events in Cato's family life in these years. His son Marcus, later known as Licinianus to distinguish him from his younger brother, fought under L. Aemilius Paullus in 168, in the final campaign of the Third Macedonian War. At the battle of Pydna he distinguished himself by his bravery in recovering his lost sword from among the enemy ranks, an exploit which his father is said to have praised in extravagant terms.[1] A little later, but before 161, Licinianus married

---

[1] Plut. *Cato Mai.* 20. 10 ff.; *Aem.* 21. 1 ff.; Justin, 33. 2. 1 ff.; cf. Cic. *De off.* 1. 37. On

Aemilia, a daughter of Paullus,[2] and later still, probably at the end of 152, he was elected to the praetorship but died before actually taking up office. Cato is said to have borne the loss with great fortitude, though this tradition may owe something to the unwonted modesty of the funeral ceremonies: it seems likely that even on this occasion Cato adhered to his own principles and avoided all extravagance.[3] By this time Cato had a second son, also named Marcus and usually known as Salonianus, after his mother Salonia. The date of Licinia's death is not known but since Salonianus was probably born in 154, the new marriage may have been about 155, when Cato was almost eighty years of age.[4] According to Plutarch Salonia was the daughter of one of Cato's clients, Salonius, who had formerly been one of his under-secretaries; she was, therefore, probably the daughter of one of his freedmen. This invites unsubstantiable speculation about the reasons for such a surprising choice, but at least it suggests that the *novus homo* no longer felt any sense of insecurity or self-consciousness about the acceptance of himself and his family among the established families of the governing aristocracy—an acceptance previously symbolized by Licinianus' marriage to the daughter of Aemilius Paullus.

2. *Defendant, Prosecutor and Advocate*

The contentiousness of Cato's censorship did not end with the censorship itself, for within a short time he was involved in a judicial dispute about 'the felicity of his *lustrum*'. The affair is specifically attested only by a single reference to Cato's speech in an anonymous panegyric of the fourth century A.D., though two fragments 'against Thermus after the censorship' are probably from the same speech and thus suggest that his adversary was from a family with which he had at least three or four major encounters in the course of his career.[5] Evidently at some time between

---

Licinianus see *RE*, s.v. *Porcius*, no. 14, cols. 167 f. His supposed service under Popillius Laenas in 173 is indicated only in Cic. *De off.* 1. 37, which is rightly bracketed by editors and is a patent error.

[2] Plut. *Cato Mai.* 20. 12; 24. 2; *Aem.* 5. 6; 21. 1; Cic. *De sen.* 15; *Verr.* 2. 4. 22; Vell. 2. 8. 1. The elder son of the marriage was consul in 118.

[3] The date: Livy, *Per.* 48. Livy and Plut. *Cato Mai.* 24. 9 say that Licinianus died as praetor, but Cic. *Tusc.* 3. 70 and Gell. 13. 20. 9, who both say praetor-designate, are to be preferred. Other refs.: Cic. *De amic.* 9; cf. *De sen.* 68; 84; *Ad fam.* 4. 6. 1.

[4] Plut. *Cato Mai.* 24. 2 ff., cf. 27. 7; Gell. 13. 20. 7 f.; Pliny, *Nat. hist.* 7. 61 f.; Solin. 1. 59; 'Victor', *De vir. ill.* 47. 9. See *RE*, s.v. *Porcius*, no. 9, col. 144; no. 15, col. 168.

[5] The fact that Cato delivered several speeches against Thermi has given rise to problems in assigning the fragments. *ORF*[3], fr. 135 is the sole fragment *de lustri sui felicitate*, but Fraccaro showed that the same speech is very probably the source of the two fragments *In*

Cato's censorship and the next (in 179/8) someone, probably a Minucius Thermus, alleged that Cato's censorship had been in some way vitiated, presumably in connection with a ritual, and consequently that the *lustrum* was 'unpropitious', *infelix*. If such an allegation had been established, whether or not it would have had practical consequences in respect of the implementation of some of the censorial acts,[6] it would certainly have been extremely damaging to Cato's standing and reputation. The proceedings probably took the form not of a prosecution but of a *sponsio*, or 'judicial wager', initiated by Thermus with a public allegation of *infelicitas* and ending with Cato vindicating himself.[7] What error was alleged is not known—there is a slight hint that it may have been connected with the ritual closure of the censorship[8]—but it is a fair guess that Cato's opponents claimed as evidence of the *infelicitas* alarming natural phenomena, such as severe and damaging storms and 'showers of blood', which induced the Senate to decree special supplications to the gods. This happened in 183 and again, with the addition of a serious plague, in the succeeding years.[9] Cato on his side, besides heaping abuse on Thermus, claimed an abundance of crops as evidence against the alleged *infelicitas*:

Cato's speech concerning the felicity of his *lustrum* is said to be brilliant. For at that time in that old republic it redounded to the praise of the censors

Thermum post censuram, 133 and 134, the latter's mention of a sacred pig almost certainly referring to the *suovetaurilia* in the *lustratio* which closed the census: 'Ricerche . . . sulla censura', *Studi storici*, 4 (1911), 61 ff. = *Opusc.* i. 458 ff. However Janzer, p. 24, suggests that the *De lustri sui felicitate* is identical with the *De suis virtutibus contra Thermum*; and Malcovati, *ORF*[3], p. 51, Scullard, *Roman Politics*[2], p. 264, and Stark, 'Catos Rede d. l. s. felicitate', *RhM* 96 (1953), 184 ff., are inclined to regard all three titles as indicating the same speech. There is, however, little reason to make this second identification and the *De virtutibus suis* (a title which suggests a different topic) more probably belongs on another occasion. Frs. 182–4, designated only *in Thermum*, cannot be assigned to any particular speech. Stark, loc. cit., attempted to argue that the words *de lustri sui felicitate* represent not a title but only a fourth-century reference to context; but his conclusion is doubtful: cf. Fraccaro, op. cit. i. 458 n. 191.

[6] Fraccaro, op. cit. i. 459, believes that it did affect the validity of the lists of citizens drawn up by the censors, but this is by no means certain.

[7] Note 'qui stulte spondet' in fr. 133. Though strictly speaking the evidence that Cato was never convicted (below) may not be applicable, since this was probably a *sponsio*, it cannot reasonably be doubted that he was successful.

[8] Fr. 134 (designated *in Thermum post censuram*) probably concerned the *suovetaurilia*; cf. n. 5 above.

[9] Livy, 39. 46. 3 ff. (183); 40. 2. 1 ff. (182); 40. 19. 1 ff. (181); 40. 36. 14–37. 3 (180). *Supplicationes* were decreed in all four years, and in 180 the near-panic caused by the plague led to the consultation of the Sibylline Books and other special measures. *A priori* the *sponsio* is unlikely to have been as late as 180, but the assignment to 183 in *ORF*[3], p. 51, seems to be arbitrary and probably too early, since Cato apparently could refer to at least one successful harvest since the censorship.

if they had established a propitious *lustrum* (*si lustrum felix condidissent*), if the crops had filled the granaries, if the vintage had been abundant, if the olive-yield had flowed plentifully.[10]

This dispute about the *lustrum* was part of a pattern of events summed up by Livy in the comment that 'Cato's censorship was full of quarrels, which occupied M. Porcius throughout his life'—a comment which surely reflects also the record number of forty-four legal cases in which Cato was defendant, always emerging successful.[11] Only a few of these cases can be identified, and, of course, some occurred earlier in Cato's career, while for those which were post-censorial Livy should not be interpreted too literally; for as the years passed connections between such judicial clashes and the events of the censorship must, with increasing frequency, have been tenuous or non-existent. Resentment and a readiness to prosecute Cato were constantly fed also by his own activity as an assiduous prosecutor, and his belabouring of the misconduct and especially the extravagance of others made him an obvious target for attempts to convict him of similar failings, such as perhaps violations of the sumptuary laws. Such an attempt gave rise to the speech 'Concerning his own expenditure', *De sumptu suo*, though nothing is known of the particular accusation or circumstances. Only one fragment—though that is a long one—is explicitly ascribed to the speech, though two other substantial passages in which Cato emphasizes his avoidance of all extravagance must come either from this speech or from one very similar in content and purpose. Since the latter passages were written in or after 164, twenty years after the censorship, in so far as there was a connection between the censorship and the case or cases concerned, it is less likely to have been as a direct consequence of particular actions than as a reflection of the general attitudes Cato had displayed and in which he had persisted.[12]

---

[10] *ORF*³, fr. 135.

[11] Livy, 39. 44. 9. Prosecuted: Plut. *Cato Mai.* 15. 4; 29. 5 = *Compar.* 2. 5; Pliny, *Nat. hist.* 7. 100; 'Victor', *De vir. ill.* 47. 7.

[12] *ORF*³, fr. 173 (with the title), and 174–5, the latter two being from Gell. 13. 24. 1 and Plut. *Cato Mai.* 4. 4 ff. (quoted above, pp. 92 f.; for 173 in full see pp. 135 f.). Some, and quite possibly all, of the Plutarch passage is drawn from the same source as Gellius quotes, beyond reasonable doubt a speech very similar to the *De sumptu suo* and generally assumed to be identical. See Fraccaro, 'L'orazione di Catone "de sumtu suo" ', *Studi storici*, 3 (1910), 378 ff. = *Opusc.* i. 257 ff.; Malcovati, *ORF*³, ad loc. Whether Fraccaro, followed by Scullard, *Roman Politics*², p. 221, is right in suggesting that Cato was obliged to defend himself before the censors of 164 is more questionable. Prosecution for violation of the sumptuary *lex Orchia* (or the *lex Fannia*, if the speech was after 161) is a more plausible guess. Fraccaro has also frequently been followed in his view that the conclusion to fr. 173 exhibits pessimism and disenchantment: 'vide sis quo loco res p. siet, uti quod rei p. bene fecissem, unde gratiam

In the speech 'Concerning his own expenditure' Cato made dramatically effective use of a passage from a previous speech which he had delivered in a case arising from a *sponsio* he had made with a certain Marcus Cornelius.[13] In this passage (and thus again in the *De sumptu suo*) he laid great emphasis on his abstention from peculation and other misdemeanours during his provincial commands, though it is not absolutely certain that in the original case—the date of which could have been at any time between 195 and the *De sumptu suo*—he was defending his own reputation, since the purpose could have been to point up the contrast of Cornelius' own misdemeanours. Two other known speeches, however, were clearly in self-defence. The one 'Concerning his own virtues against Thermus' (later than 189 but not more precisely datable) is shown by its title to have been a response to another attack similar to that which gave rise to the *De sumptu suo*, and in three of the five short fragments Cato does insist on the rugged hardihood of his early years and his strict abstention from provincial perquisites.[14] Of the speech 'On behalf of himself against Gaius Cassius' there is only a solitary and uninformative fragment and no indication of date, though it has sometimes been thought, on tenuous grounds, to belong to the case in 154 or 153 when Cato was a defendant for the last time. It was in the course of that last defence that he said, 'It is hard for one who has lived among the men of one generation to make his defence before those of another.'[15] Possibly one or two other speeches

capiebam, nunc idem illud memorare non audeo, ne invidiae siet. ita inductum est male facere impoene, bene facere non impoene licere.' It is a mistake, however, to interpret so literally a passage clearly contrived for rhetorical effect in its immediate context. The *terminus post quem* is given by the statement that Cato's villas remained unplastered up to his seventieth year. That may indicate 164 as the actual date, but the firm ascription to that year is commonly based on Fraccaro's view that it was connected with the censorship.

[13] *ORF*[3], fr. 203 (see p. 96), extracted from fr. 173 (pp. 135 f.). It has been suggested that since the *praenomen* Marcus is rare among Cornelii the Cornelius involved in this case and also in fr. 204 (*Contra Cornelium ad populum*) may be M. Cornelius Scipio Maluginensis, praetor in 176; but there are difficulties about this, especially the fact that Maluginensis did not take up his provincial command: Scullard, *Roman Politics*[2], p. 268. The speech in practice, though not explicitly, presupposes Cato's command in Spain and is therefore later than 195.

[14] *ORF*[3], frs. 128–32; the first four with title in Festus, 131 similarly in Gellius and Nonius, and as *de virtute sua* in *Schol. Bob. Pro Mil.* p. 124 Stangl; 132, designated *de innocentia sua* by Isidore, could be from a different speech: cf. Malcovati, *ORF*[3], ad loc. For the probability that it is not the same speech as the *De lustri sui felicitate* and the *In Thermum post censuram* see p. 105 n. 5.

[15] The speech: *ORF*[3], fr. 176. Prosecuted for the last time: Plut. *Cato Mai.* 15. 4; Livy, 39. 40. 11; Val. Max. 8. 7. 1. Since both Plutarch and Livy incorrectly state that Cato was 90 in 149, the date 154–153 is obtained by correcting the impossible statement in these sources that he was eighty-six or in his eighty-sixth year at the time of this prosecution. Fraccaro,

'against' particular individuals were also speeches of self-defence in such cases, but the meagre fragments give no clue as to dates or issues.[16]

The fact that Cato was so often prosecuted (though always acquitted) amply confirms that he did indeed provoke considerable resentment and animosity. Despite the paucity of details it is possible to make reasonable conjectures as to the identity of some of the individuals involved in this way. Thus Cato is known to have had major disputes with at least two Minucii Thermi on at least three, probably on four occasions.[17] He twice clashed with Ser. Sulpicius Galba and is said often to have 'torn to shreds' in the Senate Q. Fulvius Nobilior (cos. 153), whose father Marcus (cos. 189, cens. 179) he had severely criticized in a speech delivered soon after 179.[18]

Such animosities were no doubt often reciprocal, and they may have played some part in the many prosecutions which Cato himself is known to have initiated,[19] just as personal friendship and the responsibilities of a patron will often have been involved when he spoke on behalf of others. It would be unreasonable to suppose, however, that the accusations which led to all these prosecutions and speeches were only excuses to ventilate personal resentments and quarrels, that the accusations were not themselves matters of genuine concern; or that when he spoke in support or defence of others he was moved by little more than a sense of obligation. In fact the fragments of several of Cato's forensic speeches reveal glimpses of issues and arguments which are wholly in keeping with attitudes he displayed in the censorship and repeatedly throughout his career. Two such speeches are those entitled 'Against Lentulus before the censors'

'Ricerche . . . sulla censura', *Studi storici*, 4 (1911), 125 n. 385 = *Opusc.* i, 500 n. 385, hesitatingly suggested that the *Contra Cassium* might have been in defence of his censorial contracts, since C. Cassius Longinus, cos. 171, cens. 154, might have been a tribune at that time. Scullard, *Roman Politics*[2], p. 270, Malcovati, *ORF*[3], pp. 72 f., and others prefer to link it with Cassius' censorship and Cato's last defence in 154; but this is extremely speculative. The identity of the Cassius, the date, and the circumstances all remain uncertain.

[16] Notably *ORF*[3], fr. 201, *Adversum Ti. Sempronium Longum*; 204, *Contra Cornelium ad populum*.

[17] For the speeches against Quintus in 190 see p. 59 and *ORF*[3], frs. 58 ff. The other speeches are noted in this chapter. There can be little doubt that the Thermus attacked 'concerning the younger Ptolemy' (below) was Lucius, and the same man is usually assumed to have been the Thermus of the other speeches, but in no instance is a *praenomen* recorded.

[18] Galba: *ORF*[3], frs. 172 and 196–9, and below in this chapter. Q. Fulvius: Livy, *Per.* 49, 'saepe ab eo in senatu laceratus'. M. Fulvius: *ORF*[3], frs. 148–50. The joke in Cic. *De orat.* 2. 256 = *ORF*[3], fr. 151, 'Nobiliorem mobiliorem', could have been directed at either father or son.

[19] e.g. Livy, 39. 40. 8; Plut. *Cato Mai.* 15. 4; Quint. *Inst.* 12. 7. 4; 'Victor', *De vir. ill.* 47. 7; Ampel. 19. 8; cf. Nepos, *Cato* 2. 4.

and *De re Floria* (neither of which can be dated or linked to any known events). The former was probably a denunciation of Lentulus for dereliction of his duty to a ward,[20] while the *De re Floria* contained sharp comments both on sexual licence and on the impropriety of using force against a free person, though it is not certain that either was the real subject of the speech.[21] The speech 'Against M. Fulvius Nobilior'—to be dated after 179, but probably not long after—almost certainly was primarily an attack on Fulvius' censorship (179–178) which Cato discussed at length, though he also included criticisms of Fulvius' earlier conduct as a military commander.[22]

In 171 Cato delivered his speech against P. Furius Philus, and in this instance something is known about the circumstances. It was the first occasion on which use was made of a special court to try cases of alleged extortion by provincial governors. When embassies from the Spanish provinces lodged complaints against several former governors, among them Furius, the Senate arranged for tribunals of *recuperatores* to adjudicate upon the claims for redress. The Senate also permitted the Spaniards to have their cases presented to the tribunals by any patrons they chose, and among the four named was Cato. It is not clear whether he assisted in the prosecution of Marcus Titinius, who was acquitted, but he and P. Scipio Nasica (who had been his successor as governor of Hither Spain) were asked to conduct the case against Furius and did so to such effect that he went into exile without waiting for the verdict. Cato, of whose speech only one small and uninformative fragment survives, is said to have accused Furius 'on account of a most unfair valuation of grain', and new regulations now decreed confirm that major abuses had arisen

[20] *ORF*³, fr. 200. Scullard, *Roman Politics*², rightly comments on the impossibility of identifying Lentulus. Cf. Janzer, p. 29.

[21] *ORF*³, frs. 212–14; cf. Scullard, *Roman Politics*², p. 261, rightly following Malcovati, ad loc., in rejecting various conjectures as unfounded or implausible.

[22] *ORF*³, frs. 148–50 (151 may belong but need not do so). Janzer, pp. 58 ff., argues for the once widely held view that there were two speeches, supposing frs. 148 and 149, which are untitled and refer to Fulvius' consulship but not his censorship, to have come from an earlier speech, perhaps connected with the debate about Fulvius' triumph in 187. Fraccaro, 'Catoniana', *Studi storici*, 3 (1910), 272 ff. = *Opusc.* i. 247 ff., Scullard, *Roman Politics*², pp. 266 f., and Malcovati, ad loc., consider it more likely that all the fragments are from the same speech. Fraccaro and Scullard show that the speech was later than Fulvius' triumph in 187, and rightly point out that there is no real difficulty about references back to his consulship in a speech of the 170s; on the other hand their arguments that no such speech is likely to belong to the years 187–184 are weak. In this chapter the hypothesis of a single speech has been preferred because it is more plausible that with only three fragments surviving—in three different sources—they should all have come from the same speech; but it should be recognized that there is no serious objection to there having been two speeches. For the purposes of this chapter the alternative would make no significant difference.

out of the arbitrary determination by Roman officials of the price they
would pay for grain which the provincials were compelled to supply,
though evidently there had also been direct extortion of money.[23]

Nearly twenty years later, in 154 or 153, Cato again accused a Roman
official of scandalous peculation, though this time the defendant had
been serving as an envoy. In 154 Ptolemy Euergetes had come to Rome
seeking renewed support in the prosecution of his quarrel with his brother,
Ptolemy Philometor. A decade earlier this long-standing dispute had
produced an uneasy arrangement whereby Euergetes ruled Cyrene and
Philometor Egypt and Cyprus, though in 162 and 161 the Roman
Senate had given ineffective diplomatic backing to Euergetes' claim to
Cyprus. It was in pursuit of this claim that Euergetes now sought renewed
assistance. As before, the Senate responded by sending an embassy. Headed
by Cn. Cornelius Merula (who had led one of the earlier missions)
and L. Minucius Thermus, it consisted of five *legati*, each of whom was
given one warship. They were instructed to establish Euergetes in
Cyprus, and completely failed to do so. Indeed the outcome was even
more embarrassing than simple failure, for Euergetes managed to get
himself captured by his brother, who then magnanimously restored him
to his kingdom in Cyrene.[24] It is a safe inference that it was this episode
which gave rise to Cato's speech 'Concerning the younger Ptolemy
against Thermus', the fragments of which clearly come from a vigorous
attack. Precisely what Thermus was alleged to have done is not indicated,
but he was prosecuted and Cato demanded that he be punished for
outrageous and deceitful conduct inspired by greed: 'But if he did everything deceitfully, everything for the sake of avarice and money, such
abominable crimes as we have never heard of or read of, he ought to
suffer punishment for his acts.' The outcome of the case is not known.[25]

Some four years after this it was once again the abuse of public office,
this time by a provincial governor, that drew from Cato what was probably the last of his speeches. It was delivered in the final few months of

[23] ORF[3], frs. 154–5 (but 154 is not a true fragment); Livy, 43. 2. 1 ff. There is no basis for
Janzer's hints, p. 63, of factional motivation.
[24] Polyb. 33. 11. 1 ff.; 39. 7. 6; Diod. 31. 33. For the background see Scullard, *Roman
Politics*[2], pp. 230 f. and 236 f.
[25] ORF[3], frs. 177–81. The connection with the affair of 154 is widely accepted, though
Otto, *Zur Gesch. der Zeit des 6. Ptolemäers*, pp. 118 f., followed by Scullard, *Roman Politics*[2],
pp. 236 f., less plausibly associates the speech with Euergetes' proposal a year or two later to
marry Cornelia, in which he conjectures that Thermus acted as an agent for Euergetes. On
the issue of foreign affairs see further pp. 270 f. The inclusion of Thermus' *praenomen* in the
title of Cato's speech is a conjecture; it does not appear in any of the texts in which the
fragments are preserved.

his life, when, as he himself put it, 'Many things have dissuaded me from appearing here, my years, my time of life, my voice, my strength, my old age; but nevertheless when I reflected that so important a matter was being discussed . . .' The important matter was that in 150 Servius Sulpicius Galba had followed up a victory in Further Spain with the massacre of a large number of surrendered Lusitanians and the sale of others into slavery, all allegedly in violation of his pledged word. In 149 a tribune, L. Scribonius Libo, introduced a bill proposing the release of those enslaved and the setting up of a special court to try Galba.[26] It was this proposal which Cato supported 'very vehemently', while Galba's principal supporter was Q. Fulvius Nobilior, the man whom Cato had 'often torn to shreds' in the Senate and who was the son of the censor of 179–178, who had also been attacked by Cato. Against Galba's claim that his action was justifiable because the Lusitanians had intended a new rebellion Cato employed an argument similar to one he had used in 167 in the Rhodian speech: 'Yet they say they wished to rebel. I myself at the present time wish to have a thorough knowledge of the pontifical law; shall I for that reason be taken as a pontifex? If I wish to have an excellent grasp of the science of augury, would anyone on that account take me as an augur?' In view of Cato's insistence a year or two previously that the Carthaginians were already enemies because they intended war, even though they had not yet taken up arms, this may seem inconsistent or even unprincipled. It should be remembered, however, that Cato probably did not accept the truth of Galba's assertion and that this was probably only a subordinate argument.[27] The issue was bitterly contested, with Galba himself making at least three speeches, and in the end Libo's proposal was rejected by the popular assembly. There is a vivid description of methods used by Galba to arouse in the mass of voters an emotional response irrelevant to the real questions at issue:

He almost lifted on to his shoulders his ward Quintus, the son of his kinsman C. Sulpicius Galus, so that he should move the people to tears by the living memory of his illustrious father; he committed his own two sons to the guardianship of the people, and, like a soldier making his will on the eve of battle, said that he appointed the Roman people to be their guardian in their fatherless

---

[26] See esp. Livy, *Per.* 49; Cic. *Brut.* 80; 89 f.; *De orat.* 1. 227 f.; 2. 263; Val. Max. 8. 1 abs. 2; 9. 6. 2. Further refs. collected by Münzer *RE*, s.v. *Sulpicius*, no. 58 cols. 762 f. Speeches: *ORF*[3], Cato frs. 196–9; Galba frs. 12–15 (pp. 112 f.); Libo frs. 2–4 (pp. 138 f.). Discussion in Astin, *Scipio Aemilianus*, pp. 58 ff.

[27] Galba's assertion: Livy, *Per.* 49. Cato's argument: *ORF*[3], fr. 197; on Carthage, fr. 195. See further pp. 127 f.

plight. So, though at that time Galba was being overwhelmed by popular ill will and hatred, he secured his escape by means of these histrionics.[28]

That is scarcely the whole story. The rational arguments apart, there is an allegation that Galba resorted to bribery and a suspicion that his accusers sought to arouse prejudice against him by asserting that he had appropriated an excessive share of booty;[29] but it was the histrionic performance which made the greatest impression and to which Cato in particular ascribed Galba's escape. Indignant at the outcome, Cato set out an account of the affair, including the text of his own speech, in the final book of his *Origines*.[30] 'Thus', Cato complained, 'by stirring the pity of the populace for little children he snatched himself from the flames', and he declared that 'no one should bring into a hearing his own or others' children to excite pity, nor wives nor relations nor any women at all';[31] but vexed though he was by Galba's methods the heart of his complaint was that a man who had gravely abused his powers had escaped punishment, had 'snatched himself from the flames'.

3. *The* lex Voconia *and Other Internal Affairs*

In 169 Cato spoke in support of the *lex Voconia*. His speech is mentioned several times, though it is not clear whether this is because it was especially impressive or because it was associated with a law which itself attracted considerable attention.[32] This law, successfully proposed by a tribune of the plebs, Q. Voconius Saxa, had two main provisions regulating the disposal of property by will: no one whose property was valued in the census at 100,000 *asses* or more (the qualification for the centuries of the first class in the *comitia centuriata*) could name a woman as an heir; and no individual, whether man or woman, could receive more by way of legacy under a will than the amount which went to the heir or heirs.[33]

---

[28] Cic. *De orat.* 1. 228, from Rutilius Rufus.

[29] App. *Iber.* 60; cf. a possible echo in Val. Max. 6. 4. 2.

[30] Cic. *Brut.* 89; Gell. 13. 25. 15; *HRR* i², Cato frs. 106–9. See also Cic. *Brut.* 80; Livy, *Per.* 49; *Ox. epit.* 49; Val. Max. 8. 1 abs. 2; Quint. *Inst.* 2. 15. 8; *ORF*³, Cato fr. 199 = Fronto, *Ad Marcum Caes.* 3. 2 = i. 172H.

[31] Cic. *Brut.* 90; *ORF*³, Cato fr. 199 = Fronto, loc. cit.

[32] *ORF*³, frs. 156–60 (but 156 and 157 are testimonia rather than fragments). Cf. also Gelzer, *RE*, s.v. *Porcius*, no. 9, col. 132; Janzer, pp. 63 ff.; Marmorale, *Cato Maior*², pp. 121 f.; Scullard, *Roman Politics*², pp. 205 f. and 268 f.; Kienast, pp. 93 ff. Janzer, Marmorale, and Scullard are inclined to take literally the statement in Cic. *De sen.* 14 = *ORF*³, fr. 156, that Cato spoke 'magna voce et bonis lateribus'; but more probably this was Cicero's own elaboration to emphasize the fitness of the already elderly Cato. Livy, *Per.* 41, erroneously dates it to 174; see *MRR* i. 427 n. 4.

[33] Watson, *Law of Succession*, pp. 29 ff. and 167 ff.; Steinwenter, *RE*, s.v. *Lex Voconia*,

It is possible that this second provision also applied only to estates valued at 100,000 *asses* or over. Except for the general restriction imposed by this second provision the capacity of women to take legacies was unaffected and there was no change in their position in respect of intestate succession, where they ranked equally with men and hence could continue to be heirs or even, in certain cases, the sole heir.[34]

But though the date and circumstances of Cato's speech are known, there is much uncertainty about his motives, and indeed about the objectives of the law itself. In the second century A.D. the lawyer Gaius regarded the restriction on the size of legacies, by his day long since superseded, as an attempt to protect the heirs nominated in a will; for if the stipulated legacies were too generous the heirs might be left with an unduly small proportion, possibly so small as to remove the incentive to act at all. The issue was a real one in Rome long before Cato's day, and Gaius' explanation is not to be dismissed as casually as it often is.[35] Nevertheless, though protection of heirs was probably in some sense a consideration in the law,[36] it seems certain that the primary provision was the ban on naming women as heirs;[37] and there can be no reasonable doubt that the chief purpose of that prohibition was to reduce the amount of property which was passing into the legal ownership of women.

It is a plausible hypothesis that the *lex Voconia* was a response to changes which were occurring in the pattern of ownership and transmission of

cols. 2418 ff.; Gundel, s.v. *Voconius*, no. 4, cols. 696 f.; Metro, 'Il "legatum partitionis" ', *Labeo*, 9 (1963), 292 ff.; cf. *MRR* i. 425. Among many refs. see esp. Gaius, *Inst.* 2. 226 and 274; Cic. *Pro Balb.* 21; *Verr.* 2. 1. 104 ff.; Ps. Ascon. p. 248 Stangl; Livy, *Per.* 41. That application was from the first limited to the *classici* of the census (with a valuation at 100,000 *asses*) has been subject to some discussion but cannot reasonably be doubted in view of the fact that Cato had occasion to use the terms *classicus* and *infra classem*: *ORF*[3], fr. 160 = Gell. 6. 13. 3; Watson, op. cit., p. 30. Kienast, p. 93, follows an interpretation of the sum involved since shown by Walbank, *Commentary on Polybius* i. 176, to be improbable.

34 Watson, op. cit., pp. 176 f. Some qualification to this was introduced in the late Republic or early Principate, but later than the *lex Voconia*.

35 Gaius, *Inst.* 224 ff.; Watson, op. cit., pp. 163 f., discussing the earlier *lex Furia* but relevant also to the *Voconia*; cf. esp. the ruling of Coruncanius which shows that problems were being experienced in the middle of the third century: Cic. *De leg.* 2. 52.

36 This seems certain from the application of the restriction on the size of legacies to male as well as female legatees.

37 Almost all the sources characterize the law as placing restrictions on women, and though in some cases this is simply a reflection of the immediate context many have no such constraint. The passages in Cicero have a special value since, being earlier than the *lex Falcidia* of 40 B.C. which modified the rule about the size of legacies, they were written at a time when all the provisions of the *lex Voconia* were still in force (i.e. later passages might reflect only that part remaining in force after 40 B.C.).

wealth, specifically that there was a trend for an increasing number of women to have substantial wealth in their own right. Such a change could have been in part simply a reflection of the general influx and accumulation of wealth in this period, but also important is likely to have been a marked increase in the proportion of marriages which were in the less restricted form, without *manus*. In a marriage with *manus* all property received by the wife passed automatically into the ownership of her husband, whereas in a marriage without *manus* the wife was *sui iuris* (at least after the death of her father) and had full legal rights of ownership. Broadly speaking, in the latter case her property went ultimately to members of her original family, not to her husband or children. In the late third and early second centuries marriage with *manus* was probably still the most common form, and it was probably not until the first century that it became very unusual. On the other hand marriage without *manus* had probably been recognized as early as the time of the Twelve Tables and it was certainly a familiar form in Cato's time.[38] Indeed the very nature of the *lex Voconia* implies that the ownership of property by women *sui iuris* was fairly common, and such ownership is certainly presupposed in the only substantial fragment of Cato's speech.[39] Unfortunately there is no means of determining the relative proportions of these two forms of marriage in this period, let alone of testing the hypothesis that a significant change was occurring in these proportions. There are, however, two relevant considerations. First the very fact of a great influx of new wealth is likely to have increased and spread more widely the incentive for women and their fathers to arrange marriages without *manus*. Second, it would be among the wealthier sections of society that women would have not only the greater incentive to avoid *manus* but the greater opportunities, through social and economic influences, both to arrange marriages without it and to take the necessary steps subsequently to avoid the establishment of *manus* by unbroken residence with the husband.[40]

It is easy to guess at various factors which may have resulted in women owning substantial and increasing amounts of wealth; it is less easy to be confident about the particular reasons why Voconius and his supporters thought this undesirable and sought at least to slow down the trend. Explanations in terms of a desire by the powerful aristocratic families

[38] Corbett, *Roman Law of Marriage*, esp. pp. 90 f. and 108 ff.; Watson, *Law of Persons*, pp. 19 ff.

[39] *ORF*³, fr. 158, quoted below.

[40] Corbett, op. cit., pp. 85 ff.; Watson, op. cit., pp. 19 ff.

to prevent dispersal of their great wealth, or of a growing tendency for the ownership of wealth to enable women to tyrannize over their husbands or even to wield increasing political power are in various ways unsatisfactory. Reference to a dislike of 'the growing emancipation of women' is too imprecise to serve as a useful explanation of the introduction of important new restrictions on testamentary disposition, especially when one of the restrictions applied to men and women equally.[41] Nevertheless it is inescapable that in some sense the self-advantage of men at the expense of women was the objective of the law.

Probably a mixture of motives should be envisaged. For instance, if, as it seems reasonable to suppose, there was a trend for an increasing number of women to have substantial wealth in their own right, Cato and others who shared his views may well have seen this as directly related to the ostentatious displays of jewellery and expensive clothing which in their eyes were prime examples of wasteful and pernicious extravagance.[42] This, however, is more likely to have been an emotional incentive than a primary motive, for as a chosen means of attacking that particular target the provisions of the law would have been very indirect. Possibly Cato also felt that contemporary changes were resulting in a greater dispersal of inheritances and therefore were in conflict with his own conception of a duty to maintain, consolidate, and extend inherited fortunes; and one brief fragment of his speech suggests that he did indeed advance some such view: 'The land which a man has is ruined', 'agrum

---

[41] For interpretations along such lines see the works by Janzer, Kienast, and Scullard cited p. 113 n. 32. Aristocratic concern about the dispersal of estates is not a convincing explanation especially because the law took virtually no steps to control dispersal through legacies, which could be to men and women, including women *sui iuris*. Also, of course, this is precisely a period of a great influx of wealth and accumulation of estates. For evidence of concern about a growth in the domestic or political power of women reference is made to an extract from Cato's speech, fr. 158, on which see below, and to the dictum in Plut. *Cato Mai.* 8. 2: 'All other men rule their wives; we rule all other men, and our wives rule us', which, if authentic, was surely intended for a joke. (Plutarch knew it as a dictum of Themistocles, but Cato could easily have 'borrowed' it.) Neither remark ought to be taken literally as a sober statement of concern or of an allegedly common state of affairs. Against them should be set the two fragments of the *De dote* (221–2: presumably a private speech but of unknown date and circumstance), which are forceful reminders of the enormous imbalance of legal power and authority in favour of the husband. 221: 'vir cum divortium fecit, mulieri iudex pro censore est, imperium quod videtur habet, si quid perverse taetreque factum est a muliere; multatur, si vinum bibit; si cum alieno viro probri quid fecit condemnatur.' 222: 'in adulterio uxorem tuam si prehendisses, sine iudicio inpoene necares; illa te, si adulterares sive tu adulterarere, digito non auderet contingere.' Nor is fear that wealth was giving women political power a convincing explanation with regard to a state in which their total exclusion from all public office, deliberative bodies, and voting assemblies was never questioned.   [42] pp. 91 ff.

quem vir habet tollitur.'[43] A more fundamental force at work, however, may have been a feeling on the part of many husbands that it was in some way injurious to their dignity for their wives to own substantial wealth in their own right. Such an attitude would be understandable if it was only recently that this situation had become fairly common. It was an attitude which need not have arisen primarily from a rational assessment by men that there was a serious threat to their own real power and predominance; rather it is likely to have been essentially emotional, an ill-defined sense of affront to the dignity of the husband, whose role was associated in traditional concepts with an all-embracing authority. No doubt there was a tendency to rationalize, and the longest of the fragments of Cato's speech is probably best understood as reflecting and playing upon this sense of affront by means of a deliberately extreme example, perhaps intended to evoke laughter, of the indignities which could arise: 'In the beginning the woman brought you a great dowry; then she holds back a large sum of money which she does not entrust to the control of her husband but hands to him as a loan; later when she is angry with her husband she sends a slave of her own to hound him and incessantly demand the money.'[44] The appeal is to the emotions, not to reason; and such emotions are likely to have contributed much to the passage of the *lex Voconia*. Yet the drafting and presentation of a law embodying important new restrictions suggests that there were more specific considerations, more explicitly and directly concerned with the transfer and control of property, with the possession of wealth. Here it is worth considering whether the concern may have been not so much with the fact of ownership by women as with the fact that men were not now acquiring all the property which under earlier conditions would have passed to them and which they therefore regarded as in some sense due to them: in great measure it may have been not the wealth of numbers of women that aroused resentment but a sense of grievance and loss because men were conscious that under conditions prevailing until quite recently much of that wealth would have become theirs. Obviously this explanation too depends entirely on the hypothesis of a marked contemporary increase in the proportion of marriages without *manus*.

Amongst so much speculation about the purposes of the *lex Voconia*

---

[43] *ORF*³, fr. 159. Cf. p. 89.

[44] *ORF*³, fr. 158. Gellius 17. 6. 1 ff. has an interesting discussion of *servus recepticius*, here translated 'a slave of her own'. Cf. Kornhardt, 'Recipere und servus recepticius', *ZRG* 1938, pp. 162 ff.

itself, consideration of Cato's motives in supporting it is necessarily even more conjectural. As has been seen, two short fragments of his speech each hint at a line of argument he may have followed,[45] but it would be rash to assume that these were the only or even the principal arguments he used, or that they reflect his motives accurately. He could have shared in any or all of the motives which have been suggested in this discussion, and from them a plausible picture results; but that is as far as it is possible to go with any confidence.

Close in time to the speech in support of the *lex Voconia* was one 'Concerning the military tribunes'. Although strictly speaking this is undated it was almost certainly delivered between 171 and 168, during the Third Macedonian War. It is usually assumed to belong to 171, when a special arrangement was made to enable military tribunes to be selected by the commanders instead of being elected by the people; but this is not secure since each of the next three years saw events or decisions which must have been accompanied by discussion and would have provided an appropriate situation for the speech. In 170 the consul Hostilius Mancinus and the military tribunes were blaming each other for the poor state of the army in Macedonia; in 169 the consuls were not allowed to nominate tribunes for four new legions, the appointments being made by the *populus*; and in 168 the Senate decreed that half of the tribunes required should be chosen by the consuls and half by the *populus*, and added some other details. Also there were recruiting difficulties in these years. Unfortunately the two brief fragments of Cato's speech give no assistance in choosing between these occasions or identifying Cato's own opinion.[46]

When at the end of that war Aemilius Paullus returned to Rome in 167 to celebrate his victory, the proposal that he should be permitted a triumph was opposed by one of the military tribunes, Ser. Sulpicius

---

[45] The third actual fragment, 160 = Gell. 6. 13. 3, shows only that Cato had occasion to use the terms *classicus* and *infra classem* (not, as Janzer, p. 54, and Scullard, *Roman Politics*[2], p. 269, that he asked what was the difference: Gellius means that it was often asked what Cato meant by these terms).

[46] *ORF*[3], frs. 152–3; Livy, 42. 31. 5; 43. 11; 43. 12. 7; 44. 21. 2 f. Janzer, pp. 61 f., argues for 171 and that Cato opposed the decision taken in that year (similarly Scullard, *Roman Politics*[2], p. 197); but this is based on the grounds that Cato was hostile to most of the known officials of that year—an insecure conclusion from a questionable basis. Janzer also argues that fr. 152, 'expedito pauperem plebeium atque proletarium', shows Cato championing the poor and pleading for greater electoral freedom. In fact, as Kienast, p. 90, rightly argues, even if *expedito* does have the force of 'set free' (rather than e.g. 'make ready'), there is no means of knowing in what kind of context Cato used the phrase, though it would be natural to expect a military rather than a social point of view. Conceivably Cato was being sarcastic: 'If the tribunes cannot find enough recruits, let them equip *proletarii*.'

Galba (the man whose treatment of the Lusitanians was to be the subject of Cato's speech in 149). According to Livy Galba was a personal enemy, an *inimicus* of Paullus, and tried to exploit the resentment of the troops at his vigorous discipline and supposedly niggardly donatives. When the first attempt to put the matter to the vote appeared to be going against Paullus the protests of his supporters led to scenes of uproar, quietened only when the tribunes of the plebs agreed to start the proceedings afresh after allowing speeches in favour of the triumph. The lead was taken by M. Servilius Geminus, a senator of great age and distinction, but it is as good as certain that Cato also spoke; for among his speeches was one entitled 'Against Servius Galba to the soldiers', *Contra Ser. Galbam ad milites*, which it is now generally agreed belongs to this episode.[47] His son's association with Paullus suggests that personal considerations may have encouraged Cato to add his support, but there need have been nothing cynical about this. Paullus clearly merited a triumph; and there is no hint that he was accused of misappropriating booty, the vast surplus of which went into the treasury, while the donatives distributed at the triumph were the largest known down to this date and could be regarded as niggardly only in relation to the total value of all the booty.[48] Admittedly Paullus had displayed considerable brutality both in his victory celebrations at Amphipolis and in his notorious plundering of Epirus;[49] but it was not brutality *per se* that Cato objected to, but improper conduct in the performance of duties, and there is no suggestion that Paullus had abused his magisterial power or violated *fides*; and Cato will have had no sympathy at all with complaints about strict discipline.

Twelve years later, in 155, occurred the well-known affair of the 'embassy of philosophers'. The Athenians, appealing for the Senate's intervention on their behalf in a territorial dispute, sent as their envoys to Rome the heads of the three principal philosophical schools: Carneades the Academic, Diogenes the Stoic, and Critolaus the Peripatetic. On arrival at Rome each of the three proceeded to give public lectures which attracted large audiences. The Senate was slow about dealing with the embassy's business, until eventually Cato, particularly irritated by Carneades, demanded that the Senate should give an early decision so that the philosophers would depart as soon as possible. It is an episode of considerable interest and importance which will be examined in more detail in another chapter.[50]

---

[47] *ORF*[3], fr. 172 and comment ad loc.; Livy, 45. 35–9; Plut. *Aem.* 30. 2 ff.; cf. Astin, 'Scipio Aemilianus and Cato Censorius', *Latomus*, 15 (1956), 160 f.   [48] Livy, 45. 40. 5.
[49] Livy, 45. 34. 1 ff.; Polyb. 30. 15; Plut. *Aem.* 29; Val. Max. 2. 7. 14.   [50] pp. 174 ff.

After that there remains only one of Cato's interventions in internal affairs which can be dated with reasonable confidence. At the end of 153 M. Claudius Marcellus was elected to his third consulship. The choice is in one sense not difficult to explain: one of the foremost generals of the day, Marcellus almost certainly owed his election to a belief that he was the best man available to cope with a serious military crisis in Spain. Yet Marcellus' second consulship had been as recent as 155, so although respectable legal justification must have been found, his election yet again after so short a time certainly violated the intention of the rule that no individual should hold the consulship twice within ten years. Within the next few years, assuredly in reaction to this, it was laid down that no one was permitted to hold the consulship more than once; and that change was supported by Cato in a speech 'That no one be made consul a second time', *Ne quis iterum consul fieret*.[51] One of the two fragments which bear this title is part of an attack on those who indulge in private extravagance which is made possible by exploiting the opportunities of public office to acquire personal wealth, and other lines of argument are suggested by a passage of Plutarch which it is plausible to associate with this speech, though the conjecture cannot be proved:

Of those who were eager to hold office frequently he said that like men who did not know the way they were eager always to travel with lictors so as not to go astray. He censured the citizens for choosing the same men to hold office frequently. 'For you will seem', he said, 'not to rate highly the holding of office, or not to think many worthy to hold it.'[52]

All of this accords well with the general picture of Cato as a man who constantly demanded high standards in the conduct of public office and who believed in strict adherence to rules and procedures. In connection with this last point it is noteworthy that at least two undated speeches seem to reflect this interest in matters of correct procedure. One of these was entitled 'That the retiring person [i.e. magistrate or promagistrate] should not have *imperium* when the new one has come', *Ne imperium sit veteri ubi novus venerit*, and the other 'Concerning the augurs'; the one fragment of the latter is concerned with rules relating to the Vestal Virgins.[53] There was also a speech 'Concerning bribery', *De ambitu*, of

---

[51] *ORF*[3], frs. 185-6 and references ad loc.; Astin, *Scipio Aemilianus*, pp. 37 ff., esp. 39 f.; cf. p. 39 n. 2 for the possibility that the speech *Contra Annium*, fr. 109, though usually assigned to Cato's censorship, may have been directed at the consul who presided at Marcellus' election.

[52] Plut. *Cato Mai.* 8. 8 f.

[53] *ORF*[3], frs. 220 (*De aug.*) and 223 (*Ne imperium . . .*).

uncertain context and date. It is usually thought to have been in support of the first bribery law, the *lex Baebia* of 181; but other possible contexts which are known are a great scandal in 166 and another bribery law in 159. Another speech, 'That the *lex Baebia* should not be modified', *Dissuasio ne lex Baebia derogaretur*, could also have been concerned with bribery, though it is possible that it was rather in opposition to the ending of the short-lived experiment by which from 180 to 176 there were four and six praetors in alternate years.[54] Another undated speech, against a proposal to repeal part of the *lex Orchia*, may also have been linked with efforts to maintain a curb on bribery, though it was more directly concerned with the theme of private extravagance. This must have been later than 182, when the *lex Orchia* restricted the number of guests permissible at a meal, but although there are several fragments of the speech there is nothing to indicate when the modification was proposed or whether it was carried.[55] What is clear is that these speeches, despite the uncertainties about them, are very much in line with the attitudes and concerns displayed by Cato in his censorship and on other occasions.

4. Foreign Affairs[56]

From time to time it is possible to catch a glimpse of Cato's participation in foreign affairs or, to put it more accurately, in debates about foreign affairs. As it happens the earliest of these glimpses is particularly tantalizing: a speech, of which only a single word is preserved, 'Concerning the military affair of Histria', *De re Histriae militari*. This was almost certainly the Istrian campaign of 178/7, but there is nothing to show with which aspect of the affair it was concerned. If it dealt with the issues which led to the war it could have been as early as 183, but more probably it was prompted less by the question of relations with the Histrians than by the acrimonious internal disputes which sprang from the military campaign. For the mixed fortunes of the consul A. Manlius Vulso in 178 gave rise first to

[54] *ORF*[3], frs. 136, *De ambitu*, and 137, *Dissuasio ne lex Baebia* . . . . See Appendix 7.

[55] *ORF*[3], frs. 139–46. Fraccaro, 'Catoniana', *Studi storici*, 3 (1910), 250 ff. = *Opusc.* i. 233 ff., showed that despite certain contrary indications in the sources there was almost certainly only one speech, but he mistakenly argued that it must have been later than the *lex Fannia* of 161; in fact it cannot be dated. See esp. Janzer, pp. 53 ff. and Scullard, *Roman Politics*[2], pp. 264 f. Cf. also above, p. 91.

[56] For discussions embracing the events covered in this section see esp. De Sanctis, *Storia dei Romani* iv. 1[2] and 3; *CAH* viii, esp. chs. 9 and 15; Scullard, *Roman Politics*[2], chs. 12–14; Badian, *Foreign Clientelae*, chs. 4 and 5; Errington, *Dawn of Empire*, chs. 16–19; cf. Briscoe, 'Eastern Policy and Senatorial Politics,' *Historia*, 18 (1969), 49 ff.; and with special reference to Cato, Gelzer, *RE*, s.v. *Porcius*, no. 9, cols. 131 ff.; Kienast, pp. 116 ff. Janzer's comments on the speeches include many remarks about foreign affairs.

rumours of a great disaster, which induced a panic at Rome, then to an attempt by some tribunes to prevent extension of Manlius' command so that he could be recalled and prosecuted, and subsequently to a public quarrel between Manlius and his fellow consul on the one hand and his successor C. Claudius Pulcher on the other.[57]

The next glimpse is equally uninformative, though in a different way. It is reported that when king Eumenes of Pergamum visited Rome in 172 the Senate welcomed him in extravagant terms and among the leading men there was a good deal of rivalry in their attentions to him. 'But Cato', says Plutarch, 'clearly regarded him with suspicion and caution. When someone said, "But he is an excellent man and a friend of Rome", Cato replied, "That may be so, but the creature known as king is by nature a carnivore." '[58] The point of Cato's protest is almost certainly the lack of dignity, as he considered it, displayed by senators. The aphorism may reveal an authentic dislike of kings, but it throws no light on Cato's views about Roman relationships with the kingdoms of the Hellenistic East.

The next event, however, is securely dated to 167. The Third Macedonian War, which had begun in 171, ended in 168 with the victory of L. Aemilius Paullus at Pydna and the overthrow of king Perseus, so in 167 the Senate debated what kind of settlement should be imposed. This was certainly the occasion of Cato's speech 'Concerning the freeing of Macedonia', De Macedonia liberanda, in which 'he declared that the Macedonians should be free because they could not be protected.'[59] Since the Senate's solution was to leave Macedonia free, dividing it into four independent republics, there has been a tendency to assign a major role in this decision to Cato, and in particular to see Livy's account of the Senate's reasons as derived from Cato's arguments, perhaps as recorded in the Origines.[60] There is, however, no particular reason to make this

[57] ORF³, fr. 147. Livy, 39. 55. 4 ff.; 40. 18. 4; 40. 26. 2; 41. 1 ff.; 41. 7. 4 ff.; 41. 10. 1 ff. Another possible occasion for the speech is 171–170, when Istria again attracted some attention: Livy, 43. 1. 5 ff.; 43. 5. 3 f. Agnew, 'A Numbered Legion in a Fragment of the Elder Cato', AJPh 60 (1939), 214 ff., would assign ORF³, fr. inc. 245 to this speech, but the arguments are tenuous.

[58] Plut. Cato Mai. 8. 12 f.; cf. also the disapproval of kings expressed in the immediately following dictum. Eumenes had also been well received on a visit in 189 (Polyb. 21. 18. 3 ff., cf. 21. 22. 1; thence Livy, 37. 52. 3–54. 1), but the visit of 172 is the more probable occasion: Livy, 42. 11. 2 ff.; cf. App. Maced. 11. 1 f.

[59] ORF³, frs. 161 f. The suggestion of Janzer, p. 68 n. 214, that in fr. 162 tueri should be emended to teneri has not found acceptance.

[60] Livy, 45. 18. 1 ff. Jordan, p. LXXXV; Gelzer, RE, s.v. Porcius, no. 9, cols. 132 f.; Kienast, pp. 117 f. Similarly Gelzer and Kienast ascribe to Cato's influence the decision to close the Macedonian mines. Badian, Foreign Clientelae, p. 97, is rightly more circumspect.

supposition, and it is to be noted that the one argument known to have been used by Cato does not appear in Livy; indeed its highly practical character stands in marked contrast to the high-sounding sentiments about freedom which Livy records and which could well have had their origin in the senatorial decree itself. Livy provides the context for Cato's speech and shows that it was at least in general accord with the majority opinion, but his account cannot safely be used to infer more about Cato's role.

It was in this same year, 167, that Cato delivered his speech to the Senate on behalf of the Rhodians, the text of which he included in the fifth book of his *Origines*.[61] It is a speech of which several substantial fragments have survived. The prosperous island of Rhodes, long a favoured client of Rome, had remained neutral during the Third Macedonian War. Slow and seemingly unimpressive progress by the Roman forces in the first three years seems to have given encouragement and an increasing measure of popular favour to a Rhodian faction which viewed Perseus and Macedonia with considerable sympathy. By 168 this faction had actually persuaded the Rhodians to offer to arbitrate between Perseus and the Romans, a folly at any time but disastrous coming as it did on the eve of the Roman victory at Pydna; indeed the envoys to Rome arrived simultaneously with the news of the victory and were obliged hurriedly to substitute a lame and unconvincing message of congratulations. The result was that in 167 new Rhodian envoys, hastily sent in an effort to retrieve the situation, were faced with a strong move to declare war on Rhodes. One of the praetors, M'. Iuventius Thalna, went so far as to place the question before an assembly of the People without first consulting the Senate, though he was immediately thwarted by the veto of two tribunes, M. Antonius and M. Pomponius. It was Antonius who afterwards introduced the envoys to the Senate, which previously had refused to hear them or to grant official hospitality. The Senate now listened to their pleas, debated the issue, and finally decided upon a number of stern measures directed against Rhodes but not upon war. It was in

[61] For this episode see Polyb. 30. 4 f.; Livy, 45. 3. 3 ff.; 45. 20. 4–25. 4; Diod. 31. 5; Gell. 6. 3, this last including an account of the speech and the surviving fragments: *ORF*³, frs. 163–9, cf. *HRR* i², Cato fr. 95. On the speech see also pp. 137 ff. and 273 ff. A convenient modern account of the circumstances in Errington, *The Dawn of Empire*, pp. 249 ff. Gruen, 'Rome and Rhodes in the Second Century B.C.', *CQ* n.s. 25(1975), 58ff., would modify in some respects the conventional picture of the background situation. He argues that the degree both of factional strife and of pro-Macedonian sympathy has been exaggerated by *post eventum* recriminations, and that the Rhodians' difficulties sprang more from a subsequent hardening of Roman attitudes than from actions which could have been considered ill advised at the time.

this debate that Cato delivered his speech, arguing against war. The best-known of his arguments was similar to one he was to apply to the Lusi-tanians in his speech against Galba eighteen years later: whatever outcome to the war the Rhodians may have wished for, they had not committed any hostile act against Rome; and it was misdeeds, not mere wishes, that should be punished. However there are special reasons for the prominence of this feature in the surviving account and it was not necessarily the principal plea in a speech which contained a considerable variety of arguments. According to Livy Cato's speech was of great assistance to the Rhodians, but it should not be assumed too confidently that it was decisive in persuad-ing the Senate against war. In the *Origines*, to which Livy refers, Cato will have presented his contribution and his influence in the most favour-able light possible, but the very fact that an attempt was made to by-pass the Senate suggests that from the start those who wanted war were un-certain that they would be able to persuade a majority of senators.

The other known instances of Cato's involvement in foreign affairs all belong to the last few years of his life. The speech 'Concerning the younger Ptolemy' in 154 or 153 has often been regarded as one such in-stance, but this is uncertain since allegations of misconduct and peculation by Thermus could well have been the central issue. Even if they were not, there is more doubt than is usually recognized as to which Ptolemy Cato preferred.[62] Three other instances are trivial. Among the security measures taken by the Romans at the end of the Third Macedonian War had been the deportation to Italy of 1,000 leading men of the Achaean league, among them the future historian Polybius. The release of these detainees had several times been debated and rejected by the Senate. When the question was raised again in 150 Polybius' friend and patron P. Cornelius Scipio Aemilianus sought Cato's assistance on behalf of the exiles.

When there was a long debate in the Senate, with some advocating their return and some opposing it, Cato rose and said, 'As though we had nothing else to do, we sit here the whole day debating whether some old Greeks should be buried by Italian or by Achaean undertakers.' A few days after the Senate had voted that the men be allowed to return home, Polybius and his associates again sought to enter the Senate, to ask that the exiles should recover the honours they had previously had in Achaea, and they asked Cato's opinion. He smiled and said that Polybius, like Odysseus, wished to go again into the cave of the Cyclops because he had forgotten his cap and belt.

It is clear enough that Polybius regarded Cato's intervention in the

---

[62] *ORF*³, frs. 177–81; above, p. 111, and for the Ptolemies below, pp. 270 f.

debate as decisive, and as such it is a testimony to his standing and influence at this time; but equally the whole affair was, as Cato so emphatically pointed out, a minor item among the concerns of the Senate.[63]

Cato's speech to the Senate 'Concerning king Attalus and the revenues of Asia', *De rege Attalo et vectigalibus Asiae*, probably belongs at about this time. In 154 Rome had put a stop to a war between two of her allies in Asia Minor, Prusias II and Attalus II, kings of Bithynia and Pergamum respectively; and as part of the settlement Prusias had been put under obligation to pay Attalus a large indemnity in twenty annual instalments. In 151 or 150, when Prusias appealed for the cancellation of the remaining instalments, both kings sent envoys to put their cases to the Senate, which decided in favour of Attalus. This is the obvious occasion for Cato's speech, which probably, since it is termed a *dissuasio*, opposed Prusias' request, though the single fragment reveals nothing of his reasons.[64]

Almost immediately after this, in 149, the antagonism between these two kings found expression in a new disturbance in Asia Minor. Attalus encouraged and helped Prusias' son, Nicomedes, in an attempt to usurp his father's throne. The Senate decided to send an embassy to restrain Attalus and Nicomedes and chose three envoys of whom one happened to suffer badly from gout, another had received severe injuries to his head from a falling roof-tile, and the third was considered outstandingly stupid. Cato's comment was that before the embassy was finished 'not only would Prusias be dead but Nicomedes would have grown old in his kingdom. For how could the embassy hurry, or if it did hurry how could it accomplish anything when it had neither feet nor head nor heart?'[65] But although the witticism was long remembered the Bithynian affair was a relatively minor item among the preoccupations of the Senate at this time, not much more important than the release of the Achaean exiles. Both are almost insignificant beside what was unquestionably the dominating topic of these years, the crisis which led in 149 to the third and final war against Carthage.

The events which led up to this war centred around the relationship

---

[63] Plut. *Cato Mai.* 9. 2 f. = Polyb. 35. 6; cf. Paus. 7. 10. 12; *ORF*[3], frs. 187–9, showing that Cato did make a speech. For the date see Astin, *Scipio Aemilianus*, p. 245 n. 6.

[64] *ORF*[3], fr. 190; App. *Mith.* 4. The probable date of the speech was demonstrated by Fraccaro, 'Catoniana', *Studi storici*, 3 (1910), 281 ff. = *Opusc.* i. 253 ff.; cf. Scullard, *Roman Politics*[2], p. 271. For the background see, in addition to works cited on p. 121 n. 56, Magie, *Roman Rule in Asia Minor* i. 28 and 316 f.; Hansen, *The Attalids*[2], pp. 135 ff.; Vitucci, *Il regno di Bitinia*, pp. 80 ff.; McShane, *Foreign Policy of the Attalids*, pp. 189 ff.

[65] Polyb. 36. 14; Plut. *Cato Mai.* 9. 1; Livy, *Per.* 50; *Ox. epit.* 50; App. *Mith.* 6; Diod. 32. 20. Magie, op. cit., pp. 28, 317, and 1198 f. For other accounts see works cited in the preceding note and p. 121 n. 56.

between Carthage and the Numidian king Massinissa.[66] At the end of the Second Punic War, half a century earlier, Carthage had been allowed to retain all her territories in Africa, except that Massinissa was to have any territory which at any time had been held by himself or his ancestors. The failure to define these excepted areas more accurately resulted in Massinissa making encroachments which Carthage was powerless to resist; for she was prohibited from sending an army beyond her borders and thus from ejecting Massinissa from disputed territories. Appeals to Rome proved fruitless, since time after time Roman arbitrators either favoured Massinissa or did nothing—which in practice left the king in possession. A particularly blatant example of this had occurred in 161, and there was another around 158–156.[67] Inevitably feelings of impatience, resentment, anger, and distrust spread and deepened among the Carthaginians, weakening the pro-Roman and pro-Numidian factions and strengthening the more militant democrats. In 153, while the Romans were preoccupied with troubles in Spain and Massinissa was embroiled elsewhere, these feelings found expression in raids on Massinissa's settlers in disputed areas and in inciting rural Africans against the king. The consequent fighting was ended by Roman ambassadors, who nevertheless once more left Massinissa in control of the disputed territory. Soon the king raised a new dispute, again Carthage appealed to Rome, again, in 152, a Roman embassy arrived; and this time one of the envoys—surely the most senior of them—was Cato.

The presence of a senator of such eminence as Cato is an indication of the importance attached to this embassy and the seriousness with which events in Africa were viewed in Rome.[68] The experiences of the envoys

---

[66] The principal source for this episode is App. *Lib.* 68–94, supplemented by Livy, *Per.* 47–9, cf. *Ox. epit.* 49, and Plut. *Cato Mai.* 26 f., by a few fragments of Polybius and Diodorus, and by some lesser writers, notably Florus, Orosius, and Zonaras. The evidence for particular points is cited in more detail in my discussion in *Scipio Aemilianus*, pp. 49 ff., which this account follows closely. For the chronology, the motives for the destruction of Carthage, and the arguments of Scipio Nasica and his supporters see op. cit., Appendix III, pp. 270 ff. The bibliography is extensive; see esp. Kahrstedt, *Gesch. der Karthager*, pp. 613 ff.; Gsell, *Hist. anc.* iii. 312 ff.; Gelzer, 'Nasicas Widerspruch', *Philologus*, 86 (1931), 261 ff.; Adcock, 'Delenda est Carthago', *CHJ* 8 (1946), 117 ff.; Scullard, *Roman Politics*², pp. 240 ff.; Kienast, pp. 125 ff.; Badian, *Foreign Clientelae*, pp. 125 ff.; Hoffmann, 'Die römische Politik', *Historia*, 9 (1960), 309 ff.

[67] Polyb. 31. 21; Livy, *Per.* 47. Walsh, 'Massinissa', *JRS* 55 (1965), 149 ff., esp. 156 ff., discusses the encroachments and argues that Roman partiality really manifested itself after Massinissa's display of loyalty during the Third Macedonian War.

[68] Livy, *Per.* 47, says the embassy was prompted by reports that the Carthaginians had collected a large mercenary army, but this is possibly either hostile propaganda or a retrojection of later events. Reports of stocks of ship-timber at Carthage also occur in the Livian

served only to deepen that concern. In the customary manner they offered to arbitrate; but the patience of the Carthaginians had been strained too far, their distrust had grown too great: holding that Massinissa was patently in the wrong and that the task of the embassy was simply to restore to them the land which he had occupied, they refused the offer. Cato and his companions, returning to Rome with the quarrel undecided, must have been much perturbed. The refusal of Roman arbitration was a manifestation of independence and self-confidence which was probably unforeseen and which must have been most unwelcome; and the envoys themselves had seen the basis of that self-confidence in the all-too-evident prosperity and wealth of the city. If there is truth in the report that the Carthaginian senate had at first agreed to arbitration but was overridden by massive popular demonstrations the revelation of such intense and potent feelings in the mass of the population can only have added to Roman concern.[69] Whether this was so or not, the concern was such that from this point on Cato pressed for war and for the destruction of Carthage.

The driving force behind his demand was fear: fear of a Carthage economically resurgent, resentful, increasingly impatient and self-assertive.[70] His point of view was shared by other leading men, unfortunately not named, and ultimately won the support of the majority of senators; but it was Cato himself who inspired and led the agitation and did so with great vigour. The details best known are his display of a fresh Libyan fig, which he displayed in the Senate to drive home the point that Carthage was only three days sail from Rome, and his tactic of ending every contribution to senatorial debates with the opinion that Carthage should be destroyed.[71] He must have argued his case at greater length on a number of occasions, but later generations seem to have had the text of only one speech 'Concerning the Carthaginian war'. Some of the fragments show Cato stirring up emotion by painting a lurid picture of Carthaginian atrocities during the Hannibalic war. Only one preserves an argument, and that is something of a contrast with—though it does not contradict—one

account; cf. Zon. 9. 26. Walsh, op. cit., pp. 159 f., rightly notes that Massinissa seems to have deliberately played upon Roman fears of Carthaginian rearmament.

[69] Livy, *Per.* 48.

[70] Below, pp. 274 ff.; Astin, *Scipio Aemilianus*, pp. 272 ff.

[71] Fig: Plut. *Cato Mai.* 27. 1; Pliny, *Nat. hist.* 15. 74 ff. The dictum: Plut. *Cato Mai.* 27. 2; App. *Lib.* 69; Diod. 34/5. 33. 3; Florus, 1. 31. 4; cf. Pliny, loc. cit.; Vell. 1. 13. 1; 'Victor', *De vir. ill.* 47. 8. Note also the mention of Hannibal in the speech *De Achaeis*, ORF³, fr. 187. Little is added by discussions of the precise form of the dictum by Chabert, 'Le "delenda Carthago" et ses origines', *Ann. de l'Univ. de Grenoble*, 25 (1913), 49 ff., Little, 'The Authenticity and Form of Cato's Saying', *CJ* 29 (1934), 429 ff. and Thürlemann, 'Ceterum censeo Carthaginem esse delendam', *Gymnasium*, 81 (1974), 465 ff.

he had used in the Rhodian speech and was to use again against Galba:
'The Carthaginians are already our enemies; for he who prepares everything against me, so that he can make war at whatever time he wishes,
he is already my enemy even though he is not yet using weapons.'[72]

Nevertheless it took Cato more than two years of persistent pressure
to win his point. For that length of time the Senate was restrained and
Cato was thwarted by the opposition led by P. Cornelius Scipio Nasica
Corculum, who himself had probably been one of the envoys who visited
Carthage with Cato. It was argued that there was no 'just cause', that
the destruction of Carthage would have an undesirable effect on foreign
opinion, and perhaps also that to maintain her own efficiency Rome
needed Carthage as 'a counter-weight of fear'.

So determined was this opposition that Polybius, a well-informed
contemporary, commented that 'disputes about the effect on foreign
opinion very nearly made them desist from going to war.'[73] But the
ground was cut from beneath Nasica's feet by the Carthaginians themselves, whose reaction against the Numidians had acquired a momentum
which quickly carried it out of control. Late in 152 or in 151 Numidian
complaints together with reports that Carthage was rearming led to a
new Roman embassy of investigation. Cato had demanded war, and he
renewed the demand when the embassy reported military activity at
Carthage, but even in the face of that report more moderate counsels
reduced this to a threat of war unless Carthage disarmed. But before
this compromise could be tested the Carthaginians committed themselves
irrevocably. They expelled the small pro-Numidian faction, refused

[72] ORF[3], fr. 195; the other frs. are 191–4. Adcock, 'Delenda est Carthago', CHJ 8 (1946),
124, cf. Scullard, Roman Politics[2], p. 288, argues that the fragment quoted must have been
spoken before Cato could point to an unequivocal violation of the treaty of 201, thus before
the battle with Massinissa in the winter 151/0. This seems plausible but not absolutely certain.
Bilz, Die Politik des P. Cornelius Scipio Aemilianus, p. 18, and Janzer, p. 82, put the speech in
153, but Malcovati, ORF[3], p. 78, and Nenci, 'La De Bello Carthaginiensi', Critica storica, 1
(1962), 363, prefer 150. Despite the superficial impression that the argument of fr. 195 is the
opposite of that used in the Rhodian speech there is a fundamental distinction: in the Rhodian
speech Cato claims that the Rhodians refrained from hostile actions against Rome and did
not wish to go to war with her, even though they judged it in their own best interests that
she should not achieve a total victory over Perseus, whereas in fr. 195 the claim is that the
Carthaginians are actively preparing for war (i.e. not simply wishing to see Rome defeated
by someone else) and awaiting an opportunity to strike. The contrast between fr. 195 on
Carthage and fr. 197 concerning Galba is much closer to an example of double standards,
for it is known that Galba asserted that the Lusitanians were preparing to rebel: Livy, Per.
49. It is to be remembered, however, that Cato probably did not accept the truth of Galba's
assertion, so that the fragment probably reflects only a secondary argument. Cf. p. 112.

[73] Polyb. 36. 2; cf. fr. 99 BW. On Nasica's opposition see below pp. 283 f., and Astin,
Scipio Aemilianus, pp. 276 ff.

Massinissa's request for its restoration, and attacked the retinue of his son Gulussa. When Massinissa retaliated they sent out a large army which took the decisive step of pursuing him beyond the recognized frontier. The two sides met in a great battle which after a long and fierce struggle went in favour of the Numidian. The defeated Carthaginians then tried to make terms in a conference arranged at their request by the Roman Scipio Aemilianus, who happened to be on a visit to Massinissa; but although they offered large concessions they absolutely refused to hand over Numidians who had deserted to them. In renewed fighting the Punic troops were encircled and eventually compelled to surrender— most of them to be treacherously massacred by Gulussa.

The disaster was far greater than the immediate loss of a field army. Carthaginian self-assertion had violated the conditions of the treaty imposed by Rome, given Rome a pretext for war, and powerfully reinforced sentiment behind Cato. Nasica's earlier plea that there was no *iusta causa* for war had been seriously undermined. The effective decision was taken and Roman military preparations began; desperate and abject Carthaginian ambassadors were rebuffed; war was formally declared early in 149; the *deditio* of Utica (i.e. its formal surrender to Roman discretion) made available a suitable base for the expeditionary force which now set out. There quickly followed the *deditio* of Carthage itself and the successive demands by which the Romans secured first hostages and then the Carthaginian stock of arms, until the final demand for the abandonment of the city and resettlement at least ten miles inland drove a disarmed people to desperate resistance.

It is not absolutely certain that even this final demand went as far as Cato wished. When Carthage made her *deditio* Nasica attempted to secure some modification of the policy already agreed, and it is conceivable that the promise that Carthage would retain her freedom, autonomy, and territory reflects his moderating influence.[74] But if this was a compromise, nevertheless in essence Cato had prevailed: he had persuaded the Senate that Carthage must not be allowed to continue to occupy a site so politically and strategically advantageous, that she must be deprived of the magnificent coastal situation which was the key to her commercial resilience and prosperity, in effect that in the form in which she had existed and prospered Carthage should be destroyed. As matters turned out, the compromise (if such there was) made no difference. When Carthage went back on her *deditio* the Roman promise became void and its place was

---

[74] Cf. Münzer, *RE*, s.v. *Cornelius*, no. 353, col. 1500; Florus, 1. 31. 5: 'medium senatus elegit'—perhaps no more than a guess.

taken by a decision that in the fullest sense the Carthaginian state should
cease to exist and its territory be annexed.

Cato did not survive to see that decision carried out. Not until 146
was Carthage captured and destroyed; Cato died in 149, within a few
months of the outbreak of war.[75] He lived long enough to comment
acidly on the inadequacy of Roman operations in those months, singling
out as the bright exception the exploits of one of the military tribunes,
Scipio Aemilianus: 'He alone', he quoted from Homer, 'has understanding;
the rest flit like shadows.'[76] Yet scornful though he was of the early set-
backs, it is unlikely that he had doubts about the eventual outcome, or
indeed about the rightness of that outcome. In all probability he died
convinced that by ensuring Carthage would be destroyed he had rendered
to Rome one of his most valuable services.

[75] Cic. *Brut.* 61; 80; Vell. 1. 13. 1; Pliny, *Nat. hist.* 29. 15; cf. Plut. *Cato Mai.* 27. 5.
[76] Polyb. 36. 8. 7, quoting *Od.* 10. 495; also in Livy, *Per.* 49; Diod. 32. 9a; Plut. *Cato Mai.*
27. 6; *Praec. reip. ger.* 10; 'Plut.' *Apophth. Scip. Min.* 3; *Suda,* s.v. Κάτων.

7

Orator

IN the verdicts of the ancient writers there is no mistaking Cato's reputation as an orator of very considerable ability.[1] Naturally assessments vary somewhat according to the purposes, the expertise, and the personal viewpoint of individual authors, all of whom looked back on Cato from generations more sophisticated in the art of rhetoric and consciously devoted to its cultivation. Thus Quintilian was more qualified and less fulsome in his praise than Cicero before him or Fronto and Gellius after; and at least three of them, perhaps all four, were conscious that in terms of their own standards Cato had limitations. An awareness of such limitations is probably reflected in the slightly cautious *probabilis orator* of Nepos and in Plutarch's ῥήτωρ ἱκανός (itself perhaps simply taken from Nepos), a 'commendable' or 'capable' orator. Nevertheless the general verdict is enthusiastic. Plutarch himself subsequently dwells on Cato's merits and is one of three Greek authors to record that he was frequently called 'the Roman Demosthenes'. Cicero may have deliberately overstated his case when he claimed for Cato 'all the virtues of oratory' in order to make fun of the so-called 'Atticists' (why, he asked, did they model their plain style on the Greek Lysias rather than the Roman Cato?),

---

[1] This chapter is based only on the evidence which relates directly to Cato as an orator and to his speeches. Cato's other writings are discussed in Chapters 9 and 10. The number of modern works which comment on Cato as an orator is enormous. The following is a list of more important items, but the selection is necessarily to some extent arbitrary. Baumgart, *Untersuch. zu den Reden des M. Porcius Cato*; Leo, *Gesch. der röm. Literatur* i. 283 ff.; Norden, *Die antike Kunstprosa* i³. 164 ff.; Marouzeau, 'Pour mieux comprendre les textes latins', *RPh* 45 (1921), 149 ff., esp. 168 ff.; Clarke, *Rhetoric at Rome*², pp. 38 ff.; Leeman, *Orationis Ratio*, pp. 21 ff. and 43 ff.; Till–Meo, *La lingua di Catone*; von Albrecht, *Meister röm. Prosa*, pp. 24 ff.; Sblendorio, 'Note sullo stile dell'oratoria catoniana', *AFLC* 34 (1971), 5 ff.; Kennedy, *The Art of Rhetoric*, pp. 38 ff. Note also Helm, *RE*, s.v. *Porcius*, no. 9, cols. 162 ff.; Knapp, 'A Phase of the Development of Prose Writing Among the Romans', *CPh* 13 (1918), 138 ff.; Schanz–Hosius, *Gesch. der röm. Literatur* i⁴. 189 f.; Frank, *Life and Literature*, pp. 140 ff.; Marmorale, *Cato Maior*², pp. 199 ff.; Henderson, 'Cato's Pine Cones and Seneca's Plums', *TAPhA* 86 (1955), 256 ff. The discussions of Cima, *L'eloquenza latina*, pp. 17–94, and Janzer, are concerned primarily with the context and content of individual speeches. On Cicero's *Brutus* see Douglas, *Brutus*. On the inadequacies of Marcucci, *Studio critico sulle opere di Catone* i. 1 see Münzer, *WKPh*, 1903, pp. 91 ff.

but his admiration was genuine enough: Cato was as eloquent as anyone could have been at that date. To Fronto and Gellius he was an authoritative model, to be admired and studied; to Livy he was 'most eloquent', to the elder Pliny 'an excellent orator', and even to Quintilian he was 'outstanding in speaking', *in dicendo praestantissimus*. Time and again he was seen as Rome's earliest orator, or at least the earliest whose speeches could be known and studied, a key figure in the development of an art which educated Romans came to regard as one of the major cultural achievements of their society.[2]

The principal foundation for these assessments, and especially for virtually all the more specific and informative comments, was the study by later generations of the written texts of speeches, very many of which were preserved. Obvious in the cases of Gellius and Fronto, who combed the texts for words, phrases, or passages which appealed to their special tastes and interests, this is almost certainly true also of most of what was said by Cicero, Quintilian, and even Plutarch. Cicero in the *Brutus*, which contains most of his specific comments, emphasized the great number of Cato's speeches he had found and read—more than 150— while in the chapter of the *Life* in which Plutarch lists particular rhetorical qualities he evidently envisaged the supposed (and to him incomprehensible) comparison with Lysias as a matter to be resolved by reading the speeches.[3] Furthermore virtually all the qualities ascribed to Cato by these authors, even including his ability to be savage in attack, are such as could have been and in most cases are likely to have been observed in reading. By contrast, there is a notable absence of material which could have been derived only from contemporary observation and not from study of the texts—for example, about the manner of his delivery. Thus very little of the surviving comment on Cato's oratory need have stemmed from authentic contemporary accounts—not that there is any reason to suppose that contemporaries would have disagreed about its salient characteristics, though obviously they will not have assessed those

[2] Nepos, *Cato* 3. 1; Plut. *Cato Mai.* 1. 5, 2. 5 f., 4. 1 (Demosthenes), 7. 1 ff., cf. 19. 8; Diod. 34/5. 33. 3; App. *Iber.* 39; Cic. *Brut.* 63 ff., 298; id., *De orat.* 1. 171; Livy, 39. 40. 6 ff.; Pliny, *Nat. hist.* 7. 100. See also Vell. 1. 17. 3; Val. Max. 8. 7. 1. The views of Fronto and Gellius are obvious from the cumulative effect of many passages, some of which, along with more passages from Cicero and Quintilian, will be discussed below, as will the special case of the adverse judgement of Tullius Tiro on the Rhodian speech. The opinion of Sallust, though in accord with the views cited here, is likely to have been based mainly on the *Origines*.

[3] Cic. *Brut.* 65; Plut. *Cato Mai.* 7. 2 f. Hendrickson, 'Literary Sources in Cicero's Brutus', *AJPh* 27 (1906), 184 ff., makes the obvious point that Cicero is unlikely to have done the actual work of collecting himself, but that does not invalidate his statement.

characteristics in the same terms or by the same criteria. The one comment which is certainly contemporary does accord fully with later observations that his speeches were notable for *brevitas*. Curiously it was made by Cato himself. According to Plutarch he said of his speech at Athens in 191 that 'the Athenians were astonished at his speed and the swiftness of his speech; for what he himself set out briefly the interpreter repeated at length with many words.'[4]

Nor can it reasonably be doubted that among his contemporaries as well as by reputation among later generations Cato was an outstanding and exceptionally effective orator. In the first place the fact that he kept copies of so many speeches suggests that he regarded himself in some such light, and though he is no more likely to have underestimated his achievements in this field than in any other, the practice is one which is likely to have sprung from frequent success. Then a special reputation is likely to have preceded and helped to bring about the passing of so many speeches into circulation. Admittedly Cicero indicated in the *Brutus*, published in 46, that at that time the speeches were rarely read, but his words can well be taken to mean that this had not always been so, and indeed since copies of the speeches were certainly in circulation there must have been an interest at an earlier date.[5] Moreover in the 80s, long before the revival of interest in Cato's works in Cicero's later years, both Cicero himself in his *De inventione* and the author of the almost contemporary *Ad Herennium* referred to Cato in terms implying he was a great orator.[6] Finally, reference to Cato as 'the Roman Demosthenes' is more likely to have originated before rather than after Cicero established his own reputation.

Granted the fact of Cato's reputation as an orator of exceptional talent, the aim of this chapter must be to investigate more closely the character of his oratory and his role in the development of Roman oratory. Such an investigation must be concerned with two major bodies of evidence. The first of these consists of the comments made by writers in antiquity,

[4] Plut. *Cato Mai.* 12. 7. For *brevitas* in the speeches see Cic. *Brut.* 63; Pliny, *Ep.* 1. 20. 1 ff.; cf. Tac. *Dial.* 18; and below.

[5] Baumgart, *Untersuch. zu den Reden des M. Porcius Cato*, pp. 17 ff., perhaps thinking too much in terms of a corpus, argues that the speeches were largely unknown and not in circulation until Cicero developed a special interest between 55 and 46. He suggests that Cicero may have got most of the copies from his contemporary, Cato's great-grandson. This view not only relies too heavily on questionable arguments from silence but conflicts with the clear implications of Cic. *Brut.* 65; also *Ad Her.* 4. 7 implies that copies were available to the author and there is no reason to suppose that these were only of the speeches included in the *Origines*. Cf. Leo, *Gesch. der röm. Literatur* i. 284 n. 1.

[6] Cic. *De inv.* 1. 5; *Ad Her.* 4. 7.

which it has been seen were based largely upon the reading of the texts of the speeches. The volume of material available to them was large— as is evident from Cicero's knowledge of over 150 of Cato's speeches— and several of the authors who had most to say had themselves read much or all of this and were therefore giving first-hand opinions. The second major body of evidence consists of the extraordinarily numerous fragments of Cato's speeches which have been preserved—well over 200, from about eighty different speeches. The two kinds of evidence are not totally separate since a few of the fragments, including several of the more substantial, survive as quotations illustrating comments on Cato's oratorical qualities. The great majority of fragments, however, owe their survival to the antiquarians, lexicographers, grammarians, and the generally curious, for whom Cato's speeches were a rich mine of archaic, obscure, and unusual words and usages.[7]

Since both the comments and the fragments stem from the versions of Cato's speeches which were available to later generations it is pertinent to ask how close these versions were to the speeches as actually delivered. The question of 'publication', though closely related, is by comparison unimportant. It is attested that Cato included in his historical work, the *Origines*, the text of at least two of his own speeches, 'On behalf of the Rhodians' (167) and 'Against Servius Galba' (149); but there is nothing to show whether copies of other speeches were put into circulation by Cato himself or posthumously.[8] It would be interesting to know, and the answer would be an additional item to help in assessing Cato's attitude towards his own speeches, but otherwise it does not materially affect the evaluation of the two bodies of evidence. What does make a considerable difference is whether the versions were written down approximately at the time of delivery or many years later. If Cato recorded the speeches close to the time of delivery it is perhaps a slight distinction whether he wrote before or soon after delivery, but whether the record was in note form or a full text is another matter. Similarly if Cato edited many of his speeches long after the event the character of the surviving versions

[7] The fragments in *ORF*[3] are numbered to 254, but they include seventeen *testimonia* and several passages which report speeches but no actual quotation. In several others it is uncertain whether there is a quotation or only an indication of the general sense of what Cato said. For the large number of speeches preserved see also Livy, 39. 40. 7 f. As early as the time of Augustus Verrius Flaccus had enough material for at least two books *De obscuris M. Catonis*: Gell. 17. 6. 2. The numerous quotations in Festus and Paulus will have been derived mainly from Verrius' *De significatu verborum*.

[8] See pp. 155 f. for further discussion, inclining slightly against publication by Cato himself. Speeches in the *Origines*: Livy, 45. 25. 3; Gell. 6. 3. 7; id. 13. 25. 15; Cic. *De orat.* 1. 227; Livy, *Per.* 49; Val. Max. 8. 1. 2.

would have been much affected by whether he was 'polishing up' an existing text, constructing a full version from an original summary or notes, or composing simply from memory; and it has even been suggested that in many instances his posthumous editors will have found only summary versions.[9] Among the arguments advanced in favour of one view or another several are largely subjective; in reality there are only four items of evidence to be considered. First Cicero in the *De senectute*, set in the year 150, made Cato list various ways in which he was keeping his mind active, including 'At this very time I am completing [or composing: *conficio*] my speeches in the notable cases in which I spoke in defence.'[10] If taken at face value this would certainly mean that the speeches concerned were subject to some kind of *post eventum* revision, though there would remain an ambiguity about its nature and extent, and it should be noted that many speeches would not have been in the category mentioned. However, this is very thin evidence, for it is most unlikely that Cicero would have had any specific information that Cato was so occupied at this time, whereas this is just the kind of imaginative detail which Cicero could have supplied for the purposes of his argument, indeed it is precisely one of the activities in which he is likely to have envisaged himself engaging in old age. Against this statement of Cicero's is sometimes set one by Nepos: 'ab adulescentia confecit orationes.'[11] But this too is of doubtful value, for if Nepos had any basis for it at all he is likely to have had in mind the range of occasions and cases covered by the speeches, without considering when the surviving versions were actually composed. There is little to be got from Gellius' statement that following the example of his grandfather Cato's grandson left many written speeches, except that it perhaps suggests that Gellius believed the full versions to have been written by Cato himself rather than edited posthumously from summaries.[12] Lastly, there is a substantial extract from Cato's speech *De sumptu suo*, quoted verbatim by Fronto as the best example known to him of a particular rhetorical device (paraleipsis).[13] Cato describes part of the preparation of the speech he is actually delivering, an attempt to make use of material in an earlier speech, and his own comments to the scribe who was assisting him:

I ordered the book (*caudex*) to be brought out in which had been written

---

[9] Kennedy, *The Art of Rhetoric*, pp. 57 ff. A variety of views and arguments on composition and publication will be found in the following works listed on p. 131 n. 1: Baumgart, pp. 13 f.; Leo, p. 283; Norden, p. 165; Cima, pp. 30 ff.; Schanz–Hosius, p. 190; Marmorale, pp. 200 f.; also Fraccaro, *Opuscula* i. 191.

[10] Cic. *De sen.* 38.   [11] Nepos, *Cato* 3. 3.   [12] Gell. 13. 20. 10.

[13] *ORF*[3], fr. 173 = Fronto, *Ad A. Imp.* 1. 2. 9 = ii. 44–6H.

my speech on that matter concerning which I had made a judicial wager with
Marcus Cornelius. The tablets (*tabulae*) were brought out; the services of my
ancestors were read out; then those things which I had done for the state were
read. When the reading out of both of these was finished, the speech went on
as follows: 'Never have I lavished my own money or that of the allies in order
to win favour.' 'Oh no!' I said, 'Don't, don't write that.' Then he read out,
'Never have I imposed prefects on the towns of your allies, to plunder their
property and children.' 'Delete that too; they don't want to hear it. Read
further.' 'Never have I divided booty taken from the enemy or prize money
among the small circle of my friends and thus snatched it away from those who
had captured it.' 'Erase as far as that too: there is nothing they less want said
than that. It is not needed; read on.' 'Never have I granted a travel-order to
enable my friends to gain large sums by means of the warrants.' 'Get on and
delete to there too, immediately.' 'The money intended for the wine distribution
I have never shared out among my attendants and friends nor have I made them
rich to the detriment of the state.' 'Most certainly erase that, right down to the
wood. See, if you please, what condition the state is in, when for fear it should
be a cause of ill will I dare not recall the very services I performed for the state,
from which I used to gain gratitude. Thus it has become normal practice to
do ill with impunity, but not to be permitted to do well with impunity.'

The opening of this passage has often been quoted in support of the
contention that Cato kept and filed away records of his speeches in notebooks consisting of bundles of waxed tablets, presumably each speech on a
separate *caudex*; and indeed it scarcely leaves room for doubt in the matter,
even though strictly speaking it is evidence regarding only a single speech.
The full passage, however, with its quotations and instructions for erasures,
reveals even more than that. It clearly presupposes that the notebook
contained not merely notes or a summary but the continuous text, fully
written out. Furthermore the preparation of the *De sumptu suo* itself is
depicted as a careful and detailed exercise involving the assistance of a
scribe and the composition of a written text: the passage implies, in
fact, that when the speech was delivered it already existed as a detailed
written version. It would be rash to conclude that Cato never spoke
extempore or from notes, that he always prepared a full text in advance;
but when allowance is made for the dramatic element in the passage it
still contains important presuppositions about the normal method of
preparing speeches as well as about their preservation. It is much the most
significant item of evidence, and in particular is more authoritative
than Cicero's remark in the *De senectute*. Consequently it greatly encourages
the belief that in the main the versions of Cato's speeches which survived
were very close to the actual speeches which were delivered rather than

semi-literary productions or revisions considerably removed from the originals.

Despite the considerable volume of evidence available there are certain limitations to attempts to probe the character of Cato's speeches. Above all, virtually nothing can be determined about their over-all form and structure. No speech is preserved in full or in sufficiently numerous and substantial fragments to permit a convincing reconstruction (though reconstructions have been attempted),[14] and very few of the ancient comments bear upon this aspect. This is true even of the fragments of the speech 'On behalf of the Rhodians' (167) and, to a lesser extent, of the comments upon it, though these come nearest to being an exception. There is rather special information about this speech, stemming from the fact that Cicero's freedman Tullius Tiro composed a substantial monograph, in the form of a letter to one of Cicero's friends, Q. Axius, arguing that it was thoroughly bad. Although Tiro's monograph has not survived, a century and a half after it was written it roused the indignation of Aulus Gellius, who like others in the Antonine age was a fervent admirer of Cato's style and literary and rhetorical qualities. Consequently he devoted the longest single section of his miscellany, the Noctes Atticae, to a refutation of Tiro's arguments, in the course of which he quoted the introduction and six other extracts from the speech, probably in their correct sequence.[15] Nevertheless these extracts are by no means the bulk of the speech and cannot be assumed to reflect its over-all structure. All but one of them are the extracts used by Tiro to support his own particular criticisms, and one of Gellius' principal complaints is that Tiro has unfairly concentrated upon a limited area of Cato's argument and ignored much else. Indeed Gellius mentions several arguments used by Cato which do not appear at all in the extracts. Although these additional arguments and the extracts may between them cover most of the points made by Cato, Gellius does not say enough to establish the sequence or manner in which they fitted into the speech or the relative weight placed on each; and he concludes by recommending the reader 'to take in hand Cato's own speech in its entirety'. Nor are Tiro's criticisms, as reported by Gellius, of any help in this respect, for they are concerned not with structure, or even with

---

[14] Especially by Janzer; but even with so many fragments as survive from the *Dierum dictarum de consulatu suo*, ORF³, frs. 21–55, his conclusion, p. 15, that it was 'a masterpiece of construction' is unwarranted. Even the sequence of fragments is a matter of inference, and most are extremely brief.

[15] Gell. 6. 3; ORF³, frs. 163–9. Fr. 171 contains no quotation and fr. 170 is probably wrongly included: Hoffmann, 'Die römische Politik', *Historia*, 9 (1960), 309 ff., esp. 318 ff., followed by Walbank, 'Political Morality', *JRS* 55 (1965), 6.

style, but with alleged ineptitude and faulty logic in the choice of arguments; and since Gellius' principal concern is to rebut Tiro's criticisms it follows that the bulk of his comments fall in the same field. On the other hand Gellius also passes to more general comments, some of them, as will be seen later, important for consideration of style, others with some bearing on structure. They are in the following passage:[16]

It is further to be observed that in the whole of that speech of Cato's recourse is had to all the weapons and aids of the rhetorical disciplines; but we do not see it happening as we would in mock combats or battles feigned for entertainment. For the matter is not handled, I say, with over much order and ornament and measure, but just as in a doubtful battle, when the line is scattered, the fighting is in many places and with varied fortune, so then in that case, when the notorious arrogance of the Rhodians had aroused the hatred and hostility of many people, Cato used every method of protection and defence without discrimination: now he commends the Rhodians as of the highest merit, now exculpates them as if innocent, now scolds and exhorts that their goods and riches should not be coveted, now he asks for pardon as if they had done wrong, now points to them as friends of the state, now calls to mind clemency, now the mildness shown by our forefathers, now the public interest. And all those things could perhaps have been said with more order and rhythm, but it does not seem possible for them to have been said with greater vigour and vividness. It was therefore unfair of Tullius Tiro to single out from all the resources of so rich a speech, well linked to each other and coherent (*aptis inter sese et cohaerentibus*), a single and bare part to criticize as unworthy of Marcus Cato, namely that he considered that the mere desire to do wrongs which were not actually committed did not merit punishment.

Although Gellius was no dispassionate critic where Cato's writings were in question, he presumably had a reasonable basis for his opinion that the speech was coherent and well integrated. On the other hand he certainly did not mean this to be understood in the sense of an orderly, rational, and lucid exposition. Instead it was highly partisan not just in purpose but in the manner of argument, with Cato skilfully interweaving emotional pleas with rebuttals of the accusations levelled at the Rhodians (the latter especially evident in the individual extracts) and ready to argue from a variety of standpoints so diverse as to be at times mutually contradictory. Evidently one of the merits covered by *facultates aptae inter sese et cohaerentes* was the exercise of considerable skill in passing smoothly and without loss of flow from one such argument to another. A rather similar skill is indicated in Gellius' description of how in one passage within

---

[16] 6. 3. 52-4.

the speech Cato subtly obscured the weak point in an argument by a careful and gradual shift in the nature of his analogies; and such subtlety was one of the qualities noted by Cicero—'quis in docendo edisserendoque subtilior?'[17] This general comment by Cicero gives some encouragement to the inference that the qualities noted by Gellius in the Rhodian speech were fairly typical of many of Cato's orations. Otherwise there are only two points which can be added. All the speeches began with an invocation of the gods; and they were almost certainly fairly short. Although several of the allusions to Cato's well-known *brevitas*, including his own comment on his speech at Athens, refer to succinctness in expression and phraseology, there is a passage in a letter of the younger Pliny in which it is certainly to be understood as over-all brevity and in which this is treated as a recognized feature of Cato's speeches.[18]

An examination of the more detailed aspects of Cato's oratory yields a much firmer and fuller picture. The evidence is more direct, much more extensive, and largely harmonious. It is only to be expected that the comments of ancient writers should have varied somewhat according to their own interests and rhetorical ideals: for example, the predominant (though not exclusive) interest of Fronto and Marcus Aurelius was lexicographical, in the antique flavour of Cato's language and in the employment of striking and unexpected words, whereas Cicero and Quintilian, and often also Gellius, were more concerned with the harmonious and elegant use of words and figures of speech and with skill in construction.[19] Nevertheless, in spite of such different emphases, there is a considerable measure of agreement as to what were the principal characteristics, and a corresponding harmony between the comments and the direct evidence of the numerous fragments.

In general Cato was adjudged an orator of great versatility, skilful in creating a variety of effects, vivid and forceful; but one who lacked the more highly refined and polished 'ornamentation' of a later day, especially in terms of verbal elaboration, elegance of diction, and a more careful arrangement of words and rhythmical effects in accordance with principles marked out by rhetoricians. The shortcomings were indicated several times by Cicero, mainly in his *Brutus*: Cato's language was rather archaic and certain words were 'rather rough' (*horridiora*); his speeches

---

[17] Gell. 6. 3. 43 ff.; Cic. *Brut.* 65.   [18] Pliny, *Ep.* 1. 20. 1–4.

[19] On Fronto and Marcus see esp. Henderson, 'Cato's Pine Cones and Seneca's Plums', *TAPhA* 86 (1955), 256 ff.; Pepe, 'Catone Maggiore e la scuola di Frontone', *GIF* 2 (1958), 12 ff.; cf. Fronto, *Ad M. C.* 4. 3. 2 = i. 4H. The range of Gellius' interests was remarkably wide, including meaning, grammatical usage, spelling, form, and pronunciation as well as the rhetorical qualities.

were rough, unpolished (*orationes horridulae*), lacking *numeri* (rhythmical effects); the words themselves needed to be rearranged and 'so to speak cemented' in order to make his language fit more smoothly together; his orations were not sufficiently polished and perfect, his talent unpolished and raw; it lacked 'the brilliance and colour of pigments not yet invented'.[20] So Cicero, but others said much the same. Quintilian found Cato rough, meagre, and plain (*horridus*; *ieiunus*; *simplex*); Plutarch said that the outward impression (as opposed to the inner merits) of his orations was that they were raw and uncouth; while Fronto's image of pine-cones, in contrast to the 'soft and feverish plums of Seneca', indicates a plain austerity and roughness almost certainly to be understood in the same sense as the lack of polish and ornament mentioned by Cicero (whether or not Fronto regarded that as in any sense a shortcoming). Tacitus thought Cato's oratory less full and rich than that of Gaius Gracchus, and though Gellius took the opposite view he still regarded Cato as only seeking to do what Cicero afterwards perfected; and some of Gellius' comments on the Rhodian speech, quoted earlier in this chapter, are strikingly similar to certain of Cicero's remarks: 'For the matter is not handled with over much order and ornament and measure. . . . And all those things could perhaps have been said with more order and rhythm . . .'[21] It was natural for these authors to attribute such deficiencies in Cato's style—for all of them except possibly Fronto looked upon these characteristics as deficiencies—to the fact that in Cato's day Roman rhetoric was still at an early stage in its development, with the consequence that he was inevitably ignorant of the refinements to be achieved by the systematic study of rhetorical theory. That view is indicated by such remarks as those of Gellius and Cicero, mentioned above, that Cato sought to do what Cicero later perfected and that he lacked certain 'pigments not yet invented'. In other passages Cicero said that Cato 'had as much eloquence as those times and that age could produce in this state' and explicitly that, as an early figure in the development of rhetoric, he was not 'erudite' or 'learned', *eruditus* or *doctus*.[22]

The very nature of these criticisms of Cato's style is inextricably bound up with a recognition that it had considerable merits. Even Quintilian, whose attitude is the least sympathetic (perhaps because he felt himself to be combating an enthusiasm for archaism), was prepared to concede

[20] Cic. *Brut.* 68; 294; 298; *Orator* 152.
[21] Quintil. *Inst.* 2. 5. 21; 8. 5. 33; 12. 10. 10; Plut. *Cato Mai.* 7. 1; Fronto, *De orat.* 2 = ii. 102H, on which see Henderson, op. cit.; Tac. *Dial.* 18; Gell. 10. 3. 15 f.; 6. 3. 52 f.
[22] Cic. *De orat.* 1. 171; *Tusc.* 1. 5.

that Cato's style was no doubt excellent for its time, though not for the present day. He mentioned specifically as a merit only one quality, *vis*, power or forcefulness, a term used also by Gellius, but others referred to a variety of characteristics which in sum indicate a considerable versatility. This is most apparent in the assessments of Plutarch and Cicero. Plutarch referred particularly to the contrasts to be found in Cato's oratory (λόγος): 'It was both graceful and forceful, pleasant and disturbingly striking, witty and severe, aphoristic and belligerent', and despite its seeming roughness was 'full of earnestness and of matters which moved his hearers to tears and wrung their hearts'. It is possible that Plutarch's comments depended more on someone else's assessment than his own, but Cicero's certainly sprang from his personal reading. 'Who is more weighty than him in praise, more bitter in censure, more adroit in aphorism, more subtle in exposition and demonstration?' His speeches are 'full of brilliant words and matter'; if the noteworthy and praiseworthy passages are picked out they will be found to contain 'all the virtues of oratory'. Cato is keen-witted, felicitous in his choice of words, adept, and succinct; he is rich and distinguished in his use of figures of speech and his adaptations of the meaning of words.[23] Admittedly all this is drawn from that section of the *Brutus* in which for partisan purposes Cicero may have written with deliberately exaggerated enthusiasm, but elsewhere in the same work he made it clear that in essence the assessment is his true opinion, and passages in other works, both earlier and later, conform with this.[24] The correspondences with Plutarch's account are evident, and almost all the same qualities find some further mention in other authors: asperity and ferocity in attack; a readiness to resort to ridicule; the 'weightiness', *gravitas*; clarity, charm, careful and felicitous choice of words; *brevitas*; and the use of stylistic devices.[25] Also a few more specific characteristics are mentioned: the use of neologisms; a *penchant* for the word *atque*; the creation of a powerful effect by the employment of synonyms or synonymous phrases; and the example of paraleipsis quoted earlier in this chapter, though this last can scarcely be taken as typical since Fronto stated that it was quite exceptional in all the literature known to him.[26]

---

[23] Quintil. *Inst.* 2. 5. 21; 12. 10. 10; Gell. 10. 3. 15; Plut. *Cato Mai.* 7. 1; Cic. *Brut.* 63–9.

[24] Cic. *Brut.* 298; *De inv.* 1. 5; *De orat.* 1. 171 and 215; *Rep.* 2. 1; 3. 9; *Tusc.* 1. 5.

[25] Livy, 34. 5. 6; *Per.* 49; Fronto, *Ad M. C.* 4. 3. 2 = i. 4H; ibid. 2. 3. 1 = i. 128H; *Ad A. Imp.* 1. 1. 2 = ii. 48H; Apul. *Apol.* 95; Gell. 1. 23. 1; *brevitas*: Tac. *Dial.* 18; Pliny, *Ep.* 1. 20. 4; cf. Plut. *Praec. reip. ger.* 7 for the readiness to ridicule.

[26] Synonyms: Gell. 13. 25. 12 ff.; neologisms: Hor. *Ars poet.* 55 ff.; cf. Gell. 4. 9. 12; *atque*: Fronto, *Ad M. C.* 13 = i. 152H; paraleipsis: Fronto, *Ad A. Imp.* 1. 2. 9 f. = ii. 44–6H.

A great deal of this comment by ancient authors can be amply illustrated from the fragments of the speeches themselves, even though the great majority of these fragments are extremely brief.[27] The extraordinary frequency of *atque* is obvious at a glance, and in addition to the three striking passages cited by Gellius to illustrate the exploitation of synonym more than a dozen other examples can be found—such as 'egoque iam pridem cognovi atque intellexi atque arbitror . . .' (*ORF*[3], fr. 21) and 'miror audere atque religionem non tenere, statuas deorum, exempla earum facierum, signa domi pro supellectile statuere' (*ORF*[3], fr. 98).

This extensive use of synonym and pleonasm throws light also on the nature of the *brevitas* attributed to Cato, which he himself claimed for the speech at Athens. The fragments confirm that he did not indulge in extensive verbal elaboration, that he employed short expressions full of meaning rather than extended explanatory phrases, and that the effect was of rapidity and succinctness; but they also show that *brevitas* is not to be understood as a verbal economy which overrode all other considerations. Cato was not prepared to sacrifice to *brevitas* the rhetorical effects which he could achieve by synonym, or, it may be added, by the frequent use of adjectives and the repetition of key words.

Neologisms present a more difficult problem since the scarcity of earlier and contemporary material makes it difficult to know whether or not a particular word is truly a neologism. Three examples are given by Gellius, but they were not necessarily drawn from speeches.[28] In

[27] See esp. Till–Meo, *La lingua di Catone*, pp. 52 ff.; Sblendorio, 'Note sullo stile dell'oratoria catoniana', *AFLC* 34 (1971), 5 ff. The latter is a thorough and careful collection, systematically arranged, of the main stylistic devices identifiable in the fragments of the speeches, with some comparisons with the incidence of these devices in the *Origines* and the *De agricultura*. Till's book (originally in German in 1935) contains a valuable collection of material and much useful discussion. However it does have several important limitations. First, Till for the most part treats Cato's language as a uniformity, bringing together material from all his writings, whereas there is a clear case for considering the principal categories separately, at least in the first instance. Second, there is an artificiality about Till's view of Cato's language as a kind of compound drawing upon several distinct categories, an archaic element, a colloquial element, a 'poetic' element, and a very slight Greek influence, together with extensive innovation by Cato himself in all aspects of language. Discussion of this last dominates much of the book. Third, the criteria used for identifying these supposedly distinct elements seem questionable, especially in view of the lack of truly comparable material and the relatively limited amount even of material of rather different type. Broadly speaking it seems likely that Till exaggerates the innovatory and 'poetic' elements, and also the deliberate use of archaisms, in the sense that they were already archaisms to Cato. This last topic has been examined carefully by Prugni, 'Per un riesame degli arcaismi catoniani', *QIFL* 2 (1972), 25 ff., who concludes that there are some instances but that they are not numerous.

[28] Gell. 4. 9. 12. Till–Meo, *La lingua di Catone*, esp. pp. 78 ff. and 107 ff.; but see previous note.

contrast, ridicule and sarcasm are unmistakable in the censorial speech attacking the tribune M. Caelius, while the speech *De aedilibus vitio creatis* contained a remarkable example of the use of aphorism: 'I have often heard that much can intervene between mouth and morsel; but between morsel and crop, there indeed is a long interval.'[29]

As for ferocity in attack, the outstanding example, though by no means the only one, is the long extract quoted by Gellius from the speech *De falsis pugnis* directed against Q. Minucius Thermus in 190 (*ORF*[3], fr. 58). The circumstances of this speech are discussed above, in Chapter 4, and a translation of the extract will be found in Appendix 6; the Latin text is as follows:

dixit a decemviris parum bene sibi cibaria curata esse. iussit vestimenta detrahi atque flagro caedi. decemviros Bruttiani verberavere, videre multi mortales. quis hanc contumeliam, quis hoc imperium, quis hanc servitutem ferre potest? nemo hoc rex ausus est facere: eane fieri bonis, bono genere gnatis, boni consultis? ubi societas? ubi fides maiorum? insignitas iniurias, plagas, verbera, vibices, eos dolores atque carnificinas per dedecus atque maximam contumeliam, inspectantibus popularibus suis atque multis mortalibus, te facere ausum esse? set quantum luctum, quantum gemitum, quid lacrimarum, quantum fletum factum audivi! servi iniurias nimis aegre ferunt: quid illos, bono genere gnatos, magna virtute praeditos, opinamini animi habuisse atque habituros, dum vivent?

This vivid passage illustrates also many details of style characteristic of Cato's speeches but not specifically mentioned by the ancient authors, instances of those figures which Cicero said were to be found in abundance. Fragment after fragment shows a recurring use, amounting almost to addiction, of alliteration and asyndeton (e.g. '. . . verberavere, videre multi mortales') and various forms of repetition (e.g. 'quis . . . quis . . . quis . . .'; 'bonis, bono . . . boni . . .'; 'ubi . . . ubi . . .'), quite often associated with anaphora (e.g. 'quis hanc contumeliam etc. . . .'; 'set quantum luctum etc.'). Also quite common are rhetorical questions and the creation of antitheses, both exemplified by the last sentence of the extract, and the use of assonance, as in the long series of words ending in *-um*. There seems also to be some substance in the suggestion that another stylistic characteristic is that the concluding members of longer sentences are often quite short, possibly because Cato felt that this gave a powerful and dramatic effect. Examples in this extract are '. . . te facere ausum esse?' and '. . . dum vivent'.[30]

---

[29] Caelius: *ORF*[3], frs. 111–20 and above p. 86; *De aed. vit.*: *ORF*[3], fr. 217.

[30] For a detailed stylistic analysis of the Rhodian speech (the exordium, fr. 163, is cited in

Among other characteristics one that is both frequent and simple is the coupling of words in pairs or tricola, such as 'superbiam atque ferociam' (*ORF*³, fr. 163), 'bonis atque strenuis' (*ORF*³, fr. 18), 'disieci atque consedavi' (*ORF*³, fr. 49), and the witty progression in 'asinum aut musimonem aut arietem' (*ORF*³, fr. 108). There are also several instances of the so-called *figura etymologica*, in which assonance is related to common derivation, as in 'aedes aedificatae' (*ORF*³, fr. 185) and 'fures privatorum furtorum' (*ORF*³, fr. 224). Lastly, several passages show Cato making effective use of imagery and metaphor: the effluent of the sewers is termed 'cloacale flumen' (*ORF*³, fr. 126); Antiochus 'wages war with letters, he campaigns with pen and ink' (*ORF*³, fr. 20: 'Antiochus epistulis bellum gerit, calamo et atramento militat'); and, best known of all because it seems to be a reminiscence of a line of Ennius, 'you would have seen the ocean blossom with sails' (*ORF*³, fr. 29: 'mare velis florere videres').[31]

Thus far the evidence of the fragments has been used to illustrate stylistic features which were fairly clearly intended to achieve rhetorical effects. Most of these features recur frequently, so much so that the majority of fragments, including many which are very short, exhibit one or more of them. However it is possible, indeed probable that the fragments convey an exaggerated impression of stylistic richness in the speeches. These extracts are by no means a random sample. Some, including several of the more substantial, are preserved because they were selected, for example by Gellius, actually as particularly felicitous illustrations of stylistic features; while the great majority owe their survival to some unusual feature of vocabulary or usage which caught the attention of a later writer. It seems reasonable to suppose, therefore, that a complete speech of equivalent length to the fragments would be found to contain all or almost all the characteristics which have been discussed but that the incidence would be less than in the fragments. Cicero, it is to be noted, says that all the virtues of oratory are to be found in the noteworthy and praiseworthy passages which may be singled out.[32] The implication is that there was a discernible unevenness and that many passages were plainer and less effective than the surviving extracts.

full below) see von Albrecht, *Meister röm. Prosa*, pp. 24 ff., dissenting in a number of respects from Leeman, *Orationis Ratio*, pp. 45 ff.; but both bring out many features of the kind here under discussion. Some of the stylistic features discussed in these and other studies have not been taken into consideration in this chapter because they seem insufficiently secure or too controversial to be a satisfactory basis for interpretation. In particular the present author has reservations about the importance attached by von Albrecht to 'ring-form'.

[31] Till–Meo, *La lingua di Catone*, pp. 40 ff., 52 ff., 194 ff.   [32] Cic. *Brut.* 65.

Even so, the fragments, despite their selective nature, do offer some illustration of features which later writers must have looked on as shortcomings. To start with, there is, by later standards, relatively little use of grammatical subordination, and that usually only of a fairly simple kind. Cato often obtained effects by conjunctions, asyndeton, and anaphora where later orators would have used more complex methods of subordination to achieve elaborate periods; of these there are few signs in the fragments. Instead there is an inclination to use a paratactic structure, in which two members of a sentence are placed side by side, so to speak on the same level, which is the antithesis of the Ciceronian period and a form generally taken to be characteristic of early Latin. Indeed in some cases successive sentences are little more than simple 'units', sometimes with scarcely any conjunctive device, while others are clumsy in structure and expression:

aquam Anienem in sacrarium inferre oportebat. Non minus XV milia Anien abest (*ORF*³, fr. 74).

nam periniurium siet, cum mihi ob eos mores, quos prius habui, honos detur, ubi datus est, tum uti eos mutem atque alii modi sim (*ORF*³, fr. 93).

homines defoderunt in terram dimidiatos ignemque circumposuerunt: ita interfecerunt (*ORF*³, fr. 193).

Sometimes this awkwardness in structure springs from the primary purpose of the text as a passage to be spoken aloud. There is a dependence on inflexions of the voice and slight pauses in delivery to make clear relationships which are not fully conveyed, as they would have been in a Ciceronian speech, by more complex grammatical structures. One instance of this occurred in a very late speech, 'That no one be made consul a second time', in 152: 'dicere possum, quibus villae atque aedes aedificatae atque expolitae maximo opere citro atque ebore atque pavimentis Poenicis sient' (*ORF*³, fr. 185).

This same characteristic, again associated with liberal use of the simple *atque*, is to be seen also in the opening sentence of the Rhodian speech of 167; indeed the whole exordium of that speech exhibits many of the characteristic features discussed above:

scio solere plerisque hominibus rebus secundis atque prolixis atque prosperis animum excellere atque superbiam atque ferociam augescere atque crescere. quo mihi nunc magnae curae est, quod haec res tam secunde processit, ne quid in consulendo advorsi eveniat, quod nostras secundas res confutet, neve haec laetitia nimis luxuriose eveniat. advorsae res edomant et docent, quid opus siet facto, secundae res laetitia transvorsum trudere solent a recte consulendo

atque intellegendo. quo maiore opere dico suadeoque, uti haec res aliquot dies
proferatur, dum ex tanto gaudio in potestatem nostram redeamus.

The fragments also show that Cato made no deliberate effort to produce
the rhythmic effects which came to play so large a part in later oratory.
That is scarcely surprising, since to Cicero, for example, these effects were
virtually inseparable from the techniques of subordination and period-
construction which, as was observed above, were relatively undeveloped
in Cato's speeches. It has been argued that the characteristic *clausulae*
which have been studied intensively in Cicero's speeches can be detected
already in the fragments of Cato's, but in reality there is a sharp difference.
Gellius, it will be recalled, commented that the Rhodian speech might
have been more rhythmical (*numerosius*), while Cicero clearly regarded
the lack of rhythm (*numeri*) as an obvious deficiency in Cato's prose, a
judgement which has been confirmed by careful analysis of the fragments.
A comparison between these and fragments of Cicero's lost speeches shows
not only that the incidence of various metrical patterns is quite different
but also that the incidence in Cato's fragments differs scarcely at all
from the frequency established for non-metrical prose in general. Certain
rhythmic effects are found which are unrelated to the later Ciceronian
patterns—indeed, which Cicero positively avoided—notably a tendency
for several long syllables to occur in succession, especially at the end of
sentences, and some instances where paratactical phrases or clauses have a
common rhythm; but it is by no means certain that either of these was
deliberately sought and both may rather be common features of early
Latin.[33]

Turning again to the positive qualities of Cato's speeches, it cannot
reasonably be doubted that many of the stylistic effects were the product
of conscious effort, that there was a deliberate selection of words, a
deliberate arrangement of phrases, sentences, and arguments with the
intention of making a particular rhetorical impact. That seems evident
from the fragments themselves and is particularly obvious in such a phrase
as *augescere atque crescere* (from the exordium of the Rhodian speech,
quoted above), which shows one particular form of a word rather than
another being chosen to achieve a special effect. Attention has often been
drawn to the sharp contrast between the oratorical fragments, sprinkled
with alliteration, asyndeton, anaphora, pleonasm, and other stylistic
figures, and the plodding, blunt, unadorned simple sentences of the

---

[33] Primmer, 'Der Prosarhythmus in Catos Reden', *Festschrift Karl Uretska*, pp. 174 ff.,
answering Fraenkel, *Leseproben aus Reden Ciceros und Catos*, esp. pp. 156 f. See also Kennedy,
The Art of Rhetoric, p. 50.

De agricultura, a contrast epitomized in the use of the words *atque* and *et*: *atque*, notoriously common in the fragments, occurs only six or seven times in the whole of the *De agricultura*, while *et*, the standard conjunction in the latter work, is rare in the fragments. Clearly, whatever later orators may have thought, Cato felt that *atque* contributed a special tone more appropriate to the requirements of orations and consciously preferred it.[34] Similarly a sense of achievement and special merit in the speeches is implied by the practice of keeping copies and by the inclusion of at least two speeches in the *Origines*, whether or not Cato himself put into circulation the texts of any others. Cato's own comment on the succinctness of his speech at Athens shows him aware of creating a particular effect, and if his famous definition of an orator as 'a good man skilled in speaking', 'vir bonus, dicendi peritus', both raises other issues and leaves ambiguous just what is meant by *peritus*, it at least implies a recognition of skill as something which may be acquired. Plainly his third and last surviving remark about oratory, 'Keep to the subject, the words will follow', 'rem tene, verba sequentur', does not mean that the choice of words does not matter; indeed, whatever its other implications, it points to some interest in how the most suitable words are to be found.[35]

There was then in some sense a conscious artistry in Cato's speeches, and in truth this has been generally recognized; but that artistry itself raises further questions. Did Cato extend his interest to the point of a systematic study of rhetorical techniques and rhetorical theory, and in particular did he study or draw upon Greek rhetorical theory? What did he conceive the function of this artistry to be? Had it acquired already in his hands a literary value worthy of pursuit in its own right?

The question of whether or not Cato was influenced by Greek rhetorical theory has been an important aspect of discussions of his attitude towards the Greeks and their culture. That broader topic must be reserved for the next chapter, here anticipated only by noting that it will be argued that Cato probably knew Greek from a fairly early stage in his career, that he became acquainted with a fairly wide range of Greek writings, and that this too was probably not confined to the last few years of his life. The present chapter is concerned specifically with those arguments which bear directly on the supposed influence of Greek rhetorical theory. Although this is an issue about which opinion has continued to be sharply

---

[34] Leo, *Gesch. der röm. Literatur* i. 286 with n. 3; Sblendorio, 'Note sullo stile dell'oratoria catoniana', *AFLC* 34 (1971), 8, who also notes the preference for the perfect in *-ere*, which is not used in the *De agricultura*.

[35] Jordan, p. 80, *Ad Marcum filium* frs. 14 and 15. Fr. 16, though in a sense connected with speeches, simply preserves the phrase 'vires causae'.

divided it will be found that the weight of evidence suggests strongly that Cato did not engage in a serious study of Greek rhetorical theory or seek to apply it in practice.[36]

The central evidence on this issue must be the fragments of the speeches themselves and the comments of the ancient writers on them, but it will be helpful to dispose first of a number of points of a different kind. Undoubtedly the most influential of these has been the belief that in his work known as *Ad filium* Cato included a book specifically devoted to rhetorical matters. This is taken to demonstrate an interest in rhetoric from a broad and general point of view, which in turn it is supposed must at least have stimulated an examination of Greek rhetorical manuals; and more probably the composition of such a book would have owed its inspiration to those same manuals. But, as is argued elsewhere, the very foundation of these inferences is highly questionable. The very nature of the *Ad filium* has almost certainly been misunderstood and it is highly improbable that it included a specialized book devoted to rhetoric —indeed it is far from certain even that the *Ad filium* consisted of more than one book. Probably it contained a miscellany of precepts, exhortations, and observations on a variety of topics, perhaps including some remarks about making speeches. The aphoristic form of two of the three fragments usually assigned to 'the book on rhetoric' (though only one is even attested as addressed to Marcus) would accord well with this, and none of them presupposes a discussion of rhetorical theory.[37]

Much less important is the suggestion sometimes put forward that the keeping and publishing of copies of speeches was an imitation of Greek practice and an indication of a broad interest in rhetorical literature. Quite apart from the complete uncertainty as to whether Cato did in any sense 'publish' his speeches, the inference is far from compelling. It is not difficult to envisage other reasons why such a man as Cato should have formed the habit of keeping copies or even have passed some into circulation; indeed the inclusion of the text of at least two of his own speeches in his historical work, the *Origines*, was at variance with Greek practice. Even supposing he was stimulated by the discovery that Greek orators often did keep and publish speeches, this would not necessarily imply an

---

[36] Greek influence is most firmly rejected by Leo, *Gesch. der röm. Literatur* i. 279 f. and 286, Frank, *Life and Literature*, pp. 140 ff., von Albrecht, *Meister röm. Prosa*, pp. 24 ff. It is accepted especially by Norden, *Die antike Kunstprosa* i³. 165 ff., Cima, *L'eloquenza latina*, pp. 93 f., Leeman, *Orationis Ratio*, pp. 45 ff., cf. 22 f., and with some qualification by Clarke, *Rhetoric at Rome*², pp. 40 ff., cf. 11, Marmorale, *Cato Maior*², pp. 153 and 201 ff., Kennedy, *The Art of Rhetoric*, pp. 49 ff. Till–Meo, *La lingua di Catone*, pp. 46 ff. thinks it slight.

[37] Appendix 8.

interest in Greek rhetoric as such. The whole chain of inference is theoretically possible, none of it is necessary; consequently it can do nothing to resolve the question at issue.

Similarly no help is to be got from the following passage of Plutarch:

It is said that he was late in learning Greek culture (παιδεία), and further that when at a very advanced age he took Greek books in his hands he profited in a few respects in oratory from Thucydides, but more from Demosthenes. However his compositions are moderately embellished with Greek sentiments and stories.[38]

It will be observed first that if this passage were to be accepted at face value it would confine all Cato's Greek reading to his last years and thus mean that it was irrelevant to the great bulk of his speeches. However Plutarch, or rather his source, is probably wrong about this. As for the comparison itself, the basis for it is probably that some reader of the speeches believed he could discern a few resemblances to Thucydides and more to Demosthenes and inferred that Cato was influenced by those writers. There is no telling whether or not the inference was correct, nor, even if it was, what was the nature and extent of that influence. It is certainly not safe to assume that there was a conscious imitation of style or technique, particularly when Plutarch goes on, apparently on the basis of his own reading, to refer to Greek sentiments and stories (δόγματα and ἱστορίαι) in Cato's compositions. Cato was no doubt quite prepared to make use of striking or useful ideas which he came across in any source, and in fact there are two fragments which, if not quite close enough to be certain borrowings, at least bear a suspicious resemblance to passages in Demosthenes' *Philippics*, one of them being the striking fragment from the speech at Athens in 191: 'Antiochus wages war with letters, he campaigns with pen and ink.'[39] But that is not at all the same thing as an interest in rhetorical theory.[40]

The most objective evidence on the question should be the remains of the speeches themselves; and it is clear that those who have concluded that Cato was at least in some degree influenced by Greek rhetorical

[38] Plut. *Cato Mai.* 2. 5 f.

[39] *ORF*³, fr. 20, compared with Dem. *Phil.* 1. 30; also *ORF*³, fr. 195, compared with Dem. *Phil.* 3. 17, or perhaps 3. 8. Gell. 16. 1 notes the similarity between a saying of Musonius and a passage in Cato's speech at Numantia (*ORF*³, fr. 17), but it remains uncertain whether both stem from a common Greek source (so Norden, *Die antike Kunstprosa* i³, p. 168; Janzer, p. 3). On all three passages see Till–Meo, *La lingua di Catone*, pp. 46 f.; Della Corte, *Catone censore*², pp. 216, 263, and 266 f.

[40] This applies also to the argument used by Kennedy, *The Art of Rhetoric*, pp. 51 f., that actual oratory composed by Greeks was known at Rome.

theory have been persuaded above all by the numerous instances of deliberate artistry. The wealth of figures and devices skilfully and carefully employed to produce particular effects, recognized by Cicero and amply exemplified in the fragments, has seemed to many more than could be expected from 'a natural orator', more than 'mere indignant conversation',[41] and therefore to betray at least some study of manuals and theory. Yet the argument is not as formidable as it may at first appear. The frequent occurrence of figures of speech of the kind which the rhetorical manuals categorized and recommended is not proof that those manuals had been studied and followed. Rhetorical theorists do not normally invent such figures: they analyse, categorize, and seek to exploit figures which occur and which are effective in ordinary speech and in the mouth of the un-trained orator. Nor is the untrained orator necessarily a mere indignant conversationalist. He may have acquired great facility through much experience, may consciously choose his words with skill and care and use elaborate phrases to produce desired effects, without ever analysing or categorizing the linguistic forms he is using. Cato, as probably the most effective speaker of his day in Rome, would naturally have used a whole range of rhetorical figures and devices whether or not he had ever sat down to a formal study of rhetorical theory.

Thus far the evidence of the fragments is inconclusive, but they begin to take on more significance when the argument is reversed and they are viewed from a negative point of view. A considerable number of them exhibit features which would not be expected from the pen of one who had studied rhetorical theory. One or two of these, regarded by the ancient writers as deficiencies, might perhaps be explained away as due to in-experience at so early a stage in the application of rhetorical theory to the Latin language—some of the rudimentary periodizing, and the unevenness implied by Cicero—but most could not be satisfactorily accounted for in this way. The theorists counselled avoidance, for example, of frequent alliteration, of frequent repetition of the same word, and of a continuous series of words with like case endings.[42] These are relatively simple matters, yet all are characteristic in the fragments, and especially alliteration, to which, as has been seen above, Cato seems almost to have been addicted. Significantly, alliteration, as perhaps also much of Cato's sentence structure, appears to be a marked characteristic of early Latin usage. Ample examples of these various features can be found in passages already quoted in this

---

[41] Clarke, *Rhetoric at Rome*[2], p. 41.

[42] e.g. *Ad Her.* 4. 17 f.; note also the advice in 4. 42 that neologisms should be used sparingly.

chapter, spread over nearly forty years of Cato's career; for instance: 'neque mihi aedificatio neque vasum neque vestimentum ullum est manupretiosum neque pretiosus servus neque ancilla. si quid est quod utar, utor; si non est, egeo' (*ORF*[3], fr. 174) and 'set quantum luctum, quantum gemitum, quid lacrimarum, quantum fletum factum audivi' (*ORF*[3], fr. 58).[43]

Similarly, some lack of the rhythmic effects of *clausulae* could be explained by inexperience, but an incidence no greater than in non-metrical Latin would be surprising, and recurring accumulations of long syllables almost unthinkable, from an orator who had even moderate interest in Greek rhetorical theory. The same is true of such a string of *atques*, successive couplings, and awkward relationships as occur in the first sentence of the Rhodian speech: 'scio solere plerisque hominibus rebus secundis atque prolixis atque prosperis animum excellere atque superbiam atque ferociam augescere atque crescere' (*ORF*[3], fr. 163).

Other details in the fragments of this speech illustrate the same conjunction of deliberate artistry and of usages which would have seemed inept to the rhetoricians; but it also merits some individual attention, especially in respect of some broader aspects in which it has sometimes been held to betray the influence of Greek oratory.[44] In its most direct aspects the confrontation between Gellius and Tiro does little to resolve the issue of Hellenic influence, for although Tiro was judging in terms of the rhetorical standards of his own day his criticisms, as has been mentioned already, were directed at alleged ineptitude and faulty logic. Consequently even if they were correct on all points they would not show whether or not this occurred within the context of an attempt to apply rhetorical theories. To show, for example, that a particular argument is a faulty *enthymema* does nothing to determine whether Cato would have thought of it or categorized it as an *enthymema*. At first sight Tiro's criticism of the opening fragment, the exordium, seems more revealing, since he alleged that it 'ignorantly and absurdly', *inerudite et ἀναγώγως*, failed to conform with the principles which should be followed by patrons representing their clients. However Gellius answered this with the plausible argument that the speech did not belong to this category, that Tiro was therefore applying the wrong principles, and that the exordium was appropriate to the category to which the speech did belong. In other words the exordium could be held to conform to accepted rhetorical principles; but there is nothing to determine whether it was written with principles

---

[43] This is strikingly similar to some of the examples of faulty style given in *Ad Her.* 4. 18.

[44] Leeman, *Orationis Ratio*, pp. 45 ff.; Kennedy, *The Art of Rhetoric*, pp. 45 ff.

in mind or simply with a practical sense of what would be appropriate to the occasion.

Little need be said about the suggestion that the speech reflected the concepts long inculcated by Greek rhetoricians as the central aim of deliberative oratory, namely expediency, *utilitas*, with its two divisions of 'the safe', *tutum*, and 'the honourable', *honestum*. Quite apart from the fact that little trace of *tutum* survives, the appropriateness of these concepts is so obvious that their presence cannot possibly be taken to indicate the influence of Greek teaching.[45] In another way, however, the manner of argument in the speech is significant, again from a negative point of view. It was seen earlier in this chapter that the comments of Gellius and the fragments themselves leave no doubt that it was not a lucid, rational exposition of a case carefully developed from the basic facts of the issue; rather it was a vivid miscellany of emotional pleas and rebuttals of the charges levelled at the Rhodians, skilfully interwoven but by no means the orderly presentation which the product of rhetorical theory should have been. If Gellius says that throughout the speech Cato used 'all the weapons and aids of the rhetorical disciplines' (a remark which, as was pointed out long ago, would be equally applicable to the poems of Homer),[46] he goes on to say that 'the matter is not handled with over much order and ornament and measure' and that it could have been said 'with more order and rhythm'. That points to the same conclusion as has already been drawn from the general body of fragments. While the speech abounded in the ingenious arguments and devices which might be expected from the talented and experienced 'natural' orator, it was not characterized, even so relatively late in Cato's career, by such careful detail and systematic orderliness as would betray the influence of the Greek rhetoricians.[47]

The remains of Cato's speeches strongly suggest then that he did not engage in serious study of Greek rhetorical theory or seek to apply it in practice. Rather, his rhetorical artistry seems to have been primarily a personal achievement, springing from his exceptional talents and his own strong sense of linguistic effects. The resulting devices and stylistic characteristics, grounded in native Latin idiom, included much that looked forward to the more developed oratory of a later age, but also much that was to be modified, sometimes drastically, in the light of the systematic study of rhetorical theory.

45 So rightly von Albrecht, *Meister röm. Prosa*, pp. 35 f., *contra* Leeman, loc. cit., followed by Kennedy, op. cit. p. 52.   46 Leo, *Gesch. der röm. Literatur* i. 286.
    47 Cic. *De orat.* 3. 135 has much wider reference but can probably be understood to include oratory: 'Quid enim M. Catoni praeter hanc politissimam doctrinam transmarinam atque adventiciam defuit?'

Cato's independence of the Greek theorists is suggested also by his dictum 'Keep to the subject, the words will follow', 'rem tene, verba sequentur'. It has been observed already that this cannot be taken to mean that the choice of words does not require care and attention, and to that extent it might be argued that in logic it is not absolutely incompatible with the application of rhetorical theory. It is more, however, than a simple statement of priorities; it clearly implies that keeping to the subject is the principal key to finding suitable words. Though caution is always needful with an aphorism, lest it be taken too literally or too much be built upon it, this most certainly suggests an attitude of mind which would have had little use for the rhetorical theories of the Greeks.

This same dictum, however, also invites a further question. Since Cato's oratory seems not to have been significantly influenced by Greek theory, to what extent does this represent a conscious rejection on his part? His knowledge of Greek literature and Greek culture in general is a matter for the next chapter, but the evidence there discussed makes it unlikely that he can have been unaware of the existence of rhetorical theory, that he did not know, at least from the time of his visit to Athens in 191, that the Greeks studied and taught the art and techniques of oratory. It was certainly well known in Rome by 161, for in that year rhetoricians, along with philosophers, were forbidden to reside in the city; and Cato's own awareness of it is indicated by his joke (undated) that the pupils of Isocrates 'grew old in attendance upon him as though they were going to practise their arts and plead cases before Minos in Hades'.[48]

This joke and the aphorism 'rem tene, verba sequentur' can both be seen as indications of the simplest and most obvious explanation as to why Cato chose not to exploit Greek theory. They can readily be seen as reflecting an attitude of great self-satisfaction with an essentially personal and practical achievement, an attitude which regarded eloquence as the product of natural talent combined with accumulated practical experience, and which consequently scorned as remote from the realities of day-to-day oratory the minute analysis, the orderly categorizing, the proliferating technical terms that went with Greek theory and instruction.

Cato was far from being a modest man, and it is more than likely that such an attitude is indeed a major part of the explanation; yet there is reason to believe that there was something further. Rhetoric was a branch of Greek education which was relatively slow to win widespread acceptance at Rome. As late as 92, seventy years after the expulsion of rhetoricians in 161 and more than half a century after Cato's death, the

[48] Expulsion: Suet. *Rhet.* 1; Isocrates: Plut. *Cato Mai.* 23. 2.

censors of the day still thundered against the establishment of Latin
rhetorical schools.[49] Scorn and disdain are not sufficient to explain why
a majority of senators voted in 161 for the exclusion of rhetoricians
(and philosophers) from the city. Almost certainly this was linked with
the unfavourable impression formed by many Romans of at least some
aspects of the Greeks of their own day. As such it is associated with wider
issues which belong in the next chapter, but essentially it was probably
a belief that the Greeks lacked integrity and that the rhetoricians were
seeking to teach a man how to win his case even if it was a poor one.
It was an attitude—or prejudice—which long afterwards enabled even
Cicero to write of Carneades that 'he was a Greek and accustomed to
propound any view that suited his purpose.'[50] As for Cato, there is no
evidence to show whether he played any part in the exclusion of rhetoricians
in 161, but there is reason to suppose that he shared the attitude just
described. He can hardly have failed to view the role of oratory and the
purposes to which it was put within the context of that concern for
integrity which is a recurring feature of his career. That surely is the
essence of his definition of an orator as 'a good man skilled in speaking',
'vir bonus, dicendi peritus'. If such an aphorism stood alone it would be
an insecure base for weighty moral interpretations: after all, Cato applied
the same formula to the farmer—'a good man, skilled in cultivating, whose
tools gleam', 'vir bonus colendi peritus, cuius ferramenta splendent'—
and there is nothing to show which definition was the prior. But it does
not stand alone. He also said that 'the words of the Greeks came from
their lips rather than their hearts', and in 155, seeking to procure the
early dismissal of the Athenian 'embassy of philosophers', he sarcastically
censured the magistrates for keeping in suspense 'men who were so
persuasive that they could obtain anything they wished'. Few remarks
could more neatly encapsulate a compound of disdain and positive
disapproval.[51]

Such an attitude to Greek rhetorical theory and instruction is but one
aspect of the fundamentally practical, purposive character of Cato's
oratory. Throughout the Republic, and in some respects long beyond that,

[49] Suet. *Rhet.* 1; cf. Clarke, *Rhetoric at Rome*[2], pp. 11 ff., Kennedy, *The Art of Rhetoric*,
pp. 90 ff. It is not easy to believe that the censorial edict was motivated either by the political
fear that Latin schools would teach potential demagogues to speak well or, despite Cic. *De
orat.* 3. 93 ff., by concern that without Greek teachers the quality of instruction would be
low.

[50] Cic. *Rep.* 3. 8; cf. also 3. 9: 'qui saepe optimas causas ingenii calumnia ludificari solet'.
See also Guite, 'Cicero's Attitude to the Greeks', *G&R* 9 (1962), 142 ff.

[51] Farmer: Jordan, p. 78, *Ad Marcum filium* fr. 6. Other dicta: Plut. *Cato Mai.* 12. 7; 22. 6.
For fuller discussion of the episode of 155 see below, pp. 174 ff.

Roman oratory remained an exceedingly practical matter, a vital tool with which the pleader, the politician, the statesman sought to persuade audiences whose consent was necessary to his attainment of important objectives. Yet by the end of the Republic it had acquired that second role which was to be so prominent throughout the centuries of the Empire, its role as a form of literature, as an art. Side by side with its practical effects the experts savoured and judged its stylistic excellences and verbal refinements as worthy of admiration in their own right. Everything suggests that such an attitude was foreign to Cato. His definitions and priorities, his neglect of the Greek theorists, the nature and contexts of the stylistic devices he employed, the seeming unevenness of their incidence (scarcely due to an inability to sustain them), all point to the same conclusion: the conscious artistry of Cato's speeches was developed and applied not for its own sake or to achieve an artisitic quality, but with the practical purpose of producing a particular reaction in his audience and influencing opinion in the direction he wished. His practice of preserving his speeches and their subsequent survival are unquestionably important in the fact and manner of the development of oratory into a major branch of Roman culture and literature; but almost certainly Cato kept and viewed his copies as practical speeches, not as literature. The care and skill he exercised in their composition were devoted to the practical effect of particular passages, not to skill in the use and refinement of language as an achievement in itself.

Consideration of Cato's attitude to his own speeches draws attention again to the question of publication. It has been seen that there is no means of determining whether Cato himself distributed copies, either among a few friends or to a wider public: such a notion as that he put them into circulation as political pamphlets,[52] though it may be suspected of being anachronistic, is incapable of proof or disproof. Yet there is the firm fact that he 'published' (or included for publication) at least two of his own speeches in the *Origines*. This is obviously significant for the understanding of his attitude both to the *Origines* and to the speeches. For the Rhodian speech there seems no need to seek an explanation beyond Cato's readiness to highlight his own importance: inclusion of the speech was an effective means of doing this.[53] Possibly something of the same may be true of the speech against Galba, but in this case there is the important

---

[52] Leo, *Gesch. der röm. Literatur* i. 283; Frank, *Life and Literature*, p. 142.

[53] Cato may well have been given the idea of using a speech for dramatic effect by his reading of Greek authors, but that does not necessarily mean that in the *Origines* he was following Greek models in any deeper sense. See further p. 235.

difference that, however good the speech, it unquestionably failed in its purpose; furthermore Cato added angry comments on the methods used by Galba. It would be rash to assume that the inclusion of this speech and of the comments was the outcome of careful consideration, or that it necessarily conformed to a pattern already established in the *Origines*. More probably Cato, an old man bitterly angry and smarting with humiliation, on the spur of the moment added an account of what he regarded as a shocking affair to the current book which had already reached contemporary or very recent events. In any case, the effect is that in this one instance, at the very close of Cato's life, he is found taking steps to 'publish' a speech in a manner clearly related to a contemporary public issue. Even so, this still falls some way short of deliberately using the speech as a political pamphlet, as a positive attempt to influence an immediate public issue. Separate distribution of the speech would be a different matter, but on that there is no evidence. On the whole inclusion in the *Origines* might itself suggest that Cato did not distribute the text separately; indeed, if the circumstances of its inclusion were such as are suggested above, it could be taken to imply that Cato did not naturally think in terms of issuing his speech as a polemical pamphlet, that he was not accustomed to using his speeches in that way. That however is a subjective argument, far from logically unassailable. So far as the evidence goes, most questions about publication must remain unanswered.

Cato as an orator may be seen in two perspectives. The lack of earlier and contemporary material for comparison renders impossible an accurate assessment of his immediate impact on oratory as actually practised. Yet there can be no reasonable doubt that he achieved and for a very long period maintained a quite outstanding position, or that his excellence was the product of deliberate care and effort. It is highly probable, if unprovable, that the example he presented and the rivalry he aroused did much to stimulate others to try to match his influence. As for the development of Roman oratory in the longer term, the conclusions reached in this chapter confirm that Cato did not begin the application of Greek theory to Roman rhetoric, that he did not deliberately develop the written speech as a form of literature. His contribution in these fields was not intentional, but it was none the less real and significant. Almost certainly he did not write his speeches with the intention that they should be read with an eye to their artistic merits, but in due course that did happen. The level of artistry which he achieved and the practice of preserving speeches paved the way both for the synthesis with Greek theory and for the emergence of the literary role of Roman oratory.

8

Cato and the Greeks

CATO's attitude towards the Greeks and their culture is a topic critical to the understanding of his historical role. It could not be otherwise with a man who was virtually the founder of Latin prose literature and who attained great prominence in public life in an age of increasing Roman familiarity with the Greek world and of rapidly heightening awareness of its culture. The principal focus of discussion has been Cato's supposed anti-hellenism. A desire and a determination to protect Rome from the evils of Hellenic influence has frequently been taken to be a root policy, indeed the root policy, underlying many of his actions: his political conflicts with the eminent and powerful, especially the Scipios; the rigour and zeal of his censorship and the restrictions he imposed; several of his interventions in foreign affairs, as in 167 when he opposed war with Rhodes and supported a settlement for Macedonia which did not require Roman occupation; and even his extensive activity as a writer, conjectured to be an attempt to provide Roman alternatives to various Greek writings. Sometimes his attitude has been represented as an almost fanatical rejection of everything Greek—yet rarely without at least a slight qualification. For in Cato himself can be seen indications of Greek influence, its extent and nature debatable but its presence scarcely to be denied. Even when he is represented as a particularly thorough 'Greek-hater' his effort to produce Latin prose writings has itself been seen as the acceptance of concepts which were basically Greek, drawing upon Greek literary forms and even some detailed material from Greek sources. At times the paradox has been seen as sharper still: anxious to 'know his enemy', he was led to study Greek literature more intensely than many of the undiscriminating phil-hellenes about him; through the very means by which he sought to counter Hellenic influences he was unwittingly creating the basis for a true synthesis of Greek and Roman cultural values. Sometimes the qualification avoids paradox by positing change: the literary activity, the indications of some knowledge of Greek literature, have been taken as support for a belief that in his later years he moderated somewhat the stringency of his attitude.

On the other hand the facts which make such qualifications necessary also form the basis of interpretations with quite a different emphasis. The evidence for Greek influence on Cato is held to be considerable, to reveal a positive interest in various aspects of Greek culture and a ready acceptance of much that it had to offer. The uncritical antihellenism is dismissed, its place taken by a moderate and balanced attitude of careful discrimination. Such discrimination certainly implied rejection of some aspects of Greek life which Cato plausibly, though not necessarily correctly, judged potentially detrimental to Rome (moral laxity and adverse effects of the study of philosophy are usually seen as the principal areas of concern). At the same time there was much of value to be learned from the Greeks, much which it would be beneficial to welcome and adopt. Though Cato scorned uncritical and adulatory philhellenes, he himself, it is argued, was by no means their antithesis.[1]

These differences of interpretation are in considerable measure relative, contrasts in emphasis rather than absolute contradictions: virtually no account has sought to portray either the 'Greek-hater' or the philhellene without some qualification. Fundamentally this stems from apparent contradictions and paradoxes in the evidence itself. However, the diversity of views springs also from differing evaluations of the evidence, and even of what constitutes acceptable evidence. Plainly it would be misleading, in the absence of clear connecting evidence, to argue back to Cato's attitude on this subject from hypotheses about his censorship or his interventions in foreign affairs. Care is needed to avoid circularity also in arguments relating to Cato's writings, discussion of which is reserved in the main for the next chapter though some particulars must be anticipated in this. For in many respects the writings need to be considered in the light of Cato's general attitude towards the Greeks and their culture, yet they themselves constitute part of the evidence for that attitude. A further question is how

---

[1] Select bibliography: Mommsen, *History of Rome* ii. 327 ff., 381 ff., 446 ff.; Besançon, *Les Adversaires de l'hellénisme*; Leo, *Gesch. der röm. Literatur* i. 268 ff.; Rossi, 'De Catone graecarum litterarum oppugnatore', *Athenaeum*, 10 (1922), 259 ff.; Klingner, 'Cato Censorius und die Krisis des römischen Volkes', *Röm. Geisteswelt*[5], pp. 34 ff.; De Sanctis, *Storia* iv. 1[2], pp. 564 ff.; iv. 2. i, pp. 57 ff.; Smith, 'Cato Censorius', *G&R* 9 (1940), 150 ff.; Marmorale, *Cato Maior*[2], pp. 147 ff.; Della Corte, *Catone censore*[2], pp. 89 ff., 112 ff.; Scullard, *Roman Politics*[2], pp. 113, 133, 223 f.; Alfonsi, 'Catone il Censore e l'umanesimo romano', *PP* 9 (1954), 161 ff.; Kienast, pp. 101 ff.; Haffter, 'Cato der Ältere', *Röm. Politik*, pp. 158 ff.; Boscherini, *Lingua e scienza*, pp. 9 ff.; and other works cited p. 131 n. 1. Broadly speaking, and bearing in mind that all make some qualification, Mommsen, Besançon, Rossi, and Klingner may be taken as significant representatives of the antihellenist interpretation, Kienast and Haffter of the view that Cato's attitude was moderate and balanced, Della Corte of the view that his attitude changed.

much reliance is to be placed on Cicero's dialogue *De senectute*, the dramatic date of which is 150 and in which Cato, in converse with Scipio Aemilianus and Laelius, is cast as the principal speaker. The position taken in this chapter is that the dialogue cannot safely be used as evidence on this particular issue. It is certainly possible that in putting into Cato's mouth Greek allusions, and especially enthusiastic references to Xenophon, Cicero may have been developing a genuine feature of Cato rather than grossly distorting. But since Cicero said expressly that he made Cato argue more eruditely than he did in his own works and asked Atticus to imagine this to be the consequence of extensive reading of Greek literature,[2] it is simply not possible to determine the extent to which Cicero's portrait is overdrawn—or at least no reasonable estimate can be made until Cato's actual acquaintance with Greek literature has been assessed on the basis of other evidence. Hence it is quite impolitic to rely, as has sometimes been done, on such a feature as Cicero's portrayal of Cato's fondness for Xenophon.

The purpose of this chapter is to examine Cato's attitudes, but first must be considered the extent of his knowledge; and in that respect the first issue is how early in his career Cato acquired a command of the Greek language. From time to time discussion of this has been unnecessarily complicated through a misunderstanding of passages which associate the study of 'Greek letters', *litterae Graecae*, with his old age. There are a number of these, some of them containing expressions such as *perstudiosus*, 'very zealous', several the verb *disco*: he *learnt* Greek letters in his old age. Nevertheless they do not mean that Cato learned to read and write Greek in his old age; they refer to the study of Greek literature. That is sufficiently demonstrated by the passage in which Valerius Maximus wrote also of 'Latin letters': 'He desired to be educated in Greek letters; how late on we may judge from the fact that he was almost an old man when he learnt (*didicit*) even Latin letters (*litteras Latinas*).'[3] Thus while the passages obviously presuppose a facility in the Greek language, they reveal nothing about when that facility was acquired. Whether it is correct that Cato acquired an extensive knowledge of Greek literature in his old age, and first in his old age, is another matter, and one which will be taken up again later.

That Cato did at some stage acquire a command of Greek is not in question. No source casts doubt on this, and it is attested or clearly

[2] Cic. *De sen.* 3.

[3] Val. Max. 8. 7. 1; Cic. *Rep.* 5. 2 (Ziegler); *Acad.* 2. 5; *De sen.* 3; ibid. 26; Nepos, *Cato* 3. 2; Quintil. *Inst.* 12. 11. 23; cf. Plut. *Cato Mai.* 2. 5. Boscherini, *Lingua e scienza*, pp. 9 f.

presupposed in quite a number of passages, including a fragment of advice given by Cato himself to his son.[4] That advice was probably written in the 170s, but there is good evidence for a knowledge of Greek much earlier than that. On his visit to Athens in 191, it will be recalled, Cato addressed the assembly in Latin, employing an interpreter. Plutarch reports this, but adds the explicit comment that if he had wished he could have addressed the Athenians in Greek.[5] There can be no certainty that Plutarch had reliable authority for this statement, but there is no reason to question it and a strong possibility that he had excellent authority. His principal purpose in the passage was to refute the authenticity of a speech in Greek, circulating in his own day, which was alleged to have been delivered by Cato on this occasion. It is virtually certain that his firm assertion that the speech was in Latin was derived from a statement by Cato himself, almost certainly from the passage in which he commented on the speed and pungency of his own speech (which dictum Plutarch reports a few lines later); and there is therefore at least a strong possibility that the assertion that Cato could have spoken in Greek is also Cato's own. A knowledge of Greek in 191 is suggested also by the marked resemblance between the one surviving fragment of Cato's speech and a passage of Demosthenes, though this is not quite close enough for direct borrowing to be a moral certainty.[6]

Other evidence gives little help, if only because there is so little that is relevant from the earlier periods of Cato's life. One late and brief source states that Cato was instructed in 'Greek letters' by Ennius, whom Cato himself brought to Rome in 203; but few would care to treat this as reliable evidence.[7] Probably it is a conjecture, a reasonable conjecture but no more. Similarly it is a reasonable conjecture, and one often put forward, that if Cato had known no Greek previously he would have acquired some in the course of military service in Sicily during the Hannibalic war. It is plausible then to suppose that Cato had a knowledge of Greek fairly early in his career, and virtually certain that he had it before 191.

The next issue is when and to what extent Cato used his knowledge of the Greek language to acquaint himself with Greek writings—though not whether he did so, for the fact of some acquaintance is beyond question. A convenient starting-point is once again that group of passages which

---

[4] Jordan, p. 77, *Ad Marcum filium* fr. 1 = Pliny, *Nat. hist.* 29. 14, quoted below, p. 170.
[5] Plut. *Cato Mai.* 12. 5.   [6] p. 149.
[7] 'Victor', *De vir. ill.* 47. 1. The learned conversation with the Tarentine Nearchus in 209 is virtually certainly an invention by Cicero, whether or not Cato was present at the capture of Tarentum: Cic. *De sen.* 41; Plut. *Cato Mai.* 2. 3 f.; above, p. 7. For the doubtful possibility that a Greek source was cited in 195 see p. 149 n. 39.

assert that he studied 'Greek letters' intensively in his later years. It is difficult to assess the reliability of this statement. It is found first in two, perhaps three, of Cicero's dialogues and it is entirely possible that all the other versions stem from Cicero rather than from a source or tradition on which all drew; and either way there is no means of knowing whether the statement rested upon an authentic tradition—and if so, how and why it was preserved—or on an inference, possibly by Cicero himself, founded perhaps on Greek allusions in Cato's writings.[8] The latter is such an obvious possibility that the story must be treated with considerable caution. It can be taken as evidence that Greek allusions were indeed detectable in Cato's works, but that is all. Nor does Cicero himself give any reliable indication of how much knowledge of Greek literature was to be discerned in the writings of Cato. The statement in the *De senectute* that he had made Cato discourse more learnedly than he did in his own writings, which is coupled with the suggestion that Atticus could imagine this to be the consequence of the late study of Greek literature, *litterae*, might be thought to suggest that in reality there were only a few traces to be found; but on the other hand this might be only by comparison with the practices of Cicero's own day. Much the same may be said of the statement in *De oratore* 3. 135 that of all the qualities desirable in the orator in public life Cato lacked only 'this highly refined overseas and foreign learning', *hanc politissimam doctrinam transmarinam atque adventiciam*. It need refer to no more than a less deep and sophisticated knowledge than would often be found in the Ciceronian age. There is a similar imprecision about Plutarch's assessment, already noticed in Chapter 7:[9]

It is said that he was late in learning Greek culture, and further that when at a very advanced age he took Greek books in his hands he profited in a few respects in oratory from Thucydides, but more from Demosthenes. However his compositions are moderately embellished with Greek sentiments and stories.

The uncertainty surrounding the 'Greek literature in old age' tradition has been noted already, and in Chapter 7 it was observed that there is uncertainty of much the same kind about the supposed influence of Thucydides and Demosthenes. Plutarch does seem to have been commenting from his own reading when he went on to refer to moderate embellishment with Greek sentiments and stories (δόγματα and ἱστορίαι), and in so far as the recognition of these would have been more a matter of empirical

---

[8] Refs. p. 159 n. 3. It is clear that the story was not invented by Cicero for the dramatic purposes of the *De senectute* since he had previously mentioned it in *Acad.* 2. 5, and probably earlier still in *Rep.* 5. 2 (Ziegler).

[9] Plut. *Cato Mai.* 2. 5 f.; above, p. 149.

observation than of subjective inference this is firm evidence; but just
what is meant by 'moderate embellishment' is by no means clear.

There is however more direct evidence, namely the remains of Cato's
own sayings and writings. Here Greek quotations and allusions certainly
show a knowledge of Greek writings, and a knowledge which was something more than an ability to reproduce the odd item plucked from a
Greek author. Rather they point to a considerable familiarity with quite a
wide range of writings. Polybius is the secure authority that in 149 Cato
used a quotation from the *Odyssey* in order to contrast the military
exploits of Scipio Aemilianus with the ineffectiveness of other Roman
officers.[10] A year earlier easy familiarity with the *Odyssey* was evident in
a joke alluding to it. This too is reported by Polybius; and here his testimony is even more secure, for the joke was directed at him in person
when Cato said that he 'like Odysseus wished to go again into the cave of
the Cyclops because he had forgotten his cap and belt'.[11] A fragment from
the introduction to the *Origines* is so similar to the opening sentence of
Xenophon's *Symposium* that it must be a direct reminiscence: in this case
coincidental resemblance is scarcely credible.[12] Two fragments of speeches,
one the Athenian speech of 191, the other about forty years later, bear
a marked resemblance to passages in Demosthenes' *Philippics*, though they
are not quite close enough to be certain borrowings.[13] If direct Greek
influences are less evident in the *De agricultura* there are two passages
which were almost certainly taken from Greek sources. One, in chapter
127, is a medicinal recipe which stands out by reason of the use of Greek
weights and measures and other terms; the other, chapter 157, is a striking
and famous passage enthusing over the virtues and applications of cabbage,
which may well have been derived ultimately from the monograph
devoted to that vegetable by Chrysippus of Cnidus.[14] Granted that Cato is

---

[10] Polyb. 36. 8. 7, from *Suda*, s.v. ἀΐσσουσιν, quoting *Od.* 10. 495; also Livy, *Epit.* 49;
Diod. 32. 9a; Plut. *Cato Mai.* 27. 6; *Praec. reip. ger.* 10; 'Plut.' *Apophth. Scip. Min.* 3; *Suda*,
s.v. Κάτων.

[11] Polyb. 35. 6. 3 f. = Plut. *Cato Mai.* 9. 3. The occasion was when Polybius wished to
put a further request to the Senate after it had agreed to the release of the Achaean exiles
(p. 124). Cato's famous remark that 'we sit here the whole day debating whether some old
Greeks should be buried by Italian or Achaean undertakers' has sometimes been interpreted
as anti-Greek in sentiment, but clearly it need have no such implication.

[12] *HRR* i², fr. 2; cf. Xen. *Symp.* 1. 1. Attempts to identify other traces of Xenophon's
influence, especially from his *Hipparchicus* and *Peri hippices*, appear forced and are at best
inconclusive: Leo, *Gesch. der röm. Literatur* i. 275 f.; Münscher, 'Xenophon in der griech.-
röm. Literatur', *Philologus Suppb.* 13. ii. 70 ff.; Della Corte, *Catone censore*², pp. 92 f. See
Boscherini, *Lingua e scienza*, pp. 24 f.

[13] p. 149.

[14] Pliny, *Nat. hist.* 20. 78; *RE*, s.v. *Chrysippos*, no. 15, cols. 2509 f. The nature and origin

unlikely to have consulted Chrysippus or a similar author directly, it is nevertheless difficult to envisage that there was any intermediary source available to him which was not in Greek.

In addition to these passages which exhibit direct connections with particular Greek writings several of Cato's remarks imply, if not necessarily profound knowledge, at least sufficient familiarity with Greek literature or Greek affairs to enable him to refer to them easily and naturally. According to Plutarch he 'made fun of the school of Isocrates, declaring that his pupils grew old in attendance upon him as though they were going to practise their arts and plead cases before Minos in Hades'. Plutarch also records two comments upon Socrates, the first of which strongly suggests familiarity with the writings of Xenophon: 'There was nothing to admire about Socrates of old except that he was always moderate and gentle towards a difficult wife and stupid sons', and 'Socrates was a babbler and a man of violence who attempted in whatever way he could to tyrannize over his country, by destroying its customs and enticing and diverting the citizens into opinions which conflicted with the laws.' In yet another dictum reported by Plutarch Cato mentioned Epaminondas, Pericles, and Themistocles.[15] In a passage surviving from his *Origines* he referred explicitly to the stand of Leonidas and the Lacedaemonians at Thermopylae, contrasting the multitude of honours to the

of ch. 157 (and also its relationship to ch. 156, which is also concerned with cabbage and has a medical prescription in common) has been discussed extensively: see esp. Reuther, *De Catonis de agricultura libri vestigiis apud Graecos*, pp. 22 ff.; Wellmann, 'Die Georgika des Demokritos', *Abh. Preuss. Akad.* 1921, no. 4, pp. 34 ff.; Hörle, *Catos Hausbücher*, pp. 10 ff.; Mazzarino, *Introduzione*, pp. 33 ff.; Thielscher, *Belehrung*, pp. 374 ff.; Boscherini, *Lingua e scienza*, pp. 29 ff. and 62 ff.; Helm, *RE*, s.v. *Porcius*, no. 9, cols. 155 f. Most of these writers claim to identify other instances of Greek influence, and it is possible that there are some (e.g. the use of *capita* like the Greek κεφαλαί to mean roots in 33. 1, 36, and 43. 2; perhaps also 102 and 125: see Boscherini, op. cit., pp. 28 f., 37 ff., 51 ff.) but the evidence is not decisive and in many cases is unconvincing. Correspondences with the very late *Geoponica* are not a sound indication of a common origin in Greek and many of the Greek loan words which are found for the first time in Cato (Till–Meo, *La lingua di Catone*, pp. 49 ff.; Boscherini, op. cit., pp. 98 ff.) are likely to have been long current (their absence from Plautus is not remarkable, given the special character of Cato's work); cf. Kronasser, 'Nugae Catonianae', *WS* 79 (1966), 299. In fact chapters 127 and 157 stand out as decidedly different. If Cato did use Greek sources fairly extensively it would have to be said that he performed a remarkable task in translating into Latin a high proportion of terms and usages; and the question would then arise as to why he did not do so e.g. in ch. 127. The presence of a few striking instances tells against extensive use of Greek sources. For the question of Cato's acquaintance with Greek patterns of 'scientific thought' see p. 165.

The attempt of Capitani, 'Catone, De agricultura, cap. 160', *Maia*, 20 (1968), 31 ff., to demonstrate that in addition to the magical formulae ch. 160 displays medical terminology and empirico-scientific methods is not convincing.

[15] Plut. *Cato Mai.* 8. 14; 20. 3; 23. 1 ff. Note also the metaphor of the Hydra in 16. 7.

memory of Leonidas with the almost total neglect of a Roman military tribune who had performed a somewhat similar exploit.[16] A remark concerning the constitutional development of Rome, probably also drawn from the *Origines*, shows an awareness of Greek traditions about νομοθέται, lawgivers such as Lycurgus, Solon, and Cleisthenes.[17] An acid comment about a certain Postumius Albinus, reported with evident pleasure by Polybius, not only mentioned the Amphictyonic Council but employed in a simile some detailed features of Greek athletic contests. Postumius, an extreme philhellene, had gone so far as to write a history in Greek in the preface of which he asked his readers to excuse him if as a Roman he had not fully mastered Greek language and method.

In my opinion [said Polybius] Marcus Porcius answered him very properly. For he said he wondered what reason he had for making this apology. If the Amphictyonic council had ordered him to write a history, perhaps it would have been necessary to write thus and make excuses; but to write of his own accord and under no compulsion and then to ask to be pardoned if he should commit barbarisms, was evidence of utter absurdity, and was just as useless as if a man who had entered his name at the games for the boxing or the pancration, having entered the stadium, when the time came to fight should beg the spectators to excuse him if he should be unable to endure the exertion or the blows.[18]

Finally there is Cato's remark to his son, in a passage to be discussed more fully later, that he will demonstrate 'what benefit there is in looking into their [the Greeks'] literature, but not in studying it thoroughly'. If he was prepared to show the profit to be derived from looking into Greek writings, it seems a necessary inference that he had taken a fairly extensive look himself.[19]

Taken collectively this evidence shows Cato to have been sufficiently familiar with a wide range of Greek writings to quote from or allude to them easily and with moderate frequency. Some interpretations have

[16] *HRR* i², fr. 83.

[17] Cic. *Rep.* 2. 2 and 37. The point is valid even if the actual Greek examples were added by Cicero.

[18] Polyb. 39. 1. 1 ff.; thence in Plut. *Cato Mai.* 12. 6; 'Plut.' *Apophth. Cat. Mai.* 29; a paraphrase in Gell. 11. 8. 1 ff. from the lost biography by Nepos. Since Polybius had personal reasons to dislike Postumius there is the possibility of distortion, particularly in the sections which follow this extract, 9 ff., but that cannot affect the basic picture of zealous philhellenism or Cato's dictum. Münzer, RE, s.v. *Postumius*, no. 31, cols. 902 ff.

[19] The case for Cato's acquaintance with Greek writings has been deliberately limited to specific items, excluding arguments of a more general and often more controversial nature, e.g. relating to the fact or forms of written works, the title *Origines*, and a supposed awareness of Greek constitutional theory.

gone further than this, maintaining that at least in certain fields Cato was sufficiently steeped in Greek thought to be very much under its influence. Thus it has been argued that the *De agricultura* shows his thorough familiarity with Greek technical writings not only because it contains material drawn from such writings but in the manner in which various sections are arranged, the result, it is supposed, of being accustomed to Greek habits of scientific thought.[20] That is not a convincing assessment, however, either over-all or in the many particulars on the cumulative effect of which it must largely rest. Where plants or other items are grouped or differentiated (three kinds of myrtle, for example) this is more plausibly to be thought of as the result of practical observation by farmers than Greek classification.[21] Indeed it may fairly be said that one of the leading characteristics of the *De agricultura* is its remarkable concentration on immediate practicality and its particularism. So marked is this particularism that much advice is given with detail appropriate to a particular locality, with virtually no attempt to distinguish the local detail from what is more generally applicable, or to allow for a wider variety of circumstances. Such a restricted outlook is almost the antithesis of Greek schematic and theoretical thinking. It may be that in addition to the two passages already mentioned the *De agricultura* contains a few other items derived from Greek sources; but that is a very different level of Greek influence, and even it is certainly not extensive.[22]

Cato's other writings have also sometimes been seen as powerfully influenced by Greek thought, not least in his choice of topics and literary forms. It can scarcely be doubted that there was some relationship with Greek writings, at least to the extent of reproducing individual points and items of information, or of being stimulated, consciously or unconsciously, by a particular idea. There is however a considerable difference between that and being powerfully influenced in the whole structure and composition of the works. So far as the evidence makes it possible to distinguish (and in several instances it is very slender), the latter seems not to have been the case, at least in so far as Cato does not seem to have been adhering closely to Greek models. It is argued elsewhere that the *Ad filium* has been much

[20] Boscherini, *Lingua e scienza*, esp. ch. II.

[21] Cato, *De agr.* 8. 2. Similarly with several, if not most, of the other chapters (about ten in all) upon the cumulative effect of which Boscherini's case principally depends: e.g. 17, 46, 72, 125, 126. It has to be remembered that underlying all surviving material, including even various details in a 'scientific' writer like Theophrastus, is a vast continuing pool of peasant experience and methods, including herbal remedies. As Boscherini, p. 31, himself recognizes, classificatory method is nowhere else so obvious as in ch. 157, which is altogether exceptional in this and other respects. [22] p. 162 n. 14.

misunderstood and is unlikely to have been the Greek-style encyclopaedia which is often envisaged, while the idiosyncrasies of the *Origines* suggest that there was no slavish adherence to Greek concepts and methods.[23]

Oratory is a third area in which Greek thought has often been supposed to have exercised a considerable influence. It has been argued that in the fragments of Cato's speeches there are clear traces of the influence of Greek manuals of rhetoric and even that the Preface to the *De agricultura* is constructed in accordance with the principles laid down in such manuals, and is intended to be read as an address in the 'deliberative category', the *genus deliberativum*, in fact as a miniature *suasio*; but both these arguments are wrong. Careful study of the Preface, though not necessarily correct in every detail, has established that its carefully worked language and construction is firmly in a native Latin mould; and it has been seen in the previous chapter that Cato's oratory was not significantly influenced by Greek rhetorical theory.[24] Though he can hardly have been unaware of the manuals it is most unlikely that he familiarized himself with them; and the same must be true of philosophical writings, about which he knew enough to term them 'mere winding-sheets' (or 'dirges': *mera mortualia*).[25]

There were then limitations to Cato's knowledge of Greek writings and their influence upon him. Nevertheless it is clear, principally from his own words, that he did achieve a considerable familiarity with Greek literature. But when was this familiarity acquired? Was it a long process, spread over much of Cato's career and already well under way at least in his middle years, the period of his consulship and censorship? Or are those sources to be followed which suggest a new and intensive study later in life, in the years after the censorship? The trouble with statements of this latter kind is that they themselves may be no more than conjectures, the product of an ancient attempt to reconcile the apparent conflict between this familiarity with Greek literature and indications of hostility on Cato's part. As for the direct evidence of Cato's own statements, the majority of those which indicate familiarity are either undated or belong to the post-censorship years; but the survival of items which can be assigned to the later years is partly because of the presence of Polybius at that time, partly because the *Ad filium* and the *Origines* (and probably most or all of the

---

[23] See Ch. 10, *passim*, and for the *Ad filium*, Appendix 8.

[24] pp. 147 ff. On the Preface see Leeman, *Orationis Ratio*, pp. 21 ff.; Kappelmacher, 'Zum Stil Catos im De re rustica', *WS* 43 (1922/3), 168 ff.; von Albrecht, *Meister röm. Prosa*, pp. 15 ff.

[25] Gell. 18. 7. 3 = Jordan, p. 87, fr. inc. 19. As Gellius uses the phrase it is actually applied to the philosophers themselves.

other writings) were composed in that period. Nevertheless, despite the shortage of specific evidence relating to the earlier period, there are reasons for thinking that Cato's knowledge of Greek literature was already developing. There is his probable reminiscence in 191 of Demosthenes' *First Philippic*, though this cannot be held to be certain;[26] and it is difficult to believe that in the 190s and especially when he had occasion to visit Greece and Athens, one who showed such marked intellectual energy and curiosity in a variety of fields was willing to remain in incurious ignorance about the content of the prolific writings of the Greeks. That is a subjective argument, but not wholly without support since Cato himself did later attest some effort at inquiry about the Greeks while he was in Athens.[27] Similarly, though it is reasonable to suspect as conjecture the statement that his instruction in Greek literature was begun by Ennius, none the less an early association with Ennius is attested, which in turn suggests an early interest in literary matters and lends plausibility to the conjecture of an early acquaintance with Greek writings. Nor was there a problem of access. The transfer to Rome shortly after 168 of the Macedonian royal library has been suggested as a possible turning-point in Cato's experience; for Aemilius Paullus, whose daughter married Cato's son, gave it to his sons Scipio Aemilianus and Fabius Maximus Aemilianus.[28] It is quite credible that Cato could have benefited from the use of this, but a wide range of Greek material was readily available long before then. The sequence of events shows that political contacts with the Greek world quickly advanced other forms of contact; and important political contacts, though greatly expanded from around 200, stretched far back into the third century, to the domination over the Greeks of southern Italy and the acquisition of Sicily. The poets and dramatists working in Rome in the latter part of the third century patently had ready access to the Homeric poems, the classical tragedies, and numerous plays of the New Comedy. Only slightly later Ennius had access not only to all these but to a work attributed to Epicharmus, a gastronomic poem by Archestratus, and the 'Sacred Writing' of Euhemerus, and no doubt much else besides; and it is difficult to believe that Fabius Pictor and Cincius Alimentus did not have ready access to Greek historical writings. In short there is no practical obstacle to supposing that Cato began his acquaintance with Greek literature at a fairly early stage in his career, and despite the passages which

[26] p. 149, where is noted the doubtful possibility of a Greek allusion in 195.
[27] Jordan, p. 77, *Ad Marcum filium* fr. 1, quoted below, p. 170.
[28] Della Corte, *Catone censore*[2], pp. 90 ff. The library: Plut. *Aem.* 28. 11; cf. Polyb. 31. 23. 4. Isid. *Etym.* 6. 5. 1 clearly exaggerates the effect: 'Romae primus librorum copiam advexit Aemilius Paulus, Perse Macedonum rege devicto.'

associate 'Greek letters' with his old age, it seems plausible and probable that he did so.

Finally it must not be overlooked that Cato's knowledge of the Greeks was not confined to their literature. Throughout his adult life he had opportunities to observe them, both as individuals and sometimes as communities. There was the steadily increasing flow of Greeks of every degree to Rome—from kings and envoys to slaves, among the latter the *grammatistes* whom Cato himself maintained to teach other slaves to read and write.[29] But also Cato served for two substantial periods in Sicily, first under Marcellus and later as quaestor at Syracuse; and in 191–190 he visited various cities in Greece itself, including Athens where, as he himself attests, he took the opportunity to make inquiries.[30]

At this point the discussion passes from Cato's knowledge of the Greeks to the central question of his attitude to them and their culture. In fact the evidence already examined has incidentally provided some indication. On the one hand Greek influence was by no means all-pervasive; it seems unlikely, for example, that even in his later speeches he had chosen to heed the rhetoricians.[31] No doubt he was thoroughly contemptuous of those who wallowed in uncritical adulation of all things Greek, as when he poured scorn on Postumius Albinus for prefacing the history he had written in Greek with his request that his readers should pardon any failings in Greek language or method. But his scathing comments could be quoted with approval by the Greek Polybius who portrayed Postumius as an undesirable extremist:[32] 'From childhood he had set his heart on the Greek way of life and language and was excessively steeped in these, to such an extent that through him enthusiasm for what was Greek became offensive to the older and most distinguished of the Romans.'

Presumably Cato himself, to whose criticism of Postumius Polybius proceeds, was one of those 'older and most distinguished Romans', but Polybius is not to be taken to mean that they adopted an attitude of general hostility: dislike of a stupidly uncritical philhellenism does not necessarily imply an equally uncritical antihellenism. On the contrary the quotations, the allusions, the jokes, the easy familiarity all demonstrate that there was

---

[29] Plut. *Cato Mai.* 20. 5.

[30] It is not known whether Cato had much contact with Greek communities when he was sent to Fulvius Nobilior in Aetolia in 189 (*ORF*[3], Cato fr. 130) and his presence at Tarentum in 209 is controversial (p. 7).   [31] pp. 147 ff.

[32] Polyb. 39. 1. 1 ff. In Plut. *Cato Mai.* 12. 5 the comment ἐμμένων δὲ τοῖς πατρίοις καὶ καταγελῶν τῶν τὰ Ἑλληνικὰ τεθαυμακότων is to be understood in the same sense, for it is immediately illustrated by the example of Postumius, which is probably also its inspiration.

no fanatical general antihellenism, that Cato was not automatically hostile to all things Greek and did not reject them as such.

Inescapable though this conclusion is, there is also a considerable amount of apparently contradictory evidence. Almost all of this is preserved in Plutarch or the elder Pliny. According to Plutarch Cato was wholly hostile to philosophy and in rivalry spoke abusively of all Greek culture and training, πᾶσαν Ἑλληνικὴν μοῦσαν καὶ παιδείαν ὑπὸ φιλοτιμίας προπηλακίζων, while Pliny averred that Cato was always of the opinion that absolutely all Greeks, 'universos Graecos', should be expelled from Italy.[33] Obviously there is more than a little suspicion that some exaggeration is contained in such extreme generalizations, especially as both follow directly upon accounts of Cato's attempt in 155 to speed the departure of Carneades from Rome, a context which could well have tempted both these authors into ill-founded generalization. Pliny is further suspect, not only because he is making a neat antithesis with the household philosophers maintained by Cato Uticensis, but because the sentiment itself is so utterly impractical and improbable in a country which contained a substantial number of Greek cities. If it ever was uttered by Cato it cannot have been intended literally and was presumably a wild momentary hyperbole associated with his demand for the immediate dismissal of the embassy, or possibly with some such proposal as the expulsion of philosophers and rhetors from Rome in 161. Nevertheless, exaggerated though they may be, these statements prove the existence of a tradition that Cato was hostile, a tradition which has to be accounted for. Moreover there are several particulars which seem to be closely related to that tradition and which seem to indicate a hostility going beyond dislike of extremism such as Postumius displayed. These too have to be accounted for. The two references to Socrates are both sharply critical, the joke about Isocrates is sarcastic and apparently scornful. Cato expressed the opinion that whereas in general the words of the Romans came from their hearts those of the Greeks came from their lips,[34] not to mention the assertion that the Greek race was 'utterly vile and unruly', 'nequissimum et indocile'. He also delivered a devastating and uncompromising attack on Greek doctors, with whom he forbade his son to have any dealings, and in the same passage a gloomy prophecy that when the Greek race gave Rome its literature, litterae, it would corrupt everything.[35] Finally there was Cato's personal

[33] Plut. *Cato Mai.* 23. 1; Pliny, *Nat. hist.* 7. 113.
[34] Plut. *Cato Mai.* 12. 7.
[35] Jordan, p. 77, *Ad Marcum filium* fr. 1 = Pliny, *Nat. hist.* 29. 14. For the embassy see further below.

effort in 155 to speed the departure from Rome of an Athenian embassy made up of philosophers in order to cut short their public lectures, and especially those of Carneades.

A negative point will help to define the issue more precisely. This apparent contradiction in the evidence cannot be resolved satisfactorily by the hypothesis of a change in Cato's attitude during his later years. Whatever may lie behind those reports of his intensive study of Greek literature in his later years, they offer no adequate solution to the essential problem concerning his attitude. In the first place at least some of the hostile sentiments, and possibly all of them, are derived from Cato's own writings, thus from the same period and the same sources as most of the quotations and allusions. In the second place the affair of the Athenian embassy occurred only a few years before Cato's death. And in the third place several of the hostile sentiments occur in the very passage in which Cato told his son that there was good to be gained from examining Greek literature, *litterae*.

These same considerations, and especially the last, also make it impossible to explain the problem simply by positing the posthumous growth of a hostile and distorting tradition. Though almost all the information comes from two writers of the imperial age, and though both may reasonably be suspected of exaggeration in their general statements, the particulars which have to be accounted for go back to Cato himself, and in several cases to the passage addressed to his son.

A key item in the problem is clearly the passage mentioned above in which Cato gave certain advice to his son. This was quoted by the elder Pliny in the course of his own tirade against doctors. It was evidently in the work known as *Ad filium*, though probably not, as has often been supposed, in a book devoted specifically to medicine. Plutarch also cited it, though he rearranged the material to suit his own purposes and paraphrased rather than translated, whereas Pliny stated explicitly that he was quoting verbatim.[36] It is as follows:

Dicam de istis Graecis suo loco, M. fili, quid Athenis exquisitum habeam et quod bonum sit illorum litteras inspicere, non perdiscere, vincam. nequissimum et indocile genus illorum, et hoc puta vatem dixisse: quandoque ista gens suas litteras dabit, omnia conrumpet, tum etiam magis, si medicos suos hoc mittet. iurarunt inter se barbaros necare omnes medicina, et hoc ipsum mercede faciunt ut fides is sit et facile disperdant. nos quoque dictitant barbaros et spurcius nos quam alios opicon appellatione foedant. interdixi tibi de medicis.

---

[36] Pliny, *Nat. hist.* 29. 13 f.; Plut. *Cato Mai.* 23. 2 ff. On the nature of the *Ad filium* see Appendix 8.

I shall speak about those Greeks in their proper place, Marcus my son, as to what I know as the result of my inquiries at Athens, and I shall demonstrate what benefit there is in looking into their literature, but not in studying it thoroughly. Theirs is an utterly vile and unruly race; and consider that this is said by a prophet: when that race gives us its literature it will corrupt everything, and all the more so if it sends here its doctors. They have taken an oath among themselves to kill all barbarians by their medicine, and this very thing they do for a fee, so that they should be trusted and may destroy with ease. They constantly speak of us too as barbarians, and they insult us more filthily than others by calling us Opici. I have forbidden you to have dealings with doctors.

It is not difficult to find a reasonable basis for Cato's manifest and intense hostility to Greek medicine. Indeed the attitude of the Romans was always to be ambivalent on this matter. Aristocratic households were to maintain their private doctors, Greeks might make a good living, even a fortune, out of practice in Rome, and Caesar and Augustus might encourage doctors to settle there; but side by side with this there is ample evidence of a deep distrust, not to say distaste. The biting comments of the elder Pliny, for example, reveal an attitude closely akin to that of Cato himself. Along with competent doctors there came to Rome others, ill trained or plain charlatans; and the distinction was not easily drawn. One of the most popular of all, Asclepiades, went to Rome at the end of the second century B.C. to teach rhetoric but changed to the practice of medicine, for which he had no training whatsoever, as offering more lucrative prospects. On the other hand in ancient conditions the most competent inevitably had a substantial number of failures among their cases, as happened to Archagathus. Archagathus, the first Greek doctor to be officially encouraged to practise at Rome, was at first received without much enthusiasm, being awarded Roman citizenship and provided with premises at public expense; but subsequently his drastic treatments earned him the nickname *carnifex*, 'executioner', and, according to Pliny, brought doctors in general into disrepute (though this may be Pliny's own inference). Since Archagathus went to Rome in 219 Cato must have been well aware of this unfortunate decline in his reputation. It is small wonder that he, and no doubt many others of prudent disposition, preferred to rely upon traditional and familiar remedies, taking from the Greeks only a few herbal remedies similar in kind.[37]

[37] Pliny, *Nat. hist.* 29. 1–28, with Archagathus at 12 f. *RE*, s.v. *Archagathos*, no. 7, s.v. *Asklepiades*, no. 39. Note also the comments of Polybius, 12. 25 d. In general see Scarborough, *Roman Medicine*, esp. chs. 7 and 8; cf. Allbutt, *Greek Medicine at Rome*, pp. 60 ff. Some other recent discussions with different emphases but questionable arguments: Baader, 'Der ärtzliche Stand', *Acta Conventus XI Eirene*, (1968; pub. 1971) 7 ff.; Schulze, 'Die Entwicklung der Medizin in Rom', *Z. Ant.* 21 (1971), 485 ff.

Cato's rejection of Greek medicine, with its elaborate terminology, its rival theories, and its apparently insecure results, is therefore understandable as a rational conclusion: Greek doctors were unreliable and dangerous. Yet the passage from the *Ad filium* does not present a rational assessment of that kind. Instead Marcus was informed that the arrival of Greek doctors in Rome would be particularly likely to 'corrupt everything'—even more, in some mysterious way, than Greek literature—that the doctors were conspiring to kill all 'barbarians', that they charged fees to allay the suspicions of their victims, that they insulted the Romans by calling them barbarians and even more by calling them 'Opici', and that Marcus is forbidden to have anything to do with doctors. Obviously account must be taken of Cato's propensity for expressing himself in colourful hyperbole: it is not likely that he actually believed in the general oath to kill all barbarians or in the devious motive for charging fees, even if Plutarch is right in his suggestion that Cato had heard of a reply supposed to have been given by Hippocrates to Artaxerxes, that he would never put his skill at the service of barbarians who were enemies of the Greeks.[38] Nevertheless, though the underlying conviction was doubtless that Greek medicine was hazardous, it found expression not as a rational assessment but with the emotional twists and illogical conjunctions of unmistakable prejudice. Matters which were logically distinct were not kept separate in Cato's mind; rather a number of prejudices associated with the Greeks, including the prejudice against Greek doctors, impinged upon and reinforced each other.

Some other prejudices emerge clearly from the passage. In general, though Cato could appreciate Greek writings, he did not like Greeks as people. He thought the race 'nequissimum et indocile', 'utterly vile and unruly'. The latter term surely refers to the constant restlessness and political instability of Greece, the former very probably to the endemic corruption and venality which Polybius himself attests[39] and which were in total contrast to the insistence on integrity which was one of the dominating themes of Cato's public life. So too deceitfulness and fickleness are the characteristics implied in the dictum that the words of the Greeks came from their lips rather than their hearts. It is likely enough that he did not associate such failings with the Greeks of the past: he thought of Leonidas in heroic terms,[40] he said that no king of his day was worthy of comparison with Epaminondas, Pericles, Themistocles, Manius Curius, or Hamilcar Barca,[41] and was prepared to report that the Aborigines of Italy were

---

[38] Plut. *Cato Mai*. 23. 3 f.   [39] Polyb. 6. 56. 13; 18. 34. 7 f.
[40] *HRR* i², fr. 83.   [41] Plut. *Cato Mai*. 8. 14.

descended from Greeks, that Tibur was founded by three Greeks, and that certain Roman practices which he traced to the Sabines were ultimately of Spartan origin.[42] But the Greeks of his own day were a very different matter, characterized by political instability, dishonesty, and unreliability. Furthermore, he was irritated by the terms in which these people habitually spoke of the Romans: 'They refer to us too as *barbari*, and they fling more filth on us than on the others by calling us Opici.' 'Opici' was a form of 'Osci', used by the Greeks with erroneously wide reference, just as the Romans misapplied the term 'Graeci'; but in Italy, it seems, the term was already abusive and associated with obscenity.[43] Even if Cato understood how 'Opici' came to be used, to be termed *barbarus* or Opicus, particularly by people he looked down upon as corrupt and unreliable, can only have caused irritation and fed prejudice.

It may reasonably be conjectured that another reason for Cato's dislike of Greeks as people was connected with that extravagant expenditure on luxuries about which Cato complained repeatedly. Many such extravagances were adopted from Greek example—among them culinary refinements, elegant and costly forms of furniture, and the high value attached to young good-looking male slaves. In a vivid passage which at least in its essence goes back to a second century source Livy attributed such extravagance especially to the impact of the vast booty, in cash and in kind, brought to Rome from Asia in 187 by Cn. Manlius Vulso, while Polybius associated it with the aftermath of the war against Perseus, two decades later.[44] Probably both episodes had an influence, not least through the vast influx of wealth on each occasion, but earlier than that extravagant wining and dining was sufficiently associated with Greeks for Plautus to refer to it several times by the verb *pergraecari*.[45] It therefore comes as something of a surprise that in none of his attacks on extravagance is Cato known to have associated it specifically with the Greeks or Greek influence.[46] Admittedly Livy, in the speech concerning the *lex Oppia* which he puts into Cato's

[42] *HRR* i², frs. 6, 56, and 50 f.

[43] *RE*, s.v. *Osci*, cols. 1543 f.; Cugusi, *Epistolographi Lat. Min.* i. 2, p. 36. The argument of Fabbri, from modern Umbrian *opico*, that it meant 'dirty and ignorant', is unconvincing: 'Perchè Catone ritenesse ingiurioso l'appellativo di "opici" ', *BFC* 30 (1923), 105 f.

[44] Livy, 39. 6. 7 ff.; cf. *HRR* i², Piso fr. 34. Polyb. 31. 25. 3 ff. *HRR* i², Piso fr. 38 = Pliny, *Nat. hist.* 17. 244, is usually taken to indicate that Piso dated the 'overthrow of *pudicitia*' from 154, but his remark need not be taken literally and may have been no more than a severe criticism of the censors of that year.

[45] Plaut. *Poen.* 603; *Bacch.* 813; *Truc.* 87; *Most.* 22; 64; 960. Cf. Paul. *ex Fest.* 235L.

[46] The nearest to this is perhaps the dictum about young slaves and jars of pickled fish (quoted below, p. 179), but even here the weight of the comment is directed at the scale of values shown by young upper-class Romans.

mouth, does make Cato amplify his fears about growing avarice and luxury by reference to the extension of Roman power into Greece and Asia, 'filled with all the enticements of pleasures'.[47] But this is Livy's speech and Livy's conception of what would have been appropriate: it is slender evidence for Cato's views and certainly not to be pressed in detail. Otherwise no source, not even Plutarch or the elder Pliny, associates Cato's attitude towards the Greeks with this matter of luxury and extravagance. It seems possible therefore that Greek influence and the growth of extravagance were not as closely or as exclusively identified in Cato's mind as has sometimes been supposed. After all, his opposition to the repeal of the *lex Oppia* and the emphatic modesty of his own manner of life both considerably antedated the arrival of Manlius' booty in 187; and there was nothing specifically Greek about the practices prohibited by the *lex Oppia*—the use by women of carriages, gold, or multi-coloured clothing. Nevertheless various forms of luxury and extravagance were particularly associated with the Greeks, and therefore, despite the lack of evidence, it is a reasonable conjecture that such associations fortified Cato's dislike of contemporary Greeks; but it would be rash to infer that he saw Greece as the principal or fundamental source of the extravagance of which he complained.

Another important feature of the extract from the *Ad filium* is the reference to literature. Cato thought that there was benefit to be derived from examining Greek writings, but also that there was harm for the individual and for society in intensive study: the Greek race will corrupt everything through its literature. No doubt there is an element of hyperbole in this prophecy of universal corruption, but that scarcely affects the question posed by Cato's quite explicit remark. What kind of harm, what kind of corruption can Cato conceivably have seen in the intensive study of a literature which he judged it profitable to examine in a more superficial way, and from which he quoted with apparent ease and without embarrassment? The answer is to be found in terms, not so much of a rational assessment, as of an amalgam of opinions and prejudices, further aspects of which are indicated by the episode of the Athenian embassy in 155.

The bare facts of this episode are simple. The Athenians had mishandled their case in a dispute with Oropus. Faring badly under the arbitration of Sicyon, they decided to appeal to Rome to override the ruling, and to this end they appointed an embassy composed of the heads of the three principal philosophical schools: Carneades the Academic, Diogenes the Stoic,

47 Livy, 34. 4 ff. On the *lex Oppia* see pp. 25 ff.

and Critolaus the Peripatetic. On arrival at Rome each of the three proceeded to give public lectures, the novelty and brilliance of which attracted large audiences and aroused great enthusiasm. The embassy presented
its case to the Senate, which deferred its answer, until after some delay
Cato protested. He demanded that the Senate should give an early decision
in order to speed the departure of the philosophers and bring the lectures
to an end.

This action by Cato is known only from reports by the elder Pliny and
by Plutarch, both of which indicate that the principal target of Cato's
displeasure was Carneades. Other sources show that Carneades' lectures
were concerned with 'justice' and that his principal purpose was to attack
the concept of 'natural justice', to demonstrate that the concept of
justice had no foundation in nature. Following a method of inquiry often
favoured by the Academics, he delivered a brilliant discourse in favour
of justice and devoted the next day to a refutation of his own arguments.
This remarkable performance was heard by Cato.[48]

Both Pliny and Plutarch gave reasons for Cato's action. Though
Pliny's account is very brief the dictum he reported is an apt enough
comment on a man whose dexterity in argument had attracted rhetoricians
as well as philosophers and of whom Cicero said that 'he was a Greek and
accustomed to propound any view that suited his purpose.'[49] Cato
'advised that the ambassadors should be dismissed as soon as possible
because when Carneades was discoursing it was not easy to discern what
was the truth'. In contrast Plutarch's detailed version occupies a whole
chapter. He relates that Cato's reaction to the tide of enthusiasm which
swept over the Roman aristocracy, and over its younger members in
particular, was concern that 'if the young men should turn their ambitions
in this direction they might prefer a reputation based on talking to one
based on deeds and military affairs.' Plutarch continues:

And when the fame of the philosophers grew even more in the city and their
first speeches to the Senate were interpreted, at his own urgent request, by C.
Acilius, a man of great distinction, Cato decided to get rid of all the philosophers

[48] Plut. *Cato Mai.* 22. 1 ff.; Pliny, *Nat. hist.* 7. 112; Cic. *Rep.* 3. 9 = Lactant. *Inst.* 5. 14. 3;
Quintil. *Inst.* 12. 1. 35. Only these mention Cato in connection with the embassy. For the
event see also: Cic. *Acad.* 2. 137; *De orat.* 2. 155; *Tusc.* 4. 5; *Ad Att.* 12. 23; Gell. 6. 14. 8 f.;
17. 21. 48. For the circumstances: Paus. 7. 11. 4 f. Carneades' discourse was used by Cicero in
the third book of the *Republic*. Although most of this book is lost there is a summary in
Augustine, *De civ. Dei* 2. 21, and Lactantius drew fairly substantially upon it in the fifth and
sixth books of the *Divine Institutes*. For a collection of fragments, see Martino Fusco,
'L'ambasciata a Roma', *Mouseion*, 1 (1923), 189 ff. *RE*, s.v. *Karneades*, no. 1, cols. 1965 and
1978 f.
[49] Cic. *Rep.* 3. 8, cf. 9.

from the city in some respectable way. He entered the Senate and censured the magistrates for keeping in such long suspense an embassy composed of men who were easily able to obtain by persuasion anything they wanted; some decision should be reached as quickly as possible and a vote taken concerning the embassy, so that these men could go back to their schools and lecture to the sons of the Greeks, while the youth of Rome as hitherto listened to their laws and magistrates.

Then Plutarch concludes with a generalization which is probably his own and almost certainly not from the original source of the embassy story: 'This he did not, as some think, because of personal hostility to Carneades but because he was hostile to philosophy and in rivalry spoke abusively of all Greek culture and training.'

It would be a mistake to attach great weight to or to interpret too literally the reference to laws and magistrates. The metaphor is a neat and picturesque antithesis within the general topic of listening to lectures; it is not evidence that Cato considered the subject-matter of these lectures to be in a direct sense subversive of the political authority and institutions of the Roman state. On the other hand Cato's real concerns are evident. One element was probably scorn at the display of uncritical adulation, not least in a Roman senator who was so undignified as to insist on acting as an interpreter. Acilius, who was another who wrote a history in Greek, probably had enthusiasms similar to those of Aulus Postumius Albinus, who, of all people, happened to be *praetor urbanus* in this year and as such was responsible for introducing the embassy to the Senate.[50] But this was only a secondary irritant. Cato's principal concerns were with effective participation in public and military activities and with high standards of integrity. Nor are these concerns associated merely with the account of the episode of 155; their plausibility in that account is strengthened because all were prominent and enduring features of Cato's outlook. His lifelong sense that it was a duty to be active in the public interest is unmistakable, and there is ample evidence of the importance of military matters in his thinking, including good reason to believe that his concern was readily aroused when military qualities seemed to him to be threatened. Along with that he had ceaselessly upheld in public life, and had sought to enforce in the behaviour of others, high standards of conduct in terms of traditional Roman virtues—*fides*, integrity, honesty, impartiality in the administration of justice, and the insistence that public service was a duty that should not be exploited for personal gain.[51] Given the opinion that he

[50] Cic. *Acad.* 2. 137; cf. Polyb. 33. 1. 5. On Acilius see also Gell. 6. 14. 9.
[51] pp. 90 and 95 f.

held of the Greeks of his own day, together with their obvious weakness
and military incompetence, it is understandable that a man moved by such
concerns felt that too intensive a preoccupation with Greek studies might
detract from the all-important public service and militarism of the Roman
aristocracy, and equally understandable that he had no time for a philo-
sopher who could devote his energies to debating whether there was any
basis in reality for such concepts as justice and the other virtues, which
Cato assuredly regarded as self-evident and necessary ideals. A man who
judged the Greeks insincere, unreliable, and unstable may understandably
have looked askance at that rhetorical element in their training which
sought the convincing presentation of good and bad cases alike, at the
philosophical questioning and subtleties which appeared to raise doubts
about every principle of conduct, or at the combination of rhetorical
expertise and philosophical dexterity—exemplified to the full in the talents
of Carneades—which with seeming cynicism, or at least with apparent
futility, could present an elaborate argument one day and a full-scale
refutation the next. The phrase *mera mortualia*, 'mere winding-sheets' (or
'dirges') encapsulates the scorn for the futility of philosophical discussion,[52]
but there is also a deeper hostility. The criticism of Socrates as destructive[53]
confirms that the reference to the youth of Rome listening to its own laws
and magistrates may be related to a belief that philosophy was in some
sense subversive—subversive of principles and standards of conduct, subversive too of public diligence and martial qualities.

All this adds up to an attitude which, though scarcely thought through
with rigorous logic, is comprehensible as the product of observation and
emotional reaction on the part of a man devoted to those public concerns
which are apparent in Cato's career—an attitude which carried within
itself ample reason for saying that the intensive study of Greek writers
was undesirable and could be corrupting. Similarly Plutarch's comment
that 'he was wholly hostile to philosophy and in rivalry spoke abusively
of all Greek culture and training' acquires a considerable measure of
plausibility from the considerations which have been examined. In so far
as it refers to philosophy and training, παιδεία, it has a real basis in Cato's
attitude; and even the statement that he spoke slightingly of all Greek
culture could have had a factual basis in the sense that Cato was much
given to sweeping hyperbole and may have said something of the sort
when, for example, criticizing philosophical training—or Plutarch may
have interpreted the passage from the *Ad filium* in this sense. But the

[52] Gell. 18. 7. 3 = Jordan, p. 87, fr. inc. 19.
[53] Plut. *Cato Mai.* 23. 1.

implication that the hostility did in reality extend to Greek culture as a whole manifestly conflicts with the facts.

For in these attitudes and prejudices of Cato there is nothing which need imply or have inspired a general antihellenism, or conflict with the notion that there could be benefit in 'looking into' Greek literature, 'illorum litteras inspicere'. The danger to the martial spirit and to public involvement lay not in an acquaintance with Greek literature but in an excessive devotion to its study. Similarly it was not the great bulk of Greek literature and learning that was morally objectionable but, in a patently corrupt and deceitful race, an excessive devotion to verbal expertise at the expense of truth, the tireless acquisition of skill in endless and seemingly barren abstract argument, and the application of both of these to questioning the basis of what were to Cato self-evident ideals of behaviour. For these features of contemporary Greek culture Cato, like many another Roman of his day, had no use; but that did not inhibit him from enjoying or appreciating Homer, Xenophon, Demosthenes, and much else in Greek literature and learning.

But if Cato was by no means an undifferentiating antihellenist nevertheless it would be misleading to say that he took a moderate and balanced view of Hellenic culture. When all allowance is made for the exaggeration, generalization, or over-simplification which might be expected in the tradition, the evidence points to something more than scorn for the uncritical and undignified adulation of extreme philhellenes, to something other than a careful rational appraisal of Greek culture, welcoming much of it but rejecting certain features as incompatible with the essentials of Roman power and Roman society. Cato's disapproval of certain aspects of Greek culture and life has the emotional overtones of active dislike and even considerable hostility and prejudice. It is this substantial element of prejudice together with the ready indulgence in hyperbole which goes far to account for the contradictions and paradoxes in the evidence. A single comprehensive motivation, above all in terms of rational appraisal, can offer no solution, indeed would be a caricature; but if a more realistic view is taken it is possible to resolve the apparent paradoxes into the coherent picture of a single personality and to discern at least dimly how the various facets of Cato's reactions to the Greeks and their culture reflected the interaction of his personal experiences and observations, his judgements, and his various prejudices.[54]

Finally Cato is not to be envisaged as fighting a lonely defensive struggle

---

[54] See further, particularly with reference to παιδεία, Appendix 9.

against the seemingly inexorable advance of undesirable Hellenic practices. Any opposition to developments which are regarded as undesirable is in a sense defensive, but Cato was far from alone, in spite of Plutarch's implication that he was in his concern about the embassy of philosophers.[55] In fact it is not known how the Senate responded to his intervention on that occasion, but it was probably in the next year (the only possible alternative is 173) that a majority of senators could be found to vote for the expulsion of two Epicurean philosophers.[56] Six years earlier, in 161, they had authorized the praetor Marcus Pomponius to take whatever steps were necessary to exclude all philosophers and rhetoricians from the city, and as late as 92 the censors issued an edict protesting at the establishment of Latin rhetorical schools.[57] Furthermore in the later decades of Cato's life an interest in maintaining military hardihood was by no means an eccentricity on his part. It is mentioned as a motive behind both the decision in 157 to undertake the Dalmatian war, and the vote of the Senate in 151, at the instigation of P. Scipio Nasica Corculum, to order the demolition of a partially built theatre with permanent seating and the prohibition of any such structure in the city or its vicinity.[58] And whether or not Polybius is correct in attributing responsibility to the personal conduct of Aulus Postumius Albinus, he clearly attests a mood of disapproval of such unbridled enthusiasm among 'the older and most distinguished of the Romans'.[59] In view of all this, and despite the brief mass enthusiasm aroused by the embassy of philosophers, it would be unsafe to assume that Cato felt gravely threatened by the undesirable aspects of Greek culture. To take the 'prophecy' that 'when that race gives us its literature it will corrupt everything' as indicative of a sense of impending disaster is to read far more into it than can be justified—especially when it continues with the *non sequitur* 'and all the more so if it sends here its doctors'. So also with his well-known dictum, in a speech to the People, 'that they would see the state change for the worse especially when it was found that good-looking boys were being sold for more than fields and jars of pickled fish for more than a teamster'.[60] Cato undoubtedly took such matters seriously, but given his attitude to the Greeks of his own day and to those of their practices of which he disapproved, his reaction is unlikely to have been

---

[55] Plut. *Cato Mai.* 22. 4 f.   [56] Athen. 12. 547 a.   [57] Suet. *Rhet.* 1.
[58] Dalmatia: Polyb. 32. 13. 6 f. Theatre: Livy, *Epit.* 48; Oros. 4. 21. 4; Val. Max. 2. 4. 2; Vell. 1. 15. 3; Aug. *De civ. Dei* 1. 31, cf. 32 f.; see Astin, *Scipio Aemilianus*, pp. 48 and 117 f.
[59] Polyb. 39. 1. 1 ff.
[60] Polyb. 31. 25. 5 f. Other versions all probably derived from Polybius: Diod. 31. 24; 37. 3. 6; Athen. 6. 274 f–275 a; Plut. *Cato Mai.* 8. 2; *Quaest. conv.* 4. 2; 'Plut.' *Apophth. Cat. Mai.* 2.

that Rome was threatened with capture by a culture of which the merits
were so great that its vices must follow almost inevitably in their train. It
would not be surprising if he simply assumed that constant vigilance and
the evident readiness of the Senate to act would suffice to restrain or repress
what was undesirable.

Cato's lifetime covered a period in which Rome was increasingly in
contact with Greek culture, increasingly aware of it and responding to it.
It was a period of rapid cultural development, but the cultural development was also adjustment to association with an external culture with
obvious achievements to its credit. It was inevitable that Romans would
react to the new experiences in very varying ways, in terms of interest and
disinterest, likes and dislikes, approval and disapproval, involvement and
rejection. That in certain fields and on certain occasions these variations
found expression in open disagreement and controversial public action is
sufficiently demonstrated by the expulsions of philosophers and rhetoricians—for it is not to be believed that such measures had unanimous
consent or passed unopposed by those who shared the attitudes and
enthusiasms of Aulus Postumius Albinus. Yet it by no means follows—
though it has often been believed—that dispute extended beyond the
particular issues and disapproval of undue enthusiasm into profound
ideological division; that the reaction in Rome to Greek cultural influences
took the form of a deep persistent cleavage between a party of resistance
and a party of acceptance, and that this was a major and prolonged
political issue.[61]

One of the principal inducements towards such an interpretation has
been precisely the belief that Cato's own attitude and conduct were
appropriate to a partisan in just such a conflict. It is now evident, however,
and should be the cause of no surprise, that the variation in reaction was
not merely between individuals but within particular individuals, and
especially within the one individual about whom most is known and
upon whom so much interpretation has been based. Cato patently did
not react to 'Hellenism' as to a package, to be accepted or rejected in
its entirety, nor yet was his 'selective' reaction balanced, considered, and
coherent. A wide acquaintance with matters Greek extended in some

---

61 The phrase τὴν αἵρεσιν τὴν Ἑλληνικήν, used by Polybius in 39. 1. 3, where he
refers to the reaction of senior Romans to the excessive enthusiasm of Postumius Albinus,
might theoretically refer to a cultural or educational pattern which they rejected; but in
the context he almost certainly means that the aping of Greek ways became offensive to
them: ὥστε δι᾽ ἐκεῖνον καὶ τὴν αἵρεσιν τὴν Ἑλληνικὴν προσκόψαι τοῖς πρεσβυτέροις καὶ τοῖς
ἀξιολογωτάτοις τῶν Ῥωμαίων. Cf. p. 168. For supposed conflict about systems of education
see further Appendix 9.

directions to an easy familiarity, in others to a hostile prejudice. In respect of Greek culture it is more meaningful to speak of Cato's attitudes rather than his attitude; and if this is true of Cato it is reasonable to assume that it is true also, with wide variations in detail, of the Roman upper classes in general. In such a situation one can properly recognize a ferment of reaction, adaptation, and adjustment, unlikely to proceed without disagreements and controversies; and one can properly speak of the interaction of two cultures as a social and cultural phenomenon of great importance; but the central evidence of Cato's own attitudes does not accord well with the widespread belief that the process found expression in the open and sustained conflict of two sharply contrasting ideologies. Instead it was a situation and a process more complex, more confused, and more fruitful: for the outcome was not the conquest of Rome by Greek culture but a productive synthesis such that what emerged as a still distinct and unmistakably Roman culture was necessarily, consciously, yet unselfconsciously shot through with Hellenic elements.

9

The *De agricultura* and Other Writings

1. Cato's writings

'His eloquence lives and flourishes, enshrined in writings of every kind.'[1]
If Livy has here allowed enthusiasm to outweigh precision, if his claim
has too wide a sweep, the overstatement is at least understandable. The
motivations and purposes which induced Cato to write, the range, the
forms, the quality, even the basic nature of his compositions may all
be subject to debate; but the magnitude of his achievement is beyond
question. He was virtually the founder of Roman prose literature. Nor
is his achievement in any way diminished by the recognition that, like
all who make original contributions, he was not working in a vacuum,
that his writings were related to, and developed from, what others had
done. Other Romans had written historical works in prose, but in Greek,
not in Latin. Others had created literary works in the Latin language,
but in verse, not in prose. Other Romans must have noted down practical
information and assembled 'books' for private use, but Cato was the first
to prepare such books with a view to circulation, to their use by a 'public'.
And if the scope and sophistication of his compositions has sometimes
been overestimated, still they unquestionably display a remarkable
breadth of interest and variety. A summary survey will illustrate this
and provide a basis for more detailed discussion.

1. The speeches have been discussed in Chapter 7. Although they proved
to be of great significance in the development of Roman literature it is
unlikely that Cato himself thought of them in such terms. Whether
he himself 'published' any, apart from those included in the *Origines*,
is uncertain, though the balance of probability inclines slightly against.

2. Two 'books' not intended for publication and probably never
published:

(*i*) A history which, according to Plutarch, Cato stated he himself
wrote 'with his own hand in big letters, so that his son might have in his

---

[1] Livy, 39. 40. 7.

home an aid to the understanding of the old Roman traditions'. It was presumably written *c.* 185–180. Despite occasional conjectures to the contrary it is generally agreed that this work is to be distinguished from the *Origines*, except in so far as the experience of writing it could have been one of the factors encouraging the later decision to write a major historical work.[2]

(*ii*) A *commentarius* or notebook in which Cato collected prescriptions for the treatment of illnesses in his household. He mentioned this *commentarius* in his *Ad filium*, adding an indication, probably very brief, of the general nature of his treatments. Occasional modern attempts to identify this book either with part of the *Ad filium* itself or with the extant *De agricultura* are certainly erroneous.[3]

3. Writings addressed to his elder son, M. Porcius Cato Licinianus:

(*i*) The *Ad filium*. This has often been envisaged as a set of books, probably conceived as a single project, written to assist with the education of Cato's son, each book dealing with a separate topic, and including at least agriculture, medicine, and rhetoric; in fact the first Roman 'encyclopaedia'. However, there are grave objections to such a reconstruction. The most likely interpretation of the evidence is that Cato addressed to his son a collection, probably in only one book, of precepts, exhortations, and observations, many of them pithily expressed, on a variety of topics and with a marked emphasis on practical affairs. Since the son was almost certainly born in 192 or 191 such a work would probably have been put together during the 170s. Subsequently copies of the work passed into circulation, so that it was known to Pliny, Plutarch, and others, and several fragments survive. There is nothing to indicate whether Cato himself was in any way responsible for the 'publication', but in any event it is unlikely that the *Ad filium* was written with a view to this.[4]

(*ii*) A letter from Cato to his elder son, congratulating him on his bravery at the battle of Pydna in 168. This is presumably the same letter as the one in which Cato, having heard that his son had received his discharge from the army, warned him against engaging in combat unless he was first formally re-enlisted. A few other very brief fragments,

[2] Plut. *Cato Mai.* 20. 7. Cf. Peter, *HRR* i[2], pp. cxxix f.; Helm, *RE*, s.v. *Porcius*, no. 9, col. 146; Kienast's view, p. 107, that the composition of this work shows that Cato was probably already collecting material for the *Origines* goes further than the facts warrant. It is possible that Plutarch's words τῶν παλαιῶν καὶ πατρίων reflect an original reference to *mores maiorum*.

[3] Pliny, *Nat. hist.* 29. 15; Plut. *Cato Mai.* 23. 5. See Appendix 8, pp. 334 ff., esp. p. 336 n. 7; Mazzarino, *Introduzione*, chs. II and III, *passim*, esp. pp. 31 ff.

[4] Appendix 8.

including at least one usually assigned to the *Ad filium*, may come from this letter and could be taken to suggest that its contents were rather wide-ranging. That would help to account for its subsequent publication and survival until at least the time of Cicero. There is no good evidence for the survival of other letters, either to the son or to others. The letter is most unlikely to have been written originally with a view to 'publication'; whether Cato himself was in any way responsible for its passing into circulation is unknown.[5]

4. Three specialized monographs. The interpretation of the *Ad filium* as an 'encyclopaedia' gave rise to questions about the relationship between that work and these monographs. With the interpretation of the *Ad filium* adopted in this book these questions no longer arise.

(i) *De agricultura*. The only one of Cato's works to survive intact, this will be discussed in detail below. It consists of a single book.

(ii) *De re militari*. Fifteen different fragments are preserved in eighteen citations, and the work is explicitly mentioned in three further passages. There is little doubt that the correct title is *De re militari*, though other phrases are found, such as *De militari disciplina*. Despite one reference to 'books' the work virtually certainly consisted of a single book. It cannot be dated but a fragment from its preface shows that it was not merely a private notebook but was written for publication. Material drawn from it was incorporated in later military writings and transmitted as far as the *Epitoma rei militaris* of Vegetius, who refers to Cato by name, though it is virtually certain that he did not have direct access to Cato's work. There is good reason to believe that Vegetius has significantly more Catonian material than the three fragments positively established, but attempts to identify further specific passages are in varying degrees insecure.[6] The fifteen fragments of Cato's work suggest that it was a handbook of practical information about Roman military practices and methods, especially on the tactical level, ranging through such matters as the taking of *auspicia*, details of internal organization, methods of

---

[5] Plut. *Cato Mai.* 20. 11; *Quaest. Rom.* 39; Cic. *De off.* 1. 36 and 37; Cugusi, *Epistolographi latini minores* i. 1, pp. 67 ff., i. 2, pp. 34 ff.; cf. Jordan, pp. 83 f., *Epistulae* frs. 1 ff. Schmidt, 'Catos Epistula ad M. filium', *Hermes*, 100 (1972), 568 ff., argues for a wide-ranging didactic letter and also against the survival of more than one letter. Festus, p. 280L and Diom. *Gramm.* 1. 366. 13K are not good evidence for more and both passages are probably to be emended.

[6] Veget. 1. 8; 2. 3; 3. 20. A sentence in this last chapter, with no mention of Cato, is identical with a sentence cited by Nonius, p. 301, 32L, as from Cato's *De re militari*, and it is probable that the whole of Veget. 3. 20 follows Cato closely. For discussion of Cato as a source for Vegetius see esp. Schenk, *Flavius Vegetius Renatus, Klio*, Beih. 22; Neumann, *RE*, Suppb. X, s.v. *Vegetius*, cols. 1005 ff., esp. 1014 f.

maintaining discipline, formations on the march and in battle, and the uses of specialist troops such as archers. Probably the points were exemplified by accounts of particular events.[7]

(*iii*) A work dealing with aspects of civil law, perhaps more specifically with augural and pontifical law. In this case special difficulties arise because Cato's elder son, who predeceased him, wrote books on law which were evidently more extensive and more authoritative than Cato's own, the references to which are all rather indirect. It is likely that most of the citations from 'Cato' in the *Digest* and Justinian's *Institutes* are from the son's work (though at least one is probably a corruption of 'Capito').[8] The same could be true of the one fragment which is usually assigned to Cato's own work, though more probably Festus, who preserved it, and may be supposed to have taken it from the Augustan scholar Verrius Flaccus, would have added some qualification if he had believed any other Cato to have been the author.[9] The most explicit evidence is a passage of the *De senectute* in which Cicero represented Cato as busying himself in old age with various literary occupations, including, 'I am dealing with the civil law of the augurs and pontifices.'[10] Though this is not reliable evidence for the date of composition, read in its context it does show that Cicero believed Cato to have written such a work. That is implied also in not a few other references to Cato's expertise in law, several of them in lists of his skills which clearly correspond to his principal writings.[11] The paucity of fragments is presumably because this work was quickly outdated by the flood of voluminous and authoritative legal writings which followed.

5. *Carmen de moribus.* This work is known only from a single passage of Gellius (a later reference by Nonius is almost certainly taken from

---

[7] Jordan, pp. 80 ff., *De re mil.* frs. 1–15. Barwick, 'Zu den Schriften des Cornelius Celsus und des alten Cato', *WJA* 3 (1948), 126 f., is not convincing when he seeks to explain the plural *in libris* in Veget. 1. 15 (= fr. 7) by the hypothesis that in addition to the separate monograph Cato included another *in libris ad filium*. Apart from the relationship to Vegetius the monograph has aroused only slight modern interest. See Köchly and Rüstow, *Griechische Kriegschriftsteller* ii. 61 ff.; Nap, 'Ad Catonis librum de re militari', *Mn* 55 (1927), 79 ff.; Spaulding, 'The Ancient Military Writers', *CJ* 28 (1933), 660 f.

[8] Just. *Inst.* 1. 11. 12; *Dig.* 1. 2. 2. 38; 21. 1. 10. 1; 24. 3. 44 pr. (prob. Capito); 45. 1. 4. 1; cf. 34. 7; Gell. 13. 20. 9; *RE*, s.v. *Porcius*, no. 14, col. 168.

[9] Festus, p. 144, 18L, s.v. *mundus*: 'sic refert Cato in commentaris iuris civilis.'

[10] Cic. *De sen.* 38. It is conceivable that Cato's complaint recorded in Cic. *De divin.* 1. 28 = *HRR* i², fr. 132 that auguries had been lost as a result of neglect by the college is a fragment of this work, though this is not the only possible source.

[11] Livy, 39. 40. 5 f.; Nepos, *Cato* 3. 1; Quintil. *Inst.* 12. 11. 2; also Cic. *De orat.* 1. 171; 3. 135; Val. Max. 8. 7. 1; Quintil. *Inst.* 12. 3. 9. Cic. *De orat.* 2. 142 perhaps refers to the son.

Gellius), whose initial interest is in the use of the word *elegans* in a particular quotation, though he is led on to recall two further quotations.[12] He explicitly terms it 'the book of Cato which is entitled *Carmen de moribus*', and he twice more refers to it in the singular. Of the three fragments Gellius makes it clear that the second really consists of several (three?) separate quotations he has brought together. Although the term *carmen* has inspired a variety of suggestions regarding metrical form, the very diversity of conclusions encourages the belief that it was a prose work of markedly didactic tone.[13] Such a tone is certainly suggested by the fragments, though such limited material is a slender basis on which to make assertions about the book as a whole. Nevertheless they suggest that, as is only to be expected, it was concerned with *mores* not in a theoretical or philosophical sense but in the practical terms of actual behaviour. The first two fragments contrast certain features of contemporary conduct with the practice of earlier generations, by implication to the disadvantage of the former, while the third uses a simile to moralize about deterioration consequent upon idleness. It is a reasonable assumption, but no more than that, that the work was written for the purpose of circulation—rather than, for example, as a further preceptual guide for Licinianus—and that it was some kind of public exhortation to higher standards of conduct, as Cato conceived them to be.

6. A collection of 'sayings'. Cicero in the *De officiis* speaks explicitly of 'many witty sayings by many people, like those which were collected by the old Cato', 'multa multorum facete dicta, ut ea, quae a sene Catone collecta sunt'. A passage in the *De oratore*, though not quite explicit, is beyond reasonable doubt another reference to the same collection and shows that Cicero drew several of his examples from it.[14] Presumably the compilation of such a work was primarily a reflection of Cato's own sense of humour and fondness for aphorism. It would be rash to assume that it was compiled for the express purpose of circulation, but supposing it to have been made initially for private purposes it is easy to envisage Cato allowing copies to be made and the collection quickly passing into circulation. Cicero's reference to the 'old' Cato, *senex*, is not adequate evidence that Cato compiled the collection towards

---

[12] Jordan, pp. 82 f., *Carmen* frs. 1–3 = Gell. 11. 2. 1 ff.; Nonius, p. 745, 15L. Helm, *RE*, s.v. *Porcius*, no. 9, cols. 146 f., suggests that another possible fragment is in Colum. *De re rust.* 11. 1. 26. A further possibility is Jordan, p. 110, *Dict. mem.* 76 = Sen. *Epist.* 122. 2; cf. Cic. *De fin.* 2. 23; Colum. *De re rust.* 1 pr. 16.

[13] Helm, *RE*, s.v. *Porcius*, no. 9, cols. 146 ff., referring to *TLL* iii. 463, 51. For a recent argument that it was in saturnians, Pighi, 'Catonis carmen de moribus', *Latinitas*, 14 (1966), 31 ff.   [14] Cic. *De off.* 1. 104; *De orat.* 2. 271.

the end of his life, for Cicero often applies the word to Cato as a dis-
tinguishing epithet rather than as an indication of time. It is obviously
possible, though undemonstrable, that the collection was built up over
a considerable period. The only dictum certainly from the collection
was spoken by a certain C. Publicius about a P. Mummius. It is highly
probable however that the collection is the source of a dictum (quoted
twice by Cicero) addressed by Q. Fabius Maximus Cunctator to M.
Livius Macatus after the capture of Tarentum in 209, and possibly also
of a remark by Scipio Africanus which Cicero in the *Republic* says was
reported by Cato.[15] Several other remarks in the second book of the
De oratore must have been drawn from the collection. There are about
ten possibilities, but no means of establishing that any particular one of
them was taken from this source.

Inevitably there has been speculation as to whether Cato included
in this collection any sayings of his own. The question has been complicated by Plutarch's statement that 'many literal translations [sc. from
Greek] are included among his sayings and maxims', ἐν τοῖς ἀπο-
φθέγμασι καὶ ταῖς γνωμολογίαις τέτακται.[16] This however is almost certainly
a different matter. Plutarch means that there were many such translations
among the sayings attributed to Cato, and by Plutarch's time there were
available collections of such sayings independent of Cato's own collection.
One such collection was manifestly the basis of chapters 8 and 9 of
Plutarch's *Life*. Moreover a number of sayings in general circulation,
including some of Greek origin, were posthumously attached to Cato's
name and included in such collections; indeed there are a number of
such spurious attributions among the *Apophthegmata* preserved in the
Plutarch corpus.[17] Not that Cato himself is likely to have been shy of

[15] Fabius: Cic. *De orat.* 2. 271; 2. 273, cf. *De sen.* 11; *Rep.* 1. 27. Africanus: Quintil. *Inst.*
6. 3. 105, which Jordan, p. 83, cites as *Apophth.* fr. 1.

[16] Plut. *Cato Mai.* 2. 6. See esp. Rossi, 'De M. Catonis dictis et apophthegmatis', *Athenaeum*, n.s. 2 (1924), 174 ff.; Della Corte, *Catone censore*[2], pp. 246 ff.

[17] Nachstädt, Teubner edn. of Plut. *Moralia*, ii. 1, p. 81. It has been generally recognized
that this collection cannot be the one used by Plutarch. Though it has sometimes been suggested
that it was compiled by extracting dicta from Plutarch's *Life*, this too is incorrect: the order
of the common items differs too much, and there are too many striking sayings in the *Life*,
especially in chs. 8 and 9, which are not in the collection and which would scarcely have
been omitted if the latter had been based on the former. Yet there is a definite relationship
between the two, indicated by some correspondence in order and in a number of cases by
exact correspondence in much of the wording. It looks as if somewhere in the antecedents of
both works there was a common list, that the version available to Plutarch was more comprehensive (as shown (a) by chs. 8 and 9, (b) by sayings which are in both the *Life* and the
Moralia but not in the *Apophthegmata*), and that the *Apophthegmata* was based on part of the
same material but drew also upon other—and spurious—material.

using sayings translated from Greek: he was evidently quite prepared to borrow a sentence from Xenophon for the Preface to the *Origines*.[18] However that may be, it is clear that the Plutarch passage probably has no direct connection with Cato's own collection.

Nor is much help to be got from the survival of a large number of sayings attributed to Cato. Many of these, probably the majority, were culled from his speeches and other writings, and some from Polybius. There are others which could not easily be envisaged in such works, but it is perfectly possible that they were incorporated in a collection by someone else soon after—or even before—Cato's death. On the other hand it is by no means inconceivable that Cato included some of his own dicta in his own collection. The suggestion that they would no longer have had meaning or interest for him apart from the original circumstances is as much—and as little—applicable to other people's dicta as to his own. He unquestionably made a collection of the former; and he was not a man inhibited by modesty. The conclusion must be that while it is possible he included dicta of his own, it remains quite uncertain whether he actually did so.

7. *Origines*. This was a major historical work, the first in Latin, written with a view to circulation among a reading public. About 125 fragments survive from its seven books. The first book dealt with the origins and very early history of Rome, the second and third books with the origins of many other Italian peoples. The remaining four books covered the history of Rome from at least as early as the First Punic War literally down to Cato's own day: the last book included the speech against Ser. Sulpicius Galba which he delivered only shortly before his death. The *Origines* will be discussed separately in Chapter 10.

Such is the range of Cato's writings, so far as they are known. The very list highlights his remarkable versatility and the vigour with which he pursued a variety of interests. At the same time it raises fundamental questions about such matters as Cato's motives in writing, his debt to his predecessors, his methods of working, and the level of his artistry. The starting-point must be the *De agricultura*, not for its special merits—for some of the works of which only fragments remain were certainly of higher literary and intellectual quality—but because it is the only work which has survived to be judged as a full text.

---

[18] *HRR* i², fr. 2; cf. Xen. *Sympos.* 1. 1.

2. *The* De agricultura[19]

Cato's *De agricultura* is a book of moderate length—just over one hundred pages in a modern critical edition—which despite its title deals with only some aspects of agriculture.[20] It is not—and makes no pretension to be—a comprehensive treatment of the different types of agricultural production and organization. In particular it does not deal with either cereal production or animal raising as topics of central importance, according them only cursory mention as auxiliary items on farms the primary function of which was to produce wine or olive oil. Indeed, although Cato also dealt briefly with horticulture in the neighbourhood of a city, it was clearly wine and oil production that he had in the forefront of his mind as he wrote. Yet although in this sense the scope of his work is limited, in places it extends beyond strictly agricultural matters to include a number of medicinal treatments and even cooking recipes. Strongly didactic in character, with the imperative form predominating throughout, it offers little in the way of theory and generalization but a great deal of practical instruction, much of it on matters of detail, even of minute detail. With very few exceptions each of the 162 chapters deals with a single quite specific topic—such as a particular operation on the farm or a particular recipe—and this is basically true even of a few chapters, mostly in the earlier part of the book, in which the topics are rather broader and more complex. Indeed in the manuscript tradition through which the work has been preserved the point was emphasized by the rubrics indicating the contents of the individual chapters—though there is uncertainty as to whether these rubrics, which usually reproduce or paraphrase the opening words of the chapter, were part of the original work.

[19] Useful surveys of the extensive literature regarding the *De agricultura* will be found in Schanz–Hosius, *Gesch. der röm. Literatur* i⁴. 184 ff.; Helm, *RE*, s.v. *Porcius*, no. 9, cols. 147 ff.; Mazzarino, *Introduzione, passim*; White, 'Roman Agricultural Writers', in Temporini, *Aufstieg und Niedergang* i. 4, pp. 439 ff. Marmorale, *Cato Maior*², p. 162 n. 36, has a major bibliographical list; see also Zuccarelli, 'Rassegna bibliografica . . . (1940–1950)', *Paideia*, 7 (1952), 213 ff. On the aspects of the work discussed in this chapter see also esp. Gummerus, *Der röm. Gutsbetrieb, Klio,* Beih. 5 (1906), 15 ff.; Leo, *Gesch. der röm. Literatur* i. 270 ff.; Birt, 'Zum Proöm und den Summarien', *BPhW* 29 (1915), cols. 922 ff.; Hörle, *Catos Hausbücher,* §§ I and II; Brehaut, *Cato the Censor. On Farming,* pp. xiii ff.; Della Corte, *Catone censore*², pp. 100 ff.; Thielscher, *Belehrung, passim*. For bibliography more esp. concerned with social and economic aspects see p. 240 n. 1. On the agricultural material from a practical point of view see esp. White, *Roman Farming*; Brehaut, *Cato the Censor. On Farming*.

[20] The correct title is almost certainly *De agricultura*, despite the occasional occurrence of *De re rustica*: Schanz–Hosius, op. cit. p. 184; Marmorale, op. cit., p. 163. Helm, op. cit., cols. 147 ff., links the question too closely with the issue of whether Cato himself published the book.

Stylistically the *De agricultura* is plain in the extreme, consisting largely of short uncomplicated sentences and making only limited use even of a narrow range of simple conjunctions and particles. The rare flash of more vivid language and the occasional aphorism provide a tenuous link with the fragments of the speeches and other works,[21] but by the very contrast which they create these also emphasize the simple, unadorned directness which prevails. In short, Cato here employs the language of direct practical instruction, without effort to achieve literary effect or linguistic elegance. The striking exception to this is the Preface, which, whatever may be thought of its intellectual content, was manifestly composed with considerable care in order to achieve an elevated and artistic effect. It has even been suggested that its style and structure were strongly influenced by Greek rhetorical principles, but in fact its characteristics are those of the native Latin tradition, with its use of synonyms, of parallelism, of repetitions—sometimes for deliberate effect, sometimes because there was no attempt to avoid them—and the emphasis on the opening and closing elements in sentences of relatively simple structure.[22]

It has often been observed that the Preface contrasts with the main body of the work in another respect also; for it makes explicit reference to the type of the *colonus*, the peasant farmer working his own farm, whereas the book itself is not directed at all to this form of farming. Instead, although not a little of the detailed practical information would be applicable within any kind of farm organization, Cato clearly has in mind larger units belonging to, and managed on behalf of, an owner who is not normally resident on the farm.

There is no firm evidence as to when the *De agricultura* was composed. One of the early chapters contains a hint that it was probably written later than 198, but since Cato did not die until 149 that does little to help.[23] If the most literal interpretation is placed upon Cato's assertion that up to his seventieth year none of his villas was plastered and also upon the full implications of the instructions in chapter 128 'for plastering a dwelling', that chapter should have been written after 164;[24] but a date

---

[21] e.g. *De agr.* 2. 7; 4 ('frons . . . est'); 39. 2 ('cogitato . . . etc.'); 61. 1. Note also several vigorous sequences, markedly rhetorical in character, in ch. 2, dealing with the owner's inspection of the farm and his discussion with the *vilicus*.

[22] Leeman, *Orationis Ratio*, pp. 21 ff., suggests Greek influence, but see Kappelmacher, 'Zum Stil Catos im De re rustica', *WS* 43 (1922/3), 168 ff.; von Albrecht, *Meister röm. Prosa*, pp. 15 ff.

[23] *De agr.* 3. 1, with the injunction to build only at thirty-six years of age.

[24] Thielscher, *Belehrung*, pp. 14 f., who however places too much confidence in the inference. Pliny, *Nat. hist.* 14. 45, is clearly not to be taken literally as secure evidence for composition in Cato's old age, though it has sometimes been quoted to that effect.

inferred only from the literal implications of such details is scarcely a reliable basis for further argument and interpretation. That the *De agricultura* was composed in Cato's later years is certainly plausible but is not securely established.

Nevertheless this book is not only the first work on agriculture to have been written by a Roman;[25] it is also the earliest prose work in Latin to have survived and was among the earliest written. Consequently it is of exceptional interest in several different respects, including textual criticism, the history of Latin language and idiom, Roman religion, and the practical aspects of Roman agriculture; and it has also received much attention as a social and economic document. In the present study attention is focused especially on two aspects: the characteristics, methods, and processes of composition, which are considered in this chapter; and the light which the work may throw on Cato's personality and especially upon his attitudes to various social and economic matters, which is considered in Chapter 11.

Two striking features of the *De agricultura* have prompted numerous discussions about the time and manner of its composition, its publication, and possible subsequent modification. They are the seemingly disorderly presentation of the material and the occurrence of 'doublets'.

The appearance of disorder is obvious to any reader. Items appear to be introduced casually, following no systematic plan, sometimes intruding between chapters which are related to each other, sometimes in a bewildering succession of apparently disconnected individual points. Closer examination has led to a fairly widespread recognition that the first twenty-two chapters are associated with the broad theme of purchasing, managing, and developing a farm, and that the next thirty or so are based upon a calendar of farm operations beginning with the vintage and extending through to the tasks of the following summer. Yet even within these broad themes there is a general impression of interruptions and digressions and of very loose construction. In the remaining two-thirds of the book, although two or three or even more chapters in succession may be loosely connected around a single topic and in a few cases a more extended sequence can be distinguished, as in the case of the cooking recipes, the over-all impression is almost universally agreed to be that there is a lack of system, a largely haphazard arrangement, and no unifying theme. Even the person addressed is not always the same. Usually it is the owner, the *dominus*, but in at least one section and possibly in others the *vilicus*, the slave who

---

[25] Colum. *De re rust.* 1. 1. 12; cf. Pliny, *Nat. hist.* 14. 47.

manages the farm, is addressed in the second person.[26] In many chapters instructions are given in an 'impersonal' second person form for tasks which the owner is most unlikely to carry out in person; and although the imperatives which predominate throughout the book are most often in the second person, quite frequently there is a change into the third.

This sense of disorder is heightened by the occurrence within this short work of a number of 'doublets', that is to say items, in some cases whole chapters, which occur twice, usually with very little variation in content or even in wording. Not all repetitions are to be regarded as doublets or in need of special explanation; and sometimes the reckoning has perhaps been on the generous side. In some cases only a few words or a single sentence are repeated, and quite a number of doublets are merely another aspect of the relatively limited amount of over-all planning in the book. These are items which occur in two different contexts to both of which they are equally relevant and appropriate, and it is arguable that such repetitions could have been eliminated only if the organization of the material had been planned in advance with meticulous care and attention to detail, and perhaps even then only with the aid of a number of cross-references. Nevertheless several striking and apparently unnecessary doublets remain.[27] Thus instructions for the propagation of trees by layering are given first in chapters 51 and 52 and again, with only minor variations, in 133. Recommendations about the lengths of various ropes, reins, and straps given in 63 are repeated with slight differences in 135. 4, in the midst of other recommendations of the same kind. Chapters 91 and 129 are virtually identical in content and closely related (though not identical) in wording, and the relationship between 92 and 128, though not quite so close, is similar. Chapter 115 gives instructions for the preparation of a laxative wine differing only slightly from those just given in 114, without any reference back or mention that an alternative is being set out; and another prescription is found twice, with almost identical vocabulary and differing only in grammatical structure, first in 156. 5 and then in 157. 9, both of these unusually long chapters being concerned with the uses of cabbage.

---

[26] *De agr.* 143; cf. 5. 6 ff., where it is not clear whether the *vilicus* or the *dominus* is addressed, though the latter is perhaps more probable. Elsewhere many of the second-person imperatives would have been directed most appropriately to the *vilicus*, but they may have been thought of rather as 'impersonal' directions.

[27] See esp. Mazzarino, *Introduzione*, pp. 69 ff. Doublets are examined in great detail by Hörle, *Catos Hausbücher*, esp. pp. 5 and 127 ff. Thielscher, *Belehrung*, in his commentary sets out many of the passages concerned in a form which greatly facilitates comparison.

Although these features have been exciting discussion for more than a century, it has been observed with some plausibility that the numerous explanations which have been offered, despite their variations in detail, fall into two principal categories: (*i*) that Cato's original text has been distorted by subsequent revisions and interpolations; (*ii*) that the text is largely as Cato left it (except that at some stage the spelling was 'modernized') and that its disorderliness reflects the manner in which it was compiled and published.[28] However, these two approaches to the problem are not necessarily mutually exclusive, nor indeed have they always been treated as such. Moreover the second of these categories perhaps imposes a misleading unity on what are really several separate categories of argument. It would be more accurate to say that there have been four main types of explanation which, as well as varying in detail within themselves, have been brought together in a variety of combinations.[29]

(*i*) It has been argued that the *De agricultura* was substantially revised and interpolated after Cato's death, though probably before the time of the elder Pliny, who seems to have known the work in its present form.[30] One suggestion is that at a particular time, perhaps in the Augustan period, the text was subjected to a wholesale and incompetent revision which included the insertion of much material from some other work. The form of revision more frequently postulated is that because it was a practical handbook in constant use its users were inclined to add notes and

[28] See esp. Schanz–Hosius, *Gesch. der röm. Literatur* i⁴. 184 ff.; Helm, *RE*, s.v. *Porcius*, no. 9, cols. 152 ff.; Mazzarino, *Introduzione*, *passim*; White, 'Roman Agricultural Writers', in Temporini, *Aufstieg und Niedergang* i. 4, pp. 439 ff., esp. 447 ff.

[29] e.g. Mazzarino, *Introduzione*, esp. p. 57, combines three of the approaches set out below: that Cato was adapting material in *commentarii* to a literary form, that the task was incomplete at his death, and that when this unfinished work passed into circulation it was modified by annotations.

[30] So, rightly, Helm, *RE*, s.v. *Porcius*, no. 9, col. 152, citing esp. Pliny, *Nat. hist.* 19. 147. In 15. 44 and 46 Pliny states that Cato did not discuss plum-trees. On the basis of this Mazzarino, *Introduzione*, pp. 69 ff., argued that Pliny's copy of Cato's book did not include the list given in *De agr.* 133, which does mention the plum, but only the version in 8. 2, which is similar but without the plum; from which he infers that only the version of layering given in 51–2 is original, the version of layering in 133 being a gloss unknown to Pliny. He does not however account for Pliny, *Nat. hist.* 17. 96, which seems fatal to the argument, since it clearly quotes Cato's instructions on layering from the version in 133, including the reference to plums: cf. Münzer, *Beiträge zur Quellenkritik*, pp. 14 f. (though Münzer's principal argument is that much of Pliny's Catonian material is at second hand). Furthermore comparison of the sequence of ideas in 50–2 and 131–3 suggests a different explanation and that both sections are original: see Appendix 10. Aside from this question *Nat. hist.* 18. 34 seems to be the only one of the many unequivocally agricultural passages attributed by Pliny to Cato which does not correspond reasonably well to a passage in the *De agricultura*. Among a great number of quotations this is such a striking exception that the correctness of the attribution must be suspect.

glosses which sometimes were additional material, sometimes slightly modified versions of Cato's instructions, and that in due course these became incorporated in the text. A practical handbook, it is thought, would have been particularly liable to that kind of interpolation, though it perhaps occurred less in the earlier, more coherent sections, where the author's personality had imposed itself more strongly.

(*ii*) It is likely that Cato obtained at least some of his material for the *De agricultura* from 'notebooks' or *commentarii* in which useful practical information had been collected, such as a 'calendar' of farm operations, a number of cooking recipes, and various other grouped or miscellaneous notes. (Again there has been much variation in modern assessments, ranging from a simple recognition of such underlying documents as the calendar and some inventories through to a highly complex theory which seeks to identify the basic documents and the manner of their synthesis in considerable detail.[31]) It has therefore been suggested that the disorder springs partly from the unsystematic character of such notebooks, partly from a failure to integrate properly material drawn from a number of such sources. The origin of the doublets might have been that the same particulars had been recorded in more than one notebook.

(*iii*) A further suggestion is that the process of composition, especially perhaps of the later part of the book, was spread over a long period. Cato simply went on adding individual chapters or groups of chapters from time to time, when appropriate items happened to come to his attention. Hence the arrangement was haphazard, lacking theme and structure. Some information was put in twice, either by accident or because Cato did not bother to delete the earlier version when he put in a modified version. The sporadic nature of the process, perhaps spread over many years (as many as forty have been suggested), resulted in some loss of the sense of relevance and purpose, so that among the miscellaneous items added could be such items as the cookery recipes.

(*iv*) Lastly, it has been held that the book was unfinished at Cato's death. Consequently he had not completed the work of revising and rearranging a rough draft which in places may have consisted of little more than a collection of notes. Subsequently by allowing copies of the draft to be made someone in effect published it more or less in the rough unfinished state in which Cato had left it. Unfulfilled intentions might also account for the rather tenuous relationship between the Preface and the body of the work. (A variant on this, that Cato compiled the work in a rough and ready way because he did not envisage it being published, is incompatible

---

[31] Hörle, *Catos Hausbücher*, §§ I and II.

both with the existence of the Preface and with the content of the earlier chapters.[32])

These various hypotheses certainly contain some valid points. In particular it cannot reasonably be doubted that Cato drew a great deal of material from private notes and documents which were kept for practical purposes. Indeed it is highly probable that the specific recommendations given in respect of farms of different types and sizes—a suburban garden, a vineyard, and at least two farms devoted to olive-production—are based on the inventories and other particulars of actual farms belonging to Cato. The material drawn from such sources includes the inventories of farm equipment, the sample contracts, the religious formulas, the instructions on cypress trees and on brooms attributed to particular persons, and many other detailed instructions.[33] Presumably some of the sequences of closely related items, such as the cooking recipes, were obtained in this way rather than from Cato's memory, but the process was by no means wholly mechanical, even in the later sections. In the middle of chapter 157, which is certainly based on some special source, Cato's personal control of the material is revealed by the phrase 'if you use cabbage as I advise'; and the impress of his personality is particularly evident in chapters 54, 61, and 142–3, as well as in many of the earlier chapters. Similarly the possibility of intrusive glosses in a work of this kind is certainly to be taken seriously. It is, for example, the most plausible explanation for the bare statement in chapter 124 that 'dogs should be shut away during the day so that they may be keener and more watchful at night', which occurs totally unexpectedly in the middle of a sequence of chapters devoted to wine-based medicinal prescriptions. Nevertheless it is not so easy to envisage this kind of interpolation on such a scale that it was a major factor in bringing about the seeming disorder of the whole work.

Indeed, when the effort is made to envisage in detail what is actually supposed to have happened, physically, to Cato's text it may be doubted whether any of the four kinds of hypothesis outlined above is a satisfactory explanation or can account for more than a few details. A revision so incompetent that it distorted and disrupted the whole sequence and coherence of Cato's work is itself something which would require a special explanation, especially when it is supposed to have happened not at the hands of an uncomprehending medieval scribe but in the age of

---

[32] Hauler, *Zu Catos Schrift*, p. 6.

[33] Thielscher, *Belehrung*, pp. 5 ff., though he applies this type of interpretation too extensively, inferring from the text much more than is justified in the way of biographical detail concerning Cato.

Caesar or Augustus; yet a less dramatic revision which had not done this would not afford an explanation of the peculiarities of the *De agricultura*. Again, while it is easy to admit the possibility that the work is unfinished in the sense that Cato might have intended to add more material at the end, it is much less easy to envisage what kind of process of compilation and drafting would, in ancient conditions, have left the incomplete work awaiting major rearrangement and revision, yet in a sufficiently coherent form, presumably in one manuscript, for it to have been possible for it to pass into circulation. Yet if Cato was not contemplating such drastic revision a failure to finish would not itself be the explanation of the peculiarities; and if Cato left simply a collection of drafts and notes, presumably on waxed tablets, the decision to copy them into a single manuscript for publication as a book is also in need of special explanation. There is more to be said for the view that the later parts of the work were compiled without reference to any clear-cut plan or structure, in a manner which might be better described as accumulation than as composition. Whether such a process took place sporadically over a substantial period of time is more doubtful. At any rate, a sense of continuity is apparent in chapter 142, where there is an unmistakable reference back to the instructions to the *vilicus* set out in chapter 5. Moreover it is necessary to account also for the fact that the progression of thought is frequently erratic and surprising even in the earlier sections of the book, where a broad plan is observable. For these sections the explanation of sporadic accumulation is neither helpful nor probable.

Nevertheless, the view of the *De agricultura* as characterized by a lack of systematic planning is helpful in two respects. Up to a point it is valid in itself, and it points to a fifth type of explanation, one which is sometimes briefly stated or implied but which is deserving of fuller consideration, namely that the origin of the peculiarities is to be sought not so much in the mechanics of compilation or transmission as in Cato's own attitudes and preconceptions. It has been recognized, for example, that chapter 34 reveals a tolerance of digressions which would be thought inept in a modern writer, for with the words 'I return to the matter of planting' Cato resumes a topic from which he had strayed several chapters earlier and at the same time shows that the digression was his own and not a subsequent interpolation.[34] In fact the emphasis on disorder and fragmentation in the *De agricultura* has perhaps been slightly misplaced. Although there

---

[34] Leo, *Gesch. der röm. Literatur* i. 272; cf. Helm, *RE*, s.v. *Porcius*, no. 9, col. 152; Brehaut, *Cato the Censor. On Farming*, p. xix; Marmorale, *Cato Maior*², p. 164, cf. p. 184, who regards lack of planning as the simple and complete explanation.

is no strong over-all structure or rigid discipline of relevance, neither the earlier nor even the later sections are quite as fragmented as has often been supposed. A distinction must be drawn between disciplined thought and continuity of thought. Definite—though undisciplined—sequences of thought can be found more extensively and with fewer sharp breaks than has usually been assumed. Frequently, however, the sequential element does not take the form of a coherent exposition or development of a central theme. It will be as well to examine this in more detail before returning to the question of Cato's attitude in a more general sense.

In some cases the continuity of thought is simply a matter of a series of individual points which are related to each other, at times only loosely, by a particular concept or a particular farm product. In others it takes the form of a type of progression which paradoxically both establishes and tends to obscure the element of continuity: there is a tendency when a particular topic is being discussed to pick up something which has been mentioned in a subordinate or indirect manner and to make a comment directly upon this without any further direct relevance to the topic from which it sprang. In such cases there is sometimes a speedy return to the initial topic, as in chapter 3. There, in logical sequence to comments on the need for adequate buildings, there is mention of the need for good presses 'so that the work can be done well', which inspires a digression about the importance of doing the pressing as quickly as possible and the reasons why gatherers and press-operators are tempted to delay; but after a few short sentences Cato returns to the details of the pressing-equipment required.[35] The digression mentioned above which ends with the 'I return to planting' of chapter 34 is similar in kind but on a larger scale. In some other cases an earlier topic is picked up in a way which suggests not so much a resumption after a digression as the addition of an afterthought.[36]

As for groups of passages which centre on a particular theme, some are obvious enough, such as the inventories, the cookery recipes, the religious formulas, and the sample contracts. Others however are set out in such a way that the common element is not presented to the reader as a prominent feature. Thus chapters 91–101 at first sight seem to consist of a number of miscellaneous recipes and prescriptions for widely differing purposes,

---

[35] Some other examples: *De agr.* 6. 3–4, on the planting of reeds; 7–8, on fruits; 15–18, digressing from building to lime-burning and thence to woodcutting, then back to building. Note also how reference to a general activity several times provokes a digression into detailed instructions: 39 (mending pots); 40 (suitable sites for trees leads to instructions for grafting); and other instances through to 49.

[36] e.g. 128–30, uses of *amurca*, picking up from 103. For some examples in a more complicated passage see Appendix 10 on 131–50.

each introduced by reference to its purpose: e.g. 'To make a threshing-floor . . . If an olive tree is sterile . . . To keep caterpillars off vines . . . To keep scab from sheep . . . If you intend to store oil in a new jar . . .' On closer examination however all these items are found to involve the use of *amurca*, olive-lees, so that the whole group could have been entitled 'On the uses of *amurca*'. Several similar groups can be identified. Although there are some breaks in continuity where Cato changes to a completely different topic, these breaks are not as frequent as some modern accounts might suggest. In particular chapters 104 to 127, excepting only the intrusive injunction about dogs in 124, are linked together by the concept of the uses and applications of various other products of the farm; and it is likely that this idea really governs the whole block from 91 to 130, opening with uses of *amurca* and coming back to this in the last three chapters with supplementary material. Apart from the dogs in 124, only chapter 102 (a prescription for treating oxen and other animals bitten by snakes) seems to fit awkwardly into such a sequence; and for that a reasonable explanation can be conjectured if these lists were at least in part specially compiled by Cato himself. That this was so is indeed probable, for it would be surprising if in the normal course of running a farm there had been occasion to assemble a miscellany of very varied uses of, for example, *amurca*, and it seems more likely that these were brought together from other notes arranged on a different basis.[37]

The fundamental explanation for the lack of system and the lack of disciplined thought in the *De agricultura* is to be found precisely in Cato's role as the virtual founder of Latin prose literature, a role which is invariably recognized but the implications of which are easily overlooked. It is all too easy to forget how different was Cato's background and experience in this field from that of modern scholars and writers, almost all of whom have from childhood been trained and disciplined in techniques of composition; whose education and literary environment alike have constantly instilled ideals of relevance, consistency, clear and logical exposition, and avoidance of repetition; who take it for granted that the satisfactory presentation of a complicated and technical topic requires a high degree of organization and preliminary planning, not to mention the repeated revision of drafts, and who have had plenty of opportunity to observe the consequences of an insufficiency of such organization and planning. Cato had received no such training, did not live in an environment which constantly inculcated such ideals and techniques of composition, and had had little previous experience of constructing books and

[37] See p. 201 and Appendix 10.

equally little opportunity to benefit from the experience of others. Experience and skill in the composition of speeches he certainly did have, but that is a different kind of composition, presenting different problems which are of limited relevance to the *De agricultura*. A speech was not only a relatively short composition; the very circumstances which called it into being gave it a strong inherent unity and direction, in effect imposed a kind of plan and coherence—just as chronological sequence has often provided a basic framework for historical writings. Even so Gellius' comments suggest that the Rhodian speech, however forceful and vigorous, was by no means notable for disciplined thought or for clear, logical, and well-organized exposition of the arguments.[38] The Preface to the *De agricultura* does display a care and coherence in composition which may well be related to Cato's experience with speeches; but the Preface is brief and it could be argued that even within this short passage the arrangement of material is in one respect determined less by logic than by the kind of progression of ideas which was discussed above.[39] Similarly experience gained from writing the other works which may have been earlier than the *De agricultura* would have been with much simpler material. In particular the *Ad filium* was probably only a miscellany of precepts, and it is easy to imagine the *Carmen de moribus* as rather similar, loosely assembled about the theme indicated by its title. The composition of an extended didactic work devoted to a single topic and containing a mass of inter-related practical information was a much more demanding task.

It may be objected that Cato had had the literary experience of reading Greek works, often works of high quality; but this too is of doubtful relevance. In the first place his acquaintance with Greek literature by no means necessarily implies that he read it with serious attention to techniques of composition and organization. In the second place Cato is most likely to have come across works of quality, hence unlikely to have been confronted with instructive examples of glaring faults which sprang from inadequate planning and discipline. Nor is it by any means certain that he even had the opportunity to examine work similar to his own; for there is

[38] pp. 137 ff. and 151 f.

[39] Cato begins by contrasting trade and usury unfavourably with agriculture as sources of income. After indicating briefly the disadvantages of the two former he begins to expand his points by emphasizing the hostility of the *maiores* to usury. Mention of the *maiores*, however, leads him into a report of their high opinion of farming, after which he returns to the disadvantages of trade, and finally takes up again the merits of farming. Evidently the mention of the *maiores* led him to introduce at once an idea which from the point of view of orderly presentation would have been better placed after the account of the disadvantages of trade; for as it is it makes the sequence of ideas in the Preface more awkward and complicated to follow. Cf. Janson, *Latin Prose Prefaces*, p. 84.

doubt as to whether there were available Greek predecessors for the type of practical agricultural handbook he was attempting to write.[40] In any event, despite the few chapters which bear traces of being derived, directly or indirectly, from Greek sources, there are few clear signs of Greek influence in the work, and even if the idea of writing it was directly inspired by a Greek predecessor, its peculiarities make it almost impossible to believe that it was closely modelled upon any earlier work.

The *De agricultura* was probably not the first of Cato's writings. Although most of his books cannot be dated with confidence it is likely that he had already written others, such as the *Ad filium* and perhaps the *Carmen de moribus*, both of which were strongly didactic in tone (and much easier to compose). Probably encouraged by these experiments and not a little pleased with his achievements, it then occurred to him, in the same didactic spirit, to make available in writing more of his own expertise, only this time in the form not of precepts addressed to his son but of a work on a particular topic for a wider public: he would write a practical instructional book on agriculture, drawing upon his own personal knowledge and *commentarii* relating to his own properties. He commenced composition with only a sketchy and rudimentary scheme in mind, not thought out either in particular detail or at sufficient length to carry him more than a limited way through the book. He simply intended to give advice on the selection, general management, and equipment of a farm, and, since he believed it important for the owner to have sufficient knowledge to carry out frequent detailed inspections, he would supply a great deal of specific information about the tasks of the farm; probably the 'calendar' of operations through the year was envisaged as part of the initial plan. It is improbable that it ever occurred to him to think out with any precision who were his potential readers, or to put himself imaginatively in their place in order to assess what would be useful or appropriate to them. No attempt was made to relate the carefully composed Preface closely to the substance of the work—indeed the relationship is so loose that the Preface neither states nor implies the purpose of the book, while its references to

[40] On Hellenistic agricultural writings see Susemihl, *Gesch. der griech. Lit. in der Alexandriner-Zeit* i. 829 ff.; cf. Schmid–Stählin, *Gesch. der griech. Lit.* ii. i[6], pp. 289 ff.; White, *Roman Farming*, pp. 15 f. Many Greek authors are named by Varro, *De re rust.* 1. 1. 7 ff. and Columella, *De re rust.* 1. 1. 7. It is clear that some of these works were scientific and theoretical rather than practical (the majority of the authors named by Varro are termed philosophers), and that others were specialized monographs, e.g. on bee-keeping or viticulture; but about many nothing is known, though Susemihl conjectures that there was a preponderance of specialized monographs. No practical handbook comparable to Cato's is known, though it would be rash to insist that none existed. The nearest is perhaps Xenophon's *Oeconomicus*, but that differs in many major respects.

coloni and soldiers have no relationship at all to the type of farming actually described. Contrasting the merits of agriculture as a source of income with the hazards of trade and the disrepute of usury, Cato mentions a traditional attitude that to be 'a good farmer and a good *colonus*' was the height of excellence, then states the advantages of agriculture to be that 'from farmers come both the bravest men and the most energetic soldiers, the income is especially respectable and secure and the least likely to provoke resentment, and those who are engaged in that occupation are least inclined to contemplate wrongdoing.' The underlying idea is that a book on agriculture is a worthy project because agriculture itself has such merits; but this is conceived in such general terms, drawing no distinction between different types of farming or of farmer, that it was clearly not thought out with close attention either to the purpose or to the substance of the book itself.[41] In short, it is a brief self-contained essay, and it probably never occurred to Cato to take account of the specific material which was to follow, about which his ideas at this stage were in any case still for the most part rather general and vague. Then, untroubled by powerful preconceptions about the desirability of system, discipline, and strict relevance, he pressed ahead with topics largely as they came to mind, the sequence determined in part by a simple association of ideas and in the earlier sections loosely controlled by his sketchy plan.

Particularly in the later sections of the book much of the material gleaned from *commentarii*, especially the recipes and prescriptions, was reproduced more or less as it stood, without rephrasing to bring out its relationship to the new context, and in some cases the same item was found to be appropriate in more than one place. Occasionally an item was introduced into an irrelevant context because it was copied along with an adjacent item which was relevant and with which it was linked in a *commentarius* (this is almost certainly the explanation of the doublet in

---

[41] Janson, *Latin Prose Prefaces*, pp. 84 ff., distinguishes two lines of argument interwoven in the Preface: a moral argument, which is not relevant to the book, and economic arguments with which the book fits well. It is certainly the case that there is a loose, rather general relationship in so far as Cato alludes in the Preface to an income from farming of such a kind that it could be compared with an income from trade or usury; for that is the type of farming with which the book is concerned. Nevertheless by presenting Cato's treatment in terms of the interweaving of two distinct lines of argument and by overestimating the element of economic argument Janson creates the impression of a closer and more positive relationship than actually exists. Only in one point—that an income from agriculture is more secure than one from trade—can the argument be termed economic; and in the sentence just quoted in the text that point is so closely joined to 'moral' arguments that even in this respect it seems less a case of interweaving different kinds of arguments than of failing to draw a distinction. See also pp. 253 ff.

chapter 133, and probably of the ill-fitting chapter 102).[42] Such features point to a lack of concern for or of interest in careful choice of words to create a sense of unity; they may also reflect a brisk and rather impatient manner of work, and possibly even that Cato did not actually copy out the passages with his own hand but instructed a secretary to do it.[43] Moreover when Cato came across additional information appropriate to some theme which he had dealt with previously his lack of a strong concern about relevance allowed him to insert such material at the point he had now reached in his manuscript, without deleting what had intervened or attempting an insertion into the earlier section. Probably he composed a continuous text in a single manuscript, so that such an insertion would have been difficult; but it is also probable that it never occurred to him that it would be desirable to attempt it.

The heavy reliance on *commentarii* and personal knowledge had another consequence. It both reflected and powerfully reinforced the markedly particularist tendencies in Cato's attitudes, his frequent failure to distinguish details which were applicable to his own situation from information which had general validity and utility. Thus recommendations as to places at which to purchase materials, statements of prices, and even calculations of cost linked with the number of days required for transportation are expressed in terms which could not have been applicable generally.[44] Similarly particular details of Cato's own properties are transformed into general recommendations, and he really deals only with those forms of agriculture which happened to concern him at the time—even though it is certain that he did have experience of other forms, at least at some stage in his career.[45] Hence too—almost certainly—the extraordinary piece of

[42] On these chapters and also on 91–2 and 128–9 see Appendix 10.

[43] Such a procedure would fit well with the form in which many of the items are given. Cato certainly had secretaries (cf. Plut. *Cato Mai.* 24. 3) and the passage relating to the composition of the speech *De sumptu suo* (ORF[3], fr. 173; see pp. 135 f.) suggests that he may not so much have read his *commentarii* as had them read to him; for the idea of a scribe copying a passage, note in the same fragment the words *noli, noli scribere, inquam, istud*. It is a hypothesis to be approached with caution and the general interpretation set out in this chapter is not dependent upon it; for Cato's personal touch is apparent at various points even in the later parts of the *De agricultura*. Nevertheless the fragment from the *De sumptu suo* does suggest that Cato sometimes composed by dictation. Possibly Cato's own explicit statement that the 'history in big letters' was written with his own hand (Plut. *Cato Mai.* 20. 7) also indicates that this was out of the ordinary and that he often dictated. However it is also possible that the significance of this lies rather in the emphasis on Cato's personal intervention as opposed to the use of slave tutors, which is certainly the point being made a few lines before.

[44] Esp. *De agr.* 21. 5; 22. 3 f.; 135; 136. Brehaut, *Cato the Censor. On Farming*, pp. xiv f., rightly observes that despite these particularistic items Cato's intention was undoubtedly to write a book of general guidance with much wider reference.

[45] The Sabine inheritance. Note also the enthusiasm for pasturing reported in Cic. *De*

advice that an owner should commence building on his farm only from the age of thirty-six.[46]

The application of such attitudes and such methods to a mass of detailed material, not infrequently interrelated and interdependent, inevitably resulted in a degree of unevenness and disorder and an erratic progression of ideas which can only be bewildering to readers habituated to orderliness and relevance and to whom these are, quite properly, major criteria in the assessment of instructional works. The peculiarities of the *De agricultura* are the consequence of major shortcomings in method and concept; but those shortcomings must be seen and indeed can be satisfactorily understood only in the context of Cato's pioneering role in the development of Roman prose writing. They reflect not carelessness or a lack of imagination but the novelty of the situation, the lack of relevant training and experience, in short the absence of an established literary culture such as Cato himself was helping to initiate. In such a context it was a considerable imaginative achievement to have conceived of such a work, all the more so if there were no Greek models for this particular type of handbook; and for all the peculiarities and omissions it was probably also a considerable practical achievement to assemble this mass of detailed material.

3. *Other writings in relation to* De agricultura

Since the *De agricultura* is the only one of Cato's works to have survived, the scope for detailed comparison and general assessment of his writings is severely limited. The meagre fragments of the lost works offer little or no opportunity to pursue many of the questions which over the years have been so intensively studied in the *De agricultura*. The *Origines*, which is more extensively attested than the others in both *testimonia* and fragments, affords slightly greater opportunity; but since it is clearly distinctive in a number of respects and poses several problems of its own, it will be reserved for the next chapter. There it will be possible to consider how far it does or does not conform with such general conclusions as may be reached regarding Cato's other writings; for, in spite of all the limitations, certain points do seem to emerge.

---

off. 2. 89 = Jordan, p. 108, *Dicta mem.* 63, with other references. Thielscher, *Belehrung*, p. 272, wrongly rejects the authenticity of this on the ground of its similarity in form to *De agr.* 16. 1.

[46] *De agr.* 3. 1. So Thielscher, *Belehrung*, pp. 9 f. and 187, and others. Leeman, 'Cato, De Agricultura 3, 1', *Helikon*, 5 (1965), 534 ff., suggests that it may have reference to an old Greek or Etruscan belief that life is to be divided into seven-year periods. Brehaut, op. cit., p. 8, note ad loc., seeks a rational explanation in the suggestion that by that age most Romans would be approaching the end of their liability for military service.

Perhaps the most obvious characteristic is that so far as can be seen all the works which came into circulation, with the probable exception of the collection of witticisms, were essentially didactic. Admittedly this is only an assumption in the cases of the *Carmen de moribus* and the book on law, but it is an assumption which is difficult to avoid. Closely allied to the didactic aspect is the markedly practical, almost utilitarian emphasis. That was evidently the case even with the *Carmen de moribus* which, as was noted earlier, seems to have been concerned with *mores* not in a theoretical sense but in the practical terms of actual behaviour. Again, only the collection of witticisms was probably an exception.

If in some respects attention focuses naturally on characteristics which Cato's writings share in common, from other points of view these writings fall readily into distinguishable groups. One such group consists of the three works devoted respectively to agriculture, warfare, and law—each concerned with a single topic, each written with the intention of publication, and each envisaged as a kind of practical instructional handbook. Again it must be admitted that the latter two points are only assumptions —though assumptions which can scarcely be avoided—in respect of the book on law, about which it is possible to say nothing further. The *De re militari* however does offer some interesting points of comparison. As with the *De agricultura* its subject-matter was directly related to Cato's personal experience. Indeed the Preface contained a clear allusion to the relevance of that experience: 'I know that if what has been written is made public there will be many who will bring pettifogging criticisms, but for the most part they are people quite devoid of true distinction. I have allowed their pronouncements to flow past me.'[47] Such a personal declaration, condemning in advance any who might venture to disagree, is certainly different from anything in the *De agricultura*. (It is tempting to see it as a reaction to earlier criticism, hence as evidence that the *De re militari* was a relatively late work, probably later than the *De agricultura*.) On the other hand two other fragments strongly suggest that the Preface, similarly to that of the *De agricultura* but perhaps in a manner more directly related to the book itself, argued the importance of the topic;[48] and marked stylistic effects in all three fragments indicate that in this Preface too some effort was devoted to creating an impressive and high-sounding effect. In general the stylistic characteristics are such as are to be expected: sentences short and simple, with instances of asyndeton and antithesis—one of the latter

---

[47] Jordan, p. 80, *De re militari* fr. 1 = Pliny, *Nat. hist. praef.* 30. In the remainder of this chapter the fragments of this work will be indicated by the number only.

[48] Frs. 2 and 3.

particularly striking—two neologisms,[49] an epigrammatic touch, and a bold, perhaps even grandiloquent, use of the word *orationes* to indicate the pronouncements of possible critics. Most of these occur in the three fragments which are probably from the Preface. Of the remaining fragments three use the second person, which again suggests an approach similar to that of the *De agricultura*.[50] Also, though most of the fragments are such short extracts that they must be judged with caution, it does look as if the treatment was in general plain and straightforward; and one fragment heavily links together five nouns by using *aut* four times in succession.[51] It is perhaps significant that the one instance of *atque* is in a fragment which appears to be part of a narrative, where Cato may have thought it appropriate to seek a more elevated or dramatic effect.[52]

Like the *De agricultura* the *De re militari* was the first Latin book of its kind; but whereas in the case of the former there is uncertainty about the earlier existence of Greek handbooks of comparable type, there is no doubt that there were a considerable number of practical military treatises and manuals, mostly written in the Hellenistic period.[53] In view of Cato's particular interests, general curiosity, and at least moderate familiarity with Greek writings, it is scarcely conceivable that he did not know of at least some of these manuals; and it would therefore be unreasonable to suppose that there was no connection between these and his decision to write his own military book, at least to the extent of prompting the general idea of doing so. It is much less likely, however, that he followed any of them closely as a model. Much of the detail in them would have been irrelevant to Roman military practices, and both the fragments and the use made subsequently of Cato's work indicate that it dealt very specifically with Roman methods and practices. Cato, who in the *De agricultura* is so unconcerned about structure, is scarcely likely to have attempted to fit these Roman details into a pattern taken over from a Greek manual. It is impossible to tell, however, to what extent the *De re militari* exhibited the same attitudes as the *De agricultura* towards matters of composition, coherence, relevance, and structure, though the very nature of the military material may be expected to have encouraged a rather firmer structure.

---

[49] Fr. 1, *vitilitigent*; fr. 14, *disciplinosus*; said to be neologisms by Pliny, *Nat. hist. praef.* 32 and Gell. 4. 9. 12 respectively, evidently correctly in both cases. Cf. Till–Meo, *La lingua di Catone*, pp. 81, 90, 128 f.

[50] Frs. 9, 11, and 13.

[51] Fr. 11.

[52] Fr. 6: 'inde partem equitatus atque ferentarios praedatum misit.'

[53] Schmid–Stählin, *Gesch. der Griech. Literatur* ii. 1⁶, pp. 286 ff.; Kromayer–Veith, *Heerwesen und Kriegführung*, p. 13.

Other writings contrast with the three practical handbooks in various ways. The *Ad filium* and perhaps the collection of witticisms are distinctive in probably not having been written with a view to publication, and neither they nor the *Carmen de moribus* were concerned with the exposition of a single topic. The *Ad filium* was evidently a collection of precepts and exhortations covering a wide range of subjects, while a book about *mores* was scarcely dealing with a single topic in the same sense as a book of practical instruction on agriculture or warfare. In fact the *Carmen* as well as the *Ad filium* may well have been predominantly 'preceptual' in character, and in both cases, though there was no doubt a tendency for topics to occur in groups roughly determined by topic, the nature of the subject-matter probably meant that there was even less constraint to think about structure. The nature of the material explains also why striking stylistic features are more in evidence in the fragments of these works, though the features themselves are much the same as in other writings: a marked epigrammatic quality, as is only to be expected, together with brevity and succinctness, asyndeton and assonance, antitheses and paradox.[54]

4. *The development of Cato's literary activity*

There remains the most basic of the questions about Cato's writings: why did he write them? Clearly no single comprehensive answer could completely and sufficiently explain such a diversity of works. It is obvious that in an important sense the considerations which lay behind a book of miscellaneous guidance for Cato's son differed from those behind a book on agriculture intended for general circulation, and similarly in the case of each individual book. The *De agricultura* in particular, no doubt partly because it alone survives, has from time to time been seen (implausibly) as a kind of propaganda tract, usually in the sense of seeking to encourage the spread of the type of agriculture Cato describes.[55] Yet it is not sufficient to fragment the question by considering the motivation for each book separately and in isolation; there is a more general question to be answered. For Cato was an innovator, not merely in the sense of being the first Roman to write books about these particular topics but in the much more

[54] Jordan, pp. 82 f., *Carmen* frs. 1–3 = Gell. 11. 2. 1 ff.; see further p. 186 n. 12. Jordan, pp. 77–80, assigns sixteen fragments to the *Ad filium*, though five (10, 11, 13, 15, 16) have no indication that they actually belong.

[55] For the question of social and economic attitudes in the *De Agricultura* see Ch. 11. Della Corte, *Catone censore*[2], pp. 99 ff., takes the initial purpose to have been political, an attempt by Cato to restore his 'peasant image' after he had been prosecuted *de sumptu suo*.

fundamental sense of being the first to write prose books in Latin about any topic at all. An explanation is required not simply for his choice of topics but for the fact that he wrote at all.

Answers to this question have been very largely along the lines that he was attempting to create a Latin prose literature as a response to the Romans' rapidly growing awareness of Greek literature—though within this general concept it is possible to discern two rather different emphases, as well as numerous variations in detail.[56] Usually stress is laid on Cato's supposed hostility to Greek culture, or at least to certain aspects of it. Alarmed at the dangers with which he judged Rome to be threatened, yet conscious of the power of Greek literature to fascinate, not only on account of its brilliance and intellectual content but because an extensive literature was in itself an exotic novelty in Rome, he deliberately set out to create a Latin literature as an alternative. Between such an interpretation and the apparent theme of the *Carmen de moribus* it is possible to envisage a positive relationship, thus adding to the coherence of the picture; but it is the *Ad filium* which has bulked largest in such discussions. Almost universally believed to have been a kind of 'encyclopedia', in the form of a set of books with each book dealing with a separate topic, this is usually supposed to have been an attempt to provide a specifically Roman version of Greek educational programmes. Sometimes, and particularly in more recent studies, the motive for attempting to provide such an alternative has been seen not so much in outright alarm at the influence of Hellenic culture, as in a rational appraisal that certain features of Greek educational programmes were unsuited to Roman requirements and also that these programmes lacked a number of topics needed by Romans. That approach shades off into the other main category of interpretation, that Cato was not so much anxious to combat Greek literature as fired by a patriotic zeal that Rome be given a literature of its own: consciousness of cultural and literary inferiority was hurtful to the pride of the conquering Romans and was a deficiency which must be remedied. Others had already been at work in the field of verse—among them, Ennius, initially sponsored by Cato himself—and now Cato would attempt to create a prose literature.

In what follows it must be borne in mind that no account has yet been taken of the *Origines*, which has featured significantly in such assessments; but at least it is not easy to see that work, to which Cato was still making additions in the last year of his life, as having an initial or a primary role in the development of his literary activity. For the other works enough has been seen both about them and about Cato's attitudes to the Greeks for it

[56] See the bibliography at p. 158 n. 1; for the *Ad filium*, Appendix 8.

to be evident that the type of explanation outlined above is not satis-factory.[57] Cato's attitude to the Greeks and their culture, ambivalent though it was and in certain respects strongly prejudiced, was not such as would naturally have led him into attempting to create a substitute for Greek literature. It is misleading to take his hostile comments about Greek culture literally or in isolation from the other evidence which compels a different and more complex view; and it is far from clear that he was troubled by a sense of cultural inferiority, let alone afflicted with a sense of doom because he believed the fascinations of Hellenic literature threatened to hypnotize the Romans into a blind acceptance of all the worst along with the best in Greek life and culture. Profound though his dislike was of certain features of that culture, most of his writings had little or no relevance to those features. Indeed the topics about which he wrote are for the most part wholly unconvincing and implausible as the basis of a literature intended to rival that of the Greeks. So also are the unsystematic attitudes and methods displayed in the composition of the *De agricultura*, suggestive of a confident self-reliance that simply gave no thought to the Greeks, far more than of an anxious concern to produce a work that could be compared in merit. Neither does it seem likely that in these works Cato was closely following Greek models, either in detail or in structure. Above all the *Ad filium*, which for over a century has been a central feature of most discussions, has been incorrectly interpreted and was not a full-scale Latin version of a Greek educational programme. Instead it was probably simply a collection of precepts and exhortations for the guidance of Cato's son, and in the first instance was probably assembled for that purpose alone.[58]

The question 'Why did Cato write?' is deceptively simple. It appears to invite an explanation of a particular event, and thereby an answer which would almost certainly be too static, too monolithic, expressed in terms of an event rather than the growth of an idea. For it is improbable that Cato's authorship can be explained in terms of a single decision, a single moment, or even a single attitude or a single overriding purpose. It is better understood as emerging and developing, and doing so in response to his circumstances and his experience. There was a background to Cato's composition of prose works in Latin. Familiarity with the concept of books had been growing for a considerable time. Well before Cato wrote it had reached the point where some books originated in Rome and dealt with Roman subject-matter. Already the dramatists and poets, above all Ennius, had notable achievements to their credit, while Fabius Pictor and Cincius Alimentus with their histories in Greek had at least set the

---

[57] Ch. 8, *passim*, esp. pp. 178 ff.   [58] Appendix 8.

precedent for books to be written by Romans of high social standing. Furthermore the actual use of writing in Latin was of great antiquity and was certainly familiar for a wide variety of practical uses, including domestic records and communications. It is a reasonable guess that Cato's first prose books were not envisaged at all as books for a public but were intended for purely domestic, practical purposes. Possibly the 'history in big letters' written to aid the education of his elder son—itself an imaginative idea—was one of the earliest experiments and led him on to others. In due course the same basic idea of instructing his son through the medium of writing, linked with an awareness of his own talent for aphorism, produced the further development of a collection of precepts and exhortations. By its very nature, however, this was a vehicle which encouraged Cato to display his facility in the use of language, so that a work almost certainly written for the guidance of an individual could arouse sufficient interest for copies to be made and in due course for it to pass into circulation. Such experiments are likely to have stimulated not only pleasure in their success but an interest in further ventures; so increasing enthusiasm led Cato on to new and more elaborate ideas, including that of devoting a whole book to a single topic of instruction. It is indeed plausible that as he went on he was encouraged by a certain patriotic pride, for he can scarcely have been unconscious that what he was doing was novel in Rome and hitherto had been in the province of the Greeks; but the obvious relationship of his topics to his personal experience and interests suggests that his thoughts were not so much concerned with the literary background or with possible comparisons as centred on what he himself was doing as, so to speak, a self-contained activity.

If Cato's authorship did develop in some such manner as this, the question of motivation takes on a different aspect. No longer is it necessary to seek some powerful overriding purpose. That does not mean that the writing of the books was simply an end in itself, a pastime without purpose. Particular motives for individual works there must have been, perhaps especially for the *Carmen de moribus*; and linking almost all the works one with another is their common didactic character. Cato wrote his books for the purpose of instruction, probably thought automatically in those terms without seriously considering alternatives, and perhaps had a heightening sense of usefulness—and of self-importance—as he applied the concept to topic after topic. It is much less likely, however, that the purpose was carefully and precisely thought out on each occasion, or that his authorship was inspired in the first place by a burning desire to instruct the community.

If this explanation is broadly correct—and any explanation can be only a matter of interpretation and hypothesis—it may appear at first sight to somewhat diminish Cato's achievement. Unsystematic in method, deficient in discipline, relevance, and order, his initiative in Latin prose literature is no longer seen either as a sudden, dramatic step or as inspired by some great patriotic or social purpose. Furthermore, seen in the wider pattern of the development of Roman literature as a whole, the emergence of prose writings in Latin at about this time seems inevitable. Is it then little more than an accident that it was Cato who did what someone was bound to do anyway before long?

To present Cato's contribution in such subdued terms would un-questionably be misleading. What the historian, viewing in retrospect a whole historical movement, sees as an inevitable development may not have been so obvious and predictable in the contemporary context: fulfil-ment of the inevitable often requires an agent gifted with exceptional initiative and inventiveness. It is surely no accident that in this instance the agent was one of the most forceful, vigorous, and versatile personali-ties of the time. What was said before about the *De agricultura* may be said of Cato's writings in general: his innovation has to be viewed in the light of the absence of an established literary culture, with all that implies in terms of the lack of training in techniques of composition and in terms of an environment in which various concepts and standards were not yet familiar norms. In such a context Cato's contribution was a considerable imaginative achievement, no less so if it was a step-by-step development, extending and elaborating a modest initial idea, rather than a single momentary inspiration. Moreover the picture is not yet complete. The largest, the most elaborate, and probably the most sophisticated of Cato's writings, the *Origines*, has yet to be considered.

10

The *Origines*

THE *Origines* was a historical work in seven books, the first of which included an account of Aeneas and other stories about the origin of Rome, the last an episode which occurred as late as 149, the very year of Cato's death.[1] It was the first work of its kind to be written in Latin. The scale and subject-matter, distinctive among Cato's writings, raise a number of questions—about such matters as why Cato set himself to write such a work, its relationship both to his other writings and to Greek historical literature, whether it was a substantial literary achievement, and whether Cato made any special contribution in respect of historical method or insight. Such questions would probably have been by no means easy to answer even if the full text had survived. As it is the *Origines* is lost, though it is mentioned frequently by Roman and Greek writers, and well over 100 fragments have been preserved.[2] This dependence on ancient comments, which are often of an incidental nature, and upon the fragments, the majority of which are extremely brief, complicates the issues; for it poses a nexus of particular questions about composition, content, and

[1] Fragments collected by Peter, *HRR* i[2], 55 ff.; those of book 1 republished with commentary by Schröder, *M. Porcius Cato, Das erste Buch der Origines*. Useful surveys of the principal issues concerning the *Origines* and of the bibliography will be found in Schanz-Hosius, *Gesch. der röm. Literatur* i[4]. 186 ff., and Helm, *RE*, s.v. *Porcius*, no. 9, cols. 156 ff., and in three valuable recent discussions: Meister, 'Zu römischen Historikern', *Anzeiger öst. Akad. Wissens., Phil.-hist. Kl.* 101 (1964), 1 ff.; Timpe, 'Le "Origini" di Catone e la storiografia latina', *Atti e Mem. Accad. Patavina Sc. Lett.* 83 (1970–1), 5 ff.; and Cornell, 'The *Origines* of Cato and the non-Roman Historical Tradition about Ancient Italy', an unpublished doctoral thesis accepted by the University of London, 1972.

Other selected bibliography: Bormann, *M. Porcii Catonis Originum libri septem*; von Gutschmid, 'Catos Origines', *Kl. Schr.* v. 518 ff.; Leo, *Gesch. der röm. Literatur* i. 290 ff.; Peter, *HRR* i[2], pp. cxxvii ff.; Marmorale, *Cato Maior*[2], pp. 165 ff. and 224 ff.; Bömer, 'Thematik und Krise der röm. Geschichtsschreibung', *Historia*, 2 (1953), 193 ff.; De Sanctis, *Storia dei Romani* iv. 2. 1, pp. 60 ff.; Kienast, pp. 14 and 107 ff.; Leeman, *Orationis Ratio*, pp. 68 ff.; Badian, 'The Early Historians', in Dorey, *Latin Historians*, pp. 1 ff., esp. 7 ff.; Della Corte, *Catone censore*[2], pp. 78 ff. and 94 ff. Further items will be noted later in connection with particular topics.

[2] Peter, *HRR* i[2], has 125 fragments, but a number of these, though probably included correctly, are not attested as being from the *Origines*. However, he also lists another eighteen as 'uncertain', some of which are probably from this work.

structure, with which the broader questions of interpretation are necessarily linked.

By far the most important of the ancient statements about the *Origines* is the account given by Cornelius Nepos in the short biography of Cato which he wrote for his book 'Concerning Latin Historians'. After a brief eulogy of Cato's versatility and learning Nepos says:

> From his youth he composed speeches. When he was an old man he began to write history. Of that there are seven books. The first contains the deeds of the kings of the Roman people, the second and third the origin of each Italian state (*civitas*); on account of which he seems to have called them all *Origines*. In the fourth, however, is the First Punic War, in the fifth the Second. And all these matters are told in summary fashion (*capitulatim*); and he continued to follow the remaining wars in the same manner down to the praetorship of Servius Galba, who plundered the Lusitanians. And he did not name the commanders (*duces*) in these wars but recorded the events without names. In the same books he gave an account of the noteworthy (*admiranda*) happenings and sights in Italy and the Spains; in which he displayed much industry and diligence, but no learning (*nulla doctrina*).[3]

Most of Nepos' statements are supported by other evidence, including that of the fragments themselves. The title and the number of books are amply attested. Despite controversy about the time and manner of composition it is generally agreed that all of the *Origines* was written in Cato's later years, for a fragment usually assigned to book 2 which mentions the war with Perseus must have been written after *c.* 168.[4] The fragments of the first book show that it gave an account of the kings, and those of the seventh that it dealt with the affair of Sulpicius Galba, including Cato's own speech in support of the attempt to prosecute him in 149. There are many references to the origins of various peoples of Italy[5]—an innovation, for the topic was not dealt with by Fabius Pictor or other of Cato's

---

[3] Nepos, *Cato* 3. 3: 'Ab adulescentia confecit orationes. Senex historias scribere instituit. Earum sunt libri septem. Primus continet res gestas regum populi Romani, secundus et tertius unde quaeque civitas orta sit Italica, ob quam rem omnes Origines videtur appellasse. In quarto autem bellum Poenicum est primum, in quinto secundum. Atque haec omnia capitulatim sunt dicta. Reliquaque bella pari modo persecutus est usque ad praeturam Ser. Galbae, qui diripuit Lusitanos; atque horum bellorum duces non nominavit, sed sine nominibus res notavit. In eisdem exposuit quae in Italia Hispaniisque aut fierent aut uiderentur admiranda; in quibus multa industria et diligentia comparet, nulla doctrina.'

[4] *HRR* i², fr. 49 = Pliny, *Nat. hist.* 3. 114: 'Ameriam supra scriptam Cato ante Persei bellum conditam annis DCCCCLIII prodit.' That it is taken from book 2 or 3 is beyond reasonable doubt, though the ascription to 2 depends on a particular theory about how Cato arranged his material.

[5] Cf. also Dion. Hal. 1. 11. 1; Fronto, *Princ. hist.* 3 = ii. 200H; Solin. 2. 2.

Roman predecessors—and almost all such fragments which include a book-number belong to books 2 and 3. The fragments of books 4 to 7, though fewer in number, support the implication that they were predominantly concerned with wars. At the same time the note-worthy happenings and sights—the *admiranda*—are traceable throughout; . and Dionysius of Halicarnassus as well as Nepos refers to Cato's diligence.[6] The omission of names of military commanders is mentioned also by the elder Pliny and accords with the apparently pointed avoidance of names, Carthaginian as well as Roman, in certain fragments.[7]

This last feature, however, is one of several where Nepos' brief account oversimplifies the picture. Galba's name was certainly mentioned, and the use of the first person in a military fragment suggests that in accounts of his own activities Cato identified himself quite clearly, whether or not he actually referred to himself by name;[8] indeed it is more probable than not that the *Origines* is the source of Livy's highly favourable account of Cato's Spanish campaign, with his comment that Cato was 'certainly not the man to detract from his own praises'.[9] Similarly Cato can hardly have failed to be identifiable as the author of his own speech against Galba, or of the earlier speech on behalf of the Rhodians, which he included in book 5—though in neither of these cases was his role that of a commander in war.[10] It is also an oversimplification to say that the first book contained the exploits of the kings; for it also contained an account of Aeneas and the origins of Rome, and one fragment refers to an event half a century after the kings.[11] The second and third books recounted not only the origins of Italian peoples but some of their customs and various character-istics of the areas where they lived; and although most of the surviving *admiranda* can indeed be associated with Italy or Spain, one concerns Illyricum and another Carthage.[12]

The one point at which Nepos seems to pass beyond oversimplification into misleading inaccuracy is in his statement that 'in the fourth book is the First Punic War, in the fifth the Second', together with the implication

---

[6] Dion. Hal. 1. 11. 1; 1. 74. 2; cf. Solin. 2. 2.

[7] *HRR* i², fr. 88 = Pliny, *Nat. hist.* 8. 11; cf. esp. frs. 83, 86, 87.

[8] *HRR* i², fr. 99. [9] Appendix 2.

[10] Rhodians: *HRR* i², fr. 95 = *ORF*³, frs. 163 ff. Galba: *HRR* i², frs. 106 ff. = *ORF*³, frs. 196 ff. Both Nepos and Pliny refer to the omitted names specifically as those of military commanders, with no indication as to whether the principle was extended also to leading men in political or other activities. For much of Cato's predominantly military account the distinction was probably not very significant, but episodes like these must have raised the issue for him and it is not clear that his reaction was strictly consistent or logical.

[11] *HRR* i², fr. 25. The obvious interpretation is rightly defended by Cornell, *The Origines*, pp. 94 ff. [12] *HRR* i², frs. 78 (Carthage) and 97 (Illyricum); cf. also 80 and 96.

that the 'remaining wars', dealt with in books 6 and 7, were those of the following half-century. Fragments relating to the First Punic War do indeed come from the fourth book, but so do three fragments relating to the Second, one referring to its outbreak and two to Maharbal's proposal to attack Rome directly after Cannae.[13] Cannae, as has often been observed, would have been a suitable episode with which to end a book, but after Nepos' account it is something of a surprise to find that book 4 extended so far as the eventful opening years of the Second Punic War. As it happens none of the fragments attested as belonging to book 5 is unquestionably concerned with the topic mentioned by Nepos, the Second Punic War, though some could be; but it was this book which contained Cato's speech on behalf of the Rhodians, delivered in 167, twenty-four years after the end of the Second Punic War. Thus if Cato presented his material broadly in chronological sequence this book must have covered not only the later part of the Second Punic War but the three Macedonian wars, the war against Antiochus, the numerous wars against Ligurians and Gauls in northern Italy, and a series of wars in Spain, including Cato's own campaign. The issue that this raises is not merely that of Nepos' inaccuracy—for that need represent nothing more than carelessness, an undue reliance, perhaps, on faded memories from a reading of the *Origines* years before, or on an over-hasty glance at a few columns of text. More fundamental is the strikingly uneven treatment of events that seems to be implied. While books 4 and 5, and especially the latter, apparently embraced a considerable sweep of time and major wars of great length and complexity, two whole books seem to have been devoted to the final period of less than twenty years, during which Rome's wars were less dramatic and on a smaller scale. Such a distribution has frequently been judged implausible, with the result that there have been controversial but persistent suggestions that in the later books the material was arranged on the basis of theatres of war rather than on an over-all chronological basis. It has been suggested, for example, that book 5, after completing the Second Punic War, traced affairs in the East, that book 6 dealt with Italy and Cisalpine Gaul from 201 onwards, and that events in Spain in that same period were reserved for the final book.[14] Additional evidence for

[13] *HRR* i[2], frs. 84, 86, and 87; no book is cited for 86, but it clearly concerns the same episode as 87.

[14] Fraccaro, *Opusc.* i. 193 ff.; cf. Schanz–Hosius, *Gesch. der röm. Literatur* i[4]. 187 and 189; Marmorale, *Cato Maior*[2], pp. 167 f.; *Kienast*, p. 14; Badian, 'The Early Historians', in Dorey, *Latin Historians*, p. 8. For earlier attempts along these lines see Bormann, *M. Porcii Catonis Originum libri septem*, pp. 35 ff.; von Gutschmid, 'Catos Origines', *Kl. Schr.* v. 519. Such explanations are rejected by Leo, *Gesch. der röm. Literatur* i. 295; Meister, 'Zu röm. Historikern',

such a distribution has been sought in Nepos' statement that matters were related *capitulatim*, taken to mean 'arranged under headings' or 'by topic'. Also Cato's scornful comment on the material recorded on the annual tablets of the Pontifex Maximus has been seen as an indication of a deliberate rejection of an annalistic arrangement.[15]

But the distribution of material in the final four books is not the only feature of the *Origines* to have provoked discussion about its composition and structure. First, as was implied by Nepos and later stated explicitly by Festus, the title *Origines*, though an apt designation of the first three books, has no obvious relationship to the remaining four.[16] Second, Nepos makes no mention of the whole vast span of the early Republic and the conquest of Italy, down to and including the Pyrrhic War. He seems to indicate a great gap in Cato's account, from the expulsion of the kings to the First Punic War, and the fragments themselves compel a modification of this only to the extent that book 1 was carried at least to 458.

Attempts have been made to account for the Italian wars by supposing them to have been recounted in the second and third books: along with the origins of the various peoples Cato reported their conquest by Rome. Sometimes this has been associated with the supposed arrangement of the later books on the basis of theatres of war: books 2 and 3 dealt with the Italian theatre. However this view has found little favour, partly because it seems to imply a difficult and unnecessary feat of organization, but mainly because the many fragments of books 2 and 3 give no indication of such narratives. A more plausible explanation is that Cato gave only a brief outline of the history of the early Republic (probably at the beginning of book 4), the reason for this being that at this time only a relatively little material had been collected. Thus Fabius Pictor and Cincius Alimentus are reported to have dealt with this same period in summary fashion, and it occupied only three of the eighteen books of Ennius' *Annals*.[17]

AAWW 101 (1964), 4 ff.; Timpe, 'Le Origini', *Atti e Mem. Accad. Patavina Sc. Lett.* 83 (1970–1), 25 f.; Cornell, *The Origines*, pp. 22 ff. and 100 ff.

[15] HRR i², fr. 77: 'Non lubet scribere, quod in tabula apud pontificem maximum est, quotiens annona cara, quotiens lunae aut solis lumine caligo aut quid obstiterit.' The inference clearly does not follow, though, despite references to the *Origines* as *annales* in Pliny, *Nat. hist.* 8. 11, and Livy, *Per.* 49, it is most unlikely that Cato's material was arranged on a strict year-by-year basis comparable, e.g., to Livy's.

[16] Festus, p. 216L. Della Corte's view of the appositeness of the title to books 4–7 is unconvincing: *Catone censore²*, p. 95.

[17] See esp. Gabba, 'Considerazioni sulla tradizione letteraria sulle origini della Repubblica', in *Les Origines de la république romaine*, Fond. Hardt xiii. 133 ff. Fabius and Cincius: Dion. Hal. 1. 6. 2. Ennius: Vahlen, *Ennianae poesis reliquiae*, pp. CLXX ff. Recent surveys of issues and literature concerning Fabius and Ennius by Timpe and Jocelyn respectively in Temporini (ed.), *Aufstieg und Niedergang* i. 2, pp. 928 ff. and 987 ff.

Alternatively the combined silence of Nepos and the fragments has been taken to indicate that Cato omitted the early Republic altogether, the omission in turn being explained by reference either to Cato's supposed attitudes towards the Italian peoples or to the theory about the composition of the *Origines* which is most commonly advanced in order to explain the apparent inadequacy of its title.[18]

That theory is that the first three books were written as a self-contained work, for which the title *Origines* was wholly suitable. The idea of a work devoted to the origins of Rome and the Italian peoples is often thought to have been prompted by the existence of Greek works dealing with κτίσεις (*ktiseis*), stories and legends about the foundation of various cities, and it is often observed that it was probably early in the second century that Polemon of Ilium wrote a collection of 'Foundations of Italian and Sicilian Cities'. Some years after completing the three books of *Origines*, it is suggested, Cato went back to historical writing, but now with the history of his own lifetime very much in the forefront of his mind; and since he was still adding material in 149 he probably died with this additional work unfinished. Either it had been intended to be a completely separate work but in posthumous publication was tacked on to the true *Origines*, or it was written as an extension of the original work but Cato did not substitute a more appropriate title, perhaps because he had not yet finished. On the other hand it has also been asserted that there is no good evidence for the theory of composition in two distinct stages, and that the fact that the title is appropriate only to the first few books can be paralleled and requires no more special explanation than the cases of Xenophon's *Anabasis* and *Cyropaedeia*.[19]

It is obvious that many of these problems concerning composition and

---

[18] The various theories are reviewed at length by Cornell, *The Origines*, pp. 16 ff., who himself believes the early Republic to have been omitted altogether, as do most of the more recent writers mentioned on p. 211 n. 1. However, Bömer, p. 196, and Badian, p. 11, favour the 'hour-glass' explanation, while earlier writers, such as Bormann and von Gutschmid, sought one in the internal arrangement of books 2 and 3.

[19] Of the writers mentioned on p. 211 n. 1 the recent advocates of an essentially 'unitary' view are Marmorale, pp. 167 f. and 226 f., Bömer, p. 193, Timpe, pp. 14 ff. and 31 f., and Cornell, pp. 26 ff. Virtually all others accept either the two-stage theory or a view of prolonged composition which approximates to it. However this division does not correspond exactly with opinions about the title or about whether the early Republic was included: in particular Timpe and Cornell accept a unitary view but believe the early Republic was omitted. Attempts have occasionally been made, e.g. by Rosenberg, *Einleitung und Quellenkunde*, p. 166, to prove widely separated composition by claiming *HRR* i², fr. 49 (quoted above, p. 212 n. 4) as evidence that the early books were written in or soon after 168; in reality it shows only that they were written between *c.* 168 and 149.

structure are directly relevant to attempts to assess the character of the *Origines*; and here again there is much diversity and controversy, for the aims and attitudes which have been attributed to Cato, whether singly or more often in combinations, are numerous and varied. His primary purpose has most commonly been believed to have been to instruct by displaying the example of the past; but even that has been given different emphases. The most pragmatic version is that, at least in the later books, he wished to enable the generals and leaders of the future to benefit from study of the past.[20] Usually however his concern is envisaged as having been with moral rather than practical instruction: to show that traditional virtues and standards of conduct had been the indispensable foundation for Rome's successes; or to demonstrate that the power and glory of Rome was the creation not of individual leaders but of the collective effort of the citizen body, each performing whatever duty was appropriate to his rank. The latter concept is inferred especially from Cato's suppression of the names of military leaders and from his observation, probably but not certainly in the *Origines*, that the Roman constitution was not the creation of a single lawgiver or a single time but was fashioned over many genera-tions.[21] A factor often thought to have been at work here, and especially in the suppression of names, is a prejudice resulting from the fact that Cato was a *novus homo*, expressing itself as an unwillingness to celebrate the distinguished ancestors of the nobles and especially of his personal op-ponents; while the inclusion of two of Cato's own speeches has encouraged the view that self-advertisement and self-assertion played a considerable part in the later books. On the other hand it has also been thought that a major motive was the assertion of Rome's cultural merits *vis-à-vis* the Greeks, either by creating in Rome a historical literature of its own, or, more subtly, by demonstrating, especially in the first book, that the Romans were closely related to the Greeks, or even that they really were Greeks, that it was they rather than the degenerate contemporary Hellenes who had preserved what was best in Greek character and customs.[22] Yet another kind of assessment finds special significance in Cato's interest in the Italians. The devotion of books 2 and 3 to an account of their origins— an innovation which was to remain unique—has frequently given rise to suggestions that he was strongly influenced by a political conception of Italy as in some sense a unity. Cato was certainly not championing the

[20] Della Corte, *Catone censore*[2], pp. 95 f.

[21] Cic. *Rep.* 2. 2. See further pp. 225 ff. and 232 f.

[22] Esp. Kienast, p. 108; Leeman, *Orationis Ratio*, p. 70; Badian, 'The Early Historians', in Dorey, *Latin Historians*, pp. 8 f.

Italians against Rome—the *Origines* was in no way anti-Roman—but it has been suggested that he believed that the growth and achievements of Rome could be fairly and properly understood only by taking full account of the contribution made by the Italian peoples; or further that he wished to convey a conception of Italy as a fundamental unity whose history must be viewed as the interlocking history of her numerous peoples.[23] If Cato did indeed totally and deliberately omit the early Republic from a unitary history of Rome, the explanation, it has been supposed, can be found in such beliefs: he was reluctant to narrate the conquest of the Italians, for which the account of Italian origins serves as a kind of substitute.[24]

This survey of numerous theories about the *Origines* is not intended to suggest that all are equally plausible. Many rest on demonstrably insecure foundations. Thus there can be no reasonable doubt that *capitulatim*, like the Greek κεφαλαιωδῶς, means not 'arranged under headings' but 'in summary fashion' or 'outlining only the most important facts' (which does not exclude particular episodes being narrated in detail).[25] Moreover the point at which Nepos says 'All these matters are told *capitulatim*' is after his description of the first five books and before he mentions the last two; which suggests that the *Origines* did indeed display that marked contrast in the scale of treatment which is implied by the fragments but which many scholars have found hard to credit.[26] In fact the attempt to explain away that unevenness is the only reason for the theory that Cato arranged his material according to 'theatres of war'; for there is no other evidence, and the very limited fragments from the later books (only one from book 6) are just as compatible with a broadly chronological treatment. The evidence of Nepos does not disprove that theory but it does suggest that it is unnecessary.[27]

[23] Argued esp. by Cornell, *The Origines*, pp. 66 ff.; cf. Klingner, 'Cato Censorius und die Krisis des röm. Volkes', *Röm. Geisteswelt*[5], p. 59. Most discussions include some mention of a special attitude towards the Italians. Timpe, 'Le Origini', *Atti e Mem. Accad. Patavina Sc. Lett.* 83 (1970–1), 8 and 19, though allowing some place to the concept, thinks that it has been much exaggerated. Villa, 'Catone e la politica di Roma verso gli Italici', *RSC* 3 (1955), 41 ff., argues that Cato's ideas evolved even beyond an 'Italian nationalism' to a concept of the provincials as on a level with the allies.

[24] Cornell, loc. cit., citing esp. Mommsen, *History of Rome* ii. 435; De Sanctis, *Storia* iv. 2. 1, p. 63.

[25] Leo, *Gesch. der röm. Literatur* i. 294 n. 3; so also Helm, *RE*, s.v. *Porcius*, no. 9, cols. 159 f., Cornell, *The Origines*, pp. 96 f., and most others, against the view taken by von Gutschmid, 'Catos Origines', *Kl. Schr.*, p. 524, and Badian, 'The Early Historians', in Dorey, *Latin Historians*, p. 8.

[26] The argument from the position of *capitulatim* is not absolutely decisive since Nepos goes on to say that Cato treated the other wars *pari modo*.

[27] A chronological treatment seems indicated in Dion. Hal. 1. 7. 3, where Cato is one of

Similarly, though it cannot be proved that Cato did include the early Republic, it is unsafe to base interpretations of the *Origines* on a conviction that he entirely omitted it. Since Fabius Pictor himself, Cato's most likely source, dealt with that period in a summary way (κεφαλαιωδῶς),[28] there would be nothing surprising if Cato gave only a short account; and neither Nepos nor the fragments give positive ground for believing that there was no such account. In the case of Nepos that is obvious from the demonstrable imprecision and oversimplification of his statements about the content of particular books. As for the fragments, a disproportionately large number are drawn from the first three books, because the contents of those books had a special relevance to the geographical sections of the elder Pliny's *Natural History* and Servius' commentary on the *Aeneid*. Fragments from the later books which can be associated with specific events are not so numerous that significance can be attached to the absence of any associated with the early Republic, particularly as an account of that period is likely to have been brief. In short, there is no satisfactory evidence at all on the question, and no answer can be more than a guess made in the light of opinions about the general character of the *Origines*.

Again, there is no external evidence that the *Origines* was composed in two distinct stages, let alone as two separate works. A fragment from book 4 disparaging the kind of information recorded in the pontifical records could have come from a special introduction to that book and therefore would fit in with the theory of two-stage composition, but it by no means requires that theory.[29] The two-stage hypothesis is entirely a modern attempt to account for the seeming disparity between the first three books and the rest, and for a title which appears relevant only to the former. Since the *Origines* survives only in fragments and was known to all our authorities as a single work, with no hint that it was ever otherwise, such a drastic hypothesis would be acceptable only if those features remained incomprehensible on any reasonable view of unitary composition. As for the belief that the work was left unfinished, the only evidence (apart from the question of the title) is the addition of the affair of Sulpicius Galba shortly before Cato's death. That is indeed suggestive, but what it most

several early Roman historians whose works are likened to Greek *chronographiae*. Modern expectations about the scale of treatment appropriate to the eastern wars have been much influenced both by assessment of their importance from a particular historical perspective and by the volume of material diligently collected by Polybius, much of it now preserved in Livy. Since Cato almost certainly lacked the benefit of both it would be no surprise if his own account was little more than an outline except where he himself had been directly involved.

[28] Dion. Hal. 1. 6. 2.   [29] *HRR* i², fr. 77, cited above, p. 215 n. 15.

naturally suggests is that the *Origines* was unfinished in the sense that it had no predetermined point of conclusion, so that Cato was free to add new material as events occurred. In fact it points to the possibility, to which attention has sometimes been drawn,[30] that the inspiration of the work was a good deal less intellectual, its organization a good deal looser, than is presupposed by many of the theories outlined above, or indeed by some of the problems as they have been propounded. Particular ideas and particular preconceptions there must have been, and these it is proper to seek to identify; but if there is difficulty in discerning a clear-set theme to the work as a whole or an effective over-all form, the possibility must be considered that there was no well-thought-out theme, no clear-cut predetermined plan for the structure of the entire work. In the light of the *De agricultura* that is a possibility which is not in the least surprising.

It was observed in the previous chapter that although Cato's writings were produced in a society which lacked a well-established literary tradition, they did not occur in a vacuum. In the case of the *Origines* Cato's other writings are themselves part of the context; and whether the composition of the *De agricultura* was earlier or coincided in part with that of the *Origines*, the attitudes and methods displayed by the author elsewhere and especially in his one surviving work are not to be ignored in discussion of the *Origines* itself. Cato's other writings have a didactic, purposeful character, yet it is probable that as he proceeded the real impetus lay less in an anxiety to remedy ignorance than in a growing interest in the experiment of writing. It is most unlikely that the instructional intentions of the *De agricultura* were accompanied by careful preliminary thought about the potential readership or its needs. Cato evidently did start on that work with an idea as to what he would write about, but it was general and imprecise; in so far as it constituted a plan it was sketchy and in the event carried him only about a third of the way through the book. The Preface, it will be recalled, was written virtually as a self-contained essay, with no close attention to the details of what was to follow; indeed everything suggests that Cato embarked on the actual composition without attempting a preliminary survey of his material, let alone planning its organization in detail. The writing betrays a marked lack of disciplined thought and little sense of relevance; and it combines clear traces of the impact of Cato's own personality with clumsiness and infelicity in the incorporation of material from his sources.

[30] Marmorale, *Cato Maior*[2], pp. 168 f. and 224 ff.; Timpe, 'Le Origini', *Atti e Mem. Accad. Patavina Sc. Lett.* 83 (1970–1), 14 and 26 f.; cf. Bömer, '*Thematik und Krise*', *Historia*, 2 (1953), 197.

The *Origines* was a literary experiment on a much grander scale than the *De agricultura*, and in quite a different field; its antecedents included not only Cato's own innovations in Latin prose literature but the incipient Roman interest in native historical topics, as evidenced in the epic poems of Naevius and Ennius and in the prose histories of Fabius Pictor and Cincius Alimentus, written in Greek but about Roman history—and behind them lay the long tradition of Greek historiography. Yet these differences afford no reason to suppose that in the work of composition Cato's methods and attitudes were radically different from those revealed by the *De agricultura*; for the methods and attitudes were the product of Cato's own background and *milieu* much more than of the particular subject-matter. Certainly in a historical work the chronological element could be expected automatically to create a skeletal structure, whereas in the *De agricultura* the nature of the material exacerbates the consequences of inadequate planning; but the fundamental point is precisely Cato's readiness to write with only rudimentary plans in mind, and *a priori* his approach to the writing of the *Origines* is more likely to have been similar than a total contrast. In a similar way the demands of narrative imposed a style somewhat different from the instructional imperatives of the *De agricultura*, and though the language is generally simple and plain, stylistic devices such as are found in the speeches indicate that at certain points there was a conscious attempt to create a heightened effect.[31] But this too, though not without an interest and perhaps an importance of its own, does not affect the reasonable assumption that the composition of the *Origines* reflected attitudes and methods similar to those indicated by the *De agricultura*.

That assumption does much to facilitate the understanding of the *Origines*. At the very start it enables the three fragments of the Preface to be seen in better perspective. These are:

(1) an incomplete sentence, 'If there are any men to whom it gives pleasure to write down the deeds (*gestas*) of the Roman people . . .'

(2) an opinion that 'the leisure of illustrious and great men ought to be no less subject to account than their business'.

(3) a comment that Cato's preface was one of the kind which commended the value of history in general terms.[32]

---

[31] See pp. 237 ff.

[32] *HRR* i[2], frs. 1–3. Bormann, *M. Porcii Catonis Originum libri septem*, pp. 5 and 29 f., assigned to the Preface a dictum about the use of leisure which Cato is said to have attributed to Scipio Africanus (*HRR* i[2], fr. 127 = Cic. *Rep.* 1. 27 and *De off.* 3. 1), but this is generally recognized to be quite uncertain. Commentary by Schröder, *Das erste Buch der Origines*, pp. 47 ff.

The first of these fragments reveals nothing, since the missing portion of the sentence could be restored to fit in with almost any of the theories about the *Origines*. The second, however, besides being allied to Cato's persistent concept of the obligations incumbent upon public men, clearly implies the claim actually reported in the third, that history had value, and therefore that what he was doing was purposeful, not an end in itself— and presumably not a purely literary endeavour. So far as it can be recovered, therefore, the attitude adopted in this preface is in line with that suggested by Cato's other works: in his own mind the idea of purpose was closely associated with his experiments in writing, as though he took it almost for granted that prose books must be in some sense useful. Strictly speaking the fragments reveal nothing more about the particular kind of value or usefulness which Cato claimed for history, though the natural expectation is that he asserted that it was in some sense didactic. Disappointing though that loss is, however, it is doubtful if it is especially significant for the understanding of the *Origines* itself. That is not intended to suggest that Cato was hypocritical, that he did not believe in his own argument; but it need not have been a deep and dominating conviction. Given the evidence of the *De agricultura* it would be rash, even implausible to assume that the particular value and purposes (for nothing requires that there was only one) which were claimed for history in the Preface represented the principal impetus for the composition of the *Origines*; or that in the body of the work Cato constantly selected, organized, and presented his material to serve that particular purpose or purposes. It is much more likely that this preface too was written before Cato began writing the body of the work, without careful and detailed consideration of what was to follow; that this too was virtually a self-contained essay, neither profound nor rigorously relevant. Admittedly the reference in the second fragment to the obligations of 'great and illustrious men' is closely allied to a persistent trait in Cato's thinking; but the form in which it is expressed here is a borrowed contrivance, virtually a translation of the opening sentence of Xenophon's *Symposium*, the formulation of which no doubt appealed to Cato but which it would be questionable to regard as a deep conviction literally as it stands; rather it too hints at a certain artificiality.

If Cato began writing with only a general idea or a rather sketchy plan of what he was going to do, if he proceeded with no deep-rooted concern for system, order, and relevance, it is scarcely surprising if the structure of the *Origines* was in places awkward, or if the treatment of the material was markedly uneven, not only as between the different books but in the sense that some episodes were narrated at a length which could not possibly have been maintained consistently within the compass of the seven books. The example of the *De agricultura* makes it difficult to believe in the kind of planning and organization implicit in the theory that the *Origines* was arranged on the basis of 'theatres of war'. On the other hand it is wholly understandable that the composition of the later books, like the later part of the *De agricultura*, should have become rather a process of accumulation and extension, which accounts for the addition of the Galba episode, the different scale of the later books, and, in part, for the inclusion of some of Cato's own speeches. The presence of numerous *admiranda*, scattered through the work in the form of incidental information and curiosities, is precisely what is to be expected, as is Nepos' comment that in this Cato displayed much industry and diligence but *nulla doctrina*—whether this last means a lack of learned discussion or a failure to name other literary authorities. The fact that the origins of the Italian peoples occupied two whole books is less dramatic and less significant if Cato started without a detailed preliminary survey of his material or without a plan governed by a strong sense of what would be an appropriate allocation of space to particular topics—if in short a principal controlling factor was simply the amount of material he managed to find (though the inclusion of the origins of the Italians itself still requires explanation). Even the title seems less of a problem if Cato's initial general idea included beginning with an account of Roman and Italian origins and if, with that in the forefront of his mind, the title was the first thing he wrote—as seems to have been the case with the *De agricultura*.[33]

If the *Origines* is seen as basically a further extension of Cato's experiments in writing prose works in Latin, no dominating intellectual or didactic purpose is required to explain why his attention should have turned towards history. Quite apart from the fact that his reading of Greek works must already have made him familiar with the idea of historical writing, there had been in Rome since Cato's earliest years an awakening interest in the Roman past which had already found expression in various literary works: in Cato's *Origines* incipient Roman historiography and incipient Latin prose literature naturally merged. Nor is there need of any special explanation, any distinctive purpose, to account for the fact that Cato began with the origins of Rome, from the Aeneas legend onwards. His predecessors, both in Greek prose and in Latin epic, had all done this: Fabius, Cincius, Ennius, even Naevius in his *Punic War* (and they were conforming to a common Greek practice). What would have needed a special explanation would have been the omission of this material; as it

[33] Birt, 'Zum Proöm und den Summarien', *BPhW*, 29 (1915), cols. 922 ff.

was Cato was simply following previous example. Indeed Cato's version of the foundation stories was evidently largely the same as that of Fabius Pictor, leaving little doubt that Fabius was his principal source.[34] Not that Cato did nothing more than transfer Fabius' account into Latin; as is to be expected, there are some traces of Cato's own initiative. In one matter (the prodigy of the sow and her litter in connection with the foundation of Alba Longa) his version seems to have differed slightly from that of Fabius and this is presumably evidence that he also consulted some other source.[35] More interesting is that instead of giving the date of the foundation of Rome in terms of Olympiad-reckoning he expressed it as 'four hundred and thirty-two years after the Trojan War'.[36] Evidently he decided that calculation by Olympiads would mean little to Romans, so he went to the trouble of making new calculations of his own, in a form which would have meaning at least in terms of the time-span of the events he was narrating.

This close relationship between Cato and his predecessors, at least in respect of book I, means also that there is no need to read a special motive into his narration of those legends which traced the ancestry of the Romans back to Greek origins. He was simply following the established pattern, the given picture. Possibly it is significant, in relation to his supposed anti-hellenism, that he did not seek to change it; but there is nothing remarkable, nothing necessarily purposeful about his association of the Romans with Greek origins. It was an association accepted in the tradition which Cato followed, and it took that form because it originated with Greeks. Starting long before Fabius Pictor, it was developed through the attempts of Greek writers to explain and reconstruct the origins of various peoples who were on the periphery of their world or who impinged upon hellenic affairs. There was a natural tendency for such writers to seek and to speculate about supposed links between their own traditions and the

---

[34] Dion. Hal. 1. 79. 4; Leo, *Gesch. der röm. Literatur* i. 297 f.; Bömer, 'Thematik und Krise', *Historia*, 2 (1953), 196; Schanz–Hosius, *Gesch. der röm. Literatur* i⁴, p. 189; Helm, *RE*, s.v. *Porcius*, no. 9, col. 161. Schröder, *Das erste Buch der Origines*, examines the fragments individually and also surveys the problems of the relevant foundation legends. Dion. Hal. 4. 15. 1 = *HRR* i², fr. 23 on the Servian tribes presents considerable textual problems, but on any solution Cato's version, though simpler than Fabius', did not conflict with it.

[35] Schröder, op. cit., pp. 37 (fr. 13 b) and 140 ff., comparing *FGrH*, no. 809 (Fabius), fr. 2.

[36] *HRR* i², fr. 17 = Dion. Hal. 1. 74. 2; details discussed by Schröder, op. cit., pp. 167 ff.; cf. Moretti, 'Le "Origines" di Catone, Timeo ed Eratostene', *RFIC* 80 (n.s. 30) (1952), 289 ff., esp. 298. If the date is in terms of the era of Eratosthenes (probable but not actually stated) it is 751 B.C., about three years earlier than the date given by Fabius in terms of Olympiads. It is theoretically possible but in practice unlikely that Dionysius himself calculated the relationship from data given by Cato. These and other details do not affect the central point that Cato gave the date in an independent form calculated by himself.

distant past of other peoples, to try to explain such peoples—and indeed the whole world—from a predominantly hellenic-centred point of view.[37] As Rome grew in importance it more frequently came within the scope of such speculations, and as these became more elaborate efforts were made to combine them into a coherent picture. A certain Diocles of Peparethus seems to have been the first to carry the synthesizing to the point of publishing an account as a separate book, and it was his version which was followed in most respects by Fabius, who in turn was followed by Cato.[38]

Similar considerations apply to suggestions that the actual scope of book 1 may have been determined by a political concept. That concept, closely linked to Cato's belief in the obligations of public service, was that the state and its successes were the collective achievements of the Roman people, not the individual achievements of outstanding leaders, and that the exploits of individuals should not be highlighted. Hence Cato included in book 1 not only the foundation legends but the kings and even material after the kings because he was giving expression to a concept of the origin of Rome not as an event but as the creation of a state, as a collective achievement over a long period of time, a process which he perhaps believed was completed only with the Decemvirate. The contents of book 1 would thus have corresponded to the formulation of that concept which Cicero attributes to Cato: 'the condition (or form) of our state (*civitas*) excels that of the other states because in them there have usually been individual lawgivers each of whom established his own state by means of his own laws and institutions . . . but our state (*res publica*) was established by the genius not of one man but of many, nor in the lifetime of one man but over several generations.'[39]

Although such an interpretation has certain superficial attractions, it is unnecessary, insecure, and indeed improbable. The quoted statement

[37] Bickerman, 'Origines Gentium', *CPh* 47 (1952), 65 ff.

[38] Plut. *Rom.* 3. 1; 8. 9 = *FGrH*, no. 820 (Diocles), frs. 2 a and b. Strictly speaking these passages do not prove that Fabius used Diocles as a source, only that his account agreed in most respects. On the development of the tradition see esp. Gabba, 'Considerazioni sulla tradizione letteraria sulle origini della Repubblica', in *Les Origines de la république romaine*, Fond. Hardt xiii. 133 ff.; also Alföldi, *Early Rome and the Latins*, pp. 250 ff.; Schröder, *Das erste Buch der Origines*, pp. 57 ff.

[39] Cic. *Rep.* 2. 2. This view developed esp. by Kienast, pp. 109 ff., and Cornell, *The Origines* pp. 89 ff.; see also Timpe, 'Le Origini', *Atti e Mem. Accad. Patavina Sc. Lett.* 83 (1970–1), 21 ff.; Leo, *Kl. Sch.* i. 319 ff. = *Misc. Cic.*, pp. 15 ff. On the basis of *Rep.* 2. 2 f. it is sometimes held that the chronological and historical framework which Cicero used in book 2 of the *De republica* was taken from book 1 of the *Origines*. Supposing this to be correct, it would still be improper to infer Cato's views from those expressed by Cicero, as attempted by Villa, 'Il "de re publica" come fonte per la conoscenza delle idee politiche di Catone Censore', *MC* 16 (1949), 68 ff.

itself is of uncertain significance and a fragile basis for the proposed super-structure. Nothing is known of the circumstances or context in which Cato said or wrote this, nor is it known in which of his works it occurred. The idea is one to which it is conceivable that he attached considerable significance, yet it need have been no more than a casual passing obser-vation. Even if it is regarded as a carefully considered statement of a deeply held conviction, a link with leanings towards a 'collective' view of the state, or with an ideal of political conduct, or with the omission of names in the later books of the *Origines* is certainly not a necessary implication. Speculation about such links, about their implications as political concepts, and about the role of these in the *Origines* has received some encourage-ment from the belief that a remark about the government of Carthage shows Cato's thought in this work to have been influenced by political theory. (The fragment is plausibly assigned to book 4, though it is not actually attested even that it came from the *Origines*.[40]) Some awareness of political theorizing and occasional traces of a superficial influence would scarcely be surprising, are perhaps to be expected; but that is not what is in question. The simple comment that Carthage was organized (*ordinatam*) on the basis of *populus*, *optimates*, and royal power is scarcely evidence that Cato was deeply influenced by the forms and concepts of political theory or that he frequently thought in such terms[41]—let alone that he conceived of Rome itself as a 'mixed constitution' in the Polybian manner. And though at this time Polybius himself may already have been collecting material for his own interpretation of the Roman constitution, and though Cato may have been acquainted with him, it is unlikely that the relation-ship was so close as to suggest intellectual influence.[42]

All this points to the insecurity of the suggested political interpretation of book 1; but as was said above, besides being insecure it is also improb-able and unnecessary. For it is fundamentally implausible to suppose that the author of the *De agricultura* planned the first book of the *Origines* with

[40] *HRR* i[2], fr. 80.

[41] Walbank, *Polybius*, pp. 136 f., believes the basic idea to have been so widespread as to be a commonplace; and Cato's description may even simply reflect the terms used in some description he followed.

[42] Although Scipio Aemilianus was a link between them the circumstances of the release of the Achaean hostages in 150 suggests that Polybius was in no position to approach Cato directly: Plut. *Cato Mai.* 9. 2 f. = Polyb. 35. 6; for Scipio and Cato see Astin, 'Scipio Aemilianus and Cato Censorius', *Latomus*, 15 (1956), 159 ff.; id., *Scipio Aemilianus*, pp. 13 and 280 f. Kienast, pp. 110 ff., and Leeman, *Orationis Ratio*, p. 69, attach importance to supposed contacts between Polybius and Cato; Nicolet, 'Polybe et les institutions romaines', *Polybe*, Fond. Hardt xx. 209 ff., esp. 243 ff., envisages influence exercised by Cato on Polybius rather than the reverse.

such care and sophistication as to make it the deliberate expression of a political concept concerning the nature of the Roman state. It is just possible that it reflected such a political concept in a less sophisticated manner, namely that as Cato wrote his account the reason he broke off at whatever point he did was that he had reached a stage where the *res publica* seemed to him complete. It is much more likely, however, that he was simply following his sources, both in what he included and in where he stopped—that he ended book 1 where he did because he had reached the end of the topics which they had treated fairly fully. For, as was mentioned previously, Fabius Pictor and Cato's other predecessors all had what has been termed the 'hour-glass' pattern, according only short and slender treatment to the period dealt with between the ampler sections on the kings and the Punic Wars.

The heart of the issue, however, lies not in the first book of the *Origines* but in the second and third. At first sight these may appear harder to reconcile with the idea that the *Origines* was intended by Cato to be a single work, upon which he embarked with only broad general ideas of purpose and comparatively little preliminary planning, and that its primary inspiration was not an overriding intellectual theme or didactic purpose. The problem concerns their subject-matter. Why did Cato introduce an account of 'the origin of each Italian state'? Fabius Pictor had not done this, nor Cincius, Naevius, or Ennius. Does not this apparent innovation suggest that the first three books may after all have drawn their inspiration, not to mention the title, from the Greek 'foundation' literature, *ktiseis*, and at least in some degree may have been a self-contained composition?[43] Does it not suggest, additionally or alternatively, that the content and structure of the *Origines*, or at least of these books, were powerfully influenced by a distinctive attitude towards Italy and the Italians?[44] Does it not suggest an attitude so distinctive and so prominent that the expression of it must have been a major theme, probably a major purpose of the *Origines*?

It would be rash to exclude altogether the possibility that Cato was influenced by the *ktiseis* literature, especially as several writers of such works are said to have included items relating to Italy, most recently Polemon of Ilium who, probably early in the second century, wrote a work entitled 'Foundations of Italian and Sicilian Cities'.[45] On the other

[43] Some connection with the *ktiseis* literature has been widely accepted. For a clear exposition of this view see esp. Timpe, 'Le Origini', *Atti e Mem. Accad. Patavina Sc. Lett.* 83 (1970–1), 15 ff.

[44] p. 218 n. 23.

[45] *Schol. Apoll. Rhod.* 4. 324; Deichgräber, *RE*, s.v. *Polemon*, no. 9, col. 1301. Among

hand, though comparatively little is known about the literature concerned specifically with *ktiseis*, it does not seem to have been the most likely model for a historical work—and Cato's Preface leaves no doubt that he regarded the *Origines* as history. By the Hellenistic period (in contrast to its early beginnings) the genre seems to have become somewhat separate and different from history, not practised by the major historians, some of it in verse, and characterized by a mixture of antiquarianism and romantic fiction. Moreover, the assumption that the *Origines* was modelled upon *ktiseis* explains nothing, except possibly the title, which cannot be explained as well or better in terms of the main stream of Greek historical writing.[46] Even in the matter of the title it has been argued that *origo* does not mean the same as κτίσις, and it may be noted that Dionysius of Halicarnassus refers to Cato's accounts of the Italian cities as 'genealogies', not *ktiseis*.[47] However that may be, Polybius makes it quite clear that in excluding from his own history 'genealogies' and accounts of 'colonies, foundations (*ktiseis*), and ties of kinship', he himself was exceptional, departing from a practice which was nearly universal;[48] and Timaeus, the third-century historian of whose work Cato cannot have been ignorant, had followed the practice on a grand scale. His history was concerned mainly with the western Greeks, but several books, almost certainly the first five, were given over to accounts of the surrounding peoples and lands of the western Mediterranean, including the Italian peoples.[49] There is no specific evidence that Cato used Timaeus' work, though equally nothing to make it improbable;[50] but as a precursor to the character of the first three books of the *Origines* the opening section of Timaeus' history is at least as plausible as the *ktiseis*. Indeed it is more plausible, for Timaeus had written a unitary history in which the relationship between the

earlier writers Alcimos, probably late in the fourth century, included an Italian book in his *Sikelika* and Hippys of Rhegium wrote κτίσις Ἰταλίας. See further Timpe, loc. cit.

[46] These observations essentially follow Cornell, *The Origines*, pp. 137 ff., though he is more confident in rejecting the *ktiseis* model. For the *ktiseis* literature see Schmid, *Studien zu griechischen Ktisissagen*, esp. pp. 53 ff. and 90 ff.

[47] Dion. Hal. 1. 11. 1.   [48] Polyb. 9. 1. 3 ff.

[49] Jacoby, *FGrH*, commentary on no. 566 (Timaeus), pp. 542 f. and 547 ff. On Timaeus' life and writings see also Brown, *Timaeus of Tauromenium*, esp. ch. 1.

[50] It is no objection that he differed about the date of the foundation of Rome and some associated details. On the former he made his own calculation (p. 224), on the latter he was following the adaptations of the legends, notably the inclusion of the Alban kings, invented to accommodate the eighth-century foundation, first suggested by Timaeus himself without allowance for the long interval after the Trojan war: Alföldi, *Early Rome and the Latins*, pp. 125 f. Moretti, 'Le "Origines" di Catone, Timeo ed Eratostene', *RFIC* 80 (n.s. 30) (1952), 289 ff., attempts to show, largely on the basis of indirect evidence, that Cato did consult Timaeus, but the arguments are not conclusive.

opening books and the rest was very similar to that between Cato's first three books and the remainder. The relative proportions are different, but Cato's methods of working are sufficient to account for that.

The evidence of Polybius and especially of Timaeus shows that if Cato's account of the origins of various peoples is viewed as the first section of a substantial history it need not be regarded as unprecedented or extraordinary; and Timaeus' own work is likely to have been one of the principal sources from which he got the idea. Yet there still does remain a question as to why Cato chose to follow this example. For Fabius Pictor, Cato's immediate source for book 1, did not do so, or rather restricted himself to the origins of Rome itself, whereas Cato went on to deal with the origins and characteristics of Italy (thus not modelling himself exactly on Timaeus either, since his survey was much wider than Cato's). The possibility cannot be excluded that one reason for Cato's choice was that he did indeed have some concept of Italy as a unit and of the history of all its peoples being interlocked with that of Rome. On the other hand certain features suggest that if such a concept was at work it is unlikely to have been profound or far-reaching. Although it could have begun in Cato's mind with an awareness of the contribution of the Italian allies to Rome's greatness, that was certainly not a major element in any concept governing books 2 and 3, for Cato is known to have included the Ligurians, albeit with curt disparagement, and a good deal about the Cisalpine Gauls, both of them long-standing and formidable enemies only recently subjected.[51] This alone rules out a conception based on cultural unity, which in any case is virtually inconceivable at this date. It is unlikely therefore to have risen much above a sense of geographical unity, perhaps with a recognition that all the peoples within that geographical area had become involved with—or subject to—the Romans. Although such an idea could well have played a part in Cato's choice it is unlikely to have been a great inspirational theme giving shape to the *Origines*. In fact it would not have differed greatly from Timaeus' own approach. Indeed it is an obvious possibility that the main reason for Cato's survey of Italian origins is that he was simply copying what seemed to him a good idea: to write about peoples adjacent to and impinging upon those who were the principal subject of the history, in Timaeus' case the western Greeks, in Cato's the Romans. He may even have concluded from his reading of Greek historians that in this respect Fabius was deficient as a historian; and his principal idea may have been to improve upon Fabius. The actual execution of the idea is of course likely to have reflected Cato's methods of work. A similar account

[51] *HRR* i², frs. 31 ff.

of the Carthaginians appears to have come in book 4, which could be justified as a logical progress from the account of the Italians, neatly preparing the way for the treatment of the First Punic War; but more probably Cato's planning was not so systematic and its position was determined primarily by the fact that he was about to write about that war.[52] Similarly information about Spain and Spanish peoples was evidently linked with narratives of the Spanish wars. And it has already been seen that Cato's methods of work could explain why the Italians, about whom he must have found it easiest to accumulate much information, occupied two whole books.

The conclusion to be drawn from all this is not only that the character of the second and third books is no obstacle to the approach to the *Origines* here being suggested. It is also that the problems which these books have so often been felt to pose cease to be serious problems if full account is taken of the fact that the author of the *Origines* is also the author of the *De agricultura*, and that in each case his methods and attitudes in composition are likely to have been basically the same—and very unlikely to have been totally different.

Considerable light would be thrown on Cato's attitudes and methods if it were possible to form a reasonably clear picture of his sources for the information contained in books 2 and 3. Unfortunately what emerges is sketchy and imprecise, and furthermore, since it is virtually all derived from inference, it is largely at the level of probability rather than demonstrable fact. Legends involving Greeks and Trojans are frequent enough to leave no real doubt that Cato drew substantially on Greek literary sources, as is only to be expected (though it has been suggested that even some of these stories could have reached him through local traditions into which Greek reconstructions of the origins of native peoples had already been absorbed).[53] But Cato did not simply reproduce or synthesize such sources, for there are indications of his personal contribution in both the collection and the handling of material. Thus when he wrote that Ameria was founded 953 years before the war against Perseus, he had at least made the calculations required to put the date in that form, wherever he got the basic information;[54] and the remark that the origin of the Ligurians is lost to memory because 'they are illiterate and liars' seems characteristic of

[52] *HRR* i², frs. 78 and 80, the latter not attested as from the *Origines* but almost certainly correctly placed here.

[53] So Cornell, *The Origines*, esp. pp. 156 ff. and 343 ff., one of whose major contentions is that Cato drew heavily on local tradition. See further his article 'Notes on the Sources for Campanian History in the Fifth Century B.C.', *MH* 31 (1974), 193 ff.

[54] *HRR* i², fr. 49; above, p. 212 n. 4.

Cato's own sweeping judgements.[55] The note that at Arpinum 'the *sacra* do not follow the heir' is a technical point of pontifical law of such specifically Roman interest that it is most unlikely to have appeared in a Greek source.[56] Probably Cato accumulated a considerable amount of information partly by personal observation and partly by questioning persons who knew the areas and peoples concerned. Much of what survives, however, could have been drawn equally well either from local sources or from Greek writings. Since Timaeus had certainly dealt with Italy, including even the Ligurians and the Gauls,[57] there is obviously a strong possibility that in most instances the core of Cato's version of an 'origin' was taken from Timaeus and supplemented with additional material which Cato had collected; but all that can be said with confidence is that both kinds of source were used, and that Cato's personal contribution was substantially more than the mere reproduction of what was written in standard Greek histories.

There are fewer fragments from the four later books, and most of these concern either military narrative or the miscellaneous incidental information which Nepos termed *admiranda*. Most are brief, though notable exceptions, both as it happens preserved by Gellius, are the long account from book 4 of a heroic exploit by a military tribune (named by Gellius as Caedicius), and from book 5 the fragments of Cato's speech in 167 on behalf of the Rhodians; and to these could perhaps be added the several fragments concerning the affair of Sulpicius Galba in 149.[58] Despite the obvious limitations that all this implies, there is some material here for discussion of several questions about Cato's intentions and attitudes as displayed in these books.

In the first place the long account of the military tribune Caedicius, offering himself for seemingly certain death in order to serve the state, and miraculously surviving to render many more services, has an unmistakable didactic air. Cato narrated the episode at such length in order to highlight a shining and inspiring example both of Roman heroism and of complete dedication to the service of the *res publica*. It would be a wrong emphasis— and an untenable proposition—to say that the *Origines* was written for the express purpose of instruction by such edifying example, as though that were a primary motive—particularly as there is only the one clear instance.

---

[55] *HRR* i², fr. 31, cf. 32.   [56] *HRR* i², fr. 61.

[57] Polyb. 12. 28a. 3 = *FGrH*, no. 566 (Timaeus), fr. 7; cf. fr. 1; Jacoby, commentary on no. 566 pp. 542 f. and on frs. 1 and 7.

[58] *HRR* i², frs. 83 (= Gell. 3. 7: Caedicius); 95 (= *ORF*³, frs. 163 ff.: Rhodes); 106–9 (= *ORF*³, frs. 196 ff.: Galba).

But it does show that instruction, or, perhaps more accurately, exhortation by example was a feature of the *Origines*, a purpose to which Cato on occasion geared his narrative. It is a fair guess that he took it for granted that this was one of the functions of historical writing, and that in his Preface it figured in his account of the value (*bonum*) of history.

The Caedicius passage might also be held to illustrate a link which has often been suggested between Cato's concern about duty to the state and his curious idiosyncrasy of omitting the names of military commanders; for although it is not absolutely certain that Cato never named Caedicius, throughout the long surviving passage he refers to him only as 'the military tribune', and he similarly refers by office only to the consul and the Carthaginian general who figure in the story.[59] Various explanations have been offered for this strange practice. The idea that he really did name the commanders, but only at the beginning of each year in a history arranged on an annalistic basis, like Livy's, goes against the evidence at every point. The suggestion that it was really a common feature of early annalistic history is questionable in itself and in any case is explained as induced by a consideration which would not have applied to Cato.[60] That it was a polemical and partisan suppression of references to ancestors of Cato's opponents fails to account for it being general, apparently extending even to Carthaginians; and it is not credible that he felt obliged to omit all names in order to cover his determination to omit some. There is more to be said for the view that its roots lay in his outlook as a *novus homo*, that his resentment of those who could reap advantage from the fame of their ancestors encouraged him to react by suppressing the names; but the idea he actually applied in the *Origines*, even if at bottom a rationalization of such a reaction, in its universal embrace clearly went beyond an expression of resentment. The answer really does seem to be that, whatever

---

[59] *HRR* i², fr. 83 = Gell. 3. 7. At the beginning and end of his chapter Gellius says that the tribune was named Q. Caedicius, noting that Claudius Quadrigarius gave his name as Laberius. Frontinus, *Strat.* 1. 5. 15, cf. 4. 5. 10, says that some wrote that he was called Laberius, some Q. Caedicius, but most Calpurnius Flamma; and it is this last which is found in all other surviving accounts (though they are perhaps all derived from Livy). See Münzer, *RE*, s.v. *Caedicius*, no. 9, and *Calpurnius*, no. 42. Since Gellius cites no other authority for the uncommon version of the name which he actually accepts, there is at least a possibility that at some point Cato did record it.

[60] Peter, *HRR*, i², pp. cxli f.; Leo, *Gesch. der röm. Lit.* i. 296; Bömer, 'Naevius und Fabius Pictor', *SO* 29 (1952), 39 n. 4; Walbank, *Polybius*, p. 92. The suggestion is that the early records of the Pontifex Maximus noted names of officials at the beginning of each year but only the bare facts of victories and other events, without indication of which official was responsible; consequently the early historians were obliged to follow suit. Whatever may be thought of this it is plainly not applicable to the Punic wars. So De Sanctis, *Storia* iv. 2. 1, p. 63; Cornell, *The Origines*, pp. 73 f.

the underlying stimuli, it was an application of Cato's concept of duty: service for the state, not for personal glory. As such it has been linked from time to time with his remark about Rome not having been established by a single lawgiver and with his recognition of three elements in the government of Carthage, the notion being that he formulated a particular view of the nature of the state and of the individual's role in it—or rather of what those ought to be.[61] It has been seen already, however, that the evidence is very insecure for Cato having had so sophisticated a view. In fact it is doubtful if his attitude should be regarded as much more than a strong sense of duty, and a belief that others had similar obligations to serve the state. That in the *Origines* he should give expression to that belief by suppressing the names of commanders was probably a temporary enthusiasm, clumsy and extravagant, though not wholly inappropriate in one given to swift and extravagant hyperbole. In any case, though the concern with duty was genuine, it is very unlikely that this particular manifestation was deeply rooted in his beliefs. Cato was not entirely consistent about it even within the *Origines*. Quite apart from the fact that it was not applied in the earlier books and, more important, that it was either nullified or not applied in the case of Cato himself, it was in the *Origines* that Cato, apparently in approval, declared it to have been an ancient custom at banquets 'to sing the praises and virtues of illustrious men'.[62] Of course the passage is out of context and may, for example, have been contrasted with contemporary excesses as part of an explanation as to why Cato himself had decided to omit names; but it still shows that he had no absolute or fundamental objection to the praise of illustrious men.[63] And that the idea was certainly not a consistent feature of Cato's outlook is amply demonstrated by the fragment of a speech in which he asserted that 'legal rights, law, liberty and the state ought to be held in common: glory and honour, in whatever way each man builds them for himself.'[64]

Cato's interest in his own *gloria* has a particular relevance to the inclusion in the *Origines* of at least two of his own speeches. There is no satisfactory evidence to determine whether or not he included more. The known instances are not reported in such a manner that the lack of reference

---

[61] pp. 225 ff.   [62] *HRR* i², fr. 118.

[63] The conclusion of the Caedicius passage, with its comparison of the honours accorded to the tribune and to Leonidas, is usually taken to be a deprecation of extensive honours to an individual for services rendered to the state; but even this is not certain. It is possible that Cato meant that Caedicius should have been more honoured for what he did. The key sentences are ambiguous on this: 'sed idem benefactum quo in loco ponas, nimium interest . . . at tribuno militum parva laus pro factis relicta, qui idem fecerat atque rem servaverat.'

[64] *ORF*³, fr. 252.

to others is significant; and though the sole surviving fragment from book 6 does use the first person singular, it is preserved in a form which would be compatible with it being an extract either from another speech by Cato himself or from remarks attributed to someone else in Cato's narrative.[65] What is clear is that in the two certain instances, the Rhodian speech in book 5 and that against Galba in book 7, Cato's own role and authorship were completely evident in the *Origines*. Obviously the incorporation of these speeches is in part a reflection of Cato's readiness to use the *Origines* as a vehicle for the display of his own activities and importance; yet that explanation is not entirely sufficient on its own. In the first place, proud though Cato may have been of his speech against Galba, the proposal which he was supporting was rejected, an outcome on which he commented angrily, even bitterly. In the second place the inclusion of the text of speeches as actually delivered, and moreover speeches by the historian himself, was quite exceptional and probably unique, so that even if the principal aim is taken to be self-display it is still necessary to explain how Cato came to adopt this particular method.

The circumstances surrounding the speech against Galba suggest the possibility that Cato had decided to use the *Origines* as a vehicle to convey his point of view on various issues, and in the Galba case itself there may indeed be an element of truth in that. If so, the hope was presumably to influence attitudes and conduct in the future rather than effect any change in a dispute which was already decided. Yet it is at least equally likely that Cato's action was not particularly carefully considered. Since he was probably in the habit already of extending the *Origines* by accounts of recent events, the addition of the whole of the Galba episode, including Cato's own speech, may have been basically an instance of this, but one specially influenced by the immediate emotions of an old man who was bitterly angry and smarting with humiliation. Thus it may have been rather different in circumstance, motive, and manner from anything he had previously done in the *Origines*.[66] In any case, the question at issue cannot really turn on this episode, for the speech against Galba was not the first to have been included. The crucial step had been taken much earlier, no later than the incorporation of the Rhodian speech into book 5; and for this an explanation in terms of polemics is not at all convincing. If it may be doubted whether Cato expected his account of the Galba affair to have a direct effect on the dispute itself, in the case of the Rhodian episode this is

---

[65] *HRR* i², fr. 105: 'quod est scriptum a M. Catone in sexta origine: Itaque ego, inquit, cognobiliorem cognitionem esse arbitror.' For the use of *inquit*, not being part of the actual quotation, cf. fr. 101 and *ORF*³, frs. 111 and 112.   [66] pp. 155 f.

wholly implausible, since book 5 of the *Origines* is very unlikely to have been written and even more unlikely to have been published until long after the event. Nor is it plausible to suggest that Cato saw his forceful but heterogeneous and sometimes almost contradictory arguments as a statement of principles which he wished to propagate.[67] A rather different motive which has been suggested is resentment against one of the Rhodian delegates, Astymedes, because by publishing his own speech he might seem to have detracted from Cato's own role in saving Rhodes from a declaration of war;[68] but even if that did not seem an inadequate explanation the question would still remain as to why Cato responded with the novel device of incorporating his actual speech in his history.

Though Cato's inclusion of speeches which he himself had delivered is exceptional, nevertheless it is scarcely credible that it had no relationship at all to the established practice according to which Greek historians put speeches of their own composition into the mouths of historical persons. The only satisfactory explanation of Cato's action appears to be a combination of pride in his own achievement with an awareness that speeches were a normal feature of historical writing. But that awareness—or at least its application in practice—was limited, for Cato's own orations did not fulfil the established role of such speeches as devices to convey a special sense of particular historical situations and issues.[69] The Rhodian speech in particular can hardly be regarded as highlighting a situation or decision of momentous importance for Rome. Either Cato had not fully understood that role or he had no interest in reproducing it, the significance of the precedent being for him simply that it gave him the idea of displaying his own performance in this way. And either of these alternatives strongly suggests that while Cato readily took over the general concept and features of historical writing he was then much more interested in the positive work of finding and writing out his material than in conforming to Greek historiographical and literary models.

The speeches are thus an important pointer to the relationship between the *Origines* and Greek historical writing; and they indicate an attitude on Cato's part very similar to that suggested by his other writings.[70] It is a conclusion with which the rest of what is known about the *Origines* is fully compatible. The recounting of numerous Greek-centred foundation stories, and particularly those concerning Rome itself, shows not a sense of

[67] pp. 138 f. and 273 ff.
[68] Kennedy, *The Art of Rhetoric*, pp. 59 f.; cf. Polyb. 30. 4. 10 ff.
[69] Leo, *Gesch. der röm. Literatur* i. 298 f.; Marmorale, *Cato Maior*[2], p. 169; Bömer, 'Thematik und Krise', *Historia*, 2 (1953), 197.   [70] pp. 207 f.

cultural inferiority but simple acceptance of received tradition. Since both the concept and the practice of writing history were Greek in origin and it was still a predominantly Greek activity, Cato's work was necessarily a product of that tradition and reflected its forms and methods. In one respect at least, namely in his survey of Italian origins, he was almost certainly showing himself directly acquainted with Greek works, not merely with those of his Roman predecessors who wrote in Greek. Since he was aware of the background and must have been conscious that to write history in Latin was an innovation, it is a plausible, indeed a highly probable conjecture that patriotic pride played a substantial role among the motives for writing the *Origines*. Nevertheless in various particulars the imprint of his own personality is evident, and such idiosyncratic features as the speeches and the omission of names strongly suggest that even in this work he was not constantly concerned about meticulous conformity to Greek conventions or anxious about possible comparisons.

Yet in most respects Cato's personal contributions to historical writing were neither far-reaching nor influential. Except for the *admiranda* his account was probably mostly narrative, from book 4 onwards mostly military narrative, offering little in the way of analysis or a new understanding of Rome. Though the meagreness of the fragments requires that a note of caution accompany any judgement, it is doubtful if Cato contributed anything of lasting value in historical method or intellectual insight.[71] Significantly, none of his distinctive innovations became normal practice. Although many of the subsequent Roman historians were not themselves eminent in public life, none of those who were is known to have reproduced his own speeches in his history, while Nepos and Pliny clearly regarded Cato's omission of names as peculiar to himself. Nor did Roman historians see fit to discuss the origins of the Italians, preferring in this respect to follow the pattern established by Fabius Pictor and Cincius Alimentus. Possibly Cato's example did encourage other great public figures to write histories which highlighted their own activities, thus creating in Roman historiography a partisan strain which lasted to the end of the Republic and even beyond.[72] But there were some precedents for this among the Greeks—though most Greek historians were not major public figures—and it was Fabius and Cincius who had established the

[71] Bömer, 'Thematik und Krise', *Historia*, 2 (1953), 196 ff., rightly warns against allowing the powerful impress of Cato's personality to be mistaken for innovation in historical method. Also Timpe, 'Le Origini', *Atti e Mem. Accad. Patavina Sc. Lett.* 83 (1970–1), 32 f.; id., 'Fabius Pictor', in Temporini, *Aufstieg und Niedergang* i. 2, pp. 962 f.; cf. Marmorale, *Cato Maior*[2], pp. 168 and 224 ff.

[72] Badian, 'The Early Historians', in Dorey, *Latin Historians*, p. 9.

fundamental point that the writing of history was a respectable occupation for Roman senators.

The writing of the *Origines* was undoubtedly a major undertaking, but Cato's one really significant contribution as a historian was to write in Latin. Presumably he thereby made a coherent account of Rome's origin and history available to a larger audience, though just how much larger remains uncertain in view of the widespread acquaintance with Greek in the upper classes.[73] More important, however, he had added a new and important dimension to the prose literature which he himself had begun; for despite the limitations of method and intellectual insight with which he probably embarked on the composition of the *Origines*, it represents an extension of his experiments into a different type of literature, and one which had within it the potential for great artistic and intellectual development at the hands of his successors. If his own work was no more than a modest beginning in that respect, it is still remarkable that one individual should have been responsible for carrying the first experiments in Latin prose literature as far as Cato did.

Nor is that the full measure of his achievement. There is also the question of the quality of the prose writing, in the sense of the skilful and artistic use of language.[74] Here again the meagreness of the fragments is a considerable difficulty, made worse by the fact that a good proportion are paraphrases rather than quotations. Some of the passages in Cicero at first sight seem damning: to write like Cato and other early Roman historians requires no orator, merely that the author should not be a liar; the sole ornament they sought was *brevitas*; otherwise all is bare and light-weight (*exile*, sc. in style).[75] Not everything is so severe, however, and in truth Cicero's comments on the *Origines* are closely assimilated to those on Cato's speeches and his judgement is in essence the same: Cato's writing is not without merit but by Cicero's standards is gravely deficient in elaboration and ornament.[76] Essentially the same picture is implied by Sallust who, with an attitude towards ornamentation very different from Cicero's, praised Cato's *brevitas* and called him *disertissimus*, 'the most skilled of the Roman race in writing'.[77] However, the ancient sources have very few

[73] That there was a potential new readership is suggested by the fact that somewhat later the history written in Greek by Acilius was translated into Latin, and those written by Postumius Albinus and Fabius Pictor may also have been: Livy, 25. 39. 11; Timpe, 'Fabius Pictor', in Temporini, *Aufstieg und Niedergang* i. 2, p. 963 n. 89.

[74] See esp. Leo, *Gesch. der röm. Literatur* i. 299 f.; Helm, *RE*, s.v. *Porcius*, no. 9, col. 161; Leeman, *Orationis Ratio*, pp. 70 f.; von Albrecht, *Meister röm. Prosa*, pp. 38 ff. Cf. also other works cited p. 211 n. 1.   [75] Cic. *De orat.* 2. 51 ff.; *De leg.* 1. 6.

[76] Cic. *Brut.* 66 ff.; *De orat.* 2. 53; 3. 135.

[77] Sall. *Hist.* 1, fr. 4, where the reference is clearly to the *Origines*.

comments on the style specifically of the *Origines*, though various general statements are clearly to be taken to include it as well as the speeches.[78] In short, the evidence is not extensive, but such as it is it suggests a certain similarity in style to the speeches, and certainly no obvious contrast.

Much the same may be said of the fragments. Many suggest a plain, bald narrative conveyed in short sentences, simple in structure and style. Yet there is also a scattering of words and phrases which suggest that in places Cato brought into play some of those stylistic devices which can be observed in the fragments of the speeches: asyndeton, repetition, antithesis, pleonasm, coupled adjectives, the familiar *atque*.[79] Unfortunately there is a special difficulty about the fragment which is by far the longest, the account of Caedicius; for Gellius clearly implies that he is not using Cato's exact words to tell the story. In fact the narrative is so simple and plain that it is difficult to believe that Gellius had departed very far from the original; but what is uncertain is whether Gellius' paraphrasing has added to the neatness and clarity of the narrative, and whether he or Cato is responsible for some of the slightly elaborate phrases and constructions which occur.[80] At the conclusion, however, Gellius quotes a substantial section which he says is in Cato's own words, first describing Caedicius' miraculous survival and praising his achievement and service to the *res publica*, and then comparing the meagre honours he received with those showered on the memory of Leonidas for his similar exploit at Thermopylae. The stylistic elaboration of this passage is striking, working up to a climax in the comparison with Leonidas which is comparable to the more forceful passages from the speeches.

This affinity with the speeches is interesting and significant. Like the speeches the *Origines* showed an unevenness in style. Much of the narrative was simple and plain, sufficiently so to make it fairly certain that the creation of literary elegance was not a fundamental purpose or consideration in Cato's composition of the *Origines*. It has rightly been observed that his use of style was functional,[81] not an end in itself. But whereas in the *De agricultura* it was only in the Preface that he had deliberately sought a more elevated style, in the *Origines* he found incentive to do this also at

---

[78] Notably many passages in Fronto and Gellius.

[79] e.g. *HRR* i², frs. 77, 79, 83, 91, 93, 97, 99, 101, 110, 113. Sblendorio, 'Note sullo stile dell'oratoria catoniana', *AFLC* 34 (1971), 5 ff., notes and distinguishes the occurrence of such features in the *Origines*.

[80] See esp. von Albrecht, *Meister röm. Prosa*, pp. 38 ff., for a detailed assessment of the whole passage. That Gellius' text in the narrative is close to Cato's own words is suggested also by several instances of hendiadys and the considerable number of sentences lacking connectives.   [81] von Albrecht, op. cit., p. 50.

various points in the body of the work. There were probably two principal factors encouraging this. One, exemplified by the Caedicius passage,
was the wish to take didactic advantage of the climax of a story. The other
was that in the course of the narrative he was from time to time describing
events which were swift or dramatic, reminiscent of descriptive passages
in his speeches. In each type of case he would naturally have been led to
apply the formidable facility in language which he had acquired in a lifetime of successful oratory. In this way the *Origines* not only advanced his
experiments in prose writing into a new field but carried them a small but
significant way into a new dimension of literary quality.

II

The *De agricultura* as a Social Document[1]

DURING the half-century following the Second Punic War—the last fifty or so of Cato's eighty-five years—the agricultural scene in Italy underwent a profound transformation. If some aspects of that transformation remain uncertain or controversial, nevertheless its main features are clear enough. There was a rapid spread of medium- and large-scale agricultural enterprises, many, perhaps most of them worked by slave labour and managed on behalf of wealthy absentee owners by overseers who themselves were often slaves. Although there was, no doubt, much variation in the scale as well as the type of agriculture practised, considerable holdings quickly accumulated to a relatively limited number of owners. The opportunities of empire and the spoils of the major wars of the period produced a great influx of wealth, much of which passed directly into private hands and was spent on agricultural acquisitions and enterprises. At the same time the sale of numerous prisoners from the wars, together perhaps with easier access to the slave-trade of the eastern Mediterranean, facilitated the supply of slaves.[2]

[1] The following recent works contain discussions of special relevance to the central issues of this chapter: Toynbee, *Hannibal's Legacy* ii, esp. ch. 7; Dohr, *Die italischen Gutshöfe*; Brockmeyer, *Arbeitsorganisation und ökonomisches Denken*, pp. 72 ff.; White, *Roman Farming*; id., 'Roman Agricultural Writers', in Temporini (ed.), *Aufstieg und Niedergang* i. 4, pp. 439 ff. (with valuable bibliography); Martin, *Recherches sur les agronomes latins*, esp. pp. 84 ff.; Finley, *The Ancient Economy*. Additionally: Gummerus, *Der röm. Gutsbetrieb*, *Klio*, Beih. 5 (1906); Heitland, *Agricola*; Curcio, *La primitiva civiltà latina agricola*; Scalais, 'La politique agraire de Rome', *MB* 34 (1932), 196 ff.; Brehaut, *Cato the Censor. On Farming*; *ESAR* i; Yeo, 'The Development of the Roman Plantation' and 'The Economics of Roman and American Slavery', *Finanzarchiv*, 13 (1952), 321 ff. and 445 ff.; Kienast, esp. pp. 30, 35 f., 89; Foucher, 'La vie rurale', *BAGB* 1957, 2, pp. 41 ff.; Maróti, 'Zur Frage der Warenproduktion', *A. Ant. Hung.* 11 (1963), 215 ff.; Salomon, 'Essai sur les structures agraires', *Recherches d'hist. économique*, pp. 1 ff.; White, *A Bibliography of Roman Agriculture*; Šimovičová, 'Zur Erkenntis der Warenproduktion in Catos Schrift', *GLO* 3 (1971), 3 ff.; id., 'Der Warenaustausch und die Marktformen in Catos Schrift', *GLO* 4 (1972), 3 ff.; id., 'Zur Frage der Rentabilität und der Produktionskosten in M. Porcius Catos Schrift', *GLO* 5 (1973), 129 ff. Also articles in Russian by Sergeenko, *VDI* 1948, pp. 206 ff., 1949, pp. 86 ff., 1952, pp. 38 ff., 1955, pp. 31 ff., and by Kac, *VDI* 1964, pp. 81 ff. (these and other works in Russian not consulted directly in the preparation of this chapter).

[2] Astin, *Scipio Aemilianus*, pp. 161 ff.; Toynbee, *Hannibal's Legacy* ii, esp. chs. 6–8; Brunt

The changes in the pattern of Italian agriculture were to have far-reaching effects in the social, military, and political structure of the Roman state, and in particular they were to be a major factor underlying the crisis and catastrophe of the tribunate of Tiberius Gracchus in 133. In due course they began to press with growing severity upon many peasants who farmed on a small scale, whether as proprietors or as tenants; enlargement of the holdings of the wealthy, abetted by other factors, led increasingly to dispossession of the peasants. But that aspect of the process developed only with the passage of time; in the early years of the second century the expanding agricultural activities of the wealthy were not so much supplanting their poorer neighbours as filling a vacuum. The damage and more especially the disruption inflicted on southern Italy during Hannibal's invasion and its aftermath had been accompanied by the uprooting of tens of thousands of peasants, Roman and allied, for prolonged military service; and the casualties of the Second Punic War had been enormous. Consequently there was ample opportunity for the wealthy to expand their activities and acquire additional land without creating immediate widespread pressures on the peasants; indeed there are indications that so far from this producing a mass of dispossessed and destitute peasantry, great difficulty was experienced in finding sufficient settlers for Rome's various colonial ventures in the first quarter of the century.[3] Furthermore, confiscations of territories from peoples who had defected to Hannibal had greatly enlarged the Roman *ager publicus*,[4] which in turn opened up additional opportunities; for on payment of a modest rental any Roman citizen was entitled to farm or to pasture animals upon it up to the maximum extent prescribed by law. The pasturing of flocks and herds was particularly assisted by the increased availability of higher ground over which they could move freely for summer grazing.

The early history of the restrictions on the use of public land is controversial. It is not easy to believe that the *maxima* attested later in the second century—500 *iugera* of land, 100 large animals, and 500 small animals—originated in a law as old as 367 B.C. A common view is that such restrictions were first introduced in the first quarter of the second century, but

---

Roman Manpower, chs. 17 and 20, rightly attaching greater importance to the disruptive effects of the war and especially of Roman actions in its aftermath, as opposed to Toynbee's overstatement of the destruction and its long-term effects. On the spread of *latifundia* and their form see also Yeo, 'The Economics of Roman and American Slavery', *Finanzarchiv*, 13 (1952), 445 ff., esp. 459 ff.; Tibiletti, 'Lo sviluppo del latifondo', *X Congresso Internazionale di Scienze Storiche* (1955) ii. 235 ff.; White, 'Latifundia', *BICS* 14 (1967), 62 ff.

[3] Salmon, *Roman Colonization*, pp. 95 ff.
[4] Brunt, *Roman Manpower*, esp. ch. 17 and p. 371.

it is also possible that at that time earlier restrictions were modified and the limits raised to those attested.[5] Either view would imply that increasing use of public land had drawn attention to the issue, the second probably also that earlier limits were proving to be unreasonably restrictive in relation to the amount of land now available.[6] However that may be, as late as 180 it was possible to resettle 40,000 Ligurians near Beneventum, though by 173 in highly fertile Campania private encroachment on public land, compounded by administrative failure to collect the rentals, had gone so far that a consul, no less, had to be sent to determine the boundaries; and in 167 Cato could illustrate an argument in his Rhodian speech by referring to a wish to exceed the legal limits as a familiar and understandable sentiment.[7] Thus over a period of time a great deal of the *ager publicus* was brought into use, both as pasture and as cash-crop 'plantation' farms, as the fateful transformation spread across both private and public land.

Since most of the evidence for agricultural conditions in Italy during this period of change is both late and slender, Cato's *De agricultura* has special interest; for it was written during this very period and is concerned with what may be loosely termed 'investment farming'.[8] Broadly speaking its value in this context lies in what it reveals about the type—or types—of agricultural organization with which Cato deals and about the attitudes and preconceptions in respect of social and economic matters which are reflected in his approach to his material. It is necessary to keep in mind, however, three important considerations about the character of the book. First, Cato concerned himself with certain types of farms only, and made no attempt to give advice on all the forms of agriculture actually practised in Italy at this time. Second, since the idea governing his approach to the subject was to give practical advice, his whole treatment is strongly didactic and not at all descriptive. Third, as was discussed at length in a previous

---

[5] See esp. Tibiletti, 'Il possesso dell'ager publicus', *Athenaeum*, 26 (1948), 173 f., esp. 191 f., and 27 (1949), 3 ff.; 'Richerche di storia agraria romana', *Athenaeum*, 28 (1950), 245 ff.; also Toynbee, *Hannibal's Legacy* ii. 554 ff.

[6] Heavy fines on graziers in 196 and 193 could reflect the imposition of restrictions but equally could have resulted from increasing defiance of earlier restrictions which were inappropriate to the new conditions: Livy, 33. 42. 10; 35. 10. 11 f.

[7] Livy, 40. 38. 1 ff. (Ligurians); 42. 1. 6 and 19. 1 (Campania); *ORF*[3], Cato fr. 167.

[8] The type of agricultural organization dealt with by Cato has frequently been discussed. Of the more recent works listed on p. 240 n. 1 those of Dohr and White are especially useful; of the older works esp. that of Gummerus. For the technical aspects see White, *Roman Farming*, from whom (p. 19) the term 'investment farming' is borrowed. The present discussion deliberately avoids frequent use of modern financial terms because their more technical connotations and their cumulative effect might create a misleading impression; see further p. 259.

chapter, the presentation of his material is much affected by his undisciplined methods of composition and by his heavy reliance on his own personal experience and private memoranda. Consequently the insights the book affords are selective, or more accurately, patchy, certainly not systematic or comprehensive. On the other hand they have the directness and authenticity which springs from personal knowledge and from a concern with practical particulars, undistorted by attempts to create a descriptive framework or a generalized interpretation.

If the *De agricultura* is not evidence for Italian agriculture as a whole, it nevertheless yields a remarkable amount of information about a particular type of farm which, it may legitimately be inferred, was at that time common in Latium and Campania. The purpose of this type of farm was to produce a cash income for an owner who was not normally resident upon it. Although at one point Cato mentions the possibility that the owner may have only one such property, he implies that it was common to own more than one, as he himself did.[9] He has in mind farms ranging from about 100 to 240 *iugera* (roughly 60 to 150 acres). In one passage he speaks of 100 *iugera* as ideal, but there he is thinking primarily of a vineyard and that is indeed the size of the vineyard for which he later gives an inventory. The two olive-yards referred to in the text are both larger, one of them 120 and the other 240 *iugera*.[10]

The primary function of the farms which are dealt with in the *De agricultura* was to produce wine or olive oil for sale. An exception to this is found in the brief digression on the 'suburban farm', *fundus suburbanus*, which is to be used to grow a considerable variety of produce marketable in the near-by town;[11] but in general it is quite clear that Cato's attention is directed principally to wine and olive oil. That is not to say that these farms were by any means given over to monoculture. A variety of other crops was raised and animals were kept, but only in an auxiliary role. Profit might be made from the sale of surplus grain and osiers, and it is taken for granted that the sale of lambs and wool will produce some income from the flock kept on the olive-yard; but in all cases this was only incidental.[12] Grain and other crops were grown not for sale but to feed the resident labour-force and work-animals, while others, such as the osiers, were to provide materials required for various agricultural operations. The only cattle mentioned are work-oxen; a swineherd figures among the

---

[9] *De agr.* 8. 2: 'et qui eum fundum solum habebit'. That Cato himself owned several such properties is the obvious implication of the *De agricultura* itself and of the reference to several villas in Gell. 13. 24. 1 and Plut. *Cato Mai.* 4. 5; cf. Thielscher, *Belehrung*, pp. 5 ff.

[10] *De agr.* 1. 7; 11. 1; 3. 5; 10. 1.   [11] *De agr.* 7–8.

[12] *De agr.* 2. 7 (grain, lambs, wool); 9 (osiers); 150 (the flock; lambs; wool).

personnel recommended for both vineyard and olive-yard, but Cato says nothing at all about the swine themselves; and the flock of sheep to be kept on the olive-yard is small, probably of 100 sheep, tended by a single shepherd and kept primarily as a source of valuable manure and perhaps for the cheese made from the ewes' milk.[13] Thus although strictly speaking this was neither mixed farming nor subsistence farming the production of the single cash-crop was supported by an element of each.

Obviously the purpose of this quite extensive ancillary activity was to create a considerable measure of self-sufficiency. Not that Cato's properties were truly self-sufficient in the manner of some known in later periods, which were on such a scale that they included whole villages and obtained virtually all their requirements from resident craftsmen. Cato assumes that neighbouring farms will have need of each other's assistance, even if he does seek to restrict his *vilicus* to a few such contacts.[14] More important, the items which it is assumed will be obtained from various towns include not only such an exceptional and very expensive purchase as a new olive-press but practically all metal tools, ropes, and other 'manufactured' equipment.[15] On the other hand the intention is undoubtedly that so far as possible the farm should be self-supporting in consumables and materials which could be grown on it. The reason for this may be partly a desire to keep the establishment as self-contained as possible, avoiding time-consuming visits to markets—for visits to purchase need have been made only at long intervals; and possibly the less outside contact there was the fewer opportunities and temptations there would be for slaves to abscond. The principal consideration however was certainly financial, the simple belief that anything produced on the farm itself was a saving, whereas anything purchased from elsewhere involved an expenditure which had to be set against the cash profit. Whether Cato thought of this ancillary production as in itself an expense is questionable, but even supposing him to have done so he certainly did not have available accounting techniques anywhere near adequate to permit realistic comparison with purchase in the market.[16] If he thought at all in terms of

---

[13] Cheese figures in the contract in *De agr.* 150. 1 and in a number of the recipes in 75 ff.; sheep's manure in 151. 2 and 161. 4; cf. 30 and White, *Roman Farming*, pp. 134 f. The swine permitted to the sheep contractor in 150. 2 seem not to be those for whom swineherds are provided in 10. 1 and 11. 1.   [14] *De agr.* 4; 5. 3.

[15] *De agr.* 22. 3 f.; 135; conveniently classified by Toynbee, *Hannibal's Legacy* ii. 682. Gummerus, *Der röm. Gutsbetrieb*, p. 34, and Toynbee, op. cit., p. 309, point out that in addition large quantities of pitch must have been purchased, though this is not mentioned by Cato.

[16] Mickwitz, 'Economic Rationalism in Graeco-Roman Agriculture', *Eng. Hist. Review* 52 1937), 577 ff.; de Ste Croix, 'Greek and Roman Accounting', in Littleton and Yamey (edd.),

comparative cost, it was with the confident assumption that what was grown on the farm was cheaper (an assumption which may well have been correct in the prevailing conditions, especially in view of the slowness and high cost of bulk transport). More probably he thought in the more elementary terms that purchasing involved spending and growing did not.[17] However that may be, the practical effect in either case was that although such farms were not truly self-supporting communities, there was a considerable measure of self-sufficiency and consequently of isolation.

The permanent labour-force which made up this little community consisted entirely of slaves—Cato recommends thirteen for the 240-*iugera* olive-yard, sixteen for the vineyard. In both cases this includes the *vilicus* or overseer and one woman, the *vilica*, who was sometimes— probably usually—wife as well as housekeeper to the *vilicus*.[18] In one passage Cato seems to imply that some of the other slaves might have dependants, an arrangement known to and even recommended by later writers; but it is a tenuous reference and nowhere else does Cato give any indication of such a situation.[19] Several of the slaves—in fact in the olive-yard a majority—have specialized roles, such as teamster, muleteer, swineherd, shepherd, and of course the *vilicus* himself. Of the remainder, designated simply 'workmen', *operarii*, at least some were shackled, *compediti*, and the single incidental mention of this is such as to suggest that Cato regarded it as a normal state of affairs rather than a special punishment.[20] Although it is customary to emphasize Cato's concern with getting the maximum possible work out of the slaves, there is some reason to think that as a full-time, year-round labour force the provision was if anything slightly generous in relation to the tasks expected of it.[21] At exceptionally busy times, notably at harvest, it was normal to supplement the permanent establishment with temporary free labour, the availability of which Cato mentions as an important consideration in choosing a farm. No less than

Studies in the History of Accounting, pp. 14 ff., surveys accounting practices in general but adds nothing to Mickwitz on the immediate point. *De agr.* 1. 7 gives an impression of some sophistication in comparisons between different parts of the farm, but this is misleading: see Appendix 11.

[17] On the concept of self-sufficiency see also Finley, *The Ancient Economy*, pp. 109 f.; also below, pp. 260 f., for the likelihood that the concern with self-sufficiency and small savings reflects the realities of agricultural life.   [18] *De agr.* 10. 1; 11. 1; on the *vilica*, 143.

[19] *De agr.* 25: 'Quom vinum . . . legetur, facito uti servetur familiae primum suisque.' *De agr.* 138 does not give the support Thielscher seems to suppose for his acceptance that there were dependants: *Belehrung*, pp. 232 f.

[20] In other passages Cato seems to use *operarius* to indicate a free worker. The argument of Westermann, *Slave Systems*, pp. 68 f., that it has this meaning also in 10. 1 and 11. 1 is not convincing. *Compediti*: *De agr.* 56.   [21] White, *Roman Farming*, p. 373.

fifty free labourers are stipulated in the sample contract for olive-gathering. Although the hiring of day-labourers does seem to be envisaged as a possibility, most of this supplementary labour seems to have been obtained by contracting out the work.[22] Thus Cato gives a number of sample contracts but, significantly, virtually no advice about the actual conduct of harvesting or pressing. There is little doubt that he regarded it as standard practice to contract out grain harvesting, olive-gathering and pressing, and the major operations of the vintage.

In such a system the *vilicus* played a key role. Obviously major 'policy' decisions, including those relating to important contracts, were matters for the owner himself; but since he made only occasional visits the day-to-day management of the entire operation, including discipline over and adjudication among the slaves, was in the hands of the *vilicus*. Its efficiency depended almost entirely upon that person's competence, industry, reliability, and honesty, as Cato's elaborate and optimistic instructions show.[23] In practice even Cato regards it as no surprise if there are shortcomings and excuses,[24] and it is not easy to believe that great numbers of *vilici* were amply endowed with all the required skills and personal qualities. Cato envisages the owner controlling the situation and keeping up efficiency by means of rigorous inspections, careful checking of detailed accounts, and calculations of the time needed for work done in relation to the time available; all of which presupposes considerable expertise on the part of the owner himself, not to mention a task of supervision which became increasingly burdensome and complicated as the number of his properties increased.[25] All in all it may be doubted whether many of these farms were run as competently as a full and literal application of Cato's instructions would imply.

It is perhaps this problem of supervision which accounts for the presence among Cato's sample contracts of a few for the lease of long-term operations on the farm, in such a way as to give the contractor an interest in a high yield. One instance is particularly significant in that it sets out, unfortunately only very briefly, provisions for the leasing of a vineyard,

---

[22] *De agr.* 1. 3; 5. 4; 136–7; 144–50. The sample contracts have given rise to some discussion in connection with the history of certain aspects of Roman law. Some articles on this aspect are included in the general bibliography of this book, pp. 351 ff.

[23] *De agr.* 5.   [24] *De agr.* 2. 2.

[25] *De agr.* 2; 4. The problem of supervision of an increasing number of properties is emphasized by Brockmeyer, *Arbeitsorganisation*, pp. 75 ff., though he interprets not only the contracts mentioned below but much of the resort to contracts (including e.g. the sale of grapes on the vine) as a kind of compromise induced by the problem. In going so far he makes insufficient allowance for the extent to which the unevenness of labour requirements was a serious problem.

including its auxiliary elements, to a share-tenant. It is not clear whether the *vilicus* was to continue under the direction of the tenant or was to be replaced by him, but in any event this amounts to a different principle of management and operation, under which the owner presumably accepted a lower share of the return in exchange for less need to supervise in detail and possibly a higher standard of management.[26]

This matter of the share-tenant is a useful reminder that the extent to which the picture conveyed by Cato is representative must not be over-estimated. Since Cato himself thought almost entirely in terms of direct management through a *vilicus*, it is a reasonable assumption that farms of the type with which he was concerned frequently were managed in this way. On the other hand his mention of terms for a share-tenant of a vineyard (and if for a vineyard why not for an olive-yard?) shows him to have been aware of an alternative arrangement and creates a similar assumption, namely that, though he himself made little or no use of this alternative, at least it was by no means a rarity. So brief is the passage, so obviously in contrast with Cato's predominant assumption, that it is almost by chance that the share-tenant is mentioned, and there is no means at all of determining the relative proportions of the two systems. Yet this unanswerable question has direct relevance not only to agricultural management but to the composition of the rural population at the time.

All this is even more true when it comes to consideration of types of agriculture with which Cato does not concern himself. Peasant agriculture, for example, certainly continued to exist and is assumed to do so by Cato himself in his Preface to the *De agricultura*, but within the work itself it simply does not come within his purview. Consequently Cato's silence affords no evidence, even as regards Latium and Campania, about the extent to which peasant agriculture was in decline; and there is nothing in the book to help decide whether it was largely subsistence or cash-crop farming, or, if the latter, whether the products were in competition with those of farms such as Cato does deal with.[27]

---

[26] *De agr.* 137. The brevity of the passage leaves unanswered questions about the slaves and the animals as well as the *vilicus*. Any improvement in management might have been a short-term advantage only, since a tenant with no long-term interest is not usually disposed to effect long-term improvements. Minor contracts which may have a similar significance concern the *politor* who helps with the grain harvest, 136, cf. 5. 4, and the products of the flock of sheep, 150. For discussion of the precise role of the *politor* see Frank, 'An Interpretation of Cato, Agricultura 136', *AJPh* 54 (1933), 162 ff.; Brockmeyer, *Arbeitsorganisation*, pp. 81 ff.; Goujard, 'Politio, politor (Caton, Agr. 136)', *RPh* 44 (1970), 84 ff., who argues that he assists through the year and not just for a limited season.

[27] Direct competition is often assumed but is questionable, especially with regard to wine; cf. Brunt, *Roman Manpower*, pp. 708 f.

The one thing Cato does reveal about the population pattern is that a large pool of free labour was available for temporary hire in agriculture; indeed he reveals its availability because the type of agriculture which concerns him depended heavily upon it to cope with temporary seasonal needs for much additional labour. It is a plausible guess that many of these men were peasant farmers supplementing the livelihood won from their own farms; but there may also have been casual labourers and temporary migrants from towns or other areas taking advantage of the brief seasonal demand. Since Cato had no reason to mention how these people normally supported themselves there is no means of determining the actual mix or how many were normally rural dwellers in those particular localities.

Even within his own category of 'investment farming' Cato's scope is sharply restricted. His silence in no way tells against the possibility, indeed the probability, that, especially in other areas, there were many such farms which differed in organization, size, and primary product from those he does deal with; nor is his lack of interest significant evidence as to the extent to which grain was being grown for market in Italy at this time.[28] But it is the pasturing of sheep and cattle which most clearly illustrates the point. It has been mentioned already that the only cattle which Cato discusses are work-oxen, and that the small flock of sheep on the olive-yard, though yielding some marketable items, has a basically ancillary role. Meadows are mentioned several times as desirable, and there is a sample contract for leasing them for winter pasture;[29] but nowhere is advice given on pasturing as a major or principal source of income. Yet already in the early years of the second century this was sufficiently widespread to attract attention by quite considerable problems to which it gave rise.[30] If Cato did not deal with it in the *De agricultura*, that is an indication of the limits of his interests, purposes, or methods,

[28] White, *Roman Farming*, pp. 19 and 65 ff. On grain see Brunt, *Roman Manpower*, esp. pp. 128 f., 369, 705 f.

[29] *De agr.* 1. 7; 8. 1; 9; 50. 1; 149.

[30] Fines on graziers in 196 and 193: Livy, 33. 42. 10; 35. 10. 11 f. Repression of brigandage and unrest among *pastores* in 185 and 184: Livy, 39. 29. 9; 39. 41. 6. Toynbee, *Hannibal's Legacy* ii. 320 f., following Frank, 'The Bacchanalian Cult of 186 B.C.', *CQ* 21 (1927), 130, notes the close link with the aftermath of the Bacchanalian affair (cf. also Livy, 40. 19. 9 f.) and suspects that Roman action was more of a 'witch-hunt' than the suppression of rebellious movements. If that were so it would have a bearing on the nature of the problem but not on the fact that there were slave shepherds in sufficiently large numbers to be felt to present some kind of serious problem. In point of fact Toynbee's interpretation involves rejecting explicit statements by Livy. There have been numerous discussions of pasturing and its growth in this period, e.g. recently, Toynbee, op. cit. ii, ch. 7; Brunt, *Roman Manpower*, pp. 370 ff.; White, *Roman Farming*, ch. 8.

not that it was unimportant or unfamiliar. As it happens, the point is strikingly illustrated by the emphasis placed on pasturing in one of Cato's dicta:

When he was asked what was most advantageous in the management of property, he replied, 'Good pasturing' (*bene pascere*). What second? 'Fairly good pasturing.' What third? 'Poor pasturing.' What fourth? 'Ploughing' [*arare*, which must mean 'arable farming', 'cultivating crops']. And when the questioner said, 'What about usury?' Cato replied, 'What about killing a man?'[31]

The glaring discrepancy between the advice given in this dictum and the assumptions and practice displayed in the *De agricultura* is not in itself a serious problem. It is not uncommon for people to contradict themselves, shift their opinions, or give advice which they themselves have not followed; and they are perhaps all the more likely to do these things in matters in which the techniques available to them for assessment and comparison are crude and inadequate.[32] Neither the *De agricultura* nor the dictum can be dated, so it is not possible to determine which was the prior, let alone the interval between them. If the dictum were the later that would at least fit in with the mention of 'land with natural pastures' among the types of property which Plutarch says that Cato came to prefer in his later years:

As he applied himself more strenuously to money-getting he considered farming more a pastime than a source of income, and put his resources into enterprises which were safe and sure. He bought ponds, hot springs, sites given over to fullers, pitch-workings, land with natural pastures and woodland, which brought him much money and, as he himself said, could not be ruined

---

[31] Cic. *De off.* 2. 89 = Jordan, p. 108, *Dicta mem.* 63; partial versions in several later writers. Thielscher, *Belehrung*, p. 272, comparing *De agr.* 61. 1 (similar in form but not in substance), wrongly rejects the dictum as patently spurious. On usury see below and Appendix 5.

[32] At first sight *De agr.* 1. 7 seems to imply a sharp change of opinion between the time of the book and that of the dictum (or vice versa), since in the rating by merit of nine features of a farm meadows are placed only fifth. However, quite apart from the fact that the list is muddled and ill considered (Appendix 11) it is probable that Cato is here thinking not about pasturing as a primary activity but about the limited pasture required in connection with a vineyard. It is the silence of the *De agricultura* about pasturing, not a specific statement in it, that seems to contradict the dictum; and the true explanation may lie less in a change of opinion than in the particularism which is a marked feature of the book and which probably resulted in Cato concerning himself only with what he himself was immediately involved in at the time. That there may not really have been a great discrepancy in opinions after all is suggested by *De agr.* 9, where the value of meadows is briefly emphasized. Brunt, *Roman Manpower*, p. 371 n. 3, takes the explanation to be that Cato drew a sharp distinction between arable and stockbreeding, i.e. that he would have regarded the latter as irrelevant to a book *de agricultura*.

by Jupiter. He engaged also in the most criticized form of lending at interest, namely maritime loans, in the following way. He instructed the borrowers to invite many persons into a company, and when there were fifty of them and as many ships he himself held one share through Quintio, a freedman, who acted with the borrowers in their transactions and sailed with them. Thus the risk was not on the whole but on a small part, in return for great profits.[33]

Whether Cato really went so far as to refer to agriculture as a mere pastime is questionable; if he did it is more likely than not to have been another instance of overstatement for immediate effect, once again taken by Plutarch at face value as a statement of considered opinion. More probably Plutarch took the idea from Cicero's *De senectute*[34] and himself applied it to the antithesis he was making between Cato's interest in agriculture and his other activities. But at least the reference to the purchase of properties which 'could not be ruined by Jupiter', which plainly implies that they were to be preferred to crop production, is expressly attributed to Cato himself; and there is no good reason to deny the correctness either of this attribution or of the account of his maritime loans, which also could go back to Cato himself. Unfortunately there is again no satisfactory indication of chronological priority. Although at first sight Plutarch's treatment of the passage might be taken to suggest that the references are to a time after the *De agricultura* was written, an earlier date is by no means impossible.[35] What is apparent is that this passage, the dictum quoted above, and the *De agricultura* itself, interrelated by references to income, investment, agriculture, pasturing, commerce, and lending at interest, all raise questions about Cato's attitudes and motives in economic and social matters. In this connection the *De agricultura*'s Preface (in which are the book's only references to commerce and money-lending) is of particular interest. It is as follows:

Concerning agriculture.[36] It is sometimes more advantageous to seek to make money by trade, or would be if it were not so hazardous, and likewise

[33] Plut. *Cato Mai.* 21. 5 f.

[34] Esp. *De sen.* 24, which is not reliable evidence since Cicero is likely to have felt free to devise his own arguments and put them into Cato's mouth.

[35] It is argued below that there is no serious incompatibility between the activities Plutarch describes and the *De agricultura*; thus, to put it at its mildest, the assertion that there was a major change in Cato's practice may be an inference by Plutarch himself. Kienast, pp. 35 f. attempts actually to demonstrate that Cato had important commercial interests as early as the 190s; but his arguments, relating to the *Dissuasio legis Iuniae de feneratione* (on which see Appendix 5), are insufficient.

[36] Birt, 'Zum Proöm und den Summarien', *BPhW* 29 (1915), 922 ff., is almost certainly correct in his contention that Cato's sequence of thought flows on directly from the title. Previously the abruptness of the opening of the Preface had frequently aroused suspicions that a sentence was missing.

to engage in usury, if it were as respectable [sc. 'as agriculture']. Our ancestors considered it so[37] and laid it down thus in the laws: that a thief is condemned to pay twofold, a usurer fourfold. From this one may judge how much worse a citizen they considered a usurer than a thief. And when they praised a good man they praised him as 'a good farmer and a good *colonus*'. One who was so praised was considered to have been praised in the highest terms. The trader I consider to be energetic and eager to make money, but, as I said above, exposed to hazard and disaster. But from farmers come both the bravest men and the most energetic soldiers, the income is especially respectable and secure and the least likely to provoke resentment, and those who are engaged in that occupation are least inclined to contemplate wrongdoing.[38]

Within these four interrelated items—the Preface, the *De agricultura* itself, the dictum, and the Plutarch passage—are to be found several seeming inconsistencies. Cato's concern with investment farming carried out by slave-labour, and only with such farming, has often been contrasted with the high estimation of the peasant farmer in the Preface to the *De agricultura*: the whole tenor of the book, it has been thought, is at variance with this element in its own Preface, for it was just such farming which threatened the future of the peasantry. Secondly, the mention of a preference for income-producing properties 'which could not be ruined by Jupiter' can be contrasted with the assertion that income from agriculture was especially secure. Thirdly, Cato argued that trade was a less satisfactory source of income than agriculture, yet he financed maritime trade, apparently sufficiently frequently to designate a particular freedman to manage this aspect of his affairs. Fourthly, the man who made large profits from these maritime loans denounced usury in the strongest possible terms, bracketing it with murder.

This last is not really a substantial difficulty.[39] In theory the explanation might be that in his later years Cato modified his opinion, but that is neither probable nor necessary. It is not probable because Cato's hostility to usury was clearly intense—a very different matter to an opinion on the

---

[37] i.e. that usury was not *honestum*.

[38] 'De agricultura. Interdum praestare mercaturis rem quaerere, nisi tam periculosum sit, et item fenerari, si tam honestum sit. Maiores nostri sic habuerunt et ita in legibus posiverunt: furem dupli condemnari, feneratorem quadrupli. Quanto peiorem civem existimarint feneratorem quam furem, hinc licet existimare. Et virum bonum quom laudabant, ita laudabant: bonum agricolam bonumque colonum; amplissime laudari existimabatur qui ita laudabatur. Mercatorem autem strenuum studiosumque rei quaerendae existimo, verum, ut supra dixi, periculosum et calamitosum. At ex agricolis et viri fortissimi et milites strenuissimi gignuntur, maximeque pius quaestus stabilissimusque consequitur minimeque invidiosus, minimeque male cogitantes sunt qui in eo studio occupati sunt.'

[39] Appendix 5.

relative merits of pasturing and cultivation—and its expression at widely separated times in his career shows that it was no momentary outburst or ephemeral enthusiasm. The explanation that there was a change of opinion is unnecessary because to present the facts as a direct inconsistency, as was done above, is to emphasize an identity where a Roman such as Cato would almost certainly have taken for granted a distinction. It is a modern tendency to focus attention upon a similarity or identity in economic process—in this case, the lending of money at interest—and look upon that as the essential, the most meaningful feature; but the Romans, though far from naïve in financial matters, did not habitually subordinate all other aspects to this. For them there were other considerations of a social kind which could be no less or even more significant. Scale of operation, social standing, occupation, life-style, landed interests were all relevant. Quite apart from the fact that maritime loans were often regarded as distinctive, and were never subject to the legal restrictions on rates of interest, it is most unlikely that an eminent senator much of whose wealth consisted of landed property would have identified his partial financing of large-scale maritime ventures with the 'sordid' activities of the professional money-lender.

The relationship between Cato's comment on trade and his financial involvement in it likewise presents no substantial problem. Although there are some similarities to the usury issue—for in this instance also the explanation could theoretically be a change of opinion, and Roman attitudes towards trade were similarly influenced by considerations of scale, role, and status[40]—nevertheless there is an important difference. Against usury Cato expressed a strong social and moral objection, but against trade only the practical consideration that it was hazardous. The trader himself, so far from being bracketed with criminals, is regarded as respectable: he is energetic, *strenuus*, one of Cato's favourite epithets of approval, and to be 'eager to make money' is clearly viewed as a merit, not a vice. While agriculture is praised also because of certain positive social characteristics associated with it, this does not extend to mentioning by way of contrast any moral or social objection to trade. There is no compulsion therefore to treat Cato's argument for the superiority of agriculture as a declaration that all financial involvement with trade is to be avoided. There is nothing in the Preface incompatible with the notion that while Cato kept much of his wealth in the more secure form of enterprise, he also took advantage of a form which, if more hazardous, on his own statement could be more profitable; especially since a prominent

[40] p. 320.

feature of Plutarch's account is precisely Cato's elaborate care to secure his interests against the risks involved in maritime trade.

All this would be true even if the Preface to the *De agricultura* were assumed to be a carefully considered statement of Cato's judgements and principles; but in fact that assumption is highly questionable. The Preface is manifestly not one of those in which the author carefully sets out his motives for undertaking his work. Its genesis seems to have been rather that having decided to write a book about agriculture Cato thought it necessary to devise a preface; and the simple underlying idea he adopted was that a book about agriculture was a worthy project because agriculture itself had great merits as a source of income. These merits he expressed partly by pointing to the drawbacks of two other ways of acquiring wealth, partly by referring to certain positive qualities which in general terms were associated with agriculture—though some of these had no real connection with the type of agriculture with which Cato himself was concerned. In short, the argument of the Preface was devised for the occasion and was not necessarily or even probably the product of long consideration and deep conviction.[41] That does not mean that Cato did not in some sense believe what he wrote, but it does mean that it should not be interpreted too literally as an expression of beliefs and principles to which his actual conduct can be expected to have conformed closely and consistently. In view of this it is even less admissible to draw from his comment on the hazards of trade the inference that, even if only at that particular time, he himself must have eschewed it completely in favour of agriculture.

So too in this same context the word *stabilissimus* can be seen in perspective, almost certainly not as a considered and absolute judgement that agriculture was the most secure of all sources of income, but, in the slightly artificial argument of a brief *ad hoc* essay, simply as an antithesis to the characterization of trade as hazardous, *periculosa*. It is possible that Plutarch is right, that Cato did at some stage revise his opinion, changing his practice accordingly. It is at least equally possible however that if on some occasion Cato in a characteristically vivid phrase spoke of his pitch-works and so on as properties 'which could not be ruined by Jupiter', that too may have been an ephemeral comment which Plutarch too readily interpreted as a guiding principle of financial management.

The likelihood that the Preface to the *De agricultura* was more of an *ad hoc*, perhaps rather contrived construction for the book than a statement of considered judgements does not mean that it lacks value as evidence for

---

[41] See also pp. 200 f.

Cato's attitudes and preconceptions, or that its argument has no relationship at all to the *De agricultura* itself. Certainly it does not set out Cato's purpose in writing the book or indicate the character of what is to follow, let alone explain any principle according to which material is organized or selected. It does not even declare the merits of the particular type of farming with which Cato is about to deal. Nevertheless the Preface shares with the rest of the work Cato's basic attitude, his patent presupposition that a book about agriculture will be concerned with agriculture carried on as a source of income for a wealthy absentee owner. It is an assumption which is neither stated nor argued but which is taken for granted from the very first words: 'It is sometimes more advantageous to seek money by trade . . .'; and it bulks large among the positive merits of agriculture: 'the income is especially respectable and secure and the least likely to provoke resentment'.[42]

What then, in view of this underlying presupposition, is the significance of Cato's laudatory references to the peasant farmer? Among the positive merits of agriculture he includes the military excellence of peasant farmers, yet his interest is exclusively in a very different type of farming in which they have no role. In fact he does not even have occasion to mention them in the body of the book, except perhaps indirectly, concealed among the supplementary seasonal labour. In the eyes of many his references to them in the Preface have seemed at best irrelevant, at worst an inconsistency bordering on hypocrisy; for the spread of the investment farming which interests Cato was a major factor in the supplanting, the deracination of numerous peasants.[43] Nevertheless, although these references illustrate that the Preface was not closely geared to the detail which was to follow, and although at bottom there was an illogical element in Cato's thinking, it is likely that he intended the references to play a role in his argument which to his mind was neither irrelevant nor inconsistent. An examination of this will serve also to bring out in more detail the patterns and emphases of thought in the Preface.

[42] Janson, *Latin Prose Prefaces*, pp. 84 ff., gives prominence to this aspect in a discussion which draws a distinction between two types of argument in the Preface somewhat similar to that drawn below. However the present discussion is at variance with his analysis in a number of respects, especially: (*i*) he regards the non-economic element as ethical, concerned with character, whereas it is argued below that it is principally and probably entirely concerned with social esteem; (*ii*) he does not bring out the deliberate correspondences between the later and earlier parts; (*iii*) he implies that the element of economic argument is stronger than it actually is and thereby creates the impression of a closer relationship between the Preface and the book than is actually the case.

[43] e.g. Toynbee, *Hannibal's Legacy* ii. 296 f., expressing a common reaction with uncommon vividness.

As has been seen already, the underlying idea, not stated explicitly but quite evident, is that a book about agriculture is a worthy project because agriculture itself has great merits as a source of income. The actual argument is concerned with demonstrating those merits. The dominant motif is that agriculture is preferable to trade and usury, both the choice of these alternatives and the opening formulation indicating that they are being compared primarily as sources of income, not as forms of activity. In the first half of the Preface, which except for one sentence is concerned with the disadvantages of trade and usury, there are three elements in the comparison: (i) these alternatives sometimes bring in more wealth; but (ii) income from trade is exposed to hazards; (iii) usury is not *honestum*. The first of the two objections is the obvious financial consideration that the risk of loss is to be set against the prospect of greater profit; but the second, which is stated with considerable force, is in no sense financial or economic. It is social; and it is social not in the sense of social utility or of the practical advantages and inconveniences of a particular way of life, but in terms of social values, social esteem: usury is not respectable.

When Cato turns from the drawbacks of trade and usury to the positive merits of agriculture the considerations can be divided into the same two general categories, financial and social. The specific points which he makes are:

(*i*) the farmer has traditionally been held in high esteem, i.e. he was so regarded by the *maiores*;

(*ii*) from farmers come the bravest men and the most energetic soldiers, *viri fortissimi et milites strenuissimi*;

(*iii*) the income from farming is especially respectable, *maxime pius*;

(*iv*) the income is especially secure, *stabilissimus*;

(*v*) the income is the kind least likely to provoke resentment, *minime invidiosus*;

(*vi*) those engaged in farming are least (or very little) inclined to contemplate wrongdoing, *minime male cogitantes*.

It is immediately obvious that all but one of these considerations are social, not financial or economic, the one exception being (*iv*), the security of the income, which is clearly intended precisely to pick up and contrast with the earlier emphasis on the insecurity of income from trade. In the same way (*i*) directly contrasts the esteem in which the *maiores* held the farmer with their intense disapproval of the usurer; and (*iii*), the respectability of an income from agriculture, and (*v*), its freedom from resentment, pick up and contrast with the assertion that usury is not *honestum*. Thus (*i*) and (*iii*) assert the social respectability of an income from agriculture, (*v*) its freedom from one of the features which contribute to the low esteem of usury.[44] It is evident therefore that the pattern of thought which governs the majority of the positive points about the superiority of agriculture is that they should correspond to and make a direct contrast with the particular defects previously ascribed to trade and usury. Two points, however—(*ii*), the military excellence of farmers, and (*vi*) their disinclination to contemplate wrongdoing—seem at first sight to be of a different kind; and one of the main reasons why Cato gives the impression of irrelevance and inconsistency is precisely that in these points he seems to be asserting the superiority of agriculture in terms not of social esteem but of useful social consequences of its practice, yet consequences which just could not follow from the only form of agriculture with which he concerns himself.

Although these two points do indeed involve an illogicality, it is less direct, less blatant than that account of them suggests. They can and almost certainly should be interpreted in the context of the pattern of thought identified above, in which the positive points made about the superiority of agriculture correspond to the defects previously ascribed to trade and usury. Cato is attempting to argue that an income from farming is socially desirable, but not because the actual farming which produces the income will also contribute to these useful social features (which in the form he envisages it plainly will not): what is in the forefront of his mind is its respectability. That respectability, however, is associated in his thought not just with investment farming but with agriculture *in a general sense*. For Cato, part of what makes investment farming respectable is that it is a form of agriculture, and agriculture in general is respectable; the particular form enjoys by association the respectability which belongs to the whole. That he is indeed viewing the matter in these general terms may seem strange but is evident already from the sentence in which he speaks of the esteem in which the *maiores* held the farmer and the *colonus*, in direct contrast to their disapproval of usury; for though the phrase refers primarily to the peasant farmer, the approbation by the *maiores* is clearly seen by Cato as a sign of the respectability of agriculture as a whole. But among the factors which seemed to him to contribute to the respectability of agriculture in general were the desirable qualities commonly found in peasant farmers; and for

---

44 It is possible that the phrase 'minime male cogitantes' was similarly intended to make a specific contrast, e.g. with reputed dishonesty among *feneratores*; but the argument which follows has not been tied to this hypothesis.

Cato these were therefore relevant to his argument, despite their lack of connection with investment farming, because his point of view was that an income from agriculture was socially superior by virtue of the superior prestige attaching to agriculture as such. Fundamentally it all rested on an illogical association of ideas, or, to give it a different emphasis, a failure to differentiate where logic required differentiation; but preoccupation with esteem and prestige can easily obscure logic. Given that basis, and precisely because Cato was thinking primarily in terms of social esteem and not of social utility, from his point of view his references to peasant farmers were relevant and created no inconsistency.

One further point about these references to peasant farmers calls for brief comment. Cato seems to take for granted their continued existence and availability for military service; and certainly he betrays no alarm or consciousness that they were a threatened class, let alone that they were threatened by the very type of agriculture about which he himself is writing. Various explanations are conceivable. Possibly the silence is misleading: he may have thought it irrelevant to refer to such a problem. Yet his actual remarks are surprising, though not impossible, if he was conscious that a serious problem threatened. The explanation might be found in his particularism, making him slow to appreciate the general problem and to link it up with his own specific topic. More probably however there was a general lack of appreciation of what was happening, for the transformation of the agricultural scene was a developing process rather than a sudden and dramatic metamorphosis, and for a considerable time its full implications were masked by other factors. Not until the last few years of Cato's life, or even later, did the extent and import of the growing pressures on the peasantry begin to force themselves prominently to attention.[45]

Whether or not this interpretation of Cato's pattern of thought in the Preface is correct in detail, there can be no question about certain major features to which attention has been drawn. Cato automatically thought of agriculture in terms of a source of cash income for a largely absentee owner such as himself. In comparing alternative sources of income he readily thought of balancing greater security against the possibility of greater returns, preferring the former; these are economic considerations, but they are the only economic considerations he mentions. Just as readily he thought in terms which are not economic at all but of quite a different kind—principally (and probably entirely) concerned with social esteem; and he not only found it quite natural to set this

---

[45] Astin, *Scipio Aemilianus*, ch. 13, esp. pp. 161 ff. and 167 ff.

against the possibility of greater profit but regarded the non-economic consideration as patently overriding the economic, despite his proclaimed and unashamed enthusiasm for accumulating wealth.[46] There is nothing surprising in this, for it is a familiar enough attitude in the late Republic: the acquisition of wealth was important and the prospect of greater profit a major criterion, but social considerations were potent also and at times outweighed the economic.

All this does however draw attention to the question of what criteria Cato thought appropriate for the actual operation of a farm. Obviously economic considerations played a major role, but was his attitude here too influenced also by considerations or preconceptions which were not economic in character? Or was his attitude so dominated by concern with profit, did he view the farm so exclusively as a financial venture, that everything was organized, judged, and decided according to the one criterion of producing the greatest possible income?

Majority opinion leans heavily towards this latter assessment, for which a good deal of support can indeed be found in the *De agricultura*.[47] Throughout the work there is an unmistakable concern with getting the best returns and spending as little as possible. There are numbers of recommendations for small savings and avoiding waste. Care is to be taken that facilities for the storage of oil and wine are sufficient to permit the products to be held until prices are high.[48] The owner is encouraged to pay frequent visits because if he does so 'the farm will be better, there will be less wrongdoing, you will receive greater returns.'[49] A variety of ancillary crops is to be raised to ensure that so far as possible the farm will be self-sufficient and not require purchases of consumables or of materials which could be grown. All surplus items, both produce and equipment, should be sold: a substantial list of such items concludes with the injunction that the owner should be 'a seller, not a buyer'.[50] Several passages display a concern to keep the slaves and animals busy at work. Cato offers advice on work which it is permissible to undertake—and which should be undertaken—on festival days (*feriae*), and numerous suggestions for jobs which can be done in bad weather and by torch-light in the dark of winter mornings and evenings. A chapter devoted to work which can be

---

[46] Plut. *Cato Mai.* 21. 8.

[47] Among the works noted on p. 240 n. 1 see esp. those of Toynbee, Brockmeyer, White ('Roman Agricultural Writers', pp. 457 f.), Martin, Yeo, Kienast, Foucher, and Maróti. Cic. *De sen.* 24 and Plut. *Cato Mai.* 21. 5 and 25. 1 (the latter probably based on the Cicero passage) do not constitute good evidence that Cato was motivated by pleasure and sentiment.

[48] *De agr.* 3. 2.   [49] *De agr.* 4.   [50] *De agr.* 2. 7

done during bad weather ends with the reminder, 'Bear in mind that if nothing is being done none the less there will be expense.'[51]

The forcefulness usually detectable in assessments which especially emphasize this aspect of Cato often seems to be intensified by a tendency found in many modern discussions to make frequent use of such financial expressions as 'capitalist', 'capital investment', 'outlay', 'running costs', 'return on investment', 'maximizing profits'. Up to a point all these terms can be used to describe aspects of Cato's activities, provided they are understood in a simple and elementary sense; and they are undoubtedly convenient, and sometimes difficult to avoid. The drawback is that in their cumulative effect such terms tend to create the impression of a greater financial sophistication and a greater facility in financial and economic abstraction than was actually the case—the more so as in modern contexts several of them do have more complex technical connotations. The financial shrewdness of the Romans is not to be underestimated, but there is no escaping the fact that the practical and conceptual tools at their disposal had important limitations.[52] Since there was no double-entry book-keeping they lacked the essential key to accurate analytical accounting;[53] the concept of amortization was unknown; and they were not habituated to thinking or expressing themselves in terms of economic abstractions. Cato's own approach shows no consideration of investing additional capital as a means of increasing productivity; rather his aim seems to be to reduce purchases to the minimum in order to widen the margin between cash receipts and cash expenditure.

There are other qualifications to be added to the conclusion, basically correct though it is, that Cato's attitude to the operations of the farm was determined by considerations of financial profit from an 'investment'. The first of these is that the *De agricultura* itself has indications that other values, other preconceptions did influence Cato's judgement. The rate of payment recommended for a building contractor is not a matter of the lowest price at which the owner could get the work done; on the contrary, it is clearly implied that a lower price may be possible, but that the recommended rate will be paid 'by a good owner who . . . pays conscientiously', 'ab domino bono qui . . . nummos fide bona solvat'.[54] In the same chapter two more prices are given as those which will be

[51] *De agr.* 39; cf. 2. 4; 5. 2; 37. 3; 138.

[52] Finley, *The Ancient Economy*, esp. pp. 110 f. and 115 ff.

[53] Mickwitz, 'Economic Rationalism in Graeco-Roman Agriculture', *Eng. Hist. Review* 52 (1937), 577 ff.; de Ste Croix, 'Greek and Roman Accounting', in Littleton and Yamey, *Studies in the History of Accounting*, pp. 14 ff.

[54] *De agr.* 14. 3.

paid by 'a good owner', the second case being that 'in an unhealthy location, where the work cannot be done in summer, a good owner will add
a fourth to the price.' Then in an earlier passage occurs the statement that
'it is advantageous for the master to have a well-built farm-complex
(*villa rustica*), store-room for oil, and store-room for wine, with many
storage jars, so that he can await high prices: it will add to his wealth,
standing, and distinction', 'et rei et virtuti et gloriae erit'.[55] Thus *virtus*
and *gloria* stand alongside financial profit as desirable advantages accruing
from having sound and ample buildings.

Secondly the evidence of these passages is reinforced by indications
elsewhere that Cato did regard the good management of a farm as a
matter of social esteem, indeed of social responsibility, as well as of
financial advantage. One indication that this was a natural tendency in his
thought is his choice of antithesis in his complaint that good-looking
boys were being sold for more than fields and jars of pickled fish for
more than teamsters;[56] and similarly with his statement that when purchasing slaves 'he wanted not the young and dainty but the hard-working
and sturdy, such as grooms and herdsmen.'[57] The attitude is clearest,
however, in Cato's insistence that it was a reason for action by the censors
'if anyone had allowed his land to run to waste and was not giving it
sufficient attention and had neither ploughed nor weeded it, or if anyone
had neglected his orchard or vineyard'.[58]

Thirdly the constant preoccupation with small savings and self-
sufficiency is not necessarily a manifestation of extreme parsimony, of
an obsession with squeezing every tiny drop of additional income, however trivial it might be beside the profits from the main cash crops.[59] No
doubt those profits were often large; yet they were perhaps more pre-
carious than is sometimes allowed. Harvests of both olives and grapes
are liable to fluctuations; and both, but more especially grapes, are vulnerable to natural hazards. Moreover, given the slowness and high cost of
transport, and supposing neighbouring farms to have been operated on
broadly the same pattern as Cato's, so that the products Cato required as

[55] *De agr.* 3. 2.
[56] Polyb. 31. 25. 5a; thence Plut. *Cato Mai.* 8. 2; *Quaest. conv.* 4. 2; 'Plut.' *Apophth. Cat.
Mai.* 2; Diod. 31. 24; 37. 3. 6; Athen. 6. 274 f.
[57] Plut. *Cato Mai.* 4. 5, on which see further below.
[58] Gell. 4. 12. 1.
[59] On self-sufficiency see above, pp. 244 f. Plutarch, *Cato Mai.* 4, has a string of instances, not
from the *De agricultura*, which he fairly clearly regards as illustrative of niggardliness (cf. 5. 1;
compar. 4. 4 ff.); but at least some of the passage, and probably the whole of it from 4. 4 on,
comes from a speech in self-defence, probably *De sumptu suo*, so is not to be taken literally
and in detail as sober evidence of Cato's actual conduct; see pp. 92 f.

ancillaries were not being produced locally as cash crops, it could well be that even small additional purchases would have eaten significantly into the profits. Carelessness and wastefulness in a number of small matters really could have added up to a significant additional expense, and, more important still, whether or not that was actually the case, it is likely to have been assumed to be true. For, as was mentioned previously, the Roman farmer did not have available accounting techniques anywhere near adequate to permit realistic comparison of market prices with the true cost of what was produced on the farm. Thus the seeming parsimony may be a reflection of realities of agricultural life as much as of a grasping nature obsessed with 'maximizing profits'.

There is no question but that when Cato decided to write about agriculture he thought automatically in terms of agriculture as a source of income, and therefore that the dominant consideration in the advice he gave was to make the farm yield as large and as secure an income as possible. Nothing else is to be expected. But a dominant consideration is not necessarily the sole consideration; and the criteria which Cato applied to farm management were not exclusively financial, nor were they exclusively ones which would have been equally applicable to any type of income-producing enterprise. At least in some small measure his attitude was influenced also by his preconceptions about integrity, personal prestige, and the social respectability of agriculture.

Closely related to this issue of Cato's single-minded concern with profit is the topic of his attitude towards slaves.[60] Discussions of Roman slavery invariably and properly emphasize the sharp distinction between the circumstances and prospects of household slaves and those of agricultural slaves. In discussing Cato's attitude therefore it is desirable to take these two categories separately, and as it happens the evidence, mainly from the *De agricultura* and from Plutarch, divides itself fairly neatly along these lines.

When Cato claimed in a speech, probably around 164, that 'he never paid more than fifteen hundred drachmas [so Plutarch, presumably for *denarii*] for a slave, since he wanted not the young and the dainty but the hard-working and sturdy, such as grooms and herdsmen', the antithesis is rhetorical and misleading, for he owned many domestic slaves.[61] He may not have cared much about their daintiness, but he certainly

---

[60] In addition to the works cited on p. 240 n. 1, note Sicard, 'Caton et les fonctions des esclaves', *RD* 35 (1957), 177 ff. Westermann, *The Slave Systems of Greek and Roman Antiquity*, esp. pp. 76 f., and Staerman, *Die Blütezeit der Sklavenwirtschaft in der röm. Republik,* make considerable use of evidence relating to Cato.

[61] Except where otherwise indicated the material regarding Cato's domestic slaves is in Plut. *Cato Mai.* 4. 4 ff.; 10. 6; 20. 5 f.; 21. 1 ff.

bought considerable numbers of young slaves with a view to training them. He even owned a *grammatistes* to teach them to read and write. There is no evidence for the actual number he owned at any particular time, though it no doubt increased considerably along with his general success and prosperity. When he took only five with him to Spain in 195, that was patently a calculated display of restraint, not an indication of the actual size of his household.[62]

The practice of slavery, taken for granted though it was, had some attendant disadvantages for owners. Though domestic and urban slaves had to be allowed considerable freedom of movement, if they misbehaved it was the owner who was liable to pay recompense for any theft, damage, or injury they might commit; they were an obvious source of information for anyone who was unduly inquisitive about the owner's private affairs; and there was a perpetual uneasiness that silent resentment might find expression in violence. Owners sought to forestall such problems by a combination of deterrent punishment and incentives to good behaviour (the latter not to be confused with humane sympathy); and in this Cato's methods, apart perhaps from a characteristic thoroughness displayed in both directions, seem to have been in accord with what is suggested by the generality of evidence (including both the contemporary comedies of Plautus and what is known from the late Republic). His discipline seems to have been strict and severe. Punishment for negligence in the preparation of meals, and no doubt in all other cases, was inflicted without delay.[63] In some instances an offending slave was put to death, though this was clearly an exceptional penalty. The sternness with which Cato was expected to react to disobedience on a matter he judged important is illustrated by the slave in Spain who hanged himself rather than face Cato after contravening his instructions about the purchase of booty.[64] His slaves were instructed never to enter another house without the express instruction of Cato or his wife, and if they were asked what Cato was doing always to answer that they did not know. He expressed such views as that it was desirable to encourage dissensions among them and to be suspicious of harmony; that a slave should always be either at some necessary task in the house or asleep;[65] and that slaves who slept readily were

---

[62] p. 52.

[63] Plutarch's statement, *Cato Mai.* 21. 3 f., that the punishment of slaves for neglect in the preparation of meals was a development of Cato's later years is almost certainly an inference of his own from the comparison with Cato's claims about having the same food and wine as his slaves.   [64] Plut. *Cato Mai.* 10. 6; 'Plut.' *Apophth. Cat. Mai.* 27.

[65] The context of this remark shows that its point lay in keeping the slaves out of mischief, not in extracting the maximum possible work.

preferable in character and usefulness (though how far such sentiments, which are presumably drawn from particular pronouncements, are a true guide to his actual practice is perhaps uncertain). Furthermore, 'thinking that slaves were led into the most serious mischief by their sexual passions, he arranged that the males should have intercourse with the female slaves for a fixed fee, but that none should approach any other woman.' The 'fixed fee' is usually interpreted as a fee payable to Cato himself, the crowning example of his mean and grasping nature. The Greek wording, however, could equally well mean that in return for their services the females were allowed to charge a fee to be added to their own *peculium*, but that Cato laid down a fixed amount.

Side by side with this discipline, however, are indications of extensive use of incentives and the application of common sense. Plutarch says that when the possibility of capital punishment arose the accused slave was executed if he was found guilty when judged by all his fellow slaves. If one may suspect that Cato did not find it appropriate to handle every such case in this way, it is an important indication of some practical modification of absolute authority by involvement of the rest of the household community.[66] The use of manumission—the best known of the Roman incentives—is attested by the chance mention of two freedmen— one of them Quintio, who looked after the maritime loans, the other Salonius, the former under-secretary whose daughter Cato took as his second wife.[67] His first wife is said to have nursed slave children along with his son, in order to encourage a sense of loyalty. As for the *peculium*, that is money and property conventionally recognized as belonging to the slave, there are indications that Cato not only allowed but actively encouraged considerable accumulation. The offence of the unfortunate slave in Spain was that from among the prisoners-of-war he had bought three as slaves of his own. 'Also', says Plutarch, 'he used to lend money to those of his slaves who wished it. They bought boys, and then after training and teaching them for a year at Cato's expense, sold them again.

[66] It need hardly be said that such an arrangement, presumably patterned on the traditional Roman practice of consulting a *concilium* in family jurisdiction, may still have left the effective decision largely in Cato's own hands, and that he is more likely to have been motivated by a wish to secure the involvement of the other slaves than by a belief that their collective judgement might be superior to his own. Nováková, 'Litibus familia supersedeat', *Studia Antiqua A. Salac*, pp. 90 ff., argues that Plutarch's statement arises from a misunderstanding and elaboration of *De agr.* 5. 1; but the difference is too great for that to be likely, especially if Nováková's own interpretation of *De agr.* 5. 1 is correct: see p. 264 n. 70.

[67] Quintio: Plut. *Cato Mai.* 20. 6; Salonius: Plut. *Cato Mai.* 24. 3 ff.; Gell. 13. 20. 8; cf. Pliny, *Nat. hist.* 7. 61, whence Solin. 1. 59. Salonius is not actually termed a freedman but his former occupation virtually guarantees that he was.

Many of these boys Cato retained for himself, reckoning to the credit of the slave the highest price which had been bid for the boy.' Such an arrangement points not only to substantial *peculia* but to some skill and imagination in the management of slaves.

The actual experiences of agricultural slaves must have depended to no small extent on the *vilicus*, but from Cato's instructions it is clear that his intention was that they should be managed with something of the same common sense and imagination. He explicitly instructs the *vilicus* to look after them and to ensure that they do not go cold or hungry.[68] In calculating the quantities of food required he seems to allow reasonable amounts, allocating extra to the labourers when they are engaged on heavy digging.[69] A delinquent is to be punished 'in accordance with his offence and with moderation', 'pro noxa bono modo', which, whatever scales of punishment Cato thought appropriate, is certainly directed against both undue leniency and undue severity according to the prevailing standards. Slaves who do well are to receive expressions of approval, to encourage the rest; the teamsters are to be encouraged by flattery; and, most significantly, let the *vilicus* 'see to it that he knows how to do all the operations of the farm, and let him perform them often, provided he does not exhaust himself; if he does that he will know what is in the minds of the slaves, and they will work more contentedly.'[70]

All this suggests that Cato's attitude towards his agricultural as well as his domestic slaves was more complex and less crude than is often implied. Indeed, it is possible, even likely that in some points the harshness of his attitude has been somewhat overdrawn as a result of taking certain of his remarks in isolation from their context. Thus particular emphasis has been placed on his reference to reducing the food allowance of slaves when they are sick and on his statement that a sickly or an elderly slave should be sold—the selling of elderly slaves being mentioned also on

[68] *De agr.* 5. 2.

[69] *De agr.* 56; cf. 57–8. White, *Roman Farming*, pp. 360 f.; Rowland, 'Grain for Slaves', *CW* 63 (1970), 229; cf. Oates, 'A Note on Cato, *De Agri Cultura*, LVI', *AJPh* 55 (1934), 67 ff. There is a tendency apparent in a number of accounts to describe the change as a reduction in quantity for the *compediti* when they are not engaged in heavy work.

[70] All these points in *De agr.* 5. In 5. 1 'litibus familia supersedeat' has often been taken as provision for the settlement of disputes on an orderly basis, with the *vilicus* or even the *familia* itself giving judgement. There are however problems of interpretation and of text. Nováková, 'Litibus familia supersedeat', *Studia Antiqua A. Salac*, pp. 90 ff., recalls that *supersedeo* in the sense 'preside over' would be unique and argues that it has its more usual meaning of 'refrain from': 'Let the *familia* refrain from quarrels', which in the context means that the *vilicus* is to see to it that it does so. Thus far it is likely that Nováková is correct, but the further argument that Plutarch's reference to slave adjudication in *Cato Mai.* 21. 4 arises from a misunderstanding and explanatory elaboration of this passage is less convincing.

another occasion. In fact all these references occur in passages with a markedly rhetorical tone and in a manner which suggests that it may not be proper to take any of them, especially the first, as sober evidence of principles which were rigorously applied on Cato's farms.[71] Nor is it so certain that to sell an elderly or a sickly slave was necessarily any more harsh than to keep him struggling with work with which he was increasingly unable to cope, let alone than manumitting him and leaving him to fend for himself. Similarly with Cato's concern with the kind of work which could be done on *feriae*. It should go without saying that no farmer or farm labour-force could afford to be totally idle on the numerous days on which the regular types of work could not be done.[72] To interpret this as 'no holidays for the slaves' is to misrepresent its significance. No doubt slaves were allowed very few holidays, but the *De agricultura* does at least have a strong hint that Cato's agricultural slaves were allowed the normal slave holiday of the *Saturnalia* and celebrated the *Compitalia*.[73] Again, to represent the frequent concern with keeping the slaves at their work only in terms of squeezing out the last possible drop of profit may be to miss the point that on such establishments as Cato's, where the *vilicus* could not be everywhere at once, there must have been a constant inclination to slackness, idleness, and work-evasion.

Yet when all this is said, these are only reminders that perhaps not every item should have the harshest construction automatically placed upon it; they do not greatly affect the basic picture. It is not, of course, being suggested that even when Cato's instructions, as noted in the paragraph before last, were carried out to perfection—which probably they never were— the life of his agricultural slaves was a kind of rustic idyll. Some spent their days shackled, probably most were prisoners, torn and hopelessly severed from their native surroundings, and all toiled at long and laborious work. Nor is it being suggested that Cato's motives differed fundamentally from those of the farmer who takes good care of work-animals or an expensive piece of machinery. Just so Cato took good physical care of his slaves as valuable pieces of property. On the other hand his attitude towards slaves is more complex than that comparison suggests. He does in a sense view them as instruments to be used, but he is also conscious that they are human beings, and that consciousness shows itself in his approach to how they are to be used. They are to be managed, not just ordered; advantage is to be taken of their human emotional reactions by using tact, encouragement, and praise to secure co-operation and greater

---

[71] *De agr.* 2. 4; 2. 7; Plut. *Cato Mai.* 4. 5. See Appendix 12.
[72] Cf. Pliny, *Nat. hist.* 18. 40.   [73] *De agr.* 57.

effort. Most remarkable of all, the *vilicus* is to experience the tasks himself so that he may know what is in the minds of the slaves—which is surely a relatively sophisticated approach to the management of labour. And certainly the slaves are being thought of as human beings, whose reactions to their tasks and the difficulties they experience are matters which need to be understood—not just observed—and taken into account.[74] The motive is still practical, even economic: there is no reason to suppose Cato's attitude to have been influenced by sympathy or humanity. At bottom it remained an unquestioning acceptance of the right to exercise absolute control over other human beings, and to use that control to further his own interests entirely as he saw fit. Yet to reduce it to those stark terms is to ignore the insight and subtlety which Cato actually displayed in dealing with these human beings, and thereby to ignore something of the way in which slavery actually operated.

The essence of that conclusion may be applied equally to the broader issue of the emphasis frequently placed on the capitalist character of Cato's activities and attitude. It is not incorrect, but it is incomplete. Cato did think of farming, so far as it concerned himself, primarily as a financial 'investment'. The *raison d'être* of the whole enterprise—land, equipment, animals, crops, and men—was to produce an income for Cato himself, and it was organized and managed in a manner intended to maintain the size and security of that income. Yet awareness of the economic considerations and their importance for Cato's attitude should not be allowed to distract attention from other considerations and other preconceptions which also played some part—preconceptions about social prestige, personal integrity, and the social value and respectability of agriculture. To overlook these is to overlook something significant in the complex reality of Cato himself—and of the society in which he lived.

[74] Contrast Westermann, *Slave Systems*, p. 76, who speaks of 'the completely economic motivation' and asserts that 'the slave-driving in his [sc. Cato's] treatment was unmitigated by any consideration of the needs of the slave as a human being.' Other accounts are often less absolute, recognizing Cato's interest in the physical welfare of the slaves, but this usually results in an emphasis on the similarity to his attitude towards work-oxen. It is not here being suggested, of course, that Cato was concerned about the slaves' human needs and feelings *per se*.

12

Foreign Affairs

THE period in which Cato was politically prominent, from the end of the
Hannibalic war to his death in 149, was marked by a rapid and remarkable
expansion which transformed Rome, already supreme in the central
Mediterranean in consequence of the Punic Wars, into the power which
dominated the entire Mediterranean world.[1] It was, therefore, a period of
great activity and complexity in foreign affairs, the more so because in
Africa and in the Hellenistic lands to the east of the Adriatic it involved not
annexation but, before and after the great military victories, a stream of embassies and a long succession of senatorial decisions concerning numerous
sovereign states. Cato must have participated in many of those decisions,
and there can be little doubt that his personal prestige, his advancing
seniority—he was of consular standing for almost the entire period—and
his formidable powers of self-expression combined to make his potential
influence considerable, though his exercise of it happens to be attested
mainly in his later years. Furthermore, the issues and decisions with which
he is connected by the evidence—titles and fragments of speeches, a few
dicta, and in a few instances some additional narrative—exhibit considerable variety: the Histrian affair in 178–177; the visit of Eumenes of Pergamum to Rome in 172; the settlement of Macedonia in 167 and the debate
about Rhodes in the same year; the embassy of L. Minucius Thermus to
investigate the quarrels of the Ptolemies in 154; the attempt by Prusias of
Bithynia to secure a reduction in his indemnity to Attalus II of Pergamum,
and the movement, supported by Attalus, to replace Prusias by his son
Nicomedes; the release of the Achaean hostages; and the events which led
up to the Third Punic War.[2]

On closer inspection, however, the evidence is found to have considerable limitations. In the first place almost all the items relate either to the

[1] See works cited p. 121 n. 56; De Sanctis, *CAH*, Scullard, Badian, and Errington all have
valuable discussions of the whole period. The earlier part of the period in particular has given
rise to an extensive bibliography.

[2] For an account of these events see Ch. 6, § 4, pp. 121 ff. Cato's activities in Spain and in
the war against Antiochus do not come within the scope of this chapter since there is no
evidence as to his attitudes to the issues of foreign affairs involved.

year 167 or to the last five years of Cato's life—and the two exceptions reveal nothing relevant.[3] Thus not only are they confined to two brief periods in an exceptionally long career, but they have little or no connection with the momentous debates and decisions which bore directly upon the major extensions of Roman power in the first quarter of the century. What is more they amount to only a tiny proportion of the numerous issues and decisions which made up the whole complex picture; and though they are connected with a variety of topics, that very variety means that most have no direct or obvious relationship to each other. Furthermore, in most of these instances the evidence concerning Cato is slender and isolated, and in some it leaves his stance on the issues uncertain. There is certainly not enough material to permit a coherent reconstruction of his attitudes and opinions in general or of changes and developments in them.

Nevertheless, despite these limitations, views have been expressed as to what were Cato's principal concerns in foreign affairs. In particular it has been suggested that he was concerned to curtail Roman expansion, at least in the East, and that his guiding principle was that Roman involvement should be as slight as possible. Reasons put forward for this are either an anxiety to keep contacts with the Greek world to the minimum or a concern to avoid dissipation of manpower and military strength; in either event the guiding consideration behind his actions is held to be to prevent situations arising which might require Roman military intervention or, worse, direct Roman administration. A variant on this is that Cato wished to enable Rome to maintain as much control and derive as much financial advantage as was possible short of incurring significant expense or demands on manpower.[4]

At first sight the actual course of events between 167 and 149 might seem to correspond well with—and thereby give some encouragement to —the view that Cato had an active concern to avoid eastern entanglements, for whatever reason; and it might even seem to suggest that the Senate shared such a concern. For the possibility of creating a Roman province was consciously rejected by the Senate in 167 when it had to decide about the future of Macedonia; and Rome did remain without provinces and without further military commitments east of the Adriatic until after Cato's death.[5] It does not follow, however, that the avoidance of

---

[3] The speech *De re Histriae militari* and the dictum concerning Eumenes: see below, and pp. 121 f.

[4] De Sanctis, *Storia* iv. 1², p. 345; iv. 3, pp. 100 f.; Scullard, *Roman Politics*², pp. 212 and 217; Frank, *Roman Imperialism*, pp. 190 ff.; id., *CAH* viii. 369 f.; Kienast, pp. 116 ff.

[5] The exception is the short Dalmatian campaign of 157, but that is a separate matter from involvement with the Hellenistic states.

direct involvement was a live issue or a conscious concern in those years, that it was a major criterion in determining the decisions of the Senate (or indeed the stances taken by Cato, in connection with whom the decision about Macedonia will be discussed further below). Unquestionably in reaching its decisions the Senate at times allowed considerations of Roman advantage to exclude all other considerations, such as the genuine merits of requests and appeals from kings or cities, or the rights and wrongs of disputes in which it acted as arbitrator between states. Indeed the tendency was noted by Polybius as a marked characteristic of Roman decisions in these years,[6] and it found expression in a number of decisions which were undoubtedly intended to weaken kings or states of whom the senators had become suspicious or resentful.[7] That is not the same, however, as consciously seeking to avoid situations which might eventually necessitate direct administration or military involvement. It is more likely that no serious question of either arose and that the prevailing situation was, therefore, taken for granted. Neither hypothesis, however, can be either proved or disproved. As for Cato, in so far as his attitudes and opinions regarding foreign affairs can be recovered at all, they must be sought in the evidence relating directly to himself.[8]

Unfortunately, several of Cato's attested links with foreign affairs can be quickly dismissed as uninformative—though not all for the same reason. Thus the dictum connected with the visit of Eumenes to Rome in 172, though it may reflect a genuine dislike of kings, mainly reveals a sense of the eminence of Roman senators and disapproval of the flattery and lack of dignity which many of them were displaying in their dealings with the

[6] Polyb. 31. 10. 7.

[7] e.g. Polyb. 30. 19; 31. 2; 31. 6; 31. 10. 6 ff.; 32. 1. 5 ff. Briscoe, 'Eastern Policy and Senatorial Politics', *Historia*, 18 (1969), 49 ff., goes so far as to interpret this as a conscious policy of 'divide and rule' systematically pursued by a largely dominant faction in the Senate but opposed by others, including Cato. This seems to go considerably beyond the evidence, and also to depend on views which are not followed in this book regarding the nature of factional politics and their relationship to 'policy', in so far as that term may be appropriate. On the latter see further below in this chapter; also Astin, *Politics and Policies*, with particular reference to the interrelationship.

[8] Some comments on Cato's attitude, either in general or in respect of particular episodes, appear to have been influenced by a particular conception of his attitude towards Greek culture. This would in any event be a dubious basis for inferring his views on foreign affairs, especially as the known speeches and actions do not exhibit a marked pattern or other features which point strongly in this direction. The known arguments of the Rhodian speech (see below) suggest that anti-hellenism was not a consideration on that occasion. In reality Cato's attitude towards the Greeks and their culture, discussed in Ch. 8, was more complicated than a general anti-hellenism. Frank, *Roman Imperialism*, pp. 190 ff., makes confident conjectures about Cato's role in foreign affairs between 190 and 168, for which there is virtually no evidence, but, pp. 218 ff., is surprisingly cautious about the following years.

king. It is no indication of Cato's views on political arrangements regarding Eumenes and the kingdom of Pergamum, or of any difference between Cato and the majority of senators in respect of such arrangements. Similarly the slightly earlier speech 'Concerning the military affair of Histria' may have been concerned with an internal quarrel rather than with a question truly about foreign affairs; and even if it did deal with the latter, nothing whatever is known of the purpose of Cato's speech or his arguments. By contrast Cato's intervention—nearly thirty years later—to secure the release of the Achaean exiles is well attested and quite clear cut; but since what he said in the Senate was intended expressly to emphasize the unimportance and triviality of the question it is scarcely to be treated as significant evidence for his opinion about Roman policy towards Achaea.[9]

More controversial is the speech 'Concerning the younger Ptolemy, against Thermus', *De Ptolemaeo minore contra Thermum*.[10] Since Cato was evidently prosecuting Thermus and since Thermus was one of the envoys sent to reinstate the younger Ptolemy, Euergetes, as king of Cyprus in place of his brother Philometor, it is usually assumed that it is the latter whom Cato described as 'an excellent and most beneficent king'[11] and that Cato disapproved of the support given by the majority of senators to Euergetes. This, however, goes well beyond the evidence. The one feature of the speech which is quite clear is Cato's allegation that there had been gross corruption, that 'he [presumably Thermus] did everything deceitfully, everything for the sake of avarice and money.' Thus there is a strong likelihood that allegations of impropriety and corruption in the conduct of the embassy were the central issue which gave rise to the speech; in which case the prosecution of Thermus would not necessarily have had any bearing on foreign affairs as such.[12] On the other hand, even if Cato was motivated largely or partly by the actual question of the Ptolemies, while the evidence is certainly compatible with his favouring Philometor and attacking a prominent supporter of Euergetes, it is equally compatible with the possibility that he favoured Euergetes. He would then have been attacking Thermus in connection with the embarrassing failure of the

---

[9] For these three events see pp. 121 f. and 124 f.

[10] *ORF*[3], frs. 177–81. See also pp. 111 and 124.

[11] *ORF*[3], fr. 180. So Bouché-Leclercq, *Histoire des Lagides* ii. 44 f.; Scullard, *Roman Politics*[2], p. 237; Gelzer, *RE*, s.v. *Porcius*, no. 9, col. 138; Kienast, pp. 124 f.; De Sanctis, *Storia* iv. 3, pp. 100 f.; Briscoe, 'Eastern Policy and Senatorial Politics', *Historia*, 18 (1969), 61 f.

[12] Implied by Malcovati, *ORF*[3], p. 73; otherwise it seems to be generally assumed that an issue of foreign affairs was the principal concern.

mission (Philometor captured Euergetes and then magnanimously restored him to his kingdom of Cyrene), alleging that the débâcle was due to Thermus' corruption. To cap such uncertainties with speculation about why Cato may have favoured one Ptolemy rather than the other is obviously pointless.

The two items concerning the kingdoms of Bithynia and Pergamum are also tenuous, though in both disputes it is fairly clear which side Cato supported.[13] At first sight it is tempting to see a significant contrast between his opposition to Prusias' request for a reduction in his indemnity to Attalus and his approval, just a year or two later, of the attempt to save Prusias from the insurrection organized by Nicomedes and Attalus: Cato, it will be recalled, commented sarcastically upon the inadequacy of the envoys assigned to this task. The seeming contrast in his attitude on these occasions invites speculation that he shifted his position because he was anxious to maintain a balance between the two rival kings; but the contrast is artificial and such speculation goes well beyond legitimate inference from evidence which is equally open to other explanations. Cato did oppose the reduction of Prusias' indemnity to Attalus, but his reasons for doing so are almost totally unattested.[14] The outcome of the debate was the rejection of Prusias' request, which amounted to a declaration that he had not produced adequate reasons why the Senate should modify its own decision of some three years before. Given that the Senate is likely to have been reluctant to make such a modification unless the arguments were very powerful indeed, this could perfectly well have been the genuine reason for the present decision—and for Cato's advocacy of it. Ulterior motives relating to power politics may have entered in, but whether they actually did so, and, if so, in what form and to what extent, is entirely unknown. No such additional explanation is required to account for the attitude adopted by Cato and the Senate.

Similarly there is no need to suppose that there were 'balance of power' considerations behind Cato's sarcastic comment on the embassy sent to save Prusias. Since the comment seems to have been made in the Senate in response to a request for his opinion, it is reasonable to infer that he genuinely believed that a real effort should be made to save Prusias; but again his reasons are entirely a matter for conjecture. What is certain is that the majority of senators favoured giving public support to Prusias, and

[13] p. 125.

[14] The single fragment, ORF[3], fr. 190, refers to Roman citizens conscripted to serve as rowers in the war against Perseus. A possible guess is that Cato was contrasting this with Prusias' neutrality in that war, though this does not seem to have been held against him at the time.

there is no good reason to doubt that they—and Cato—gave that support because Prusias was patently in the right—all the more so if it is true that dislike of Prusias made much of the support reluctant.[15] It is conceivable that Cato was anxious for quick action to save Prusias because he wanted tension to continue between Bithynia and Pergamum, whereas the accession of Nicomedes with Attalus' support was likely to end in a friendly alliance; but that is a purely hypothetical explanation for a stance which is entirely comprehensible without it. In short, in regard to both the indemnity and Attalus' support for Nicomedes Cato's attitude can be adequately accounted for by the assumption that he judged the issues on their merits. There is nothing to show that he was not influenced by more selfish or more cynical considerations but nothing at all to show that he was.

A far more important issue than any of those so far considered was what was to be done about Macedonia after the defeat and overthrow of Perseus. Cato's speech 'Concerning the freeing of Macedonia', *De Macedonia liberanda*, shows that he did declare himself against the creation of a Roman province. In this he shared the majority view among the senators: whether anyone took the contrary view is not known. It is a reasonable guess that Cato also agreed with the arrangements actually imposed on Macedonia, but the evidence does not go that far. As has been observed elsewhere, the fact that Cato spoke as he did is not sufficient reason to attribute to him a particularly influential role in formulating either these arrangements or the sentiments which Livy attributes to the Senate—which is not to deny the possibility that he did have significant influence.[16] As for his reasons against creating a province, one argument only is mentioned: 'he declared that the Macedonians should be free because they could not be protected.' Whether he—or the Senate—also had other reasons, spoken or unspoken, is simply not known, but there is no reason to doubt the implication that Cato believed that the effort to hold and defend Macedonia as a province would make unacceptable demands on Roman resources, and that, therefore, the Macedonians should be left free to defend themselves with local levies. If a similar question had presented itself in the following years, perhaps Cato would have again taken the same view, but this does not necessarily follow in his case any more than in that of the Senate as a whole—which shortly after his death was led by

[15] App. *Mith.* 6, blaming the urban praetor for first delaying the Senate's reception of Prusias' embassy and then selecting incompetent envoys.

[16] *ORF*[3], frs. 161 f.; Livy, 45. 18. 1 ff. See pp. 122 f., and for some further discussions of the settlement De Sanctis, *Storia* iv. 1[2], pp. 327 ff.; Scullard, *Roman Politics*[2], pp. 212 f.; Meloni, *Perseo*, pp. 412 ff.; Errington, *Dawn of Empire*, pp. 222 f.; cf. Janzer, pp. 67 f.

new circumstances to convert Macedonia into a province. The fact is that in 167 the future of Macedonia had to be decided and, since the monarchy was to be abolished, the possibility of making it a province was bound to come under consideration, even if only to be quickly dismissed. It happens to be known that in that situation Cato expressed his own opinion on the possibility. That opinion may have rested on such deeply held convictions about the long-term considerations that they amounted to a virtually immutable policy; but equally it may not have done so. Instead it may have been a judgement much more closely related to the specific situation, reached in the light of the contingent circumstances and readily modifiable if a change in circumstances should alter the relevant considerations. Cato's attitude to Macedonia in 167 neither implies nor in itself supports the hypothesis that over almost the next twenty years he was so deeply and constantly concerned to avoid entanglements in the East that this was the principal consideration which guided his reactions to the various questions which arose. It would be a different matter if several other instances were known of Cato speaking against direct involvement east of the Adriatic; there would then be a strong case for seeking to explain the common pattern by some such hypothesis. As it is, only one other instance is known, namely the speech about the Rhodians, also of 167.

The Rhodian speech and the agitation against Carthage are the two instances of Cato's involvement with foreign affairs about which most is known—much more than in any of the other instances—and it is these which are most revealing. The two cases differ greatly not only in the area and the type of problem with which they are concerned but in the kind of information preserved. In the case of Carthage, which will be discussed later, there are a few short fragments from one speech but also quite a number of statements and comments about Cato's role. In the case of Rhodes, however, although the circumstances are fairly fully reported, the significant information about Cato consists virtually entirely of the account of his speech given by Gellius (who reports all seven surviving fragments).[17] Otherwise the speech is mentioned briefly by

---

[17] Gell. 6. 3, cf. 13. 25. 14; *ORF*[3], frs. 163–9; 171 is a *testimonium*, not a fragment, and Hoffmann, 'Die röm. Politik', *Historia*, 9 (1960), 318 ff., is almost certainly correct in arguing that App. *Lib.* 65 = fr. 170 is not a separate fragment but combines a comment by Appian with an allusion to the exordium = fr. 163. For the circumstances see pp. 123 f. There are numerous discussions which comment on the motives of Cato and the Senate, e.g.: De Sanctis, *Storia* iv. i[2], pp. 343 ff.; Janzer, pp. 69 ff.; Gelzer, *RE*, s.v. *Porcius*, no. 9, cols. 133 ff.; Scullard, *Roman Politics*[2], pp. 216 ff.; Kienast, pp. 119 ff.; Schmitt, *Rom und Rhodos*, pp. 151 ff.; Badian, *Foreign Clientelae*, pp. 100 ff.; Della Corte, *Catone censore*[2], pp. 73 ff.; Briscoe, 'Eastern Policy and Senatorial Politics', *Historia*, 18 (1969), 49 ff., esp. 57 f.; Gruen, 'Rome and Rhodes in the Second Century B.C.', *CQ* n.s. 25 (1975), 58 ff., esp. 77 ff.

Appian and by Livy, the latter saying in the course of his account of the Senate's debate:

The cause of the Rhodians was greatly aided by M. Porcius Cato, who, though harsh by temperament, on this occasion conducted himself as a moderate and mild senator. I shall not introduce a pale shadow of this eloquent man by reporting what he said: his own speech is preserved in writing, included in the fifth book of his *Origines*.[18]

Just how decisive Cato's speech really was is hard to tell. Polybius does not mention it,[19] and Livy's estimate is no more than a reflection of the prominence of the speech in the *Origines*, though its inclusion there suggests that Cato ascribed to himself a substantial role in influencing the Senate's decision not to go to war.[20] However, the extent to which his speech actually influenced the outcome is much less important than the fact that Gellius says a good deal about the arguments it contained.[21]

[18] Livy, 45. 25. 2 f.

[19] Polyb. 30. 4. 9 says that the reply given to the Rhodians included a warning that they would have been treated more severely 'if it had not been for a few persons who were their friends', but no names are given.

[20] The exordium, fr. 163, contains a plea that a decision be delayed some days, which seems not to have happened; but Cato may have been more concerned with the rhetorical effect than the actual proposal. There is no indication of Cato's attitude to the subsequent measures which were clearly intended to punish and restrict Rhodes; his argument was specifically against war.

[21] His comments occur throughout 6. 3, but in addition to the fragments themselves two passages are particularly important. A translation of section 52 will be found in Ch. 7, p. 138; a translation of 43–7 is given here:

These are the criticisms which Tiro passed upon Cato, not altogether pointless or wholly unreasonable; (44) but as a matter of fact, Cato did not leave this ἐπαγωγή bare, isolated, and unsupported, but he propped it up in various ways and clothed it with many other arguments. Furthermore, since he had an eye as much to the interests of the state as to those of the Rhodians, he regarded nothing that he said or did in that matter as discreditable, provided he strove by every kind of argument to save our allies. (45) And first of all, he very cleverly sought to find actions which are prohibited, not by natural or by international law, but by statutes passed to remedy some evil or meet an emergency; such for example as the one which limited the number of cattle or the amount of land. (46) In such cases that which is forbidden cannot lawfully be done; but to wish to do it, if it should be allowed, is not dishonourable. (47) And then he gradually compared and connected such actions as these with that which in itself it is not honourable either to do or to wish to do. Then finally, in order that the impropriety of the comparison may not become evident, he defends it by numerous bulwarks, not laying great stress on those trivial and ideal censures of unlawful desires, such as form the arguments of philosophers in their leisure moments, but striving with might and main for one single end, namely, that the cause of the Rhodians, the retention of whose friendship was in the interests of the state, should be shown either to be just, or, in any event, at least pardonable. Accordingly, he now affirms that the Rhodians did not make war and did not desire to do so; but again he declares that only acts should be considered and judged, and that mere empty wishes are liable neither to laws nor punishment; sometimes, however, as if

The purpose of Gellius' discussion, it will be recalled, is to refute Tiro's criticisms of the speech, criticisms which amount to assertions that the opening, the exordium, was inept and that certain passages were faulty in logic or were misleading.[22] Consequently Gellius does not give close and precise attention to the historical circumstances of the speech, nor is he concerned to give a clear and balanced summary of its arguments. On the contrary, a great deal of his comment is naturally directed to that aspect of the speech on which Tiro's arguments had especially been focused. That aspect was Cato's argument that though the Rhodians may have wished the Romans not to win a decisive victory over Perseus, nevertheless they made no attempt to translate their wishes into reality; and that no guilt is to be attached to a mere wish. Five of the six passages quoted by Gellius because they had been discussed by Tiro are concerned with this aspect (the other being the exordium); and since one of Gellius' complaints is that Tiro has unfairly singled out a small part of a rich and varied speech,[23] it is clear that neither these fragments nor the focus of Tiro's argument are truly representative of the speech as a whole. Fortunately, however, Gellius did not limit his defence of the speech to arguing that Tiro's criticisms of the individual passages were themselves faulty and misleading interpretations. Because one of his major contentions is that the aspect which Tiro singled out was only one of many varied arguments, he goes on to mention others that Cato actually used. Consequently, although Gellius refers to these only in summary fashion (only one is illustrated with a brief quotation from the speech), rather unsystematically and with some repetition, nevertheless he indicates several lines of argument employed by Cato.

When these lines of argument are extracted from their context in Gellius, separated from each other, and listed, as they are below, it is necessary to bear in mind the limitations of Gellius' discussion and also that on Gellius' evidence the original speech was itself not systematic and orderly but a skilful intermixture of arguments so diverse as to be at times mutually contradictory. Consequently what follows does not represent the interrelationship, the relative prominence, or indeed the original sequence of the particular items in the speech itself. It simply identifies the

conceding that they had done wrong, he urges that they should be pardoned, and he shows that the granting of pardon is expedient in human affairs and stirs up fear of upheaval in the state if they [sc. the senators] do not exercise forgiveness; but on the other hand, he demonstrates that if pardon is granted the greatness of the Roman people will be maintained.

[22] pp. 137 f. and 151.
[23] 6. 3. 54.

lines of argument which Cato is shown by Gellius to have used in his speech.

1. Success and prosperity induce euphoria and arrogance and are apt to cause errors of judgement; therefore Cato fears that an erroneous judgement may curtail the present success. A decision should be postponed for a few days (6. 3. 14 = ORF^3, Cato fr. 163).

2. The Rhodians are of the highest merit. (It is possible that this led up to and was closely linked with point 3a (below), which it immediately precedes in 6. 3. 52.)

3. The Rhodians are blameless:
   (a) They neither made war nor wished to make war against Rome.
   (b) They did not act against Rome, and only acts, not mere wishes, call for punishment. The most serious allegation is that they wished to be enemies, which may be true but is not punishable (6. 3. 15 f., 22 ff., 47, 52, 54).

4. Cato protests at the motives of those whose objective is the wealth and property of the Rhodians (6. 3. 52).[24]

5. The arrogance of the Rhodians is not a reason for anger and for punishing them (6. 3. 48 ff.).

6. Cato urges that the Rhodians should be pardoned (as if he was conceding that they had done wrong: 6. 3. 47 and 52).
   (a) (6. 3. 47)
      (i) The granting of pardon is expedient (*utile*) in human affairs.
      (ii) He stirs up a fear of upheavals in the state 'if they [the senators] do not exercise forgiveness', 'metus in republica rerum novarum movet'.
      (iii) On the other hand, if pardon is granted the greatness, *magnitudo*, of the Roman people will be maintained.

[24] There is reason to suspect that this point did play a larger role in the speech itself than the brief mention in 6. 3. 52 would suggest. At 6. 3. 7, briefly explaining the circumstances, Gellius says that when some senators wanted war because the Rhodians were *male animatos*, Cato defended 'these excellent and faithful allies towards whom many of the leading men were hostile, being intent on plundering and possessing their wealth'—which suggests that this aspect impressed itself on Gellius because it was a marked feature of the speech. Another possibility is that he was influenced by Cato's own account in the *Origines*, which would also be significant.

(*b*) (6. 3. 52). There is a Roman tradition of clemency and mildness, 'nunc clementiae, nunc mansuetudinis maiorum . . . commonefacit.'

7. 'He reminds them of public expediency.' (This is closely bracketed with *clementia* and *mansuetudo* in 6. 3. 52, the complete phrase being 'nunc clementiae, nunc mansuetudinis maiorum, nunc utilitatis publicae commonefacit.' This conjunction, and indeed the sequence of the sentence to which it is the conclusion, suggest that public advantage is being urged as one of the reasons why the Rhodians should be pardoned. It is probably another reference to the arguments mentioned in 6. 3. 47, set out in 6*a* above, where the concept of *utile* is also found.)

8. The Rhodians are friends and clients:
   (*a*) (6. 3. 52). They are *necessarii* of the state, 'nunc ut necessarios reipublicae ostendat' (the position of this phrase immediately after a reference to a plea for pardon suggests that here Gellius had in mind a passage where this was urged as a reason for granting pardon).
   (*b*) (6. 3. 26). 'Shall we now suddenly abandon such great services given and received, so great a friendship? Shall we be the first actually to do what we say they wished to do?' (Both the second sentence and the context in Gellius show that this was not part of a separate assessment of the advantages to be gained from maintaining the *amicitia*. Instead it was part of Cato's argument that it was deeds, not wishes, which were culpable and punishable. The appeal to past services and *amicitia* was an emotional reinforcement of this, pointing up the impropriety implicit in the intended attack on Rhodes when it was viewed as Cato presented it: Rome punishing Rhodes by actually doing what she complained Rhodes had wished to do.)
   (*c*) In 6. 3. 47 Gellius, referring to Cato's efforts to secure a favourable judgement on the Rhodians, says, 'the retention of whose friendship was in the interests of the state', 'quorum amicitiam retineri ex re publica fuit'. This, however, is Gellius' passing comment to reinforce his explanation that Cato was ready to resort to any argument which might be effective, whether or not it was sound. It probably reflects Gellius' superficial notion of the circumstances rather than the contents of the speech, and it would be wrong to treat it as a carefully considered judgement. It is

certainly not strong evidence that 'the importance of retaining the friendship of the Rhodians' was the dominating theme of the speech or even that there was a section devoted to the practical advantages of retaining the *amicitia*. On the other hand, it is clear that in a looser sense the notion of public advantage and the long-standing relationship with Rhodes were both introduced into various parts of the speech.

It is not possible to be absolutely certain that Gellius mentioned every line of argument used by Cato, but it is unlikely that he has passed over any which were at all prominent. Obviously there may have been more than one aspect to the treatment of some of them and no doubt considerable elaboration, as the fragments show was the case with the particular argument attacked by Tiro. But since Gellius' contention in the later part of his discussion is that Tiro misrepresented Cato by his exclusive concentration on one argument, he has a positive interest in supporting his case by reference to as many other arguments used by Cato as possible. It is, therefore, reasonable to suppose that he does indicate, though mostly in a summary way, all the arguments which figured significantly in the original speech.

A question which presents much greater difficulty is that of the relationship between these arguments and Cato's real reasons for opposing military action against Rhodes. For it is immediately apparent not only that these arguments cannot all have weighed equally with him but that he himself could not have regarded them all as valid and did not do so. Some of them are mutually contradictory, or virtually so, and Gellius clearly regarded the full speech as showing that Cato considered there to be nothing discreditable in using all possible arguments which might help to bring about the desired result, even if they were not equally sound.[25] It is improbable, though not inconceivable, that he omitted all mention of the reasons which weighed most with himself; but Gellius' comments suggest that it cannot be taken for granted that they were those which were given the greatest prominence in the speech, and therefore that it might not have been possible to identify them with confidence even if the full text had survived. It is a plausible guess, for example, that a powerful consideration in Cato's mind was a belief that much of the impetus for war sprang from hopes of rich booty; but what makes this plausible is not so much the suspicion that it may have been quite prominent in the speech (see

---

[25] Gell. 6. 3. 44 (see p. 274 n. 21):'nihil sibi dictu factuque in ea re turpe duxit, quin omni sententiarum via servatum ire socios niteretur.'

item 4, above, and footnote) as the fact that disapproval of such behaviour is a recurring feature of Cato's career.

There is, however, another way of looking at this question. The arguments advanced by Cato, both those which had really determined his own attitude and those which were additional, were employed because he believed they would carry weight with many senators; and though he could have misjudged details, it is most unlikely that his judgement was seriously at fault about the types of argument which were likely to be effective. Thus the arguments of the speech are at least a useful indication of the kinds of consideration which senators were likely to take into account in reaching decisions about foreign affairs.

From this point of view the striking feature of Cato's arguments is that overwhelmingly they are moral in character—taking 'moral' in a broad sense.[26] It is even doubtful if there was any reference at all to considerations of *Realpolitik*—such as strategic interests, the policing role of the Rhodian navy, the balance between the Greek states, manpower resources, and practical objections to further Roman commitments in the East (or, for that matter, any objection on the score of the undesirability of closer cultural contacts). There is no definite mention of any considerations of this kind, though it is possible that some such underlie the reference to *utilitas publica* as one of the reasons for pardoning the Rhodians, and it is to be remembered that this could have been more prominent in the original than Gellius' brief mention might suggest at first sight. Even if this were so, however, *utilitas publica* in such a sense was patently not the principal theme of the speech, most of the arguments being of quite a different kind; and if anything it is more probable than not that the *utilitas publica* mentioned in 6. 3. 52 was conceived in less concrete and specific terms. This is probably a second reference to the arguments previously indicated in 6. 3. 47 (see items 6a and 7, above), where the expediency of granting pardon is mentioned first in general terms (*utile rebus humanis*), followed by a warning that unwillingness to grant pardon is liable to lead to internal upheavals;[27] and where finally what it is said will be maintained by

[26] Kienast, pp. 123 f., wrongly sees the moral elements as subordinate to the idea of *utilitas*, which he regards as the dominating idea in a speech of which the striking feature is sober practicality. Nevertheless, as will appear below, 'moral' is not to be understood as totally divorced from 'practical' or 'expedient'.

[27] This must be connected with a general attitude of unwillingness to pardon, not with the particular case of Rhodes. 'Metus in republica rerum novarum movet' must mean 'in Rome', and it would surely have been beyond even Cato's talents to argue that a failure to pardon Rhodes would provoke upheavals in the Roman state. Gelzer, *RE*, s.v. *Porcius*, no. 9, cols. 134 f.; Kienast, pp. 122 f.; and Schmitt, *Rom und Rhodos*, p. 154, take the sentence to be a reference to Iuventius Thalna's attempt to secure a declaration of war without consulting

granting pardon is the *magnitudo*, the greatness, of the Roman people. It is significant indication of the kind of *utilitas* envisaged that what is mentioned is greatness—rather than safety, power, or supremacy. Obviously Cato sought to present his case as expedient and in the interests of the Roman people—as he surely believed it to be: indeed that is essentially the appeal of the exordium itself, with its implication that a hasty decision to go to war might turn out to mar the success Rome was currently enjoying. But his concept of expediency, of what would be to the advantage or disadvantage of the Roman people, was not confined to calculated strategic and political considerations. It is not that these were totally disregarded, for whether or not they played a role in the Rhodian affair they certainly did on other occasions, as is illustrated by the fragment of Cato's own speech on Macedonia; but the arguments used in Cato's Rhodian speech do show that the senators in general were not habituated to judging foreign affairs exclusively or even predominantly in terms of such considerations. Nor perhaps is it adequate to say simply that account was taken of moral and other considerations alongside those of expediency; rather, it seems that there was no strong sense that these various considerations were to be separated into different categories.

It is usually possible to rationalize a moral argument or a principle in terms of calculated advantage, as Cato himself did in this speech when he argued that an unwillingness to grant pardon was an attitude which could bring about internal upheaval. The prevailing tendency of his arguments, however, was to assume that it was to the advantage of Rome to do what was right, not merely in the sense that it would induce in others favourable attitudes which would facilitate Rome's aims, but also in the sense that to act rightly, to adhere to proprieties and traditional standards of conduct, maintained the quality of Rome and was thereby a source of strength and prosperity. So to Cato it was both 'right' and in the public interest—the latter partly following from the former—not to make war without a just cause, not to punish where there was no misdeed, not to attack a guiltless state for the sake of plunder, not to subordinate to an outburst of anger the clemency and moderation which a dutiful client was entitled to expect from a responsible patron. So it was that as a serious argument for pardoning the Rhodians the clemency and moderation of the *maiores* could

the Senate, and in varying degrees they regard this as a major argument in Cato's case. This seems unlikely, however. Since Thalna had already been thwarted and the matter brought before the Senate the constitutional issue was already resolved and would not be reopened if the Senate itself decided on war. Gellius' sentence about the fear of *res novae* should almost certainly be taken closely with the general ideas which precede and follow it—usefulness in human affairs and *magnitudo*.

appear alongside public expediency (which at that point may or may not imply arguments of *Realpolitik*); and so it was that if the granting of pardon would maintain Rome's greatness that did not have to be expressed in terms of political and strategic particulars but was a sufficient concept in itself. Thus in the speech the categories of argument intermingled and overlapped—moralistic, legalistic, looking to the general welfare of Rome, perhaps also to calculated political and strategic advantage, and appealing to sentiment and tradition. These arguments, as was observed before, were expected to carry weight, and their nature and variety show that the Senate, though unquestionably it often did take account of arguments of calculated expediency, did not habitually reach its decisions on that basis alone but was readily influenced by 'moral', legalistic, and emotional considerations.[28]

In theory it does not follow that the same was true of Cato himself: it would not be possible actually to disprove a contention that he was a calculating realist, deliberately playing upon tendencies which he observed in his fellow senators but did not himself share. But that would be, to put it mildly, a rash and unsupported assumption which becomes incredible in the face of the recurrent evidence for his concern with propriety and correct conduct in other matters during his career. Though in the case of Rhodes there can be no certainty as to which of his arguments counted for most in his own mind, and though like other senators he will have formed his own opinion about the force and relative merits of particular arguments, there is no reason to suppose that he differed fundamentally from other senators in the way he assessed questions relating to foreign affairs.

All of this has implications, in respect both of Cato and of the Senate, as to the use of the word 'policy' in relation to the conduct of foreign affairs. The ready acceptance of 'moral', legalistic, and emotional considerations implies that to a significant extent attention was liable to be focused on the immediate merits of a particular question, and by no means exclusively or even predominantly on its relationship to longer-term political or strategic interests. Consequently, though obviously in reaching a decision account was taken of its likely consequences, unless a common pattern is

---

[28] It is to be noted also that the accounts of the Rhodian episode represent those who wanted war as motivated by indignation and in some cases by greed. Cato's exordium, fr. 163, is essentially a plea not to allow the emotion of the moment to lead to an unwise decision, and in fr. 169 his rhetorical question, 'idne irascimini, si quis superbior est quam nos?' indicates that indignation at Rhodian arrogance really was a factor. The only indication of possible calculation of the public interest is Polyb. 29. 19. 5, where in rebuffing the original embassy the Senate is said to have wished to make an example of the Rhodians.

very obvious it is a mistake to try to link together a succession of decisions by the Senate—or of stances by Cato—by the hypothesis that the calculation of such interests was the dominant factor, and especially by the hypothesis of consistent pursuit of clearly defined objectives.

There is nothing surprising about this. The Senate was ill suited in size, structure, and method of operation, to formulate long-term policies of any complexity, let alone to apply them in detail effectively and consistently over a substantial period.[29] No doubt the thinking of senators was often influenced by underlying prejudices and presuppositions which could produce a discernible pattern in a series of decisions, as could a tendency to follow the precedents of earlier decisions which had worked out well.[30] But that is not the same as consciously, consistently, and with careful calculation subordinating particular decisions to broad principles and long-term objectives. For doing that successfully the Roman Senate was too large, its practices of delegation too rudimentary and too unsystematic; and it was almost totally without support from anything resembling a civil or diplomatic service. There was some expertise among senators who had visited various states as members of the admittedly frequent embassies sent out by the Senate, and some of these exercised considerable influence,[31] but the flow of reliable information was necessarily slow and uneven, and probably often superficial. Above all there was no body of persons whose task it was, as happens in the foreign office of a modern state, to undertake an objective, cool, and calculating examination of all the factors, possibilities, and implications in a given situation, relating that situation to the long-term objectives currently laid down, disregarding their own emotional reactions and moral judgements and regarding those of others essentially as factors to be allowed for in their assessment. Moral judgements and emotional reactions, along with some modification of the long-term objectives, may enter in when the authoritative decisions are taken; but where there is a competent foreign affairs service they do so in the face of and clearly distinguishable from an assessment of various alternatives in terms of objective calculations, which, therefore, carry great weight. In Rome there was no organization to service the Senate in this way. The whole process of assessment and decision was a single operation (even if it was sometimes spread over more than one occasion)

[29] Astin, Politics and Policies, esp. pp. 14 ff.

[30] Similarly changes in prevailing moods or attitudes might produce a discernible trend in such a series of decisions.

[31] e.g. Ti. Sempronius Gracchus (cos. 177): Polyb. 30. 27. 1 ff.; 30. 30. 7 f.; 30. 31. 19 f.; 31. 15. 9 ff. (where the import is clear despite a lacuna in the text). The best-known example is Flamininus earlier in the century. Kienast, p. 153 n. 125, notes some others.

performed by an assembly of some 300 persons. It is scarcely a matter for surprise, therefore, if in such circumstances considerations of 'morality',[32] legalism, expediency, and emotion readily intermingled, or if there was a tendency for a good deal of attention to be focused on the immediate merits of a question rather than its relationship to long-term objectives, which in any case are likely at best to have been ill defined and fluctuating and may never have been thought out at all.

All this is illustrated again in the dispute which led up to the Third Punic War.[33] This time, in contrast to his role in the Rhodian debate, Cato was the principal advocate of action, sustaining his calls for the destruction of Carthage through a controversy which lasted well over two years despite tenacious opposition led by Scipio Nasica Corculum. There are in fact interesting similarities between some of Nasica's arguments (so far as they are known) and certain of those used by Cato in 167.[34] In the earlier stages Nasica, much like Cato in the exordium of the Rhodian speech, urged that nothing should be done rashly, implying, as had Cato, that there was a danger of the emotion of the moment (in this case probably fear rather than indignation) precipitating a wrong decision. When reports that Carthage had acquired both an army and a fleet led Cato to intensify his calls for war, Nasica obtained a compromise decision by urging that there was not yet a 'just cause', *iusta causa*, for war, and Cato's own words show that one of the arguments he was contesting was that the Carthaginians had not yet committed any hostile actions against Rome.[35] Closely related to this was the dispute about how the destruction of Carthage would be viewed by foreign opinion—a consideration which Polybius asserts came close to tipping the decision against war[36] and which was possibly the heart of Nasica's continued opposition even after the Carthaginian invasion of Numidia, openly violating the treaty with Rome, had formally settled the question of a *iusta causa*. It is possible, of course, that Nasica and his supporters meant this in the sense of the effect on Rome's political and strategic interests, encouraging, for example, Hellenistic states to unite to resist her wishes; but it is at least as probable that they

[32] A well-known instance involving both short-term expediency and 'morality' is the divided reaction in 172 to Q. Marcius Philippus' deceitful truce with Perseus: Livy, 42. 47; cf. Diod. 30. 7. 1. According to Livy, evidently following Polybius, a number of older senators protested, though the majority approved Philippus' action. It is a plausible guess, but no more, that Cato was among the protesters.

[33] For an account see pp. 125 ff.; also Astin, *Scipio Aemilianus*, pp. 49 ff. and Appendix III.

[34] There is nothing in Cato's arguments, however, which corresponds closely to Nasica's argument that Rome needed a 'counterweight of fear' to maintain her effectiveness. On the variations with which that argument is reported see Astin, *Scipio Aemilianus*, pp. 276 ff.

[35] *ORF*[3], fr. 195, quoted below.   [36] Polyb. 36. 2. 4.

argued in terms of the esteem and prestige enjoyed by Rome, much as Cato had related the granting of pardon to Rome's greatness.

On the other side Cato is consistently represented as actuated by the belief that the Carthaginians were a danger to Rome, a belief reinforced by his own observation of their prosperity and by their increasing self-assertion and intransigence over their disputes with Massinissa.[37] The few fragments surviving from his speech 'Concerning a Carthaginian war', *De bello Carthaginiensi*, are in accord with this. Nothing emerges from a brief reference to the foundation of Carthage, but the one fragment which preserves a rational argument in effect declares that since the Carthaginians are equipping themselves to make war on Rome it is necessary to strike first: 'The Carthaginians are already our enemies; for he who prepares everything against me, so that he can make war at whatever time he wishes, is already my enemy even though he is not yet using weapons.'[38] The proximity of this enemy he dramatized on one occasion by his display of a fig gathered only three days before in the territory of Carthage.[39] Three other fragments show Cato using stories of Punic atrocities to play upon the emotions of the senators[40]—which does not necessarily mean that he was doing so cynically and was himself undisturbed by them: anger and horror experienced as a young man may easily have revived as potent and obsessive forces in the mind of an octogenarian.

Fear of a resurgent Carthage was the principal motive which led to the destruction of the city. By and large, little difficulty has been felt about accepting this in the case of the aged Cato himself, but there has been some reluctance to accept it as the principal motive for the decision of the Senate as a whole.[41] Carthage, it has sometimes been thought, was too weak ever again to be a menace to Rome, and hard-headed Roman politicians could not seriously have feared her. Hence various suggestions have been made as to more subtle, calculating motives, in which the destruction of Carthage was not an end in itself (in the sense of the removal of a threat) but a means to some further objective: the furtherance of Roman commerce by the elimination of a major competitor; the annexation of the territory of Carthage before it fell to Numidia, thus forestalling the emergence of Numidia as a major power; or the conscious adoption of a policy of direct rule in face of constant instability and resentment resulting from the inadequacies of a previous policy of paternalist predominance. The last of

---

[37] App. *Lib.* 69; Plut. *Cato Mai.* 26 f.; Livy, *Per.* 48–9; Cic. *De sen.* 18; Pliny, *Nat. hist.* 15. 74 f.; Florus, 1. 31. 4 ff.   [38] *ORF*[3], fr. 195.

[39] Plut. *Cato Mai.* 27. 1; Pliny, *Nat. hist.* 15. 74 ff.   [40] *ORF*[3], frs. 191–3.

[41] On this reluctance and suggested alternative motives see Astin, *Scipio Aemilianus*, pp. 272 ff.

these does have some basis in a change of attitude which seems to have been taking place in this period, displaying less patience and a readier resort to harshness for deterrent example, and reflected in the creation of three new provinces within the space of fifteen years, two of them east of the Adriatic. A change in attitude, however, is not the same as a deliberate decision of policy. Of all such explanations it can be said that there is no evidence for them, that what evidence there is tells against them, and that they are unnecessary. There is no hint in the sources of commercial motivation, and not until many years after the destruction of Carthage was there any attempt to occupy or utilize its splendid site and harbour—indeed, far from seeking it for themselves the conquerors imposed solemn imprecations against resettlement. Serious fear of Numidia is most improbable—far less probable than fear of Carthage—and if the Senate, acting from careful political calculation, had wished to halt Numidian occupations of Carthaginian territory it would have had little difficulty in doing so. Moreover there is no justification for supposing that the demand in 149 for abandonment of the city of Carthage and the building of a new city at least ten miles inland was not genuinely the last demand, or that the Senate did not mean what it said when it promised that if the Carthaginians obeyed instructions they would retain their lands, their freedom, and their autonomy. In other words, in deciding upon the destruction of the city the Senate probably did not decide to create a new province, and it was probably only the Carthaginians' final desperate resistance in breach of their *deditio* that made the latter virtually inevitable.

Behind all the 'superimposed' explanations lies a belief that fear of the Carthaginians is an insufficient explanation for the decision to destroy the city, that the Senate cannot at this date have so feared them; but that assumption is mistaken. Even on the basis of rational, unemotional calculation a belief that a resurgent Carthage was a danger was not so unreasonable as has sometimes been thought. There was certainly a spirit of restive self-assertion among the Carthaginians. In consequence, through most of the crisis period the majority were prepared to support military leaders who advocated responding with military action to the pressures from Massinissa. Not only did they show their resentment of past Roman conduct by refusing Roman arbitration but even before that there had been raids on Massinissa's territory, and in the winter of 151/150 they mobilized a large army to undertake a full-scale expedition into Numidia, in blatant violation of the treaty imposed by Rome at the end of the Second Punic War. Even when the disastrous outcome of that campaign had induced a temporary panic-stricken subservience, one of the militant leaders, Hasdrubal, escaped and collected a large rebel army. Moreover the kingdom of Numidia was exhibiting signs of internal disaffection which the Carthaginians were already exploiting. If Massinissa were to die or become incapacitated—and he was nearly ninety years of age—swift intervention might easily give the Carthaginians control; and if Rome had not decided to act that could have remained a possibility even after the Carthaginian disaster in the winter of 151/150. Cato and his supporters could reasonably have concluded that if nothing were done soon the increasing militancy and self-assertion in Carthage would result in an increasing defiance of the restrictions on rearmament, that her favourable site and commercial prosperity gave her great military and naval potential, that intervention to enforce disarmament would become an increasingly formidable and costly operation, and that the alternative to such intervention was the alarming prospect of a people which had every reason to hate Rome being left free to rearm and strengthen themselves as they wished.

There was, therefore, a rational basis for the fear expressed by Cato and his supporters; none the less, it was the emotion of fear that was at work, not only a rational appraisal of the likely implications of different courses of action or inaction. Cato is known to have played on emotions, and the final decision to demand the abandonment of the site of Carthage reflected emotion—fear, and perhaps hatred—as well as reason. True, it had the ruthless logic of destroying the ultimate basis of the prosperity which might be used for military strength, but it went well beyond the dictates of rational calculation alone as to what was necessary and advantageous—particularly in a situation where the likely effect on foreign opinion is said to have nearly induced the senators not to go to war. The decision to destroy the city is readily understandable, but only in the context of a genuine if exaggerated fear. The Senate, as the discussion earlier in this chapter indicates, was a body which it is not difficult to imagine being swayed by such fear; and indeed it is scarcely conceivable that it could have debated the allegations of rearmament and signs of self-assertion by this terrible enemy of the past without engendering a great deal of emotion.

The Carthaginian controversy exhibited, therefore, not the same arguments and sentiments as the Rhodian affair, but a similar mixture of different types of argument and consideration: considerations of 'right' and legalism connected with a *iusta causa*, of Rome's standing in the eyes of others, of expediency and security, and of emotion. Furthermore, everything suggests that this question was considered largely as a self-contained issue, taking account of the likely consequences of alternative possibilities, but not with reference to broader policies or more distant goals. All of which seems to support the inference that the Senate frequently approached questions relating to foreign affairs in this way.

There is no reason to suppose that as an individual senator Cato's own approach was significantly different. It is impossible to prove that strong convictions about carefully considered long-term foreign policy were not an important factor in determining his stance on particular issues; but there is no evidence and no necessity for that hypothesis. There is no succession of coincidences to be accounted for, and no instance in which his known attitude cannot be explained satisfactorily in terms of opinion about the merits of the immediate issue; and in the two instances relating to Rhodes and Carthage enough is known to leave little doubt that this was how he viewed the issues. That is not to say that in foreign affairs he was merely a short-term pragmatist, despite the domination of his attitude in the Carthaginian issue by his determination to eradicate the supposed danger. Wider considerations are evident in the Rhodian speech, and it must not be assumed too readily that Cato simply dismissed them in regard to Carthage (the argument is likely to have been about whether there was a *iusta causa*, not whether Rome should go to war without one); but these are considerations of correct conduct and of legalism and they are intermingled with other types of consideration, seemingly without a sharp and conscious distinction into categories; and certainly no one type of consideration is treated as overriding.

Two points remain. First, although, as was said before, it is a reasonable guess that Cato increasingly exercised significant influence in debates about foreign affairs, there are only two or three instances in which he is actually known to have done so. Of those the release of the Achaean hostages was a minor matter, while there is some uncertainty about just how important his role was in the decision about Rhodes—which in any case, despite the heat it evidently generated, was scarcely to be regarded as momentous. Only in the matter of Carthage, in the last few years of his life, can it be positively affirmed that Cato played a major role in an issue of foreign affairs. Second, although there are only a few instances in which Cato's stance on an issue of foreign affairs is known, in each of these instances he was in agreement with the decision ultimately taken by the Senate (though in the earlier stages of the Carthaginian controversy the Senate had preferred more moderate proposals than his).[42] There

---

[42] But it is a plausible guess that in 172 he was among the minority of senators who were reluctant to set the stamp of senatorial approval on the truce with Perseus deceitfully negotiated by Q. Marcius Philippus: p. 283 n. 32.

are not enough instances to justify pressing this point too strongly, but it does seem to suggest that here again, in foreign affairs as in other matters, Cato is not to be thought of as a lone and idiosyncratic figure but as an influential senator who, if exceptionally forceful and colourful, was reasonably representative of the views and attitudes of many of his fellow senators.

13

Conclusion

IN a personal sense the career of Marcus Porcius Cato was a brilliant success. Winning fame as soldier and as orator, the 'new man' not only became a senator but, having made his way into an aristocracy sharply competitive for office and honour, scaled the heights of the consulship, celebrated a military triumph, and went on to the even more exclusive distinction of the censorship. The latter office, it will be recalled, could be held by only four Romans in each decade. Nor was that the end. For a further thirty-four years, surviving numerous disputes and prosecutions, Cato continued influential and vigorous in public affairs. Indeed he was already in his eighties when he took to himself the role for which he is probably most widely known today, that of principal author of the destruction of Carthage, leading the long sustained and ultimately successful calls for military action against the old enemy.

In antiquity he was long remembered, and by no means only—or even predominantly—for the destruction of Carthage. For centuries after his death not merely his success but his versatility, the range of his achievement, and in some respects his pioneering role, are mirrored in the ability of a remarkable variety of writers to find him relevant to their diverse interests and purposes. He could be seen as an exemplar of military talent, as a pioneering but skilful and powerful orator, as a symbol of personal austerity, or as a champion of severe integrity in public life. His works could be treated as ideal models of a rugged, antique style, as treasuries of curious words and phrases, or as mines from which to quarry pithy sayings or nuggets of information about early Italy or agriculture or military affairs; or again, as innovatory works in the Latin prose tradition, especially in the emergence of Latin historical writing. Above all he could appear—or be presented—as an idealized public figure, as a wise counsellor, as one of the outstanding senators of the Roman Republic.

Yet personal success and posthumous fame do not necessarily indicate historical significance; and whether Cato's life and achievement were historically significant is a question by no means simple to interpret or to answer. Patently they were not of that kind which may be likened to 'an erratic block which has diverted the stream of human history'.[1] Even of his role in the creation of a Latin prose literature it could be held that, innovator though he was, he is to be seen as no more than the particular agent of a development which had become inevitable and could not have been long delayed. For all their novelty and interest in their Roman setting, his writings seem to have had marked stylistic and intellectual limitations and could scarcely have been matched against the standards of Greek literary achievement, increasing awareness of which certainly was a key factor in the evolution of Roman literature. On the other hand, as was pointed out elsewhere,[2] that which the historian in retrospect sees as inevitable often requires for its realization an agent gifted with exceptional initiative and inventiveness; and in their context the extent of Cato's achievement and the range of his contributions are alike remarkable. No one can know how the sequel would have been modified if what Cato did had been brought about instead by a different personality, or in more piecemeal fashion, perhaps by several persons, or more gradually, or slightly later in time; but there can be no doubt that in the actual course of events the versatile personality of Cato played a direct, substantial, and unique role in the emergence of Latin prose literature. Cato may not have been an erratic block diverting the stream of Roman literary development into new and scarcely predictable directions, but he was undoubtedly responsible for the stream taking a considerable surge forward and he perhaps helped to shape some of the channels along which it was to flow.

The significance of Cato's military activity is more easily assessed. Undoubtedly his abilities were considerable and his services valuable. In 195 his wide-ranging successes, reversing the tide of the Spanish rebellion, did much to restore the Roman hold in the Iberian peninsula, while four years later at Thermopylae his outflanking movement played an important part in the Roman victory and may well have been decisive. Nevertheless, a single year of command in Spain and a single spectacular exploit in Greece were scarcely likely to have—and did not have—the kind of far-reaching significance associated with the achievements of such commanders as Scipio Africanus or Julius Caesar.

The difficulty of assessment reappears, however, as soon as attention is turned from military operations to central decisions about foreign affairs. To start with, there are the gaping deficiencies in information about Cato's contributions to such decisions, so that even about several of the most momentous issues of the period, let alone numerous minor ones,

---

[1] Baynes, with reference to Constantine, in *Constantine and the Christian Church*[2]; p. 3.
[2] p. 210.

nothing is known of his attitude—though in some cases this may be a hint that his was not a decisive voice. Even so, enough is known to suggest that it would be an error to discuss the question in terms of 'Cato's foreign policy'. In those few instances where his intervention is attested the evidence suggests a tendency to deal with individual issues on their merits, rather than to subordinate them to the dictates of long-term policy or considered principles; and that Cato, like other senators, was apt to be swayed by a wide variety of motives and arguments. But even in terms of particular decisions the extent of his influence is not easy to determine. It is true that in each instance in which Cato's personal opinion is known it coincides with that ultimately adopted by the Senate; but that may mean only that he was usually in harmony with the majority rather than that he took the lead, and in any case most of the issues involved were relatively minor. In practice it is likely that as time went on he did exercise an important influence on decisions about foreign affairs; but the fact is that there are only two or three specific matters about which it can be confidently affirmed that he actually did so, and only one of those was a major issue.

But that one issue was the great controversy which culminated in the Third Punic War and the destruction of Carthage; and in this there is every likelihood that Cato's role was indeed decisive. Whether it is also to be judged historically significant depends upon conjectures as to what would have happened if Cato had not pressed his case, or had failed in the face of Nasica's opposition. Would it have meant no more than a short delay, until another crisis arose, its outcome essentially the same as that which actually occurred? Or would Roman inaction have allowed Carthage to husband her wealth and her strength, until she could indeed have well-founded hopes of asserting her independence of action, perhaps drawing Rome into yet another massive struggle for supremacy? Or would the Punic city have subsided into submissiveness as a client state? How long then before Rome had an African province? What would have happened about the veterans and settlers who later on poured into the province, or the grain and wealth which flowed out? What turn might the struggle between Jugurtha and his brothers have taken if Carthage had still been there to complicate the issue? If the Roman Senate had not determined on the destruction of Carthage how would Rome and other Mediterranean peoples have behaved towards each other in the following years?—for, direct physical consequences apart, the psychological and symbolic impact of the Third Punic War was undoubtedly considerable. The questions are virtually unanswerable, the potential for speculation immense; yet, if there can be no certainty, plainly there is a strong possibility that by bringing about the annihilation of Carthage Cato did substantially influence the subsequent history of the Roman state and the Roman empire.

From a more general point of view, and especially in the field of domestic politics, it is easy to interpret Cato's activity, long and vigorous though it was, as ultimately ineffective. That 'Cato's political efficiency did not make him an historically significant figure'[3] is an unequivocal but by no means unorthodox modern verdict. The political destruction of Africanus, perhaps the most dramatic of Cato's domestic political achievements, was probably of little consequence in the wider perspective. Historians conscious of the eventual collapse of the Roman Republic can readily compile formidable lists of incipient problems with which Cato failed to grapple, for which (so far as is known) he put forward no solutions (though such lists are apt to include items which no Roman of Cato's time is likely to have foreseen or to have recognized as problems).[4] Moreover, when attention is turned to Cato's attested actions and to the concerns which he did display, though it is necessary to beware of underestimating his pertinacity and of unduly emphasizing the 'backward-looking' element in his approach, a strong case can still be made for an essentially negative judgement. Neither his censorship nor his forensic activities nor his frequent exhortations and complaints halted misconduct in office or the growing readiness to acquire private wealth by the abuse of public position or the rapidly increasing private expenditure on costly and 'luxurious' appurtenances of life. Nor did Cato's complaints against some aspects of Greek practice and culture effectively discourage Romans of succeeding generations from taking a greater interest in philosophy and rhetorical training, or from sending their sons to study in Athens or Rhodes.

Cato is often presented as championing the values of a past which was fast fading and beyond recall. No doubt there is an element of truth in this: the most ardent and rigid upholders of traditional values, particularly the values of exclusive groups, are frequently to be found among the 'new men' who have recently achieved association with them. But in other respects the picture is misleading. The issues which aroused Cato's concern were contemporary and important; and if he saw them essentially as questions of personal *mores* and of a climate of social opinion, that was not wholly unrealistic and in any case was virtually inevitable in a Roman of Cato's time. Moreover he was by no means an isolated curiosity. No doubt his opinions were sometimes distinctive in detail, and frequently distinctive in the manner and effectiveness with which they were

---

[3] Toynbee, *Hannibal's Legacy*, ii. 516.   [4] pp. 98 f.

expressed—for he was a man of exceptional determination and exceptional talents; but his general attitudes, his concern with standards of public conduct and his disapproval of luxury and extravagance, evidently found much support. Similarly it was a general Roman problem of adjustment to Greek cultural influences which was mirrored in the curious complex of Cato's attitudes and prejudices towards the Greeks—which in broad terms, if not in every detail, was probably a more typical reaction than was the uncritical enthusiasm of Aulus Postumius Albinus. In short, exceptional though he was in talents and in personality, Cato was probably broadly representative of a substantial body of contemporary opinion and attitudes. In that sense, at least, he has considerable historical significance, and all the more so if it be supposed that such attitudes are likely to have been fortified and more effectively articulated in consequence of being championed by so formidable a representative.

Nor should it be assumed too readily that these attitudes and opinions proved entirely irrelevant to the future. Although in the government of its provincial subjects the later Republic frequently failed lamentably to apply in practice the standards for which Cato had striven, it adopted and repeatedly strengthened legislative measures and judicial machinery specifically designed to enforce those very standards. Likewise despite—or perhaps because of—the rapid growth of wealth and extravagance sumptuary legislation was a recurring feature to the time of Augustus. As for Cato's attitudes towards the Greeks, it can be argued that in some respects these not only had contemporary significance but foreshadowed what was to come, even in certain of their negative aspects. Thus although Greek medicine was to win greater acceptance, Roman attitudes remained ambivalent and displayed considerable distrust and prejudice. A dislike of contemporary Greeks, characterized as unscrupulous and decadent, was to persist alongside acceptance and absorption of the Greek cultural heritage. Undue devotion to study long continued to be looked upon as undignified, as unworthy of a Roman senator: what was judged excessive changed, but the basic attitude remained. Similarly with philosophy. Up to a point its study became acceptable and respectable; but philosophy in Roman hands became something very different from the imaginative, critical, questioning pursuit which it had been in Greek hands alone. Cato would surely have disapproved of Lucretius as much as he did of Carneades; but if philosophy had been presented to him in the guise in which it appears in the writings of Seneca or of Marcus Aurelius it is far from certain that he would have reacted with the same hostility.

It would be flagrantly implausible to suppose that a man who lived to the age of eighty-five never found himself out of tune with the times, any more than that he was never inconsistent with himself or never modified his attitudes. Nevertheless, though the patchiness of the evidence no doubt obscures some contradictions, it does appear that in important respects there was a broad continuity and consistency; and so far from standing in lonely opposition to the tide of opinion and the inexorable course of events, Cato had a much more positive relationship than has often been envisaged both to the contemporary and to the future history of Rome. Neither an eccentric nor an anachronism, he was extraordinary yet in no small degree representative, a remarkable Roman but none the less a Roman of his time.

APPENDIX 1

Sources

THE ancient literary sources for the study of Cato are numerous and extremely varied. Whether as a symbolic figure, as the subject of useful, striking, or uplifting anecdotes, or as orator or author, many writers found some mention of him relevant to their widely differing interests and purposes.[1] However, the material is by no means evenly distributed, a considerable proportion of it, including much that is especially informative, being contributed by about a dozen of these writers; and of these several, such as Quintilian, Fronto, Aulus Gellius, Seneca, Columella, and the elder Pliny, require no special discussion. Naturally there are problems about certain particular passages in them, and their remarks have always to be understood in relation to their individual standpoints and purposes; but in general they are relatively straightforward. In some instances it simply happens to be their works which have preserved facts or ideas which were probably generally current in the literary tradition, while in many other instances their interest is in Cato's style in his speeches and writings, or they cite him as a source of information. The discussion which follows is therefore limited to a brief survey of six others among the dozen or so major contributors: Cato himself, Polybius, Livy, Cicero, Cornelius Nepos, and Plutarch.[2]

Cato's own speeches and writings are important in two senses. First, since many of them survived throughout antiquity, directly or indirectly they underlie much of the information and comment in later writers. Thus, though contamination and distortion are to be expected, there are also substantial elements which are ultimately derived from Cato himself. Second, the remnants still available to the modern scholar, fragmentary though they are, yield many valuable facts and insights. That is true even of the *De agricultura* (the only work

---

[1] The attitudes of many writers towards Cato are discussed extensively by Della Corte, *Catone censore*[2], pp. 123 ff.

[2] On these sources and their possible interrelationships see esp. Nissen, *Kritische Untersuchungen*, esp. pp. 292 ff.; Soltau, 'Nepos und Plutarchos', *Neue Jahrb. für Philologie* 153 (1896), 123 ff.; Leo, *Die griech.-röm. Biographie*, pp. 165 ff. and 212; Fraccaro, 'Sulla biografia di Catone Maggiore', *Opusc.* i. 139 ff. (with supplements to original publication in *Atti e mem. della Accad. Virgiliana* n.s. 3 (1910), 99 ff.); id., 'Le fonti per il consolato di M. Porcio Catone', *Studi storici*, 3 (1910), 129 ff. = *Opusc.* i. 177 ff.; id., 'Ricerche storiche e letterarie sulla censura del 184–183', *Studi storici*, 4 (1911), 1 ff. = *Opusc.* i. 417 ff.; Smith, 'Plutarch's Biographical Sources in the Roman Lives' and 'The Cato Censorius of Plutarch', *CQ* 34 (1940), 1 ff. and 105 ff.; Kienast, pp. 10 ff.; Tränkle, *Cato in der vierten und fünften Dekade des Livius*; Ruebel, *The Political Development of Cato Censorius*, pp. 9 ff.

to survive *in extenso*); for although it is a practical manual with little direct biographical information, it does throw useful light on certain features of the society in which Cato lived and on some of his own attitudes and preconceptions. Of his other works, especially his speeches and the historical work, the *Origines*, numerous fragments are preserved as quotations by later authors, frequently because they were interested in his style, or his antique vocabulary and grammar, or his version of the early traditions of Rome and Italy. In many instances the purpose for which these quotations were made gives good ground for supposing them to be verbatim. The fragments of the speeches in particular—well over 200 fragments have been identified from about eighty different speeches— provide a considerable amount of information about Cato and his activities.[3]

Of the other authors the Greek historian Polybius was undoubtedly the best informed. One of the Achaean leaders who were deported to Italy in 167, Polybius was living in Rome, much interested in political affairs, for most of the last eighteen years of Cato's life; and on one occasion, when in 150 Cato advocated the release of the remaining detainees, Polybius is attested as having had direct dealings with him. Moreover Polybius' close relationship with his patron Scipio Aemilianus, whose sister was married to Cato's son, possibly afforded him other personal contacts with Cato, and almost certainly a good deal of information about him.[4] In view of this it is unfortunate that there are references to Cato in only six of the extant extracts from Polybius' history and that, while a few passages in other authors may have been derived from this work, very little of the surviving tradition about Cato can be traced back to him with confidence. However, each of the extant extracts is a useful piece of evidence, one being an anecdote about Cato in Spain and the others all being centred around sayings of Cato which Polybius records with obvious appreciation.

The most substantial surviving narrative of the period is that of Livy. This covers much of Cato's lifetime, though not the whole of it since Livy's text breaks off after the year 167, the remainder of his history being known only through brief epitomes. Cato is mentioned in a considerable number of passages, six or seven of which are substantial, including an unusually vivid character-sketch. While Livy could have taken some of these from Polybius the general nature of his methods in dealing with the kind of information involved points rather to various annalists, such as Valerius Antias. Even the annalists were presumably reworking a good deal of information which ultimately went back to Cato's own writings, but there are also indications that at least a few of Livy's passages may have quite a close relationship with those writings. In this respect Livy's account of Cato's Spanish campaign is particularly striking.

---

[3] The fragments of the speeches are collected by Malcovati in *ORF*[3], pp. 12 ff., those of the *Origines* by Peter in *HRR* i[2], 55 ff. Both supersede the corresponding sections of Jordan's collection, which remains standard for the fragments of the other works and includes a collection of dicta.

[4] Astin, 'Scipio Aemilianus and Cato Censorius', *Latomus*, 15 (1956), 159 ff.; id., *Scipio Aemilianus*, pp. 3 f. For the Achaean detainees, above, pp. 124 f.

Although this does raise some special questions, which are discussed in Appendix 2, there can be no serious doubt that much of it represents Cato's own version of events. In five other passages speeches by Cato are said to be extant, including several from the censorship.[5] The censorial speech against Lucius Flamininus is actually appealed to as evidence against a version of events given by Valerius Antias; and in the case of the speech about Rhodes in 167 Livy says that he will not introduce an imitation of what Cato said: the speech itself is extant in the fifth book of Cato's *Origines*. It still does not follow with absolute certainty that Livy had actually read these speeches, but there is obviously a strong possibility that he had done so; and since both the Rhodian speech and the speech against Ser. Sulpicius Galba in 149 are stated to have been included in the *Origines* it is possible that some of Livy's information is drawn directly from that work.

Cicero's many references to Cato fall into three broad categories. First, anecdotes, quotations, and general characterizing remarks are found in his works of every kind. For the most part these are used to illustrate or to reinforce Cicero's assertions, frequently by supplying the authority of an eminent— and idealized—example from the past. Cicero's readiness to use Cato in this way is no doubt enhanced by a certain sense of self-identification with a *novus homo* of municipal origin who attained great distinction, though in only a few passages are these aspects explicitly mentioned, and they are sufficiently accounted for by their relevance to the immediate context.

The second category consists of comments, mostly in Cicero's rhetorical writings, upon Cato's qualities as orator and writer. These are first-hand comments, based upon Cicero's own reading of Cato's speeches—very many of which were available to him—and of the *Origines*.[6] Thus, while allowance must be made for Cicero's own preconceptions about rhetorical and stylistic ideals, this evidence has a valuable directness.

The third category consists of the material in Cicero's dialogue *De senectute*, in which he cast Cato in his last years as his principal dramatic spokesman on the subject of old age, in conversation with Scipio Aemilianus and Laelius. Consequently the dialogue contains not only sentiments about old age which may reasonably be assumed to be Cicero's rather than Cato's, but a good deal of empirical information about Cato's career and a measure of characterization. Although this last feature has given rise to some discussion the basic assumptions to be made in using the dialogue as evidence about Cato seem to be obvious and to admit of no serious alternative. Cicero is likely to have made considerable efforts to get right the factual biographical statements and to give his dialogue a setting which would not strike the reader as implausible;[7] but for the

---

[5] Livy, 38. 54. 11 (on the money of Antiochus); 39. 42. 6–43. 5 (censorship); 42. 25. 2 f. (on behalf of the Rhodians); *Per.* 41 (for the *lex Voconia*); *Per.* 49 (against Galba). However, it is probable that no authentic text underlies the speech against repeal of the *lex Oppia* which Livy puts into Cato's mouth: 34. 2. 1 ff.; see pp. 25 f.

[6] Cic. *Brut.* 65. See esp. Ch. 7, *passim*.   [7] Astin, *Scipio Aemilianus*, pp. 9 ff.

sentiments about old age Cato is no more than a dramatic mouthpiece for Cicero. As for the characterization, though it may contain authentic elements, it almost certainly owes more to Cicero's idealization and immediate purposes than to a considered assessment of the historical Cato. Cicero selected Cato because he was a famous senator who had lived to a great age and remained active and influential to the end. In so far as the historical Cato happened to have had some opinions and characteristics which Cicero wished to commend, so much the better; but these did not determine his choice and where necessary could be supplemented extensively. Consequently authentic elements can be securely identified only by reference to external evidence, with the result that Cicero's characterization of Cato in the dialogue cannot safely be used as evidence. For the empirical material, however, Cicero was able to draw upon good sources, not only Cato's own writings but the recently completed *liber annalis* of his friend Atticus. It does not follow that he was beyond making mistakes, but in practice the only substantial point on which he has been seriously challenged is his story that Cato was present at the capture of Tarentum by Fabius Maximus in 209; and even here, though Cicero adds some patently fictitious material for the purposes of his dialogue, it is not so certain as has sometimes been supposed that the basic fact is wrong.[8]

There remains some uncertainty in connection with the first of the three categories of Ciceronian evidence, especially in respect of particular qualities and characteristics ascribed to Cato; for these raise interrelated questions concerning Cicero's conception of Cato and the amount of reliable information available to him. Studies of these topics, while indicating that the essence of Cicero's conception of Cato remained largely unchanged, have tended to emphasize a radical development in his knowledge and interest.[9] In his early years, it is suggested, Cato's works, being out of fashion, were not readily available to him; hence he had almost no direct knowledge and his remarks simply reflect a generalized and already idealized oral tradition. Only in his later works, in consequence of his own increased interest in Cato and his personal efforts at collecting Cato's works, does he display a growing acquaintance with the speeches and writings and a more detailed knowledge of his career. Hence the characterization which is found in the earlier works and which continued to colour his conception of Cato does not rest upon a reliable basis.

Such arguments go considerably beyond what may legitimately be inferred from the evidence, even though it is obviously likely that Cicero's knowledge of Cato grew over the years. In the first place, since a passage in the *Ad Herennium* shows that at least some of Cato's speeches were well known in the 80s, there is no difficulty in supposing Cicero to have had direct knowledge of them—especially as his *De inventione*, in which Cato's eloquence is mentioned, was

---

[8] p. 7.
[9] Padberg, *Cicero und Cato Censorius*; Gnauk, *Die Bedeutung des Marius und Cato maior für Cicero*; Kammer, *Untersuch. zu Ciceros Bild von Cato Censorius.*

written in that same period.[10] More central is the distinction which must be made between Cicero's speeches and his various treatises. It is scarcely surprising that references to Cato in the former tend to be general and less precise, those in the latter markedly more specific; but this distinction happens also to coincide with a temporal one. With the exception of the very early *De inventione* (and some of the letters), all Cicero's surviving works from before his exile are speeches, so that inevitably pre-exile references to Cato are almost all found in speeches, whereas all but one of the references in the treatises are *ipso facto* from his later years. Therefore the apparent difference of kind between earlier and later references, which itself has perhaps been overstated, is at the least magnified by the contrast in the nature of the works and possibly may have no other basis.

Thus in assessing the reliability of Cicero's remarks about Cato this difference between speeches and other works is almost certainly a much more significant consideration than any supposed radical change in the extent and basis of his knowledge. In composing speeches he is less likely to have checked details of argumentative allusions, more likely, having accepted the general idea of Cato as an admirable citizen, to ascribe to him whatever quality or talent was appropriate to the immediate argument, without stopping to consider whether or not this could be justified by reference to historical evidence. Thus the emphasis in *Pro Murena* 66 on *moderatio*, *comitas*, and *facilitas* induces caution and even scepticism, since the purpose is to place in an unfavourable light the asperity of Cicero's principal opponent, who was Cato's great-grandson. On the other hand even the evidence of the speeches is not to be dismissed lightly, especially when a particular point recurs several times; for Cicero's basic attitude is likely to have had a reasonable foundation of familiarity both with the facts of Cato's career and with some of his writings.

The surviving contribution of Cornelius Nepos is a short biography of Cato, only three chapters long. It would be unrealistic to attempt to identify Nepos' particular sources, but in general he seems to be well informed. The biography has first a brief account of Cato's personal background and the main steps in his public career, followed by a few general comments. A statement of his varied expertise (which in fact reflects the topics about which he wrote) leads into a summary but extremely valuable account of the *Origines*. Nepos concludes by referring readers who desire more information to the fuller account of Cato which he gave in a separate book, written at the request of Atticus. The surviving biography, which is an extract from a work about Latin historians, seems to have been produced by summarizing the longer biography and adding a description of the *Origines*.

The fact that this larger biography once existed has excited a considerable amount of elaborate conjecture about its relationship to Plutarch's 'Life', which is the longest and most detailed single account of Cato to have survived.

---

[10] *Ad Her.* 4. 7; Cic. *De inv.* 1. 5.

(There are also frequent references to Cato in Plutarch's other writings, but these supply very little information which is not found also in the 'Life'.) Moreover there is a remarkable similarity between Plutarch's opening sentence and that of Nepos' extant biography. However, it is also relevant to the question of Plutarch's sources that in connection with particular stories he names Polybius, Cicero, and Livy once each, that other remarks appear to be closely linked to passages in Livy's history and Cicero's *De senectute* but also to have points of difference, and that Plutarch frequently attributes statements to Cato himself. Many modern discussions have inclined to the view that although Plutarch perhaps introduced some additional material, such as the large group of dicta in chapters 8 and 9, he drew mainly upon a single principal source which was itself in the form of a biography, and that he was citing the named authors at second hand, not directly from his own reading. It has often been thought that this source was Nepos' lost biography, though it has also been suggested that there was an earlier biography, nowhere attested in the surviving literature, which was used by Cicero and Nepos as well as by Plutarch.

It is more likely, however, that Plutarch was not so heavily dependent upon a single source. The fact that his account of an event does not coincide in all particulars with that of an author he names does not demonstrate that he himself had not consulted that author. It is wrong to assume that he must have followed slavishly one account *in toto*, rather than modifying it by accepting details from other versions. He was after all a wealthy, cultured, and curious man who could be expected to have had access to and to have consulted a wide range of books—though consultation of an author such as Livy could have taken the form of instructing an assistant to collect extracts dealing with Cato.[11] That Nepos' biography was among the works consulted is probable, especially in view of the coincidence of the opening sentences; but that it was closely followed is not easy to reconcile with Plutarch's failure to mention Cato's services in the battle of the Metaurus and his aedileship, both of which appear in Nepos' shorter biography and presumably were in the longer. Indeed these omissions and some other features cast doubt on whether Plutarch can have followed at all closely any source in biographical form. Admittedly the 'Life' is constructed around certain events in Cato's career which are introduced in chronological order. Nevertheless, a high proportion of the material consists of sayings, sentiments, and stories, so that the total effect is markedly anecdotal and the factual, chronological structure is relatively slight. Only a few episodes—notably the exploit at Thermopylae, the censorship, and the affair of Carneades—receive the kind of narrative treatment which might be expected in a descriptive biography; and in addition to the battle of the Metaurus and the aedileship there are several other items the omission of which is surprising if Plutarch was closely adhering to such a source. Among the latter are Cato's opposition to the repeal of the *lex Oppia*, his first candidature for the censorship, and his

---

[11] Jones, *Plutarch and Rome*, pp. 81 ff.

Rhodian speech. Particularly remarkable is the absence of a narrative of Cato's Spanish campaign, which is dealt with by a series of anecdotes. All this can be seen as reflecting Plutarch's own interests and methods of delineating character, and is understandable if he himself drew from a number of works and did a significant amount of compilation; but it is not what would be expected if Plutarch's method was essentially to follow and embellish one main source. Thus, while there is much uncertainty about the sources of most of Plutarch's material, the probability is that they are varied and complex; and therefore each item must be considered on its merits.

The remaining aspect of this question concerns the large amount of material which is attributed to Cato himself. Much of this is found only in Plutarch, though several of the dicta are also recorded elsewhere and two important passages are directly associated with fragments which are attested independently.[12] Moreover it is likely that some of the passages which attribute to Cato certain opinions and forms of conduct are really particular statements by Cato reproduced by Plutarch in generalized form. Indeed it seems probable that in handling such material Plutarch was inclined to place a literal and general interpretation upon statements which, even if phrased in general terms, were originally directed to a particular context, a particular form of this being the literal acceptance of remarks which more probably display Cato's talent for hyperbole. Some of this material almost certainly reached Plutarch through intermediate sources, notably many of the anecdotes and dicta, especially those in chapters 8 and 9, which he probably took from a collection which was in circulation;[13] and in other cases also it is conceivable that he obtained the quotations indirectly, from other authors whom he was using. On the other hand there is no great difficulty in supposing Plutarch to have drawn material directly from some of Cato's writings, particularly since much of the collection and translation of extracts might have been entrusted to an assistant;[14] and his remarks about Cato's oratory are most naturally understood to imply that he was acquainted with some of the speeches.[15]

However, whether or not Plutarch incorporated material which he had extracted directly from Cato's works is less important than that by and large there is no reason to doubt the authenticity of the material in question, in the sense that it is ultimately derived from Cato himself.

[12] Plut. *Cato Mai.* 4. 4 ff., cf. Gell. 13. 24. 1 = *ORF*³, Cato fr. 174; 23. 3 ff., cf. Jordan, pp. 77 f., *Ad Marcum filium*, frs. 1–3. See further pp. 92 f., 107, and 334 f.

[13] p. 187, with n. 17.

[14] Jones, loc. cit.

[15] Plut. *Cato Mai.* 7. 1 ff., esp. 3.

Livy's Sources for Cato's Spanish Campaign

THERE is universal agreement that Livy's extended and realistic account of Cato's Spanish campaign (34. 8–21) is in great measure derived from Cato's own writings. Nevertheless, within this consensus certain points are open to discussion. The three main questions which have arisen will be examined in turn, although the complexity of certain of the arguments which have been advanced makes some overlap unavoidable.

1. *Where Livy has material derived from Cato's writings, did this come from Cato's speeches (notably the* De consulatu suo) *or from the* Origines?

The primary fact here is that there are several brief but close correspondences, some verbal and some factual, between Livy's account and fragments of Cato's speech *De consulatu suo*. Although these correspondences have led several scholars, notably Fraccaro and Janzer, to the conclusion that Livy's material is derived principally from this speech,[1] it is doubtful if they justify any inference beyond the basic fact that some of Livy's material stems from Cato himself. If Cato wrote about the campaign several times there would inevitably have been close factual correspondences and very probably verbal correspondences between his various versions. Thus if Livy's material was derived from, for example, the *Origines*, this could still have resulted in the correspondences with the fragments of the *De consulatu suo*.[2] Two other points have a bearing on this possibility. First, while some of the fragments of the speech correspond with words or phrases in the account of Cato's journey to Spain in Livy, 34. 8, there are other features of the fragments concerning this journey which find no echo in Livy—notably the speed of Cato's preparations, some place-names, and some touches of poetic language.[3] This is what would be expected if Livy used a version similar to that in the speech but not the speech itself (though that is not the only possible explanation). Second, Livy's account of Cato's journey

---

[1] Fraccaro, 'Le fonti per il consolato', *Studi storici*, 3 (1910), 165–75 = *Opusc.* i. 201–7 (this for all references to Fraccaro in this appendix); Janzer, pp. 8–16, esp. 15–16; cf. Gelzer, *RE*, s.v. *Porcius*, no. 9, col. 112; Scullard, *Roman Politics*[2], p. 258. Janzer and Scullard have a list of correspondences (some very close, others rather slender), to which might be added *ORF*[3], Cato fr. 31, compared with Livy, 34. 9. 10. The speech, *ORF*[3], Cato frs. 21–55, was probably delivered *c.* 189: see p. 60.

[2] So Tränkle, *Cato in der vierten und fünften Dekade des Livius*, p. 28.

[3] Observed by Fraccaro, op. cit., p. 202, who took this as evidence that there was an intermediate source. Of the three points mentioned the first is much the most significant and the last carries almost no weight.

is followed in the next chapter, 9. 1–10, naturally and logically by an elaborate description of Emporiae. It is unlikely, though perhaps not inconceivable, that this description originally formed part of a speech. Fraccaro, convinced that the original source of Livy's material in chapter 8 was the *De consulatu suo*, concluded that the description was drawn from some other source—ultimately perhaps the *Origines*;[4] but if it is admitted that despite the correspondences, the 'Catonian' material in chapter 8 need not have come from that speech there emerges an obvious possibility that both this material and the description of Emporiae may have been derived from the *Origines*.[5]

2. *Did Livy draw his 'Catonian' material directly from Cato's writings or from one or more annalists who had followed Cato closely but had already incorporated some additional material?*

That Livy did not use Cato directly is asserted by Fraccaro, who has two main reasons.[6] The first is that, as was mentioned above, Livy in his account of Cato's journey to Spain omits certain features which are found in the fragments of the *De consulatu suo*, which Fraccaro holds to be the origin of Livy's material about the journey. Yet even if Fraccaro is right about this last point the conclusion scarcely follows; for if someone worked from the speech and omitted certain details, that person could just as well have been Livy as some predecessor. Moreover, it has been seen already that there is at least the possibility that the reason for the omissions is that Livy's material is derived from some other version by Cato himself.

Fraccaro's other reason lies in his analysis of Livy's narrative, in which he believes that there can be detected a complex structure resulting from the conflation of various sources. In particular he holds that two sections which are both derived from Cato overlap and bear clear signs of conflation; from which he concludes that the material reached Livy through intermediate sources. The validity of this argument, then, depends in great measure upon the extent to

---

[4] There is an obvious gloss by Livy himself at 34. 9. 3, but Fraccaro rightly notes that the description as a whole is probably based on an account written not long after the Roman conquest. Fraccaro's further conclusions that it had reached Livy indirectly and that 'philosophical reflections' in Livy indicate a source after the manner of Poseidonius are highly subjective.

[5] Tränkle, op. cit., pp. 27 ff., Peter, *HRR* i², p. cliii, and Walsh, *Livy*, pp. 134 f., favour the *Origines* as the source of Livy's material.

[6] Gelzer, *RE*, s.v. *Porcius*, no. 9, col. 112, allows that the correspondences suggest that Livy may have consulted Cato directly but holds that the bulk of his narrative is drawn from two late annalistic sources, probably Claudius Quadrigarius and Valerius Antias. Della Corte, *Catone censore*², pp. 167 f. and 208 f., takes a similar view but with more emphasis on direct consultation; Klotz, *Livius*, pp. 33 ff., believes Livy used the annalists only. Tränkle, op. cit., pp. 20 ff., argues that it is unnecessary to posit an intermediate source, but his arguments are unnecessarily linked with his view on the chronology of Cato's campaign, on which see Appendix 3.

which Fraccaro's dissection of the narrative may be regarded as proven. This will be considered in the following section.

3. To what extent does Livy's narrative show signs of having been conflated from several different sources?

It will be useful first to set out a summary showing the sequence of material in Livy, 34. 8–21, as follows:

8. 4–7. Cato's preparations and journey to Spain; his arrival at Emporiae.

9.　　　Description of Emporiae, ending (9. 10–13) with Cato setting out from Emporiae to ravage the enemy's fields.

10.　　The march of Helvius across Spain and his return to Rome.

11–12. Cato, encamped near Emporiae, deals with the problem of the Ilergetes; embarkation of a force which apparently was to be sent to their aid.

13–16. Disembarkation of this force, establishment of a *castra hiberna*, and the Emporiae campaign, ending with two rebellions of Bergistani.

17. 1–4. Activities and victory of the praetors Manlius and Claudius; the Turduli hire Celtiberian mercenaries.

17. 5–12. Cato destroys the walls of towns north of the Ebro.

18.　　Disquisition on the achievements and qualities of Cato in this campaign.

19.　　Cato's campaign in the south.

20–1. Cato's activities after his return to the north, including the capture of Bergium.

That there has been at least a little conflation is established by two undisputed facts: chapter 10 (the march of Helvius) is patently an intrusion into the main body of Livy's narrative and is shown by 10. 2 to have been drawn from Valerius Antias (which implies that the main narrative was not); and at 15. 9 Livy contrasts statements by Valerius Antias and by Cato himself about Spanish casualties at the battle of Emporiae, thus proving that two sources were used at some stage in the tradition. Several scholars, however, have claimed to detect other indications of conflation.

One assertion frequently made (though not by Fraccaro) is that the rebellion of Bergium in chapter 21 is a doublet of one or both of the rebellions of Bergistani recorded in 16. 9–10. This is unquestionably the aspect of the source problem which has the most far-reaching implications for the reconstruction of Cato's actions. Nissen, for example, seems to have been led to the improbable view that the whole of chapters 20 and 21 are to be rejected as repetition, from a different source, of material already covered by Livy. De Sanctis and Gelzer more plausibly identify the rebellion of chapter 21, after the return from Turdetania, with the second rebellion in 16. 10. They therefore infer that in 16 Livy was following a source which omitted the Turdetanian campaign altogether, passing at 16. 9–10 direct from a rebellion which occurred before that campaign to one which followed it. But since 17. 5 ('consul interim rebellione Bergistanorum ictus') patently picks up 16. 10, they are led further to the view that the whole episode of disarming the towns north of the Ebro also occurred after the Turdetanian campaign.[7]

In theory it is possible that the rebellion in chapter 21 might be a doublet of that in 16. 10, if the two passages were considered in isolation, but there are definite differences between the accounts and there is no compelling similarity.[8] On the other hand Livy's language in 16. 9–10 leaves no doubt at all that he believed the second rebellion to have occurred almost immediately after the first, which itself was inspired by reports of Cato's plans to march south. In particular the words with which Livy introduces the second rebellion, 'haud ita multo post eidem, regresso Tarraconem consule, priusquam inde quoquam procederet, defecerunt', must naturally be taken in the context to mean that it occurred before Cato set out for Turdetania.[9] To reject this, to regard it as the product of gross distortion by Livy or his source would require substantially more powerful arguments than have been advanced, and even so it would be difficult to believe that a source which had already introduced explicitly Cato's projected march to Turdetania omitted entirely the campaign itself. The discussion of these episodes in Chapter 3 of this book rests on the firm conviction that there is no doublet and that Cato disarmed the towns north of the Ebro before his southern campaign.

Fraccaro himself rejects the notion that there is a doublet, but instead he claims to find several other signs of conflation. As was mentioned in the preceding section, he believes that, among other complexities, there are signs of two separate sources which both contain information derived from Cato himself. These complexities he explains by supposing Livy to have used as his principal source one in which all the material except chapter 10 had already been conflated; the only section intruded by Livy himself was chapter 10.

One of the passages cited by Fraccaro—17. 1–4—certainly could be an

---

[7] Nissen, *Kritische Untersuchungen*, pp. 156 ff., followed by Kahrstedt, *Die Annalistik von Livius*, pp. 8 ff. and 105; De Sanctis, *Storia* iv. 1², pp. 436 ff., esp. n. 157; Gelzer, *RE*, s.v. *Porcius*, no. 9, cols. 112 and 114 f.; cf. also Della Corte, *Catone censore²*, p. 32. Kienast, pp. 44 f., also thinks a doublet probable and therefore that the Bergistani rebelled only once prior to the Turdetanian campaign; but he does not postpone the disarming of the towns.

[8] In 16. 9–10 the rebellion is said to have been by seven *castella* of the *civitas* of the Bergistani, whereas in 21 the operation is against the *Bergium castrum*, clearly a formidable fortress; and in 16 there is no hint of the internal quarrels and upheavals of the Bergistani described in 21.

[9] 34. 16. 8–10: 'Fama deinde volgatur consulem in Turdetaniam exercitum ducturum, et ad devios montanos "profectum etiam" falso perlatum est. Ad hunc vanum et sine auctore ullo rumorem Bergistanorum civitatis septem castella defecerunt: eos deducto exercitu consul sine memorando proelio in potestatem redegit. Haud ita multo post eidem, regresso Tarraconem consule, priusquam inde quoquam procederet, defecerunt. Iterum subacti; sed non eadem venia victis fuit: sub corona veniere omnes, ne saepius pacem sollicitarent.'

intrusion. It separates 16. 10 and 17. 5, which are very closely linked in language and substance, and unlike the material in which it is set it is not concerned with the activities of Cato but with the successes of other generals against the Turdetani. It looks suspiciously like an inept insertion, whether by Livy or by some predecessor. On the other hand the conclusion of this passage, that the Turdetani secured the help of Celtiberian mercenaries, is picked up in chapter 19, which is fairly certainly derived from Cato's narrative.

Fraccaro's other suggestions are less convincing. One of them is that the description of Emporiae in chapter 9. 1–10 is an intrusion; but it has been seen already that this stems from his belief that the Catonian origin underlying chapter 8 was a speech, and that this belief is not necessarily correct. The possibility that chapters 8 and 9 are both derived from the *Origines* is reinforced by their coherence. Not only does the description of Emporiae come at the logical place in Livy's account but it leads smoothly into the concluding sentences of chapter 9, which concern Cato's preliminary movements and which Fraccaro himself regards as derived from the same source as chapter 8.

At the end of chapter 9 Livy relates Cato's reception at Emporiae, a delay of a few days, and some associated points; and he concludes (9. 13): 'profectus ab Emporiis agros hostium urit vastatque, omnia fuga et terrore complet.' Chapter 10 is agreed to be an intrusion, but Fraccaro holds that 9. 13 is picked up not in chapter 11 but in 13. 2: 'ipse, cum iam id tempus anni appeteret quo geri res possent, castra hiberna . . . posuit.' Chapters 11 and 12, which describe Cato's dealings with the Ilergetes, he regards as another intrusion, even though they are patently derived from Cato himself: hence his belief that Livy's material is here derived from two intermediate traditions which both go back to Cato. He points to the opening words of chapter 11—'consul haud procul Emporiis castra habebat'—and argues that this episode took place while Cato was still at Emporiae; and that the concluding words of 9. 13 had already taken the narrative past this stage. From this it would follow that 11 and 12 must have come from a different source.

In reality there is no need at all for this hypothesis. A fragment of Cato's *De consulatu suo* proves that after reaching Emporiae he moved about and constructed several camps before establishing a *castra hiberna* (which is obviously the same as the *castra hiberna* of 13. 2).[10] The conclusion of chapter 9, 'profectus ab Emporiis . . . etc.', is most naturally taken to refer to the commencement of this phase, and it would seem eminently reasonable to suppose that Cato's dealings with the Ilergetes occurred during this phase—not when he was actually at Emporiae but when, as Livy says, he had a camp not far from it. If this simple assumption is made there is no difficulty in supposing that the contents of chapters 11 and 12 were derived from the same source as the conclusion of

---

[10] *ORF*³, Cato, fr. 35: 'interea unamquamque turmam manipulum cohortem temptabam quid facere possent; proeliis levibus spectabam cuiusmodi quisque esset . . . interea aliquot ⟨p⟩au⟨ca⟩ castra feci. sed ubi anni tempus venit, castra hiberna . . .'

chapter 9 and the commencement of chapter 13; for the affair of the Ilergetes occurs at the right place, between Cato's initial departure from Emporiae and the establishment of the *castra hiberna*.

4. Conclusion

The evidence that Livy's narrative reflects the conflation of differing or overlapping accounts is much less extensive than has sometimes been supposed. Certainly there is no compelling necessity to posit a complex history of several intermediate stages between Cato and Livy, or the conflation of two or more intermediate accounts which were both drawing heavily on Cato himself— though no one can actually disprove such elaborate hypotheses. Given the general character of Livy's account, the references to Valerias Antias, and the explicit comparison at 34. 15. 9 of statements by Valerius and Cato, the obvious inference is that Livy had in front of him both Valerius and an account stemming from Cato himself. For the most part he followed the Catonian version, but at 15. 9 he explicitly compared the two and earlier he had inserted chapter 10 (the march of Helvius) from Valerius. The best and simplest explanation of the apparently intrusive passage at 34. 17. 1–4 is probably that Livy also took from Valerius a reference to the victory of Manlius and Claudius over the Turdetani, yet in setting this down had in mind what was to come in his own narrative. Hence his concluding sentence: 'Yet the war was not ended by that battle; the Turduli hired ten thousand Celtiberi and prepared to carry on the war with the arms of strangers.'[11]

There is no way of deciding whether Livy used Cato's account directly or through an intermediate source. All that can be said is that the arguments which seemed actually to require one or more intermediate sources are not convincing, and there is no obvious objection to the simple view that he did use Cato directly. In view of the character of the Roman historical tradition and of Livy's own methods, the question must be left open. Similarly no certain answer can be given as to whether the bulk of Livy's narrative was derived from one of Cato's speeches or from the *Origines*, though the latter seems much the more probable. In any event there is no reason to doubt that with few exceptions both the particular episodes and their sequence in Livy are derived from Cato himself.

[11] 'Nec tamen ea pugna debellatum est: decem milia Celtiberum mercede Turduli conducunt alienisque armis parabant bellum.'

APPENDIX 3

Some Notes on the Chronology of Cato's Spanish Campaign

THE principal items of evidence bearing upon the chronology of Cato's departure for Spain and his operations near Emporiae are as follows:

(*i*) Livy states that he set out immediately (extemplo) after the affair of the *lex Oppia* (34. 8. 4), though that episode is not itself dated to a specific time in the year.

(*ii*) Cato himself claimed that the preparations were carried out speedily (*ORF*³, fr. 28).

(*iii*) The fleet was not hindered by adverse conditions and reached the rendezvous at portus Pyrenaei on the day appointed (*ORF*³, Cato fr. 29; Livy, 34. 8. 6).

(*iv*) Cato reached Emporiae at 'the time of year when the Spaniards had grain on the threshing-floors' (*in areis*; Livy, 34. 9. 12).

(*v*) After 'a few days' actually at Emporiae Cato spent an unspecified period of time in minor operations, constructing several temporary camps (Livy, 34. 9. 11 and 13; *ORF*³, Cato fr. 35).

(*vi*) At an appropriate time Cato established a more permanent camp three miles from Emporiae:

> (*a*) 'ipse, cum iam id tempus anni appeteret quo geri res possent, castra hiberna tria milia passuum ab Emporiis posuit' (Livy, 34. 13. 2).
>
> (*b*) 'sed ubi anni tempus venit, castra hiberna . . .' (*ORF*³, Cato fr. 35, at the end of the fragment describing how the troops were tested and given experience).

(*vii*) According to Livy Cato launched from this camp a series of training and probing forays, culminating in the initiative to provoke the full-scale battle (34. 13. 2 ff.).

(*viii*) Livy reports that news of victories won by Cato reached Rome at almost the same time as news of Flamininus' success at Sparta against Nabis, i.e. in the autumn of 195.[1]

The reference to grain on the threshing-floors should mean that Cato reached Emporiae between late May and early July; and since the evidence

---

[1] Livy, 34. 42. 1; De Sanctis, *Storia*, iv. 1², p. 377. Confirmatory evidence is the report in Livy, 34. 43. 1, that envoys sent by Nabis after he had come to terms with Flamininus reached Rome at the beginning of the next consular year, i.e. late in 195. On the relationship at this time between the Roman calendar and the Julian year see p. 33 n. 13.

suggests some urgency and certainly no excessive delay, and since moreover Cato had been in office from late in 196, it is reasonable to place his arrival in Spain early in the possible period. Hence his departure from Luna may be placed in April, the expedition assembling there early in the recognized sailing season, though perhaps not at the earliest possible date. On this basis the battle of Emporiae and Cato's advance to the Ebro are usually and rightly believed to have taken place later in the summer of 195, and the *castra hiberna* is taken to mean a strongly built, more permanent camp rather than literally a camp for the winter. In the first place Livy himself clearly uses *castra hiberna* in this sense, since he associates its construction with the beginning, not the end, of a campaigning period. In the second place, if Cato arrived in May (Julian) or even in June of 195, it is extremely unlikely that his first serious offensive move was delayed until the spring of 194. In the third place, if Livy is to be believed, news of victories won by Cato was received in Rome at almost the same time as news of Flamininus' successes against Nabis, thus in the later months of 195.

The interpretation and arguments set out above are essentially those put forward, with some variations in detail, by Fraccaro and De Sanctis.[2] Beloch, however, in accordance with his erroneous theory that the Roman calendar was several months *behind* the notional Julian, held that Cato must have arrived in late summer or early autumn, that the *castra hiberna* was literally a winter camp, and that the campaign really began in the spring of 194.[3] The essence of this view has been revived by Tränkle, who holds that although Beloch was certainly wrong about the calendar he was right about the date of Cato's arrival and the start of the campaign.[4] The reference to threshing-floors he explains by the hypothesis of a second harvest, in September, but his principal argument is that *castra hiberna*—the term used by Cato as well as Livy—does not mean *castra stativa* and therefore is to be taken literally. Livy's words 'id tempus anni appeteret quo geri res possent' he explains as a misunderstanding, an erroneous gloss expanding Cato's own phrase 'ubi anni tempus venit, castra hiberna . . .', which, he holds, really refers to the beginning of winter. He concedes that this implies a long delay before Cato went to his province, but asserts, rightly, that this was not incompatible with Roman practice.

The counter-arguments concerning the indications of a fairly speedy departure and also the reporting of victories won by Cato have already been noted above. The issue really turns on the meaning of *castra hiberna* and Livy's alleged misunderstanding. In fact, however, Livy's unmistakable interpretation of the expression as an equivalent of *castra stativa* is very strong evidence. Without

[2] Fraccaro, 'Le fonti per il consolato', *Studi storici*, 3 (1910), 192 ff. = *Opusc.* i. 219 ff.; De Sanctis, *Storia* iv. 1², pp. 376 f. and 435 n. 149; cf. also Schulten, *Numantia* (1905), p. 75. Previously Weissenborn–Müller, commentary on Livy ad loc., and Nissen, *Kritische Untersuchungen*, p. 155, had placed Cato's arrival in the winter months; Weissenborn even suggested that *in areis* really means *in horreis*.

[3] 'Der röm. Kalender von 218–168', *Klio*, 15 (1918), 385 f.

[4] *Cato in der vierten und fünften Dekade des Livius*, pp. 22 ff.

anything else to guide him Livy would surely have taken it to mean 'winter camp'. But Livy was not a lexicographer, dealing with an isolated expression; he had a narrative in front of him. The very fact that he does not take *castra hiberna* in its literal sense is a strong indication that this narrative gave him positive reason to take it otherwise.

The one question remaining is whether Cato's operations in the south occurred in the late summer and autumn of 195 or in the spring of 194. The former seems much the more probable. First, there is no hint of a break in Cato's activities but rather an implication that his response to Manlius' appeal followed directly upon his northern victories. Second, Cato's successor evidently made every effort to succeed him as early as possible (p. 51), thus leaving little time in the spring for the operations described. Third, if Cato arrived late in May his initial northern campaign could have been completed early enough to allow for the southern campaign in 195. Fourth, the limitation on time imposed by the imminence of winter may well be part of the explanation for the limited nature of what he attempted.

Possible Sites for the Battle of Emporiae

THE battle of Emporiae is recorded in sufficient detail to offer at least a possibility of identifying its location. Although certain features of Livy's account may owe something to his own artistic elaboration most of the essential facts are derived from Cato himself and therefore constitute a sound basis for discussion.[1]

1. *The environs of Emporiae*

The flat and fertile plain of Ampurdán extends inland from Emporiae for several kilometres. It is bounded on the west by a line of hills, the highest of them being Puig Cegalá at 179 m, which stretches for most of the 15 kilometres from the river Fluvia in the north to the river Ter in the south. For the most part these hills are now heavily overgrown with conifers and scrub. Behind this line the country continues to be hilly and broken. In antiquity the northern and southern ends of the plain were probably slightly more restricted than now by the two rivers, both of which have evidently changed their courses. The lower reaches of the Ter have shifted considerably, now passing south of the group of hills dominated by Santa Catalina, whereas in antiquity the river seems to have taken a northwards turn, following the general line of the modern Canal de Riego around the west and north of these hills and reaching the sea between Emporiae and La Escala. However, except that this brings into consideration the site discussed in § 6 below, the changes in the courses of the rivers do not materially affect the present discussion.[2]

2. *Distance from Emporiae*

Cato's march to the field of battle began from his *castra hiberna*, situated about 3 Roman miles, i.e. about 4·5 km, from Emporiae.[3] He marched by

---

[1] Livy, 34. 13–16. Unless othewise indicated, all data discussed in this Appendix will be found in those chapters. Their derivation is discussed in Appendix 2. In studying the terrain around Emporiae I have made use of maps published by the Servicio Geográfico del Ejército of Spain. I was able to spend several days in the area in the summer of 1970 and again in 1972. Also I am grateful for the assistance of Col. C. E. Thompson, who read a draft of this Appendix and discussed it with me.

[2] For the rivers see Almagro, *Las fuentes escritas referentes a Ampurias*, pp. 80–2, 85–6, 91; Schulten, *Iberische Landeskunde*, pp. 303 f.

[3] The site of this camp cannot be identified. Almagro, op. cit., pp. 72 f., thinks that it was probably near modern Armentera, close to the Fluvia. He mentions also Albóns, which would be incompatible with two of the sites for the battle discussed below, and a site near the beach of Mongó, which seems unduly isolated. For Schulten's suggestion that it was on Puig Cegalá see p. 315 n. 9.

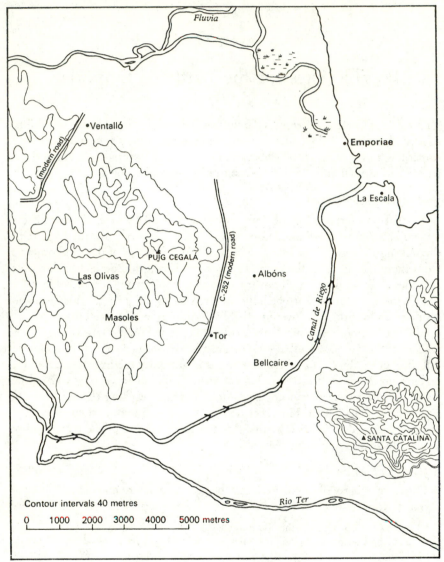

MAP 2. The Environs of Emporiae

night, starting after nightfall and having his army deployed on his chosen
ground by dawn. In midsummer at this latitude the interval from sunset to
sunrise is under nine hours and the period of actual darkness no more than
seven hours. Although Cato's reconnaissance is likely to have been thorough,
an army of perhaps 20,000 men cannot have moved very rapidly in the dark,
over what were at best rough tracks. Moreover, the distance covered is most
unlikely to have been in a direct line and unless one of the rivers was crossed

(on which see below) the march cannot have exceeded about 8 kilometres from any conceivable starting-point without entering the hilly terrain to the west, which, in turn, would have ensured both a winding route and slower rate of march. Allowance must also be made for the time-lapse between the van and the rear of the army, which would have been substantial even if it was able to move in several columns; and if it had to move in a single column, then this time-lapse could have been as much as two hours.[4] Furthermore Cato had sufficient time to deploy his army before dawn, and he is likely to have allowed time to spare both as a margin of safety and to rest his troops. The distance marched is therefore most unlikely to have exceeded 15 kilometres and was probably less. This means that, theoretically, the maximum possible distance of the battle-field from Emporiae itself was 20 kilometres, but in practice it must have been substantially less as the crow flies.

The area of search is further narrowed by the rivers. To the south the Ter is a considerable obstacle even at the height of summer. No doubt there were places where it could be forded, but the operation would not have been easy or speedy in the dark and would make it unlikely that Cato could have reached before dawn any plausible site for the battle other than the one near Bellcaire, on the western edge of the Santa Catalina hills, which is discussed below in § 6. The Fluvia, to the north, is less of an obstacle in itself and in summer could probably have been forded at a number of points—though the marshy ground around its mouth, especially to the north, was probably much more extensive in antiquity than it is today. If less certainly than the Ter, it still represents a probable limit, and in any event to the north of it there is no likely site for the battle within the acceptable distance from Emporiae.

3. Features of the site

Cato's line of battle faced roughly towards the sea, with the Spanish camp on an eminence of some kind between him and the sea.[5] Since Cato plainly selected his own position for the battle its general characteristics can safely be assumed to have been favourable to him: at least a gentle downward slope and probably some protection given to flanks by the configuration of the ground, yet with sufficient room on his left for an outflanking march by two infantry cohorts. Further, this favourable ground must have been sufficiently wide to accommodate Cato's line of battle. Although the length of this line cannot be determined, it is possible to establish approximately the minimum space required.

[4] See Kromayer-Veith, *Heerwesen und Kriegführung*, p. 352, for some observations on the length of columns.

[5] It is nowhere stated explicitly that the Spanish camp was on an eminence, but it would be very suprising if it had not been, particularly since the hills clearly dominate the plain. Also Cato's choice of ground, behind the enemy's camp and facing broadly east (i.e. into the rising sun), would not be easy to explain if the Spaniards had positioned themselves out on the level plain.

The forces allocated to Cato totalled about 25,000 men (two Roman legions, 15,000 allies, and 800 cavalry).[6] Even if these had been at full strength initially, there must have been some casualties prior to the battle, and also a detachment was left to guard the Roman camp. Thus a figure of about 20,000 cannot be far out for the army which Cato actually deployed. Not all of these were in the line of battle: one whole legion was held in reserve until the assault on the enemy's camp and two cohorts were used for the outflanking march, so that the number deployed along the frontage was not more than about 15,000. Possibly it was less, if other units also were held in reserve, but it is unlikely to have been very much less.[7]

Calculation of the frontage of a Roman army is always bedevilled by the disputes and uncertainties about standard dispositions, and in the present instance it is complicated further by the possible use of formations and tactics specially devised to meet the exigencies of the Spanish wars. Nevertheless only if one of two improbable assumptions is made could Cato's frontage have been as short as just under 1 kilometre: either that hardly more than 10,000 men were used in the battle line; or that the entire force (except the units in reserve), drawn up fifteen deep, was packed shoulder to shoulder at 3 feet per man, constituting one gigantic phalanx. In practice, quite apart from the possibility that the spacing of individuals may sometimes have been greater, there will certainly have been intervals between major units, and whether or not the manipular *quincunx* formation was used in its traditional form, the course of the battle suggests at least an adaptation of it by which some intervals were left between sub-units.[8]

[6] Livy, 33. 43. 3.

[7] Cato ultimately broke the Spanish line by bringing into action fresh troops 'ex secunda acie': Livy, 34. 15. 1–2; cf. App. *Iber.* 40. These, however, were not necessarily units held in reserve in the same manner as the second legion; they could have been a reserve line of the legion already engaged, in which case they are to be reckoned among the troops deployed in the line of battle. Bell, 'Tactical Reform in the Roman Republican Army', *Historia*, 14 (1965), 406, suggests that Appian's three τάξεις are to be understood as three cohorts and that these could have been the rear line of a legion in *triplex acies*.

[8] For the dispute about the standard tactical disposition see esp. Kromayer–Veith, *Heerwesen und Kriegführung*, pp. 356–73, and Walbank, *Commentary on Polybius* ii. 588 ff., on Polyb. 18. 30. 5 ff., which is central to the issue. The question usually posed is how maniples drawn up for a shock assault in close order, at 3 feet per man, rearranged themselves with a front of 6 feet per man to allow room for individual swordsmanship. Perhaps a more realistic solution might be found if it were posited that the basic disposition allowed 6 feet per man and that there was a drill to form close order for an assault. The normal total depth may have been fifteen ranks: Kromayer–Veith, op. cit., pp. 287 f. Bell, 'Tactical Reform in the Roman Republican Army', *Historia*, 14 (1965), 404 ff., argues strongly that the frequent references to cohorts in the Spanish wars reflect the development of tactical units larger and more concentrated than the traditional maniples because the *quincunx* formation was proving inadequate in the theatre. Livy's account of Cato's battle has several references to cohorts, though they are not stated explicitly to be Roman rather than allied. In any event Cato's decisive charge with fresh troops looks remarkably like exploitation of intervals of the usual kind, and Bell himself, p. 405 with n. 6, rightly observes that the second legion is referred to in the traditional terms *principes* and *hastati* (Livy, 34. 15. 6).

Thus the actual frontage is unlikely to have been much under 1·5 km and could have been considerably more.

To sum up, the site occupied by Cato's army had a downward incline in the direction of the sea, extended laterally for at least 1 kilometre of favourable ground, and probably more, and faced the Spanish camp which is likely to have been on a hill or incline opposite. Further, it was less than 20 kilometres distant from Emporiae, and north of the present course of the river Ter. These conclusions regarding the general orientation of the battle, its probable situation between the rivers, and its proximity to Emporiae find some support in the fact that many fugitives from the battle took refuge in the Spanish settlement at Emporiae.

The number of sites which meet the criteria set out above is very small. The present writer found only four which appear to justify serious consideration. These four will now be discussed in turn.

4. Ventalló

At the northern end of the line of hills which dominate this part of the plain of Ampurdán is the Sierra de Ventalló, rising to 172 m, with a direct view towards Emporiae and with an excellent slope for deployment into the plain. This is a possible site for the Spanish camp. Behind the Sierra is a long valley at the mouth of which is situated the village of Ventalló. This valley, running from north-east to south-west, is so level and straight that the modern road extends along it for 2 kilometres without a bend of any kind, and for a considerable distance the farther (i.e. north-west) side of the valley presents an incline suitable for the deployment of Cato's army, facing the Sierra de Ventalló.[9]

Against these promising features must be set others which raise considerable doubts. First, although the incline on the north-west side of the valley is suitable, projecting spurs would have restricted a line facing the Sierra de Ventalló to little more than the bare minimum of 1 kilometre, and certainly to less than 1·5 km. Second, and more seriously, the Sierra de Ventalló slopes very steeply into this valley. It must be asked whether such a steep incline would have permitted three different movements which occurred during the battle: the advance of three cohorts *sub ipsum vallum* and their simulated flight; the unexpectedly rapid and efficient Spanish deployment; and the orderly march, apparently in line rather than in column, of Cato's second legion against the Spanish camp. The Spanish deployment and the advance of the legion, which was unopposed, are just conceivable, though the former in particular would have

[9] Schulten found on Puig Cegalá the remains of some ancient walls which he cautiously suggested might be part of Cato's *castra hiberna*: 'Forschungen in Spanien', *AA* (1940), 94. Of the four sites under discussion for the battle only those at Ventalló and Bellcaire would be plausible if this identification were correct; but the identification is much too tentative to serve as the basis of argument. See also p. 311 n. 3 concerning the site of the camp.

been very difficult; but in the face of such a slope the feint attack and simulated
flight of the three cohorts would seem extraordinarily dangerous and most
improbable. Finally, it is doubtful whether a large Spanish encampment on the
Sierra de Ventalló would have had sufficient access to an adequate supply of
water.

5. Albóns

The village of Albóns is situated a little over four kilometres south-west of
Emporiae, on a small hill rising out of the plain, a short distance from the forward
slopes of Puig Cegalá. At first sight it would seem possible that the Spanish
camp was on the hillock of Albóns, and that Cato drew up his army on a
north–south line, roughly corresponding to that of the modern road C-252,
along the lower slopes of Puig Cegalá. On closer inspection, however, this
appears less plausible.

In the first place, it is doubtful if the hillock of Albóns is large enough to have
accommodated the Spanish camp. Although there is no reliable figure for
the size of the Spanish army it is most unlikely that it was smaller than Cato's.[10]
The carefully planned camp of a Roman consular army seems to have required
an area of between 40 and 60 hectares,[11] yet the area of the hill at Albóns
does not exceed 36 hectares.

In the second place the configuration of the slopes opposite Albóns does
not provide quite what is required. To have had his army facing a camp at
Albóns Cato would have been obliged to place the bulk of it on level ground,
with virtually no special advantage of incline and with no natural features
to cover his right flank. Yet he would have placed his men facing the rising
sun, and it would be surprising if he had done this without any special advantage
in compensation. In point of fact on the other side of Albóns, to the east and
east-south-east, there is a very slight incline towards the village. It seems that
if the Spaniards had been at Albóns Cato could have deployed his troops on
this side with no significant loss of advantage as regards terrain and with the
rising sun at their backs.

6. The hills east of Bellcaire

The most striking feature of this group of hills is the ridge of high hills
which runs roughly south-eastwards from the village of Bellcaire and which
is dominated by Santa Catalina. There is no possibility that the Spanish camp

---

[10] App. *Iber.* 40 states that there were 40,000 Spaniards, while Valerius Antias asserted that
more than 40,000 were killed (Livy, 34. 15. 9). Livy says explicitly that Cato himself did not
specify the number slain; whether the figure used by Appian and Valerius is derived from
an authentic estimate of the total Spanish army is uncertain and perhaps improbable.

[11] Schulten, 'Forschungen in Spanien', *AA* (1940), 94, based especially on his studies of
the camps at Numantia. The dimensions of the consular camp described in Polyb. 6. 27 ff.
imply an area approaching 49 ha. See esp. Walbank, *Commentary on Polybius* i. 714 f.

was situated on this ridge: the major part of it is far too high and precipitous while the lower hills at the western extremity are not sufficiently extensive and have their view to the north seriously impeded. However, to the north of the main ridge lies a lower and rather wider group of hills, also in the form of a ridge, running parallel to the main Santa Catalina ridge. The central and higher parts of this ridge can be ruled out entirely, firstly because the sides of the hill, especially on the southern side, are too steep, secondly because the general configuration of these hills on their southern side would not permit the movements described in the account of the battle, and thirdly because the valley between this ridge and the main ridge to the south is far too narrow and circumscribed to permit the operations described in Livy. The only portion of this ridge which can be considered seriously as a possible site for the Spanish camp is the western end, just east of the village of Bellcaire. Here the sides are less steep and the hill is possibly broad enough to have served as a camp for the Spanish army. The site has good visibility and since in antiquity the river Ter seems to have followed the general line of the modern Canal de Riego, it would have been close to a major source of water. It is only about 7 or 8 kilometres from Emporiae. The crucial question is whether the terrain to the south of this part of the ridge would have permitted the deployment of the Roman army and the events of the battle as described in Livy. The Roman army could not have been deployed directly parallel to the ridge and facing it on its southern side because this would have meant that its right flank would have been a considerable way up the narrow valley between the two ridges. Other considerations apart, this is simply not compatible with the cavalry operations described as having occurred on the right flank. There is however another possibility: the Roman army might have been drawn up roughly across the entrance to the valley, that is facing the south-west side of the ridge. From the western end of the main Santa Catalina massif a low ridge, which might rather be regarded as a slight rise in the ground, runs down to the village of Bellcaire. If the Roman forces had been drawn up along this it would have given a slight slope in their favour, and this is a possible reason why Cato should have chosen to have come round to this side of the camp. If the Roman forces had been drawn up in this manner there would probably have been room for the cavalry action on the right flank.

Nevertheless, there are reasons for doubt. First, the possible line along which the Romans could have been drawn up is not really long enough; it is less than 1 kilometre and therefore only just reaches the minimum possible length. Second, though the cavalry action on the right would have been possible there would have been little room for the cavalry action on the left. Third, it is particularly difficult to envisage the flanking march of the Roman troops from the left of their own line round the Spanish right wing and coming in behind the Spanish line; such a march would have taken them right up to, if not actually through, the possible site of the Spanish camp.

7. *Masoles and the Valley of Las Olivas*

At the southern end of the line of hills which dominate the plain is a broad shoulder of Puig Cegalá, the highest point of which is named Masoles, 93 metres high. Masoles and its extension to the south-south-west (beyond a broad saddle the elevation rises again to 83 metres) certainly constitute a possible site for the Spanish camp. Behind them (i.e. to the west) a broad valley runs for several kilometres almost due north from the Ter to the village of Las Olivas. This valley meets all the requirements for the deployment of Cato's army and for the action of the battle. The only area of doubt is whether Masoles is not only a possible but a likely site for the Spanish camp. It appears to have two disadvantages. First, there might have been some danger if the Romans had succeeded in occupying higher ground to the north, on other parts of Puig Cegalá. Second, a ridge which runs down south-eastwards from Puig Cegalá to the modern village of Tor obscures the view from the site itself towards the north-east, in the direction of Emporiae, though the Spaniards could easily have maintained entirely satisfactory observation from the hills to the north of Masoles. Clearly these are only minor drawbacks, easily off-set by simple precautions.

8. *Conclusion*

Uncertainties remain. There can be no final assurance, for example, that the Spaniards did not camp on level ground on the plain, or that Cato did not launch his feint attack up an unexpectedly steep incline, or that he did not see some advantage not now apparent in a position which faced the rising sun. It may be, too, that there are possible sites which have been overlooked, and none of the four sites considered in this Appendix can be excluded as totally impossible. The fact remains, however, that the plateau of Masoles, for the Spanish camp, and the valley of Las Olivas, for the battle, accord with both the given data and the probabilities of the situation, and appear to do so much better than any other site within the maximum acceptable distance from Emporiae.

APPENDIX 5

Cato, Usury, and the *Lex Iunia*

AMONG the sayings of Cato cited by Cicero there is a particularly sharp comment about usury: 'When he was asked what was most advantageous in the management of property, he replied: "Good pasturing." What second? "Fairly good pasturing." What third? "Poor pasturing." What fourth? "Ploughing." And when the questioner said, "What about usury?" Cato replied, "What about killing a man?" '[1]

There is always the possibility that such an anecdote incorporates some elaboration of the original saying, but even so it must reflect a strong tradition regarding Cato's attitude to usury. The same intense dislike is apparent in the preface to the *De agricultura*, which first states rather mildly that usury is not so respectable (*honestum*) as agriculture but immediately continues: 'Our ancestors considered it so and laid down thus in the laws: that a thief is condemned to pay twofold, a usurer fourfold. From this one may judge how much worse a citizen they considered a usurer than a thief.'

There was at least one occasion when Cato gave practical expression to this attitude. Livy (32. 27. 3) records that when in 198 Cato went as praetor to Sardinia he was considered 'rather harsh in the restraint of usury: usurers were expelled from the island'.

Hostility to *feneratores* is an attitude found commonly enough in Roman sources. Cicero stated bluntly that their means of livelihood was considered *sordidus* and was regarded with disapproval because it was one of those 'which incur people's ill will'. At an early date legal restraint had actually been carried so far as to ban usury, a ban which inevitably it had proved impossible to maintain.[2] Cato's bracketing of theft and usury, though no doubt no more to be taken literally than his rhetorical equation of murder and usury, suggests an attitude of mind, imprecise and emotionally based but marked by strong conviction, which regarded *feneratio* as akin to robbery—a sentiment by no means unknown in other societies; and his comment later in the Preface of the *De agricultura* that an income from agriculture is 'the least likely to provoke resentment' (*minime invidiosus*) clearly refers back to his disapproval of usury and shows an attitude almost identical with Cicero's view that *feneratio* was an occupation which incurs ill will. So far, then, there is nothing especially remarkable

---

[1] Cic. *De off.* 2. 89 = Jordan, p. 108, *Dicta mem.* 63; partial versions in later writers.
[2] Cic. *De off.* 1. 150. See further Crook, *Law and Life of Rome*, pp. 211 f. For the ban see below, p. 322.

about Cato's attitude, except perhaps the characteristic sharpness and hyperbole with which he expressed it; nor was he the only Roman magistrate of the period to take public action against usurers, for in 192 the curule aediles, M. Tuccius and P. Iunius Brutus, imposed such heavy fines that they were able to pay for substantial public works out of the proceeds.[3]

A new element enters into the discussion with Plutarch's report that Cato 'engaged in the most criticized form of lending at interest, namely maritime loans'. Plutarch goes on to describe how by insisting on financing a large fleet of vessels rather than individual ships Cato minimized the risk of serious losses and ensured great profits for himself.[4] The seeming inconsistency has prompted the suggestion that Cato's attitudes changed with the passage of time—a suggestion to which some other comments by Plutarch might afford a certain plausibility.[5] The suggestion fails to carry conviction, however, on three counts: it has a distinctly *ad hoc* character; it seems to accept the total reversal of a strongly held view to which Cato gave expression on several widely separated occasions and which therefore was not a mere ephemeral outburst; and the authentic and forceful statement which opens the *De agricultura* was probably itself composed in the later years of Cato's life. A more likely explanation is that a Roman of Cato's standing was probably not conscious of any inconsistency, that he would have drawn a distinction which to us may seem artificial and illogical but which was none the less real and important in the Roman mind. It is revealed clearly enough by Cicero, who views as *sordidus* the occupation of the *fenerator*, making his living by lending money at interest; yet Cicero provides ample evidence that numerous respectable senators regularly increased their fortunes by lending money at interest. Closely related is Cicero's notorious opinion that trade, *mercatura*, is *sordida* if it is on a small scale but is not altogether to be disparaged if it is on a large scale, and becomes eminently praiseworthy if it produces a large fortune to be invested in land.[6]

The obvious conclusion to be drawn is that this dichotomy of view, nonsensical in economic terms but highly significant socially, was prevalent also in Cato's day. Cato would not see as applicable to his own activities his prejudices against *feneratio* as a principal form of livelihood or source of income. It was a very different matter to be a Roman senator loaning part of the great wealth derived from one's landed property to finance large-scale maritime ventures—a type of loan which in any event was often thought of as distinctive and in a class apart, and which was never subject to the legal limit on rates of interest.[7]

[3] Livy 35. 41. 9 f.

[4] Plut. *Cato Mai.* 21. 6 f.; on the technicalities of the arrangement see Rougé, *Recherches sur l'organisation du commerce maritime en Méditerranée sous l'empire romain*, pp. 426 ff.

[5] Scullard, *Roman Politics*², p. 222; Plut. *Cato Mai.* 21. 3 ff.

[6] Cic. *De off.* 1. 150–1; Finley, *The Ancient Economy*, pp. 53 ff.; Crook, loc. cit., for the prevalence of lending at interest.

[7] Klingmüller, *RE*, s.v. *Fenus*, cols. 2200 ff. (*fenus nauticum*), esp. 2203; Billeter, *Geschichte des Zinsfusses*, pp. 242 f.; de Ste Croix, 'Ancient Greek and Roman Maritime Loans', in

There is a further piece of evidence which bears upon this matter. Two fragments survive of a speech in which Cato expressed opposition to a proposed *lex Iunia* concerning usury, *Dissuasio legis Iuniae de feneratione*. From the absence of any other reference to such a *lex Iunia* it is generally inferred that the proposal was rejected. There is no specific evidence concerning the date of this episode, the identity of the Iunius, or the content of the proposal, but it is widely assumed that there is some connection with the events of 193 and 192. In 193 special measures had to be taken on the initiative of the Senate to prevent the legal restrictions on usury being circumvented by the placing of loans through members of the Latin or Italian allied states, a practice which had given rise to complaints about the accumulated burden of debt; and in 192 P. Iunius Brutus was one of the aediles who exacted heavy fines from usurers. Hence it is commonly presumed that this Iunius was closely associated with the proposed *lex Iunia* and was perhaps the actual author, either as tribune in 195 or as praetor in 190; an alternative sometimes mentioned is the praetor of 191, M. Iunius Brutus, in the immediate aftermath of the prosecutions of 192. Hence also the presumption that the proposal was for an extension of legal restrictions on usury.[8]

All this poses the obvious question as to why Cato, notoriously hostile to usury, should have opposed a law seemingly directed to controlling and restricting it, the more so as one of the fragments of his speech, referring to *fenus* as having been a source of discord, certainly suggests that his hostility was maintained on this occasion. Three explanations have been suggested, none of which is wholly convincing. First, that the title of the speech should be understood as '*Dissuasio legis Iuniae. De feneratione*', implying that the *lex Iunia* itself was not necessarily concerned with usury but that Cato took the opportunity to speak against usury. This is too much like special pleading designed to explain away the evidence; and if it is argued that some slender support might be found in the form of the title given by Festus, *Cato de feneratione ⟨in dissuasione⟩* (?) *legis Iuniae*, the version of Nonius says bluntly *in dissuasione de feneratione*.

The second suggestion is that Cato may have objected to the *lex Iunia* on the ground that it was not sufficiently severe. Though a possible reason for

---

Edey and Yamey (edd.), *Debits, Credits, Finance and Profits*, p. 55. It is not clear what Plutarch means when he refers to this as 'the most criticized kind of loan' (τῷ διαβεβλημένῳ μάλιστα τῶν δανεισμῶν ἐπὶ ναυτικοῖς). Presumably the remark in part reflects the tendency to disparage maritime commerce (which itself was compounded of a variety of prejudices: see esp. Rougé, op. cit. pp. 11 ff.) and, like that tendency, is closely related to the high element of risk: the risk is certainly Cato's criticism of commerce in *De agr. praef.* 2. Nor is it by any means certain that Plutarch is reflecting a widespread attitude; his remark must be set beside Cicero's (*De off.* 1. 151) that under certain circumstances trade *videtur iure optimo posse laudari*. On Cato's attitude to involvement in trade see pp. 252 ff.

[8] *ORF*[3], Cato frs. 56 and 57. Principal discussions: Münzer, *RE*, s.v. *Iunius*, no. 54, col. 1020; Janzer, pp. 17 f.; Rotondi, *Leges Publicae*[2], p. 273; Marmorale, *Cato Maior*[2], pp. 48 f. and 69 f.; Scullard, *Roman Politics*[2], p. 257; Gelzer, *RE*, s.v. *Porcius*, no. 9, col. 119; Kienast, pp. 35 f. The events of 193: Livy, 35. 7. 2–5.

opposing the bill, this is hardly what we should normally expect, and this explanation also seems too much of a special plea to carry conviction.[9]

Thirdly, Kienast has suggested that the true explanation must be that the law would have been damaging to Cato's own interests in respect of his profitable maritime loans, hence that his opposition was selfish and hypocritical. To avoid the difficulty of supposing that Cato brazenly spoke in open contradiction to his proclaimed sentiments about usury, Kienast adopts the view already mentioned that the stated objection was probably that the proposals were insufficiently severe.[10] This difficulty apart, Kienast's view implies a degree of conscious cynicism and hypocrisy which does not accord well with the general run of evidence about Cato, and it ignores the probability that Cato will have thought of his maritime loans as being in quite a different category from *feneratio*.

At this point it is worth recalling that there is no specific evidence to link the *lex Iunia* with the events of 193 and 192 or with either the aedile of 192 or the praetor of 191—for there were plenty of other Iunii in public life in Rome during the period of Cato's career. Nevertheless, the coincidence of subject would make it rash to fall back on an interpretation which positively excluded a connection; but the inference commonly drawn from this identification about the content of Iunius' proposals deserves re-examination in the light of what the state of the law regarding *feneratio* may have been at this time.

It has been mentioned already that at an early date usury was prohibited altogether by law. Livy says that according to certain writers this was done by a *lex Genucia* in 342, but whether or not the date is correct there seems no doubt that the prohibition existed.[11] It may be doubted whether it was ever enforceable, and certainly it cannot have remained effective in practice in the face of the growing scale and complexity of Roman affairs during the third century. By Cato's day the audiences of Plautus were familiar enough with *feneratio*, and Cato's own remarks show that it was a possible, though in his view a most undesirable, source of income. What is less clear, however, is whether the total prohibition had been formally modified or had simply been allowed to fall into disuse.

Appian (*B.C.* 1. 54) states explicitly that as late as 89 B.C. the total prohibition was still technically in force, and indeed that at that moment of economic stress the sharp discrepancy between the law and established practice led to grave disputes and public violence. On the other hand, if Appian's statement did not exist Livy's account of the issue in 193 would almost certainly be taken

[9] Janzer, followed by Marmorale and Scullard, suggested the first explanation but offers the second as an alternative; Gelzer favours the second (refs. in previous note).

[10] Kienast, pp. 35 f. So convinced is he that this explanation must be correct that he treats it as clear evidence that Cato was involved in maritime operations no later than the 190s.

[11] Livy, 7. 42. 1; Tac. *Ann.* 6. 16; App. *B.C.* 1. 54; Klingmüller, *RE*, s.v. *Fenus*, cols. 2192 f.; Billeter, *Geschichte des Zinsfusses*, pp. 135 ff.

as virtual proof that usury, subject to a legal limit on the rate of interest, had been legalized by that date. 'The state was burdened by interest payments, and although avarice had been restrained by numerous laws governing usury, a fraudulent course had been adopted, namely that accounts were transferred to members of the allied states, who were not bound by the laws; thus debtors were overwhelmed by unrestricted interest (*libero faenore*).' The steps taken to deal with the problem were first to ensure that such arrangements were made public, then to give debtors, notwithstanding the non-Roman status of creditors, the option of settling under Roman law, and finally the promotion of a *lex Sempronia* which laid down that the law respecting money lent in transactions with members of the allied or Latin states should be the same as that applicable to transactions involving Roman citizens. Admittedly most of Livy's account could be held to be logically compatible with a situation in which the Roman laws which were being circumvented were those which forbade the taking of interest, but the phrase *libero faenore* strongly suggests that Livy himself envisages rather a strictly limited rate.[12] However, it may well be that full resolution of this particular problem is not essential to a satisfactory interpretation of the *lex Iunia* and Cato's opposition.

Livy's account shows that, whether interest was prohibited or severely restricted, the legal provisions in 193 simply did not correspond to the economic realities of the situation or cater for a pressing and widespread need for loans. There is a strong probability that in plugging the loophole the *lex Sempronia* had the effect of imposing, if not an absolute ban on interest, a maximum rate of interest which was unrealistically low in relation to this heavy demand. The inevitable consequence would have been a mixture of hardship, an eager search for further loopholes, and a spate of illegal transactions. It is hardly a coincidence that in the next year the aediles are found mounting numerous prosecutions against *feneratores*. It is therefore an attractive hypothesis that the proposed *lex Iunia* was 'an attempt to set a maximum rate which was realistic and enforceable. If the author of the law was indeed the Iunius who had been the aedile in 192, such a move is quite conceivable as a result of his experiences in attempting to enforce the existing law.

If that was indeed the purport of Iunius' proposal Cato's opposition is not difficult to explain. However modest the proposed new maximum, Cato could well have regarded any modification of the prevailing restriction as a dangerous concession, a weakening of the authority of law, as a positive encouragement to a disreputable practice. A demand for more rigorous enforcement of the existing law and opposition to any relaxation would seem wholly in character. It must be recognized that the fragments tell us so little that neither this nor any other explanation can be more than highly conjectural, but this particular hypothesis does at least avoid the need to posit serious inconsistency in an aspect of Cato's behaviour where this seems unlikely.

[12] Livy 35. 7. 2–5; cf. Frank, *ESAR* i. 206 ff.

Some Interpretations related to Cato's Censorship

THIS appendix examines briefly a number of views relating to Cato's censorship which have some claim to be important or to have been influential. In Chapter 5 these were not discussed specifically but were rejected by implication.

In the first place there is the view that Cato was using the office of censor in pursuit of a policy of hostility towards the senatorial aristocracy. It was argued in Chapter 4, however, that there are no good grounds for supposing him to have pursued such a policy in his career in general,[1] and there is no reason to see it at work in the censorship in particular. Certainly he took severe action against a number of distinguished senators, but that stemmed naturally from the strict and conscientious performance of the normal functions of the office; and Livy says explicitly that in the general registration the censorship was stern and harsh towards *all* orders. Similarly it is evident that neither Cato's measures against luxury nor his efforts to establish (or re-establish) stricter standards of conduct need in any way presuppose an 'anti-aristocratic' policy, or an attempt to impose on the governing aristocracy the influence and ethic of a resentful 'Italian middle class'.[2]

Nor is there good ground for supposing Cato's actions as censor to have been strongly influenced by personal or political hostilities or by factional rivalries. While it would be rash to assume that he was never influenced by such considerations, the only case in which this is suggested by the ancient writers is the removal of Lucius Scipio Asiaticus from the equestrian order.[3] It is easy to believe that in the aftermath of his great quarrel with the Scipios Cato was not sorry to find some reason for removing Lucius, but it is questionable whether this amounted to a serious political attack; for Lucius remained in the Senate and it is highly probable that the withdrawal of his horse was *sine ignominia* and the consequence of his physical infirmity—a logical outcome, in fact, of Cato's strict application of the requirements for equestrian service. Otherwise there is no suggestion of a partisan approach, and no need of the hypothesis to explain Cato's actions. Even the nomination of his friend and colleague Valerius as *princeps senatus* cannot confidently be interpreted as partisan, since there is

[1] pp. 66 ff.
[2] Such a view permeates many of the studies by Fraccaro collected in his *Opuscula* i, including the study of the censorship, pp. 393–508. Cf. also Marmorale, *Cato Maior*[2], pp. 89 f.
[3] p. 81.

a very real possibility that in terms of the traditional requirements Valerius was the only eligible candidate.[4]

A very different view of the censorship has been put forward by Kienast,[5] who believes that Cato's political activity in general and much of his work as censor was conducted in the interests of the senatorial aristocracy. Noting that the next three censorships were to have many resemblances to that of 184, he infers that Cato, though contributing a special personal drive and insight, was essentially representative of a large group of senators. In particular he sees him as on the watch against the growing power of wealthy financiers who undertook state contracts, and he interprets the dispute over the censorial contracts in this light. He holds that while the censors of 184 saw the urgent necessity of extensive new building works (supposedly to modernize Rome and fit her to be the ruling city of a great empire) the Senate must have known that every large building project conferred more influence on the class of contractors; in consequence the censors, while making advantageous arrangements with the contractors, had to be careful to leave them not too powerful and therefore tried to limit the profit margins. In a sense this approach is the converse of the theory that Cato pursued an 'anti-aristocratic' policy; indeed Kienast's interpretations of Cato's words and actions as in the interest of the nobles are often presented as a direct rebuttal of such a view. Yet both approaches perhaps presuppose too readily an issue which may have had relatively little importance in this period. While there may have been occasional resentment when particular nobles attained exceptional prominence and influence, there is little reason to think that at this date the senatorial aristocracy was consciously concerned that it might lose power and influence to some other class in the state, and especially not to a cohesive class of powerful financiers and contractors with a strongly developed sense of identity. Badian[6] has rightly pointed out that there is no reason to regard Cato as hostile to *publicani* as such (indeed his arrangements for the Spanish mines must have benefited them greatly), that the obvious explanation of the affair of 184 is that the censors regarded it as their duty to arrange contracts which were the best possible from the point of view of public funds, and above all that the events of 184 themselves suggest that as yet the *publicani* wielded little power and were by no means a cohesive class or force. Neither the original low margins nor the reletting at margins still low even after the exclusion of the original contractors nor the fact that these could be excluded is comprehensible except on the premiss that there were numerous competitors. Moreover few if any of them could have been dealing exclusively with state contracts, they were working for fairly low returns, and they were incapable

---

[4] It is generally supposed that Cato passed over Titus Flamininus; e.g. Fraccaro, *Opusc.* i. 482 f.; Marmorale, *Cato Maior*[2], pp. 90 f.; Kienast, p. 74. But Kienast, p. 149 n. 72, also notes cautiously the possibility that Flamininus may not have been eligible, and this is indeed probable: Mommsen, *Röm. Staats.* iii. 31.

[5] Kienast, pp. 68 ff.   [6] *Publicans and Sinners*, pp. 35 ff.

of sufficient cooperation to organize a boycott of the contract auctions, the one really effective means of pressure potentially open to them.

Yet another view is that an important factor at work was Cato's social conscience, that in his censorship and on other occasions Cato was combating the rich few and the profiteers, and consciously trying to help the poor and excluded many.[7] At first sight it seems that a fair amount of evidence might be marshalled to support this. Cato was associated with the *lex Porcia* which introduced penalties to protect the rights of citizens under the *provocatio* laws; he disapproved of officers enriching themselves from war booty and he favoured extensive distributions to the rank and file; he repeatedly showed hostility to usury, and in a speech 'Concerning the military tribunes' (*c.* 171–169) he used the words 'expedito pauperem plebeium atque proletarium', which at least one scholar has taken as a call for greater electoral freedom for the poor. Attention might be drawn also to his vigorous protests at the abuses of power by Q. Minucius Thermus and L. Flamininus. In the censorship itself, it could be argued, he showed stern persistence in restricting the profits of financiers, placed a 10 per cent tax on the real capital value of luxury possessions, stopped wealthy men diverting to private establishments water intended for the citizens at large, and by initiating vast expenditure on the sewer system must have greatly improved the living conditions of thousands of ordinary people.

On closer inspection, however, the case proves to be superficial. In the first place, his tax was aimed not at wealth or at valuable property as such but at a limited group of luxuries which in his eyes resulted from a frivolous and undesirable misuse of wealth. Far from viewing the wealthy with hostility, he held that it was their duty to increase their wealth and he actively amassed a considerable fortune of his own.[8] His dispute with the *publicani* had little relevance to the poor. If the contractors can be termed profiteers in any sense—which seems very doubtful—it was at the expense not of the poor but of the state, and it was the public treasury that Cato was protecting. In the absence of any context whatsoever except its title the extract from the speech 'Concerning the military tribunes' is of little value, open as it is to a variety of unverifiable conjectures: a reference to voting procedures is no more likely than a recommendation that in an emergency situation men of the poorer classes should be conscripted into the army.

And most of the other items are more plausibly to be seen as expressions of other values than a 'social conscience' in the sense of a sympathetic championing of the poor. Thus his attitude to usury—by no means a subject of concern only to the poor—almost certainly emanated from a deep social prejudice, fortified by a conviction that what was required by law should be carried out.[9] The rigorous application of this latter conviction, embracing the scrupulous observance of procedures and fulfilment of duties, can be seen as a recurrent theme in many of Cato's actions. It goes far to account for his approach to his

[7] Della Corte, *Catone censore*[2], p. 58.   [8] pp. 89 and 94.   [9] Appendix 5.

censorship as a whole and to many of the particular tasks; it explains his support for sanctions to enforce the existing laws on *provocatio*, his action against unauthorized diversion of water from the public system, even his attitude to booty —where his concern was at least as much that the state should gets its due as that the troops should get theirs. In the latter case another concept was also at work, the belief that public office should be regarded as public service and in no way allowed to become the occasion of private gain. It was the improper use of magisterial authority, probably with particular emphasis on a breach of *fides*, which was the substance of the complaint against L. Flamininus. *Fides* appears again, though it is not the main element, in one of the attacks on Q. Minucius Thermus, while in that concerned with the execution of ten men the principal emphasis of the main surviving fragment is on the total lack of judicial process prior to the execution of free men.[10] It should be noticed also that there is no reason to suppose these victims to have been of the lower classes. It is at least as likely that they were local officials, men of high status and considerable wealth. Such were certainly the *decemviri* whose maltreatment is complained of in the other speech against Thermus.

An insistence on such concepts as *fides*, integrity, public service, on strict adherence to judicial procedures, in sum on the scrupulous observance of propriety and fulfilment of duties in public office, would often work to the benefit of the poor, protecting them against arbitrary and illegal abuse; but the primary emphasis of Cato's thought was on the former rather than the latter. There is no sign that he conceived one of his major roles to have been the protection of the poor and the improvement of their condition, to be pursued as ends in themselves. In this respect the fact that he did not hold the tribunate of the plebs, and presumably did not seek it, is a significant pointer. Particularly illuminating is the long fragment from his speech against Q. Minucius Thermus, *De falsis pugnis*, in which he complained about the beating of allied officials—*decemviri*. It reveals, almost incidentally but unmistakably, that like virtually all Roman senators—perhaps one should say virtually all Romans—Cato took for granted the importance of social rank and the automatic association of privilege with birth into a 'good' family. It was a special cause of shame and humiliation that men of such status were punished in public, in the presence of their own citizens.

He said that his supplies had been inadequately attended to by the *decemviri*. He ordered that their clothes be dragged off and that they be scourged. The Bruttiani beat the decemvirs; many men saw it done. Who can endure such insult, such tyranny, such servitude? No king has dared to act thus; are these things to be inflicted upon good men, born of good family, men of good counsel? Where is our alliance? Where the *fides* of our ancestors? How comes it that you have dared to inflict signal injuries, blows, lashes, stripes, these pains and tortures, with disgrace and extreme ignominy, since their own

---

[10] *ORF*[3], Cato frs. 58; 59. See pp. 59 and 63.

people and many persons were looking on? But how much grief, how much groaning, what tears, how much weeping have I heard were caused! Even slaves bitterly resent injuries: what feeling do you think those men, sprung from good families, endowed with great excellence, had and will have so long as they live?[11]

[11] *ORF*[3], Cato fr. 58.

Cato's Speeches *De ambitu* and *Dissuasio ne lex Baebia derogaretur*

THE context and purpose of Cato's two speeches 'Concerning bribery', *De ambitu*, and 'That the *lex Baebia* should not be partially repealed', *Dissuasio ne lex Baebia derogaretur*, are the subject of an important discussion by Fraccaro, whose conclusions have been widely accepted.[1] The purpose of the present discussion is not to refute Fraccaro's conclusions, which could all be correct, but to serve as a reminder that they are hypothetical and that there are alternative possibilities. In one respect in particular there is no reason to prefer any one of three quite different possibilities to the others, though Fraccaro considers only one.

The brief fragments from these speeches add nothing in respect of date and circumstances beyond what is indicated by the titles themselves, nor is there any independent reference to Cato having made a speech or intervened on an occasion which would have been appropriate for either of these speeches. The only method of inquiry open, therefore, is to consider whether any known events or circumstances, though not explicitly connected with Cato, would have provided appropriate or likely contexts. Fraccaro argues that such contexts are provided by certain legislative events in 181 and the following few years.

Livy states explicitly that the consuls of 181, P. Cornelius Cethegus and M. Baebius Tamphilus, were the authors of legislation against electoral corruption: 'et legem de ambitu consules ex auctoritate senatus ad populum tulerunt.'[2] Then in his account of the elections held in 180 for the magistrates of 179 he states that four praetors were appointed (there had been six each year from 197 onwards) in accordance with the *lex Baebia*, which laid down that in alternate years four were to be appointed (i.e. as opposed to six in the intervening years): 'praetores quattuor post multos annos lege Baebia creati, quae alternis quaternos iubebat creari.'[3] This alternation was soon ended in favour of a return to six praetors in each year. Since the last college of four was probably in 177 the

---

[1] *ORF*[3], frs. 136 and 137–8. Fraccaro, 'Catoniana', *Studi storici*, 3 (1910), pp. 241 ff. = *Opusc.* i. 227 ff.; cf. Janzer, pp. 52 ff.; Scullard, *Roman Politics*[2], pp. 172 f.; Kienast, pp. 92 f.; Malcovati, *ORF*[3], ad loc.

[2] Livy, 40. 19. 11. It is usual to emend *leges* to *legem*, though Fraccaro would retain the former on the ground that it is appropriate to a law with a variety of provisions, such as he conceives this law to have been.

[3] Livy, 40. 44. 2.

change in the provisions of the *lex Baebia* was evidently made in 177 or 176.[4] Fraccaro argues plausibly that the law itself was probably passed in 181 rather than 180, partly because there is a known Baebius in office in that year, partly because, to avoid undue disruption, the law is likely to have started the system by allowing six praetors to be appointed at the elections held in the year in which the law itself was passed.

Fraccaro's interpretation of Cato's speeches in conjunction with these circumstances leads him to the following conclusions:

(*i*) In 181 there were not two separate *leges Baebiae*—*de ambitu* and *de praetoribus* —but one. That one, proposed by the two consuls with the support of the Senate, included among its provisions to combat *ambitus* a device for reducing the number of praetors, and thus the number of contestants for the consulship.[5]

(*ii*) Cato probably supported this law in his speech *De ambitu*.[6]

(*iii*) A few years later there was a *derogatio*, i.e. a partial repeal, of the *lex Baebia*, removing the restriction to four praetorships in the alternate years. This change was opposed by Cato in his *Dissuasio ne lex Baebia derogaretur*.

Underlying these conclusions is the argument that the 'nobles', though resentful at the restrictions on bribery, would not have dared to propose their abolition. Therefore, it is inferred, the proposed *derogatio* against which Cato spoke must have concerned a *lex Baebia* in connection with the number of praetorships, not with *ambitus*; and since a *derogatio* implies partial, not total repeal, that provision must have been part of a law with wider scope, for which the obvious candidate is the law against *ambitus* reported by Livy to have been passed in the very year when the provision for alternating numbers of praetors is likely to have been carried.

The most obvious point of uncertainty in all this concerns the date and circumstances of the speech *De ambitu*, which Fraccaro associates with the law of 181 without discussing alternatives. Yet Obsequens mentions an omen which occurred in 166 'comitia cum ambitiosissime fierent et ob hoc senatus in Capitolio haberetur'; and another *lex de ambitu* was passed in 159.[7] Since virtually nothing is known about Cato's speech beyond its title and a few words which might come from any discussion of *ambitus*, it could have been associated with any one of the three occasions and there is no good reason for preferring 181 to 166 or 159.

---

[4] Fraccaro himself and Malcovati (refs. above) date this to 179 or 178 in the belief that here were six praetors in 177; but Scullard, op. cit., p. 173 n. 2, points out that there were probably only four in that year; cf. *MRR* i. 398 f.

[5] In this Fraccaro is developing a suggestion put forward by Mommsen, *Röm. Staatsrecht* ii³, 198 f.

[6] Fraccaro writes of Cato making this speech to the *populus*, but though others have followed him, and though he could well be correct, there is no obvious reason to insist on this. The point is irrelevant, however, to the main issue.

[7] Obsequ. 12; Livy, *Per.* 47.

There are also uncertainties about other aspects of Fraccaro's argument. Thus it is rash to assume that no one would have attempted to repeal part of the provisions of a law against bribery. It might have been argued, for example, that some provisions were producing results which had not been intended, or the practical consequences may have given rise to popular resentment. Again, not only a bribery law but also one concerned with the number of praetors may have had several provisions of which only some were annulled in 177 or 176, so that the attempt at a *derogatio* indicated by Cato's *dissuasio* is not a strong reason for rejecting the idea of a separate law. Furthermore, it is not immediately obvious that the reduction from six to five in the average number of persons qualified to seek the consulship is likely to have had a great bearing on the issue of electoral corruption.[8] There is little doubt that the initial increase from four praetors to six had been connected with the decision to form two permanent provinces out of the Spanish territories which had been won from the Carthaginians; and since, in the following years, it had frequently been found desirable to leave the same magistrates in charge for two years, there is at least a possibility that the whole short-lived experiment of alternating six and four was prompted by practical administrative considerations and had nothing to do with *ambitus* or political issues. Finally it cannot be taken as beyond question that there was no *lex Baebia* other than the one or two mentioned by Livy. Several Baebii are known, holding various offices, including tribunates, within Cato's lifetime, and the silence of the sources is no impediment to one of them having been the author of some other law. Consequently, though it remains an attractive hypothesis that Cato's *dissuasio* was in opposition to the restoration of the number of praetors to six the whole question is fraught with uncertainties.

[8] The fact that the difference was an average of only one praetorship per year is an obvious reason for doubting the interpretation offered by Kienast, loc. cit., following Afzelius, 'Zur Definition der röm. Nobilität', *C & M* 7 (1945), 189 ff., esp. 197 f. Kienast suggests that the *lex Baebia* restricted the number of praetors in order to hinder an increase in the number of new families reaching 'the nobility' (since the losses suffered by established families during the Second Punic War made it difficult for them to find enough candidates). Accepting that Cato's *dissuasio* was against the return to six per year, he interprets this as motivated by a fear that an influx of new people would enlarge the *clientelae* of particular powerful families.

APPENDIX 8

The Nature of Cato's *Ad filium*

AMONG the fragments of Cato's writings are some which are shown either by their content or by their context to have been addressed to his son—obviously to his elder son, Licinianus, since the younger, Salonianus, was born only a few years before Cato's death. Some of these fragments come from one or more letters to the son, but others have such indications as *in libris quos scripsit ad filium*, or simply *ad filium*. In 1850 Jahn argued that these latter fragments come from a set of books written to assist with the education of the son, each book dealing with a special topic, such as medicine or agriculture. These *libri ad filium* would therefore have constituted the first Roman 'encyclopedia', a major literary innovation and the model to be followed in a later age by Celsus. Subsequent scholars have differed on certain points of detail and interpretation—such as whether or not there were books dealing with military science and jurisprudence, whether the *Carmen de moribus* was a section of this work, what relationship the medical and agricultural books may have had to the extant *De agricultura*, whether the project was to any degree modelled on Greek encyclopedic education, or may have been a conscious attempt to create a Roman alternative, whether certain of the fragments collected under this heading by Jordan really belong there. Nevertheless in its essentials Jahn's interpretation has been almost universally accepted.[1] There is a fairly general agreement that the *libri ad filium*, though possibly written at intervals, were probably conceived as a single project; that they must have been composed in the period *c.* 180–*c.* 173; that the 'history' which Plutarch says Cato wrote 'in big letters' for his son[2] was an earlier and separate work; that at least three topics were dealt with—agriculture, medicine, and rhetoric (later Celsus was to treat these three and also military science); and that the manner of expression was strongly didactic, such that Cato's admonitions could later be characterized as 'precepts' or even as 'oracular'.

This concept of a coherent group of books, created as a well-organized

---

[1] Jahn, 'Über römische Encyclopädien', *Ber. d. Königlich Sächsischen Ges. d. Wiss., Phil.-hist. Klasse* 2 (1850), 263 ff.; Gerosa, *La prima enciclopedia romana*; Leo, *Gesch. der röm. Literatur* i. 276 ff.; Schanz–Hosius, *Gesch. der röm. Literatur* i⁴. 181 f.; Klingner, 'Cato Censorius und die Krisis des römischen Volkes', *Röm. Geisteswelt*⁵, pp. 50 ff.; Della Corte, 'Catone Maggiore e i Libri ad Marcum', *RFIC* 19 (1941), 81–96; id., *Catone censore*², pp. 107 ff.; Barwick, 'Zu den Schriften des Cornelius Celsus und des alten Cato', *WJA* 3 (1948), 117 ff.; Marmorale, *Cato Maior*², pp. 156 ff.; Helm, *RE*, s.v. *Porcius*, no. 9, cols. 146 f.; Kienast, pp. 104 f.; Grimal, 'Encyclopédies antiques', *CHM* 9 (1965–6), 459 ff., esp. 464 ff. The fragments are collected by Jordan, pp. 77–80; see also his discussion on pp. xcix–cii.

[2] Plut. *Cato Mai.* 20. 7.

educational project and systematically treating several major topics in turn, seems to have been seriously doubted only by Mazzarino;[3] which is surprising, since the evidence exhibits several curious features. To start with, of the sixteen fragments assigned by Jordan to this work five (10, 11, 13, 15, 16) have no indication of an addressee and no indication of the title or subject of the work or works from which they came: they have been so assigned by Jordan largely on the assumption that there was an 'encyclopedia' which treated the postulated subjects, and that these fragments would be appropriate in such a context. Five of the remainder reveal no more than that they are comments addressed to Cato's son (1, 2, 5, 12, 14); and the other six exhibit a marked variety in the descriptions of the work or works from which they are taken:

> . . . *ad filium vel de oratore* . . . (fr. 3, Diomedes)
> . . . *in epistula ad filium* . . . (fr. 4, Priscian)
> . . . *in praeceptis ad filium* . . . (fr. 7, Nonius)
> . . . *in oratione ad filium* . . . (fr. 6, Servius)
> . . . *in libris quos scripsit ad filium* . . . (fr. 8, Servius)
> . . . *in libris ad filium de agricultura* . . . (fr. 9, Servius).

It will be noticed that one of these designations is actually *in epistula*, though there has been a marked unwillingness to take this literally. But the problems go much deeper than this variety, this lack of consistency as to title or subject. Jordan assigned three fragments (14–16) to the supposed book on rhetoric, but only one of these (14) is attested even as addressed to Marcus, and though all three do have reference to rhetoric, none is stated to be drawn from a book devoted to that topic. Indeed, there is some cause for uneasiness about the very notion that the man whose advice was 'rem tene, verba sequentur' (fr. 15) saw fit to compose a whole book specifically about rhetoric. A passage by Quintilian and another in a later work on rhetoric have been taken to imply that Cato did write such a book, but they do not necessarily do so and would be equally compatible with the inclusion of some observations about rhetorical matters in more general contexts.[4] Moreover the silence of Cicero, especially in the *Brutus* and the *De oratore*, strongly suggests that he knew of no such book by Cato, for he has much to say about Cato in both these works dealing with Roman oratory.

---

[3] *Introduzione*, ch. 2, esp. pp. 23 ff.

[4] (i) Quintil. *Inst.* 3. 1. 19: 'Romanorum primus, quantum ego quidem sciam, condidit aliqua in hanc materiam M. Cato, post M. Antonius inchoavit.' It is arguable that Quintilian's phrase is more appropriate to a number of well-known observations than to a book (Cato's definition of an orator was so well known that it is found in at least seven passages, in six writers, as well as in a humorous adaptation recorded in Pliny, *Epist.* 4. 7. 5).

(ii) 'Victorinus', in Halm, *Rhetores Latini*, p. 308 lines 25 f. (Jordan, p. 80, *Ad Marcum filium* fr. 16), explaining the *propositio* or *summa* of a case, says: 'et haec est, quam Cato in libro suo appellat vires causae.' It is possible that a book on rhetoric is meant and that the phrase is part of a technical exposition and definition. It is at least as likely however that the author has chosen to illustrate his own point by picking out Cato's phrase, which need not have been used in so specialized a context.

The only specific evidence for a full specialized book is in the words of Diomedes, *vel de oratore* (emended by one scholar to *de aratore*!), which introduce a fragment asserting that 'hare brings much sleep to him who eats it' (fr. 3). The difficulty of imagining the role of this sentiment in a discussion *de oratore* has led inevitably, and in defiance of Diomedes' words, to the assignment of this fragment to the supposed book on medicine—and indeed the elder Pliny mentions the same fragment in the context of a passage devoted to medical prescriptions (*Nat. hist.* 28. 260). Moreover it is fairly certain from a passage in Plutarch that in its original context this fragment was closely linked to the well-known fragment which preserves Cato's biting attack on Greek doctors—which in turn is usually held to be evidence for the existence of a book *ad filium* specifically devoted to medicine (both passages will be quoted shortly).

Yet the evidence of a book devoted to medicine is itself a matter of doubt. First, the only medical book actually attributed to Cato is the *commentarius* in which he recorded prescriptions and remedies used in the treatment of his family and household; but in the fragment which mentions this it is referred to in a manner which shows clearly that it was a separate and different work from the work *ad filium* from which the fragment itself is taken (fr. 2, quoted below). Thus there is no explicit reference to a book *ad filium* concerned with medicine. Second, of the five fragments assigned by Jordan to this supposed book (1–5, and of those 1 and 2 are so closely related as to be almost one continuous piece), it has already been seen that one (3) is designated *de oratore*, and another (4; perhaps the most plausibly medical in content) is said to be 'in a letter to his son', *in epistula ad filium*. Third, it has already been mentioned that the passage which constitutes fragments 1 and 2 (the criticism of Greek doctors) was almost certainly closely linked with the passage about eating hare—which is the one designated *de oratore*. Nor is there anything about the fragments collected by Jordan which compels the inference that they are drawn from a medical treatise. They could have been, but it is not difficult to imagine them in other contexts, and this is especially so with fragments 1, 2, and 5—the very ones which are not cited as *de oratore* or *in epistula*. In this connection it will be as well to examine a little more closely fragments 1 and 2.

Fragment 1 = Pliny, *Nat. hist.* 29. 14:

Dicam de istis Graecis suo loco, M. fili, quid Athenis exquisitum habeam et quod bonum sit illorum litteras inspicere, non perdiscere, vincam. nequissimum et indocile genus illorum, et hoc puta vatem dixisse: quandoque ista gens suas litteras dabit, omnia conrumpet, tum etiam magis, si medicos suos hoc mittet. iurarunt inter se barbaros necare omnes medicina, et hoc ipsum mercede faciunt ut fides is sit et facile disperdant. nos quoque dictitant barbaros et spurcius nos quam alios opicon appellatione foedant. interdixi tibi de medicis.[5]

Pliny, anxious to emphasize that the objection is not to the practice of medicine

---

[5] The wider significance of this passage is discussed in Ch. 8, esp. pp. 170 ff.

and healing but to its profession, especially for money, continues a few lines later (29. 15–16):

Quid ergo? damnatam ab eo rem utilissimam credimus? minime, Hercules. subicit enim qua medicina se et coniugem usque ad longam senectam perduxerit, his ipsis scilicet quae nunc nos trademus, profiteturque esse commentarium sibi quo medeatur filio, servis, familiaribus, quem nos per genera usus sui digerimus. non rem antiqui damnabant, sed artem, maxime vero quaestum esse manipretio vitae recusabant.

The words *subicit* to *perduxerit* and *profiteturque* to *digerimus* constitute fragment 2.

It is evident that the first fragment could have come from a context of general exhortation to the son about his conduct just as well as from a book setting out practical medical treatment, with which subject indeed it has no necessary connection. Whether the same is true of the second fragment depends upon whether or not the words 'subicit qua medicina se et coniugem usque ad longam senectam perduxerit' indicate that Cato proceeded to a full exposition of his methods and remedies. The probability however is that he did not do so, since he saw fit to support his assertions by mention of the fact that he possessed a *commentarius* containing remedies, clearly not repeated in the work *ad filium* and not superseded by it. It is to be noted too that none of the supposedly 'medical' fragments lends positive support to belief in such an exposition of remedies, for none of these fragments is such that it must necessarily refer to a specific remedy. In fact Cato need have said little or nothing more than is reported by Plutarch in his account of the same passage:

He said that there was a notebook (*hypomnema*) written by himself, and that those who were sick in his household he cared for and treated in accordance with this, never requiring anyone to fast, but feeding them on vegetables or pieces of duck, pigeon, or hare; for he said that this diet was light and good for sick people, except that it often fell out that those who ate it dreamed. He said that by using such care and treatment he had good health himself, and kept his family in good health.[6]

In the *ad filium* Cato, making his point that highly successful medical treatment was possible without the assistance of unscrupulous and profiteering Greek doctors, instanced the efficacy of his own private collection of remedies, indicated their general characteristics, and noted the one drawback that they tended to induce sleep; but there is no reason to suppose and no likelihood that he went on to expound his remedies in detail.

At first sight Pliny's words 'his ipsis scilicet quae nunc nos trademus [or *tractamus*]', where 'his ipsis' is in apposition with 'qua medicina', might seem to run counter to this view, to suggest that many of the remedies which Pliny expounds

---

[6] *Cato Mai.* 23. 5 f. The reference to excessive dreaming clearly stems from a confusion of the Latin words *somnus* and *somnium*, and corresponds to the *multum somni* said to result from eating hare (Jordan, p. 78, *Ad Marcum filium* fr. 3). Most of the points in fragments 1 and 2 as given by Pliny recur in this chapter, though Plutarch uses them in a different order.

he has drawn from Cato's account in the *ad filium*; in other words that in that work Cato did set out his *medicina* in detail. It is entirely plausible, however, to take Pliny to mean that the general character of Cato's remedies (i.e. the 'traditional', 'non-professional' methods) corresponded to the character of those set out by Pliny himself. Plausible and moreover preferable: for everything suggests that Pliny neither drew upon nor had access to any substantial collection of remedies by Cato. In the first place it is striking how infrequently Pliny cites Cato in his medical books (20–32), in contrast to the frequency of citation in books 3 and 14–18, for which Pliny did have available writings by Cato which were relevant to his topics. Indeed in his own introductory summary in book 1 Pliny indicates Cato as one of his sources for only four of the thirteen medical books, which suggests that even allowing for inaccuracies on Pliny's part Cato cannot have figured prominently in this field. Furthermore, those few remedies which Pliny does cite as derived from Cato are all to be found in the *De agricultura*, which suggests that the small groups of medical recipes in that work were the only such items by Cato available to Pliny. This general picture is strengthened also by a statement Pliny makes at 25. 4. Commenting that the medicinal use of herbs was a topic long neglected by Roman writers, he observes that Cato 'merely touched on a few matters, not omitting the treatment of cattle also', 'paucis dumtaxat attigit, boum etiam medicina non omissa.' This is an entirely apt description of what is to be found in the *De agricultura*, but hardly of what may reasonably be supposed to have been in either the private *commentarius* or in an alleged complete book *ad filium* devoted to medical matters; which in turn suggests that no such books were available to Pliny.[7] So far as the *ad filium* is concerned that would surely mean either that Pliny did not have access to a copy and was citing from it only at second hand, or that it did not contain an extended exposition *de medicina*. Since Pliny cites

---

[7] That Pliny had access to the *commentarius* is held by Schönberger, 'Versuch der Gewinnung eines Cato-Fragmentes', *Philologus*, 113 (1969), 283 ff. He argues first that in *Nat. hist.* 20. 80 ff. Pliny's account of Cato's opinions about cabbage has some elements which are not in the *De agricultura* and therefore is drawn from another work by Cato; but when account is taken of Pliny's paraphrasing the only substantial item which is in question is 'tantamque esse vim ut qui terat haec validiorem fieri se sentiat'—which could well be a joke about Cato's extravagant claims for his universal panacea. Schönberger also argues that the words 'quem nos per genera usus sui digerimus' in 29. 15 mean that Pliny incorporated the contents of the *commentarius* in his own work, distributing the particular remedies according to his own arrangement of subjects. Leo, *Gesch. der röm. Literatur* i. 279 n. 1, though uncertain about the precise meaning of the clause, also took it to indicate that Pliny knew the *commentarius* (as did Reuther, *De Catonis de agri cult. vestigiis apud Graecos*, pp. 31 f., wrongly identifying it with the extant *De agricultura*). Mazzarino, *Introduzione*, pp. 21 ff., esp. 28 f., rightly emphasizes the incompatibility between this interpretation and the comment in *Nat. hist.* 25. 4, as well as the improbability of the private *commentarius* surviving to be available to Pliny, and the fact that its very existence is known only from Cato's own reference to it in his *ad filium*. Nor am I convinced by the principal contention of Schönberger's article, that another fragment of Cato, probably from the *commentarius*, is preserved in Gargilius Martialis, 30.

from the *ad filium* in three separate passages (one of them far removed from the medical books)[8] it seems more likely that he did have access to a copy, and therefore that there was no extended exposition of remedies.

It seems then that the evidence of Pliny does nothing to provide a sound basis for the hypothesis of a book *ad filium de medicina*, indeed that it actually suggests that the book cited by Pliny as *ad filium* did not have that specialized character. In view of the total inadequacy of the other evidence and the curious features it exhibits, the only reasonable conclusion seems to be to abandon the hypothesis itself.

There remains the supposed book on agriculture. For this the case is stronger, resting on two main points: first, there are some fragments with a markedly agricultural content which do not correspond to anything in the extant *De agricultura*; second, Servius comments upon a sentiment in Vergil, 'hoc etiam Cato ait in libris ad filium de agri cultura.'[9] Even so, there are some difficulties similar to those which arise in respect of the supposed books on rhetoric and medicine. To start with, the character of the extant *De agricultura*, in one book, makes it difficult to believe that Cato composed for his son a much longer work on the same subject, in two or more books. Hence scholars have often felt obliged to place a rather forced interpretation upon the words of Servius cited above, taking *libri ad filium* as the title of the 'encyclopedia' and *de agricultura* as that of the particular book to which Servius is referring. It would be equally plausible and perhaps preferable to suppose that *de agricultura* refers to the subject not of the book but only of this particular fragment, which is how one must interpret the similar *de validis ad filium* with which Pliny, *Nat. hist.* 7. 171, designates a fragment usually assigned to the supposed *De medicina*. Again, of the eight fragments assigned by Jordan to this heading three (10, 11, 13) have no indication at all of title or addressee; of the five attested as directed to Marcus only the one has the designation *de agricultura* and of these same five one (6) is designated *in oratione ad filium* and another (7) *in praeceptis ad filium*. All of the eight fragments could have found a reasonably appropriate place in a work on agriculture, but most could equally easily have come from a collection of *dicta* or of general exhortations; and three (10, 12, 13) with no special agricultural content have evidently been placed under this heading simply because it seemed the most appropriate of the three postulated topics of the 'encyclopedia'. Furthermore it is remarkable and suggestive that although, as has been seen, the elder Pliny quotes from the *ad filium* and almost certainly had access to a copy, virtually all the numerous remarks on agricultural topics which he attributes to Cato could have been derived from the extant *De agricultura*.[10]

---

[8] *Nat. hist.* 7. 171; 28. 260 (author but no title, but corresponds closely to fr. 3 *ad filium*); 29. 14 f.

[9] Servius ad Verg. *Georg.* 2. 412. Jordan, pp. 78 f., cites the 'agricultural' fragments as 6–13.

[10] p. 193 n. 30.

In some respects then even the supposed *De agricultura* relates somewhat awkwardly to the evidence; the hypothesis of a book on rhetoric, for which the positive evidence is very slender, relates still more awkwardly; while the hypothesis of a book *ad filium de medicina* lacks all positive attestation, imposes a forced interpretation on some of the supposed citations, and is contradicted by certain evidence some of which actually suggests that such a book probably never existed. The obvious conclusion to be drawn from all this is that the basic hypothesis of an 'encyclopedia', itself entirely without positive attestation, is unsatisfactory. What seems to be needed is a more modest appraisal of the evidence and fewer conjectural elaborations.

The principal considerations of which account has to be taken are as follows:

(*i*) There is a significant number of fragments attested as addressed by Cato to his son, mostly so indicated by the phrase *Cato ad filium*, and evidently distinct from the fragments of a letter (or letters).

(*ii*) In respect of their subject-matter the fragments show considerable variation and appear to touch on a wide range of topics; no obvious coherence emerges.

(*iii*) Five of the fragments have no more specific indication of the title or nature of the parent work than *ad filium*, but those six which either do have or can be linked to such indications show marked variations, as set out above, and no two are alike. (Two of these six (3, 4) are each found in two separate passages, but in each case the indication occurs once only.)

(*iv*) Most of the fragments have a markedly didactic or hortatory tone, and several are briskly epigrammatic. While the modern notion that the contents of the *ad filium* were regarded in antiquity as 'oracular' in manner has only a tenuous basis,[11] Nonius' phrase *in praeceptis* (fr. 7) is certainly apposite to the majority of fragments, as has often been recognized.

One further point of considerable importance is so far unresolved: whether there was one book *ad filium* or more than one. The existence of several books is one possible explanation for the variations in designation, and as can be seen above Servius does twice use the plural *libri*. On the other hand in another passage, almost certainly referring to the same work by Cato, Servius himself

---

[11] The passages most frequently cited are Pliny, *Nat. hist.* 29. 14 (fr. 1, cited above) and 7. 171 (fr. 5); but in the first of these Cato himself introduces the image of the *vates* to strengthen the impact of the particular prediction he is making; and in the second the idea of the oracle has clearly been introduced by Pliny because Cato, addressing the son who was to die comparatively early, comments on a characteristic supposed to point to early death. Seneca, *Controv.* i, *praef.* 9, describes Cato's definition of an orator (fr. 14) as 'the voice not of Cato but of an oracle'. Otherwise Pliny twice (*Nat. hist.* 18. 174 and 200) refers in such terms to quotations from the *De agricultura*, and Columella once to a dictum without specifying the source, while Julius Victor terms as 'praeceptum paene divinum' a fragment (15) listed by Jordan as from the *ad filium*, though the source is not actually attested. Thus there is only slender evidence that such terms were a widespread reaction to Cato's manner of expression or were especially induced by the *ad filium*.

uses the phrase *in oratione ad filium*; no other source gives any indication of more than one book;[12] and since none of the variations in designation occurs more than once they could be accounted for equally well, and probably better, if the work lacked any title beyond *ad filium* and its contents were miscellaneous in character, though with particularly frequent reference to certain topics. It is therefore quite possible and on balance more likely that there was only one book and that Servius' use of the plural is the result of loose or careless writing—just as Vegetius once uses the plural *libri* of Cato's *De re militari*, whereas other evidence leaves no reasonable doubt that there was only one book.[13]

The facts appear to call for a relatively simple explanation, broadly along the lines already suggested by Mazzarino:[14] that Cato addressed to his son a collection, probably in one book, of precepts, exhortations, instructions, and observations, some in the form of pithy sayings, others perhaps more extended; that the primary emphasis was on practical affairs; that to judge from the extant *De agricultura*, there was probably no rigid and strictly systematic grouping by subject-matter, though it is reasonable to assume a natural tendency for items in particular fields to occur in rough groups simply as the result of the association of ideas, and also to assume that certain broad topics tended to be the subject of a fairly large proportion of the precepts. Probably the only title was *ad filium*, and individuals quoting from it added descriptive phrases such as 'in the precepts', 'in the discourse' (*in oratione*), or perhaps even *in epistula*. Diomedes' *vel de oratore* (if the text is correct) may simply reflect his awareness of a substantial number of observations regarding 'the orator', and Servius' *De agricultura* might be explained similarly, though here the explanation suggested above is perhaps more likely.

If this was indeed the character of the *ad filium*, it may well be the source of some of the many dicta and sententiae attributed to Cato without indication of provenance—including those assigned to this work by Jordan, but also others. Prime examples are the remarks about Socrates and Isocrates recorded by Plutarch in a chapter which otherwise seems to be derived entirely from the *ad filium*—remarks which would follow well in the wake of the opening sentences of fragment 1 (above).[15]

For a Roman father to make extensive use of somewhat authoritarian *praecepta* and *sententiae* in the education of a son was probably no novelty.[16] No doubt

---

[12] The opening words of fr. 1, 'dicam de istis Graecis suo loco', are often taken to indicate an intention to deal with the matter in a separate book. That inference rests, however, on the belief that the fragment is from a book devoted to medicine, and if that premiss is rejected the reference may just as well be to a later part of the same book.

[13] p. 185.   [14] *Introduzione*, ch. 2, esp. pp. 23 ff.

[15] Plut. *Cato Mai.* 23.

[16] Paulus exc. Fest. p. 82. 19L is sometimes quoted in illustration: 'sicut habetur in antiquo carmine, cum pater filio de agricultura praeciperet: "Hiberno pulvere, verno luto, grandia farra, camille, metes."' Leo, *Gesch. der röm. Literatur* i, p. 276; Mazzarino, *Introduzione*, pp. 51 f.

those imparted by Cato were distinctive by reason of his exceptional wit and his alert and perceptive intelligence; but in so far as there was real innovation in the *ad filium* it probably lay not so much in the content as in reducing a large body of precepts to writing and subsequently allowing the collection to pass into general circulation.

If the concept of a learned 'encyclopedia' must yield to that of an assemblage of hortatory precepts, other long-discussed notions must also be abandoned. On any view the range of Cato's interests and writings was wide for a Roman of his time, but he no longer appears as quite such a polymath, no longer is he to be seen as extending his intellectual and literary activity to the composition of specialized books on rhetoric and medicine. Nor does the question now arise of the extent of Greek influence behind the genesis of the 'encyclopedia', of whether the *ad filium* was an imitation and adaptation to Roman needs of a Greek model, or perhaps was an attempt to create a purely Roman substitute in a reactionary struggle against the extension of Greek methods of education. No more can the *ad filium* be rated as a major creative contribution to the forms and traditions of Roman literature, or its author as the precursor and exemplar to Varro, Celsus, and the elder Pliny. Yet there is gain as well as loss, gain above all in the coherence of the over-all picture of Cato and his achievement. The modest concept of the *ad filium* as here proposed is more in character with the authoritarian, paternalistic Roman as he appears in other contexts, more akin to the manner of the extant *De agricultura*, and more appropriate to this early phase of the development of Roman prose literature.

Additional Note to Chapter 8: Cato and Education

IT is argued in Chapter 8 that the evidence concerning Cato's attitude to the Greeks and their culture does not accord well with the long-dominant notion of Cato leading a strong opposition to the extension of Hellenic influence, or with the view that a struggle between philhellenes and 'anti-hellenes' was one of the major public and social issues of the period. Belief in an ideological division of that kind has often focused especially upon a supposed confrontation between two opposing systems of education, the traditional Roman and the 'new', much more intellectual Greek. It has been seen that Cato was indeed strongly opposed to certain important aspects of Greek παιδεία, but there is no good ground to suppose that the issue was normally seen in terms of a stark choice between two systems, rather than the accretion of Greek practices to Roman. Plutarch's assertion that Cato 'spoke slightingly of all Greek culture and training', when considered in its context, is certainly not adequate evidence for the former view.[1]

Belief in the conflict of educational ideologies both gave rise to and drew considerable support from the interpretation of Cato's *Ad filium* as a Roman version of the Greek 'encyclopedia', substituting various Roman-oriented treatises for some of those of conventional Greek type. The 'encyclopedia' is sometimes envisaged simply as an adaptation of a Greek model to Roman needs, often as an attempt to provide an ordered and comprehensive programme of specifically Roman character to compete with the attractions of the Greek. However, it is argued in Appendix 8 that such an interpretation of the *Ad filium* is misconceived and that it was probably no more than a miscellany of hortatory precepts.

The other main argument adduced for a polarizing conflict about educational methods is the contrast between the education provided for their respective sons by Cato and L. Aemilius Paullus, in both cases as described by Plutarch.[2] In this matter the relationship which was established between the families has always been an awkward feature for those who attempt to represent Cato and Paullus as champions of conflicting ideals which were a major divisive factor in Roman life; but it is the case that Plutarch reports Paullus as 'bringing up his sons in the traditional native training (παιδεία) as he himself had been brought

---

[1] See esp. pp. 176 ff.   [2] *Cato Mai.* 20. 5 ff.; *Aem.* 6. 8 f.

up, but also, and more zealously, in the Greek. For the young men were sur-
rounded not only by Greek teachers, scholars, and rhetoricians but also by
Greek sculptors, painters, overseers of horses and hounds, and instructors in
hunting.' No doubt Plutarch's own sympathies have led him to colour the
Greek element, and part of the difference from what Cato did lies in a different
attitude to the use of slaves and freedmen. Cato would not allow his son to
be taught by his *grammatistes* Chilon, but the reason stated is not that Chilon
was a Greek but that it would be wrong for the boy to be disciplined by a slave.
That there is also a more substantial difference than this is undeniable, and no
doubt some of the subsequent interests of Scipio Aemilianus are in part a
consequence of Hellenic features of his education; but still the difference concerns
the addition, not the substitution of the Greek elements. Plutarch states expressly
that Paullus' sons were educated in the traditional native way; and later, if Scipio
Aemilianus took a different view from Cato of philosophy, he was certainly
no uncritical or unrestrained philhellene such as Polybius represents A. Postumius
Albinus to have been.[3]

Finally, it should be mentioned that the belief that a cultural clash was a
major issue in public life in the period has several times been made the basis of
interpretations of the comedies of Terence; in particular the *Adelphi* has been
interpreted as a reflection of the supposed conflict of educational ideals, with
Demea approximating to Cato, Micio to Paullus.[4] In the view of the present
author such interpretations do not carry conviction, in the first place because
of the grave doubts about the basic assumption that there was a conflict of the
kind supposed, and in the second place because, although differences about the
upbringing of sons are a major element in the play, they are differences of quite
a different kind, essentially irrelevant to the supposed cultural clash. It is to be
noted also that of all Terence's plays this is the one which is supposed to adhere
most closely to its Greek model, and also that its supposed 'liberal' leanings and
mockery of Cato are not easily reconciled with the final twist to the plot.[5]

[3] Astin, *Scipio Aemilianus*, pp. 15 f.
[4] Lana, 'Terenzio e il movimento filellenico in Roma', *RFIC* 25 (1947), 44 ff. and 155 ff.;
MacKendrick, 'Demetrius of Phalerum, Cato and the Adelphoe', *RFIC* 32 (1954), 18 ff.;
Trencsényi-Waldapfel, 'Une comédie de Térence jouée aux funérailles de L. Aemilius
Paullus', *A. Ant. Hung.* 5 (1957), 129 ff.; Della Corte, *Catone censore*[2], pp. 137 ff.
[5] Attempts to demonstrate a similarity of social views between Cato and Plautus similarly
presuppose a 'traditional' anti-hellenic interpretation of Cato's attitude, as well as raising
debatable issues as regards the interpretation of Plautus: e.g. Jurewicz, 'Plautus, Cato der
ältere und die röm. Gesellschaft', *Aus der altertumwiss. Arbeit Volkspolen* (ed. Irmscher),
pp. 52 ff.; Della Corte, *Catone censore*[2], pp. 131 ff.; Grimal, 'Il Trinummus . . .', *Dioniso*, 43
(1969), 363 ff.

Notes on Some Passages in the *De agricultura* (102; 131–50; 91–2 and 128–9)

Chapter 102

It is suggested on p. 201 that occasionally an item was introduced into an irrelevant context because it was copied along with an adjacent item which was relevant and with which it was linked in a *commentarius*. The awkwardness of the prescription set out in chapter 102 is that it does not use *amurca*, and thus interrupts a sequence. However the prescription has primary reference to oxen, and the immediately following chapter, 103, is a recommendation that *amurca* be fed to cattle to keep them healthy. Thus if Cato himself was responsible for compiling the collection of uses of *amurca*, and did not simply reproduce an existing collection, the two items in 102 and 103 could have been taken together from a collection of notes concerned with the care of oxen. For another probable instance of the same process at work, see below on chapter 133. In both cases what happened is all the more understandable if Cato was making some use of an *amanuensis*, though the explanation offered here does not depend on this additional hypothesis. On this see p. 202 with n. 43.

Chapters 131 to 150

The group of chapters from 131 to 150 is of particular interest in relation to Cato's attitudes and methods in the composition of the *De agricultura*. Although at first sight the confusing arrangement of these chapters appears to stem from chance rather than from design, on closer inspection it seems possible to trace a complicated process of composition which illustrates several of the major factors at work. The exposition which follows is necessarily interpretative and may not be correct in every detail; yet it does show that the sequence is much more likely to reflect the progression of a single author's thought than haphazard compilation or subsequent interpolation or confusion.

Chapter 130 concludes a large group of chapters devoted to useful applications of various farm products. With chapter 131 Cato begins a brief section concerning some religious festivals and rites. He starts by specifying the correct time for the sacrifice for the oxen, the procedure for which is set out in 132. But to find this he evidently consulted the same source as for his calendar of operations, and he copied from it some adjacent and linked material which is not relevant to the present context. Thus, since the festival is the signal for the commencement of the spring ploughing, he follows his opening remark about the correct time with some advice on the ploughing itself; and in 133 instructions are set out for the propagation of trees by means of layering. Excepting the actual procedure for the festival as set out in 132, precisely this sequence—and much the same wording—is to be found in chapters 50. 2–52, towards the end of the 'calendar'. Then in chapter 134 Cato sets out the procedure for another festival, this time one preceding the harvest, obviously matching the pre-ploughing festival he has already described.

Here Cato evidently thought he had finished with festivals (perhaps because those which he discusses a little later were not dealt with in the same source as these two). He therefore passes to a new topic, devoting the unusually long chapter 135 to advice as to where to purchase certain commodities and to recommendations about the dimensions of various equipment. There can be little doubt that all of this is based on records of acquisitions for his own properties. Since the following items, in chapters 136–7, are sample contracts it is at least plausible that the choice of contracts as the next topic was determined by their presence in the same set of notes as the records of the acquisitions. At this point however Cato recollected several further religious items, which are set out in 138–41, interrupting the sequence concerned with contracts. It is possible that something quite accidental or external brought these additional items to his attention, but it is at least equally possible that his recollection was triggered by the reference to oxen (*boves*) in the contract in 137; for 138 opens with an instruction about oxen (*boves* is the first word) on festival days.[1]

These additional religious items led Cato into a further digression. Two of them and especially the last, in chapter 141, envisage parts of the ceremonies being performed on the instructions of the *dominus* by someone else, almost certainly his *vilicus*.[2] This prompted thoughts about the *vilicus* and a realization that nothing had been said previously about the *vilica*; so in 142 Cato briefly recalls the instructions set out for the *vilicus* in 5 and proceeds in 143 to give further instructions which relate to the duties of the *vilica*. Then in 144–50 he returns to the contracts which he began to set out in 136 and from which he digressed after 137.

Chapters 91–2 and 128–9

Chapter 91 is virtually identical to 129, and 92 is very similar to 128. 91–2 are the first in the group concerned with the uses of *amurca*, being concerned respectively with making a threshing-floor and making a mixture for plastering a granary. Chapters 128–9 are separated from that group by chapters devoted to

[1] Another possible indication of the continuity of thought is the reference to a preliminary oblation to Ianus and Iuppiter in 141. 2. Petersmann, 'Zu einem altrömischen Opferritual', *RhM* 116 (1973), 241, suggests that it presupposes an awareness of details given in 134.

[2] *De agr.* 139 and 141. However Petersmann, op. cit., p. 239, is certainly correct in arguing that the name Manius in 141 is for illustration only and has no reference to a particular person, despite attempts to link it with the name Manlius in 144 and 152 and to infer that Cato had a *vilicus* of that name.

wine and other products, but are followed by another chapter specifying a use for *amurca*. Clearly 128–9 are part of what was in some sense a supplementary list: the only question is whether it was added by Cato himself or by someone later, presumably first as a marginal gloss. In either case it has to be explained why two of the three items should repeat formulas already given at the very start of the '*amurca* section'. There is also the curious fact that in the supplementary list these two formulas are given in reverse order. That is indeed a significant point, for in that section the formula which comes first is the one which differs from the earlier version more substantially than does its partner. More precisely, chapter 92 begins 'To keep weevils and mice from injuring grain', and although that idea does recur in 128, the purpose stated at the beginning of that version is 'To plaster a dwelling'. The formula for the plaster is the same, but the principal application is different, and it is the application which introduces the chapter in each case. It is this difference which has led to the repetition, the formula in 129 being repeated simply because in some source it was closely linked with the other. And that is just as likely to have been done by Cato himself as by some later annotator—indeed more likely. For given the difference in stated application the likely explanation for the very close similarity in the formulas and in the vocabulary used in each place is that the same formulas had been recorded in two different *commentarii* of Cato's, perhaps from different farms, perhaps compiled for different purposes.

Cato's Priorities in *De agricultura* 1. 7

THE first chapter of the *De agricultura* contains advice on the considerations to be borne in mind when buying a farm. At the end of the chapter Cato writes:

If you ask me what is the best kind of farm (*praedium quod primum siet*) I will say this: a hundred *iugera* of land, comprising every sort of soil (*de omnibus agris*) and in an excellent situation: a vineyard is first, provided it produces much wine; in second place is a watered garden; in third an osier-bed; in fourth an olive-yard; in fifth a meadow; in sixth grain land (*campus frumentarius*); in seventh woodland for foliage; in eighth an orchard [or possibly 'a vineyard trained on trees'; *arbustum*]; in ninth an acorn wood.[1]

Since Cato here places nine items in an order of priority[2] the questions which immediately present themselves are 'What is the criterion of comparison?' and 'On how sound a basis are the priorities determined?' It seems clear that the starting-point is the hypothesis of the 100 *iugera* farm with every kind of soil: thus it is reasonable to expect that what follows is a ranking of the different elements which are expected to be within that farm. The criterion which Cato is usually supposed to be applying is the relative profitability of the various items, and that indeed is how Varro and Pliny seem to have understood the passage.[3] Since Cato's subsequent account envisages several of the items as producing only crops for consumption on the farm, i.e. not cash crops the value of which would be established by sale, such an interpretation might suggest that Cato thought in quite sophisticated terms about the contribution of each to the over-all profit of the farm. Such a conclusion, however, immediately encounters formidable objections, not least the glaring weaknesses which Finley has pointed out in a ranking intended to be on such a basis: 'no consideration of the location of the farm with respect to available markets or to export possibilities; nothing about the nature of the soil beyond the single phrase, "if the wine is good and the yield is great"; no cost accounting of even a rudimentary nature.'[4] It is not even possible to save part of this by pointing to the introductory hypothesis of all kinds of soil and an excellent location and suppos-

---

[1] *De agr.* 1. 7.

[2] Salomon's attempt to avoid the difficulties of the passage by the assumption that no order of priority is intended is patently impossible: 'Essai sur les structures agraires', in *Recherches d'hist. économique*, pp. 46 ff., rejecting an even more unlikely explanation by Sergeenko.

[3] Varro, *De re rust.* 1. 7. 9 f.; 1. 8. 1; Pliny, *Nat. hist.* 17. 176; 18. 26 ff.

[4] *The Ancient Economy*, p. 111. Finley follows the reading *si vino bono et multo est*, but the words *bono et* are omitted by Mazzarino from the Teubner text.

ing the ranking is based on the premiss that these are ideal; for then the qualification about the yield from the vineyard is nonsense. Furthermore, the fact is that Cato did not have at his disposal accounting techniques anywhere near adequate to make meaningful comparisons of profitability in this way, let alone to make a sensible ranking of no less than nine items.[5]

In the context a possible way out of this might be to suppose that Cato was thinking not so much of quantifiable profitability but of general usefulness. The buyer should bear these items in mind in order of importance or usefulness when he is inspecting a farm: thus if the seventh or eighth item were lacking or of poor quality or size it would matter less than if it were the second or third. But there is another objection which this explanation meets no better than the first; it is in fact a difficulty about the very notion of the list as setting out priorities within the 100-*iugera* farm. For the list itself then conflicts with the actual organization of his farms that Cato envisages in subsequent chapters. Three items —the garden, the *arbustum*, and the acorn wood—do not reappear in connection with those farms; and the garden and *arbustum* are particularly significant, for while they have no role in the farms which are the major interest, such as the vineyard which heads this list, they both figure prominently in the 'suburban farm'. Furthermore, the high ranking of the osier-bed is surprising in view of what is said later.[6]

At first sight this seems to point to another possibility, as does the stated condition for the primacy of the vineyard in the list. For what is the effect on the list if the condition is not met? Does the second item, the garden, then become first? In so far as the garden itself is concerned, that would be compatible with the importance given to the garden on a suburban farm provided it is close to a town. But that would imply that the list ranks the items according to quite a different criterion from that envisaged above: each item is being compared as a source of profit in its own right—'If it is not possible to obtain a vineyard with the best soils and location, the next most profitable would be a garden which does meet these conditions', and so on. If this were correct the listing of pasturage in fifth place would be particularly striking, especially in contrast to the dictum in Cic. *De off.* 2. 89.[7] However, this interpretation too seems out of the question. Quite apart from the questionable ability of Cato to make so many meaningful comparisons, and the extraordinary position of the olive-yard in fourth place despite its subsequent prominence in the *De agricultura*, there are two decisive objections. It is incredible that Cato should have envisaged some of these items in a primary role; and this criterion is irreconcilable with the words with which Cato introduces the list.

[5] Mickwitz, 'Economic Rationalism in Graeco-Roman Agriculture', *Eng. Hist. Review* 52 (1937), 577 ff. As it happens Varro, *De re rust.* 1. 7. 10 and 1. 8. 1, queries whether Cato is correct even to put the vineyard in first place, on the ground that some think the profits are consumed by high expenses.

[6] *De agr.* 7. 1; 8. 2; 9.   [7] p. 249.

The conclusion seems inescapable. Cato simply did not think clearly and precisely what he was doing or what his list meant; he did not distinguish properly in his own mind between priority within a particular farm and the relative merits of different kinds of farms, so that the list is a muddle of both; and in neither case did he have any clear—let alone sound—criterion in mind. The list therefore does the very opposite of indicating sophisticated economic thought and it has no value as reliable evidence for the economic realities of Cato's Italy. It is however an indication of his unsystematic method of composition, since there is no clear considered relationship between it and the advice which follows.

APPENDIX 12

Three Passages concerning Cato's Treatment of Slaves[1]

(*i*) The mention of reducing the food allowance of sick slaves is found in *De agr.* 2. 4. The chapter instructs the owner on what to do when he visits the farm. After inspecting it he compares the work which should have been done with what has actually been done. If there is a discrepancy it is assumed the *vilicus* will offer excuses (2. 2): 'he has acted diligently, [but] slaves have not been well, the weather has been bad, slaves have run away, he has carried out public work.' Sections 3 and 4 contain the answers with which the owner will 'recall him to the reckoning': (*a*) in wet weather jobs which could be done in the rain should have been done—and a list is given; (*b*) on *feriae* various jobs, including mending the public road, could have been done; (*c*) when slaves were sick such large food allowances should not have been given: 'cum servi aegrotarint, cibaria tanta dari non oportuisse'. The owner is to deal with all this calmly, *aequo animo*.

It is obvious that each of the excuses is picked up in the answers, except the runaway slaves, who are difficult to comment on. Indeed the spirit of the passage seems to be that the *vilicus'* excuses must be countered; the owner must keep the upper hand and not give the impression that he will accept excuses. Hence it is necessary to find something to say about the slaves, though assuming the sickness to have been genuine it is not possible to saying anything truly *ad rem*; hence the point about reduced allowances is brought in. It is possible that such reductions were normally required by Cato, but the artificial role of the remark in this contrived context is such that it may be a mistake to take it seriously as evidence for Cato's normal principle and practice. It is suggestive, though not decisive, that there is no mention of such reductions in *De agr.* 56, where the normal allowances are set out.

(*ii*) Reference to the sale of elderly and sickly slaves occurs at the end of the same chapter, 2. 7, where advice about the visit concludes with a recommendation to hold a sale: 'auctionem uti faciat: vendat oleum, si pretium habeat; vinum frumentum quod supersit, vendat; boves vetulos, armenta delicula, oves deliculas, lanam, pelles, plostrum vetus, ferramenta vetera, servum senem, servum morbosum, et si quid aliut supersit, vendat. patrem familias vendacem, non emacem esse oportet.'

[1] See pp. 264 f.

The rhetorical momentum of the passage is evident (perhaps even more so when read in its full context), building up to the concluding aphorism. A list of possible items is amassed for effect, and it is at least as likely that Cato was thinking around for items to put in as that he was stating a carefully considered policy. Undoubtedly he did at times sell off sickly and old slaves, but such a passage is not strong evidence that it was a practice pursued regularly, systematically, and ruthlessly on his farms.

(*iii*) The fourth chapter of Plutarch's *Life* of Cato is concerned with various austerities which he is said to have practised. In 4.5 Plutarch says that according to Cato himself 'he never paid more than 1,500 drachmas (= *denarii*?) for a slave, since he wanted not the young and dainty but the hard-working and sturdy, such as grooms and herdsmen; and these he thought it necessary to sell when they became rather old and not to feed them when they were useless.'

This last comment, which Plutarch thought disgraceful, again leaves no doubt that on occasion Cato sold off elderly slaves—the more so because it is virtually certain that it was not taken by Plutarch from the *De agricultura* and therefore that Cato twice referred to the selling of such slaves. However, this passage too needs to be treated with some caution. It is pointed out elsewhere that some of the other comments which come in the same sequence as this originated in one of Cato's speeches in defence of himself, probably the *De sumptu suo*;[2] and it is very likely that the present passage also originated there. Thus it is probably from a context in which Cato had every incentive to emphasize his austerity as forcefully and dramatically as possible. Furthermore, as also is pointed out elsewhere, the antithesis between dainty young slaves and Cato's purchase of tough teamsters is rhetorical and misleading,[3] so that the organically related remark about selling elderly slaves may reasonably be suspected of itself being influenced by rhetorical requirements. Overstatement is more probable than not, so that this passage too proves to be weak evidence for regular and systematic practice.

[2] p. 92.   [3] pp. 261 f.

Bibliography

THIS bibliography lists primarily books and articles cited in footnotes, excepting (i) a few peripheral items, (ii) items listed under 'Abbreviations' (p. xi). Some other items have been included, but the literature pertaining to Cato is vast and there is therefore a strong subjective element in the selection. In particular most of the numerous articles dealing with textual, linguistic, or technical aspects of the *De agricultura* have been omitted. Works in Russian, Polish, and Romanian have not been consulted directly.

ADCOCK, F. E., 'Delenda est Carthago', *CHJ* 8 (1944–6), 117 ff.

AFZELIUS, A., *Die römische Kriegsmacht während der Auseinandersetzung mit den hellenistischen Grossmächten*, Copenhagen, 1944.

AGNEW, M. E., 'A Numbered Legion in a Fragment of the Elder Cato', *AJPh* 60 (1939), 214 ff.

ALBERTARIO, E., 'Contratti agrari nel De agri cultura di Catone', *Rivista di diritto agrario*, Jan.–Mar. 1936, 2 ff.

ALBRECHT, M. von, *Meister römischer Prosa von Cato bis Apuleius*, Heidelberg, 1971.

ALFÖLDI, A., *Early Rome and the Latins*, Ann Arbor, 1965.

ALFONSI, L., 'Catone il Censore e l'umanesimo romano', *PP* 9 (1954), 161 ff.

ALLBUTT, T. C., *Greek Medicine in Rome*, London, 1921.

ALMAGRO, M., *Las fuentes escritas referentes a Ampurias*, Barcelona, 1951.

ARCANGELI, A., 'I contratti agrari nel *de agri cultura* di Catone', *Studi ded. alla mem. di P. P. Zanzucchi* (Milan, 1927), pp. 67 ff.

ASTIN, A. E., 'Scipio Aemilianus and Cato Censorius', *Latomus*, 15 (1956), 159 ff.

—— *The Lex Annalis before Sulla*, Collection Latomus XXXII, Brussels, 1958.

—— *Scipio Aemilianus*, Oxford, 1967.

—— *Politics and Policies in the Roman Republic* (Inaugural lecture), Belfast, 1968.

—— 'Cato Tusculanus and the Capitoline Fasti', *JRS* 62 (1972), 20 ff.

BAADER, G., 'Der ärtzliche Stande in der römischen Republik', *Acta Conventus XI Eirene* (Warsaw, 1971), pp. 7 ff.

BADIAN, E., *Foreign Clientelae (264–70 B.C.)*, Oxford, 1958.

—— 'Rome and Antiochus the Great. A Study in Cold War', *CPh* 54 (1959), 81 ff. (= *Studies in Greek and Roman History* (Oxford, 1964), pp. 112 ff.).

—— 'The Early Historians', *Latin Historians* (London, 1966; ed. T. A. Dorey), pp. 1 ff.

—— 'Ennius and his Friends', *Ennius*, Fondation Hardt, *Entretiens* xvii (Geneva, 1972), pp. 149 ff.

—— *Publicans and Sinners*, Oxford, 1972.

BALSDON, J. P. V. D., 'L. Cornelius Scipio: a Salvage Operation', *Historia*, 21 (1972), 224 ff.

BARWICK, K., 'Zu den Schriften des Cornelius Celsus und des alten Cato', *WJA* 3 (1948), 117 ff.

BAUMAN, R. A., 'The Lex Valeria de Provocatione of 300 B.C.', *Historia*, 22 (1973), 34 ff.

BAUMGART, M. O., *Untersuchungen zu den Reden des M. Porcius Cato Censorius*, Breslau, 1905.

BELL, M. J. V., 'Tactical Reform in the Roman Republican Army', *Historia*, 14 (1965), 404 ff.

BELOCH, K. J., 'Der römische Kalender von 218–168', *Klio*, 15 (1918), 382 ff.

BESANÇON, A., *Les Adversaires de l'hellénisme à Rome pendant la période républicaine*, Paris and Lausanne, 1910.

BICKERMAN, E. J., 'Origines Gentium', *CPh* 47 (1952), 65 ff.

BILLETER, G., *Geschichte des Zinsfusses im griechisch-römischen Altertum bis auf Justinian*, Leipzig, 1898.

BILZ, K., *Die Politik des P. Cornelius Scipio Aemilianus*, Stuttgart, 1936.

BIRT, T., 'Zum Proöm und den Summarien der Catonischen Schrift *de agri cultura*', *BPhW* 29 (1915), 922 ff.

BÖMER, F., 'Naevius und Fabius Pictor', *SO* 29 (1952), 34 ff.

—— 'Thematik und Krise der römischen Geschichtsschreibung im 2. Jahrhundert v. Chr.', *Historia*, 2 (1953), 189 ff.

BORMANN, A., *M. Porcii Catonis Originum libri septem*, Brandenburg, 1858.

BOSCHERINI, S., 'Grecismi nel libro di Catone De agri cultura', *A & R* 4 (1959), 145 ff.

—— *Lingua e scienza greca nel 'De agri cultura' di Catone*, Rome, 1970.

—— 'Due probabili cachi greci in Catone', *I debattiti del Circ. ling. Fiorentino 1945–1970* (Florence, 1970; ed. Mille), pp. 27 ff.

BOSCH GIMPERA, P., *see* Schulten, A.

BOUCHÉ-LECLERCQ, A., *Histoire des Lagides*, 4 vols., Paris, 1903–7.

BREHAUT, E., *Cato the Censor. On Farming*, New York, 1933.

BRISCOE, J., 'Eastern Policy and Senatorial Politics, 168–146 B.C.', *Historia*, 18 (1969), 49 ff.

—— A Commentary on Livy, Books XXXI–XXXIII, Oxford, 1973.

BROCKMEYER, N., *Arbeitsorganisation und ökonomisches Denken in der Gutswirtschaft des römischen Reiches*, Bochum, 1968.

BROWN, T. S., *Timaeus of Tauromenium*, Berkeley, 1958.

BRUNT, P. A., *Italian Manpower 225 B.C.–A.D. 14*, Oxford, 1971.

CAPITANI, U., 'Catone, De agricultura, cap. 160', *Maia*, 20 (1968), 31 ff.

CHABERT, S., 'Le "delenda Carthago" et ses origines', *Annales de l'Université de Grenoble*, 25 (1913), 49 ff.

CIMA, A., *L'eloquenza latina prima di Cicerone*, Rome, 1903.

CLARKE, M. L., *Rhetoric at Rome²*, London, 1962.

COLIN, G., *Rome et la Grèce de 200 à 146 av. J.-C.*, Paris, 1905.

CORBETT, P. E., *The Roman Law of Marriage*, Oxford, 1930.

CORNELL, T. J., 'The *Origines* of Cato and the non-Roman Historical Tradition about Ancient Italy', Unpublished doctoral thesis accepted by the University of London in 1972.

—— 'Notes on the Sources for Campanian History in the Fifth Century B.C.', *MH* 31 (1974), 193 ff.

COVA, P. V., 'Livio e la repressione dei Baccanali', *Athenaeum*, n.s. 52 (1974), 82 ff.

CROOK, J. A., *Law and Life of Rome*, London, 1967.

—— 'Intestacy in Roman Society', *Proceedings of the Cambridge Philological Society*, 199 (n.s. 19) (1973), 38 ff.

CUGUSI, P., *Epistolographi Latini Minores* i. 1 & 2, Turin, 1970.

CURCIO, G., *La primitiva civiltà latina agricola e il libro dell'agricoltura di M. Porcio Catone*, Florence, 1929.

DELLA CORTE, F., 'Catone Maggiore e i *Libri ad Marcum filium*', *RFIC* 19 (1941), 81 ff.

—— *Plutarch. Detti e vita di Catone*, Turin, 1952.

—— *Catone censore. La vita e la fortuna*[2], Florence, 1969.

DEL MORO, I., 'Le guerre dei Romani nella Spagna dalla fine della II Punica alla metà del secondo secolo a. Cr.', *Atti della R. Università di Genova*, 20 (1913), 319 ff.

DEL POZZO, F., *Il console M. Porcio Catone in Spagna nel 195 a. C.*, Vicenza, 1921 (not seen).

DEROW, P. S., 'The Roman Calendar, 190–168 B.C.', *Phoenix*, 27 (1973), 345 ff.

DE SANCTIS, G., *Storia dei Romani*, 4 vols., Turin and Florence, 1953–68.

DOHR, H., *Die italischen Gutshöfe nach den Schriften Catos und Varros*, Cologne, 1965.

DOUGLAS, A. E., *M. Tulli Ciceronis Brutus*, Oxford, 1966.

ELMER, H. C., '*Que, et, atque* in the Inscriptions of the Republic, in Terence, and in Cato', *AJPh* 8 (1887), 292 ff.

ERRINGTON, R. M., *The Dawn of Empire: Rome's Rise to World Power*, London, 1971.

FABBRI, P., 'Perchè Catone ritenesse ingiurioso l'appellativo di "opici" ', *BFC* 30 (1923), 105 f.

FATÁS CABEZA, G., 'Sobre Suessetanos y Sedetanos', *AEA* 44 (1971), 109 ff.

FINLEY, M. I., *The Ancient Economy*, London, 1973.

FLACELIÈRE, R., 'Le troisième remords de Caton', *REG* 80 (1967), 195 ff.

FORNI, G., 'Manio Curio Dentato uomo democratico', *Athenaeum*, n.s. 31 (1953), 170 ff.

FOUCHER, A., 'La vie rurale à l'époque de Caton d'après le *De agricultura*', *BAGB* 1957. 2, pp. 41 ff.

FRACCARO, P., 'Sulla biografia di Catone Maggiore sino al consolato e le sue fonti', *Atti e mem. dell'Accad. Virgiliana di Mantova* 3 (1910), 99 ff. = *Opuscula* i. 139 ff. (with two additional excursuses).

—— 'Le fonti per il consolato di M. Porcio Catone', *Studi storici per l'antichità classica*, 3 (1910), 129 ff. = *Opuscula* i. 177 ff.

—— 'Catoniana', *Studi storici per l'antichità classica*, 3 (1910), 241 ff. = *Opuscula* i. 227 ff.

—— 'L'orazione di Catone "de sumtu suo" ', *Studi storici per l'antichità classica*, 3 (1910), 378 ff. = *Opuscula* i. 257 ff.

—— 'Sull'orazione di Catone Maggiore "de lustri sui felicitate" ', *BFC* 17 (1910–11), 59 ff.

Fraccaro, P., 'Ricerche storiche e letterarie sulla censura del 184–183 (M. Porcio Catone L. Valerio Flacco)', *Studi storici per l'antichità classica*, 4 (1911), 1 ff. = *Opuscula* i. 417 ff.

—— 'I processi degli Scipioni', *Studi storici per l'antichità classica*, 4 (1911), 217 ff. = *Opuscula* i. 263 ff.

—— 'Catone il Censore in Tito Livio', *Studi Liviani* (Rome, 1934; L'Ist. di Studi Romani), pp. 209 ff. = *Opuscula* i. 115 ff.

—— 'Ancora sui processi degli Scipioni', *Athenaeum* ,27 (1939), 3 ff. = *Opuscula* i. 393 ff.

—— *Opuscula*, 3 vols., Pavia, 1956–7.

Fraenkel, E., *Leseproben aus Reden Ciceros und Catos*, Rome, 1968.

Frank, T., 'On Rome's Conquest of Sabinum, Picenum and Etruria', *Klio*, 11 (1911), 365 ff.

—— *Roman Imperialism*, New York, 1914.

—— 'The Bacchanalian Cult of 186 B.C.', *CQ* 21 (1927), 128 ff.

—— *Life and Literature in the Roman Republic*, Berkeley, 1930.

—— 'An Interpretation of Cato, Agricultura, 136' *AJPh* 54 (1933), 162 ff.

Frezza, P., 'I formulari catoniani e le forme della protezione del creditore pignoratizio', *Studi E. Betti* ii (Milan, 1962), 433 ff.

Gabba, E., 'Considerazioni sulla tradizione letteraria sulle origini della Repubblica', *Les Origines de la république romaine*, Fondation Hardt, *Entretiens* xiii (Geneva, 1966), pp. 133 ff.

Gagé, J., 'La rogatio Petillia et le procès de P. Scipion', *RPh* 27 (1953), 34 ff.

Gelzer, M., 'Nasicas Widerspruch gegen die Zerstörung Karthagos', *Philologus*, 86 (1931), 261 ff. = *Kleine Schriften* ii (Wiesbaden, 1963), 39 ff.

Gentilli, G., 'Catoniana', *A & R* 7 (1904), cols. 298 ff.

Gerosa, M., *La prima enciclopedia romana. I 'libri ad Marcum filium' di Catone Censore*, Pavia, 1910.

Gnauk, R., *Die Bedeutung des Marius und Cato maior für Cicero*, Berlin, 1936.

Götzfried, K., *Annalen der röm. Provinzen beider Spanien 218–154*, Erlangen, 1907.

Goujard, R., 'Politio, politor (Caton, Agr. 136)', *RPh* 44 (1970), 84 ff.

Gouron, A., 'Gage confirmatoire et gage pénitential en droit romain', *RD* 39 (1961), 5 ff. and 197 ff.

Grandis, A., 'A proposito dei giudizi del Mommsen sull'opera letteraria di Catone', *A & R* 20 (1917), 203 ff.

Grimal, P., 'Encyclopédies antiques', *CHM* 9 (1965–6), 459 ff.

—— 'Il Trinummus e gli albori della filosofia in Roma', *Dioniso*, 43 (1969), 363 ff.

Grosso, F., 'Il caso di Pleminio', *GIF* 5 (1952), 119 ff. and 234 ff.

Grosso, G., 'Il fr. 77 D 17, 2 e i formulari di locazioni del *De agri cultura* di Catone', *SDHI* 3 (1937), 440 ff.

Gruen, E. S., 'Rome and Rhodes in the Second Century B.C.', *CQ* n.s. 25 (1975), 58 ff.

Gsell, S., *Histoire ancienne de l'Afrique du Nord*, iii and vii, Paris, 1918 and 1928.

Guite, H. F., 'Cicero's Attitude to the Greeks', *G & R* 9 (1962), 142 ff.

GUMMERUS, H., *Der römische Gutsbetrieb als wirtschaftlicher Organismus nach den Werken des Cato, Varro und Columella, Klio*, Beiheft 5, Leipzig, 1906.

GUTSCHMID, A. von, 'Catos Origines', *Kleine Schriften* v (Leipzig, 1894), 518 ff.

HAFFTER, H., *Römische Politik und römische Politiker*, Heidelberg, 1967.

HANSEN, E. V., *The Attalids of Pergamum*[2], London, 1971.

HANSSEN, J. S. Th., 'Les diminutifs chez Caton', *SO* 18 (1938), 89 ff.

HAULER, E., *Zu Catos Schrift über das Landwesen*, Vienna, 1896.

HEITLAND, W. E., *Agricola*, Cambridge, 1921.

HELLMANN, F., 'Zur Cato- und Valerius-Rede (Liv. xxxiv, 1–7)', *NJAB* 1940, 81 ff.

HENDERSON, C., 'Cato's Pine Cones and Seneca's Plums. Fronto p. 149 vdH.', *TAPhA* 86 (1955), 256 ff.

HENDRICKSON, G. L., 'Literary Sources in Cicero's Brutus and the Technique of Citation in Dialogue', *AJPh* 27 (1906), 184 ff.

HEURGON, J., 'Caton et la Gaule Cisalpine', *Mélanges d'hist. anc. offerts à W. Seston* (Paris, 1974), pp. 231 ff.

HÖRLE, J., *Catos Hausbücher: Analyse seiner Schrift De Agricultura nebst Wiederstellung seines Kelterhauses und Gutshofes*, Paderborn, 1929.

HOFFMANN, W., 'Die römische Politik des 2. Jahrhunderts und das Ende Karthagos', *Historia*, 9 (1960), 309 ff.

HOLLEAUX, M., 'Le consul M. Fulvius et le siège de Samé', *BCH* 54 (1930), 1 ff. = *Études d'épigraphie* v (Paris, 1957), 249 ff.

HOSIUS, C., see Schanz, M.

ILBERG, J., 'A. Cornelius Celsus und die Medizin in Rom', *Neue Jahrbücher*, 10 (1907), 377 ff.

JAHN, O., 'Über römische Encyclopädien', *Ber. d. Königlich Sächsischen Ges. d. Wiss., Phil.-hist. Klasse* 2 (1850), 263 ff.

JANSON, T., *Latin Prose Prefaces*, Stockholm, 1964.

JOCELYN, H. D., 'The Poems of Quintus Ennius', *Aufstieg und Niedergang* i. 2 (Berlin, 1972; ed. Temporini, H.), 987 ff.

JONES, C. P., *Plutarch and Rome*, Oxford, 1971.

JUREWICZ, O., 'De Plauto et Catone apud populum Romanum agentibus', *Meander*, 11 (1956), 437 ff. (in Polish, résumé in Latin).

—— 'Plautus, Cato der ältere und die römische Gesellschaft', *Aus der altertumswissenschaftlichen Arbeit Volkspolen* (Berlin, 1959; ed. Irmscher, J.), pp. 52 ff.

KAC, A. L., 'Le problème de l'esclavage chez Plaute et Caton', *VDI* 89 (1964), 81 ff. (in Russian).

KAHRSTEDT, U., *Die Annalistik von Livius, B. xxxi–xlv*, Berlin, 1913.

—— *Geschichte der Karthager von 218–146* (vol. iii of O. Meltzer, *Geschichte der Karthager*), Berlin, 1913.

KAMMER, U., *Untersuchungen zu Ciceros Bild von Cato Censorius*, Giessen, 1964.

KAPPELMACHER, A., 'Zum Stil Catos im De re rustica', *WS* 43 (1922–3), 168 ff.

KENNEDY, G., *The Art of Rhetoric in the Roman World*, Princeton, 1972.

KLINGNER, F., 'Cato Censorius und die Krisis des römischen Volkes', *Die Antike*, 1934, pp. 239 ff. = *Römische Geisteswelt*[5] (Munich, 1965), pp. 34 ff.

KLOTZ, A., *Livius und seine Vorgänger*, Leipzig–Berlin, 1940.

KNAPP, C., 'A Phase of the Development of Prose Writing among the Romans', *CPh* 13 (1918), 138 ff.

KÖCHLY, H., and RÜSTOW, W., *Griechische Kriegschriftsteller* ii, Leipzig, 1885.

KORNHARDT, H., 'Recipere und servus recepticius', *ZRG* 1938, pp. 162 ff.

KROMAYER, J., and VEITH, G., *Heerwesen und Kriegführung der Griechen und Römer*, Munich, 1928.

KRONASSER, H., 'Nugae Catonianae', *WS* 79 (1966), 298 ff.

KRÜGER, M., 'Die Abschaffung der lex Oppia (Liv. xxxiv, 1–8, 3)', *NJAB* 1940, pp. 65 ff.

KUZIŠCIN, V. I., 'La date du De agricultura de Caton', *VDI* 96 (1966), 54 ff. (in Russian).

LABRUNA, L., 'Plauto, Manilio, Catone. Premesse allo studio dell'emptio consensuale', *Labeo*, 14 (1968), 24 ff.

LANA, I., 'Terenzio e il movimento filellenico in Roma', *RFIC* 25 (1947), 44 ff. and 155 ff.

LEEMAN, A. D., *Orationis ratio*, 2 vols., Amsterdam, 1963.

—— 'Cato, De Agricultura 3, 1', *Helikon*, 5 (1965), 534 f.

LEO, F., *Miscella Ciceroniana*, Göttingen, 1892 = *Ausgewählte kleine Schriften* i (Rome, 1960), 301 ff.

—— *Die griechisch-römische Biographie nach ihrer literarischen Form*, Leipzig, 1901.

—— *Geschichte der römischen Literatur* i, Berlin, 1913.

LEPORE, U., 'Catoniana', *GIF* 7 (1954), 193 ff.

LINTOTT, A. W., 'Provocatio from the Struggle of the Orders to the Principate', *Aufstieg und Niedergang der römischen Welt* 1. 2 (Berlin, 1972; ed. Temporini, H.), pp. 226 ff.

—— 'Imperial Expansion and Moral Decline in the Roman Republic', *Historia*, 21 (1972), 626 ff.

LITTLE, C. E., 'The Authenticity and Form of Cato's Saying: Carthago delenda est', *CJ* 29 (1934), 429 ff.

LOŚ, S., *Rome au carrefour. Étude monographique de Caton l'Ancien*, Warsaw, 1960 (in Polish).

McDONALD, A. H., 'Scipio Africanus and Roman Politics in the Second Century B.C.', *JRS* 28 (1938), 153 ff.

—— 'Rome and the Italian Confederation (200–186 B.C.)', *JRS* 34 (1944), 11 ff.

MacKENDRICK, P., 'Demetrius of Phalerum, Cato and the Adelphoe', *RFIC* 32 (1954), 18 ff.

McSHANE, R. B., *The Foreign Policy of the Attalids of Pergamum*, Urbana, 1964.

MAGIE, D., *Roman Rule in Asia Minor*, 2 vols., Princeton, 1950.

MARCHETTI, P., 'La marche du calendrier romain de 203 à 190', *L'Antiquité classique*, 42 (1973), 473 ff.

MARCUCCI, F., *Studio critico sulle opere di Catone* i. 1, Pisa, 1902.

MARMORALE, E. V., 'Catoniana', *Paideia*, 2 (1947), 141 ff. (also in the Preface to *Cato Maior²*).

—— *Cato Maior²*, Bari, 1949.

MARÓTI, E., 'Zur Frage der Warenproduktion in Catos De Agri Cultura', *A. Ant. Hung.* 11 (1963), 215 ff.

—— 'Zum Problem der Ausgestaltung des überlieferten Cato-Bilde', *Acta Univ Debrecen. de L. Kossuth nomin.* Ser. hist. 3 (1964), 3 ff.

—— 'Feriae in familia. Zur Interpretation von Cato De agricultura c. 138', *Acta Conventus XI Eirene* (Warsaw, 1971), pp. 63 ff.

MAROUZEAU, J., 'Pour mieux comprendre les textes latins', *RPh* 45 (1921), 149 ff.

MARTIN, J., 'Die Provokation in der klassischen und späten Republik', *Hermes*, 98 (1970), 72 ff.

MARTIN, R., *Recherches sur les agronomes latins*, Paris, 1971.

MARTINO FUSCO, M. Di, 'L'ambasciata a Roma del 156 da parte di Atene per la riduzione delle riparazione', *Mous.* 1 (1923), 189 ff.

MAZZARINO, A., *Introduzione al* De agri cultura *di Catone*, Rome, 1952.

—— 'Tarquinio Prisco e la guerra coi Sabini nelle Origines di Catone', *Helikon*, 8 (1968), 444 ff.

MEISTER, R., 'Zu römischen Historikern', *AAWW* 101 (1964), 1 ff.

MELONI, P., *Perseo e la fine della monarchia macedone*, Rome, 1953.

MEO, C. de, *see* Till, R.

METRO, A., 'Il "legatum partitionis" ', *Labeo*, 9 (1963), 291 ff.

MICKWITZ, G., 'Economic Rationalism in Graeco-Roman Agriculture', *Eng. Hist. Review*, 52 (1937), 577 ff.

MIHAESCU, H., 'L'économie agricole chez Caton', *Studii și Cerc. Istorie Veche* 1 (1950), 187 ff. (in Romanian).

MOMMSEN, T., *Römisches Staatsrecht*, 3 vols., Leipzig, 1887–8.

—— *The History of Rome*, English translation by W. P. Dickson², London, 1912–13.

MORETTI, L., 'Le "Origines" di Catone, Timeo ed Eratostene', *RFIC* 30 (1952), 289 ff.

MÜNSCHER, K., *Xenophon in der griechisch-römischen Literatur. Philologus*, Supp. 13, Heft ii, Leipzig, 1920.

MÜNZER, F., *Beiträge zur Quellenkritik der Naturgeschichte des Plinius*, Berlin, 1897.

—— 'Atticus als Geschichtsschreiber', *Hermes*, 40 (1905), 50 ff.

NAP, J. M., 'Ad Catonis librum de re militari', *Mn* 55 (1927), 79 ff.

NENCI, G., 'La De bello Carthaginiensi di Catone Censore', *Critica storica*, 1 (1962), 363 ff.

NEWMAN, J. K., 'Ennius the Mystic', *G & R* 10 (1963), 132 ff.; 12 (1965), pp. 42 ff.; 14 (1967), 44 ff.

NICOLET, C., 'Polybe et les institutions romaines', *Polybe*, Fondation Hardt, *Entretiens* xx (Geneva, 1974), 209 ff.

NISSEN, H., *Kritische Untersuchungen über die Quellen der vierten und fünften Dekade des Livius*, Berlin, 1863.

NITZSCH, K. W., 'Über Catos Buch vom Landbau', *Zeitschr. f. die Altertumswiss.*, 1845, pp. 493 ff.

NORDEN, E., *Die antike Kunstprosa* i³, Leipzig, 1915.

NOVÁKOVÁ, J., 'Litibus familia supersedeat', *Studi antiqua A. Salac* (Prague, 1955), pp. 90 ff.

OATES, W. J., 'A Note on Cato, *De Agri Cultura*, LVI', *AJPh* 55 (1934), 67 ff.

OLSON, L., 'Cato's Views on the Farmer's Obligation to the Land', *Agricultural History*, 19 (1945), 129 ff.

OTTO, W., *Zur Geschichte der Zeit des 6. Ptolemäers*, Munich, 1934.

PADBERG, F., *Cicero und Cato Censorius, ein Beitrag zu Ciceros Bildungsgang*, Münster, 1933.

PAIS, E., 'L'orazione di Catone a favore della Lex Oppia', *Atti d. R. Accad. di Arch., Lett. e Belle Arti di Napoli* 1 (1910), 123 ff.

PEPE, L., 'Catone Maggiore e la scuola di Frontone', *GIF* 11 (1958), 12 ff.

PETERSMANN, H., 'Zu einem altrömischen Opferritual (Cato de agricultura c. 141)', *RhM* 116 (1973), 238 ff.

PIGHI, G. B., 'Catonis carmen de moribus', *Latinitas*, 14 (1966), 31 ff.

POUCET, J., 'Les origines mythiques des Sabins à travers l'œuvre de Caton, de Cn. Gellius, de Varron, d'Hygin et de Strabon', *Études étrusco-italiques* (Louvain, 1963), 155 ff.

PRIMMER, A., 'Der Prosarhythmus in Catos Reden', *Festschrift Karl Vretska* (Heidelberg, 1970), pp. 174 ff.

PRITCHETT, W. K., *Studies in Ancient Greek Topography* i, Berkeley and Los Angeles, 1965.

PRUGNI, G., 'Per un riesame degli arcaismi catoniani', *QIFL* 2 (1972), 25 ff.

REGIBUS, L. de, *Il processo degli Scipioni*, Turin, 1921.

—— *Il Censore e l'Africano*, Genoa, 1959.

REITZENSTEIN, R., Review of P. Weise, *Quaestionum Catonianarum Capita V, WKlPh* 1888, cols. 587 ff.

REUTHER, P., *De Catonis De agri cultura libri vestigiis apud Graecos*, Leipzig, 1903.

RIBBECK, O., 'M. Porcius Cato als Schriftsteller', *Neues schweizerischen Museum*, 1 (1861), 7 ff. = *Reden und Vorträge* (Leipzig, 1899), pp. 236 ff.

ROSENBERG, A., *Einleitung und Quellenkunde zur römischen Geschichte*, Berlin, 1921.

ROSSETTI, S., 'La Numidia e Cartagine fra la II e la III guerra punica', *PP* 15 (1960), 336 ff.

ROSSI, O., 'De Catone graecarum litterarum oppugnatore, latinitatis acerrimo defensore', *Athenaeum*, 10 (1922), 259 ff.

—— 'De Catonis dictis et apophthegmatis', *Athenaeum*, n.s. 2 (1924), 174 ff.

ROTONDI, G., *Leges Publicae Populi Romani*², Hildesheim, 1962.

ROUGÉ, J., *Recherches sur l'organisation du commerce maritime en Méditerranée sous l'empire romain*, Paris, 1966.

ROWLAND, R. J., 'Grain for Slaves. A Note on Cato, *De Agri Cultura*', *CW* 63 (1970), 229.

RUEBEL, J. S., *The Political Development of Cato Censorius. The Man and the Image*, Diss. University of Cincinnati, 1972 (pub. Univ. Microfilms, Ann Arbor).

RÜSTOW, W., *see* Köchly, H.

SAINT-DENIS, E. de, 'Caton l'Ancien vu par Cicéron', *IL* 8 (1956), 93 ff.

SAINTE-CROIX, G. E. M. de, 'Greek and Roman Accounting', *Studies in the History of Accounting* (London, 1956; edd. Littleton, A. D. and Yamey, B. S.) pp. 14 ff.

—— 'Ancient Greek and Roman Maritime Loans', *Debits, Credits, Finance and Profits. Essays in Honour of W. T. Baxter* (London, 1974; edd. Edey, H. and Yamey, B. S.), pp. 41 ff.

SALMON, E. T., *Roman Colonization under the Republic*, London, 1970.

SALOMON, P., 'Essai sur les structures agraires de l'Italie centrale au IIe siècle avant J.-C.', *Recherches d'histoire économique* (Paris, 1964), pp. 1 ff.

SANDER, E., 'Die antiqua ordinatio legionis des Vegetius', *Klio*, N.F. 14 (1939), 382 ff.

SARGENTI, M., 'Il *De agri cultura* di Catone e le origini dell'ipoteca romana', *SDHI* 22 (1956), 158 ff.

SAUMAGNE, C., 'Les prétextes juridiques de la IIIe guerre punique', *RH* 167 (1931), 225 ff. and 168 (1931), 1 ff.

SBLENDORIO, M. T., 'Note sullo stile dell'oratoria catoniana', *AFLC* 34 (1971), 5 ff.

SCALAIS, R., 'La politique agraire de Rome depuis les guerres puniques jusqu'aux Gracques', *MB* 34 (1930), 195 ff.

SCARBOROUGH, J., *Roman Medicine*, London, 1969.

SCHANZ, M., and HOSIUS, C., *Geschichte der römischen Literatur* i⁴, Munich, 1927.

SCHATZMAN, I., 'The Roman General's Authority over Booty', *Historia*, 21 (1972), 177 ff.

SCHENK, D., *Flavius Vegetius Renatus. Klio*, Beiheft 22, Wiesbaden, 1930.

SCHLAG, U., *Regnum in Senatu*, Stuttgart, 1968.

SCHMAELING, E., *Die Sittenaufsicht der Censoren*, Stuttgart, 1938.

SCHMID, B., *Studien zu griechischen Ktisissagen*, Freiburg, 1947.

SCHMID, W., and STÄHLIN, O., *Geschichte der griechischen Literatur* ii. 1⁶, Munich, 1920.

SCHMIDT, P. L., 'Catos Epistula ad M.filium und die Anfänge der römischen Briefliteratur', *Hermes*, 100 (1972), 568 ff.

SCHMITT, H. H., *Rom und Rhodos*, Munich, 1957.

SCHOELL, F., 'Vir bonus dicendi peritus', *RhM* 57 (1902), 312 ff.

SCHÖNBERGER, O., 'Der glückliche Cato', *RhM* 112 (1969), 190.

—— 'Versuch der Gewinnung eines Cato-Fragmentes', *Philologus*, 113 (1969), 283 ff.

SCHOENDOERFFER, O., *De genuina Catonis de agricultura libri forma, I. De Syntaxi Catonis*, Königsberg, 1885.

SCHRÖDER, W. A., *M. Porcius Cato. Das erste Buch der Origines*, Meisenheim am Glan, 1971.

SCHULTEN, A., *Numantia*, Berlin, 1905.

—— *Numantia*, 4 vols., Munich, 1914–31.

—— 'Iliturgi', *Hermes*, 63 (1928), 288–301.

SCHULTEN, A., *Geschichte von Numantia*, Munich, 1933.

—— 'Forschungen in Spanien 1933–1939', *AA* 1940, pp. 75 ff.

—— *Iberische Landeskunde* i, Strasbourg, 1955.

—— and BOSCH GIMPERA, P., *Fontes Hispaniae Antiquae* iii, *Las guerras de 237–154 a. de J. C.*, Barcelona, 1935.

SCHULZE, J. F., 'Die Entwicklung der Medizin in Rom und das Verhältnis der Römer gegenüber der ärtzlichen Tätigkeit von den anfängen bis zum Beginn der Kaiserzeit', *Z. Ant.* 21 (1971), 485 ff.

SCIVOLETTO, N., 'L'oratio contra Galbam e le Origines di Catone', *GIF* 14 (1961), 63 ff.

SCULLARD, H. H., *Scipio Africanus: Soldier and Politician*, London, 1970.

—— *Roman Politics 220–150 B.C.*², Oxford, 1973.

SERGEENKO, M. E., 'L'agriculture chez Caton', *VDI* 26 (1948), 206 ff. (in Russian).

—— 'L' "échelle de rapports" des terrains cultivés chez Caton', *VDI* 27 (1949), 86 ff. (in Russian).

—— 'Caractéristiques de la vie des agriculteurs dans l'Italie centrale au IIᵉ siècle av. J.-C.', *VDI* 42 (1952), 38 ff. (in Russian).

—— 'L'agriculture dans la *suburbana* italique', *VDI* 51 (1955), 31 ff. (in Russian).

SICARD, G., 'Caton et les fonctions des esclaves', *RD* 35 (1957), 177 ff.

SIENA, E., 'A proposito di una nuova interpretazione delle fonti sul processo dell'Africano', *RFIC* 35 (1957), 175 ff.

ŠIMOVIČOVÁ, E., 'Zur Erkenntnis der Warenproduktion in Catos Schrift De Agricultura vom Standpunkt der herrschenden Wirtschaftstheorien', *GLO* 3 (1971), 3 ff.

—— 'Der Warenaustausch und die Marktformen in Catos Schrift De Agri Cultura', *GLO* 4 (1972), 3 ff.

—— 'Zur Frage der Rentabilität und der Produktionskosten in M. Porcius Catos Schrift "De Agri Cultura" ', *GLO* 5 (1973), 129 ff.

SMITH, R. E., 'Cato Censorius', *G & R* 9 (1940), 150 ff.

—— 'Plutarch's Biographical Sources in the Roman Lives', *CQ* 34 (1940), 1 ff.

—— 'The Cato Censorius of Plutarch', *CQ* 34 (1940), 105 ff.

SOLTAU, W., 'Nepos und Plutarch', *Neue Jahrb. für Philol. und Paed.* 153 (= *Jahrb. für class. Phil.* 42) (1896), 123 ff.

SPAULDING, O. L., 'The Ancient Military Writers', *CJ* 28 (1933), 657 ff.

STABILE, F., 'Costruzione paratattica appositiva in Cato?', *RFIC* 49 (1921), 336 ff.

STÄHLIN, O., *see* Schmid, W.

ŠTAERMAN, E. M., *Die Blütezeit der Sklavenwirtschaft in der römischen Republik*, Wiesbaden, 1969.

STARK, R., 'Catos Rede de lustri sui felicitate', *RhM* 96 (1953), 184 ff.

STIER, H. E., *Roms Aufstieg zur Weltmacht und die griechische Welt*, Cologne, 1957.

SUMNER, G. V., 'Proconsuls and *Provinciae* in Spain, 218/7–196/5 B.C.', *Arethusa*, 3 (1970), 85 ff.

SUSEMIHL, F., *Geschichte der griechischen Litteratur in der Alexandrinerzeit*, 2 vols., Leipzig, 1891–2.

TARDITI, G., 'La questione dei Baccanali a Roma nel 186 a.C.', *PP* 9 (1954), 265 ff.

TAYLOR, L. R., *The Voting Districts of the Roman Republic*, Rome, 1960.

THIELSCHER, P., *Des Marcus Cato Belehrung über die Landwirtschaft*, Berlin, 1963.

THÜRLEMANN, S., 'Ceterum censeo Carthaginem esse delendam', *Gymnasium*, 81 (1974), 465 ff.

TIBILETTI, G., 'Il possesso dell'*ager publicus* e le nome *de modo agrorum* sino ai Gracchi', *Athenaeum*, 26 (1948), 173 ff., and 27 (1949), 3 ff.

—— 'Ricerche di storia agraria romana', *Athenaeum*, 28 (1950), 183 ff.

—— 'Lo sviluppo del latifundo in Italia dall'epoca graccana al principio dell'impero', *X Congresso Internazionale di Scienze Storiche* ii (Florence, 1955), 235 ff.

TILL, R., *La lingua di Catone* (Rome, 1968), translation, with supplementary notes, by C. de Meo of *Die Sprache Catos* (Leipzig, 1935; *Philologus*, Supp. 28. 2).

—— 'Zu Plutarchs Biographie des älteren Cato', *Hermes*, 81 (1953), 438 ff.

TIMPE, D., 'Le "Origini" di Catone e la storiografia latina', *Atti e Mem. dell'Accad. Patavina di Sc. Lett. ed Arti* 83 (1970–1), Parte 3, 5 ff.

—— 'Fabius Pictor und die Anfänge der römischen Historiographie', *Aufstieg und Niedergang* i. 2 (Berlin, 1972; ed. Temporini), 928 ff.

TOYNBEE, A. J., *Hannibal's Legacy*, 2 vols., Oxford, 1965.

TRÄNKLE, H., 'Catos Origines im Geschichtswerk des Livius', *Forschungen zur röm. Literatur. Festschrift K. Büchner* (Wiesbaden, 1970), pp. 274 ff.

—— *Cato in der vierten und fünften Dekade des Livius*, Mainz, 1971.

TRENCSÉNYI-WALDAPFEL, I., 'Une comédie de Térence jouée aux funérailles de L. Aemilius Paulus', *A. Ant. Hung.* 5 (1957), 129 ff.

VAHLEN, J., *Ennianae poesis reliquiae*[3], Leipzig, 1928.

VALLEJO, J., 'Cuestiones hispánicas en las fuentes griegas y latinas', *Emerita*, 11 (1943), 142 ff.

VEITH, G., *see* Kromayer, J.

VILLA, E., 'Il "de re publica" come fonte per la conoscenza delle idee politiche di Catone il Censore', *MC* 16 (1949), 68 ff.

—— 'Attualità e tradizione nell'ideale politico e sociale di *vir bonus* in Catone', *RSC* 1 (1952–3), 96 ff.

—— 'Catone e la Saturnia terra', *RSC* 2 (1954), 114 ff.

—— 'Catone e la politica di Roma verso gli Italici', *RSC* 3 (1955), 41 ff.

VITUCCI, G., *Il regno di Bitinia*, Rome, 1953.

WAITE, S. V. F., 'Approaches to the Analysis of Latin Prose, Applied to Cato, Sallust and Livy', *RELO* 2 (1970), 91 ff.

—— 'A Computer-assisted Study of the Style of Cato the Elder with Reference to Sallust and Livy', *HSCPh* 74 (1970), 348 f.

WALBANK, F. W., *A Historical Commentary on Polybius*, vols. i and ii, Oxford, 1957 and 1967.

WALBANK, F. W., 'Political Morality and the Friends of Scipio', *JRS* 55 (1965), 1 ff.

—— *Polybius*, Berkeley, 1972.

WALSH, P. G., *Livy. His Historical Aims and Methods*, Cambridge, 1961.

—— 'Massinissa', *JRS* 55 (1965), 149 ff.

WALTHER, W., 'Catos De agricultura im Unterricht', *NJAB* 1940, pp. 208 ff.

WATSON, A., *The Law of Persons in the Later Roman Republic*, Oxford, 1967.

—— *The Law of Succession in the Later Roman Republic*, Oxford, 1971.

WEISE, P., *Quaestionum Catonianarum capita V*, Göttingen, 1886.

WELLMANN, M., *Die Georgika des Demokritos*, Berlin, 1921.

WESTERMANN, W. L., *The Slave Systems of Greek and Roman Antiquity*, Philadelphia, 1955.

WHITE, K. D., 'Latifundia', *BICS* 14 (1967), 62 ff.

—— *Roman Farming*, London, 1970.

—— *A Bibliography of Roman Agriculture*, Reading, 1970.

—— 'Roman Agricultural Writers I: Varro and his Predecessors', *Aufstieg und Niedergang* i. 4 (Berlin, 1973; ed. Temporini), 439 ff.

WÓJCIK, A., 'Fabula de Catone et Scipione inter se dissentientibus quo modo ex civilibus discidiis orta sit', *Eos*, 53 (1963), 341 ff. (in Polish with résumé in Latin).

—— 'De Catonis Maioris fabula ab ipso aliisque antiquitus tradita', *Eos*, 55 (1965 [1968]), 296 ff. (in Polish with résumé in Latin).

—— 'De Catone Maiore Censorii cognomine appellato', *Eos*, 59 (1971), 309 ff. (in Polish with résumé in Latin).

YEO, C. A., 'The Development of the Roman Plantation and Marketing of Farm Products', *Finanzarchiv*, 13 (1952), 321 ff.

—— 'The Economics of Roman and American Slavery', *Finanzarchiv*, 13 (1952), 445 ff.

ZANCAN, L., 'Le cause della terza guerra punica', *AIV* 95 (1935–6), 529 ff.

ZUCCARELLI, U., 'Rassegna bibliografica di studi e pubblicazioni su Catone (1940–1950)', *Paideia*, 7 (1952), 213 ff.

General Index

THIS index, which is selective, is mainly of proper names. Romans who attained consular rank are identified by date of first consulship (and only the first), irrespective of whether that office features in this book. Other Romans who are known to have held public office are normally identified by reference to one relevant office.

Index of Passages from Cato's Writings

THE passages are identified and numbered in accordance with the standard collections and editions. For convenience the titles of speeches have been included in the form given by Malcovati in ORF³, even in instances where some reservation is expressed in this book about title, assignment of fragments, or date. Items recorded only as dicta are not indexed.

SPEECHES. (Fragments in ORF³)
Oratio quam dixit Numantiae apud equites
  17: 45 n. 44, 149 n. 39.
  18: 144.
De triumpho ad populum
  19: 47 n. 51, 52 n. 4.
Apud Athenienses
  20: 57, 144, 149, 160, 162.
Dierum dictarum de consulatu suo
  21–55: 28 f., 60, 64, 137 n. 14, 302 ff.
  21: 87 n. 42, 142.
  22: 64 n. 43.
  23: 64 n. 43.
  24: 64 n. 43.
  28: 34 f., 308.
  29: 35 n. 18, 144, 308.
  30: 35 n. 18.
  31: 302 n. 1.
  35: 30 n. 6, 36 n. 21, 37, 308.
  36: 37 n. 28.
  37: 37 n. 28.
  38: 37 n. 28.
  40: 34 n. 15, 41 nn. 32 *and* 33, 43.
  41: 34 n. 15, 41 n. 32.
  42: 44.
  49: 57 n. 19, 60, 144.
  50: 60 n. 30, 64 f., 87 f.
  51: 36 n. 23, 53 n. 5.
Dissuasio legis Iuniae de feneratione
  56–7: 54 f., 250 n. 35, 321 ff.
In Q. Minucium Thermum de falsis pugnis
  58: 59 n. 27, 63, 90 nn. 51 *and* 52, 100 n.
    85, 109, 143, 151, 327 f.
In Q. Minucium Thermum de decem hominibus
  59–63: 59 n. 27, 63, 109.
  59: 63, 90 n. 52, 327.
Orationum in Q. Minucium Thermum reliquiae incertae sedis
  64: 59 n. 27, 87 n. 42.
  65: 59 n. 27.
In M'. Acilium Glabrionem
  66: 36 n. 21, 59 f.
De pecunia regis Antiochi
  67: 70 f., 297 n. 5.

De coniuratione
  68: 74.
In L. Quinctium Flamininum
  71: 80 n. 6.
In L. Veturium de sacrificio commisso cum ei equum ademit
  72–82: 82.
  74: 145.
  78: 82, 97.
  79: 82.
  80: 82.
De moribus Claudii Neronis
  83–4: 81.
  83: 87 n. 42.
Ut plura aera equestria fierent
  85–6: 82 n. 18.
Uti basilica aedificaretur
  87: 84.
De Indigitibus
  88: 86.
De agna musta pascenda
  89–92: 86.
De vestitu et vehiculis
  93: 83, 93.
De signis et tabulis
  94–5: 83.
In Lepidum
  96: 91.
Ne spolia figerentur nisi de hoste capta
  97: 86.
Uti praeda in publicum referatur
  98: 53 n. 7, 86, 87 n. 42, 90 n. 52, 96, 142.
In L. Furium de aqua
  99–105: 84.
  102: 84 n. 26.
  103: 84 n. 25.
Contra Oppium
  106: 85.
De fundo oleario
  107: 86.
De Laetorio
  108: 18 n. 13, 82 n. 17, 144.
Contra Annium
  109: 82, 120 n. 51.

* Fragments possibly from the *Origines* but not attested as taken from that work.